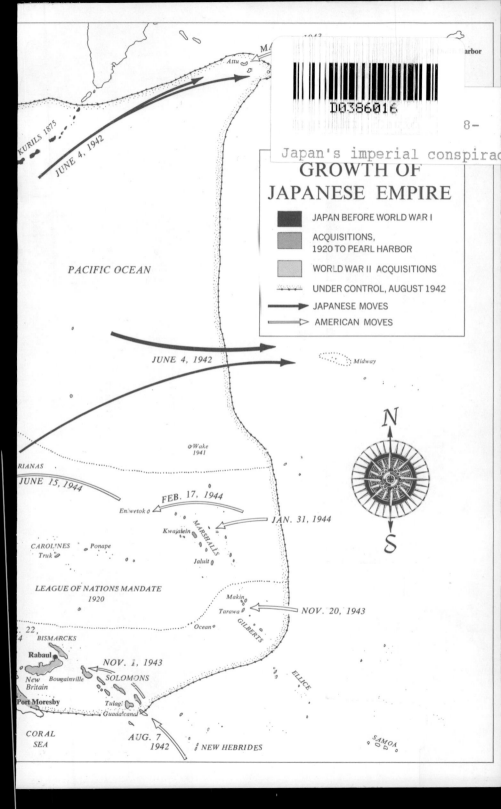

GROWTH OF JAPANESE EMPIRE

JAPAN BEFORE WORLD WAR I

ACQUISITIONS,
1920 TO PEARL HARBOR

WORLD WAR II ACQUISITIONS

UNDER CONTROL, AUGUST 1942

JAPANESE MOVES

AMERICAN MOVES

PACIFIC OCEAN

JUNE 4, 1942

JUNE 4, 1942

Midway

Attu

KURILS 1875

JUNE 4, 1942

N

S

Wake 1941

RIANAS

JUNE 15, 1944

FEB. 17, 1944

Eniwetok

JAN. 31, 1944

Kwajalein

MARSHALLS

CAROLINES
Truk *Ponape*

Jaluit

LEAGUE OF NATIONS MANDATE
1920

Makin
Tarawa *NOV. 20, 1943*

Ocean *GILBERTS*

22,
4 *BISMARCKS*

Rabaul

NOV. 1, 1943

New Bougainville SOLOMONS
Britain

Port Moresby

Tulagi
Guadalcanal

ELLICE

CORAL
SEA

AUG. 7
1942

NEW HEBRIDES

SAMOA

JAPAN'S
IMPERIAL
CONSPIRACY

VOLUME I

JAPAN'S
IMPERIAL
CONSPIRACY

❧

BY DAVID BERGAMINI

VOLUME I

William Morrow and Company, Inc., New York

Copyright © 1971 by David Bergamini

Grateful acknowledgment is made to Little, Brown and Company for
permission to reprint "The Japanese," from *Verses from 1929 On,*
by Ogden Nash, copyright 1935 by The Curtis Publishing Company.

Printed in the United States of America.

Maps by Dyno Lowenstein

To Jack, a U.S. Marine, and Kino-san, a Japanese nursemaid, who both perished in a clash of cultures and aspirations which might have been averted but for the proud deceptions and lazy ignorance of many on both sides.

CONTENTS

VOLUME I

PART FIVE—DISCIPLINING THE LEGIONS

VOLUME II

PART SIX—TRIUMVIR OF ASIA

PART SEVEN—ARMAGEDDON

INTRODUCTION

The work at hand resurveys an area of history which I once explored in a judicial capacity. Whilst Chief Justice of the Australian state of Queensland and later a justice of the High Court of Australia, I headed the bench of eleven judges from eleven nations known as the International Military Tribunal for the Far East, which sat in Tokyo from May 1946 to November 1948. After that two-and-a-half-years' trial, which was commended for its fairness even by the Japanese vernacular press, the Tribunal sentenced twenty-five Japanese leaders to death or imprisonment for having conspired to wage aggressive war and for being responsible for the conventional war crimes—the atrocities—which had been committed by their subordinates.

When David Bergamini's manuscript, *Japan's Imperial Conspiracy*, arrived in my mail I picked it up with alacrity. I had been led to expect much from the author because of his journalistic and scholarly qualifications and his years of research with source documents. Now, on reading the result of his labors, I find that my expectations have been exceeded.

Japan's Imperial Conspiracy is a tremendous achievement. I have read few histories which weave so many intricate situations into an engrossing story and at the same time present, with logic and lucidity, a challenging thesis as to the nature of the historical process. The author's insistence upon dealing with history as the

deeds of men and women, and not as the dark workings of complex sociological and economic pressures, is refreshing. It may take
years for this work to find its proper place in the evaluation of
scholars. More than half the information in it is new to the
English-speaking public and some of the interpretation is sure to
be controversial. I would judge, however, that the book has the
highest importance and will cause a major readjustment in Western views of Oriental history.

To a large extent, *Japan's Imperial Conspiracy* supplements
and complements the findings of the Tribunal of which I was
president. Indeed it indicates that those findings could have been
based on evidence of guilt even more convincing than that tendered by the Prosecution. This is not surprising, as the trial began on May 3, 1946, only eight months after Japan's surrender,
and a large part of the author's source materials did not become
available in Japan until after 1960. The judges at the Tribunal
could be sure that much evidence existed which was not tendered
by the Prosecution or the Defense and which was not readily accessible to the Prosecution or Defense; but the Tribunal had no
power of its own motion to order investigations and researches.

The work at hand departs from the facts known to the Tribunal
in its appreciation of the role of the Emperor. With much fasci-
nating detail drawn from the diaries of Hirohito's courtiers, Mr.
Bergamini holds the Emperor responsible not only for authorizing Japan's 1941 attack upon the West, but also for instigating it.
I can comment on this point of view, without acting extrajudi-
cially, because the Emperor was not on trial before the Tribunal.

The Tribunal used the Anglo-American form of trial. That
form had, for centuries, worked well in English-speaking countries and seemed likely to ensure just results. In Anglo-American
jurisprudence, however, the right to present an indictment belonged exclusively to the prosecution. The Prosecution at the Tribunal indicted lesser Japanese leaders but specifically exempted
the Emperor from the Tribunal's jurisdiction.

Before the trial began I took the view that the Emperor, as an
absolute monarch, was responsible prima facie for authorizing the
war, and at the request of my government I advised accordingly.

I added that if the Emperor were indicted I would have to disbar myself because I gave that advice. The evidence brought out at the trial confirmed my a priori finding and revealed that the Emperor had, indeed, authorized the war and so was responsible for it.

The question of the Emperor's part became an important matter when it came time to award punishment to the accused. Inasmuch as the accused were only subordinates who had obeyed orders and inasmuch as their leader had escaped trial, strongly extenuating circumstances had to be taken into account in awarding punishment. The Prosecution's evidence left room to believe that the Emperor had authorized the war with reluctance. I was not entirely convinced by this evidence, but it had some probative value.

An entry made on November 30, 1941, in the diary of Marquis Kido, the Emperor's Lord Privy Seal, revealed that the Emperor authorized the war with some hesitation. It also revealed that this hesitation was not due to his dedication to peace but to a fear of defeat which was dispelled by what the Emperor called "the altogether satisfactory assurances" given by the Navy Minister and the Navy Chief of Staff.

Japan's 1941 Prime Minister, General Tojo, who was one of the accused at the trial, first testified that he had never acted against the wishes of the Emperor and then returned to the stand to say that he had done his best to persuade the Emperor to authorize the war. Neither of his statements added much to the effect of Marquis Kido's diary entry.

Admiral Okada, who as Prime Minister in 1936 had barely survived an assassination attempt by military extremists, gave evidence to the effect that the Emperor was a man of peace. Had the Emperor been in the dock, Okada's statement would certainly have been received in mitigation as going to the general character of the Emperor.

Since the extent of the Emperor's guilt or innocence lay outside the competence of the Tribunal, these shreds of evidence were incidental. Nevertheless the Prosecution had opened a wide church door of doubt as to the authority of the accused in initiating the crimes with which they were charged. To avoid any possibility of injustice, I proposed that no capital punishment be imposed on any of the accused, and that they be sentenced instead to imprisonment under conditions of hardship in some place or places outside Japan. However, seven of the accused were sentenced to death by hanging.

As I could not say that the death sentences were manifestly excessive—the test applied by the High Court of Australia in reviewing sentences on appeal—I did not press my dissent, and pronounced the death sentences as well as the sentences of imprisonment.

Japan's Imperial Conspiracy reassures me that, with the possible exception of the hanging of Matsui Iwane, none of these sentences was a miscarriage of justice and that the men hanged were indeed responsible for, although they might have deplored, the wanton murders and barbarous inhumanities which they did little or nothing to prevent. In regard to the Emperor himself, the decision not to try him had been reached, at a high political level, in the U.S. and other Allied governments. At my government's request for advice on the Emperor's case, I advised that it should be dealt with at the political or diplomatic level.

It may seem rather quaint for an alliance of democratic governments to wage war upon an autocratic government at great expense in life and material, and then leave the chief autocrat of that government in a position of leadership. But Hirohito was not only an individual; he was a symbol. However culpable he may have been individually, he was also the spiritual embodiment of his entire nation. In 1945 a majority of Japanese believed, as a matter of religious faith, that Japan and the Emperor were indivisible and must live or die together.

During the thirty months in which I sat upon the bench in Tokyo, I was frequently struck by the solicitude and reverence of witnesses toward the Japanese monarch, and by their earnestness and sense of rectitude in pleading their case. I sometimes asked myself what right we had to condemn Japan for having resorted to belligerency in 1941. I perceived much justice and extenuation in the able arguments of Defense counsel that Japan was a tiny land of 90,000,000 and 15 per cent cultivable soil, and that she had been subjected to severe trade restrictions and limitations from without. I pondered how the United States or Britain would have reacted in that situation, and indeed how their peoples would have wanted them to react.

The United States and Britain in a situation like Japan's in 1941 might well have had recourse to war. I recall Daniel Webster's address to the Bar Association in London over a century ago in which that notable American jurist acclaimed the expansion of little England into a great empire in these words:

Her morning drumbeats beginning with the Sun and keeping company with the hours encircle the globe with one unbroken strain of the martial airs of England.

The expansion was not wholly the result of peaceful negotiation.

Until the twentieth century the right to wage war was a sovereign right exercised by all nations without any check except the fear of defeat. Losers paid indemnities in money or territory, and rough rules of chivalry were applied in judging international right and wrong. After World War I, however, all the major powers made an effort to agree upon standards of war conduct and upon principles of international law which might be used in judging those who initiated war. Finally in 1928 sixty-three nations signed the Pact of Paris condemning recourse to war as an instrument of national policy except in self-defense. Japan was one of these nations. Ironically her government specifically informed fellow signatories that she was signing in the name of the Imperial Throne and not, as others had done, in the name of her people.

The Pact of Paris did not explicitly state that the war leaders of a signatory nation could be held individually responsible if that nation broke the pact. Some international jurists of standing have taken the view that the Pact did not impose individual liability. However, I cannot attribute to sixty-three nations—some of whom signed the Pact only after years of deep consideration of their national interests—such futility as to subscribe to an international law for the breach of which no individual human being could be punished. In any case Japan explicitly acknowledged, in the Instrument of Surrender which was signed on behalf of Emperor Hirohito on September 2, 1945, that the Allied nations had the right to try individual Japanese war leaders for crimes against international law. Entries for August 1945 in the diary of Marquis Kido, the Emperor's Lord Privy Seal, reveal that Hirohito understood "war criminals" to include all those responsible for the war, even, perhaps, himself.

Briefly and simply then this was the legal position at the opening of the Tribunal: if Japan was guilty of aggressive war according to the Pact of Paris and the Instrument of Surrender of Japan which she had signed, her political, military and other war leaders were individually liable. The only defense which she could make was "self-defense." The Tribunal considered this defense and rejected it; it could not succeed. Japan had attacked nations like Thailand and the Commonwealth of the Philippines which had never in any way threatened her. In short her making of war was not merely an Act of State for which the customary punishment was indemnity or cession of territory. It was a Delict of State for which we could find her war leaders guilty as criminals.

After hearing evidence, pro and con, for two and a half years the Tribunal did so find. Tempering justice with mercy, we saw sufficient extenuation in 18 of the 25 cases before us to impose only prison terms. In the other seven cases the Tribunal imposed capital punishment because, on the basis of the evidence, the accused were responsible not only for aggressive war but also for leadership which had allowed otherwise well disciplined Japanese troops to commit pillage, rape and murder in areas outside the forward field of battle.

It is Mr. Bergamini's view, implicit if not stated, that we should have sentenced no Japanese leader to death without also trying the Emperor. I can sympathize with this view even though I do not concur in it. The Emperor, by Mr. Bergamini's account, had a somewhat theoretical, scientific and cloistered appreciation of the realities. He may have been, as the author suggests, no puppet but a robust and intelligent leader of his gifted and energetic people. He lived, however, on a plane above some of his ministers. He seems to have been a patriot, acting in a spirit of self-sacrifice and for the good of his people. He may have played the role of a hawk and may have plotted war on the West for decades before 1941. But I suspect that, had Hirohito sat in the dock in 1946–1948, I would have had a higher regard for his character than I had for that of most of the other Japanese war leaders. Indeed the worth of Hirohito as a statesman appears from the position of his nation today which, under his rule, has reacted to war and defeat by making herself the third industrial power on earth.

Offenders who turn King's evidence or otherwise assist the rule of law have always been treated with a degree of leniency. So it was with Hirohito. He survived the threat of indictment and the humiliation of defeat to make Japan a stable force in Asia. He asserted his supreme authority as an absolute monarch to terminate hostilities which had escalated into nuclear warfare. It is true that he did so only as Japan reeled in the shock of the atomic blasts at Hiroshima and Nagasaki; but he did it at some personal risk as is revealed by Mr. Bergamini's account of the curious happenings in and about the Palace on the night of August 14–15, 1945.

Mr. Bergamini presents a strong case for believing that Hirohito schemed and plotted to lead Japan to the conquest of Asia. Under the circumstances my feeling that the Emperor was worth saving may seem cynical and Machiavellian. But so may the author's evident admiration for Hirohito. And so may the decision to grant the Emperor immunity which was concurred in by statesmen of such disparate views as Truman, Churchill, Attlee and Stalin.

Hirohito was Japanese. He grew up in a peculiarly insular world which had developed for centuries in isolation from other nations. Anthropologists, poets, priests and diplomats, each in their own fields, have found, on study, that the Japanese world contains a logic and a beauty of its own. Now Mr. Bergamini, after long research in source documents, presents the political side of that world. He does so in lucid Western terms but he succeeds in projecting the Japanese viewpoint. On putting down his book, I was convinced that any Japanese who had grown up in the Imperial Palace would have tried to do what Hirohito did and that few would have succeeded in doing it so well. In short, having tried war and nearly succeeded in it, Hirohito was better qualified to profit by the lessons of defeat and to lead his people in new directions than any other Japanese.

In driving the reader to this realization, Mr. Bergamini adopts a realism toward Japan which, in my experience, is new. On the one hand he rejects the wartime hate of the Japanese as cold and calculating schemers. On the other hand he deplores the postwar apology for the Japanese as fanatic emotional blunderers. In Mr. Bergamini's view, the Japanese were always rational and succeeded in terrifying the rest of the world by using well the few material resources which they possessed. At the same time they were loving parents and children and fought for a way of life which to them was all firelight and comfort. It included the matting floor, the scalding tub, the backlighted paper-screened doorways and windows, the pickled radishes and steaming rice. In my years in Tokyo I never adopted any of those Japanese institutions but Mr. Bergamini almost makes me wish that I had. In reading his pages I found myself identifying so well with the protagonists of his story that I was hanging upon the success of their enterprises.

Because of his insistence upon appreciating Japanese values and Japanese accomplishments, without accepting obfuscations or apologies, Mr. Bergamini has had to reinterpret Japanese history. His pages offer fresh ideas about events A.D. 50 as well as A.D. 1945. I find his insights extraordinarily coherent and persuasive and I can only say: "Reader, read on."

SIR WILLIAM FLOOD WEBB

Brisbane, Australia

AUTHOR TO READER

"Of course I want the Japanese to win," I said. "The Japanese are clean and the Chinese are dirty. The Japanese work and the Chinese beg. The Japs make machines and the Chinese only break them."

"I should say you're a bloody Nazi," remarked the English boy. And at that, the two of us were rolling on the playground, muddying our gray flannel shorts and school blazers and knocking our heads against the sandbag emplacement put up a week earlier after the first Japanese air raid. It was October of 1937. We were both nine-year-old students at a small British school for white boys in the central Chinese city of Hankow. The fight was my first at Hankow Private and it was to be repeated with other members of my class, for the same cause, several times in the next two months. I had been born in Japan and my family had brought me to China from Japan less than a year earlier. Now Japan had attacked China and Japanese troops were driving swiftly on Nanking, the Chinese capital.

Almost a year later, in September of 1938, I sat with my father at the mouth of a cave used as a temple by the chanting, sandaled, Buddhist monks of the sacred Chinese mountain of Lushan. In summertime Lushan—halfway down the Yangtze River from Hankow toward Nanking—was a resort for Westerners. Through our field glasses, my father and I looked down the steep slopes, 5,000 feet, into the front lines of Japanese-occupied China. At our distance we could just make out individual Japanese soldiers. They were conducting a reprisal raid against a Chinese farm village, bayoneting its inhabitants and systematically burning its huts. The smoke of the village streamed into the sky, blotting out the plumes from the fires of the charcoal makers who worked rain or shine, war or peace, in the wooded foothills. Tomorrow there would be a fresh influx of refugees to our mountaintop, orphaned children for the most part, toddlers with cruel bayonet wounds carried piggyback by elder sisters only a few years older than they were. And then tomorrow night the Chinese guerrillas who held the summit of the mountain would make a fresh sortie into the flatlands and bring back a few Japanese heads to mount on bamboo poles and carry in their victory parade.

I was no longer a Japanese sympathizer. The gentle, thoughtful, courteous, good-natured people among whom I had grown to boyhood were now transformed, hideously and most puzzlingly. Here on the battlefield, the Japanese soldiers did not merely wage war: they strutted and slapped faces; they commandeered food from the starving, bedrolls from the homeless, coppers from the destitute; they raped little girls, cut open pregnant women, threw infants into the air and caught them on bayonets; they recognized no truth except the confessions of the tortured, no art of government except intimidation. I did not understand why they acted as they did but I came to take Japanese behavior for granted. Some of my father's friends blamed the famous "Japanese inferiority complex." The Chinese general who lived down the street said it was Japanese leadership that was at fault. Japan, he said, was governed by an unworthy emperor who hoped to conquer the world. I tended to accept the general's explanation because it was simple.

In early 1939 my family and other Westerners were evacuated from the mountaintop of Lushan, through the Chinese and Japanese lines, and taken on a Japanese ship to Shanghai. During the three-day voyage down the Yangtze River, the Japanese commissary served nothing but bread, butter, sardines, and coffee. I discovered that there was plenty of Japanese-style food aboard and was soon eating rice, soya sauce, and pickled radish with the cooks and the guards in the kitchen. Outside the war zone I found with surprise that the Japanese soldiers were the same cheerful, considerate people that I remembered. Most of them knew the big Tokyo hospital of St. Luke's which my father had built. They seemed genuinely grateful for the years he had devoted to architecture in Japan.

Two days after Christmas, 1941, I was once again on a mountaintop with my family—this time in the resort town of Baguio in the Philippines. Again we were refugees, living from suitcases. We were waiting at the local American school, in a body with some 300 other Americans, to be officially captured by the Japanese and declared prisoners of war. A local Japanese immigrant who had worked for my father as a carpenter came to the headmaster's home, where my family was camped out on mattresses on the floor, and informed us with great politeness that at last the Japanese Army had arrived. We gathered to greet it on one of the school tennis courts.

A sound truck, escorted by two weapons carriers, screeched up the drive in the dusk and lurched to a halt. Light machine guns turned back and forth to cover us. A Japanese Methodist minister leapt from the sound truck and began a harangue. By the heroism of the Japanese Army, he announced, an Asia for the Asiatics had at last been realized. We were prisoners of the Co-Prosperity Sphere of Greater East Asia. "You wirru prease surrender your guns." Our elected spokesman told him that we had already made sure that none of us had any guns. The minister did not believe us. He threatened to have his men conduct a search and shoot a man for every gun they found. Then he threatened to shoot ten men for every gun found. Finally he declared: "If we find one gun, we wirru shoot orr of you."

A second-grader came forward trembling, holding out an air-compression BB pistol. "Please," he sobbed, "don't shoot Mom." The Japanese soldiers in the weapons carriers guffawed. The rest of us relaxed. The Methodist minister scowled and turned away. We were herded into one of the school dormitories and left there, hungry but unmolested, for two days while the Japanese secured the town of Baguio and decided where to intern us for the duration. As a thirteen-year-old, I made a mental note of the fact that, even in a war zone, Japanese soldiers might retain some of their sentimental fondness for children.

It also struck me that we were to be treated with speeches rather than bayonets—not at all like Japanese prisoners in China. Was Japanese brutality all calculated, all obedience to policy dictated from above? My question was answered a few days later when Baguio's community of expatriate Chinese shopkeepers was interned in a building next to ours. In a matter of hours the same Japanese soldiers who were guarding us had tied one of the Chinese to a post and beaten him senseless in front of his fellow nationals. The Chinese, I perceived, fell under internal Asian policy whereas we were items classified under external policy toward the West.

Eventually we settled in a former U.S. Army post. There we learned to grow thin on two bowls of rice and one serving of vegetable stew a day and became accustomed to living communally on one six-by-three-foot oblong of barracks floor apiece. One day a Japanese guard approached our Executive Committee, suggesting that arrangements might be made for opening a school in the camp. Like most of the adult internees, the members of the committee anticipated a short war. Preoccupied with immediate problems of survival, they paid little attention to the suggestion. The guard, however, was persistent. He approached one of the older teen-age boys in camp and offered to help get books. Finally he loaded five of us into a truck, covered us with a tarpaulin, and secretly drove past his own guardhouse to Brent School where we had studied before the war.

We found the doors sealed with notices which announced: "Property of the Imperial Japanese Army. Looters will be shot." We broke the seals, loaded the truck with school books, and took them back into the concentration camp. Finding that our assumed birthright of an education might be denied us, most of us read those school books dog-eared in the years which followed. As a result, only one of the score of high-school-age internees lost much educational ground because of his three years in camp, and two of us actually managed to gain a year. After five hours on a work gang each day, our stomachs empty, we had little strength left anyway for anything but reading. I remember lying on my bunk with a geometry book, slightly dizzy as usual before the afternoon meal, puzzling over the fanatic belief in education which gave Japan a literacy rate of over 99 per cent and which had prompted our guard to conspire with us in getting the books.

Mine and a dozen other families which had been registered residents of Baguio before the war were released from camp for a few months in 1942 in a Japanese attempt to make the native Filipinos feel that life had returned to normal. In those months of liberation, we borrowed money, bought food, and had enough to eat. Baguio had been made a convalescent center for Japanese troops wounded on Bataan. The town crawled with soldiers, and most of us stayed close to home except for a weekly expedition to the stalls of the open-air food market in the town plaza. On those trips downtown I made a hobby of collecting proclamations written in English and posted in the market by the Japanese high command. I did not dare to be seen transcribing them in public so I read and reread them until I had memorized the words, then wrote them down as soon as I was home in the little house where we were living. These proclamations struck me because they showed the gulf between Japanese and other languages and the awkward light in which the Japanese appeared whenever they tried to express themselves in English. I remember one poster in particular:

Still the Igorot peoples living in and about Baguio continue to put the fire on or to loot something from the properties in and about Baguio. This is not good behaviour anyway. When the Imperial Japanese Army finds out those who intend to do so, it will shoot them by guns.

> signed,
> Affectionately yours,
> Lt. Col. Kanmori

A year and a half later I was sitting after dark on the split-cane porch of one of the huts satellite to the barracks of our concen-

tration camp. Each of us had just received our first and only Red
Cross package of the war. Mine contained ten packages of cigarettes which were not edible. That afternoon, during my daily
chore and privilege of passing through the fence to remove the
garbage from the kitchen in the Japanese guardhouse, I had spoken to one of the guards—a clean-looking, open-faced mechanic
from the Japanese city of Nagoya—offering him a pack of cigarettes for two hands of bananas. I had given him ten cigarettes
in advance and he had secreted one hand of bananas at the bottom of one of the garbage cans I was to carry away. Now, as
I sat on the tiny porch, I heard a hiss in the darkness beyond. I
moved out warily from the puddle of light surrounding the hut
and there in the darkness confronted the guard from Nagoya,
thrusting a huge hand of bananas at me.

"We have been ordered out," he said.

"Can you come back to the men's barracks with me?" I asked.
"I have the cigarettes at my bunk there."

"Do not think of them," he assured me. "We are already equal.
I have a son in Japan who is also hungry."

I thanked him and asked him where he was going.

"To the Southern Area," he replied.

That probably meant New Guinea, so I wished him health.

"No," he said fatalistically, "we must all die. There is no way
but to die for the Emperor." He bobbed his head in a short but
punctilious bow and hurried toward the guardhouse before he
could be caught fraternizing. The sadness and despair of his voice
lingered after him. Most of them, I thought, hated it as much as
we did. They were just waiting to have it over with, to obey the
final order and die. If the guard had had the orders, he would
probably have killed his own son. With a baffled tug, I ad-
justed the G string, which was all I was wearing, settled my toes
firmly against the soles of my clumsy wooden clogs, and turned
my mind to the problem of smuggling my bananas into the men's
barracks.

In early 1944 a new commandant was sent to us from Tokyo.
He let it be known that he suffered from tertiary syphilis and
was subject to savage fits of temper. He quickly showed us that

he liked nothing better than to belabor a man about the head with a baseball bat. He might have killed some of us with his beatings if it had not been for the presence of a Japanese civilian attached to our camp as an observer. This civilian was the son of the famous General Mazaki who had sponsored a rebellion against Emperor Hirohito in 1936 and earlier had opposed an imperial policy decision to "Strike South," that is, to prepare for ultimate seizure of the British colony of Malaya, the Dutch colony of the East Indies, and if necessary the U.S. colony of the Philippines. Because of his father's opposition to imperial wishes, our young Mazaki had not been allowed to join the Army, but because of his father's former prestige, he knew how to talk to Army men. His ability to stand up to our mad commandant saved us many concussions and at least one death.

One day while tending to the garbage at the officers' quarters near the gate, I overheard Mazaki pleading with the commandant about our right to have light bulbs with which to read until lights-out at 9:30 P.M. The commandant said that he had orders from Tokyo to be tough, that there was no place for us in the New Order, that we must ultimately die. Mazaki replied that of course we might die under those circumstances, but that if wrong was done there might some day, after the war, come a time of payment. Then, sternly, he reminded the commandant that the name of the Imperial Throne must never be sullied by impropriety in international dealings.

Young Mazaki, our benefactor, was later killed when an American plane strafed a Japanese truck convoy. The convoy had just delivered a life-saving shipment of food to 6,000 interned Westerners at a camp south of Manila. The camp had been cut off from supplies during the confusion which followed the first American landings in Luzon in 1945. In later years, when I knew the history of the Mazaki family, I was impressed by the fact that those who had tried to keep Japan from waging an unjust war were brave men who had continued their struggle to the end.

In December of 1944 our concentration camp was moved in trucks to Manila for the denouement of the war. We lived on chicken corn, weeds, and snails for a month and a half. And then,

unexpectedly, came the U.S. 1st Cavalry. MacArthur had received
a tip from an unknown Japanese—a correct tip as we were told
later by a member of our camp committee—that Tokyo had ordered concentration camp commandants to dispose of their
prisoners rather than surrender them. Our executions were scheduled for Monday morning, February 5, 1945. On Saturday
afternoon, February 3, the 1st Cavalry tanks made a dash across
the swamps north of Manila. They arrived in the city at dusk. We
were housed on the concrete floors of the Bilibid Prison hospital, a
bleak white building shuttered with sheets of corrugated iron and
surrounded by the thick mossy walls of an old Spanish fortress.
From our roof the Disney cartoon emblems on the sides of the
tanks could not be made out for what they were. They looked like
Japanese characters. Only scattered rifle fire greeted the tanks at
first, but then a Japanese battery on a building across the avenue
opened up and sent us all scuttling downstairs to lie low on the
concrete ground floor. No one could tell whether the Americans
had finally arrived or whether the Japanese were putting down a
guerrilla insurrection. A few wealthy internees laid bets pro and
con with their last hoarded ounces of Philippine tobacco and
peanut butter.

Four objectives were red-circled on the tank crews' maps: our
Bilibid Prison, the bigger internment center at Santo Tomas University, and two breweries. While waiting for reinforcements, the
tanks began circling the four city blocks containing these four objectives. Only a skeleton force of Japanese soldiers remained in
the city, and they were concentrated in the old Spanish citadel to
the south of us. This skeleton force had been supplemented at the
last minute by a landing party of Imperial Marines—aristocratic
kinsmen of the Emperor—and at the instigation of these newcomers was now preoccupied with a death-throe orgy of rape and
murder in the Filipino slums. As a result, except for fires set by in-
filtrators and a few small shells lobbed in from knee mortars, action in our area was light. A Japanese munitions dump which was
being destroyed several blocks away lit the night with carnival fire-
works. The tanks went round and round our compound with a
monotonous grinding sound. We still did not know for sure that
they were American.

Then, one of the gold miners of the Benguet Company, who was interned with us, crawled upstairs and peered over the parapet on the roof to see what the tanks were doing. While he stood watch, two of the tanks stopped and opened up their turrets for the men to smoke a cigarette. One of the drivers yelled something to the other. The miner crawled back downstairs and passed on his story. It reached me by an excited missionary spinster in her fifties: "Hey, Casey, haven't we been up this fricking street before?" And so we knew that bets could be paid off, that the last little hoards of food could be eaten, that the tanks were American.

Next morning the Japanese officers in charge of our Formosan and Korean guards carried machine guns and Molotov cocktails up the stairs to our roof where they prepared to make a last stand. My father was asked by the chairman of our Executive Committee to stand watch over the meager possessions we had left on the deserted second floor. After shooting at the tanks for a while, the officers of the guard were signaled from the prison gate that the tank crews outside had agreed to Japanese terms: release of all P.O.W.'s and internees unharmed in exchange for a jeep ride to the city limits and freedom to join Japanese forces outside Manila. Our Japanese officers then came down from the roof. They found my father sitting alone at the head of the stairs on the second floor. Knowing nothing of the agreement made at the gate, he assumed that they were going out to die and might well shoot him in passing. In his confusion he politely muttered *sayonara*, goodbye. The first of the retreating officers turned on him with a look of hate. "Hope I see you all soon in Tokyo," added my father brightly. The second officer smiled, opened his coat, took something from an inner pocket, and thrust into my father's lap a bottle of beer.

In a moment the Japanese had withdrawn from the building. My dazed father was left surrounded by half-empty flasks of brandy and bottles of beer—tokens of the Japanese hopes for the future. Our own American tankmen drove the Japanese guard out into the suburbs and let them off at a place where Filipino irregulars were waiting to gun them down. I did not feel sorry for the officers at the time, but I was grateful for their bureaucratic propriety. They had let us live because our executions were not scheduled for another twenty-four hours.

Twenty years later, with degrees from Dartmouth and Oxford and ten years of experience on *Life* magazine, I was finishing my fifth book, a volume about the philosophy of science. My agent suggested to me that the editors of William Morrow and Company would be interested in a book about the Japanese side of World War II, based on Japanese documents.

The thought of unriddling my childhood puzzlement about the double nature of the Japanese appealed to me strongly. I spent almost a year studying in U.S. libraries. I learned how to speak Japanese again, still badly, and for the first time how to read it— slowly. I worked my way through 140,000 pages of collateral reading in English, French, and German, 50,000 pages of testimony presented at the postwar Tokyo war crimes trials, and another 30,000 pages of captured Japanese documents and U.S. Intelligence reports. Then I moved my wife, my four children, and 272 reference books to a small Japanese-style house overlooking the experimental fields of the agricultural faculty of the old Imperial University in Kyoto, the ancient capital of Japan.

On an afternoon in September of 1965, I was eating seaweed-wrapped rolls of vinegared rice and raw fish across a table from a retired Japanese Naval Air Force commander. He was one of a handful of air aces who had survived both Japan's war with China and her war with the United States. I had had an uneasy feeling ever since my arrival a few weeks earlier that nothing had changed in Japan except the size of the buildings, and I was prepared to dislike the commander cordially. Half his face had been blown away and was covered with purple scar tissue. He was gentle and spoke English. Learning that I had spent thirty-nine months in a Japanese concentration camp, he said that he was ready to help me in any way that he could, for his people "owed me a debt." He told me that he had dive-bombed over both the mountaintops where I had seen Japanese fire as a child. We compared dates and discovered that I had probably seen his plane hurtling down out of the sky on both occasions: once in 1938 and again in 1941. He had even spent time on Guam, where my elder brother, a U.S.

Marine on his way to liberate the concentration camps in the Philippines, had died before a Japanese machine-gun blast in 1944.

Strangely, I soon found myself talking animatedly with this former enemy. Despite his blasted face, he had no bitterness. War was a profession and a game to him. He interested me in it and gave me introductions to several old retired generals who had not already been bored with interviews and interrogations. I became something of an authority on Japanese battlegrounds and Japanese World War II strategic concepts. Soon I realized that I was being passed from hand to hand to hear incidental stories of Japanese heroism and tactical genuis. I was not bored by the stories, nor did I disbelieve them, but I came to feel more and more strongly that anecdotes and actions do not a war make. I was still haunted by my childhood question: What had made the delightful, intelligent, artistic Japanese people turn to war and run amok over half of Asia?

The stock answer to my question was militarism, a mass madness which was supposed to have been stirred up in the Japanese public during the 1930's by a handful of conniving, ambitious generals. I studied the soldiers I was interviewing. Most of them had ended the war as lieutenant generals. All of them were intelligent men who had gone on to staff college after military academy and so had served for years in the nerve center of Japanese militarism, the offices of the Army General Staff in Tokyo. All of them were enthusiastic military technicians, full of recommendations about the conduct of the war in Viet Nam. None of them seemed to be gifted politically. When they felt they could not give straightforward answers to my questions, they said nothing: they looked blank and professed ignorance, or they looked arch and pleaded continuing security restrictions.

On occasion they let slip previously unknown facts of great significance. A retired general of seventy-six, for instance, proudly told me that in August of 1938 he had been put in charge of devising air-to-ground communications and given detailed maps of the terrain for the Nomonhan war with Russia. Evidently he did not realize that this war, which began in May of 1939, was still represented officially by the Japanese government as a spontaneous border incident and his superiors had testified at the war crimes trials to being unable, at the outbreak of the "incident," to find a map in the files of the General Staff which would show them where Nomonhan was.

I could hardly believe, I said, that there were no radios in most Army Air Force planes before 1938. Was the general absolutely sure of his dates? He rummaged in his papers in the next room and triumphantly returned with a volume of his diary. He showed me the dated entry in it where he had recorded his assignment. Two Japanese witnesses were present at my interview with him, and when it was over, I questioned them both to make sure that I had made no mistake about what he had said. They assured me that I had not, but one of them showed curiosity as to why I laid such stress on the date.

Later that week the seventy-six-year-old general traveled over 500 miles, up to Tokyo and back, to see an aged colleague who was a consultant for Japan's modern Self-Defense Forces. When he returned he called me to say that he had been mistaken, that he had carelessly confused the 1938 and 1939 volumes of his diary. Since I had seen the year, *Showa jusannen,* clearly written outside and inside the volume in question, I dismissed the matter as trivial and did my best to save the general's face.

I had an opportunity to see most of my generals in the company of a man of aristocratic birth. I was impressed by their deference to him. They knew their place. Clearly they had been mere cogs in the machine of Japanese society. They did not have the social caste and with it the self-assurance to have forced militarism on Japan—not without the tacit support of their betters in Japan's social hierarchy.

With all of my generals I discussed the atrocities which I had seen committed by Japanese soldiers in China and to a lesser extent in the Philippines. I wanted to discover whether they stemmed from a latent vengeful cruelty in the Japanese or from a well-considered policy of terror which the Japanese soldier carried out under orders. Most of my generals had little to say on the subject except to insist that Japanese troops committed no more casual brutalities than the troops of any other nation. They cited old military police reports and Chinese newspapers to persuade me that, ordinarily, in taking a town Japanese soldiers had committed about two murders and twenty rapes for every thousand troops engaged. I was prepared to believe that similar figures might hold for any army.

In addition to casual brutalities, however, the Japanese had frequently massacred entire villages in China. One of my generals admitted that this was true. He explained that every realistic commander, who had to hold a wide territory with a few troops, was forced on occasion to conduct disciplined reprisals against villages as object lessons to neighboring villages. He maintained cynically that this practice, too, was common to all armies. Indeed, a good commander, he said, kept his special "dirty" reprisal units apart from the rest of his men so that corruption would not spread through the ranks.

I persisted that there had been occasions like the Bataan death march and the rape of Nanking on which the Japanese Army had committed at one time not ten murders out of casual brutality and not a hundred murders in a reprisal raid but thousands and even tens of thousands of murders. All of my generals confessed that they had heard of such "bad things" but only my one exceptionally candid general would make a comment. "Those were the politicians' murders." He wrinkled his face and would say no more.

It was the "politicians'" murders which interested me and I began to study seriously the machinery of prewar Japanese civilian decision making.

In Kyoto I had acquired an excellent research assistant, an honest, politically moderate young student leader taking a master's degree at Doshisha University. Hijino Shigeki bought and read and underlined for me some 30,000 pages of Japanese memoirs and background histories. He worked for me purely in a research capacity and is not responsible for any of the views or judgments expressed herein. A born politician, he gave me insights into Japanese politics. He recruited for me an army of research assistants which I would never have been able to mobilize for myself. His indefatigable staff scanned and culled for me the whole of Japan's voluminous war literature. In the editorials and novels of the late 1920's which my research group collected, I found no evidence of any trend toward militarism. On the contrary I found a popular desire for peace, a repudiation of the hoary warrior cult of the samurai. In the staid economic and military journals of the period, however, I found every evidence of planning for war—planning without popular support but directed and centralized from the pinnacles of the Japanese aristocracy.

I had an introduction at the Imperial Court from General MacArthur's nephew, Douglas MacArthur II, a former U.S. ambassador to Tokyo. I used it to test my growing suspicions in interviews with courtiers who had been close to Hirohito. What a contrast they were to my generals: charming, devious, knowledgeable, never at a loss. Surely here were the real leaders of Japan.

Two of the courtiers inserted into their conversations with me a number of stories about the ruler of Japan since 1926, Emperor Hirohito. These stories had never been reported in print, and I dismissed them at first as Court gossip. But they assumed considerable importance when I later assembled the full context for them. I was told, for instance, that Hirohito had listened to shortwave transmissions from Malaya on the night of Pearl Harbor; that he had once been induced to have a son by artificial insemination; that his own birth was rumored to have taken place a year earlier than commonly stated.

In the anecdotes told to me, I perceived that Hirohito, at the very least, was not the passive dupe of history that he had been made out to be. From the mouths of his own chamberlains he emerged as a powerful autocratic protagonist. He was said to have extraordinary intelligence. Until 1945 he was said to have kept up with every detail of government, to have consulted constantly with officials of all sorts, and to have maintained always an over-all view of world affairs. His powers—civil, military, and religious— were acknowledged to have been absolute, but he was said to have exercised them only ceremonially and to have rubber-stamped the recommendations of his state ministers. Yet in anecdote after anecdote he was shown keeping abreast of his ministers' deliberations and putting in a word now and then to steer them toward recommendations which would be acceptable to him. It was even admitted that he had occasionally decided between opposing viewpoints, accepted a minority viewpoint, or disregarded a recommendation altogether.

I realized that I must go back to the beginning of my research and start all over again. Emperor Hirohito had signed the declaration of war with the United States. It was said that he had done so unwillingly, but this assertion did not appear in the record until made by a retired prime minister, Prince Konoye, many months after the war had started. It was also said that Hirohito might have been assassinated if he had tried to prevent the war. This assertion seemed farfetched, for it was generally admitted that privates and generals were all ready to die for him and that the only Japanese irreverent enough to assassinate him would have been the few Westernized bankers and diplomats who opposed the war.

Emperor Hirohito had stamped the orders sending troops into north China in 1937. It was later said that he did so unwillingly, yet he went on two months later to stamp orders for the dispatch of troops to central and south China as well. He reluctantly postponed execution of the south-China orders on the advice of hesitant "militarists" in the Japanese General Staff. He opened an Imperial Headquarters in his palace so that he could personally supervise the fighting. He became so immersed in war planning that the prime minister at the time complained of his preoccupation. Finally his own uncle assumed command of the attack in Nanking, the Chinese capital, and moved into a hotel in Nanking, to look on while his troops murdered over 100,000 defenseless military and civilian prisoners there. It was the first act of genocide in World War II, but when the uncle returned to Tokyo, Hirohito went out of his way to confer decorations and honors upon him.

Earlier still, in 1931–32, Hirohito had sanctioned the conquest of Manchuria. Again it was said afterward that he had acted reluctantly, but the records of the time simply indicated that he had been reluctant to have the full responsibility for the venture borne by the sacred institution of the Throne which he represented. Again, when the conquest was complete, he honored the conquerors, making the general in charge his chief aide-de-camp and military advisor.

From such obvious facts, I concluded that there was a great disparity between the deeds of Emperor Hirohito and the words which were said about him in later years. I reviewed and reconsidered all the notes I had taken in my reading of source documents, and I became convinced that the modern history of Japan, as presented since World War II, was a skillfully contrived illusion fabricated late in the war, partly by counterintelligence specialists in the General Staff and partly by high-ranking palace courtiers.

The logic of the Japanese cover story was so topsy-turvy that sequels were sometimes cited as causes for what had already happened. Again and again the documents of the time showed that events attributed to chance or spontaneous mass action had actually been discussed at high official levels months or years in advance. The Emperor's chief political advisor, the lord privy seal, routinely named the next prime minister and described "his mission" weeks or months before the onset of the Cabinet crisis which would topple the prime minister already in office. Conversations were even on record in which the lord privy seal correctly foresaw the personnel and accomplishments of the next two governments.

I began to meet my Japanese contacts with a fresh attitude, interviewing them informally and asking for flesh-and-blood details of the countless stick figures who scurried across the pages of the testimony, the diaries, the reminiscences which I had read. I was rewarded with responsive answers, still cautious and indirect, but now full of anecdote and illustration. The vignettes given to me were subtle and ironic, as fragile as butterfly wings, as difficult to pin down as the snide remarks of a consummate hostess. But I began to glimpse the real world inside Japan's closed prewar society.

It was a nightmare world in which everyone spoke politely in well-modulated voices while living with the secrecy and involuted double-thinking of eternal intrigue. The men in the limelight always represented more powerful figures in the shadow. In assessing the role a man played, his deeds had to be counted for more than his words and his associations and loyalties for more than his personal character. State policy was framed in back rooms behind back rooms and the people had no voice in it. Even the party politicians, even the great industrial magnates were usually out on the edges of the national web of string pulling and influence peddling. The masses were nothing more than a mob, swayed this way and that by a venal press and a system of public relations and rumor mongering which had been in use for more than a thousand years.

As my understanding of prewar Japanese society grew, I became increasingly uncomfortable in the Japanese society of 1966. I harbored blasphemous thoughts about the man who from 1926 to 1945 had been worshipped by all Japanese as a god. It did not ease my sense of dangerous knowledge to discover that most of the Japanese who befriended me in Kyoto had been World War II intelligence agents. Two of my best informants in Tokyo asked to have their final interviews with me surreptitiously in small out-of-the-way cafés where they would not be known. My mail from the United States showed signs of having been opened by the local postmaster. While my luggage lay awaiting shipment on a Kobe dock, two notebooks and a roll of film marked "Rape of Nanking" disappeared from one of my six book lockers.

When our ship cleared harbor, taking my family and me on the first leg of our journey home to the United States, I watched the receding coastline of Japan with mingled relief and regret: relief from the oppressive feeling that I was being watched; regret that the book I envisaged writing would not make me welcome again in the land of my birth.

I had with me eight thick loose-leaf folders of cards inscribed with the personnel records of 932 leading Japanese bureaucrats and military officers, 2,000 pages of closely scribbled notebooks, a hundred issues of various Japanese magazines, 60 volumes of Japanese diaries and reminiscences, and 240 hours of interviews and impressions on magnetic tape.

I added to this mass of material by interrupting our journey home for ten days in Singapore and five weeks in Australia. In Singapore I was able to read the complete files of a wartime newspaper, the *Syonan Times*, published by the Japanese occupation authorities in English. In Canberra, Australia, I was kindly given access to some World War II Australian civil intelligence reports; to the papers of the Far Eastern Commission, which was supposed to advise General Douglas MacArthur in the postwar administration of Japan; and to the memoranda and letters of Queensland's Chief Justice Sir William Webb who had presided over the eleven-nation Allied tribunal which had tried Japan's Class-A war criminals in Tokyo from 1946 to 1948. I was relieved to discover in the Canberra archives that at war's end Australian, New Zealand, and Chinese officials had all agreed that Emperor Hirohito was the master of Japan and should head any list of Japanese responsible for the war. They had later bowed to a decision by General Mac-Arthur—a decision which I myself thought sensible—to use the Emperor for the rehabilitation of Japan rather than try him as a criminal under international law.

On return to my home in Connecticut, I began to assimilate and arrange the mountain of half digested information I had brought back with me from abroad. From my eight volumes of individual personnel records I distilled a large wall chart of the men who had occupied key posts in the Army, the Court, and the bureaucracy. From Japanese biographical dictionaries I drew up scores of pedigrees of aristocratic families.* From old Japanese newspapers and from 5,613 pages of diaries kept by the highest officials in the Japanese state, I compiled a day-by-day chronology of events, covering 8,125 days of the most intimate Japanese history. Gradually I learned to separate spear carriers from principals. Patterns emerged—factions and tongs which maintained consistent positions year after year and decade after decade. Countless "incidents" which had once seemed unfathomably Oriental began to make hard, rational sense. Everything fell into place and reinforced my simple perception of the obvious: that Hirohito had, indeed, been Emperor.

The picture of Hirohito which emerged from my evidence differed from the official portrait of biographers as a photographic negative from a photographic positive. By my account Hirohito was a formidable war leader: tireless, dedicated, meticulous,

---

* I discovered with wonderment that neither in Japanese nor English had a complete list ever been printed of the living members of the imperial family. Even during World War II, when Japanese were calling their Emperor a god and committing suicide for him by the legion, no Western analyst had traced the careers of the Japanese generals who were his uncles and cousins.

clever, and patient. He had inherited from his great-grandfather a mission, which was to rid Asia of white men. Since his people were reluctant and backward, he had skillfully manipulated them for twenty years before the war in order to prepare them psychologically and militarily for their task. By contrast the official portrait—in many ways less attractive—represented Hirohito as a cultured, secluded biologist who left the management of his realm to generals and admirals and devoted all his energy to puttering about with fungi and small wormlike marine organisms.

Skillful mythmaking, of which I had uncovered many examples in Imperial Court press releases, could account for the imprinting of a false image, but I was perplexed by the ease with which the true image had been obliterated. It was difficult for me to believe that an entire people, plus foreign observers, could suffer consistently from mass blindness. Could an Emperor really strut about naked while everyone, including envoys from other nations, admired the quality and refinement of his clothes? Apparently he could, for in 1967 I witnessed a convincing demonstration of the phenomenon.

In January of that year, as I neared the end of my researches, a small Tokyo publishing firm, Hara Shobo, came out with the memoranda of Japan's wartime Army Chief of Staff, General Sugiyama Hajime, as jotted down in his daybook between 1940 and 1944. Here was an unimpeachable handwritten source document by the highest military official in the Japanese state. Sugiyama had committed suicide in 1945, at the time of Japan's surrender, and had had no opportunity to dress up his notes in any way. Most of them were concerned with dull military details or duller militaristic cant. A few of them, however, were verbatim accounts of conversations with Hirohito. They revealed Hirohito asking detailed questions about military and economic planning in the months before Pearl Harbor. They directly refuted statements which General Douglas MacArthur said that Hirohito had made to him after the war, professing ignorance of all military and economic matters in 1941.

Most surprising, the *Sugiyama Memoranda* stated that in January 1941, eleven months before the outbreak of war with the United States, Hirohito had personally ordered a secret evaluation to be made of the feasibility of a surprise attack on Pearl Harbor. Previously Western historians had believed that Hirohito had known nothing of the surprise-attack plan until at least November 1941. The 1941 grand chamberlain, Admiral Suzuki Kantaro, was even on record stating flatly, after the war, that Hirohito had been ignorant of the Pearl Harbor plan until it had been already executed.

The *Sugiyama Memoranda* revealed that Hirohito had participated in the Pearl Harbor planning a full six months before any of his official military advisors were informed of it. Evidence taken before the Allied judges of the International Military Tribunal for the Far East, and verified by witnesses under oath and cross-examination, demonstrated conclusively that none of the "militarists" who were supposed to have dragged Hirohito to war knew of the Pearl Harbor plan until August 1941. General Tojo, the arch "militarist" who headed Japan's wartime Cabinet, was not told of the plan until November 1941.

This, then, was a major historical revelation. Its hypothetical equivalent in U.S. terms would be a newly discovered note in the handwriting of Secretary of War Henry L. Stimson asserting that in the summer of 1941 President Roosevelt had secretly ordered a study to be made of the possibility of keeping obsolescent battleships at conspicuously ill-protected moorings in Pearl Harbor in order to lure Japan into making an attack and providing an excuse for American entry into World War II.

I could imagine what a front-page sensation such a documentary discovery would create in the United States, and I watched with fascination the Japanese reaction to the publication of the *Sugiyama Memoranda*. The leading Japanese newspapers all noted, on back pages, that Chief of Staff Sugiyama's papers had been published in two handsome volumes. But not one newspaper carried a review of the set or commented on it in any way. As a result U.S. newspapers never got the story, and Hirohito's personal part in the Pearl Harbor planning had not yet reached the pages of *The New York Times* as this book went to press in 1971.

The silence which greeted the *Sugiyama Memoranda* convinced me that the Japanese, even today, remain extraordinarily discreet in matters touching the Emperor, and that Western observers in

Japan, beset as ever by linguistic and cultural confusions, can fail to notice anything that is not deliberately pointed out to them. To see this demonstrated erased a last doubt in my mind. It was the summer of 1967. I had just finished reviewing the last of the plots and assassinations of the 1930's and had satisfied myself that Hirohito had had a hand in many of them. I wrote finis to a 300,000-word rough draft which I had been writing of all that was new and problematic in my research. It was not a book but a legal brief which examined all the evidence available to me. It assured me that all events fitted my interpretation and that all the historic protagonists were consistently motivated.

I laid my rough draft aside for a month to consider its implications. The story that emerged from its densely packed pages was strange and new. It was unkind to both Japanese and Americans. More than half of my information had never before been reported in English. And the burden of it all was that Hirohito had not only led his nation into war by stamping military orders but, through his coterie, had also intimidated those who opposed him by conniving in bizarre Oriental intrigues, including religious frauds, blackmails, and assassinations.

I realized that it would be difficult for anyone to believe that what I had written was true when it was largely unknown to Western specialists on Japan and when much of it would be new even to well-informed Japanese. So many prior considerations had to be taken into account by the incredulous reader before he could suspend his disbelief. He had to know that ancient religious taboos still clung to the person of the Japanese Emperor; that until 1945 no Japanese plebeian ever dared utter the syllables *Hi-ro-hi-to*; that until 1945 Japanese commoners never looked at the Emperor except slyly from an almost prostrate position on the curb beside an imperial progress; that Japanese courtiers from time immemorial had been inventing artful stories to conceal the active participation of their masters in controversial affairs of state. The concept of god-king had passed out of memory in the West centuries ago, and Western observers in Japan had never had reason to put together all available scraps of information about the imperial family; they had readily accepted the conventional assertion that Hirohito was a ceremonial figurehead, for they had preconceptions about "constitutional monarchs" based on such figures as Queen Victoria. No firsthand records of day-to-day dealings with Hirohito had been published in Japan until 1966. And most important, General Douglas MacArthur, in hopes of recasting Japanese character in an American mold, had decided in 1945 to use the Emperor and to whitewash him rather than depose and expose him.

It would take pages of particulars, I felt, to make others understand these bizarre circumstances, and I foresaw that my pages might be roundly abused before the general reader would have a chance to look at them. Only twenty-five years ago millions of Japanese had died with a prayer on their lips of *Banzai*, "May the Emperor live ten thousand years." Since then Japan in 1967 had passed West Germany in gross national product to become the third-ranking nation on earth.

Yet as late as 1961, when a Japanese magazine published a fantasy about a robber who broke into a palace and beheaded a fictional emperor, the publisher found himself terrorized for having committed lèse majesté. Hired "patriots" from one of the underworld gangs forced their way into his print shop and smashed up his presses. Then they went on to his home, shot one of his servants dead, and wounded his wife. The Grub Street scribbler who had written the fantasy disappeared. Reportedly he went underground and some say that he emigrated to Brazil.

Through no virtue of my own, I had happened to revisit Japan during a period of historical re-evaluation in which some of the first important papers of the Imperial Court were published. These cast a new light on the rest of the documentation, a light which was particularly illuminating to anyone like me, going over the whole mass of materials freshly at one time.

The re-evaluation—so I was told later by a senior Japanese diplomat—had been launched by Hirohito himself. In the fall of 1963, at a palace banquet in support of literature, Hirohito had suggested to the writers at his end of the table that it was time to overleap the trauma of Hiroshima and to begin re-creating the true spirit of Japan's prewar and wartime history. World War II no longer seemed the colossal blunder it had in 1946 but a positive piece of statesmanship which had hastened the complete industrialization of Japan. The year 1965 would be the twentieth anniversary of the end of that war, and 1966 would be the twenty-fifth anniversary of the beginning of that war.

The historical re-evaluation begun in Japan in 1965 was conducted with extreme circumspection and aimed mainly at the knowledgeable Japanese audience. I had to make its implications explicit for the American audience. I had to explain feelings and motives which Japanese took for granted—especially the feelings and motives of Emperor Hirohito. In so doing, I would have to enter dark corners of Hirohito's life wherein I would have to hunt down clues and rely on circumstantial, as well as verbal and documentary, evidence.

Moreover, since history is continuous, I would have to offer to fit my interpretation into the whole course of Japanese history. I could not possibly make myself as much of an authority on the years 1866 to 1911 as I was on the years 1931 to 1945, but I would have to say what I knew about those years because it had not been said before and because the burden of my book related as much to the nineteenth, the seventeenth, or the twenty-first centuries as it did to the twentieth.

Also, I would have to present Hirohito as the leader of a "conspiracy," a word which, through overuse and jingoism, had become universally suspect. The International Military Tribunal for the Far East had handed down a verdict of "conspiracy to wage aggressive war" against Japanese war leaders and had uncovered no less than eight important conspiracies which had directed the course of Japan between 1928 and 1936. Conspiracy had an old and honored place in Japanese culture. Each of Japan's territorial armies in prewar days had had a team of staff officers which was officially called "the plot section." I had added six conspiracies to the list compiled by the Allied judges and had connected them all with Hirohito's central, imperial-family conspiracy. Hirohito had worked with a minority, in secret, first to lead Japan to war with the West and then, in defeat, to obscure the record.

Resolutely I entitled my work *Japan's Imperial Conspiracy*. I set out to select the most pivotal events from my research and to bring them alive with light and color. Wherever I felt I had enough information to work with, I did my best to make the

xl   *Author to Reader*

reader feel that he was present. If I knew from my own experience what a landscape looked like at a certain time of year, I re-created that landscape if it came up at that time of year. If I knew what brand of cigarettes a man smoked, I mentioned it when I reported that he was smoking. If I knew a man cracked his knuckles idiosyncratically, I took the liberty of saying that he cracked his knuckles at this or that juncture.

I also used certain rhetorical devices which may irritate some readers already familiar with Japan. To overcome the difficulty and confusion of Japanese names I tagged some of them, repetitively, with touchstone adjectives. I did this because I found that even specialists often lost track of minor characters in the cast of Japanese history and kept in mind no over-all picture of their careers.

Between 1967 and 1970, while I worked on my final manuscript, I received much help from Japanese who came to see me. I was honored by visits from an influential banker's son, a leading publicist, an in-law of the Japanese imperial family, and an important diplomat. All of these men were friends or children of Hirohito's closest advisors. Passing through New York, they breathed the freedom—or the social informality—of the United States and spoke much more candidly than even the best of my informants in Japan. Only one of them volunteered information to me, but I now had detailed knowledge of many of their relatives and close associates, and I was able to draw them out. In response to trivial questions they unburdened themselves.

They gave me many of the grace notes I needed and, more important, they assured me that I was right. They corroborated my interpretation and encouraged me to think that I was presenting a true view of an Oriental ideology during an era when Americans were preoccupied with European communism and fascism.

It seems to me that Western historians have gone too far in portraying the Japanese as creatures of mass hysteria. Japan's economic record belies such a patronizing attitude. Only a century ago, in 1868, Japan's economic development resembled that of England when Henry VII came to the throne in 1485. The transformation of the last century was not wrought by inscrutable mad-

men but by a most industrious and intelligent people. I have
had the awe and pleasure of knowing them all my life. It is a
basic premise of this book that Japanese leaders—and their Western counterparts also—have been very smart men.

When Allied armies overran Germany in 1945, they captured
millions of pages of the highest state papers. By contrast, when
the Allies began their negotiated Occupation of Japan, the war
had been over for two weeks and the only papers of any consequence which fell into American hands were placed there voluntarily by the Japanese themselves. The minutes of the meetings
of Imperial Headquarters, presided over by Emperor Hirohito in
his palace from 1937 to 1945, had all, it was said, been incinerated.
So had most of the files of the Army General Staff, the Navy
General Staff, and the secret police.

In my bibliography and source notes I have cited about a thousand books and documents which have provided me with items
of information. Most of them, however, have given me a single
detail or a single insight. Only a score of them have been exten-
sively helpful and all but two of that score were not published in
Japan until after 1960.

The only significant primary source documents turned over after the war to Allied Occupation authorities were diaries. Every
Japanese in an important position kept a record of his official life
in order to defend himself against the threats of blackmail or
charges of irresponsibility which were likely to be made against
him in the normal course of Japanese politics. All such daybooks
were of course written with an eye to the public and to posterity.
They might at any time be seized and produced in chambers by
the secret police. They might in later years be published by im-
pecunious grandchildren. And in the case of palace officials they
might always be requisitioned for research or recreational reading
by Hirohito himself.

Two of these carefully written journals, by men in the highest
policy-making circles, were placed in American hands during the
first two years of the Occupation. One was the *Kido Diary*, 1930–
1945, written by Marquis Kido Koichi who had been lord privy
seal and chief civilian advisor to Hirohito in the years 1940–

1945. Less than a tenth of it, selected for point-making reasons, was translated either by the prosecution or the defense and placed in evidence at the International Military Tribunal for the Far East. Another nine tenths of the diary, as it is presently available, were not released until 1966 when they were published by Tokyo University Press. Even in this form the diary still seems to be incomplete because the most eventful days in the period which it covers are filled with the notation "nothing to report."*

The second journal made available to the American Occupation forces has come to be known as the "Saionji-Harada Memoirs." These were ostensibly the notes of Japan's most eminent liberal statesman, Prince Saionji, who had the duty, until November 1940, when he was ninety-one years old, of recommending to the Emperor the name of the man to appoint as prime minister in each successive Japanese government. Actually the memoirs were composed by Saionji's political secretary, Baron Harada, a sly gossip and opportunist who acted as agent for Hirohito in Saionji's staff.

An English version of the Saionji-Harada memoirs was produced in twenty-five mimeographed volumes by a volunteer Japanese task force in 1946–47 for use by the defense at the International Military Tribunal. The translation was stylish but inexact. For instance, at several critical junctures it converted the lord privy seal or *naidaijin*, the Emperor's chief civilian advisor, into the home minister or *naimudaijin*, a Cabinet bureaucrat in charge of police.

The Japanese text of the Saionji-Harada memoirs was published in eight volumes in Tokyo between 1952 and 1956 under the title *Saionji-ko to Seikyoku* [Prince Saionji and the Political Situation]. The British scholar who undertook to read it on behalf of the Western academic community apparently glanced at it and then wrote two books which quote exclusively from the careless translation prepared for the defense section of the International Military Tribunal.

---

* As far as I have been able to discover, no one except for myself has read the complete text of the diary critically, comparing the terse entries with events recorded elsewhere. A graduate student of Japanese ancestry at the University of Washington has translated the previously untranslated bulk of the diary and his gloss, which I have not seen, will no doubt be put out by a university press in due course.

In 1956 a ninth volume of the Saionji-Harada memoirs was published in Japan, in a limited edition. It contained the notes of Harada on which the other eight volumes were based, and an index which made the other eight volumes useful. So far as I have been able to determine, few Western scholars except myself have made much use of this expensive, difficult-to-obtain ninth volume.

Twenty-two years after the end of the war, in 1967, two more important journals were published in Japan: the diaries of General Honjo Shigeru, written during the years 1931–1936 in which he led the conquest of Manchuria and in which he served Hirohito as chief aide-de-camp and military advisor; and the memoranda of General Sugiyama Hajime, written in the years 1940–1944 when he served at Imperial Headquarters as chief of the Japanese Army General Staff. Until 1970, neither of these primary source documents had been digested by Western scholars of Japan or much cited in Western scholarly journals. Yet they contained the stories of Hirohito's military advisors and greatly supplemented the two journals of the civilian advisors, Kido and Harada, which had been partially available since 1946.

These four diaries, of Kido, Harada, Honjo, and Sugiyama, contain more than half of all that is known of the highest deliberations of Japanese leaders in the years 1930–1945.

In addition I have reviewed most of the police files, personnel records, position papers, and military orders which were captured by American intelligence officers during the opening months of the Occupation. I have been through the 200,000-odd pages of testimony, proceedings, and collateral documentation put in the record by Japanese and Western sources at the International Military Tribunal for the Far East. I have scanned bushel-baskets of subsidiary exposés and reminiscences published in Tokyo in the late 1940's and early 1950's.

With more care, I have also examined some 300,000 pages of memoirs, journalistic reconstructions, and "lost" documents in anthologies which have emerged from Japanese presses since the end of the Occupation in 1952. I have found several thousand pages of this material worth reading word by word, especially the journalistic reconstructions based on extensive interviewing. I believe that the best of the Japanese secondary evidence stems from highly authoritative sources and is more honest than some of the primary material.* In addition there is a wealth of information available verbally from old men of importance who survived the war and are still alive.

I made wary but exhaustive use of all these materials. In handling them I gave high credence to chronology and cause-and-effect logic. I relied heavily on the indisputable record of deeds done by Japanese, as recorded in back files of newspapers, and of positions occupied by Japanese, as recorded in personnel records.† The color and much of the explanation with which I filled in my narrative were supplied almost entirely by word of mouth. Some of my informants pledged me to nonattribution, some did not. A few asked me to conceal the fact that I had interviewed them at all. I have kept these promises because of the danger which still exists for those who speak too freely in modern Japan.

There was one extraordinary Japanese aristocrat in his sixties who said to me, in English: "Why, I believe you are leading me on. What do you wish me to say? I knew Hirohito as a boy. He was a romantic warlike idiot then and I suppose he still is. But I have been out of things for several decades. I do not wish to be disturbed in my old age. If you quote me by name I shall deny that I ever met you."

Strict historians do not approve of using information from privileged sources. In dealing with American or European history they are certainly right in so feeling. For Japanese history—and perhaps for all Asiatic history—a case can be made for greater latitude. In most parts of the Orient, the very idea of a public record does not exist. To a far greater degree than in the West, state records belong to the statesmen who made them. The tradi-

* In particular the two volumes of reminiscences by retired Major General Ohtani Keijiro of the secret police; a short tract privately printed by the Empress's brother; an as yet unpublished 5,000-page opus by retired Lieutenant General Tanaka Takayoshi of Army Intelligence; and the volumes of Murofushi Tetsuro, Takahashi Masae, Fujishima Taisuke, Shimada Toshihiko, Hata Ikuhiko, Oyake Soichi, Agawa Hiroshi, and Kuroda Hisata.

† Most of the latter were kindly made available to me by Hata Ikuhiko, a civilian employee of Japan's modern Self-Defense Forces. Mr. Hata is the author of *Nichu Senso-shi*, The History of the Sino-Japanese War, and of *Gun Fuashizumu Undoshi*, The Record of Fascist Movements in the Japanese Army.

tion of a free press has no deep roots. Even the written contract in financial transactions has only begun to supplant the verbal agreement based on word of honor.

However, I think that any thoughtful scholar who takes the trouble to go through the source notes at the end of this volume will find that the essential facts of the story which I have told come from written diaries, memoranda, and memoirs. I have relied on privileged word-of-mouth sources primarily to corroborate my assessments of the facts, characters, and motives revealed in the primary source documents and to re-create as closely as possible the physical settings in which events took place. I have invented nothing but I have put together much. And I trust that from total immersion in the day-to-day, week-by-week record of Japanese history, I have gained an understanding of circumstances and nuances which has enabled me to shed more insights than I have committed errors.

So many people have helped me with this book that I cannot list them without fear of forgetting a few. I am especially grateful to the librarians of the Beinecke and Law School libraries at Yale, of the Doshisha and Kyoto University libraries in Kyoto, of the War Memorial Museum in Canberra, Australia, of the Fergusson Library in Stamford, Connecticut, and of the U.S. National Archives' War Documents Center in Alexandria, Virginia. There I would like to call attention to Thomas E. Hohmann as the most knowledgeable, unbureaucratic expediter of information flow whom I have ever encountered inside or outside of government.

Kitagawa Hiroshi, Koizumi Shinzo, Henry R. Luce, Douglas Mac-Arthur II, and my father were all particularly helpful in opening doors to me in Japan. Historian Hata Ikuhiko made available to me personal notebooks which he had compiled over a fifteen-year period. Retired Major General Tanaka Takayoshi allowed me to read part of his 5,000-page unpublished memoirs. Aso Shigeru, Lester Brooks, Don Brown, Robert J. C. Butow, Chiang Kai-shek, Otis Cary, William Craig, James Crowley, Grace Fox, Fujimoto Kazu, Fujisawa Shigezo, Frank Gibney, Giga Soichiro, Hashimoto Hirotoshi, Arthur Hummel, Inoki Masamichi, Inoue Ichiro, Kajiura Ginjiro, Kagami Mideo, Kawamata Yoshiya, Kobayashi Yoshiaki, Kotani Hidejiro, Matsumoto Shigeharu, Morishige Yoshi, Walter

Nichols, R. K. Ochiai, Ogawa Masao, Okumiya Masatake, Oya Soichi, Edwin O. Reischauer, Sato Yoshijiro, Osamu Shimizu, Roy Smith, Sung Yueh, Tachibana Yoshimori, Takahashi Shun, Takata Ichitaro, Takata Motosaburo, Tanaka Katsumi, Tsurumi Shunsuke, Uemura Kazuhiko, Elizabeth Gray Vining, William P. Woodard, Chitoshi Yanaga, all have given me their time and their kind and courteous attention. I am indebted to Hillel Black, John Cuneo, Alan Fraser, Lawrence Hughes, Peter Leavitt, Elizabeth Lucas, and Mary Newman for invaluable help and criticism in reducing my manuscript to its present form. My dear wife has lived with me and typed each of these pages more than once in the last six years. Finally I wish to express particular gratitude to a Buddhist priest and an innkeeper in Kyoto, to four retired Japanese generals, to three former members of Hirohito's Court, and to three second-generation members of Hirohito's circle of intimates without whose information this book would have been stillborn.

In writing the names of Japanese citizens, I have followed the native Oriental custom: that is, last name first and first name last. To do otherwise would be inconsistent, for the ruler of Republican China is known as Chiang Kai-shek, and it would be confusing to Westernize the order of his names by calling him Kai-shek Chiang. In dealing with Westerners, modern Japanese usually reverse the order of their names whereas most modern Chinese do not. In these pages the reader is asked to remember that family names are given first and personal names second according to the familiar bureaucratic formula, "Doe, John."

In daily life the second or personal name of a Japanese male adult is almost never spoken. Even good friends do not address one another as Jim or Harry but always as Mr. Jones or Mr. Smith. Moreover, the ideographs in which given names are written often have exotic pronunciations. In every case there is a right reading which was used by the man's parents when he was a child, but even the man's close associates in later life may not know what it is. The notorious World War II prime minister, Tojo, for instance, was listed for years in *Who's Who in Japan* as Tojo Eiki when in fact his name was Tojo Hideki. Many of these misreadings have become permanent fixtures of the historical record as it is set down in English. In the chapter which follows, for example, Lieutenant General Tada Hayao is known in most other books as Tada Shun. Throughout this work I have tried to give people the names their mothers actually called them. I have undoubtedly made or perpetuated some mistakes, for which I apologize in advance both to readers and to mothers.

Finally, I dedicate this work to a rather simple, old-fashioned proposition: that history is not determined by blind economic and demographic forces; that the much maligned masses of countries play little part in it; that the responsibility for it belongs primarily to a few willful individuals who take upon themselves the professional duties of government. Except in tiny city-state democracies or in broken-down societies, prey to anarchy, the people do not make policy. The leaders who do make policy are, I believe, enthusiastic patriots who come to identify their personal advancement with the national interest. They are open to persuasion only when they hope to get the best of a bargain or when they fear that their leadership position may be destroyed before the eyes of their followers. My story deals with leaders who recognize such homely truths; with leaders who look upon themselves as institutions rather than individuals; with leaders of a society which has a longer record of uninterrupted successful domestic political development than any other in the world.

PART ONE

✣

VENGEANCE
OF WAR

" 'The Emperor is sacred and inviolable' (Constitution, Art. 3). He cannot be removed from the Throne for any reason, and he is not to be held responsible for over-stepping the limitations of law in the exercise of his sovereignty. All responsibility for the exercise of his sovereignty must be assumed by the Ministers of State and other organs. Thus, no criticism can be directed against the Emperor, but only against the instruments of his sovereignty. Laws are not to be applied to the Emperor as a principle especially criminal laws, for no court of law can try the Emperor himself and he is not subject to any law."

Page 117, *The Japan Yearbook 1944-45*, published by The Foreign Affairs Association of Japan, an organization financed by the Japanese government.

1

RAPE OF NANKING

SHRINE OF REMORSE

High on a green hillside of gnarled pines and weathered rocks, some fifty miles down the coast from Tokyo, stands a more-than-life-sized statue of Kanon, the Buddhist goddess of mercy. She looks southwest toward China across the blue waters and white sands of Atami, a beach resort celebrated for its baths and its courtesans. She is made crudely of clay baked to a mud-gold glaze. Half of the clay is native Japanese soil; the other half came in sacks from China in 1938, dug from the banks of the great muddy Yangtze River. If you scramble up the rock on which the goddess stands and work your way around her pedestal, you find a four-foot clearing in the underbrush immediately behind her flowing robes. There, where they cannot be seen from the path below, seven slender boards of graying unpainted wood are stuck in the earth, each with a name lettered on it in black Japanese characters: Tojo Hideki, Itagaki Seishiro, Doihara Kenji, Hirota Koki, Kimura Heitaro, Muto Akira, Matsui Iwane. They are the names of the men hanged by the Allies after a two-year trial in 1948 as the Hitlers, Himmlers, and Goerings of Japan.

Nearby, on a terrace poised over the sparkling bay a thousand feet below, stands a small shrine. Its eaves are hung with ropes of colored paper—token presents to the spirits of the dead. On a lectern, at one end of the prayer rail that runs across the shrine entrance, is a guest book. Members of the families of each of the hanged men on the hill have signed it every month or two since the early 1950's. Inside the shrine, mementos of Japanese war dead hang on one wall and of Chinese war dead on the opposite wall. Between them at the altar, on most days most of the time, kneels the shrine priestess chanting prayers and lamentations. As she chants she strikes musically on a polished stick and weeps. She says, if you speak to her, that it is her duty to weep and that she has been weeping since 1938.

Beside the shrine is a tea pavilion for pilgrims who need to catch their breath after the steep climb up the hillside. It is hung with testimonials to the ideal of Pan-Asianism and with posterlike paintings of Chinese and Japanese toiling together in harmony. Along one wall of the tea pavilion runs a minutely detailed panorama of the monumental roofs and towers which once adorned the skyline of the Chinese city of Nanking. It was for Nanking that the priestess first began to weep—Nanking which for a decade in the 1920's and 1930's was the showpiece capital of China, Nanking where a brief experiment in republicanism intervened between the totalitarian eras of old Imperial Peking and new Communist Peking. The priestess weeps for Nanking because she is engaged to do so by her family, the Matsuis, on whose estate the shrine stands; because the name of her kinsman, General Matsui Iwane, is one of those on the markers up on the rock behind the goddess of mercy; because it was for Nanking that Matsui was hanged in 1948.

In 1937 Matsui's army, in a brilliant, brutal four-month campaign, smashed its way 170 miles up the Yangtze Valley from the port of Shanghai, captured Nanking, and subjected it to six weeks of gruesome, graduated terror. Between 100,000 and 200,000 Chinese were executed. At least 5,000 women, girls, and children were raped before they were killed. Everything of value in the city was pillaged and whole sections of it were systematically put to the torch. Before Warsaw, before Buchenwald, Nanking was the great atrocity. It convinced many Americans, for the first time, that the governments siding with Germany in the Anti-Comintern Pact were genuinely evil.

The goddess of mercy on the slope above Atami, built half of Yangtze and half of native clay, was already standing, in 1938, in acknowledgment of Japan's national guilt for Nanking. A decade later, after many more atrocities and the war with the United States, the markers for the seven hanged men were added secretly behind the statue. The markers were put there not to condemn the shades of the men to eternal penitence for Nanking but rather to signify that Japan's war criminals, like the Chinese murdered in Nanking, were considered sacrificial victims. In the eyes of most Japanese, they were not guilty in the sense charged by the international tribunal of jurists which had sentenced them. They were not evil conspirators who had forced Japan to war, not mad individualists like Hitler and his cohorts, but loyal servants of the Emperor, responsible officials of the government, symbolic scapegoats elected from the ruling circle to satisfy the requirements of Western justice. As such they deserved the mercy of the goddess and the special prayers of all those pilgrims who felt that they too had participated in the nation's crime.

Although Japanese almost unanimously condemn the sentence handed down at the war crimes trial in 1948, they do not therefore maintain that Japan went to war by majority choice or even that Japanese soldiers raped and killed without official encouragement. They say only that Japan is a collective family society and that it is impossible for any seven men to have been mainly responsible. They say that Japan is a hierarchic society and that none of the seven men hanged came from the topmost layers of the aristocracy. They say that Emperor Hirohito declared the war and that he is still the master of the Japanese nation. The priestess at Atami says that her shrine is a reminder "to the Emperor and the great vassals of the debt which they owe the people and the dead."

"It is not only for the former time," she explains, "but for today and the time to come that I remain at my post in prayer."

JAPAN AND CHINA

In 1937, when the crime of Nanking did not yet burden the Japanese conscience, Japan had been wresting territory from China for over forty years: the island of Taiwan and the penin-

sula of Korea in 1896; a New-England-sized piece of Manchuria
in 1931; the remaining Texas-sized piece of Manchuria in 1932;
the Kansas-sized province of Jehol in 1933; and Montana-sized
Inner Mongolia in 1935. Then in the summer of 1937 Japan
went on to launch a full-scale invasion of all that was left of
China, the populous heartland of some 500 million souls extending from the Great Wall in the north to the borders of Indochina,
Siam, Burma, and India to the south. First, in July, Japanese armies captured Peking, the old imperial capital in North China.
Then, in August, Japanese forces began to fight at the mouth of
the Yangtze River for the huge port of Shanghai which laid claim,
with New York, London, and Tokyo, to being the largest city
in the world. Shanghai was the doorway to Central China. Once
unlocked, it would open an easy passage to Nanking, the Chinese
capital, which lay 170 miles inland up the Yangtze River.

Ostensibly the war with China began because a Japanese private
left his unit for a few minutes while he went into the bushes to
urinate. While he was gone his comrades heard shooting. They
were men of the Japanese regiment garrisoned by treaty in the
northern Chinese city of Tientsin. They were out on night maneuvers near the ancient Marco Polo Bridge outside Peking.[1]
Their commander said, "I heard Chinese Communist shots"—and
ordered a roll call. Finding that the soldier who was urinating did
not answer the roll call, the commander advanced on the Chinese
fort at one end of the Marco Polo Bridge and demanded that it
open its gates so that the Japanese could search it for their missing comrade. When the Chinese commander refused, the Japanese
commander started shelling the fort. The absent soldier had long
since rejoined his battalion, but the war had begun.

Although two million Chinese were to die in it and one million Japanese were to fight in it, the Japanese government insisted, throughout the eight years that it lasted, on calling the
war the "China Incident." To this day, some Western historians
maintain that it really was an incident, beginning in an accidental brush between Chinese and Japanese troops and escalating
into a major conflict as a matter of military honor on both sides.

[1] A bridge decorated with stone lions which the Venetian traveler, six hundred and fifty years earlier, had called "unequaled by any other in the world."

In reality Emperor Hirohito of Japan had directed his General Staff to plan the war in early 1935. In March of 1936, still more than a year before the war broke out, Hirohito reviewed the plans which had been made. They were so detailed that they included even a description of the provocation which would be staged at the Marco Polo Bridge.

In the inner circles of Japanese government, the war was a controversial issue from the moment it was first planned. It was opposed, in particular, by the Japanese Army. A majority of the officers in the General Staff wanted to fight Russia, not China. The most zealous of them sought to change Hirohito's views by supporting an insurrection of junior officers in the streets of Tokyo in February of 1936. Hirohito refused to be swayed. Exercising his full powers as commander-in-chief, national high priest, and divine descendant of the sun goddess, he put down the insurrection and dismissed from the Army the ringleaders of the Strike-North or Fight-Russia faction.

Hirohito insisted on fighting China not because he bore any animosity toward the Chinese but because war with China had become a necessary part of the national program which he had inherited from his grandfather and great-grandfather. After Commodore Perry of the United States in 1853 had forced Japan at gun point to open her ports to Western commerce and settlement, Hirohito's great-grandfather had sworn an oath with his great vassals. The "redheaded barbarians" must be driven from Japan's sacred soil and Japan must "expand overseas" in order to create a buffer zone which would prevent any further profanation.

By the 1920's, Hirohito and his own great vassals had decided that the national program could not be fulfilled until Japan had added the East Indies to her empire. Except in the East Indies there was no adequate source of petroleum in Asia. And without petroleum for ships and airplanes, Japan could not hope to keep the "barbarians" at bay. To control the East Indies Japan needed ports and staging areas along the South China coast.

In the early 1930's Chiang Kai-shek, the ruler of China and a former protégé of Japan, ceased to co-operate with Hirohito. Like the Japanese Army, he insisted that the first enemy of Asian traditionalists was Russia and communism. It followed as the night the day that the necessary staging areas and dock facilities in southern China must be taken by force. At first Hirohito and his intimates thought to bring Chiang Kai-shek to reason by only threatening war. But in December of 1936, on a visit to a town in western China, Chiang Kai-shek was kidnapped by a group of his own soldiers. As a condition for his release, Chiang agreed to stand up to Japan and grant the Japanese no more concessions.

When the urinating soldier disappeared and Japan began pouring troops into North China, Chiang held to the political pledge he had made to his kidnappers and refused Hirohito's offered terms of peace. When Japan extended the fighting from the Peking area in North China to Shanghai in Central China, Chiang committed his best divisions to an all-out defense of Shanghai. At that point Hirohito and his advisors decided to make China get rid of Chiang Kai-shek and accept a more accommodating leader. The capture of Nanking was planned in the innermost recesses of the Imperial Palace in Tokyo to bring about Chiang's ouster.

MATSUI'S COMMAND

The eerie arrangements for the rape of Nanking began to be made on August 15, 1937. On that day General Matsui Iwane, the kinsman of the weeping priestess at the shrine for war criminals in Atami, the man who would go down in history as "the butcher of Nanking," was summoned by Emperor Hirohito to the Imperial Palace in Tokyo. Matsui's official car approached the great moat from the southwest. Beyond it rose a massive, mortarless, fifty-foot wall of gray granite erected in the sixteenth century. Atop the battlements grew pine trees. The corners of the tile-and-copper roofs on the white watchtowers curved up at their tips like wings about to fly. Beyond could be seen the crowns of giant hardwoods in the Emperor's private park, the Fukiage Gardens. There in a landscape of trees and rocks and ponds—perhaps the most carefully tended garden in the world—rambled the one-story buildings of unpainted weathered wood in which Emperor Hirohito lived. General Matsui had never seen them at close quarters. He had been no farther into the Inner Palace than the courtyard of white pebbles and the ghostly white wood Shrine of the Sacred Mirror where Hirohito worshipped his ancestors. Few but servants and members of the imperial family went farther.

Matsui's car threaded its way between the office buildings of government ministries on his right and the southwest wall of the palace on his left. Rounding the southernmost corner of the wall he crossed through Cherry Field Gate into the imperial public gardens. Thence across the moat, through Foot-of-the-Slope Gate, he arrived at the cluster of office buildings where clerks of the Imperial Household Ministry toiled over investment of the Emperor's hundred-million-dollar private fortune. Outside the office of the imperial aides-de-camp, Matsui alighted and saluted a fellow officer, an aide, who would lead him into the Imperial Presence. His samurai sword knocking against his ankle, Matsui followed the aide through a checkerboard of raked pebble courtyards, miniature gardens of dwarfed trees, and sundry outbuildings. Some of these unpretentious palace shacks were only kitchens; others were tiny research centers and libraries, the repositories of imperial family codes, genealogies, and contracts.

Emerging once more into open park, Matsui and the Emperor's aide passed the sprawling banquet hall and Privy Council chamber and came to the east entrance of the Outer Palace reserved for ceremonial functions. Here, a quarter of a mile from Hirohito's residence and from the Western-style study where he did most of his paper work, were the official audience chambers and anterooms in which Japanese history was, if not made, at least formalized.

General Matsui mounted a flight of stone steps, passed through a quiet reception area of muted gold screens and coffered ceilings, marched down a plain straight corridor, and stiffly saluted the Emperor's chief aide-de-camp who stood at the door of the Emperor's audience chamber. In accordance with ancient custom, Matsui untied his ancestral samurai sword and handed it to his guide, the junior aide, to keep for him while he was in the Emperor's presence. Then, he strode forward into the magnificent audience chamber, the Phoenix Hall. It was so named for the motif of fiery mythological birds which could be picked out everywhere in the parquet, brocade, lacquer, chased silver, and carved wood of its floors, walls, and ceilings.

The Phoenix Hall was empty. Matsui bowed double and remained bowing while he waited for Emperor Hirohito to show himself. In this room Hirohito was a god-king who could make no mistakes. In this room Hirohito never exercised the absolute power he was acknowledged to possess. In this room Hirohito acted only on the advice of his advisors. Beside Matsui bowed the chief aide-de-camp, waiting to advise.

Matsui had been sounded out by the chief aide-de-camp the previous day and knew that Hirohito was about to offer him a command in China. It was a great honor for him to be reactivated from the reserve for such an appointment. It was especially gratifying to him because he was a proponent of friendship with China. Only two months ago he had been hatching subversive plots to prevent an all-out war with China. He did not know it, but a secret-police report to that effect had recently crossed the Emperor's desk.[2] Two years ago, in August of 1933, when Matsui had first heard about the proposed conquest of China, he had asked to be retired from active Army command and had gone on a tour of Asiatic capitals seeking leaders who would support his personal dream of a united Asia. In Peking, he had tried vainly to establish a local branch of the *Toa Renmei* or East Asia League, a society which he had helped to found in Japan two years earlier.

Now that war between China and Japan was a reality, Matsui felt compelled, out of patriotism, to change his line somewhat. For the past month, in his public speeches for the East Asia League, he had been advocating a bold drive up the Yangtze River on Nanking, the Chinese capital. Swift capture of Nanking, he said, followed by humane occupation policies and an honest municipal administration, would persuade the Chinese masses to forsake Chiang Kai-shek and throw in their lot with the leaders of Japan.

---

2 His fellow conspirator, according to the secret-police report, was General Honjo Shigeru who will be met with in the pages that follow as the conqueror of Manchuria, then as the Emperor's chief aide-de-camp, then as a sympathizer with the Army rebels who tried unsuccessfully in 1936 to change the Emperor's mind.

That Hirohito, knowing Matsui's convictions, should be giving him a command in China was a good sign—a sign, perhaps, that Hirohito was beginning to understand the advantages of a negotiated settlement with China. Matsui would have felt happier, however, if his impending audience with the Emperor had been called in the concrete Imperial Library on the fringe of the Inner Palace. There in his workroom Hirohito was acknowledged to be a man and fallible. There he talked to other men. There he expressed opinions and invited discussion. Here in the magnificent Phoenix Hall he usually uttered only predictable formulas in the high-pitched official voice belonging to his position as national Shinto high priest.

As a devout Buddhist, the sixth son of a wealthy scholar of Chinese classics, Matsui paid only lip service to the state religion of Shinto ancestor worship. This bowing and waiting in the August heat made him feel older than his sixty years. After all, he was not a well man. His weight was down to one hundred pounds and that was too little even for his slight, five-foot frame. His medal-encrusted full-dress uniform stifled him. The humiliating tics in his right face and arm began to work uncontrollably. He felt as if one of his fevers might be coming on. His mind drifted. He entertained a brief vision of East Asia awakening under benevolent Japanese leadership—and felt somewhat better.

Suddenly the Emperor was present. With words of extraordinary solicitude he begged Matsui to stand at ease and come forward. He regretted that he had kept the general waiting and asked him how he was recuperating from his tuberculosis. Matsui straightened and marched unsteadily ahead. He saw his thirty-seven-year-old monarch standing before him in a plain unadorned khaki uniform, rumpled and slightly sweat-stained but buttoned to the neck. Hirohito had not been seen out of military uniform, now, for a year and a half.

Before Matsui had begun to answer the Emperor's question about his health, the chief aide-de-camp interrupted to remind Hirohito of his next appointment. Hirohito nodded and told Matsui that the latest flare-up of fighting in the port city of Shanghai, the gateway to Nanking, had reached a critical juncture. Hirohito had decided to dispatch a relief force of two divisions to assist the Marine garrison which was endeavoring to protect Japanese property in the port. He understood, he said, that General Matsui would be willing to lead such an expedition.

Matsui bowed low and, still feeling faint, began to explain the honor that he felt and also the convictions that he held as to the enlightened methods which must be used in bringing the Chinese over to the Japanese cause. Hirohito nodded approvingly and unrolled an official scroll of rice-paper parchment. At Matsui's first pause, the Emperor began to read in his high-pitched official voice. At a nudge from the chief aide-de-camp Matsui knelt. Hirohito proclaimed him commander-in-chief of Japanese forces in Central China and bestowed upon him a baton symbolic of his new command.

Matsui might have reflected that a retired general in his state of health, with his nervous frailties and somewhat mystic convictions, was an extraordinary choice for the duty which Hirohito had conferred upon him. Matsui, however, was in a daze. A few moments later he found himself riding out of the palace grounds sharing a car with the highest ranking of Hirohito's hereditary counselors, the lanky, cynical, effete Prince Konoye. At forty-six, after seventeen years as Hirohito's chief back-room crony, Prince Konoye had finally been appointed by Hirohito, just two months previously, as the nation's constitutional figurehead, the prime minister.

"There is no solution," said little General Matsui to Konoye in the car, "except to break the power of Chiang Kai-shek by capturing Nanking. That is what I must do."

At a farewell dinner given by his fellow directors of the East Asia League on the eve of his departure for China two days later, General Matsui explained, "I am going to the front not to fight an enemy but in the state of mind of one who sets out to pacify his brother."

MIRED IN SHANGHAI

As Japanese Intelligence well knew, Matsui would have a hard time of it. Chiang Kai-shek had saved his best troops from commitment in the war in North China and was pouring them into the action in Central China at Shanghai. Ordinary tactical considerations were complicated by the fact that Shanghai was the world's most cosmopolitan city. The United States, Great Britain, and France all maintained military garrisons there in addition to the Japanese and Chinese. English clubs, American hotels, French cafés, Russian bakeries, German rathskellers, and Japanese geisha houses, together with branch offices of all the largest commercial concerns on earth, rubbed walls with opium dens and brothels— the unparalleled poverty of China's worst slums.

When Matsui received his orders from Emperor Hirohito, the Japanese Marines stationed in Shanghai were fighting for their lives. Chiang Kai-shek's troops outnumbered the Marines ten to one and had collectively about half the fire power of the Marines. A Japanese fleet of destroyers, cruisers, and battleships lay out in the mouth of the Yangtze River pouring shells into the Chinese rear. A tiny Chinese air force, commanded by Madame Chiang Kai-shek, was doing its best to sink the Japanese fleet with ten- and twenty-pound bombs. A minority of the Chinese pilots had been trained in America and were harassing the Japanese fleet effectively. A majority of the Chinese pilots had been trained by an Italian mission sent to Chiang Kai-shek by Mussolini. They were greatly confusing issues by dropping bombs near Western ships in the harbor and even on the crowded streets of the International Settlement. The pursuit planes of the Japanese Naval Air Force were fighting back effectively and gradually knocking the Chinese pilots out of the sky. The bombers of the Japanese Army Air Force were raining down explosives on the Chinese slums with a carnage that was appalling.

By international agreement Japan was pledged, in waging war, to avoid all deliberate killing of civilian noncombatants. Quaint as it may seem today, the bombing of civilians was a novelty, little practiced before except in Spain's civil war and in Mussolini's aggression in Ethiopia. Japan's violation of the convention had begun on August 14, 1937. On August 13 Emperor Hirohito's uncle, Prince Higashikuni, had been appointed chief of the Japanese Army Air Force. In aristocratic Japanese circles, Prince Higashikuni was known as one of the boldest and most unscrupulous of Hirohito's retinue—a man with a long, unsavory record of Army Intelligence work, blackmail, and religious fraud.

Into this complicated military, political, and diplomatic situation, little General Matsui brought some 35,000 fresh troops on
August 23, eight days after his audience with Hirohito. As he
was landing his men, a hidden Chinese artillery emplacement
opened fire on the Japanese docks and killed several hundred
Japanese before it was silenced. One of those who fell was a cousin
of Hirohito's wife, Empress Nagako.[3] It was little General Matsui's
first setback and a foretaste of things to come. Chiang Kai-shek's
troops fought with a reckless courage that was unexpected. Against
their human-sea tactics every step of advance was taken over a
hill of corpses. After five days of action General Matsui had to
be reinforced by another regular division and two reservist divisions which had been forehandedly reactivated months earlier.

Even with five divisions at his disposal, Matsui could not break
out of the street fighting in Shanghai to drive upriver on Nanking. His progress was made doubly cautious by the presence of
the English, American, and French forces nearby who were
entrusted with protection of their own nationals in Shanghai's
International Settlement and French Concession. Japanese intellectuals in Army uniform who hoped to incite Western intervention caused almost daily incidents with Western Marines and
policemen along the borders of the various zones of foreign settlement. The Chinese Air Force, in the same spirit, had already
bombed two of the largest Western hotels and, with remarkable
accuracy, had killed some forty-odd foreign nationals.

General Matsui took extreme pains to keep his men from lob-
bing shells over the foreign settlements or from taking tactical
advantage of foreign leasehold soil. Although he spoke pigeon
English haltingly and pronounced French unintelligibly, he became a favorite source of Western newsmen and was invited to
dinner at some of the best homes in the foreign community. Little
by little his five divisions advanced out of the Japanese sector and
moved on, street by street and barricade by barricade, into the
native slums to the west. But it took time, and when two months

[3] Prince Fushimi Hiroyoshi. He recovered from his wounds but died of
complications a year later. The Chinese exulted, for his father, a cousin once
removed of Empress Nagako, was the chief of the Japanese Navy General
Staff.

had passed, Matsui was still battling his way out through the suburbs.

From the beginning Matsui's sluggish pace disappointed Hirohito and he began to feel that he must take more personal charge of the war. Up to that time he had supervised operations through two channels: over-all strategy through his wife's great-uncle Prince Kanin, chief of the Army General Staff; and detailed tactics through his cadre of aides-de-camp who shuttled back and forth between the palace and the General Staff Operations office three hundred yards from the palace wall. All divisional movement orders had to be signed by him ultimately, and he liked to be in on tactical deliberations before they arrived on his desk as fully developed plans. He had found in the past that unless he expressed his wishes early in every process of policy formulation he could not object to a detail later without making some underling lose face and tender his resignation.

In early September, Hirohito requested the creation of a Grand Imperial Headquarters inside the palace at which he could supervise staff planning personally. The membership and protocol of the headquarters, doing business as it would in the Imperial Presence—the presence of a god—naturally took some working out, and the Imperial H.Q. did not become a reality until mid-November. Hirohito insisted on it partly because of the stalemate in Shanghai and partly because he had learned in early September that some of his instructions to the General Staff were being filed and forgotten in the in-basket of the chief of the Operations Department, Major General Ishiwara Kanji.

Ishiwara was a brilliant strategist and had drawn up the plans for the conquest of Manchuria six years earlier, but he was also an idealist. With Matsui, the little tubercular general in Shanghai, he was co-founder of the East Asia League, the *Toa Renmei*. The League espoused war in order to create a united Asia in which Japanese would be equal partners with other Asian nationals. It stood in contrast to the Asia Development Union, the *Koa Domei*, which espoused absolute Japanese mastery and exploitation of Asia for "war eternal" with the other races. The founder of the Asia Development Union was Tojo, chief of staff of Japanese forces in Manchuria and later notorious as Japan's prime minister in World War II. Tojo was Ishiwara's most bitter enemy. Five days after Hirohito discovered that Ishiwara was not transmitting all his imperial instructions, Ishiwara was posted to Manchuria to become Tojo's assistant.

In the weeks that followed, a new chief of operations—appropriately named Shimomura Sadamu, or Shimomura the "Peace-Fixer"—drew up plans for a second expeditionary force to Central China which would outflank the stubborn Chinese defense of Shanghai and push on to Nanking. The development and realization of these plans were entrusted to members of the Emperor's own cabal of officers. These were colonels and generals in their forties who had become liegemen of one or another of the Emperor's uncles at the Military Academy and Staff College between 1905 and 1915.[4] Most of them had pledged themselves to Hirohito personally in 1921 in Europe when they were embassy Intelligence officers and he was a crown prince on a grand tour. Most of them had attended political indoctrination classes at a school in the palace in 1922–1924 and had become converts there to the idea that Japan's destiny lay to the south in the Indies.

As soon as plans for the Nanking operation were completed in October, the two young officers on the cabal who had been responsible for drafting the plans were assigned as assistants to General Matsui's staff in Shanghai to see that the plans were well understood and executed. At the same time one of the Emperor's kinsmen, his favorite aide-de-camp,[5] left Hirohito's side to take charge of the all-powerful Military Affairs Bureau which ran the War Ministry. Also at the same time, the most talented of the Emperor's cabal, Major General Suzuki Tei-ichi, was attached to the command of the 16th Division which would actually conduct the great rape.

Suzuki was one of the two or three young Army men whom Hirohito knew best and relied on most. His name will crop up so

---

[4] Emperor Hirohito had no true blood uncles, but Empress Nagako, his wife and distant cousin, had six uncles and nine avuncular first cousins. Two of her uncles and two of her uncle-cousins married Hirohito's blood aunts. The term "Hirohito's uncle" as used in these pages refers regularly to one or the other of his two double-uncles-in-law.

[5] Machijiri Kazumoto. He and the Emperor's uncle, Prince Higashikuni, on a trip to Paris in 1920, had been the two original founders of the cabal.

often in these pages that, to distinguish him from other Suzukis (other Smiths), he will be called the "ubiquitous" Suzuki. He had the keen, lean, professorial air of many successful stockbrokers: long face, high forehead, close-cropped hair, spectacles, and thoughtful creases around the jaw. As chief of the Cabinet Planning Board, he would become the czar of Japan's legislation and economic mobilization during World War II. After ten years in Allied prison, he remains at eighty-one, in 1970, one of Japan's best dressed, best spoken, best informed citizens.

The ubiquitous Suzuki supervised the rape of Nanking largely by radio from a desk at the home headquarters of the 16th Division in the old Japanese capital city of Kyoto. He probably supplemented his desk work by lightning plane trips to and from the front lines, but testimony as to the times and frequency of his inspections is confused and contradictory. He had known Chiang Kai-shek at Military Academy in Tokyo thirty years ago, and he had been used as Hirohito's personal emissary to Chiang on several past occasions. In addition he was the Army's leading economic expert. Thus he was equipped to fulfill a double function. On the one hand he would play the intermediary in secret radio negotiations between Chiang Kai-shek and Prime Minister Prince Konoye while the rape of Nanking was in progress. On the other hand, to defray invasion costs, he would direct his 16th Division in a systematic looting of Nanking.

When his most trusted minions in the Army had taken their ominous places, Hirohito issued an imperial rescript in October explaining that Japan was unleashing her military might "to urge grave self-reflection upon China and to establish peace in the East without delay." Prince Konoye and little General Matsui, the commander in Shanghai, both expanded on this thesis to itemize the political objectives of a drive on Nanking. They made two principal points: the Chinese must appreciate "the price they will have to pay" for "continued nationalism" and "anti-Japanese sentiments"; they must forsake the cause of Chiang Kai-shek and of his party, the Kuomintang or KMT.

RED TENTS

When the fourteenth-century Mongol conqueror Tamerlane invested a city, he is supposed to have camped before it in a white tent on the first day of the siege as a sign of mercy, in a red tent on the second day as a sign of mercy to women and children, in a black tent on the third day as a sign of mercy to no one. Matsui's expeditionary force to Shanghai had been Japan's white tent. Now in late October, when Chiang Kai-shek did not respond to Hirohito's edict, a second flotilla gathered in North Chinese and Japanese ports. It carried four and a half fresh divisions, some 80,000 men. It sailed in two shifts, a "red" and a "black." It struck at two ill-protected shorelines, the first well south and the last well north of the fighting in Shanghai. Logistically both landings were triumphs of amphibious technique on hostile beaches and deserve place in military annals beside the exploits of Napoleon in Egypt or of Caesar in Britain. They foreshadowed the landings of the later war in the Pacific.

The experts who presided over the amphibious technicalities had been working in Taiwan for three years, assigned to study the problems associated with the possibility of a Japanese attack on offshore islands like Java or Luzon. Half the men in the two armadas had been purged from the Army by Hirohito's order in the ideological struggles of the previous twelve years. The overall commander, who personally led the major southern prong of the task force, was himself a reactivated general, a small, bald, studious-looking strategist named Yanagawa Heisuke. He had been cast into the reserve as one of the three Army figureheads of the unsuccessful rebellion against Hirohito in 1936. General Yanagawa had been in Paris to greet Hirohito in 1921 when the then crown prince had made his first and only trip beyond the borders of his homeland. Yanagawa had been in and out of the palace at all hours as the vice minister of war between 1932 and 1934. In late 1935 he had taken charge of the Japanese army stationed in Taiwan and had superintended the development of many of the amphibious techniques which were to be tried out this day. Like most of his men he was hungry to re-establish himself in imperial

favor. When recalled to command in September, he had written
to his wife: "It is as if I were recrossing the Styx out of Hades; I
can see light ahead."

Early on the morning of November 5, 1937, Yanagawa's task
force steamed under radio silence into Hangchow Bay, a finger of
the China Sea some 40 miles south of Shanghai which reached
into the China coastline along the underbelly of Chiang Kai-
shek's southern flank. The transports, with over 60,000 men aboard,
hove to and waited for dawn off the waterfront of the little walled
town of Chin-shan-wei, Bastion of the Golden Mountain. On the
muted ships, over the grumble of taut anchor chains and the
squeak of the winches which were lowering assault boats, could
be heard the work chants of the awakening town, the "heya-hoa"
of coolies shouldering produce and refuse to and from the central
market place.

First light revealed a dawn fog clinging to the yellow waters
of the bay. General Yanagawa decided to wait for it to lift. This
low-lying green shore beyond the fog was the southern edge of
the swarming, industrious bayou land of the Yangtze River delta;
it was laced with sampan canals which would cause confusion
and casualties unless his men could see the whole lay of the terrain. To the rhythmic knocking of the assault boats against the
metal hull of the ship, Yanagawa wrote two bleak *tanka* (thirty-
one-syllable poems):

> The mist of morning
> has still not dissipated.
> Enveloped by it,
> I wait out ninety minutes
> that seem interminable.
>
> By the Emperor's
> inexorable mandate,
> the road that I take
> is like today's scenery
> washed entirely in tears.

When the effluvia of the bay began to melt under the rising
sun, Yanagawa donned a white surgical mask, such as Japanese

regularly wore in those days to prevent the catching or spreading
of colds. His common soldiers, hastily mustered under his command, did not yet know that he was the former vice minister of
war, and he thought it best that they should not recognize him
now. Yanagawa stepped onto the nets above the waiting assault
boats and ordered the first wave to cast off and make for the
beaches.

The Chinese soldiers in the area were taken completely unawares. By noon most of Yanagawa's three and a half divisions
were ashore and had invested the Bastion of the Golden Mountain. The next morning Yanagawa had clouds of advertising bal-
loons wafted aloft on an onshore breeze. They dangled scrolls of
false intelligence: "A million Japanese soldiers have landed at
Hangchow Bay." Provincial Chinese levies melted away before
the news. Those that stayed at their posts were quickly overrun
by the Japanese 6th Division which spearheaded the thrust north
from the beachheads. Its commander, Lieutenant General Tani
Hisao, later executed as a war criminal, is described by a contemporary Army commentator as beginning the advance by "gal-
loping off in eight directions in the fog with the fury of the demon
Ashura."

Three days after the landing, the 6th Division had burned and
blasted its way twenty-five of the forty miles to the outskirts of
Shanghai. On the third day it occupied the suburban city of Pine
Bay or Sungchiang. Nine weeks later a British correspondent managed to see what was left of Pine Bay. "There is hardly a building
standing," he wrote, "which has not been gutted by fire. Smoulder-
ing ruins and deserted streets present an eerie spectacle, the only
living creatures being dogs unnaturally fattened by feasting on
corpses. In the whole of Sungchiang, which should contain a
densely packed population of approximately 100,000, I saw only
five Chinese, who were old men, hiding in a French mission compound in tears."

BLACK TENTS

With their southern flank turned, the Chinese outside of Shanghai began to pull back to a line of pillboxes across the Yangtze

delta which had been planned by Chiang Kai-shek's German military aides for this very eventuality. Then the Japanese 16th Division, the "black" fleet from North China, steamed up the Yangtze estuary under cover of darkness and landed at a place called Paimou Inlet on the Chinese northern flank just behind the line of pillboxes. The second "black" half of Japan's seaborne pincer had closed. The executioners of Nanking had arrived. The new division was commanded from Kyoto by the ubiquitous Suzuki and in the field by Lieutenant General Nakajima Kesago, fifty-five, a small Himmler of a man, a specialist in thought control, intimidation, and torture. It was Nakajima who would superintend in detail over the Nanking atrocities. Like most of the other officers recently reposted to take charge of the Nanking operation, Nakajima had been in France as a member of Army Intelligence in 1921 and had then had the honor of being presented to Crown Prince Hirohito. Since the Army mutiny in Tokyo in 1936, Hirohito had employed Nakajima to keep peace in the capital as chief of the secret police or *kempei*.

Although Japanese officers rarely criticize one another in front of foreigners, they make an exception in Nakajima's case. In their words, Nakajima was a "hard man of sadistic personality."

"He is such an expert marksman," wrote one, "that he finds duckhunting 'ridiculous' and prefers to stand by a waterfall shooting robins as they come over in the downdraft. Now [in 1939] in North Manchuria, where he has been sent to preserve peace after the sacred war with China, there are no more 'bandits' to suppress and . . . he is no doubt morose. It must be a catastrophe for the robins of Manchuria."

"Nakajima drank too much French civilization," said another. "He fancied himself a Robespierre or Danton. He came to Nanking bringing special Peking oil for burning bodies."

"After we broke out of Shanghai," recalled a third, "my 11th Division advanced on a parallel course with Nakajima's 16th which had just landed. Every night from my sleeping floor I could see the glare of the villages they were firing. . . . Burned houses make bad billets. Only cowards are involved in such incidents."

After the war, Chiang Kai-shek's government charged that Nakajima's 16th Division, together with the 6th under "demon Ashura" Tani, took 390,000 lives in their advance on Nanking.

STOP LINE FARCE

In the trident of Nakajima hooking down from the north, Yanagawa stabbing up from the south, and Matsui thrusting out towards Nanking from Shanghai to the east, the retreat of Chiang Kai-shek's troops turned into a rout. The necklace of pillboxes scientifically strung across the Yangtze delta by German military engineers was abandoned with hardly a fight. Dark rumors circulated in China that it had been bought out with Japanese gold, and so in part it may have been, but in an over-all sense it fell to Japanese technique and daring.

After the Chinese retreat began, the Japanese divisions in the field did not pause in their pursuit. The General Staff in Tokyo made a great show for the Western press of drawing lines on the map and announcing that here the advance was to stop. At each line the men regrouped and then moved on as soon as they received secret orders from the Emperor to do so. The existence of such orders was not revealed until their publication by a group of retired generals in 1964.

At the time an impression was carefully created for foreign observers that the men at the front were out of hand and could not be controlled. The truth was that they had never been more scrupulously obedient, for they knew that a Grand Imperial Headquarters was being established in the palace and that their deeds would be watched by the sacred Emperor in person. The first stop line was drawn across the Yangtze delta on November 7. When all divisions had arrived at it on November 24, it was dissolved by the Emperor's order. The General Staff drew a second stop line that same day fifty miles farther west. Hirohito dissolved it unofficially three days later and officially seven days later.

By that four-day interval between unofficial and official orders hangs a typical palace tale. The vice chief of the General Staff in Tokyo, Lieutenant General Tada Hayao, disapproved of the attack on Nanking because he knew of the campaign of terror that was planned for the Chinese capital and felt that it would under-

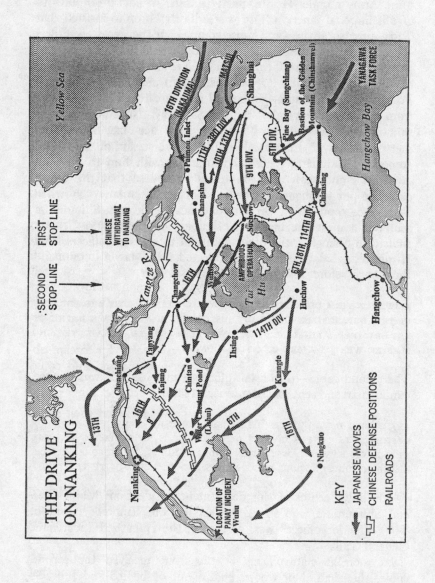

THE DRIVE ON NANKING

KEY

JAPANESE MOVES

CHINESE DEFENSE POSITIONS

RAILROADS

Yellow Sea

Yangtze R.

Hangchow Bay

SECOND STOP LINE

FIRST STOP LINE

CHINESE WITHDRAWAL TO NANKING

16TH DIVISION (NAKAJIMA)

Paimon Inlet

11TH · 3RD DIV.

10TH · 13TH

MATSUI

Shanghai

9TH DIV.

6TH DIV.

Pine Bay (Sungchiang)

Bastion of the Golden Mountain (Chinshanwei)

YANAGAWA TASK FORCE

Changshu

Changchow

16TH

Wusih

Suchow

Tai Hu

AMPHIBIOUS OPERATION

Chianging

6TH, 18TH, 114TH DIV.

Huchow

Hangchow

Tayyang

Chenchiang

Kajung

Chintan

Water Chestnut Pond (Lishui)

Ihsing

114TH DIV.

Kuangfe

Nanking

16TH

6TH

18TH

LOCATION OF PANAY INCIDENT

Wuhu

Ningkuo

13TH

mine Army morale. He steadfastly refused to advise Hirohito to give it imperial sanction. Just as steadfastly Hirohito insisted that Tada must so advise—and must countersign the necessary orders —because he was the vice chief of the General Staff. The task of persuading Lieutenant General Tada fell to the new, biddable chief of the General Staff's Operations Department, Major General Peace-Fixer Shimomura. He coaxed and threatened all week long from Monday, November 22, to Saturday, November 27. At midweek, on Wednesday, November 24, Peace-Fixer Shimomura met privately with Emperor Hirohito after a session of the Grand Imperial Headquarters staff and arranged with him to have all formalities and seals and counterseals ready so that the orders could be put through the Court machinery instantaneously when Tada once capitulated. On Saturday, nearing despair, Shimomura sent out a most irregular pair of cables, one official to General Matsui in Shanghai, the other unofficial to the staff officers from Hirohito's cabal who had been injected into Matsui's command the month before. The first cable to Matsui said:

KEEPING A FIRM DETERMINATION TO ATTACK NANKING WE ARE ENGAGED IN THIS DEPARTMENT IN STEADY DISCUSSION. HOWEVER, WE HAVE NOT YET OBTAINED A FINAL DECISION. ONLY REST ASSURED, PLEASE, THAT NO MATTER WHAT, WE ARE COMING AROUND.

The second cable—to the staff officers under Matsui—was marked confidential and sent special priority. It said:

ALTHOUGH I HAVE NOT YET OBTAINED A DECISION FROM OUR SUPERIOR OFFICER, THE CENTER OF THIS DEPARTMENT IS ENTHUSIASTIC FOR THE ATTACK ON NANKING. WITH THIS UNDERSTANDING, THEREFORE, PLEASE ABANDON YOUR PREVIOUS OCCUPATIONS AND GO AHEAD WITH IT.

The only "center of this department," aside from Major General Shimomura who signed the cables, was Emperor Hirohito. The "superior officer" was, of course, the embattled Lieutenant General Tada.

As soon as staff officers at the front received the second cable, they had their troops bugled out of bistros and brothels in the two principal cities on the second stop line and made ready to plunge onward. The stubborn Tada in Tokyo was threatened with the possibility that the troops would move without orders—a stain on Army honor for which he, as vice chief of staff, would be made to take the responsibility. Faced with retirement and disgrace on the one hand and on the other promises of a prosperous future, Tada gave in on the evening of the day the cables were sent. He stipulated that the orders be dated December 1, four days hence—a peculiarly Japanese way of putting on record the fact that he was acting under duress. He also asked that Emperor Hirohito acknowledge his responsibility for the orders by promulgating them in the form of an imperial edict to the whole people of Japan.

Tada conceded that he would carry the orders to the front himself and that they need not mention the second stop line but should merely say, "Take Nanking." An imperial edict required imprimatur by the Great Seal of State and by the counterseals of chamberlains who were ordinarily scattered about in villas and spas all over Japan. Usually the formalities took a week or more. Now, to Tada's astonishment, all arrangements had been made in advance; Emperor Hirohito, in perfect propriety, was able to affix the Great Seal to them the next morning, Sunday, November 28. Tada then completed his demonstration of dissent by taking three days to deliver the written orders to Shanghai, a one-day flight away. However, the orders were radioed to the front immediately, and the troops poured over the second stop line minutes after receiving them. Some of the men were under the impression that they were ordered to "take Nanking, effective December 1," which meant that they had more than 100 miles to go in three days.

The "white" divisions of Matsui and the "red" divisions of Yanagawa now began a race to see which could reach Nanking first. Matsui's men made a brilliant start by an amphibious flanking thrust across the Tai-Hu or Big Lake which lies just west of the Yangtze delta, about halfway between Shanghai and Nanking. Yanagawa's men, skirting the same lake on the south, more than kept pace. On the northernmost front, the "black" 16th Division of the sadistic Nakajima, who was to conduct the Rape, loafed along in the rear. On December 1, when the Emperor's orders to take Nanking arrived officially, all forces were running well but all had over fifty miles to go before they could comply.

The campaign had cost the Japanese 70,000 casualties already and would cost them another 40,000 before Nanking was taken. In the decimated forward regiments battle fever propelled the men on nerves alone. Inter-unit rivalries had always run fierce in the Japanese Army, making mortal combat out of the traditional barroom brawl. But now, according to surviving veterans, the chase up the Yangtze delta had brought the men to such a competitive pitch that they were burning villages, slaughtering cattle, and carrying off girls solely to deprive men from other units of billets, food, and entertainment. Their mood may be gauged from an item passed by the censor and printed on December 7 by the *Japan Advertiser*.

SUB-LIEUTENANTS IN RACE
TO FELL 100 CHINESE
RUNNING CLOSE CONTEST

Sub-Lieutenant Toshiaki Mukai and Sub-Lieutenant Takeshi Noda, both of the Katagiri unit at Kuyung, in a friendly contest to see which of them will first fell 100 Chinese in individual sword combat before the Japanese forces completely occupy Nanking, are well in the final phase of their race, running almost neck to neck. On Sunday [December 5th] . . . the "score," according to the *Asahi*, was: Sub-Lieutenant Mukai, 89, and Sub-Lieutenant Noda, 78.

A week later, the day after Nanking had already fallen, the *Advertiser* went on to tell that the goal had been extended to 150 because referees had not been able to determine which contestant had reached 100 first. "Mukai's blade," it reported, "was slightly damaged in the competition. He explained that this was the result of cutting a Chinese in half, helmet and all. The contest was 'fun' he declared."

After moving 120 miles in a week, against the grain of the few motor roads in the region, the "red" men of the eager, disgraced Yanagawa occupied Lishiu, or Water-Chestnut Pond, on Saturday, December 4. From there it was only thirty miles north along a good highway to the Nanking city walls. There, however, a last-ditch line of resistance had been improvised by fresh provincial Chinese levies who were defending their own homes and paddies. Yanagawa's weary soldiers could not make a breakthrough and were held up for almost three days. Farther north, Matsui's "white" troops reached the same stubborn line two days later and proceeded to blast through the Chinese entrenchments with a salvo of all-out infantry charges. Still farther north, the sadistic Nakajima and his "black" forces cut out cross-country after a ride along the Shanghai-Nanking railway tracks and, meeting little resistance, began to catch up with their fellow runners.

CHIANG CORNERED

Within the walls of Nanking, Chiang Kai-shek had lived through a month of bitter disillusionment. At his request, on September 12, the League of Nations had called a conference of law-professing nations which had met from November 4 to November 24 in Brussels. The conference had closed without taking action except to censure Japan mildly. Chiang Kai-shek's German advisors had asked for more support from Berlin and had learned that the faction of Foreign Minister Ribbentrop, favoring Japan, had won Hitler's ear. Russia, caught in the toils of Stalin's latest purge, could send only a few more planes and pilots to Chiang. The United States sent retired Air Force General Claire Chennault and a score of flying adventurers, but American planes, already bought and shipped, were being off-loaded and held in Californian ports. On December 2 Chiang Kai-shek met with his generals and agreed to accede to Japanese terms. From a Japanese point of view, they were moderate, amounting to no more than official Chinese recognition of *de facto* realities: an autonomous Inner Mongolia; an enlargement of the international demilitarized zone around Shanghai; an alliance with Japan against Russia; demilitarization of a two-hundred-mile-wide strip along the Manchurian frontier which would include the old capital of Peking; appointment therein of officials friendly to Japan.

On accepting the terms in principle, Chiang learned on December 5 that the situation had changed and that Japan was no longer willing to offer any peace terms. Chiang therefore told his neutral negotiator, the German ambassador to China, Oscar Traut- mann, that further negotiations were impossible in the military predicament of the moment. Chiang proceeded to evacuate the last skeletal bureaus of his government from Nanking. He and his staff followed on December 7, when he flew to Hankow, 350 miles farther upriver, and there established a new temporary cap- ital.

HIROHITO'S UNCLE

By December 7, 1937, the 300,000 troops remaining between the Japanese forces and their goal, Nanking, were in complete disarray, and the Chinese capital was effectively naked of any de- fense except its own ancient brick walls. Four divisions of weary, overstrung Japanese soldiers were converging on the city across a cold, ravaged countryside: Yanagawa's "red" 6th and 114th, Mat- sui's "white" 9th and Nakajima's "black" 16th. As the bloodthirsty troops closed in, General Matsui lay bedridden with a tuber- cular fever at his field headquarters in Suchow in the Yangtze delta. On December 2, five days earlier, Emperor Hirohito had relieved him of personal supervision of the men in the field and had moved him up to over-all command of the Central China theater. In his place as commander-in-chief of the Army around Nanking, Hirohito appointed his own uncle, Prince Asaka.

Despite the fact that he was a member of the imperial family, Prince Asaka was a tough professional soldier and in his thirty- year rise from cadet to lieutenant general had enjoyed few favors or sinecures. A lean, silent aristocrat of fifty, he walked with a pronounced limp which he had acquired in a car crash outside of Paris in 1923 during his three-year posting there—with his present helpmeets Yanagawa and Nakajima—as a military intelligence of- ficer. Once a versatile athlete, he had concentrated on golf since his accident and now played one of the best games in Japan. He used it along with his fluent French to entertain most of the lu- minaries who visited Tokyo from Paris in the 1930's. During the Army mutiny of February 1936, at an emergency meeting of the Council of Princes of the Blood, he had sided with Emperor Hirohito's brother Chichibu in urging consideration of the grievances of the Army's Strike-North or Fight-Russia faction. Afterwards, in a memorandum for the palace rolls, Hirohito had singled him out for censure as the one imperial kinsman whose attitude was "not good." He had been given this present disagreeable duty at Nanking as an opportunity to make amends. When he had performed it, as he would perform it, all too well, he would return to imperial favor.

Prince Asaka's appointment to the front, overriding all other authority in a wave of imperial influence, gave the sick General Matsui premonitions that his command was about to be abused. He ordered his armies to pull up and regroup three to four kilometers outside the Nanking city walls, to go into the city with only a few well-disciplined battalions, and to make sure that the occupation was carried out in such a way as "to sparkle before the eyes of the Chinese and make them place confidence in Japan." Then he called the staff officers of his legions together at his sickbed in Suchow and issued them a most extraordinary tablet of moral commandments:

The entry of the Imperial Army into a foreign capital is a great event in our history . . . attracting the attention of the world. Therefore let no unit enter the city in a disorderly fashion. . . . The units entering the walled city shall be the ones especially chosen for that purpose by the divisional commanders concerned. Let them know beforehand the matters to be remembered and the position of foreign rights and interests in the walled city. Let them be absolutely free from plunder. Dispose sentries as needed. Plundering and causing fires, even carelessly, shall be punished severely. Together with the troops let many military police and auxiliary military police enter the walled city and thereby prevent unlawful conduct.

Prince Asaka left Tokyo by plane on Sunday, December 5, and arrived to take command at the front three days later. He found his old companion of Paris days, the sadistic Nakajima, installed in an abandoned Chinese country villa near advanced field headquarters some ten miles southeast of Nanking. Nakajima was laid up with a painful flesh wound in the left buttock received that Sunday. He reported to his former princely patron that the Japanese forces had broken through everywhere at the outer Nanking perimeter and that some 300,000 Chinese troops were about to be surrounded and pinned against the Nanking city walls. Preliminary negotiations indicated that they were ready to surrender. After Prince Asaka had heard this summary, a set of orders went out from his headquarters, under his personal seal, marked "secret, to be destroyed." They said simply, "Kill all captives." The Chinese soldiers sensed a change in attitude and fled for the walls of Nanking. At least three quarters of them lived to fight another day. The remaining 75,000 men were later trapped in Nanking and contributed substantially to the fatality statistics compiled by Western observers in the city during the rape. Prince Asaka's staff officer for Intelligence, a lieutenant colonel, claimed to friends that he had forged the "kill" orders on his own initiative. If he did, it is remarkable that he was not courtmartialed but continued his fighting career until June of 1945 when he died, a lieutenant general, in the caves of Okinawa.[6]

THE PANAY DIVERSION

After Prince Asaka's dispatch to the front, during the final days before the capture of Nanking, Emperor Hirohito is described by one of his courtiers as "taking no recreation and exercising a wide intensive supervision of military operations." Prince Konoye, the prime minister and long the specialist in domestic politics within Hirohito's coterie of young men, feared that the Emperor might be losing his perspective in a welter of military detail. Though a prince, the lanky cynical Konoye belonged not to the imperial family but to the equally ancient and aristocratic Fujiwara clan whose duty it had been for thirteen hundred years to stand around the Throne as "ministers on the left" and "ministers on the right" and protect emperors from the consequences of their own cloistered enthusiasms. No courtier knew better than Konoye how to humor Hirohito. With no other palace familiar did the young

[6] Cho Isamu. Earlier, in 1931, he had helped to organize, under palace auspices, a pair of fake coups d'etat which served to confuse issues and ease settlements during the domestic political crises attendant upon the conquest of Manchuria.

Emperor feel more equal—more free to argue, to talk personalities, to bandy criticism.

On November 20, when Hirohito established his Grand Imperial Headquarters, Prince Konoye had stormed into the palace to protest the fact that he was not included in the headquarters even as an observer. Hirohito assured him that it would be a purely military conclave, of great stiffness, in which a politician would have no interest. Konoye replied that military decisions were always of political interest. "I would like to resign," he declared, "before this second strategy in China begins." Accustomed to such dramatic outbursts from his favorite, Hirohito begged Konoye to remain in office and soothed him with a promise: "I myself will keep you fully informed on military operations."

Konoye had voiced no previous objections to the war with China. On the contrary, if Japan became embroiled deeply enough in China she might be prevented from making a disastrously premature attack on Russia to the north or on the United States and Great Britain to the south. All autumn long Konoye had been fighting a running battle with officers in the General Staff who wished to fight Russia and avoid involvement in China. They had opposed the expeditionary force to Shanghai, opposed reinforcing it, opposed the additional landings south and north of Shanghai, and opposed the orders to take Nanking. Most recently they had sought to accept Chiang Kai-shek's offer of conditional capitulation, and Konoye had been hard put to it to increase the severity of Japanese demands so that Chiang would not accept them. It was difficult for a politician to stand against militarists when they wanted to make peace.

Now "this second strategy in China" threatened Konoye's objectives in a different way. He had helped to persuade Hirohito that no acceptable deal could be worked out with Chiang. He had urged, without much personal conviction, that the capture of Nanking would cause Chiang's generals to desert him and would make possible the establishment of a puppet Chinese regime co-operative toward long-range Japanese aims. But this new strategy which was to be pursued at Nanking gave Konoye pause. He may not have known much about it, but he knew enough to feel squeamish about presiding over it as prime minister. If terror and destruction at Nanking were carried far enough, they might even succeed in toppling Chiang Kai-shek. Then the problem would be to prevent Hirohito and the Navy from proceeding too fast with plans for an attack on Malaya and the Indies.

On December 7, after another audience with the Emperor, Konoye felt that his worst fears were coming true. He knew from his sources in Chiang Kai-shek's suite that the Chinese leader had fled Nanking that day. The troops were closing in. And Hirohito was entirely absorbed in long-term military planning. Konoye complained to Marquis Kido, another of the Emperor's intimates: "I just met with the Emperor and he is talking of strategy all the way up to next March. He mentioned sending a division to Canton, which surprised me because I had heard nothing of such a strike before." Canton lay only fifty-seven miles from the British crown colony of Hong Kong. Hirohito had already signed the orders to attack it. "If things go on this way," continued Konoye, "I cannot take the full responsibility. I told the Emperor that after observing the results of the capture of Nanking, I may have to ask for a change of Cabinet. The Emperor seems to have no objections."

Five days after Konoye's audience with Hirohito, an old crony of the prime minister, a reactivated reserve colonel of artillery named Hashimoto Kingoro, torpedoed the plans to attack Canton by singlehandedly instigating a celebrated international incident, the sinking of the U.S. gunboat *Panay*. Shortly after Chiang Kai-shek fled his capital, Hashimoto's artillery regiment had reached the Yangtze by an overland route sixty miles upstream from Nanking. There, near the town of Wuhu, he had laid out a two-mile gauntlet of heavy field pieces along the river bank in order to cut off fugitives attempting to escape up the river from Nanking. Late on Saturday, December 11, he had shelled a ferryboat load of British refugees and a British gunboat, the *Lady Bird*, and killed a British sailor. On the following morning he learned that a second convoy of Western refugees, consisting of three Socony-Vacuum tankers and the little U.S. gunboat *Panay*, was waiting out the occupation of Nanking at a safe anchorage downriver, halfway between the battery and the beleaguered city. Colonel Hashimoto commanded a squadron of naval aircraft which had been attached to his unit to help him blockade the river. He ordered his naval pilots to attack the U.S. ships. The pilots, although they were not commissioned officers, questioned Colonel Hashimoto's orders and took off only after long argument.

At 1:30 P.M. ordinary Sunday routine was being observed aboard the *Panay*. Eight of her officers were off visiting with the civilians on the three nearby tankers. It was a fine clear day. The two huge American flags painted on the *Panay*'s decks glistened in the bright sunlight. At 1:38 three twin-motor planes in V-formation were seen coming in at a considerable height from the southwest. Red circles on their underwings proclaimed them Japanese, which was reassuring, because the Japanese had been notified of the *Panay*'s position, and Japanese pilots, unlike their Chinese counterparts, were not known for dropping bombs by mistake. Then suddenly black dots detached themselves from the bellies of the three planes and a moment later, in what was for that time a miracle of precision bombing, the *Panay* was mortally damaged. One bomb scored a direct hit on her bow and a second stove a hole in her starboard side. The engines were knocked out. The three-inch gun was disabled. The pilot house, sick bay, and radio shack were demolished. The captain went out of action with a hipful of shrapnel.

Before the crew could recover from this instant devastation, six single-engine biplane fighters bore in from the south, unloading smaller anti-personnel bombs. The executive officer, who had just assumed command, took a piece of shrapnel in the throat and could not speak. He continued to issue orders, scribbling them on slips of paper. The slow biplane fighters wheeled and climbed and came in singly for a second and third run of dive bombing. The crew of the 30-caliber machine gun on the afterdeck collected itself and began to return fire. Two of the planes answered in kind. After twenty minutes of bombing and strafing, the *Panay* was listing to starboard and slowly settling, and the attacking planes turned their attention to the three Socony tankers.

Every one of the *Panay*'s line officers was wounded along with almost every member of the crew. At 2:00 P.M. the mute executive officer scrawled an order to abandon ship. As the wounded

were being ferried ashore, one of the planes returned briefly to
strafe the open lifeboat. By 3:00 P.M. the decks of the *Panay*
had been emptied and were awash with the yellow waters of the
great septic river. When she did not sink at once, two mates
rowed back to her to take off provisions and medical supplies.
A Japanese launch approached the *Panay*, swept her decks with
machine-gun fire, and put aboard an inspection crew. A moment
later the Japanese seamen could be seen leaping back into their
boat and hurrying away. Five minutes later, at 3:54 P.M., the
Panay rolled onto her starboard side and sank. Two of the tankers were burning and the third had been grounded on a mud
bank. Their passengers and crews, together with the men of the
Panay, hid out for three days in the rushes of the riverbank. They
were finally rescued by the U.S. gunboat *Oahu*. In all, two Americans were dead, one dying and fourteen others critical litter
cases. A considerable number of the Chinese crewmen of the
tankers had also been killed or wounded but could not be counted
because many of the survivors had fled into the countryside.

On the day after the sinking of the *Panay*, President Roosevelt
unofficially requested the Japanese ambassador in Washington to
transmit his "shock and concern" directly to Emperor Hirohito.
It was an unprecedented step which disregarded the façade of
Japan's official government. Chamberlains with diplomatic experience encouraged Hirohito to think that it might presage a declaration of war by the United States. Ambassador Joseph Grew in
the American Embassy a few blocks from the palace had servants
start packing his trunks and let it be known that the situation
reminded him of Berlin in 1915 when the *Lusitania* had been
sunk. Japanese Foreign Minister Hirota Koki immediately offered
apologies and promised an indemnity for the families of the bereaved and wounded. Japanese private citizens flocked to the
American Embassy and stopped embassy staff members on the
streets to express their regrets. One well-dressed Japanese woman
cut off a tress of her hair in the embassy lobby and submitted it
with a carnation to signify that she felt as if she had lost a husband. So much unsolicited condolence money poured in to the
embassy that Grew finally rounded it out and contributed $5,000,-
000 to Japanese charity. Vice Navy Minister Yamamoto Isoroku,

who would later lead the attack on Pearl Harbor, publicly accepted the full responsibility for the incident and privately fumed because he could not force the Army to discipline its Colonel Hashimoto who had ordered the *Panay* to be sunk.

Through Konoye's patronage, the guilty Hashimoto enjoyed impunity. He continued in command of his artillery regiment until March of 1939. When he finally doffed his uniform, Prince Konoye was organizing a one-party system for Japan—an Imperial Rule Assistance Association which would serve as a reasonable facsimile of the Nazi party in Germany or of the Communist party in Russia. Konoye made Hashimoto executive director of the new monolithic party.

By sinking the U.S.S. *Panay* and shelling H.M.S. *Lady Bird*, Colonel Hashimoto did succeed in making the planned attack on the Hong Kong area too dangerous for execution. On December 20, eight days after the *Panay* incident, 30,000 Japanese troops were embarked on transports in harbors along the southwestern coast of Taiwan. Two days later, at Konoye's urging, Hirohito reluctantly ordered them back ashore and postponed the attack on Canton for ten months. A strong presumption exists that Konoye sent a messenger to China to ask Hashimoto to sink the *Panay*. It is reinforced by the fact that a few days after the *Panay* sinking, an emissary of Konoye, sent to feel out Chinese politicians on a puppet regime which might replace Chiang Kai-shek's government, was mistakenly apprehended by the Japanese secret police in the port of Osaka and prevented from leaving Japan in time to keep his appointments on the continent.

On the day of the *Panay* sinking, December 12, Konoye moved into a new villa in the suburb of Ogikubo. At the housewarming he told one of his guests, "I can no longer bear it. When Nanking falls, Chiang Kai-shek's government must fall. If it does not, I am to issue a statement of nonrecognition of Chiang and to refuse to deal with him. I think that is the time for me to withdraw. I shall resign then." A statement to the effect that Japan would refuse to deal with Chiang Kai-shek and would found its own puppet government in China had already been drafted by Hirohito's kinsman and favorite aide-de-camp, Machijiri. Konoye did finally issue a version of the statement a month later when the rape of Nanking was reaching its final stages. But neither Konoye nor Chiang Kai-shek resigned, and Konoye's new home at Ogikubo came to be known in the Japanese vernacular as the "Hate-China" Villa. By the uninformed Japanese masses, in short, Konoye was held responsible as prime minister for the butchery at Nanking.

THE ELEVENTH HOUR

In the bleak winter landscape of resting rice paddies outside Nanking, the little mud-walled villages of farmers' huts were almost empty. By December 10, three days after Chiang Kai-shek had left the capital, almost 800,000 of the 1,000,000-odd inhabitants of the city had fled upriver. Eighteen million refugees from the Yangtze delta had passed through the environs of the city and most of them, too, were now on their way into the hinterlands. The Chinese rearguard of about 100,000 soldiers bundled any civilians remaining in the suburbs inside the city walls; in accordance with "a scorched-earth policy of resistance" enunciated two months earlier by Chiang Kai-shek, they proceeded to burn every outlying field and roof that might be of use to the invader.

As the sound of cannon fire approached, the Chinese troops manned the great brick walls and waited. Twenty feet thick and fifty feet high, the notched medieval battlements presented a substantial impediment even to modern artillery. Within them the old medieval city had been razed during a peasant rebellion eighty years earlier. Now, except for several dense Chinese residential and commercial areas, it was a monumental government park, studded with new public buildings and full of open vistas in which pheasants nested. As the Chinese troops waited to be attacked, they respected the republican dream embodied in the city. They stole a few bicycles and broke into a few shops but connoisseurs of warfare in China were struck by their exemplary discipline, their solemn good behavior.

American, German, and British residents remaining in the city organized a safety zone, a noncombatant area of one and a half square miles around the major missionary, university, and hospital properties. The fleeing Chinese government had turned over to the zone's administrative committee of foreigners 450 policemen, 10,000 sacks of flour, $400,000 in cash, and four million pounds of rice. It was hoped that in the zone Chinese civilians might find refuge for a few nights until the Japanese had completed their occupation and re-established law and order. Such a scheme had been tried in Shanghai and had been welcomed by the Japanese. General Matsui had contributed almost $3,000 out of his own pocket to help defray its expenses.

But in the case of Nanking, the Japanese refused in advance to sanction a safety zone. And before attacking, they advised that all non-Chinese should leave the area. Consular officials and most Western businessmen complied under orders from their head offices. Some retired to Western gunboats on the river like the *Panay*, others to a huge floating wharf of transit sheds and checkout shacks maintained by the British Jardine-Matheson Steamship Company. Twenty-two university professors, doctors, missionaries, and businessmen, however, remained inside the walls, including fifteen Americans and six Germans. Because of their presence the occupation of Nanking was carefully documented as the occupation of other cities west of Shanghai had not been. The Germans in particular had a chance to see all, for they felt protected by the Anti-Comintern Pact and walked about freely wearing swastika arm bands.

On Thursday, December 9, two battalions of Matsui's 9th Division drove to within a trench line of the southeastern walls. General Matsui had leaflets dropped from planes, promising clemency and suggesting truce procedures for handing over the reins of civil government. At midday on Friday two of Matsui's staff officers stood for three hours outside the Mountain Gate in the eastern wall, waiting to see if the Chinese would send out a delegation under flag of truce to cede the city. When none came, Hirohito's uncle Prince Asaka ordered a general assault. According to Tokyo's *Asahi* newspaper, the next day, Prince Asaka stood Napoleonic on a hill to the east and "watched the fall of the city surrounded by clouds of gunsmoke." In the morning commoners in Tokyo were rewarded with the opportunity of eating specially decorated dishes of *Nanking soba*, Nanking noodles.

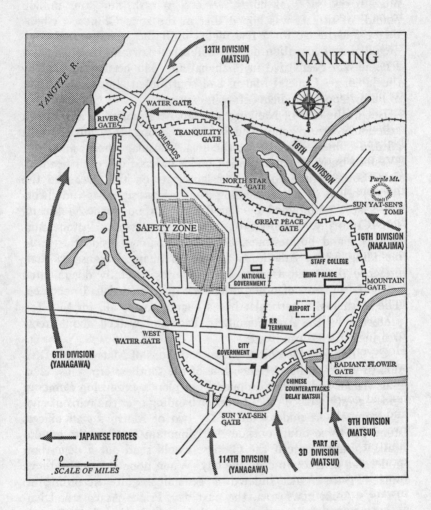

The news and noodles were premature, however. Late on Friday, December 10, the men of Matsui's 9th Division had managed to plant the flag of the rising sun on the southeastern walls only to be driven off by counterattacks during the night. Prince Asaka ordered the three other divisions under his command to cut short their mopping-up activities in outlying areas and make a thorough investiture of the city. The terrible 16th under secret-police sadist Nakajima was to circle around on the eastern side, the brutal 6th to fight its way up the western side along the river, and the reservist 114th to join the attack on the southern walls.

Black-booted but still limping from the bullet in his buttock, Nakajima was detained during Saturday, December 11, by resistance on the hump of the Purple Mountain northeast of the walls. It was a wooded suburban area noted for its fine villas and for the acre-large, granite-stepped mausoleum of Sun Yat-sen. The mausoleum was laid out on the upper slopes of the mountain in the shape of an ancient Chinese crossbow pointing toward the summit. Sun Yat-sen, once a protégé of Japan, was revered by Chinese republicans as a George Washington. With the aid of spotters in two blimps which hovered unmolested over his head, Nakajima was able to capture the tomb unscratched and to burn the nearby homes of China's rich on a selective political basis.

Yanagawa's 6th and 114th Divisions were also held up that day, by a bloody action on the Rain Flower Plateau south of Nanking. However, by Sunday, the following day, all units had fought their way clear. Nakajima spurred his men west toward the Yangtze along the northern walls of the city while Yanagawa's 6th Division hunted down Chinese soldiers in the marshes along the riverbank and headed north along the western walls. When the pincer of the two divisions closed at the northwest corner of town, it would shut off Nanking from the Yangtze and block the last avenue of escape. Chinese troops manning the walls began to desert their posts in panic. The Chinese commander made belated gestures toward arranging a truce through German intermediation, then abruptly joined the fugitives.

The last way out of the city was the Ichiang or Water Gate on the Yangtze to the northwest. In the approaches to this gate, according to a letter written twelve days later by Nanking's regional

Y.M.C.A. secretary George Fitch, "Trucks and cars jammed, were overturned, caught fire; at the gate more cars jammed and were burned—a terrible holocaust—and the dead lay feet deep. The gate blocked, terror-mad soldiers scaled the wall and let themselves down on the other side with ropes, puttees and belts tied together, clothing torn to strips. Many fell and were killed. But at the river was perhaps the most appalling scene of all. A fleet of junks was there. It was totally inadequate for the horde that was now in a frenzy to cross to the north side. The overcrowded junks capsized, then sank; thousands drowned."

Some of the fugitive junks and sampans survived the panic at the Water Gate to make a start upstream. Above Nanking they were overhauled by fast Japanese naval launches which had followed the Army's advance all the way up the Yangtze from Shanghai. The duck hunt which ensued was not in the finest traditions of the aristocratic British-style Japanese Navy, and on some of the boats generous rations of saké were issued to keep the sailors happy with their work. In and out the launches darted, ramming and machine-gunning until the river was clear.

FALL OF THE CITY

That night, Sunday, December 12, Nanking was captured at last. The storming of the walls resembled some scene from the brush of Hieronymus Bosch. It was not yet moonrise, and the only light was the hellish flicker of grenade bursts and flares. The Chinese fought with antiquated muskets and great two-handed Manchurian swords from a parapet that had been deeply furrowed by artillery fire; the Japanese machine-gunned their way up scaling ladders which were set up, overthrown, and set up again. The cadences of rattling, whining, thudding high explosive were punctuated by the splashes of bodies falling into the waters of the ancient moat. At about midnight men of the 114th Division—most of them disgraced rebels like their commander, Yanagawa—scrambled to a slippery foothold atop the battlements, raised a Japanese flag, and fought their way down the stairs within to open the Sun Yat-sen Gate at the southernmost extremity of the city. A few minutes later the Wakizaki unit of Matsui's 9th Division blasted their way through the Radiant Flower Gate farther to the east.

By early Monday morning retreating Chinese soldiers, with nowhere to run, were taking off their uniforms and begging the German businessmen and American professors in charge of the unrecognized safety zone for admission and concealment. The innocent Westerners disarmed several hundred of them, assured them that they would be treated as war prisoners by the Japanese, and quartered them all together in one building where they could be turned over to the occupation troops in a body. Many of them then proceeded to filter out of the building and mingle with the rest of the refugee throng in the safety zone.

According to a report unearthed years later in occupied Berlin —a report written by General Alexander Ernst von Falkenhausen who was attached to the German Embassy as a military advisor for Chiang Kai-shek—the attitude of the first Japanese soldiers entering the city that Monday was "very correct."[7] Pushing north, unresisted through the half-deserted slums in the southern part of town, men of Yanagawa's division were first reported in the safety zone at eleven o'clock on Monday morning. Three members of the zone committee met them and explained to them the purpose of the zone. According to the American Y.M.C.A. man Fitch, "They showed no hostility, though a few moments later they killed twenty refugees who were frightened by their presence and ran away from them."

Throughout the rest of the day patrols from Matsui's and Yanagawa's divisions wandered through the city exploring, sightseeing, and occasionally shooting. One of Matsui's staff officers entered the Mountain Gate on the east and checked the route over which Matsui would ride on horseback when he presided at the official triumphal entry planned for four days later. Around the Radiant Flower Gate where fighting had been heaviest, the Wakizaki unit tidied up, cremating Chinese corpses and assem-

[7] Falkenhausen was a Prussian Junker who had his own strict views as to what was correct and what not. He served as military governor for the Third Reich in Belgium in World War II, conspired in the plot to assassinate Hitler, and ended the war first in Gestapo prison, then in Allied prison. He was judged guilty of war crimes at Nuremberg but because of extenuating circumstances the execution of his prison sentence was indefinitely suspended.

bling and marking Japanese ones. All day and through the night Buddhist chaplains chanted prayers beside the rows of bodies.

That night a few picked garrison battalions and a number of AWOL drunks remained in the city. The bulk of the men who had entered in the morning returned as ordered to the 9th and 114th Division encampments outside the walls—to cold tents, poor food, and scarce water. They took with them as solace about a dozen Chinese women whom they had seized in the city. During the night the patrols left in the town shot at any Chinese seen abroad, and the drunk and disorderly went on a bender in the southern slums in the course of which they murdered eight men and boys in one household and raped, murdered, and mutilated a woman and two girls in a family of thirteen. The next day an American missionary, on a walk through the downtown area, was disgusted to find a "civilian Chinese corpse on almost every block."

According to a survey made three months later by an American sociologist, three hundred civilians had died during the capture of the city, fifty of them by stray bullets, bombs, and shells in the military action, the rest by wanton shooting and bayoneting after the military action was over. As war went in China in those days it was an ordinary toll. A few hundred killed, a few dozen raped—such had been the statistics in Tientsin, Peking, Shanghai, and all other major cities occupied in China by Japanese troops in previous weeks.

Not knowing that the casualties would be deliberately multiplied a hundredfold in the month to come, Western newsmen made plans that Monday night to return to Shanghai and file their stories. A dozen of them left the city walls early the next morning and fretted out the next few days on docks or over beer in Japanese regimental field H.Q.s waiting for transportation. Only one, Yates McDaniel of the Associated Press, remained in the city long enough to witness the onset of the terror.

THE RAPE BEGINS

Late on Tuesday morning, when Nanking had been in Japanese hands for thirty-six hours, former Tokyo secret-police chief Nakajima and his 16th Division rolled into town through the Water

Gate in trucks and armored cars. He had been delayed by the capture of some 10,000 prisoners at the last moment. All through the night his men had been busy herding the prisoners drove by drove to the edge of the Yangtze. They had worn their fingers to the bone pressing machine-gun triggers. At least 6,000 of the prisoners had died. Now in the flat drear light of the next noon, Nakajima's men began a systematic search inside Nanking for Chinese soldiers who had run away, taken off their uniforms, and vanished. The orders from Prince Asaka, the Emperor's uncle, were explicit: kill all captives. There were supposed to be 300,000 captives; less than 10,000 had been killed. Chiang Kai-shek's advisor, the Junker General von Falkenhausen, in his report to Berlin, notes that thereafter he saw a "complete change in attitude" in the Japanese.

"The Japanese troops," he wrote, "which had been insufficiently supplied because of their rapid advance were let loose in the town and behaved in a manner which was almost indescribable for regular troops."

Secret policeman Nakajima came to Nanking with an appointment in his pocket from Prince Asaka putting him in charge of the "maintenance of public peace." Thereafter public peace was sedulously destroyed. With Nakajima came Colonel Muto Akira, a member of the imperial cabal; he was charged by Prince Asaka with the "responsibility for billeting Japanese troops in the Nanking area." Thereafter the troops found their own billets. Muto announced that their camps outside the walls were inadequate and invited all hands in all four divisions to enter town and bed down where they pleased.

In defense of the Muto-Nakajima administration it was submitted at war crime tribunals a decade later that Nakajima had only fourteen secret policemen to assist him in maintaining public peace. The facts are that he had just come from the supreme command of all the secret police in Tokyo; that he had planes available for transporting staff officers to and from the homeland; and that Western observers saw those secret policemen which he did have in Nanking supervising looting and standing guard for soldiers who had entered homes to rape the women.

Colonel Muto, at his trial, made cynical fun of the proceedings by an equally absurd excuse; he pleaded that divisional encampments outside the city on the banks of the great Yangtze were "inadequate due to shortage of water." When the horde of soldiers were moved into town, they subsisted largely on water which they boiled and filtered and which was carried in to them by coolies from the Yangtze. The Nanking municipal water plant had been put out of commission by a bomb or shell on December 9. Damage to it was described as slight. Muto had at his disposal the 6th Field Epidemic Control Unit and a part of the 8th Field Engineers. Yet water was not turned on again in Nanking until January 7 when the Japanese had been there for over three weeks.

The 80,000-odd soldiers turned loose in Nanking by Muto, Nakajima, and Prince Asaka would have raped, killed, stolen, and burned if left to their own devices. In the event they acted under the guidance of their officers; they worked at being drunk and disorderly; they ran amok, but systematically. Their rape of Nanking began when Nakajima entered the city on December 14; it continued for six weeks; and it was not stopped, despite worldwide protest, until Prince Konoye admitted to Hirohito that there was no longer any hope of it unseating Chiang Kai-shek.

The full tale of crimes conveys a numbing insistent horror which beggars summation. It is recorded in some four thousand pages of notes, letters, and diaries written at the time by Y.M.C.A. man Fitch, General von Falkenhausen, and several others including an American surgeon and two American university professors. In addition the Safety Zone Committee filed 444 carefully authenticated "cases" of murder, mass murder, rape, arson, and pillage with Prince Asaka's staff officers while the terror was in progress. Finally the Reverend John Magee, postwar chaplain of Yale University and father of Ian Magee, the war poet, documented the sights he saw with a movie camera. His black-and-white film—which he later protested did not do justice to the "black-and-red realities"—was smuggled home to the United States. Its parade of mutilated corpses, blood-spattered rooms, and babies on bayonets was considered too revolting to exhibit except to a few limited audiences. Ironically enough, sections of the film were given their widest circulation by America First organizations intent on demonstrating the futility of foreign involvements.

On the afternoon of his arrival in town, Tuesday, December 14, sadist Nakajima had bills posted advising Chinese soldiers who had gone into hiding to give themselves up and trust to "the mercy of the Imperial Japanese Army." One of Nakajima's subordinates called on the Safety Zone Committee to inform it that 6,000 discarded Chinese uniforms had been found inside the walls. Unless the soldiers who had worn them surrendered quickly, they would sacrifice their rights as prisoners of war and would be subject to the death penalty as spies. The Western committeemen circulated the Japanese argument by word of mouth through the zone shelters and advised Chinese that it was legally correct. The next day thousands of Chinese soldiers and coolies who had served in labor battalions gave themselves up. "How foolish I had been," wrote Y.M.C.A. man Fitch a fortnight later, "to tell them the Japanese would spare their lives."

Throughout Wednesday, December 15, the prisoners of war were assembled in city squares, trussed hand to hand and man to man with signal corps telephone wire, and marched off to pens along the riverbank to be "interned." That night a command orgy was held beside the pens. The captives were brought out group by group, surrounded on all sides by soldiers, and used as dummies for bayonet charges. Kerosene was poured on the heaps of bodies and ignited. More prisoners were led out to be prodded into the flames of the pyres. Officers with sabers gave decapitation demonstrations. A trial was made of old samurai swords in which it was demonstrated that none had the virtue of being able to split a man from pate to groin at a stroke.

On Thursday the performance was repeated. For lack of military prisoners Nakajima's men requisitioned any able-bodied Chinese civilian they could lay hands on. They took the staff which was laboring to turn on the power again at the electrical plant. They took ninety policemen and forty-seven volunteer policemen employed by the safety zone. They took a quota of fathers and sons from most of the refugee camps. Once again novel forms of execution were tried out in an effort to heighten the terror and relieve the sickening monotony of bayonet and bonfire. According to photographs snapped by Japanese officers —and later copied by Chinese technicians in Shanghai studios where the films were brazenly brought for development—men were bound hand and foot and planted neck deep in earth. In the third century B.C., the Chinese emperor who built the Great Wall of China had executed a band of proscribed Confucian scholars in this way. Generations of Chinese and Japanese schoolboys had read the old horror tale with flesh crawling. Its re-enactment at Nanking must have struck some staff officer as a clever way to exploit cultural traditions, but in the staging the psychological effect was mitigated by overembellishment and impatience. In antiquity the protruding heads of the victims had had to endure the kicks and catcalls of passers-by until the bodies below ground began to waste away. In 1937 the victims were all dead long before the onset of starvation and maggots—some jabbed with bayonets, some trampled by horses, some doused with boiling water, some crushed under tank tracks.

Between their nocturnal duties as devils on the riverbank, the Japanese soldiers were employed by day for looting. According to sociologist Lewis Smythe, one of the American professors in Nanking, the pillage began as private enterprise. "Japanese soldiers," he wrote, "needed private carriers to help them struggle along under great loads." But already on the day after Nakajima's arrival, Smythe also saw "systematic destruction of shop-front after shop-front under the eyes of Japanese officers." He added, "Scores of refugees in camps and shelters had money and valuables removed from their slight possessions during mass searches." The great bulk of the booty found its way not into privates' knapsacks but into official Army warehouses. Three months later one of the zone committee tried to track down a piano which had been looted from his home. He was politely conducted by a Japanese officer to an Army storage shed containing two hundred pianos. Other warehouses were filled with rugs and paintings, mattresses and blankets, antique screens and chests. Some high officers, including Nakajima, were able to keep small fortunes for themselves in jade and porcelain and silver, but most of the plunder was later sold and the money used to defray over-all Army expenses.

It was the same day, December 15, that the crime for which Nanking is most remembered became an organized pastime. The raping started when trucks commanded by well-spoken officers made the rounds of the safety-zone refugee camps and took away loads of young women for "questioning." In some instances the pretext was belied on the spot by the soldiers who raped the girls in full public view even before loading them on the trucks. Women of beauty and some education were usually culled from each catch to serve with others of their own quality in the harems of colonels or major generals. Less fortunate creatures were shipped off to the various public buildings and auditoriums where soldiers were barracked. Some were raped for a night by ten or twenty men and then released in the morning, to be called for again and again by other trucks in days to come. Some were violated and then executed. Many immature girls were turned loose in such a man-handled condition that they died a day or two later. Sturdy wives were often assigned as slaves to platoons or entire companies and were expected to wash clothes all day and perform as prostitutes all night. Many young women were simply tied to beds as permanent fixtures accessible to any and all comers. When they became too weepy or too diseased to arouse desire, they were disposed of. In alleys and parks lay the corpses of women who had been dishonored even after death by mutilation and stuffing.

The mass abductions of December 15 and 16 caused panic and wholesale immigration of women and children into the safety zone. Most came stealthily by night; some painted sores and rashes on their faces and skulked in along back alleys by day. The population of the zone climbed from 50,000 to 200,000 in seventy-two hours. Only a quarter of the refugees could fit into the various schools and dormitories where the Zone Committee had organized staffs and kitchens. The rest camped where they could, as close to the organized shelters as possible. They thereby gained a little protection from the zone's policemen and from the nearby presence of Nanking's twenty-two Westerners.

Nevertheless, the Japanese raided the buildings of the zone regularly for more victims. Night after night soldiers climbed over walls into the various compounds, brandished pistols, and had their way with as many cowed women as they wanted. Westerners retained remarkable authority under the circumstances and could usually prevent rape when they came on it in person. Thus Minor

Searle Bates, a history professor with degrees from Oxford, Yale, and Harvard, succeeded on five occasions in breaking up acts of rape already in progress. But there were many women in the zone, many buildings, many lascivious soldiers, and the indignant Western missionaries and professors could not be everywhere. Moreover they themselves were sometimes held at bayonet point and made to look on helplessly.

On Thursday night, when the rabble of unkempt, laughing, drunken conquerors had unbuttoned their collective lust for two full days, the members of the Safety Zone Committee met to compare notes. Some of them broke down and wept while trying to tell what they had seen. They estimated that a thousand women were being raped that night and that almost as many had been raped that day. The next morning one of them took into his compound a dazed creature who said that she had been abused by thirty-seven men in turn. Another decided to leave on his lawn undisturbed a baby who had cried and been smothered by a soldier who was raping the child's mother.

In Nakajima's first three days of terror, his men had been ruthless but not efficient in the later Nazi sense. To save machine-gun bullets they had used bayonets for most of the killing, and an astonishing number of victims crawled away to recover. So many thousands of men and women had been submitted to the crude Japanese techniques of genocide that the hundreds who survived are not statistically surprising. But individually the tales of hardihood which some of them recounted at postwar tribunals seem miraculous. Men who quickly threw themselves flat sometimes survived machine-gunning, bayoneting, and burning with kerosene. Men run through with bayonets and "buried" in the river clung to reeds for hours, waiting for the Japanese to go away. Men "beheaded"—their thick carrying-pole shoulder muscles severed but not their spinal cords—recovered untended in riverbank hovels. A few men even lived to tell of scrabbling up out of shallow mass graves. The Chinese peasant who survived his septic childhood had a hardy constitution and an uncomplicated will to live.

TRIUMPHAL ENTRY

On Friday morning, December 17, the rape of Nanking slackened during the ceremonial entry into the city of little General Matsui. Still feverish after the latest flare-up of his chronic tuberculosis, Matsui was brought upriver in a naval launch, put into a car, and driven around to the battered triple archway of the Mountain Gate on the eastern side of the city. There he mounted a fine chestnut with a narrow white stripe or race on its nose. While he waited at the gate for the triumphal procession to form up behind him, he mused sorrowfully on his old friend Sun Yatsen, the founder of Republican China, who lay buried in the great mausoleum up the hill to his rear. It was more than twenty years now since Matsui and Sun had first talked dreams together of Oriental unity and brotherhood. It was already eight years since Sun's entombment there on the Purple Mountain. The other Japanese who had attended the entombment as mourners were all dead or discredited. Of all the old group espousing Sino-Japanese cooperation only Matsui still held a position of authority.

Matsui was distracted in his meditations by a stir behind him. He turned and saw that the second place in his cavalcade had been taken by Colonel Hashimoto Kingoro who had sunk the *Panay*. It was a calculated insult. Matsui had tried to discipline Hashimoto after the *Panay* attack only to discover that he was protected by influential friends and that Prince Asaka would not even reprimand him. To make the indignity more pointed, Hashimoto rode a larger, finer horse than Matsui's, a thoroughbred bay with a full blaze on its nostrils. The pleasure went out of the afternoon; the laurels of the conqueror seemed faded and empty. This was Prince Asaka's command territory, and Matsui could do nothing about the affront without merely calling attention to his own loss of face. He was reduced to complaining of the incident a week later to—of all people—the American correspondent of *The New York Times*.

A fanfare of ill-blown bugles sounded and General Matsui led Hashimoto and the entourage of Prince Asaka into the conquered capital. The boulevard before him was lined with tens of thousands of soldiers. He reared his horse and wheeled it smartly to face the palace in Tokyo far and away to the northeast. Nearby the announcer for Japan Radio quickly, softly, tensely told his microphone: "General Matsui will lead a triple banzai for the Emperor."

General Matsui broke in at once in a thin straining voice: "Dai Gen-sui Heika (Great Field Marshal on the Steps of Heaven)— banzai—ten thousand years of life."

A great banzai came roaring back but it ended—he could hardly believe it of Japanese troops on review—in a hideous cackle of drunken laughter.

"Banzai," he ventured more shrilly—and a thousand voices shouted.

"Banzai," he quavered a third time—and a radio technician had to turn down his controls to avoid overloading and distortion. The words were conventional enough but the voices of the men, preserved on tape by Japan's National Broadcasting Company, would have done credit to the legions of Genghis Khan or Attila. Matsui headed his horse down the boulevard and proceeded along a carefully cleared route, past thousands of cheering soldiers, until he arrived at the Metropolitan Hotel in the north of town.

From the shouts and look of the men at the parade and from hints dropped during the feasting at the Metropolitan that evening, Matsui gleaned a shrewd suspicion of what had been happening in Nanking. His specific instructions to quarter only a few picked battalions in the city had been flagrantly disregarded. He cut short the banquet and called a staff conference. According to officers who were present, he dressed down Nakajima and Muto and ordered them to have all unnecessary troops moved out of the city. Billeting officer Muto promised to take a fresh look at accommodations in the countryside.

On awakening in the Metropolitan next morning, Matsui was melancholy. One of his civilian aides asked him why and he replied, "I now realize that we have unknowingly wrought a most grievous effect on this city. When I think of the feelings and sentiments of many of my Chinese friends who have fled from Nanking and of the future of the two countries, I cannot but feel depressed. I am very lonely and can never get in a mood to rejoice about this victory."

Even in his press release that morning, though he dutifully trumpeted official Tokyo policy, Matsui let a note of sadness creep into the bombast: "Future Army operations will depend entirely on what attitude Chiang Kai-shek and the Nationalist Government take. I personally feel sorry for the tragedies to the people, but the Army must continue unless China repents. Now, in the winter, the season gives time to reflect. I offer my sympathy, with deep emotion, to a million innocent people."

All that day Matsui remained lugubriously intent upon the dead. He visited the tomb of Sun Yat-sen, on the Purple Mountain, and sat for hours at a memorial service at the Nanking city airport just inside the southeastern walls. During the ceremony, he composed one of those short, cryptogrammic "Chinese poems" which have been cultivated as a separate art by Japanese literati for so many centuries that they are difficult to understand either for a Japanese or a Chinese. It was addressed to the soul of Sun Yat-sen:

> In the gold-purple tomb
> was he present or absent
> the departed spirit,
> my friend of former years,
> in the ghastly
> field-colors of the dusk?
>
> Memories of past meetings
> on the battlefield
> came back to pierce my heart
> as I sat, head bowed,
> astride my war horse
> under the Mountain Gate.

In the latter part of the memorial service, Matsui delivered a substantial address on the awakening of "Greater East Asia" and the brotherhood of Chinese and Japanese. He spoke of conducting a service for the dead Chinese warriors which would immediately follow the ceremony for the fallen Japanese. However, Prince Asaka told him that since it was growing late the service for the Chinese would have to be held some other time. Matsui was upset;

according to the account he gave to his Buddhist confessor shortly before his hanging in 1948: "Immediately after the memorial services, I assembled the higher officers and wept tears of anger before them. . . . Both Prince Asaka and Lieutenant General Yanagawa . . . were there. . . . I told them . . . everything had been lost in one moment through the brutalities of the soldiers. And can you imagine it, even after that, these soldiers laughed at me."

The next day billeting expert Muto reported that he still could find no adequate facilities for troops outside Nanking. And so Matsui, exercising his full powers as commander of the Central China Theater, issued operational orders which would send three of the four divisions in Nanking out on new campaigns across the Yangtze or back toward the coast. The remaining division was Nakajima's "black" 16th, and that Matsui could not touch because it was already assigned to Nanking by Imperial Headquarters in Tokyo. Prince Asaka's retinue of European-educated staff officers, thinking it best to humor Matsui, assured him that his orders would be carried out promptly.

Later that Sunday morning, when Matsui expressed a wish to inspect the whole of Nanking, a group of them drove him up to the observatory on Chinling Hill. There he made them "look curiously at one another"; he studied the destroyed areas of the city intently through field glasses and said, "If General Chiang [Kai-shek] had been patient for a few years longer and avoided hostilities, Japan would have understood the disadvantage of trying to solve the issue between the two countries by the use of arms." On the way down the hill from the observatory, Matsui abruptly asked to talk to some of the Chinese refugees in Nanking. After a brief delay a suitable group was herded together for him, and he went about among them asking questions and offering words of comfort and reassurance.

That afternoon Matsui was removed to Prince Asaka's headquarters outside of Nanking, to be put on a destroyer a day later and sent back to Shanghai.

RAPE RENEWED

While Matsui conducted his sentimental visit to the conquered capital, the terror had subsided. Even in the western half of town which he did not visit, only a few dozen men were executed during his stay and only a few score women raped. As soon as he had left the city, however, terror was resumed. And by midnight the committeemen of the safety zone had set down that Sunday as "the worst yet." For the first time they themselves felt threatened. They continued with impunity to haul soldiers from the bodies of Chinese women, but they were also forced to watch Chinese husbands, who had stirred in defense of their wives, killed out of hand. Matsui in reproving his staff officers had said too much about the danger of antagonizing foreign powers and about the shame of Japan before the world. The men involved in the shame felt compelled to flaunt their indifference. They made a hero out of Colonel Hashimoto who had sunk the *Panay*. They went out of their way to dare the West to intervene. One American was shot at that day and several others were jostled and shoved. Western homes marked and sealed as neutral property were broken into and looted. Chinese caretakers at deserted Western embassies were killed. Star-Spangled Banners and Union Jacks were torn down and trampled. Uniformed Japanese toughs went out of their way to murder in front of white witnesses. A mandarin in a long silk gown was overtaken by two Japanese soldiers under a balcony where two Americans and two Russians were standing watching. One of the Americans later testified: "He was trying to get away, hastened his pace to get away, around a corner in a bamboo fence, but there was no opening. The soldiers walked in front of him and shot him in the face. . . . They were both laughing and talking as if nothing had happened, never stopped smoking their cigarettes and talking, killed him with no more feeling than one taking a shot at a wild duck."

That night the confused devil soldiers were rallied and regimented for a new destructive duty that could be laid out for them in plans like a campaign of battle. The objective was to complete the looting of Nanking's shops and home industries and then, alley by alley and section by section, to burn them systematically to the ground. The arson squads were given trucks in which to load everything of value before a building was put to the torch. For kindling they were issued black sticks of Thermit and strips of paper impregnated with another incendiary chemical. It was cold in Nanking and the men went to work with a will. The first fires bloomed at dusk a few hours after Matsui had left the city. By the next night Y.M.C.A. man Fitch, looking from his bedroom window, could count fourteen districts all blazing at once.

If anyone doubted that the rape was to continue, he was disabused on Friday morning, December 24, when Nakajima advised the Safety Zone Committee that the number of Chinese soldiers who had doffed their uniforms and gone into hiding was not 6,000 as previously estimated but 20,000. Equally ominous, it was noted that the molestation of women had begun to take new and extreme forms—grandmothers over seventy, girls under twelve, and mothers in the last month of pregnancy.

After Matsui had gone, his staff officer Colonel Muto, the billeting expert, stayed on in Nanking "overseeing the enforcement of Matsui's orders." There was "some delay" in withdrawing the surplus divisions. By Thursday, December 23, Yanagawa's renegade 114th, the brutal 6th, and Matsui's own 9th had withdrawn from the city. Thereafter only Nakajima's 16th was left to superintend over the longest, most disciplined stage of the rape. Nanking was already a picked carcass; only a sharp knife could cut more flesh from it.

ASAKA'S LAST OUNCE

Prince Asaka, the Emperor's uncle, moved his headquarters into Nanking on Christmas Day. He remained within the walls all through January while rape and murder continued to ladle off blood from the city into a graduated chemical flask. It was not until the last hope of frightening or shaming the Chinese into capitulation had vanished—the last little girl been violated—that he finally started back toward Tokyo on February 10.

In Shanghai little General Matsui heard of new atrocities in Nanking every day. He remained powerless to stop them and so he "worried greatly" about Prince Asaka's reputation. On Christmas, the day that Asaka moved into Nanking, Matsui voiced his worries in an interview with *New York Times* correspondent Hallett Abend—whom he struck as "likeable" and "pathetic." Having little hope that this indirect plea to Emperor Hirohito, through the pages of *The New York Times*, would do any good, he followed it up the next day by sending a message to Prince Asaka's chief of staff. "It is rumored," he wrote, "that unlawful acts continue. . . . Especially because Prince Asaka is our commander, military discipline and morals must be that much more strictly maintained. Anyone who misconducts himself must be severely punished." Privately, over a New Year's toast, Matsui told a Japanese diplomat, "My men have done something very wrong and extremely regrettable." Asked later if the men had thrown over the traces and gone berserk, he pointedly said, "I considered that the discipline was excellent but the guidance and behavior were not."

Despite Matsui's protests it remained a commonplace to stumble on new bodies in the fetid streets or to see queues of soldiers waiting their turn outside a doorway where some Chinese woman had at last been run to earth. All the men remaining in the city were registered by Nakajima's secret police, and a few score of them were selected each afternoon for that night's beheading party. The city remained without light, water, garbage disposal, police, or firemen. The Safety Zone Committee warned Prince Asaka's headquarters of the danger of plague. Asaka's staff officers replied by offering to take over the feeding of the 100,000 Chinese who were being kept alive by the zone's daily rice dole. With this responsibility, of course, the Japanese Army would assume control of the zone's rice warehouses and international relief funds. The Zone Committee refused the offer. Western newspapers were beginning to print their first eyewitness accounts of what had happened in Nanking.

Prince Asaka's engineers finally turned on the city's public utilities on January 7. Three days later Prince Kaya, a cousin of Hirohito's Empress—one who had served in previous years as an admiring emissary to Adolf Hitler—paid Nanking a ceremonial visit and "talked earnestly to second lieutenants." On January 16, after Prince Kaya's report home to the Throne, the lanky, cynical Prince Konoye played his last trump and announced that the Japanese people no longer recognized Chiang Kai-shek as the representative of the Chinese people, that war to the death would continue to be waged against the Chiang regime, and that a Japanese-sponsored government would soon be available to all

Chinese who wished to give their allegiance to peace and Pan-Asianism.

Konoye's threat to continue the war indefinitely was a threat to kill China; the rape of Nanking had been the preliminary torture supposed to make Chinese believe the threat and fear it. But police technique, usually so successful against individual Chinese, failed to work on the Chinese nation as a whole. Konoye's declaration elicited no response. Indeed the Chiang Kai-shek government had never been more popular than in its present fugitive state in Hankow. And so the unsuccessful policy was gradually abandoned. Corpses were cleared from the streets and ponds and the systematic burning of the city ceased. The last abuse protested by the Safety Zone Committee—the rape of a twelve-year-old girl—took place on February 7, fifty-seven days after the Japanese had completely occupied the city and quelled all resistance. General von Falkenhausen, the German, continued his meticulous account a little further, up to March 19 when he noted that a girl was raped by a Japanese soldier in the U.S. missionary compound.

FINAL TOLL

In all, according to figures accepted after two years of hearings by a panel of eminent jurists from many lands, the International Military Tribunal for the Far East which sat in Tokyo from 1946 to 1948, 20,000 women were raped in Nanking and its vicinity and over 200,000 men, at least a quarter of them civilians, were murdered.[8] A third of the city was destroyed by fire. Everything of value was removed from the ruins and placed in Japanese Army warehouses. The Nanking shopkeeper and the farmer outside the walls were economically wiped out. According to a survey conducted in March 1938 by sociologist Smythe and his university students on a 2 per cent sample of the population, the farmer had lost in money and goods the equivalent of 278 days of labor, the

[8] Many Japanese maintain that the figures accepted by the tribunal are grossly exaggerated, being based in part on Chinese claims. The author, after reviewing the original data and weeding out Chinese statistics, believes it fair to say that not less than 100,000 war prisoners and 50,000 civilians were executed within thirty-seven miles of Nanking and that at least 5,000 women were raped, many of them repeatedly or on several occasions.

city dweller the equivalent of 681 days of labor. Since both at the best of times lived at subsistence level, the wherewithal to begin life anew did not exist. There were few stores of seed grain for replanting, few savings with which to stock shops. Thousands of utterly hopeless women and children had no future except the day-to-day dole of rice provided by international relief funds. It would be a year before capital filtering back into Nanking from other parts of China began to create employment opportunities and a semblance of economic revival.

REWARD AND PAYMENT

The tally of lives taken at Nanking was obviously no accident. It would not be easy for 100,000 men to kill 200,000 in the course of routine carelessness, drunkenness, and disorder. But despite world-wide protest against the crime, none of the criminals were in any way punished by the Japanese government of the time. It was official Tokyo doctrine that the troops in the field had gone berserk and that nothing could be done about them. When the Nanking veterans first returned home, however, many of them told a different story—a story of disgust at what they had seen and done. They complained that they had "learned nothing in the Army but rape and burglary"; that they had had to shoot prisoners merely to test the efficiency of machine guns; that they had been ordered by their officers, in dealing with Chinese girls, "Either pay them money or kill them in some out-of-the-way place after you have finished." In February 1939, the War Ministry issued orders to suppress such "improper talk" which may "give rise to rumors" and "impair the trust of the people in the Army." Even today Nanking is regularly referred to by retired Japanese Army officers as "the ten-year shame" or "the great dishonor." Except in the most vague theoretical terms, it remains impossible to talk about Nanking with any Japanese who participated in the deeds done there.

After Japan's defeat in 1945, Japanese government spokesmen claimed at the war crime tribunals that an Army officer had been court-martialed and put to death for responsibility in the Nanking fiasco. They did not give his name or rank. They said that a noncommissioned officer had even been sentenced to prison "for stealing a Chinese lady's slipper." They said that many of the principals in the rape had been "severely reprimanded."

True 1937 Japanese attitudes toward Nanking are not reflected in such dubious latter-day assertions. More relevant facts are these: that on the day after the capture of Nanking Emperor Hirohito expressed his "extreme satisfaction" to Prince Kanin, his wife's grand-uncle, who was chief of the Army General Staff; that Prince Kanin sent a telegram of congratulations to General Matsui, telling him that "not since history began has there been such an extraordinary military exploit"; that in late January Prince Kaya, the Empress's fascistic cousin, returned from Nanking and gave the Emperor a full report on what he had seen there; that a month later, on February 26, Emperor Hirohito received the febrile Matsui, the princely Asaka, and the eager Yanagawa at the imperial summer villa in Hayama and rewarded each of them with a pair of silver vases embossed with the imperial chrysanthemum.

Matsui retired to build his shrine of remorse at Atami, Prince Asaka to play golf. No longer in disgrace, General Yanagawa was appointed by the Emperor to run the economy of occupied China and then serve as minister of justice, no less, in the Japanese Cabinet. He finally died of disease as proconsul in Sumatra in 1944. Billeting expert Muto rose steadily to become a major general and chief of the powerful Military Affairs Bureau in 1939, lieutenant general and commander of the 2d Imperial Guards in 1942, and later Yamashita's chief of staff in the Philippines in 1944–45. The ubiquitous Major General Suzuki Tei-ichi, who had done the cerebral desk work in Kyoto for the terrible 16th Division in the field, remained as always Hirohito's personal envoy and troubleshooter in the Army, moving about with breathtaking versatility from one delicate appointment to the next. As for the sadistic Nakajima, who had dirtied himself most in the rape, he was allowed to retire from the Army in 1939 and to live out his life in comfort on the spoils which he had brought back from Nanking.

Hirohito honored all the criminals, punished none of them, and remains to this day on cordial terms with his kinsman Prince Asaka. If Hirohito had any feeling at the time that Prince Asaka had sullied the family name, he gave no sign of it. He continued to play golf with Asaka, to attend weekly showings of newsreels with him, to grant him private audiences, to sit with him on the exclusive *Gokazoku Kaigi* or Council of Princes of the Blood. If Hirohito had any feeling that Prince Asaka had been deceived or exploited by his Army subordinates at Nanking, he gave no sign of that either. On the contrary he appointed three other members of the imperial family to important Army commands in the six months after the rape of Nanking.

It is the crowning irony of Nanking that the man who finally shouldered all the blame was little tubercular General Matsui. He was tried, along with the other six leaders enshrined at Atami, by the International Military Tribunal for the Far East. Scattered through the 150,000-page record of the trial may be found the gist of Matsui's part in the rape as it has been recounted here. Nowhere in the record is there any evidence that Matsui issued secret orders for the rape to take place. Nowhere did the Allied attorneys for the prosecution ever impeach his sincerity or catch him out in even one lie.

On the other hand, there is also no explicit statement by Matsui or his defense lawyers that his authority as Central China commander-in-chief was overridden at Nanking by the imperial authority of Prince Asaka. Instead, in one of the most fuzzy defense presentations in the annals of jurisprudence, Matsui's lawyers allowed him to discourse about Sino-Japanese friendship in a windy manner that could only impress his judges as hypocritical. He wound himself in a noose of Buddhist piety and mysticism. He buried himself in pompous platitudes. His judges were naturally impressed by eyewitness accounts of Nanking bestialities. When they heard him offer no adequate excuses for the fact that he had been in over-all command in Central China they assumed that he must be worthy of hanging. Matsui himself did not disagree. After a decade of introspection, he felt that he should have done more to guide Prince Asaka and the Emperor and that it was his religious duty now to die in protection of the Throne.

"I am happy to end this way," he said. "After things turning out this way, I am really eager to die at any time."

Memoirs, orders, and diaries which have come to light in Japan since the trial tend to corroborate Matsui's story. Moreover, the conduct of the trial itself, as an honest quest for truth, is open to question, and has been questioned by every single Western historian who has since had occasion to review it. It is an incredible fact of the Matsui case that Prince Asaka, who was in direct command at Nanking and physically present there during most of the rape, was never summoned into court to testify even as a witness, much less as a defendant. The judges, who knew his position of command and listened to many less important stories at tedious length, would not have been averse to hearing his account of the rape of Nanking. They were prevented from doing so by the terms of the political equation which held in Japan immediately after the dropping of the atomic bombs and the Japanese surrender.[9]

History is not merely enacted and recorded but made and remade by later events and later points of view. After Nanking, Japan went on to invade South China and then Russian Mongolia. In the year that followed, 1940, Japan remodeled herself domestically as a one-party police state totally mobilized for modern warfare. In early 1941, Japan made a satellite of French Indochina and began to train troops seriously for the conquest of British Malaya, of the Dutch East Indies, and, contingently, of the Philippines. That summer President Roosevelt cut off Japan's supplies of strategic materials, particularly oil. In the negotiations which followed, Japan expressed herself willing to accept all of Roosevelt's conditions, except the most important: withdrawal from China and from the bases there which could be used against the Philippines and other points south. Emperor Hirohito ordered the attack on Pearl Harbor to be prepared, and when Roosevelt persisted in calling the Japanese hand, Hirohito overrode voices of caution and procrastination and ordered the attack to be launched.

In the next six months Singapore, the Philippines, Borneo, Sumatra, Java, and a dozen other islands of immense natural wealth fell to Japan in an Army-Navy operation of unexpected brilliance and ferocity. The atrocities of Nanking were repeated again and again—at the Bataan Death March, in the building of

9 This point is taken up in detail in Chapter 3.

the Burma-Thailand railway, in the final desperate rape of Manila in 1945. Then came the counter-atrocities, the appalling incendiary raids on the wood-and-paper cities of civilian Japan, and the atomic bombings of Hiroshima and Nagasaki.

When Japan had been effectively defeated, the Japanese dream of an Asiatic empire lay buried under four million corpses. If the Emperor ordered it, the Japanese people were prepared to add their own seventy million bodies to the carnage heap before admitting the defeat. America's war, however, had been waged against fascism, not the Japanese people. To stay the slaying, peace had to be made at any price. How it was made will be told in the next two chapters. The price paid was a polite international lie, a falsification of history. It was not a high price, but historical lies have to be corrected if anything is to be learned from the lessons of life on earth. From the fourth chapter onward, this book presents a previously untold story: the inner workings of the Japanese government during its attempt to conquer the world.

If a grievous miscarriage of justice was delivered by the United States and her Allies in the hanging of General Matsui in 1948, it is at least not thought of that way by most Japanese today. Rather, they see Matsui's death as a noble suicidal sacrifice in the interests of peace and the saving of Japanese and American face. The musical stick of lamentation, struck daily by the weeping priestess at the shrine in Atami, tolls in her own ears not merely for her kinsman general, nor merely for the other war criminals on the hill above her, not merely for Japan alone, but for all men everywhere.

2

A-BOMB

HIROSHIMA

You will proceed to a rendezvous at Iwo with two other B-29's. One plane will carry it.

The other planes will carry instruments and photographic equipment. You three will not contact each other, but will maintain the strictest radio silence.

Weather observation planes will be returning from over the Empire and the area of the targets. They will not address you directly, but speak as if addressing the base at Tinian. You will naturally take extreme care in hearing their reports. If they are not understood you will not break radio silence to ask repeat. They will be repeated as prearranged.

You will approach the target at a ground speed around 300 mph, and maintain a steady bombing platform at about 30,000 feet.

Bombing will be visual. If the city of choice is not clear, proceed at your discretion to another target.

As bomb is released, you will immediately turn at a 150-degree angle.

You must not, repeat, not follow standard bombing procedure by proceeding as usual to fly over the target . . . You will not fly over this explosion.

After bombs away, turn sharply so as not to be over Ground Zero when the device explodes. You may even wish to lose altitude to put more distance between yourself and zero.

Following these specifications, planes of the 509th Composite Group had practiced for seventeen days dropping oddly shaped "punkins" of Torpex explosives on various Japanese cities. Japanese plane spotters had grown used to the sight of B-29's that came in harmless threesomes and dropped a single bomb. Japanese radio propagandists had even picked up enough idle radio chatter from American ground crews in Tinian to taunt the 509th because its men put on airs of importance and secrecy. Tokyo Rose said that they had been trained in America's last desperate resort: "magic."

On August 6, 1945, however, the 509th's *Enola Gay* was not carrying magic or pumpkins but a "Thin Boy," a long slender container in which small pieces of uranium-235 waited at one end to be fired at a large piece held at the other—in short, an atomic bomb. Six and a half hours from take-off in Tinian, at exactly 8:15:17 A.M. Hiroshima time, the special bomb-bay doors opened and the bomb and its parachute were toggled out. Colonel Paul W. Tibbets took back the control from bomb-run pilot Major Thomas W. Ferebee, put the plane into a violent turn, and at full throttle headed down and out. About two minutes later—fifteen miles away—the fleeing *Enola Gay* leapt like a bronco. Captain Robert Lewis who was keeping the flight log had last written, "There will be a short intermission while we bomb our target." Now he entered the simple exclamation, "My God!"

The bomb had burst in a clear blue sky about 1,500 feet over the northwest center of the city and of its 245,000 inhabitants. For an instant a ball of fire 250 feet in diameter had hung in the air like a piece out of the heart of the sun. And in the next instant some 64,000 Japanese civilians had been set aflame or crushed. Another 26,000-odd were scorched and riddled with neutrons and gamma rays. They died within the following minutes, days, weeks, and months.

A great light sparked the land out to 100 miles. An intense thud of sound leveled 6,820 buildings at a clap and could be heard over ten miles away. The whole center of the city, a mile wide, burst into flame. A titanic spout of air and ashes—ash of buildings, ash of people—shot into the upper atmosphere and flattened into a mushroom head against the floor of space. Around the foot of the fiery cloud, cold air rushed in to fill the vacuum, gradually picking up speed until two and three hours after the explosion it roared in to fan the flames with a 30- to 40-mph gale. Around the outer eddies of the fire storm, where the initial heat wave had parched everything to tinder, more fires sprang up as if licks of flame were breaking through the earth from below. In a few hours four square miles were burning.

The pall of airborne rubbish hanging over the city darkened the crackling streets. Hail-sized drops of muddy water, taken up as vapor from Hiroshima's rivers, sporadically fell out of the cloud in a kind of rain. The ionized air had a pervasive electric smell such as one scents near a lightning stroke or a welder's arc. Small tornadoes played around the edges of the storm, disturbing the ruins and toppling still-standing trees.

Stunned human beings, finding escape holes from collapsed buildings near the center of the blast, joined processions of horribly burned ghosts who had been caught in the open but were still alive enough to try to walk away. Mildly burned and irradiated outsiders hovered on the perimeter of the inferno looking for relatives. They saw and never forgot the bodies stumbling out, flayed by the heat, skin black or bubbled or hanging in gray strips. The three rivers flowing out of the heart of the city became clogged with corpses of adults and notably of children who had quenched their seared lives in the water.

As the fire spread it caught many mildly injured people trapped under wreckage. Passing evacuees extricated some and ignored others. Men in search of their own families were even said to have stopped and apologized for obeying what they considered to be their first duty. Some sections of the city became entirely ringed with flames and the survivors in them huddled in open parks and gardens. In these sanctuaries, the dying died. Those destined to live fought fires that crept in on them, went about distributing cups of water from broken pipes and running streams, told stories for the children, swapped theories about what had happened, and spread rumors about what would happen next. A low-flying plane caused terror of strafing. The queerness of the rain suggested that the city was being sprayed with gasoline for final immolation. Soldiers went about searching for American parachutists.

For the first thirty hours most survivors wandered about digging in ashes, staring at horrors, unwittingly picking up roentgens. Electricity was out, water pipes had been broken in 70,000 places. Of forty-five hospitals, three were left standing and of their staffs only twenty-eight out of 290 doctors and 126 out of 1,780 nurses remained uninjured. Yet life did go on. It was determined later that earthworms, even in the immediate area of ground zero, continued to crawl only a few inches beneath the surface of the soil.

Gradually above ground, too, a semblance of order was restored. On the day after the bomb the governor of the prefecture called for "rehabilitation of the stricken city and an aroused fighting spirit to exterminate the devilish Americans." The Japanese Army, which for all its faults was a relatively modern and efficient organization, took charge of relief. Casualties were herded into hospitals. Army stockpiles of food and blankets were distributed. Heaps of corpses were soaked with gasoline and incinerated. The fires burned out in three days, the embers smouldered for a few days more.

By final count six months later, over 90,000 civilians and almost 10,000 soldiers had perished. Another thousand-odd were to die in the decade ahead of leukemia and other radiation diseases.

NAGASAKI

The U.S. had a second type of atomic bomb ready to drop on Japan: "Fat Boy." A prototype of it had already been exploded atop a test tower in the New Mexican desert. Fat Boy depended for its power on an extremely fissile element, plutonium, which was not found in nature but was man-made at a plant on the Columbia River in the state of Washington. Atoms of the plutonium were distributed more or less evenly throughout a compressible medium which kept them apart and prevented them from engaging in chain reactions. They were encased on the outside in a spherical shell of conventional explosive charges. When the charges were sparked and detonated, the plutonium atoms would be blown in on one another and for a fraction of a second would be held together so tightly that a far more universal splitting of the atoms would take place than in the shotgun type of uranium bomb used at Hiroshima. Indeed, the Fat Boy was expected to pack at least three times the bang of the Thin Boy.

Since Fat Boy was the second atomic bomb, everyone involved in dropping it knew that he was making awesome history. Casualty estimates had already been broadcast concerning Hiroshima. Radios crackled with commentary and speculation about the significance of the atomic age a-dawning. Japan must surrender soon. Not even the suicidal kamikaze pilot could stand on his honor while his entire homeland was being erased city by city. Moreover, the U.S.S.R. was massing tanks on the Russo-Manchurian border in order to snap up the continental fragments of Japan's collapsing empire. The Soviet offensive was launched at midnight on August 8, Tokyo time. President Truman was informed of it an hour later, and the news was broadcast. Bomb crews in the Pacific, preparing for early morning take-offs, took it in with their coffee and briefings.

Fat Boy was scheduled to be dropped on Japan on August 11. A few hours before the Russian drive started, on the afternoon of August 8, the Fat Boy bomb crew were out dropping a practice "punkin" in the Pacific. That evening when their B-29, named *Bock's Car*, touched down at the U.S. air base on the Pacific island of Tinian, the crew were abruptly notified to be ready to fly again that night—this time in earnest. A wide storm center was forming out in the Pacific. Southern Japan was expected to cloud over the next day and to remain closed in for five days thereafter. To avoid any chance of a mistake, President Truman had ordered that the Fat Boy be cast visually, not by radar. General Thomas Farrell, the Tinian commander who had discretionary powers as to when the next A-bomb should be dropped, had decided to move up the date from the eleventh to the morning of the ninth. William Laurence, *The New York Times* science reporter who was to accompany *Bock's Car* in one of its attendant camera planes, observed dryly, "I'll bet those weather forecasts came all the way from Potsdam."

From the beginning the crew members of *Bock's Car* seemed dogged by hard luck. To be ready for early morning take-off they were allowed only two hours of sleep. Awakened at 11 P.M., they were briefed until midnight, then ate a light meal and stood by

during the loading of the bomb and the complex checkout of all
its mechanisms. At the last minute the flight engineer discovered
that an auxiliary fuel pump was out of action and that a 600-gallon
tank of reserve gasoline would not be available for use during the
long flight home. "To hell with it," decided Major Charles
Sweeney, the *Bock's Car's* pilot. He took off at 1:56 A.M., Tokyo
time.

An hour later the crew of the *Bock's Car* were disturbed by an
extraordinary breach of radio silence from headquarters in Tinian.
One of the two attendant photographic planes had left behind a
physicist who was supposed to run a scientifically important high-
speed camera. For thirty excruciating minutes everyone including,
it was feared, Japanese radio monitors listened while the operation manual for the unmanned camera was read out over the air-
waves. An hour and a half later, the black box which monitored
and controlled the Fat Boy began to flash a red light which indicated that all firing circuits were closed. For another tense half
hour the crew waited in fear of fission while the lieutenant in
charge of electronics delved into the black box. It turned out that
a faulty switch had lit the warning light meaninglessly. Another
hour and a half of napping and routine passed. Then at 8:12 A.M.
Bock's Car rendezvoused with one of its two camera planes off
the southern tip of Japan. The second camera plane, the one
which had left behind its physicist, was cruising at a higher altitude a little to the north. For forty minutes the planes circled in
search of one another, passing again and again just out of sight.
At 8:56 Pilot Sweeney decided that the fuel supply was too short
for further search and headed north toward his target. Weather
planes up ahead reported conditions excellent: dawn haze clearing, blue skies shining through.

The primary target that morning was not Nagasaki but Kokura,
a manufacturing town of 170,000 inhabitants on the north coast
of Kyushu, the southernmost of Japan's main islands. Kokura had
been little bombed previously and was an ideal target. It lay in a
plain and nudged so closely against the industrial cities of Tobata,
Wakamatsu, and Yawata that the four have since been amalga-
mated as a single megalopolis, Kitakyushu, the fifth city of Japan.

Had *Bock's Car* unloaded Fat Boy on Kokura that morning, it is estimated that at least 300,000 of the 610,000 people in the four cities would have been killed.

As Major Sweeney approached Kokura at 9:30 A.M., he was pleased to see that the weather held, the sky was clear, the visibility excellent. As the plane passed over its target, however, Bombardier Kermit Beahan reported that he could not see the arsenal which he was supposed to use as aiming point; it was obscured by the smoke of factory chimneys.[1] Major Sweeney circled and came in for a second bomb run. Once again the city fled past below. Once again the river and other landmarks near point zero could be seen clearly but not the arsenal. Once again Bombardier Beahan called out, "No drop." On the third bomb run members of the crew murmured that Japanese antiaircraft gunners were beginning to get the range and that Japanese fighters were climbing from below. For the third time Bombardier Beahan failed to see his bull's-eye and shouted, "No drop." Circling and surveying the white puffs of the flak over the city, Major Sweeney announced that he was giving up and proceeding to the secondary target, Nagasaki, ninety miles to the southwest. By now the fuel situation was critical. There was no possibility of returning to Tinian. The plane would have to refuel at Iwo Jima or at the airstrip on recently secured Okinawa.

Bock's Car thundered in toward Nagasaki a few minutes before eleven in the morning. The edgy crew saw clouds ahead and begged for a radar drop. Navy Commander Fred Ashworth, who had over-all charge of the bomb, at first refused. Major Sweeney assured him, "I'll guarantee we come within a thousand feet of the target." As there was not enough fuel left to carry the heavy bomb back to Okinawa the only alternative would be to jettison Fat Boy over the ocean. After a moment's hesitation Commander

[1] *New York Times* correspondent William L. Laurence, in an eyewitness account which was delayed by censorship and not printed until September 9, wrote that there was "no opening in the thick umbrella of clouds that covered" Kokura. This was the official story for many years but now crewmen of the bomb plane deny it. By September 1945, when his article appeared, Mr. Laurence was extremely busy, being given a whirlwind Air Force tour of atomic installations in the United States as background for an exclusive series of articles on the manufacture and testing of atomic bombs.

Ashworth decided to disregard President Truman's orders and gave his consent.

Nagasaki stands at the head of a V-shaped bay. Its two heavily built-up strips of harbor front meet at the center of the city and extend inland up two narrow valleys. The distinctive X-shape of the city showed up clearly on the radarscope. Ground zero was supposed to be the center of the X. But as *Bock's Car* bore in on it, Bombardier Beahan suddenly sighted a stadium through a rift in the clouds, a stadium which he recognized from reconnaissance photographs. "I'll take it," he shouted. He asked for a correction to the right and received it. Less than a minute later, at 10:58 A.M., Tokyo time, he released the bomb visually and *Bock's Car* jumped as Fat Boy fell from the bomb bay. Major Sweeney banked his plane sharply and hared away to the south toward a forced landing on Okinawa two hours later.

Behind him, dangling from its parachute, drifted the "gimmick" as it was known to the fliers—the *pikadon* or "thunder-and-lightning" as it would be dubbed by the men on the ground. It had been released not 1,000 feet off target but 11,000 feet or more than two miles. It was descending over the bowl-shaped valley of Urakami, which housed Nagasaki's most important war factory, the Mitsubishi Ordnance Works. Through the valley ran another valuable objective, the railway line which linked the big peninsular port city to the rest of Japan. All of the dozen Japanese who looked up, and lived to write about it later, remember searching a clear blue sky. Several of them saw the plane; two of them saw the bomb and its parachute. At their lathes, turning out torpedoes and small arms, the workers in the Mitsubishi plant heard nothing. The congregation at the Friday morning mass in the nearby Our Lady of the Immaculate Conception, the largest Roman Catholic cathedral in the Orient, saw nothing. The roar of machinery, the opacity of stained glass saved them from fear before they died.

Four minutes after release, at a point approximately 1,540 feet above the ground and 200 feet east of the railway line, the bomb went off. Directly under it, destruction was complete, more complete than at Hiroshima, and death was instantaneous. But the bowl of the Urakami Valley shielded the rest of Nagasaki from direct radiation. There were no fire storms, no strange falls of muddy rain. The valley's two-mile strip of city had simply been crushed flat. The immense thunderclap echoed from the surrounding hills, overtaking the fleeing *Bock's Car* and jolting it with no less than five separate head-jerking shocks. By a count made six months later, 39,214 men, women, and children had died.[2]

ATOMIC DECISION MAKING

The two atomic bombings took 140,000 lives in all. The rape of Nanking, eight years earlier, had taken approximately the same number. Japan's conquest of Asia had begun and ended in horror. An eye for an eye and a tooth for a tooth had been meted out to an uncanny jot and tittle by the whirling scythe of war. Unlike Nanking, the A-bomb has become one of the most completely documented events in history. The unknown terrors of radiation, the horror of death by flame, the large number of victims who lingered on to die weeks later have all combined to give humane men and women everywhere an uneasy conscience. Many have wondered whether an act of vengeance or even cold-blooded racism was not committed. Bertrand Russell, the British mathematician and political idealist, went so far as to call Hiroshima "a wanton act of mass murder." It is difficult to face the skulls of Hiroshima and Nagasaki objectively. Cautious Ph.D.'s, however, have searched and searched again through the records of the decision-making process which led to the A-bombing of Hiroshima and Nagasaki, and have found little to cavil with.

At the time of the bomb decision the statesmen of three na-

[2] Had it not been for Bombardier Beahan's lucky two-mile miss, another 50,000 to 75,000 would have been killed. Beahan does not maintain that the miss was entirely accidental. He says guardedly that he knew where he was dropping the bomb and that the stadium which he sighted through the rift in the clouds was an "alternate aiming point." It may be, then, that the humane miss was authorized at a high level in General Carl Spaatz's Strategic Air Command. Wasting the kill power of such an expensive weapon would have been sufficient reason at that time for hushing up the story. Five minutes after dropping the bomb the radio operator on *Bock's Car* flashed Tinian: "Results technically successful but other factors involved make conference necessary before taking further steps."

tions were pitted against one another in a triangular negotiation, conducted through curtains of national security and self-interest. For U.S. leaders the concern was to find a surrender formula that would make it possible after the war to revolutionize Japanese culture, root out the cherished cults of samurai and Emperor worship, and cure Japan of the wish to spread ruin, ever again, through the Far East. The Emperor and the men around him had narrower objectives. They wanted to keep as much as possible of the Japanese Empire, to protect themselves from execution or imprisonment as war criminals, and above all to preserve the institution of the imperial family which had become, in modern Shinto, the be-all and end-all of Japan's spiritual life. The third party in the surrender struggle was Russia, represented by Stalin. And in Stalin's eyes the self-interest of the U.S.S.R. lay simply in acquiring for communism as much territory and influence as possible.

To achieve its ends each of the three parties had certain powers which encouraged it and certain fears which inhibited it. The United States had the strength to invade and crush Japan utterly, but could not revolutionize the governing process in Japan without the co-operation of the people and particularly of their leader and god, the Emperor. Consequently the United States needed not only to keep the Emperor as an agent but also to keep him in doubt about his future status so that he would be a helpful agent. Where Russia was concerned, the United States was in a position either to offer or withhold sanction for land grabs which the Soviet Army could and would make, with or without authorization, among the pieces of Japan's vast continental empire. The United States also had some power, through threat of landing troops on the China coast, to see that the government of China was turned back to Chiang Kai-shek rather than to Communist Mao Tse-tung.

The power of Japan's leaders lay in their ability to command a fanatic last-ditch battle from hill to hill and cave to cave which would have cost the United States 250,000 to 1,000,000 G.I. lives, would have decimated Japan, and for the future, would have deprived U.S. policy of the most viable, most stable, and most progressive nation in postwar Asia. In addition the Japanese could, at last resort, give the U.S.S.R., unopposed, the fair provinces of Manchuria, Korea, and China in return for continued neutrality and war materials with which to fight U.S. invasion.

As for the U.S.S.R., her veteran armies, in co-operation with those of Mao Tse-tung, had the brute strength to make Manchuria and most of China safe for communism. She might do this without casualties and without honor by making a deal with "fascist" Japan, or if the war lasted long enough, she might gain Anglo-American blessing to do it by force. Though depleted, the Japanese armies on the Continent were still dangerous. To defeat them would take manpower needed for the reconstruction of war-ravaged western Russia. Moreover, the U.S.S.R. had a nonaggression treaty with Japan which would not expire until 1946. On the other hand, to make a deal with Japan would be to incur the disapproval of Communists everywhere and the instant antagonism of the United States and Britain. Russia could, in fact, do nothing at all if she wished. She had much to gain and nothing to lose simply by a policy of watchful opportunism. Therefore, when Berlin fell in May 1945, the U.S.S.R. began to move the Red Army east to await developments on the doorstep of the Japanese Empire.

When the bomb burst in this triangle of power politics, it disrupted all the equations of statesmanship. Japanese leaders had no inkling of its presence until Hiroshima was actually hit in August. Stalin was far better informed. Soviet espionage had revealed to him the existence of the bomb project in early 1945. He knew that it was nearing success. When his troops had captured atomic research laboratories in Germany, he had been briefed on their purpose and told the potential military significance of the bomb. But as subsequent events were to show, Stalin did not fully appreciate the new weapon until it was used. To him it was only a bigger bomb. And in his lifetime he had seen bombs enlarged from one kilogram to a thousand without upsetting the basic power balances between nations.

As the guardians and bankers for the international group of

physicists who had built the bomb, U.S. leaders had been the first to wrestle with the implications of the new weapon. The far-sighted War Secretary Henry Stimson notified the new President Harry S Truman on April 25, 1945: "The world in its present state of moral advancement, compared with its technical development, would be eventually at the mercy of such a weapon. In other words, modern civilization might be completely destroyed." Truman noted in his memoirs that Stimson "seemed at least as much concerned with the role of the atomic bomb in the shaping of history as in its capacity to shorten this war."

On April 7 a new Cabinet had taken office in Japan. The State Department had analyzed it as a "peace cabinet," but as yet it had sounded no overtures to peace. On May 1 Under Secretary Joseph C. Grew, the prewar ambassador to Japan, met with the Navy and War Secretaries to urge that the United States offer some face-saving token that would serve as an opening for negotiations. Both Stimson and Navy Secretary James Forrestal were sympathetic. "How far and how thoroughly," asked Forrestal, "do we want to beat Japan?" Enough to make Japan a law-abiding nation was the accepted answer, but no one was sure how much of a thrashing that answer implied. Former Ambassador Grew wished to assure the Japanese that they could keep their Emperor, but a number of other State Department officials, including Assistant Secretaries Dean Acheson and Archibald MacLeish, the poet, argued that the ills of Japan might not be curable as long as the Emperor remained even as titular head of state.

After Grew's meeting with Stimson and Forrestal on May 1, President Truman on May 8 faced up to the obdurate belligerence of Japan and told the press that the United States would fight on "until the Japanese military and naval forces lay down their arms in unconditional surrender." He called for "termination of the influence of the military leaders who have brought Japan to the present brink of disaster." He promised that the United States did not want "extermination or enslavement of the Japanese people" but only a "return of soldiers and sailors to their families, their farms, their jobs." His words were, of course, beamed to Japan by radio and were dismissed by many of the

Japanese privileged to hear them as mere propaganda. A few days later Truman wrote home to his family:

I know that Japan is a terribly cruel nation in warfare but I can't bring myself to believe that, because they are cruel, we should ourselves act in the same manner. For myself, I certainly regret the necessity of wiping out whole populations because of the "pigheadedness" of the leaders of a nation and, for your information, I am not going to do it unless it becomes absolutely necessary. My object is to save as many American lives as possible, but I also have a humane feeling for the women and children in Japan.

Throughout May, the humane Truman waited in vain for any Japanese response. In Moscow, on May 28, Stalin suggested to Presidential Envoy Harry Hopkins that it might be possible to accept a conditional surrender from the Japanese and then, after occupying Japan, to escalate gradually the severity of American demands; in other words, according to Hopkins, "to agree to milder peace terms but once we get into Japan to give them the works."

This was the world of sharks and gentlemen in which, on May 31 and June 1, the leading political strategists of the United States met with the top atomic scientists of the United States to discuss policy regarding the big new bomb being perfected at Los Alamos. The group was called the Interim Committee and included Presidential representative James Byrnes, War Secretary Stimson, Chief of Staff George C. Marshall, A-bomb Project Director Major General Leslie R. Groves, and representatives of the Navy and State Departments.

On the scientific side, the meeting was staffed by Vannevar Bush, James Conant, and Karl Compton and was assisted by the expert testimony of three Nobel Prize winners: Karl's brother Arthur Compton, Enrico Fermi, and Ernest O. Lawrence, the cyclotron builder. All three advisors were pioneers in nuclear research, fission, and chain reactions, and they had been living with the vague theoretical threat of the bomb since the early 1930's. They had with them J. Robert Oppenheimer, the physicist whose charm and political ability had played a major role in enabling generals, scientists, and industrialists to pull together in production of the bomb.

Stimson, the white-haired Secretary of War who had shaped U.S. policy in the Orient since the Japanese conquest of Manchuria in 1931, swept the gathering with his burning eyes and declared the purpose of the meeting:

> Our great task is to bring this war to a prompt and successful conclusion. We may assume that our new weapon puts in our hands overwhelming power. It is our obligation to use this power with the best wisdom we can command. . . . To us now the matter of first importance is how our use of this new weapon will appear in the long view of history.

Technical questions followed Stimson's opening. Though still untested, the bomb would almost certainly work. Two bombs would be available for use early in August. Thereafter an additional bomb would be ready for delivery every few weeks.

Throughout the morning session, it was assumed that the bomb would be used. At lunch Arthur Compton suggested that it might be most humane to hold a demonstration of the bomb for the Japanese before using it on a target. War Secretary Stimson enthusiastically agreed. But over dessert the idea foundered in a sea of practical difficulties. Without killing anyone or devastating a city, what demonstration in America would impress an observation team of Japanese generals? On a mesa or bleak salt flat, the big firecracker would be startling but it would do little visible harm to the surface of the earth. How make the generals pace off the distances, learn to trust the wind gauges and seismographs, and compute the difference between this bomb and other bombs? How persuade them that it was not all some kind of gigantic materialistic Yankee stunt?

To stage an announced demonstration in an uninhabited section of Japan also seemed futile and quixotic. Under combat conditions many things could go wrong: the bomb might not work or the plane and its bomb load might be captured by the enemy. The President's representative, James Byrnes, feared with good reason that the Japanese, if warned in advance, might assemble an army of American and British P.O.W.'s to stand shackled as viewers and victims of any demonstration.

For the statesmen present, time was of the essence. If the scientists could really deliver their goods, Japan might surrender before Russia gobbled up China. The daily toll of Japanese lives taken by conventional bombs—80,000 in a single incendiary raid over Tokyo on May 10—might cease. The bomb offered an opportunity, in Churchill's words, to "end the whole war in one or two violent shocks"; and in Stimson's words, to "save many times the number of lives, both American and Japanese, that it would cost."

The Interim Committee, including all the scientists present, finally voted against demonstration and for military use of the bomb. At the same time the scientists were asked by Stimson to consider the matter further and "prepare a report as to whether we could devise any kind of demonstration that would seem likely to bring the war to an end without using the bomb against a live target." The scientists' answer was delivered on June 16. It said, in a sentence that Stimson underlined in his own copy, "We can propose no technical demonstration likely to bring an end to the war; we see no acceptable alternative to direct military use."

A group of equally distinguished atomic physicists, who did not sit on the Interim Committee but had also worked on the bomb, disagreed vehemently. At a series of meetings conducted by Nobel Prize winner James O. Franck at the University of Chicago, they drew up the Franck report, a strong idealistic plea not to use the bomb in warfare. Their protest, which was submitted in Washington but never reached the highest levels of government, was couched in strategic, moral, and political terms. They foresaw the possibility of "suitcase warfare," that is "a Pearl Harbor disaster repeated in thousandfold magnification in every one of our major cities." They recommended that the United States demonstrate the bomb before representatives of the United Nations and then turn it over to an international control commission. After demonstration, they said, the bomb might be used against Japan with the sanction of the United Nations.

At a time when the United Nations was just being organized and the Russians were beginning to show their postwar colors, internationalization of the bomb was not an idea calculated to appeal to U.S. statesmen. The one scientific question at issue, that of staging an effective demonstration of the bomb for Japanese leaders, was begged by the Franck report. It should perhaps have been considered more deeply. That perennial political loner, Edward Teller, who later masterminded the H-bomb, has since asserted: "I was positive then and I am positive now, that we made a mistake dropping the bomb without a previous bloodless demonstration. We could have used the bomb to end the war without bloodshed by exploding it high over Tokyo at night without prior warning. If it had been exploded at an altitude of 20,000 feet, instead of the low altitude of 2,000 feet . . . there would have been a minimum loss of life, if any, and hardly any damage to property, but there would have been tremendous sound and light effects. We could then have said to the Japanese leaders: 'This was an atomic bomb. One of them can destroy a city. Surrender or be destroyed!' "

Such a demonstration might very well have been effective. Indeed it might have impressed the leaders in Tokyo more than the actual obliteration of provincial Hiroshima. The technical difficulties of getting the drop-plane away from the burst at such an altitude could have been solved readily. The uncertainties of a night attack, so long as it were made without warning, would have been minimal. The fact is, however, that the suggestion was never put forward in government circles.

After the Interim Committee had met on June 1 and voted to use the bomb militarily, the decision was never changed. It was, however, kept open to change. In the six weeks that followed, President Truman was preparing for the last of the wartime conferences with Stalin and Churchill. It was to be held at Potsdam in the Soviet Zone of Germany. There the decision to use the bomb would be made final. Up to the last minute Truman watched Japan. Through radio monitoring and code breaking, he had access to all messages which passed between Tokyo and Japanese embassies in neutral countries. He was also privy to the reports of Army, Navy, and O.S.S. agents. Though not all of this intelligence has yet been made public, he cannot have found in it much hope that Japan was about to accept unconditional surrender because the actual deliberations in Tokyo at that time were a study in procrastination and bluff.

JAPAN'S DILEMMA

The majority of Japanese officials had long recognized the need to surrender but their will to act was frozen. They did not know how to admit to one another that they were beaten. They only knew what they had done in their own conquests, and they feared vengeance in kind. Theirs was not the Washington world of brusque, explicit proposals and of statesmen concerned with moral issues but a murky political atmosphere of guarded allusions and feudal allegiances, of time-consuming etiquette and prickly samurai honor.

Emperor Hirohito had been reminding his ministers to miss no chance for concluding an advantageous peace ever since the Japanese capture of Singapore in February 1942. Indeed, a Navy peace mission, equipped with special code machines and clerks, had been installed in Switzerland in 1941 even before the attack on Pearl Harbor. It was charged with keeping channels of negotiations open and maintaining contact with U.S. Intelligence. To Hirohito's dismay, however, the Japanese mission discovered that U.S. leaders had no interest in a negotiated peace. The Americans remained confident of final victory even at the lowest ebb in their fortunes. They took the position that they had been forced into war by Japan's surprise attack and that they did not mean to cease fighting until they had divested Japan of her empire and made her into a peace-loving nation. In October of 1942, Hirohito had the Army dispatch to Europe its own corps of peace experts. The major general in charge of the mission, Okamoto Kiyotomi, was an intimate friend of the Emperor's brother Prince Chichibu, who enjoyed a reputation in the West for pro-British attitudes. Nevertheless, in Sofia, Ankara, Vichy, and Berne, Okamoto and his three fellow officers found that neutral mediators held out little hope.

Six months before Pearl Harbor Hirohito had had the Naval General Staff make a study of war prospects. When the results were submitted to him, he had ordered that the study be made again by a separate group of staff officers. The second analysis corroborated the conclusion of the first: that Japan could wage war successfully on the United States for eighteen months, or until June of 1943. After that Japan must negotiate a peace or she would gradually lose everything. When the deadline passed and Japanese envoys still reported no hope of arranging a settlement, both Army and Navy had new studies made of the war outlook. By the end of 1943 the Navy's had been completed and the Army's was nearing final draft. The Navy's concluded that Japan had lost the war and would be forced to give up all the territorial acquisitions which she had made since 1880. The Army study concurred and went a step further: Japan might be able to attach only two conditions to surrender, that the homeland be spared from ravage and that the imperial dynasty be left on the Throne.

The chilling conclusions of the two staff studies were difficult to accept. Hirohito's forces still held a vast empire, an area of the globe wider than Canada and almost as long as South America. Prime Minister Tojo assured Hirohito that the cold figures of war production and war losses could lie; much could happen. But Hirohito understood figures. The staff conclusions might not be inevitable but he must still make some provision for the eventuality of defeat. He therefore asked his closest civilian advisor, Lord Privy Seal Marquis Kido Koichi, to study the problems of peace from his standpoint as a specialist in opinion making and domestic political control.

Kido committed his first thoughts to paper on January 6, 1944, precisely nineteen months before the bomb fell on Hiroshima. The war, he conceded in essence, is lost. We must make a realistic peace proposal before Germany capitulates. We should ask the U.S.S.R., as a neutral in the Pacific War, to act as our go-between and convoke a "commission of the principal Pacific nations" to dispose of our conquests. We must be ready to let them all go, either returning them to China or giving them their independence as "permanent neutral nations like Switzerland." Then, "in view of the terrible attrition we have suffered," we must "preserve and cultivate our power for one hundred years." Above all we must "keep the Anglo-Saxons from destroying us as a colored

REGENT HIROHITO

This photograph was released by the Imperial Household Ministry on December 18, 1926, a week before Emperor Taisho died. Having governed Japan for five years during his father's illness, Hirohito already knew what he wanted for Japan and how to go about effecting it.

天皇

毎日グラフ別冊
「皇室の100年」から

THE WEIGHT OF TRADITION

On his way home from Peers' School on a day in 1913 (above left) Hirohito could tussle and laugh with one of the chamberlains who constantly attended him, but he already took seriously the burdens of ancestry and tradition which lay upon his shoulders. He had to live up to the expectations of his domineering grandfather, Emperor Meiji (above); live down the eccentric reputation of his weak, vain father, Emperor Taisho (below left); and live through years of disapproval from his religious pacifist mother, Empress Dowager Sadako (below). At his coronation ceremonies in 1928 he and his bride, Nagako, (above right) would have to wear robes almost as ancient as the huge tomb of the fifth-century Emperor Nintoku (below right). The tomb took up valuable land in the suburbs of commercial Osaka, but because it was sacred no one complained of it or even pretended to notice its existence. By the same taboo Japanese would overlook many of Hirohito's activities during the years ahead.

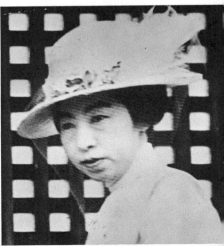

TRIP ABROAD

While still Crown Prince in 1921, Hirohito made a memorable visit to Europe. He did so over the objections of Army strongman Field Marshal Yamagata Aritomo (above left). In Europe Hirohito founded an anti-Yamagata movement in the ranks of military attachés at Japanese embassies. It was headed by his uncles Prince Higashikuni (above right) and Prince Asaka (below right). It suffered a temporary check in 1923 when Prince Kitashirakawa died in the car wreck below. Prince Asaka, too, was in the crash and broke his left leg. A brace is still visible as a bulge in his pants leg in the 1924 picture at far right. At near right he recuperates mountain climbing in the Rockies. In one further outcome of the tour, Edward Prince of Wales accepted an invitation to visit Japan in 1922 and finish a game of golf (above). Hirohito greatly admired and envied Edward's stylish dash and self-composure.

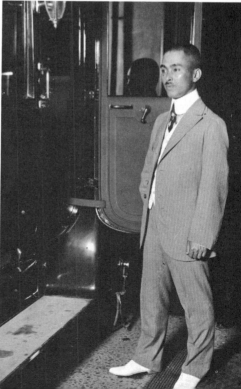

HELPFUL KINSMEN

Top left: Prince Kanin, great-uncle o Hirohito's wife, Nagako, and Army chie of staff, 1931–40. Mid-left: Princ Fushimi, Nagako's cousin and Navy chie of staff, 1932–41. Bottom left: anothe of Nagako's cousins, Prince Yamashina after an audience with Hirohito in 192 He helped develop torpedo planes as Navy test pilot. Above: Nagako's fathe Prince Kuni, and mother, Shimazu Ch kako, in 1927. Kuni communicated t Hirohito a lasting enthusiasm for ai planes, tanks, and biological warfare. A right: Prince Kaya, also a cousin o Nagako, and his wife, Toshiko, a firs cousin of Hirohito. They are shown pas ing through Los Angeles in 1934 after goodwill visit to Hitler. Above righ Hirohito's own three brothers: Princ Chichibu, the eldest, in 1937 in Londo below him, Prince Takamatsu of th Navy, in 1931; and at far right, youn Prince Mikasa of the Army, as he a peared in 1935.

FAVORITE ADVISORS

Above left: World War II Chief of Staff Sugiya[m]
on his way home as a colonel in 1922 after a year a[nd]
a half as an observer and aviation specialist at [the]
League of Nations in Geneva. Above: Admiral Yam[a-]
moto Isoroku when he was a captain attached to [the]
embassy in Washington in 1925. At left: Lord Pr[ivy]
Seal Makino shortly before his retirement in 19[.]
Below left: Lord Privy Seal Kido after his retirem[ent]
in 1945. Below: Economic co-ordinator Suzuki Tei-i[chi]
during his trial in 1947 as a war criminal. Oppo[site]
page, at top, Prewar Prime Minister Konoye sitting [in]
the guise of his ally Hitler at a fancy-dress party; be[low]
left, after his suicide from poison in 1945. Below rig[ht,]
Wartime Prime Minister Tojo.

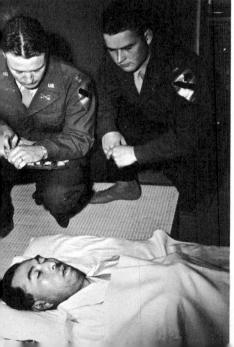

皇太子殿下御降誕奉祝記念撮影

LOYAL OPPOSITION

Of those who fought Hirohito hardest behind the scenes and then accepted defeat in silence, the most notable were General Araki Sadao, far left above; General Ugaki Kazushige, left above; Toyama Mitsuru, the lord of the Black Dragon Society, shown in 1927 with Chiang Kai-shek, far left; General Honjo Shigeru, left, Hirohito's chief aide-de-camp from 1933 to 1936; and finally Japan's tragic old liberal, the most long-lived of Emperor Meiji's advisors, Prince Saionji Kinmochi. Eyes ablaze with indignation, Saionji is shown above arriving at his Tokyo villa after one of the assassinations of 1932. He is greeted by Baron Harada Kumao, the Court spy who acted as his political secretary and Boswell.

VILLAINS AND VICTIMS

At left: Japan's girl spy, Eastern Jewel, and her lover, Tanaka Takayoshi, shortly after they had successfully touched off the 1932 "Fake War" in Shanghai. Below left: Eastern Jewel with one of the Japanese planes in which she prepared for her missions behind Chinese lines. Above right, from left to right: Kita Ikki, the ideologist of the Strike-North Faction; Dr. Okawa Shumei, the ideologist of the Strike-South Faction and palace go-between with assassins during the terror of 1932; his minion Inoue Nisho, the leader of the Blood Brotherhood; and Tatekawa Yoshiji, the Army emissary who successfully failed to prevent the seizure of Mukden by Japanese troops in September 1931. Below: Nagata Tetsuzan, the Army leader whom Hirohito's uncles first sponsored and then, in 1935, allowed to be assassinated. At right: In a remarkable picture taken early in 1932, Prime Minister Inukai stands in the clothes and posture he had at the moment of his shooting later that spring.

JAPANESE AGGRESSION

The siege gun above, emplaced to bomba[rd] Port Arthur in the 1905 war with Russia, was la[ter] smuggled into Mukden in 1931, mounted in [a] recreation shed, and used to shell Chinese positi[ons] on the night of September 18. At left: Ts[uji] Masanobu, the staff officer who masterminded [the] conquest of Singapore and the Bataan De[ath] March in 1941. Below: Japanese troops w[ent] through the "back door" from Malaya to Sin[ga]pore across an easily bridged gap in the causew[ay] left by British demolition experts. Above right: [the] three commanders who took Nanking in 193[7—] General Matsui, Prince Asaka, and General Ya[na]gawa—confer at field headquarters. Asaka, [the] Emperor's uncle, was in local command wh[ile] scenes like the one at right were enacted a[nd] thousands of Chinese prisoners were bayone[ted] beside Nanking's walls.

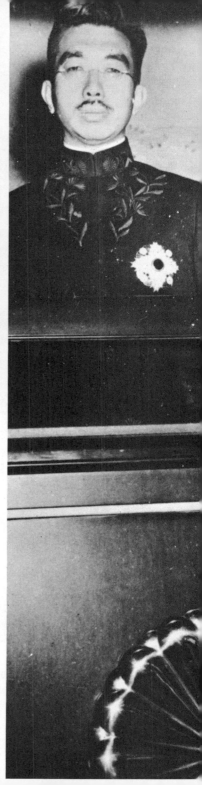

TRIUMPH AND DEFEAT

At the fall of Singapore on February 19, 1942, in a rare spontaneous popular appearance (left), Hirohito rode his horse White Snow out onto one of the palace bridges and remained motionless in the saddle for most of an hour while crowds gathered to share his moment of victory. Just as silently three years later Hirohito acknowledged imperial fault for the lost war by making his uncle Prince Higashikuni take the humiliating post of surrender prime minister. In token of his humble and contrite position Higashikuni (above) stood on a lower step out in front of his ministers in the official Cabinet portrait. In November 1945, as soon as the Occupation began to look as if it would be a success, Hirohito (right) went by train as a pilgrim to the shrine of the sun goddess at Ise. Cutting a lonely figure at the window of his imperial carriage, he wore a modified naval uniform stripped of all badges of rank save his Order of Merit, First Class.

SARTOR RESARTUS

It was years after the war before Hirohito would buy a new suit. When he did buy one, it was cut to an American pattern. Here, with Pearl Harbor now in the distant past and Japan once more a world power, Emperor Hirohito strolls in his new suit through his palace gardens.

race." We around the Throne "will have to retain our actual power in the state secretly."

If the Throne was to keep its power in secret and Japan was to lie low for one hundred years, the people of the country would have to be carefully prepared. The fighting men had staked their honor on victory or suicide, and hundreds of thousands had died in the Emperor's name. If peace were declared prematurely, patriots would say that Hirohito lacked courage to fight the war through. Widows and orphans would blame him for letting their loved ones die in vain. To save the nation's face, then, the war must be continued until everyone had suffered from it and was eager to see it finished. At that point the people could be made to feel that they had fought poorly and let the Emperor down. At that point, if Hirohito declared peace, the people would feel obligated to him.

Kido discussed his ideas with other members of the Emperor's Young Set—all in their fifties now—and found that they had been thinking along similar lines. According to an ancient metaphor, the Emperor lived "above the clouds like a crane," surveying the whole state of his nation and leaving the routine of government to his appointed officials. On those rare occasions of national crisis when he felt compelled to issue direct commands to his people, his intervention was known as "the Voice of the Crane." The members of the imperial cabal all agreed that, when the right moment came to announce a surrender, the Emperor should do it personally and suddenly, as if on an impulse of pity for the sufferings of his subjects. Then his act could be romanticized at home and abroad as "a sacred decision" enunciated by the Voice of the Crane. It might even be effective to break with all precedent and broadcast his voice on the radio.

To make Japanese absolve Hirohito would be difficult, but to make the democratizing conquerors accept the Emperor would be a problem of incalculable difficulty. Personally Hirohito did not care what happened to himself. If he lost the war—and he did not admit that he had lost it yet—he would gladly abdicate. It was the imperial institution, the bequest of his divine ancestors, which must be protected. With this one proviso, Hirohito encouraged Kido in his peace plans and returned to his preoccupation of the moment, the defense of the Marshall Islands.

Having gained the tacit consent of the Emperor, Kido delegated the task of contingency planning for defeat to a group headed by the lanky, cynical Prince Konoye, the prime minister at the time of the rape of Nanking. The group called itself the "Peace Faction." It included Japan's living ex-prime ministers, half a dozen of her leading diplomats, and several of her best strategic minds from the Army and Navy General Staffs. It met secretly at first in Konoye's home, the "Hate-China" Villa, where he had lived since the fall of Nanking in 1937. Later in 1944 it hired a regular secretarial staff and rented space in the Dai Ichi Insurance Building overlooking the southeastern gate of the palace. This location was ideal. In the basement Japan Broadcasting Corporation had its secret emergency radio station. On the sixth floor were the headquarters of the Tokyo Area Army and a switchboard controlling direct lines to the palace, to the various police headquarters, and to all military barracks in the city.

The duty of the Peace Faction was not to promote peace, as its name implied, but to salvage as much as possible from surrender. Analysis of American propaganda broadcasts to Japan revealed that Americans tended to exaggerate the dominance of "the military clique" in Japan. As a former foreign minister explained it to Lord Privy Seal Kido: "In the United States they think there is a confrontation between moderates and extremists. They think the extreme group suppresses the moderate one." Hoping to exploit this misapprehension, the Peace Faction created cover stories and remade public images for the century of enforced quiescence which Kido envisaged after defeat. Army and Navy officers were sought out who would be willing to take the part of extremists and lead mock mutinies against the Emperor when it came time for him to surrender. Men with reputations as moderates were coached in the roles they would have to play as postwar cabinet ministers. Still other moderates were recruited from the business world to take charge of hidden imperial assets and care for them as their own property. Since true moderates were in short supply, make-believe moderates were manufactured by the simple expedient of having the secret police keep dossiers on them as possible subversives. In this fashion even Prince Konoye, who had led the nation to war in 1937, hoped to create dove's clothing for himself.

In early 1945, Lord Privy Seal Kido had the secret police imprison four hundred members of the Peace Faction and keep them in detention for forty days. He apparently did so without consulting them, but as they were well treated they did not hold it against him. Many of them had once been leading advocates of war with the United States and Great Britain. Now they were cleared in Western eyes and would be enabled to hold government posts during the American Occupation. Indeed one of them, Yoshida Shigeru, was to serve for seven years as a postwar prime minister. Since 1933 he had been an unabashed proponent of the Strike-South policy, against the United States, Britain, and the Netherlands. Now, overnight, in a well-appointed prison cell, he became a certifiable hero of the resistance movement. His sudden transformation was all the more bewildering to the silent populace because he was the son-in-law of Count Makino, the Emperor's chief advisor from 1926 to 1935. Makino had been implicated in all of the assassinations and fake coups d'etat of that era which had turned Japan's military zeal from the U.S.S.R. towards the United States.

The staff officers of the Peace Faction saw the second great weakness in American political psychology as an obsessive fear of communism. By playing on it, they felt that they could make Americans look at modern Japanese history in a new and more sympathetic light. The assignment fell to Prince Konoye. He qualified as something of an expert because his son, "Butch," who later died as a prisoner of war in Russia, had attended Princeton. Konoye set about his task by creating "notes" and "diaries" which would explain the events of his own three years as prime minister. He discovered that the forgeries were more difficult to write than he had anticipated. He knew too much about the complexities of Japanese politics to frame straightforward arguments. Throughout the summer of 1944 his false starts piled up in his secretary's files. One of them, a specially composed "diary," turned up as late as 1967 at one of the inns to which he used to take assorted male and female companions.[3]

Finally Prince Konoye wrote a long, implausible "memorial to the Throne" which he later turned over to Allied Intelligence. To give it standing as a document of state, he actually read the memorial to Hirohito on February 14, 1945. He and the Emperor must have chuckled over some of the allegations in it. Konoye accused the Communists, "as part of a purposeful plan," of inciting militarism in Japan "ever since the Manchurian incident" of 1931. The Reds, he said, had brought "the country to its present plight" in order to create conditions for lower-class revolution in "the confusion that will arise out of defeat." Unfortunately for Konoye's thesis, all Communists and most leftists of any description in Japan had been in prison since the late 1920's. The only civilians agitating for militarism had always been hired bullies belonging to Court-sponsored "patriotic societies." To cope with these awkward facts, Konoye went on to explain that "our right-wingers are nothing more than Communists masquerading."

Throughout the planning of peace, Lord Privy Seal Kido encouraged Hirohito to maintain a bold public front of fight-to-the-finish. Only thus could the honor of the samurai be satisfied. Only thus could the people be kept at their jobs. Only thus could the enemy be made to appreciate the expense involved in reducing Japan's island strongholds. Only thus, finally, could the Americans be persuaded that the real power in Japan lay not with calculating civilians of the highest caste but with soldier fanatics from one of the lower castes.

In the spring of 1944 Hirohito approved construction of a labyrinth of tunnels under three mountains in the wild Nagano Alps. He let it be believed that there, if worst came to worst, he would preside over the final Imperial Headquarters and fight to the death with his best troops. Six miles of concrete galleries were ultimately completed and 75,000 men employed on them at a cost of $20

[3] Japanese, who are ordinarily tolerant about such matters, shake their heads over Konoye's sex life. They complain that he had a taste for men and women of the lowest classes and that he would give entire weekends to the bizarre experiences which they devised for him. A geisha who knew him has defended his aberrations as "a natural expression of his speculative mind."

million. Even Hirohito's personal bathtub was installed. But he
never expected to use it. He acknowledged to intimates that if he
ever left Tokyo the people's will to resist would collapse.

Later, in the autumn of 1944, Hirohito sanctioned the manufacture of "special attack weapons," kamikaze planes and torpedoes designed specifically for suicide missions. He put his seal on
plans for fire lanes across the major cities, swathes of houses cut
down to minimize the effectiveness of incendiary bombing. He
supported, in his edicts and rescripts, a campaign of domestic
propaganda calculated to persuade the people that the U.S. government meant to rape and destroy Japan thoroughly in the event
of defeat.

A year passed in which Japan lost battle after desperate battle.
When Saipan and the Marianas fell in June of 1944, Hirohito was
persuaded that perhaps a new prime minister would tempt the
U.S. government into making a peace offer. Hirohito therefore
withdrew his support from Prime Minister Tojo, who was supposed in the United States to be the archmilitarist, and smoothly
replaced him with a less notorious member of the imperial cabal,
reserve General Koiso Kuniaki. Although he had masterminded
much of the plotting for the conquest of Manchuria in 1931, Koiso
was little known outside Japan. Wizened and narrow-eyed, the
new prime minister looked more like a Chinese opium den pro-
prietor than a Japanese head of state. He was known in Japan as
a man of guile, a specialist in counterespionage rather than combat. His appointment signified that Japan was no longer trying to
win by conventional force of arms but only to salvage what she
could by intrigue. It was under Prime Minister Koiso's guidance
that Japan now resorted to human bombs, human torpedoes, and
banzai charges. Though they made U.S. victories costly, the
kamikaze tactics could do no more than slow the leapfrog approach of American task forces.

THE GREAT BLUFF

On January 6, 1945, exactly a year after admitting to his diary
that the war could not be won, Lord Privy Seal Kido, the Emper-
or's chief civilian advisor, was thumbing papers and digesting

lunch in his book-lined study on the third floor of the Imperial Household Administration Building. He was a slightly built, owlish man of fifty-five—short sparse hair, spidery utilitarian glasses, a Hitler mustache. To those who were his friends he was known for his dapper grooming, his light-colored waistcoats, and his "hunted animal look," a disarming expression of puzzled astonishment with which he greeted all news, whether of rain outside or of a city destroyed. To those who were not his friends, Kido was known for theatrical fits of hysteria in which he would shriek threats at social inferiors who thwarted him. His detractors liked to point out that he kept a pack of savage chows and police dogs locked in separate cages along the front of his villa and that he had fed them red meat throughout the period of wartime rationing. Behind the mask of Kido's driven personality worked a mind which friend and foe alike conceded to be the coolest, quickest, and soundest in the counsels of government. Emperor Hirohito, who had known Kido all his life and had worked with him closely since 1922, valued his judgment and held a genuine affection for him. When Kido was put on trial as a war criminal in 1946, Hirohito let it be known that he would abdicate if Kido were sentenced to death.[4]

Now, when the telephone rang, it was the Emperor asking Kido to come over and talk to him. Kido summoned his charcoal-burning limousine and went downstairs to wait for it. The Imperial Household Building, once a dazzling concrete symbol of Court modernization, looked dingy under its protective wartime stripes. The watery winter sun did not flatter it. When the car came, it drove Kido along the northern outbuildings of the ceremonial Outer Palace where Matsui had received his baton of command for the offensive against Nanking in 1937. The car continued up a drive flanked on the left by the moat and wall of the Inner Palace enclosure. On the other side of the wall were scattered the facilities dedicated to the personal use of the Emperor and Empress: Hirohito's biological laboratory and experimental

---

[4] Kido was released from Allied prison in 1956. Thereafter he lived in a villa outside the palace, shunning all publicity. As late as 1968 neighbors said that he looked as frail and aristocratic as fine rice parchment but remained lively, saw many visitors, and read many books.

rice field; Empress Nagako's silkworm house; the Imperial Shrine in its courtyard of white pebbles; the severely Japanese Residential Palace in which Hirohito no longer lived. All were surrounded by an artful sea of vegetation, the woodland of the Fukiage Gardens. It had suffered little from the austerity care of wartime. Its surprise turnings still surprised; its perfect vistas still satisfied. Fewer cranes and peacocks strutted the paths but there remained the arching bridges, the rock gardens, the hidden lotus pools, the tiny greenhouses containing dwarf trees, some a thousand years old.

Kido's car took a sharp left, crossed the moat on a causeway, and passed through a gate into the inner enclosure. A short driveway did scant justice to the wonders of the gardens. Through the trees on the left Kido could glimpse the gables of the English-style country house where the Empress and her chief ladies had their wartime quarters and where Emperor and Empress entertained close personal friends. It was known officially by the colorful old name of Ka-in Tei, the Pavilion of Concubines, but no concubines had been kept there during the two decades of Hirohito's reign.

Straight ahead at the end of the drive rose a squat rectangle of concrete known as *Obunko*, the Honorable Imperial Library. Hirohito had built it as a work place and over the busy years it had become his home. Now, in addition to his office, it consisted of a complex of anterooms, and sixty feet below, in the hill on which it stood, an air raid shelter. The concrete walls of the bunker, twenty feet thick, enclosed ventilating machinery, cubby-holes for attendants, a comfortable Western-style living room and bath, and a long monastically furnished audience chamber. The walls were pierced by two sloping shafts. The tunnel from the audience chamber led up a staircase to a steel bulkhead in the hillside behind the library. The shaft from the living quarters came out to a concealed door in Hirohito's above-ground workroom.

As Kido made his way into the library, past guards and chamberlains, he reviewed the arrangements with satisfaction. Hirohito was waiting for him. "The American fleet," Hirohito said, without prologue, "has begun to shell the beaches of Lingayen Gulf. I am told that they will land and that it will be difficult to defend Luzon." Luzon was the main island of the Philippines, and Hiro-

hito's information was accurate and up-to-date. Softening up of
the beaches had begun that morning in preparation for a landing
three days later. "The situation," continued the Emperor, "is extremely grave and I wonder if the time has not come for me to
consult the elder statesmen. What do you think?"

Hirohito was telling Kido that he was ready to order his government and people to surrender. He never consulted the elder
statesmen, the former prime ministers of Japan, unless he was
about to take a momentous step. The last time he had seen them
had been before Pearl Harbor. The majority of them then had
advised him against war with the United States and he had disregarded their counsel. In offering to consult them again now, he
was admitting that his course of conquest had been wrong from
the beginning; that his life, in effect, was a failure. Kido knew how
difficult it must be for him. The forty-three-year-old Hirohito was
no longer the taut ambitious prince of 1922. He felt himself
middle-aged now, growing fat and puffy from overwork and lack
of exercise. His people murmured against him. As he paced his
study, his drooping mustache quivered and his short legs shuffled
jerkily as they always did when he was nervous. He cut a sad figure,
as symbolic of Japan in defeat as he had once been, in his scrubbed
callow youth, symbolic of the aspiring opportunistic Japan.

"As you say," said Kido, "the war situation in the Philippines is
extremely grave, and as it develops we may have to reconsider
seriously our guidance of the war. But before we do I beg of you to
stand back and await developments for a while. I think you should
sound out the real convictions of the two chiefs of staff on a
thoroughly informal basis. Then later call in the members of the
Cabinet. Finally, if you deem it necessary to decide on a change
in the fundamental imperial policy, summon a joint meeting of
the Cabinet and the elder statesmen in the Imperial Presence."

It was no part of Kido's peace plan to have the Emperor admit
his mistakes or blurt out his declaration of peace prematurely.
First he must give up his direct personal supervision of military
operations and ask the chiefs of staff to take all the responsibility
for further defeats. Then he must warn the members of the
Cabinet of his change of heart so that they could make necessary
political arrangements. Then finally, when the public mind was

prepared, he should simply announce his decision to the elders. Hirohito gladly took Kido's advice and from that day on he became a willing cog in the machinery which Kido had been designing for the past year.

Lord Privy Seal Kido, as chief advisor to the Throne, had assumed the dread responsibility of deciding when the moment was ripe for the imperial decision. His final meticulous arrangements went forward at an excruciating snail's pace. It would be disastrous to declare for peace too early. Kido could not be sure that his plan would work at all. It must have the benefit of perfect timing. The nation must be reduced to war-weariness. The soldiers must sate their sense of honor. If possible, the enemy must begin to feel shame and pity.

The B-29's came almost nightly. Men on whom Kido counted disappeared in the air raids. Men lost sleep in shelters. Men had to be pushed. Hirohito, himself, sometimes wavered and had to be encouraged. On January 22, 1945, Kido wrote a heartening poem for him:

> If a hedge of plum
> can survive a winter
> of sear and fallow,
> the heart of the warrior
> can also bloom again.

While Kido waited for the perfect moment, 200,000 Japanese died.

From the last week of January until early in April, 1945, Hirohito gave private audiences, one by one, to each of the admirals and generals in the top echelons of the military bureaucracy, to each of Japan's former prime ministers, and to a number of lawyers, professors, cartel owners, and mouthpieces for slum gang lords. By mid-March there was hardly a man of influence who had not pledged his silent unselfish co-operation in the plan for national survival. As each of them emerged from the Imperial Library or from the audience chamber in the bunker below, he had further conversation with Lord Privy Seal Kido and learned what specific service he might render.

While the political muster continued, so did the military bluster and bluff. Nine thousand obsolescent planes were hidden in forest airstrips. Suicide pilots were put in training to man them. Gangs of peasant volunteers drove stakes and dug entrenchments along Japan's sacred beaches. Exhibits of hoes, rakes, axes, bamboo spears, and other rustic secret weapons were mounted in such public places as the lobby of the prime minister's residence. The last concrete was poured at the headquarters of final resort under the Japanese Alps. The Americans were promised a "final decisive battle" if they ventured to land, as anticipated, in the coming autumn.

On March 24, 1945, the wizened Prime Minister Koiso, in whose help Hirohito had been led to expect subtlety and sophistication, came to the library, in agitation after a stormy Cabinet session. He requested an immediate audience, and asked Hirohito's approval for plans to make the government a complete military dictatorship. Hirohito did not intend to give the Army more power than it already possessed. He feared that if he did Japan would be committed to a suicide course. He had hoped that Prime Minister Koiso would be able to remain in power until the summer, by which time the nation and the armed forces might be fully prepared for peace. But events had moved too swiftly and Koiso already found the political pressures on him intolerable. The Emperor, he said, must either let him prepare for war to the last or replace him with a true surrender Cabinet.

Hirohito listened in silence while his prime minister described the deterioration of national morale and the psychological need for drastic political reorganization. Out the window it was another fine spring afternoon. The sun smiled down as if in mockery on the Fukiage Gardens. It had been a month of unrelieved disaster. In two weeks more than 100,000 Tokyo residents had burned to death in the great fires of the enemy's first incendiary raids. In four weeks Iwo Jima had fallen. It was the first island to be lost on Japan's inner defense perimeter, the first home island where Japanese fishermen had lived for centuries. With Iwo had perished 20,000 soldiers and any hope that the new kamikaze tactic of despair would do more than postpone the inevitable. All those 20,000 men had vowed to die and take as many Americans with them as possible. They had had eight months to dig tunnels and develop the natural caves of the rocky island. And in the end they had killed less than 7,000 Americans and held out for less than five weeks. Their failure was a preview of the fate in store for Hirohito if he accepted the Army's plan and became a chieftain of guerrilla werewolves in the Nagano Alps. Prime Minister Koiso came to the end of his report.

"I appreciate the painful service that you have rendered," said Hirohito. "Since you have offered it, I will accept your resignation. But I must ask you to keep it confidential and remain at your post until I have appointed a suitable successor for you."

Imperial advisor Kido spent the next two weeks in difficult negotiations. The prime minister and principal Cabinet members who were to succeed the Koiso government had been chosen tentatively, as part of the peace plan, during the previous autumn. But now many of them felt that it was too early for their appointment. The high command of the secret police could give no assurance that the armed forces were ready yet to accept a peace cabinet. The government might discover on surrendering that it spoke for only a part of the country and had become a "Badoglio regime" like the one in Italy. Nevertheless, having weighed the risks and consulted the elders, Lord Privy Seal Kido finally advised the Emperor to proceed according to plan.

Hirohito accepted Kido's recommendation and on April 7, 1945, invested as the next prime minister Suzuki Kan-taro, a retired admiral of eighty. Mrs. Suzuki had helped to take care of Hirohito as a little boy and the admiral himself had served from 1929 to 1936 as Hirohito's grand chamberlain, one of his four principal advisors.[5] No man had done more to turn the Emperor's eyes south toward the wealth of the Indies. No man had done more to furnish him with an image as a peace-loving constitutional monarch. No man knew him more intimately. "To Suzuki," Hirohito once said, "I could pour out my heart."

[5] The other three were the lord privy seal, who specialized in domestic political intrigue; the chief aide-de-camp, who handled liaison with the Army; and the imperial household minister who took care of the Emperor's intricate finances. It was the grand chamberlain's function to counsel the Emperor in personal, religious, and diplomatic matters.

Despite his years, the old admiral-chamberlain maintained a droll façade of youth. He had big ears, a puckish face, and an elfin sense of humor. He smoked as many cigars as the defense effort would allow him. Whenever he had a spare moment, he produced a volume of Taoist philosophy and appeared to immerse himself in it. He larded his talk with ancient Chinese aphorisms. He never disagreed with anyone and almost never expressed an opinion. "The art of government," he liked to say, "lies in non-government."

Prime Minister Suzuki opened his term of office with a call on the people to fight and die to the last. His words, as he later explained, were an exercise in *haragei*, belly acting or belly talk, the art of saying one thing and meaning the opposite which has been cultivated by Japanese ever since the nation became an efficient police state in the tenth century A.D. Suzuki knew that he would be considered at home and abroad "a peace prime minister." At his investiture ceremony, according to his recollection later, he was "given to understand" that he must end the war.

After searching his soul and talking with Lord Privy Seal Kido, Suzuki saw his mission in the terms of an old Japanese romance. A baron who had been defeated in battle and had lost the flower of his knights was called on by the enemy to surrender his castle. His surviving retainer besought him to seek terms and save his life. He refused. He retreated to the castle, dismissed the retainers, opened the gates wide, and stood exposed on the drawbridge all alone. When the enemy came in sight, he shouted, "If you want to come, come." The enemy, fearing a trick, retired, and the shrewd baron was left to rebuild his fief. This was the stratagem which Hirohito was to use in surrendering his Imperial Throne to the conquering Americans.

In Washington former Ambassador Grew correctly interpreted the appointment of the Suzuki Cabinet as a peace gesture. He responded, as Suzuki would have wished, by asking for Japan to be reassured that she could keep her Emperor system. When the suggestion was not accepted by President Truman, Prime Minister Suzuki's vigil on the drawbridge became a nightmarish test of nerve. Japan's ally, the Third Reich, was collapsing with terrifying abruptness. By mid-April 1945, a month after crossing the

Rhine into German territory, Eisenhower's armies had driven to within sixty miles of Berlin. To the east the Red Army had broken out from its bridgeheads on the Oder River and was even closer to the German capital. The idea that troops could perform miracles when fighting on their native soil lay exposed. Japan's hope of winning a decisive battle on her home beaches began to look foolish. The home minister in charge of police and the education minister in charge of propaganda consulted with Lord Privy Seal Kido on means of suppressing popular unrest. On April 29 Hirohito's forty-fourth birthday was marred by news that his former ally Mussolini had been executed at Lake Como the day before and his corpse mutilated and left in the gutter by a mob of angry Italians.

On May 1, Hirohito warned Lord Privy Seal Kido of the imminent capitulation of Germany and discussed it with him for fifty minutes. On the following day they discussed the suicide of Adolf Hitler. In his initial peace planning sixteen months earlier, Kido had hoped to negotiate a peace before the fall of Germany. Now that the Allies had both hands free to strangle Japan, the last hope of negotiating terms had vanished and unconditional surrender became inevitable. But Japan must appear to be an irrational nation. Otherwise there would be no need for the Emperor to intervene and speak with the Voice of the Crane. More than ever, therefore, Japan must show that she was ready to hold out insanely. On May 7, the day of Germany's official surrender, Kido went through his family strong room to remove from it all documents and mementos which might incriminate the Throne.

Two days later an operational dispatch in code, stamped "urgent, confidential, top military secret," arrived at the Navy Building across the street from the plaza outside the main south gate of the palace. It came from Commander Fujimura Yoshiro who had sat out the war as the head of the Navy's peace-seeking mission in Switzerland. Desperately worried about his nation's plight, Fujimura had recently redoubled his efforts. Now he proudly reported that Allen Dulles, the head of O.S.S. in Europe, had offered his services in case Japan should wish to arrange a termination of hostilities. Fujimura followed his first cable with six others in the next ten days. He described the havoc which

Nazi diehards had brought to Germany. He enumerated the Allied forces which were being diverted from Europe to the Pacific Theater. He relayed intelligence that Russia would soon join in the war against Japan. He described the part which Allen Dulles had played in bringing peace to northern Italy and preserving it from destruction.

Fujimura's cables from Switzerland continued to arrive at the Navy Building. Pressure mounted on the two principal officers of the Navy General Staff to give some kind of answers. On May 18, when five cables had accumulated in in-baskets, Hirohito's brother Prince Takamatsu, a captain on the Navy General Staff, came to the palace to discuss the cables with Hirohito and Lord Privy Seal Kido. It was unthinkable for the Emperor to make peace directly with the Americans—not after ordering the attack on Pearl Harbor, not after the Americans had scorned earlier offers of negotiated peace. But perhaps—and Prince Takamatsu merely raised the possibility—perhaps, after all, Hirohito should abdicate in favor of his eleven-year-old son and leave others to assume the responsibility and chagrin of capitulating to the Americans. Kido disagreed sharply. Abdication would be not only cowardice but an admission of guilt. It would discredit the Throne in the eyes of the people and make democratization easy for the conquerors. Hirohito agreed.

Rumors that an American peace feeler had been rejected brought Hirohito's popularity in the Tokyo bureaucracy to an all-time ebb. When the senior member of the imperial family, Prince Kanin, died on May 21, three days after Prince Takamatsu's visit to the palace, the cause of his death—hemorrhoids—was the subject of disrespectful jokes. Nevertheless, the next day, Commander Fujimura in Switzerland was sent a cable warning him that the O.S.S. offer "contains certain points indicative of an enemy plot. Therefore we advise you to be extremely cautious."[6]

[6] Later, on June 20, when a month had passed, the zealous Fujimura was informed that his problem had been referred to the foreign ministry and that in future he would kindly submit his proposals through channels at the Japanese diplomatic office in Berne. The O.S.S. at once dropped Fujimura as a cold contact. The Japanese diplomatic codes had been broken by every major nation. To deal further with Fujimura would be to talk to Tokyo over a line tapped in Moscow.

In a week during which 193 kamikaze pilots were hurling themselves to death at Okinawa, the chief and vice chief of the Navy General Staff felt that they could not shoulder the responsibility for refusing Dulles's mediation. Hirohito accepted their resignations on May 25 and replaced them a few days later with admirals tough enough to ignore further cables from Switzerland.

On the evening of the resignations, May 25, wagging tongues were stilled by catastrophe. American bombardiers, who had a fine record for missing hospitals, universities, and the palace, neatly cleaned out an area south of the palace walls with incendiaries. It was a calculated escalation. Other fire raids had taken more lives but this one burned out the aristocracy and singed the Throne. It destroyed the principal ministries of the government and ninety-one villas belonging to the most distinguished families in Japan. Seven Imperial Princes and uncounted chamberlains had to flee their burning homes and take refuge within the palace moat.

Hours after the raid was over the ceremonial Outer Palace caught fire. Chamberlains explain, with a snide sense of poetic justice, that during the burning of the War Ministry half a mile away, old contingency planning papers were lofted into the night air and came down smoldering on the tiled palace roofs. Some 5,000 Imperial Guardsmen and several hundred officials were encamped within the moat that night, but the flames spread quickly. Hastily organized bucket brigades succeeded in wetting down the Imperial Household Ministry and preserving it untouched, but the older buildings which stood wall to wall with it were all burned to the ground: the lovely Phoenix Hall and banqueting chamber, the villa of the crown prince, and many outbuildings including several storehouses for imperial records. Some firemen who took all the responsibility for failing to check the flames were later found shot nearby. As the embers cooled, Hirohito announced from his concrete library in the Fukiage woods, "I am glad to share the sufferings of my people."

The American attempt to bring the war home to Japan's richest and most influential citizens only caused the great feudal vassal families to draw in closer to the Throne. It was clear now that the Americans were ready, if need be, to topple the entire social hierarchy. They would not consider Hirohito's personal abdication an adequate expiation of war guilt. The elite must survive or perish together. Lord Privy Seal Kido, the Emperor's principal advisor, discovered that he had new supporters. A dawn of comprehension gleamed in other aristocratic eyes when he spoke of the elaborate deceptions envisaged in his peace plan. Three days after the fire, when the minister of war sought to resign in apology for the destruction of the palace, Hirohito was widely quoted, with approval, as saying, "Please stay at your post; you will be needed this fall when it comes time for the survival or obliteration of our nation."

Now, at last, in the first week of June, the official leaders of the Japanese government were recruited to carry out the first phase of Kido's peace plan and to decide publicly on the need for surrender. Their performance, as staged, was a masterpiece of belly acting which said one thing to the world audience and another to the exclusive audience of political connoisseurs on the domestic front. On June 7 the Cabinet resolved not to desert the capital before the final decisive battle. This meant that Hirohito had given up the idea of fighting to the last in the Nagano Alps. It meant that there would be no final battle because Japan would surrender first.

With this understanding the Cabinet and representatives of the General Staff met at the Imperial Household Ministry on the following day for a full-dress council in the Imperial Presence. Before the meeting each man present was handed a pair of documents prepared by the General Staff. One reviewed the "World Situation," the other "The Present State of Our National Power." In the most pessimistic phrases, the most chilling statistics, the two studies revealed that the war had taken "an ominous turn" and that "insurmountable difficulties" stood in the way of continuing it.

After the Emperor and the others in the room had glanced through the two gloomy background papers, a declaration was read aloud and passed unanimously. It called on the nation to fight to the last of its 70 million men, women, and children. It announced that this was the "fundamental policy to be pursued henceforth in the prosecution of the war." Then it gave one minuscule hint that the policy being decided was really one for prosecution of the peace: "The enemy is also facing its own concealed difficulties and is desperate in its efforts to terminate the war soon. . . . We must resolutely take every political and military step to grasp the god-sent opportunity." In other words, Japan must exploit the distrust between the United States and Russia in order to negotiate a surrender. Without a word being said explicitly about peace, everyone in the room understood that peace was the issue. As Hirohito later explained to one of his chamberlains: "A concealed clause, which we may call clause X, was contained in the proposals laid before the imperial conference of June 8. This clause was a peace clause."

As soon as the meeting had adjourned imperial advisor Kido drafted a written plan for implementing the peace resolution. His idea was that the United States could be made to concede terms out of fear that, otherwise, Japan would give China to Russia. He proposed therefore that Japan should begin conversations with Russia at once on two separate topics: what bribe Russia would take to remain a neutral; and what terms Russia, as mediator, would be willing to try to get for Japan in a peace settlement. Kido proposed that Japan should hold out for two conditions: preservation of the Emperor system of government and some face-saving statement by the enemy that Japan had won peace with honor. Hirohito approved Kido's plan the next day, June 9, and Foreign Minister Togo[7] at once promised to press home negotiations with the Russian ambassador in Tokyo. Hirohito urged Togo "not to be too prudent." One of Togo's envoys had been talking to Russia's Ambassador Malik for a week. As yet the two men had not passed the point of drinking tea together and swapping stories about the lack of understanding for the Russian character in Japanese provincial areas.

POTSDAM ULTIMATUM

This was the state of cold fear and colder cunning which immobilized Japan in June when President Truman began to pre-

[7] Not to be confused with Japan's notorious World War II Prime Minister Tojo, spelled with a *j*.

pare for the Potsdam Conference in mid-July. It was a state unknown to any American at the time and not one which would have
aroused much sympathy if it had been known. As yet the Japanese
government had made no official offer to surrender. On June 18,
President Truman approved plans for Operation Olympic which
would have sent a million Americans into the beachheads of
southern Japan in the coming November. To support the invasion
Chief of Staff Marshall in Washington was expecting to need—for
"tactical use"—no less than nine of the new untried atomic bombs.

By coincidence, on that same day, June 18, Hirohito began to
feel that his ministers were dawdling over the task of salvaging
an honorable peace. That afternoon Lord Privy Seal Kido arranged a meeting of the Big Six—the chiefs of staff; Army, Navy,
foreign, and prime ministers—and had them adopt a timetable for
ending the war. They agreed that negotiations must be opened
in Moscow before the middle of July and that the target date for
cease-fire should be September. Their plan was confirmed at a
meeting in the Imperial Presence four days later. It was an unusual meeting in that Hirohito spoke individually to the ministers
requiring their active co-operation in the humiliating task ahead.
The next day Hirohito asked his advisor Kido to have work begun
on the imperial rescript which would have to be issued explaining
defeat to the people.

A week later, on June 29, the Japanese foreign ministry finally
made its first written proposal to the U.S.S.R. Through an intermediary,[8] Foreign Minister Togo offered Soviet Ambassador Malik a neutral Manchuria, no more special Japanese fishing
privileges, favorable consideration of other Russian requests—this
pittance in exchange for a pledge by Russia that she would refrain
from joining in the war against Japan. No mention was made of
Japan surrendering. On the contrary the Japanese emissary suggested that perhaps the U.S.S.R. would like to throw in some oil
and aviation gas in order to weaken the common enemy, the
United States. Soviet Ambassador Malik fidgeted and seemed
hardly to be listening. The Japanese were not offering enough to
tempt Russia nor asking enough to help themselves. Malik stifled

[8] Hirota Koki, a former prime and foreign minister.

a yawn and promised routinely to study the proposal. For the next two weeks he put off increasingly desperate Japanese representations. He was sick in bed, he said, with Japanese dysentery.

On Independence Day, the British government concurred jovially in what it termed the "independent" U.S. decision to use the bomb.

In Tokyo that day leaders were discussing fresh intelligence from Switzerland. It came this time from Lieutenant General Okamoto, the head of the Army "peace mission" there. Through a third party Okamoto had sounded out Allen Dulles, the chief of the O.S.S. in Europe, as to what terms, if any, the United States would give Japan. Dulles had replied that "if Japan surrenders" it was the "understanding" of the United States that the Allies would allow the Emperor system of government to be continued. It was the one condition which Japanese leaders months earlier had agreed to settle for if worst came to worst. But no one knew how much trust to put in it. Japanese spy agencies had offered such reassurances routinely in China without any intention of honoring them. Moreover, on July 2, Senator Homer Capehart of Indiana had told Congress that "Japan's capitulation is imminent" and that "only the Emperor's status remains to be decided."

Analysis of foreign broadcasts had brought it home to Hirohito that Allied leaders at their scheduled Potsdam meeting in mid-July were about to decide the fate of the Orient. To save American lives, Truman might invite Russia and even China to contribute troops for the assault on Japan. The thought of a Russian invasion was terrifying enough, but the thought of a Chinese revenge raised cold sweats. Hirohito decided to go over the head of "sick" Ambassador Malik in Tokyo and begin direct conversations with Molotov in Moscow. He summoned Prime Minister Suzuki on July 7 and told him, "We are wasting precious time feeling out the belly of Russia. How would it be if we ask her frankly to act as go-between and offer to send an envoy to Moscow with an imperial letter?" Suzuki accepted the suggestion "gratefully."

Hirohito, anguished over the decision he had made, began to have second thoughts. On July 10 his old Army minion, the ubiquitous Suzuki Tei-ichi, who had manned the home headquarters of the division which raped Nanking, came to the palace to discuss Japan's ability "to end and start again." Finally, two days later, imperial advisor Kido noted that "the Emperor has now reached a state of determination." Kido at once arranged a private audience for Prince Konoye. Konoye assured Hirohito that the nation must, indeed, surrender. In his description of conditions outside the palace, he went so far as to say, "The people all want to find a way out. Some are even of the opinion that the Emperor should be rebuked."

"Is it your conviction then that we should end the war at once?" asked Hirohito bleakly.

"It is," replied Konoye.

"So be it," said Hirohito. "There may be occasion to send you to Russia. Please be ready to act on your convictions." And with that the Emperor left the room.

Prince Konoye went directly to a meeting with Foreign Minister Togo and Togo cabled at once to Ambassador Sato in MOSCOW: SEE MOLOTOV BEFORE HIS DEPARTURE FOR POTSDAM. . . . CONVEY HIS MAJESTY'S STRONG DESIRE TO SECURE A TERMINATION OF THE WAR. . . . UNCONDITIONAL SURRENDER IS THE ONLY OBSTACLE TO PEACE. . . .

That night at 11:25 Ambassador Sato cabled back: THERE IS NO CHANCE OF WINNING THE SOVIET UNION TO OUR SIDE AND OF OBTAINING HER SUPPORT ON THE BASIS SET FORTH IN YOUR CABLES. . . . JAPAN IS DEFEATED. . . . WE MUST FACE THAT FACT AND ACT ACCORDINGLY. . . .

Sato's message crossed en route with a second cable from Foreign Minister Togo. It contained the news that Prince Konoye, bearing a letter in Hirohito's own hand, would come to Moscow to work out the details of surrender: PLEASE ARRANGE IMMEDIATELY TO OBTAIN AN ENTRY PERMIT FOR PRINCE KONOYE AND HIS PARTY. . . . HAVE A SOVIET PLANE MEET THEM AT TSITSIHAR OR MANCHOULI.[9]

There followed as sad a correspondence with death as history has ever recorded. Ambassador Sato Naotake in Moscow cabled

[9] Manchouli or Lupin is a town on the Russo-Manchurian border near the eastern corner of Mongolia. Tsitsihar or Lungkiang, which is inside of Manchuria 220 miles from the border, had a better airport.

home on July 13 that Molotov "could not find time to see me." So Sato saw Molotov's subordinate instead and begged him for a quick response to the proposed Konoye visit. Late that night Ambassador Sato was told over the phone that "the Soviet answer will be delayed because of the departure of Stalin and Molotov" for Potsdam. Throughout the Potsdam Conference Sato called every morning at the Soviet Foreign Ministry to relay further clarifications from Tokyo as to the purpose of Konoye's mission. Every afternoon and evening he composed cables itemizing the latest Soviet requests for still more clarification. Hirohito seemed relieved at the Russian procrastination. When he received Foreign Minister Togo in audience on July 18, he said, "The fate of our proposal is now beyond your control. It depends on the response of the other side and on the national destiny ordained by the divine ancestors."

On July 19 Ambassador Sato in Moscow finally received an ordinary postal letter from a member of Molotov's staff, stating that the Japanese proposals, as yet, were too vague to warrant an answer. Sato relayed this opinion to Tokyo and accompanied it with an impassioned plea for a realistic surrender note which would spare his beloved country. Foreign Minister Togo consulted with Hirohito and felt able to give Sato little further clarification. It was Prince Konoye's mission, he cabled, to bring specific surrender proposals to Moscow and to arrange a peace short of unconditional surrender.

Unknown to Stalin, unknown to Hirohito, the telegraphic correspondence between Togo and Sato was being intercepted by U.S. Intelligence; it was decoded, translated, and submitted to Secretary of State Byrnes. It revealed clearly that Japan was desperate to surrender. It did not reveal the minimal face-saving terms which Lord Privy Seal Kido and members of the General Staff had agreed to accept months earlier. It did not show any willingness on the part of the Japanese to settle for the one condition which had already been granted through O.S.S. Chief Dulles. U.S. Intelligence analysts tended to see Japan as a brutal police state under the control of a few tough fanatic generals like Tojo. The analysts did not know that Tojo was only an obedient servant of the Throne. They did not know that the Emperor's civilian advisors were at least as influential as his military aides. The power of the Japanese Army was judged by its arrogant totalitarian behavior in conquered countries overseas. It was not fully appreciated that most Japanese soldiers were of humble birth and that this made them subservient to aristocratic civilians at home.

Secretary of State Byrnes was advised, accordingly, that the Togo-Sato cables appeared to be an attempt on the part of the Japanese military to make a deal with Russia and thereby attach conditions to surrender, conditions which might enable the military clique to evade punishment and stay in power. Russian analysts took an equally inappropriate view: that Japanese capitalism was attempting to perpetuate its hold on the Japanese proletariat. The fact that capitalists had given their factories and that generals had given their lives in order to serve Hirohito as a god-king seemed beyond understanding in the practical-minded West.

In the U.S. State Department a group of men around former Ambassador Grew shared an affection for Japan and understood some of the complexities of Japan's savage heart. They demanded that the unconditional surrender policy enunciated at the height of the war be restudied so that American statesmen might know the various interpretations which could be placed on it. They succeeded in securing an agreement that unconditional surrender should be explained as unconditional surrender of soldiers and guns, not of women and private property. Before President Truman left for Potsdam, they also exacted from him a reassurance that he would try to incorporate in the Potsdam Declaration a warning of the atomic holocaust which would be visited on Japan if she did not surrender soon. Grew, and to some extent Stimson, wanted to include in the warning a clear statement of the bomb's existence and a reassurance as to the person of the Emperor. But other presidential advisors saw no reason to tell Russia, in effect, we are going to A-bomb Japan, so you had better hurry in your attack on Manchuria. And still others saw no reason to assure the Emperor that he and his family could remain in the saddle, riding out a token Allied Occupation that would make no basic changes in Japan's class and power structure.

On July 14, Washington time, when the Allied leaders were all in transit to Potsdam, the first A-bomb was hoisted atop a tower in the New Mexico desert for a test. Early on July 17, the morning of the Potsdam Conference, Truman heard the first news of results: "Baby satisfactorily born." On the following day details came in: "Baby's scream" was strong enough to be heard from the Capitol in Washington to Interim Committee Secretary George Harrison's house in Upperville, Virginia. The "light in baby's eyes" was bright enough to shine from the Capitol to Stimson's home in Highhold, Long Island. The bomb was far more powerful than anyone had anticipated. In a pre-test pool conducted by the physicists in New Mexico, guesses as to the yield of the explosion in terms of TNT equivalent had ranged from 18,000 tons down to a skeptical "zero" tossed in by Dr. Lee DuBridge, director of U.S. wartime radar research. The actual yield was 20,000 tons. After reading the full report of the test, Churchill on July 22 leaned forward in his chair, waved his cigar in emphasis, and rumbled oracularly: "Stimson! What was gunpowder? Trivial. What was electricity? Meaningless. This atomic bomb is the Second Coming in wrath."

Churchill was to add later: "The decision whether or not to use the atomic bomb to compel the surrender of Japan was never even an issue." In Truman's mind, however, it was a source of uneasiness. On July 18, the day the President received details of what the bomb could do, he consulted with his military advisors and with anyone else whose opinion might be valuable. General Eisenhower, who was visiting in Potsdam that day, remembered in later years that he had been sounded out by the President and had "expressed the hope that we would never have to use such a thing . . . take the lead in introducing into war something as horrible and destructive."

Stimson, however, maintained that the bomb might be the excuse the Japanese were waiting for, and he urged that it be used "in the manner best calculated to persuade the Emperor to submit to our demand for what is essentially unconditional surrender." Churchill and other statesmen sided with Stimson. And so on July 24, while still at Potsdam, the President issued the operational order to General Carl Spaatz that the first "special bomb" should be dropped by the "509 Composite Group as soon as weather will permit" after about August 3.

The same day, as Truman recalled later, "I casually mentioned to Stalin that we had a new weapon of unusual destructive force. The Russian premier showed no particular interest. All he said was that he was glad to hear it and hoped we would make 'good use of it against the Japanese.'" Stalin almost certainly knew that this was the atomic bomb which Red Army Intelligence had been warning him about, but he gave no sign of knowing; later, when the bomb was used at Hiroshima, the Red Army was to require almost two days before it was ready to scramble across the border into Manchuria. Instead of commenting on the bomb, Stalin four days later revealed to Truman that he had been asked by Tokyo to act as a peace mediator. He added, more or less truthfully, that Tokyo had not made any specific proposal. It was Truman's turn to look innocent, and he agreed that the Japanese peace feelers as yet had been too tentative to warrant much attention.

On July 26, after the wording had been hammered out between the Allied leaders and their staffs, Japan was given the warning of the Potsdam Declaration: "We call upon the government of Japan to proclaim the unconditional surrender of all Japanese armed forces. . . . The alternative for Japan is prompt and utter destruction." Japanese Foreign Office analysts noticed with appreciation that the Allies had defined unconditional surrender as applying only to the "armed forces." They did not notice anything more than ordinary propaganda in the phrase "prompt and utter destruction." Two days after the Potsdam Declaration had been issued, Prime Minister Suzuki declared that it offered no change in the Roosevelt policy of unconditional surrender laid down at the Cairo Conference in December 1943 and that "to us its meaning does not seem of great worth, just something to be ignored."

Several historians and several participants in the history of that decade, including General Eisenhower, have complained that the Potsdam Declaration was inadequate. It did not tell the Japanese why destruction would be "prompt and utter" nor how relatively pleasant might be the prospect of unconditional surrender and U.S. occupation. Captain Ellis M. Zacharias of U.S. Naval Intelligence did as well as he was permitted in a Japanese and English broadcast on July 28 that was beamed into Japan on the medium wave band which could be picked up by the radio sets of ordinary Japanese citizens.[10] "Japan," he said, "must make a choice. One alternative is prompt and utter destruction. . . . Centuries of sweat and toil will be brought to naught in a cataclysmic end. . . . The other alternative is the end of war. One simple decision will allow tranquility again to return to the city and the countryside. . . . The homeland of Japan will be saved to continue a sovereign existence under a peacefully inclined and responsible government."

On August 2, Foreign Minister Togo begged his ambassador in Moscow to extract from the Soviet government some answer to the proposal that Prince Konoye fly to Russia for talks. Togo now promised that Konoye would be empowered to accept the Potsdam Declaration as "the basis for a study regarding terms." At the Soviet Foreign Ministry, Japanese Ambassador Sato learned that Molotov was still on his way home from Potsdam and would see him in a few days. Russia delayed. Japan waited. The Thin Boy was flown to Tinian and assembled. On August 6 Ambassador Sato was informed that Molotov had returned and would see him two days later at 5:00 P.M. That same morning, August 6, Ambassador Sato heard that Hiroshima had disappeared in a puff of flame.

THE GOD SPEAKS

When most of Hiroshima vanished from the map, it was the switchboard operators in Tokyo who first noticed that something was missing. Minutes later incoherent phone calls began to come in from the Hiroshima area. The Army General Staff at once responded by sending out wires for more information. On the following morning, Tuesday, the vice chief of staff received an angry, terrifying confirmation of his worst fears: "The whole city of Hiroshima was destroyed instantly by a single bomb." The Army General Staff sent out more wires, and planes as well, to find out

---

[10] All radios were registered by the secret police and periodically inspected to see that they could not pick up short wave. Zacharias's broadcasts were made possible only by U.S. relay ships steaming in perilously close to the Japanese coast.

what sort of bomb had been dropped and how many had been killed.

While the generals waited, Emperor Hirohito and his advisor Lord Privy Seal Kido already knew the answers. When they met in the Imperial Library that afternoon, both had seen Naval Intelligence analyses and reports from physicists at Tokyo Imperial University. The claims being broadcast from the United States were almost certainly honest. It had been an atomic bomb. Emperor Hirohito had received remarkably accurate statistics as to the casualties: "130,000 killed and wounded." Unlike most of his countrymen Hirohito understood what *genshi bakudan*, atomic bomb, signified. Until a few months previously, he had patronized Japan's own atomic research effort. It had come to a disastrous end when a physicist, some technicians, and two buildings full of apparatus had been mysteriously blown up. Under pressure to save Japan from defeat, the work had been pushed ahead too fast and safety precautions had been neglected.[11]

In the glare of Hiroshima, Kido and Hirohito knew that they could conspire to delay no longer: the time had come to put Kido's peace plot to its final test. Man and god, they set to work that afternoon seeing key functionaries and giving them final instructions. By the next afternoon, Wednesday, August 8, the machinery was primed and ready. Kido took advantage of an air alert to join the Emperor in his bunker under the Imperial Library. Kido urged the Emperor to speak the word which would set the machinery in motion. Hirohito at once summoned Foreign Minister Togo and told him, "Now that a weapon of this devastating power has been used against us, we should not let slip the opportunity. . . . Tell Prime Minister Suzuki that it is my wish that the war be ended as soon as possible on the basis of the Potsdam Declaration." In the unforeseen and unanswerable bomb, Hirohito saw a face-saving excuse for Japan's fighting men, one which could be used to ease the humiliation of defeat and smooth the pathway to surrender.

It was that Wednesday night, six hours after Hirohito had spoken, that the bomb, in the words of Wisconsin's Senator Alex-

---

[11] The physicist was named Odan, thirty-eight years old; the explosion was probably caused by careless handling of liquid gases.

ander Wiley, "blew Joey off the fence." Japan's Ambassador Sato
in Moscow had an appointment at 11 P.M. Tokyo time, 5 P.M.
Moscow time, to see Foreign Minister Molotov. He went to the
appointment expecting to learn at last whether Russia would receive Konoye and help in arranging Japan's surrender. Instead, he
was handed a declaration of war. Molotov coolly explained to him
that the Russo-Japanese nonaggression treaty had been canceled
years before by Japan's assistance of Germany. Stalin had promised Truman at Potsdam that, before entering the Pacific war,
he would reach agreement with Chiang Kai-shek on the future of
China. The Red Army chief of staff had told his opposite number
at Potsdam that Russian operations would not begin against Japan
until the second half of August. Now, ahead of schedule on all
counts, after only two days of preparation, the Soviet forces were
surging forward into Manchuria. It was the next morning, eighteen hours after Hirohito had spoken, that the bomb fell, tragically, on Urakami—and blessedly spared Kokura and most of
Nagasaki. The Japanese had had three full days to think since
Hiroshima. No American knew that Emperor Hirohito had already
decided to accept the Potsdam Declaration.

On Thursday morning, August 9, when the second bomb was
scoring its merciful two-mile miss, the Big Six of the Japanese
Government had just gathered in the prime minister's air raid
shelter outside the palace to debate the Emperor's wish to accept
unconditional surrender. They had been summoned the previous
evening, but some of the military members of the group had made
themselves unreachable. During the night, however, pressure for
instant action had mounted when the secret police circulated news
of a "confession" made by a B-29 pilot shot down the day before
off Osaka.

Already bruised and bloodied by his interrogators, Lieutenant
Marcus McDilda had been threatened with death unless he revealed what he knew about the atomic bomb. Knowing nothing,
he decided to tell all. "As you know," he began in his Florida
drawl, "when atoms are split, there are a lot of plusses and minuses released. Well, we've taken these and put them in a huge
container and separated them from each other with a lead shield.
When the box is dropped out of a plane, we melt the lead shield

and the plusses and minuses come together. When that happens, it causes a tremendous bolt of lightning and all the atmosphere over a city is pushed back. Then when the atmosphere rolls in again, it brings about a tremendous thunderclap, which knocks down everything beneath it.

"I believe," added McDilda under prodding, "that the next two targets are to be Kyoto and Tokyo. Tokyo is supposed to be bombed in the next few days."

As the war minister and the two chiefs of staff sat down with the other members of the Big Six to discuss Hirohito's request in the sweltering air raid shelter, they exchanged information about McDilda's confession and felt oppressed by the thought that Tokyo and the Emperor, or Kyoto and the tombs of past Emperors, might soon be turned to ash. At the same time, they also feared an end to the war. They still had at their disposal in the home islands 2.5 million combat-equipped troops and 9,000 kamikaze planes. These men had been told for years that death was preferable to surrender. For months they had been promised "a final decisive battle" on the shores of Japan, a battle so costly to the enemy that it might be possible afterwards to negotiate a conditional surrender and win an honorable peace. To surrender these men without a fight evoked visions of unbearable future shame—of the veteran in rags who would spit on any general he passed on the street and feel justified in doing so.

General Anami, the war minister, carried the argument for his fellow soldiers. The Emperor wished to surrender. Japan must surrender. But it was foolish not to bargain. Japan should signify her willingness to accept the Potsdam Declaration on four conditions: that her soil be spared the tread of occupation troops; that her fighting men be disarmed and disbanded by their own officers; that her war criminals be tried in her own courts; and most important, that the Emperor system of government be guaranteed. Everyone agreed to the last proviso as an unquestionable article of religious faith. Only the two chiefs of staff, however, would back the war minister on the other three provisos. The prime, foreign, and Navy ministers argued that to surrender unconditionally on one condition might be possible but that to surrender unconditionally on four conditions could only invite an

atomic attack on Tokyo. The 3–3 deadlock was not broken when
news of the Nagasaki bombing was brought into the council chamber about 11:30 A.M. At one in the afternoon Prime Minister Suzuki opened his eyes, pushed away his teacup, stamped out his
cigar, and recessed the meeting for an hour.

War Minister Anami returned to his own ministry to see if
anything important had come up in the business of the morning.
A group of his most militant subordinates clustered around him
to ask about the Big Six meeting. He put them off with general-
ities and a promise that he had taken a strong stand. One of
them, his own brother-in-law, warned him, in a loud voice, "If
you are going to accept the Potsdam Declaration, you had better
commit hara-kiri."

"A cruel thing to say," remarked Anami to his secretary as they
climbed back into the car. "They don't know how easy hara-kiri
is for an old man of sixty like me." His secretary thought he looked
tired and deflated as he spoke. The car drove on to the official
residence supplied Anami by the government. There he took out
his old samurai bow and target and tested the state of his nerves
in the back yard. It took him seventeen shots to group five arrows
in the center of the mark. Usually ten or eleven sufficed. Aware
of his tension and his limitations, he went inside for a hurried
lunch of rice and pickles and returned to the prime minister's
residence.

For the afternoon session Prime Minister Suzuki had called in
the rest of the Cabinet. Now instead of six there were fourteen
at the deliberations. Two voted with War Minister Anami for the
stiffest conditions, five with Foreign Minister Togo for a moderate
response, and five others opted to accept unconditional surrender
in any wording that would still leave a little room for bargaining.
The meeting continued from 2:30 P.M. to 5:30 P.M. and resumed
after dinner at 6:30 P.M.

As the sun moved over the lotus pools and lengthened the shadows of the artfully grotesque trees in the palace garden, Hirohito
waited in the Imperial Library to give the divine command which
would end all argument. It was his unique privilege to vouchsafe
peace to the war-weary, his dangerous responsibility to withhold
honor from the fanatics. At intervals during the afternoon Lord

Privy Seal Kido came to the library to reassure him and beg him to be patient. It was a matter of plan that the meeting in progress should fail to reach unanimous agreement, but the ministers were duty bound to exhaust every avenue of argument before conceding a deadlock. Only then could they legitimately appeal to Hirohito and invoke the Voice of the Crane.

The task of protracting the proceedings and of preventing the weary negotiators from reaching a compromise rested on the broad shoulders of War Minister Anami. He performed it willingly enough because it helped him save face before his subordinates. He was known as an advocate of surrender, but of conditional surrender. For months he had been promising his men that he would wrest an honorable peace from the Allies or die in the attempt. He had made a similar pledge to the Emperor.

Of the cabal of young officers who had served Hirohito since the early 1920's, the sleek, burly Anami was the most dedicated and loyal, the most perfect exemplar of the samurai ideal. His archery was only one of the ancient knightly exercises by which he kept himself fit; he had also attained the fifth degree in *kendo*, the traditional Japanese swordsmanship. Contemptuous of money, careless of personal comfort, he cultivated a relaxed frame of mind, what the Japanese call "a belly that knows how to sit down." He was no intellectual and had twice failed the entrance examinations for military academy. But he knew how to lead men. In combat he was renowned for his nerves of steel. Out of combat he was beloved for his even temper, his affable storytelling, and his hard drinking.

Having gone through military academy with Prince Asaka and Prince Higashikuni, the Emperor's uncles, Anami had come into the palace circle naturally at the outset of his career and had been a part of it ever since. He had served as an aide-de-camp for the Emperor from 1926 to 1932. On the very day of Hirohito's accession to the Throne, December 25, 1926, Anami had represented the palace at a meeting with Tojo and other members of the cabal, a meeting which had resolved on the "liberation" of Manchuria from Chinese sovereignty. Many sensitive assignments later, Anami had found himself in 1944 attempting to perform miracles in New Guinea where the Japanese garrisons were cut off from outside help. When the situation had become equally desperate in Tokyo in December 1944, Hirohito, at the instigation of his two uncles, had had Anami flown home.

At 10:00 P.M., eleven hours after the second atomic bomb had been dropped, the sturdy Anami was still finding arguments against unconditional surrender. His opponents, who did not fight a bout and fill a clout each day, were all exhausted. Prime Minister Suzuki, Hirohito's old grand chamberlain, decided that enough of a gesture had been made. He called a recess and left the other members of his government to enjoy the hospitality of his residence while he drove to the palace. It was a clear night. The moon had not yet risen. Tokyo lay blacked out. As his car groped along behind its hooded headlights, Suzuki admired the silhouettes of the great trees on either side of the palace malls.

The old admiral-chamberlain-prime minister found Hirohito sitting up waiting for him in the library. He reported the deadlock in deliberations and advised the Emperor to break it by calling an immediate council in the Imperial Presence. Hirohito consented instantly and asked his attendants to phone Lord Privy Seal Kido and make the necessary arrangements. By prior agreement with Kido, Suzuki then asked the Emperor if Baron Hiranuma might be invited to the council. Hirohito winced and nodded his assent with downcast eyes. Few men in Japan had tried harder than Baron Hiranuma to turn Hirohito from the path to Pearl Harbor; few had more right to say, "I told you so."

At eighty, Baron Hiranuma represented the traditional prefascist variety of right-wing nationalism in Japan. He had the backing of other mossback aristocrats and also of many slum gang leaders and shape-up bosses. From 1929 to 1936 he had directed the affluent National Foundation Society or Kokuhonsha, an equivalent in U.S. terms of a combined Mafia headquarters and New York Athletic Club. Through his underworld connections he claimed to represent labor, and through labor, the people. In the early years of Hirohito's reign, Baron Hiranuma had supported the Strike-North faction in the Army which wished to direct Japanese aggression against Russia. In addition, as a legal authority, he had taken the position that Hirohito should not be above the law in act unless he were willing to avow himself above the law in name as well. After long conflict, Hirohito had conceded the point in 1936 when he personally and openly purged the Strike-North faction from the Army and turned on China. At the same time he had reached an understanding with Hiranuma and appointed him to the presidency of the Privy Council, an advisory body which met with Hirohito every Wednesday morning. In 1939 Baron Hiranuma had gone on to preside as prime minister over the Nomonhan Incident, a limited exploratory attack on Russia. It had turned into a fiasco and Baron Hiranuma had withdrawn into brief retirement. He had sprung back as a Cabinet minister in 1941 and had survived an assassination attempt by a hired gunman who tried to murder him for his outspoken opposition to war with America. Since then he had helped Prince Konoye to organize the Peace Faction.

When Lord Privy Seal Kido arrived at the library a few minutes later, he assured Hirohito that Baron Hiranuma would cause no trouble. He and Kido had had a long talk the day before; there was an understanding. Hirohito nodded gratefully. The baron certainly had a sharp legal mind. And he had proved his pertinacious loyalty even as an opponent. It was probably no more than just that he should assist at these final fateful deliberations. Hirohito waited restlessly for them to begin. It was 11:00 P.M. before the members of the Cabinet and High Command began to arrive at the library. Lord Privy Seal Kido bustled about having a word with each of them. Chamberlains and equerries then escorted them one by one around to the hillside entrance of the imperial bunker and down the steps into the hill, sixty feet into it horizontally, fifty feet into it vertically, to the anteroom outside the subterranean audience chamber. It was 11:20 P.M. before they were all briefed and assembled.

At 11:25 P.M. Kido had a last twelve-minute meeting with Hirohito, and then the Emperor proceeded down into the bunker through his own private door by his own stairway. He looked into the subterranean living room where some of his children and nieces and nephews were camped out asleep on the rugs and sofas. He spoke briefly with his chief aide-de-camp. He passed inspection by his wife, Empress Nagako. Then at ten minutes to midnight, his hair noticeably unkempt, his eyes unusually deep-set and haggard-looking, he entered the hot, damp 30-by-18-foot chamber. Voices hushed and there were sighs of astonishment at his disheveled appearance. He sat down behind a table, covered like an altar with a cloth of golden chrysanthemum brocade.

At Hirohito's back extended a magnificent, six-gate, golden screen. Before him, behind two narrow tables along the walls, sat eleven tired men. Four were civilians, four were generals, and three were admirals. The gathering was an accurate cross-section of the hierarchy which took turns administering Hirohito's police state. All were of the inner clique and had been privy to high conspiratorial affairs since the late 1920's. All knew now that the great gamble of war had been lost. Suicide or prison closed in ahead of them. The stuffy air of the shelter seemed, in the words of one of them, "to buzz with the spirits of the dead." A mood of bitter spiritualistic *Weltschmerz* engulfed the room.

Prime Minister Suzuki's secretary, Sakomizu Hisatsune, had the uncanny feeling that he and his companions in the bunker had already passed over into the other world. A nimbus seemed to surround the Emperor. Military Affairs Bureau Chief Yoshizumi Masao, sitting next to Sakomizu, bore an eerie resemblance to another Military Affairs Bureau chief, Nagata Tetsuzan, who had been stabbed to death exactly ten years ago by an assassin sent to him from Hirohito's two uncles, Prince Asaka and Prince Higashikuni. It seemed only right that Nagata should have returned now. Until a month before his murder, he had been the leader of the Emperor's Army cabal. He had fallen out with Hirohito over plans for the war with China and had embarrassed Hirohito through security leaks. He had been offered a chance to save himself by resigning or taking a leave of absence, but he had chosen instead to remain at his post and to become a sacrificial victim.

The haunting presence of Nagata's spirit in the bunker seized so strongly on Secretary Sakomizu's mind that years later his vision was incorporated in a painting of the surrender scene which he commissioned for the memorial museum to Prime Minister Suzuki. By subtly strengthening the chin and filling out the lips of the real man in the bunker, the artist recreated a startling likeness of Nagata as he looked at a conference in 1935 shortly before his death. The men across from him seem to be eyeing him warily but he does not look back at them. His eyes appear to be closed. And on his full lips plays a distant half smile, half sneer of sardonic satisfaction. Thousands of Japanese visit the Suzuki Museum each year and silently file past the painting.

In the real bunker, that evening of August 9, 1945, the cynical, impressionable Secretary Sakomizu saw the ghostly proceedings open with a ceremonial recitation of all the anguished arguments of the preceding days. Hirohito sat listening mute and immobile, ramrod stiff at the altar before the golden screen. Foreign Minister Togo and Navy Minister Yonai reviewed the inescapable reasons for accepting unconditional surrender. War Minister Anami and Army Chief of Staff Umezu begged—for the honor of the living and the dead—to fight a final battle.

Then Prime Minister Suzuki called on the octogenarian lawyer, Baron Hiranuma. The room rustled as the others in it whispered to one another, asking why Baron Hiranuma should speak and what he was doing there in the first place. They soon learned. Baron Hiranuma was to act as prosecutor on behalf of Japan. He was to remind each of them, even Hirohito, of his responsibilities and past irresponsibilities. As the old man rose, his long equine face was blank, then he pursed his lips judiciously, narrowed his eyes, and began.

"Have you ever made proposals to the U.S.S.R. on concrete matters?" he demanded in his cross-examination of Foreign Minister Togo. "Is a defense against these bombs possible?" he asked War Minister Anami. "It seems to me that the enemy do as they please and that there are absolutely no counterattacks against enemy air raids." He turned on the Navy minister and naval chief of staff: "Does the Navy have any countermeasures against enemy task forces?" Having no ships left to speak of, Naval Chief of Staff Toyoda spoke lamely of new types of kamikaze planes. "In view of the present deterioration of the general situation in Japan," cut in Hiranuma relentlessly, "we can suppose that continuation of the war will create greater domestic disturbance then ending of the war."

Finally, Hiranuma turned his eyes on the Emperor. "The wording of the reservation to be sent to the Allies must be revised. To accept the Potsdam Declaration '*on the understanding that it does not include any demand for a change in the status of the Emperor under the national laws'* is inappropriate. . . . The sovereignty of the Emperor is not derived through state law, nor is it provided for by the Constitution. It is only referred to in the Constitution. If the wording is changed to read 'the said declaration does not comprise any demand which prejudices the prerogatives of His Majesty as a sovereign ruler,' I would then have no objection."

When Hirohito had nodded his assent to Foreign Minister Togo that he would accept this definition of his power and responsibility in the surrender note, Hiranuma closed his case: "In accordance with the legacy bequeathed by the ancestors, Your Imperial Majesty is also responsible for preventing unrest in the nation. I should like to ask Your Majesty to make your decision with this point in mind."

Baron Hiranuma sat down. The naval chief of staff briefly took the floor. Then Prime Minister Suzuki seconded the suggestion of Hiranuma: "For hours we have discussed these matters and come to no decision. We cannot afford to waste even a minute. I propose to seek the imperial guidance. His Majesty's wish must settle the issue." Suzuki took a step toward the altar where Hirohito sat and there was a gasp at his boldness.

Without rising Hirohito replied in the high-pitched, senile-sounding Court monotone which was reserved for state pronouncements: "I will state my opinion. I agree with the foreign minister. My reasons are as follows: I have concluded that to continue this war can only mean destruction of the homeland. I cannot bear to have my innocent people suffer further. I was told by the Army chief of staff that in June the defenses at Ninety-nine League Beach would be complete. . . . It is now August and the fortifications are not complete. It was officially reported to me that one of the newly created divisions had been fully equipped. I find that as yet the men have not been supplied even with bayonets. . . . Some advocate a decisive battle in the homeland. . . . In my experience, however, there has been a discrepancy between the plans and the achievements of the fighting services. . . . I am afraid that in the face of present circumstances the Japanese people may be doomed. But I wish to hand on the country of Japan to our descendants; I wish to see as many as possible of our people survive and rise again. . . . It gives me great pain to think of the faithful soldiers and sailors who have been wounded or killed on distant battlefields and of the families who have lost everything in air raids at home. . . . Disarmament of my brave and loyal men is painful to me. Painful, too, that my devoted vassals should be considered war criminals. . . . But the time has come to bear the unbearable. . . . It does not matter what happens to me. . . . I have decided to bring the war to an end. That is why I agree with the foreign minister's proposal."

The men in the bunker were all weeping. Hirohito rose. Prime Minister Suzuki quickly said, "The imperial decision has been expressed and is thereby made the conclusion of this conference. Meeting adjourned."

It was 2:20 A.M. Hirohito turned to the door which was opened for him by his chief aide-de-camp, who had remained standing in a corner throughout the proceedings. When the Emperor had returned into the depths of the bunker, the other leaders mounted the steps into the Fukiage Gardens. The moon had risen during their stay underground, and the beauty of the garden in the moonbeams somewhat restored their despondent spirits. Hirohito reported briefly to his wife and Lord Privy Seal Kido. The Cabinet adjourned to Prime Minister Suzuki's residence where with food and drink, in a fourth and last meeting of a long and bitter day, they voted unanimously to accept the imperial decision. They broke up and went home about 4:00 A.M. Foreign Minister Togo worked on until 7:00 A.M. when his diplomatic note to Sweden and Switzerland, announcing Japan's unconditional surrender on one condition, had been duly coded and tapped out.

AMERICA RESPONDS

Seven o'clock in the morning in Tokyo is eleven o'clock the night before in Stockholm and Berne. By the time Japan's surrender offer had been decoded by Japanese diplomats in those capitals, it was past midnight. The diplomats waited politely until morning before transmitting the note to Swiss and Swedish foreign offices. By then it was past midnight in Washington. Thus when Truman and his advisors met to discuss the note at 9:00 A.M. on Friday, August 10, Washington time, sixteen anxious hours had passed in Tokyo. Moreover in Australia, which had been the most important fighting ally of the United States in the Pacific War, it was once again midnight. Japan was trying to surrender against the clock. Her note to the Allies stated:

THE JAPANESE GOVERNMENT ARE READY TO ACCEPT THE TERMS ENUMERATED IN THE JOINT DECLARATION WHICH WAS ISSUED AT POTSDAM ON JULY 26, 1945 . . . WITH THE UNDERSTANDING THAT THE SAID DECLARATION DOES NOT COMPRISE ANY DEMAND WHICH PREJUDICES THE PREROGATIVES OF HIS MAJESTY AS A SOVEREIGN RULER.

THE JAPANESE GOVERNMENT SINCERELY HOPE THAT THIS UNDERSTANDING IS WARRANTED AND DESIRE KEENLY THAT AN EXPLICIT INDICATION TO THAT EFFECT WILL BE SPEEDILY FORTHCOMING.

Truman and the new British Prime Minister Clement Attlee were disposed to accept the Japanese reservation about the Emperor. As far as anyone knew in the West, the Emperor was only a figurehead. Later that afternoon, however, when dawn came "down under," Australia was heard from. First Canberra cabled London:

WE WOULD INSIST THAT THE EMPEROR AS HEAD OF STATE AND COMMANDER IN CHIEF OF THE ARMED FORCES SHOULD BE HELD RESPONSIBLE FOR THE JAPANESE ACTS OF AGGRESSION AND WAR CRIMES AND WOULD THUS DEMAND HIS REMOVAL.

As the motherland of the British Commonwealth, the United Kingdom had been allowed hitherto to speak for Australia in most wartime policy making. Now, however, when London replied with vague reassurances, the Australian government was not to be reassured. It rebelliously shot off a second cable, this time directly to Washington:

. . . THE EMPEROR SHOULD HAVE NO IMMUNITY FROM RESPONSIBILITY FOR JAPAN'S ACTS OF AGGRESSION. . . . THE VISIBLE DETHRONEMENT OF THE SYSTEM IS A PRIMARY MEANS OF SHAKING THE FAITH OF THE JAPANESE IN THE HEAVENLY CHARACTER OF THE EMPEROR IN

WHOSE NAME THEY HAVE COMMITTED MANY ATROCITIES. UNLESS THE
SYSTEM GOES, THE JAPANESE WILL REMAIN UNCHANGED AND RECRU-
DESCENCE OF AGGRESSION IN THE PACIFIC WILL ONLY BE POSTPONED
TO A LATER GENERATION.

AT YOUR REQUEST WE POSTPONED PUBLICATION OF THE REPORT
WHICH IS NOW BEFORE THE WAR CRIMES COMMISSION. . . . IN OUR
VIEW IT DISCLOSES A DELIBERATE SYSTEM OF TERRORISM AND ATROCITY
WHICH MUST HAVE BEEN KNOWN TO THE SUPREME AUTHORITIES IN
JAPAN NOT EXCLUDING THE EMPEROR. IT WOULD BE A VERY DIFFICULT
MATTER TO JUSTIFY DISCRIMINATION IN THIS RESPECT AS BETWEEN
HITLER AND HIS ASSOCIATES ON THE ONE HAND AND HIROHITO AND HIS
ASSOCIATES ON THE OTHER.

FOR THESE REASONS WE ARE OPPOSED TO THE ACCEPTANCE OF SUR-
RENDER ON THE UNDERSTANDING WHICH THE JAPANESE ARE ATTEMPT-
ING TO ATTACH TO THE POTSDAM TERMS. . . . IT SHOULD BE CLEARLY
UNDERSTOOD BY THE JAPANESE . . . THAT THE PERSON OF THE EMPEROR
IS TO BE REGARDED AS AT THE DISPOSAL OF THE ALLIED GOVERNMENTS
IN THE SAME WAY AS EACH AND EVERY OTHER PERSON OF THE SURRENDER-
ING ENEMY STATE.

Truman and his Secretary of State James Byrnes wished to humor Australia if at all possible. Australia had contributed almost
as much sweat and blood to the defeat of Japan as had the United
States. Moreover, Australia had been excluded from the inner
counsels at Potsdam. On the other hand, Great Britain and China
had already approved a U.S. draft of the reply to Japan. So had the
Soviet Union, but with a warning that the Red Army would continue its drive into Manchuria until Japan ceased to fight. Secretary of State Byrnes, therefore, made minor modifications in the
U.S. note on the evening of August 10 and, pleading the urgency
of the situation, begged the Australian government to be satisfied
with them. The two significant paragraphs, over which Japanese
would agonize, were the second and fifth:

FROM THE MOMENT OF SURRENDER, THE AUTHORITY OF THE EMPEROR
AND THE JAPANESE GOVERNMENT TO RULE THE STATE SHALL BE SUBJECT
TO THE SUPREME COMMANDER OF THE ALLIED POWERS, WHO WILL TAKE
SUCH STEPS AS HE DEEMS PROPER TO EFFECTUATE THE SURRENDER
TERMS. . . .

THE ULTIMATE FORM OF GOVERNMENT OF JAPAN SHALL, IN ACCORD-

ANCE WITH THE POTSDAM DECLARATION, BE ESTABLISHED BY THE FREELY
EXPRESSED WILL OF THE JAPANESE PEOPLE.

The phrasing was masterful. On the one hand it assured Japanese that the Emperor would retain authority "to rule the state";
on the other it assured Australians that he would be "subject" to
the Allied commander, MacArthur. Early on the morning of August 11, Byrnes received grudging approval of his wording from
the Australian government, and at 10:45 A.M., Washington time,
the note was broadcast to Japan. There it was now a quarter to
one, Sunday morning, August 12, exactly forty-one hours forty-five
minutes since Japan had announced her surrender.

In Tokyo the vice foreign minister and half a dozen seasoned
diplomats with knowledge of English were at once routed from
their beds and set to work translating the note and studying it.
Their initial reaction was gloomy. The wording seemed excessively harsh and straightforward. There were none of those polite
hypocrisies with which Japan had always honeyed her communications to conquered peoples. The note stated flatly that "the armed
forces of the Allied Powers will remain in Japan until the purposes
set forth in the Potsdam Declaration are achieved." Those purposes included complete disarmament, removal of all obstacles to
democracy, "exaction of just reparations," and "stern justice . . .
to all war criminals." Not even before the capture of Nanking had
Japan sent a note of such severe tone. Anyone without firsthand
experience of gruff Western ways would be led to expect wholesale rape, pillage, and butchery. The people might not accept the
prospect without civil strife.

For the time being, then, the text of the note would have to
be kept out of the newspapers. It could not be prevented, however, from circulating in the upper levels of the bureaucracy.
There, the vice foreign minister observed, the problem would be
to have the note "swallowed without chewing." The troublesome
phrase would be the one, "government . . . established by the
freely expressed will of the . . . people." That was arrant republicanism. It went against the ancestral precepts handed down in
every family of the warrior caste. Rather than submit to it, there
were those who would prefer to see the whole Japanese race pass

over into the spirit world. From a Valhalla in Hades, said some devout Shintoists, the ghosts of samurai would wreak vengeance for the rest of eternity, causing fearful accidents to befall barbarians who ventured to set foot in the empty sacred isles of the homeland.

At 5:30 A.M. that morning the ranking officials of the Foreign Office took the American note, and the problems which they felt it presented, to Foreign Minister Togo at his residence. In the car one of them suggested that perhaps a diversion could be created to distract patrician attention from the "will of the people" clause. Togo's German wife was away in the mountains, and the foreign minister greeted them personally in his sleeping kimono. In this informal Japanese attire he seemed more relaxed than usual—more approachable than in the striped shirts, French cuffs, and Savile Row suits he wore to the office. Nevertheless his subordinates bowed to him with a depth and formality that exceeded required courtesy. Their feelings for him ranged from fearful respect to cool dislike. One of them noticed that his hand, as he took the American note, was completely steady.

Until a few years ago Foreign Minister Togo had been a heavy drinker and had smoked three packs of Turkish cigarettes a day. Then, at a word from his doctor, as he neared his sixtieth birthday, he had given up both in a single stroke of self-discipline. He was, without doubt, an intellectual of great brilliance and considerable inward sensitivity, but the walls of his psyche bristled with spears. His sarcasms punctured and his punctilios drew blood. His one failure as an ambassador had been scored in Germany during the mid-Thirties when he persistently referred to Hitler as "that upstart." One of the principal reasons that Hirohito had appointed him foreign minister in the Suzuki Cabinet was that he had the daring to call generals "idiots" to their faces. Now, as Togo patted out the wrinkles in his kimono and fitted on his heavy black-rimmed spectacles, he had never looked more human.

Togo read the note once, slowly. "This is the problem," he said, putting his finger on the "will of the people" clause. "In the long run it will not be an insurmountable problem from a practical standpoint, but emotionally it is difficult to accept. I do not think that the people will vote against the Emperor in a plebiscite, and until then the Emperor's 'authority to rule the state' is specifically acknowledged." Togo knew that the concept of free will was religious anathema to all but the tiny minority of Japan's 300,000 Christians. As for free expression, it had been successfully controlled for more than a thousand years.

"On this basis," continued Togo, "I think the Emperor will rise above personal feelings and accept the humiliation of being declared 'subject' to a foreigner. Still, it is an extremely hard note. Do any of you have any suggestions for softening its impact? At this time of crisis, it is most important for the whole nation to maintain perfect harmony and a united front."

The other foreign officers present broached the idea of creating a distraction. Vice Foreign Minister Matsumoto suggested that the Emperor's submission to "subject" status could be considered from one point of view as an awesome act of self-sacrifice made for the sake of the nation. Indeed the supreme humiliation could be used to make him seem a hero in his own eyes and in the eyes of the people. Togo seized on the idea with enthusiasm. All attention must be focused on the pathos and nobility of the Emperor's position. The meeting broke up shortly after dawn, and before breakfast the necessary diversion was being created.

Within the hour a captain in the Navy's Political Strategy Section, who happened also to be a minor member of the imperial family, called on the foreign editor of Domei, the state-controlled press service.[12] Despite the fact that the press had not published —and for three days would not publish—anything about the surrender negotiations, the captain asked the editor for a translation of the American note. The Navy, he said, did not feel sure enough of its own English to make a correct translation. Since hundreds of Naval officers had studied in England and even served as midshipmen in the British fleet, Domei's editor understood that a game was being played. After feeling out the requirements of the captain, he gave him a Domei News translation of the American note which described the Occupation status of the Emperor as that of "a menial belonging to the Supreme Allied Commander."

At the same time the Foreign Office was running off a transla-

[12] Captain Arima Takayasu and Editor Hasegawa Saiji.

tion of the note which described the Emperor's Occupation status as "limited by the Supreme Allied Commander." The foreign editor at Domei immediately sent a special messenger with the translation he had made for the Navy to Prime Minister Suzuki's office. The prime minister's secretary proceeded to call key offices throughout the bureaucracy in order to advise them that the Navy was circulating an unauthorized translation of the note which differed from the official one put out by the Foreign Ministry. By the time that most bureaucrats arrived at their offices to face another day of shortages and air alarms, it was common knowledge in official Tokyo that the Americans were turning all their spite on Hirohito personally and that the men in striped pants at the Foreign Ministry were trying to hide the fact.

At 8:20 A.M., that same Sunday morning, Army and Navy chiefs of staff met with one another to discuss the situation and went on to call at the Imperial Library. They told Hirohito that in their view the U.S. note was rude in the extreme and that the Army and Navy stood ready to a man to die if Hirohito wished to reject it. Hirohito's chief aide-de-camp noted that the chiefs of staff seemed uncomfortable in their protestations, as if they were making a polite gesture suggested by their subordinates. Hirohito thanked them for their loyalty and assured them that he would study the note carefully when he received the official text from Sweden. At 11:00 A.M., while the Tokyo grapevine buzzed with gossip and concern over the Emperor's humiliation, Foreign Minister Togo motored to the palace. He reported to the Throne that, in his view as a diplomat, the American note was honest and as lenient as could be expected. Hirohito agreed and asked that the Cabinet officially endorse his acceptance of it.

SAMURAI'S COMPACT

The Cabinet and the chiefs of staff debated the American note throughout Sunday afternoon and all day Monday. War Minister Anami, who had had a lengthy audience with Hirohito on Saturday, once again led the anti-surrender faction. Baron Hiranuma, who had previously played peace advocate, was received in audience by Hirohito on Sunday and had thereafter supported Anami and supplied him with legal arguments. U.S. aircraft had not bombed Japan since Friday, and both men could be reasonably sure that there would be no more atomic attacks for the time being.

The Japanese masses, however, had no such certainty. They were forbidden by law to listen to foreign broadcasts. And as yet the domestic press, though it had mentioned "the new type of bomb," and finally "the atomic bomb," dropped on Hiroshima and Nagasaki, had printed not a word about the surrender note sent to Washington. Dark rumors spread of atomic horrors, and the inhabitants of every city wondered fatalistically if they would be next. While Anami sought to impress the enemy with Japan's continuing will to fight, the fierce kamikaze spirit was, in reality, oozing from the nation's heart and leaving only apathy and despair.

In addition to reasons of state, War Minister Anami had a strong personal motive for prolonging the surrender debate. He had encouraged a group of his favorite subordinates to stage a rebellion at the moment of Japan's surrender, and he had tacitly promised them that, if they would make this last suicidal gesture, he would go with them to the spirit world by committing harakiri. It was a feudal bargain of a type unknown in the West since the days of chivalry—a death pact between a knight and his liegemen in service to their king. In Japan such romantic deeds of self-sacrifice had a recognized place in government, and careful preparations were made to see that the victims were honored and their lives were not wasted.

War Minister Anami's suicide plan had first acquired official standing on July 27, a few hours after Japan received the Potsdam Declaration. That day orders under Anami's seal were radioed out to Taiwan recalling to Japan a lieutenant colonel of the secret police, Tsukamoto Makoto. Tsukamoto had recommended himself to imperial attention in 1934 when he had helped other Court agents uncover a subversive plot of the Strike-North or Fight-Russia faction at the military academy. He had then served under the Emperor's uncle Prince Higashikuni in various intrigues in Osaka during 1935, one of them the murder of the Military Affairs Bureau chief who appears as a ghostly anachronism in the

Suzuki Museum's painting of Hirohito's bunker. Promoted to the
rank of captain—a high one in the secret police—Tsukamoto had
gone on in 1937 to assist Prince Asaka, the other of the Emperor's
uncles, at the rape of Nanking. Now, when Lieutenant Colonel
Tsukamoto received his orders in Taiwan he saw that they contained a built-in official disclaimer of the type reserved for special
assignments. That is, they attached him, for the record, to the
secret-police force in Kyoto, but they asked him to report in
Tokyo. Moreover, they gave him top transportation priority.

Planes out of Taiwan were almost nonexistent and Okinawa
blocked any direct flights to Japan. Tsukamoto had to proceed by
many short hops, first to Canton, then up the China coast to
Shanghai, then across to Kyushu and along the main island of
Honshu. It was August 6 before he was able to report in Tokyo to
the supreme commandant of the secret police. The commandant
professed complete bafflement as to why Tsukamoto had been
ordered home but added, "Since you are here you may as well take
a temporary assignment. The other day War Minister Anami was
over worrying about unrest among his subordinates. He instructed
me to look into talk of a coup d'etat. He wants me to watch over
these people and report on their plans." Old plotter Tsukamoto
understood at once. He renewed acquaintance with a former mess-
mate on Anami's staff and through him made friends with Anami's
other subordinates.

The arrival of Tsukamoto gave the fanatics on Anami's staff an
official witness. This was important to them because it meant that
their deeds would be recorded, and, if they died, they would be
given a fair hearing by their ancestors in the spirit world. In Japan's tightly organized homogeneous family society, it was common for political plotters to end their cell meetings with a report
to the local police box. Like the priests or psychiatrists of other
lands, the police could be relied on to treat such confessions as
privileged communications. They would advise as to penalties and
even sound out superiors as to official policy and attitudes. But
their meticulous records would not be accessible except to other
policemen. The act of confession and its recording on the tablets
of life were considered a sacramental end unto itself. The crime
and the punishment, being ordained by fate, were secondary. If a

confession was made before the fact, that was a sign of sincerity and was usually considered mitigating. If a confession was made after the fact, that was satisfactory and gave a man a place again in the family of his ancestors. But if a confession was not made voluntarily, then one had to be extorted even if it meant torturing a man to death. The best Japanese police took the same attitude and assumed the same heavy responsibility as the inquisitors of the Church in medieval Europe.

Having been joined by police witness Tsukamoto, a group of the most patriotic majors and lieutenant colonels at the War Ministry now did begin, in earnest, to plot a coup d'etat. Before surrender became final they would seize the palace, they said, and save the Emperor from the evil counselors who advised him to accept dishonor. War Minister Anami's brother-in-law assured them that Anami supported them and would commit suicide if their plot failed. On several occasions they discussed their ideas with Anami directly. Though always noncommittal, he took pains to seem sympathetic to their cause. They also sounded out the commander of the Imperial Guards Division and the commander of the Tokyo Area Army. These two generals responded with appropriate remarks about the importance of Army discipline but otherwise did nothing to stop the conspirators. On Sunday, August 12, when the U.S. reply was received, the plotters drew up final plans for a rising on the following night. Secret-police Colonel Tsukamoto at once reported the plans in full to his chief, the supreme commandant. When the appointed evening arrived, the rebels came to War Minister Anami to tell him that they planned to act that night. They begged him to join them. Anami reviewed their schemes and found fault with their arrangements for cutting palace telephone lines. He advised them to wait a day and they agreed that they would.

JAPAN'S LONGEST DAY

On Tuesday morning, as the Emperor's chief advisor, Lord Privy Seal Kido, was surfacing from the last dreams of the night, a chamberlain burst into his study on the third floor of the Imperial Household Building and shook him where he lay on his pallet on the floor. The chamberlain was waving a leaflet which had just been dropped in the palace grounds. It was one of five million which had been unloaded by B-29's over Japan's principal cities that morning. It informed the populace that "the Japanese government has offered to surrender." Kido sprang to his feet and, according to his own account, was "stricken with consternation." He ordered that the chief of the civilian police be phoned immediately to make sure that they were having the leaflets picked up as fast as possible. The people had standing orders to turn in the devilish B-29 pamphlets without reading them and most citizens obeyed, but there were always those who kept the pamphlets and spread the rumors they contained. Right now was the worst possible moment for the masses to learn that Japan had surrendered. They must hear it from the Emperor's own mouth. Otherwise the doves would not feel grateful to him and the hawks might rise in unsolicited rebellions.

Kido phoned the library and was received in audience at 8:30 A.M. Hirohito agreed that the great gesture of debate must be stopped at once. Prime Minister Suzuki arrived at the library while Hirohito and Kido were talking, and at 8:45 A.M. Hirohito instructed him to call together Japan's leaders at once for a conference in the Imperial Presence. Imperial advisor Kido emphasized the urgency of the situation by stipulating that the usual Court attire of frock coat or cutaway would not be required. Two hours later, wearing the most presentable coats and ties which they could borrow in the offices where the summons reached them, the ministers and generals gathered.

Presiding once more in the underground audience chamber—a sweltering inferno that fine August morning—Hirohito again overrode all differences of opinion and ordered his vassals to accept surrender. He spoke so movingly of the unbearable humiliation which he and Japan must endure for the sake of national survival that he began to weep. With him wept the leaders who had ravaged half of Asia.

When Hirohito emerged at noon from the bunker, up the private staircase into his study, he found Lord Privy Seal Kido waiting for him. Still wracked by sobs, Hirohito asked that the remarks he had just made be used as the basis for the imperial rescript of surrender which he would read over the radio on August 15, the next day. Kido relayed the Emperor's thoughts to the secretary of the Cabinet and he in turn wrote up a draft. Two scholars translated it into suitable archaic Chinese-style Japanese and labored to give it the required singsong cadences.

Before the meeting in Hirohito's air raid shelter, that Tuesday morning, August 14, War Minister Anami had told his subordinates to abandon their coup d'etat plans. During the meeting, however, Lord Privy Seal Kido received a visit from Hirohito's brother, twenty-nine-year-old Prince Mikasa, an Army lieutenant colonel. And after the meeting, when the senior members of the conspiracy refused to have anything to do with the coup plans, a major who had been a close friend of Prince Mikasa at the military academy tried to revive the plot. He spent the rest of the afternoon making the rounds of important generals' offices in an effort to muster support.

Late that afternoon Prince Konoye got wind of the coup in the air and called on Lord Privy Seal Kido to discuss rumors of "unrest in the First Imperial Guards Division." The commander of the guards, Lieutenant General Mori Takeshi, was a friend, protégé, and distant in-law of Prince Konoye. He was one of those who had been sounded out by the rebels and asked to give his support to the rebellion. At 6:00 P.M. Lieutenant General Mori came himself to the palace to find out what was expected of him. As he drove down the mall from guard headquarters to the Imperial Household Building he saw his men posted outside every one of the gates to the Fukiage Gardens. It was all most unprecedented. Two of the three guards battalions had been called out together to stand watch in the Inner Palace Enclosure and he, their commander, did not know why. He had a shrewd suspicion that Japan was facing the crisis of surrender, for he had seen the pamphlets dropped that morning by the B-29's, but he knew nothing specific. At the Imperial Household Ministry he saw the Emperor's chief aide-de-camp and sought to feel him out as to what was brewing. The most that he could elicit from Hirohito's chief military advisor, however, was a typical piece of Court advice: "The ultimate test has come. Unless it is made to go with great circumspection, it will not go at all." Mori, who was a simple, stu-

dious man, went on to see General Tanaka, in charge of Tokyo
Area Defense. Tanaka told him frankly of the Emperor's decision
to surrender. Imperial Guards Commander Mori returned to his
headquarters in the north of the palace immersed in thought. Late
that night he was to behave so circumspectly that it was to cost
him his life.

General Tojo, the former prime minister, was also worried by
rumors of a coup. His son-in-law Major Koga Hidemasa was involved in it. The day before, son-in-law Koga had paid a brief visit
to his suburban home next door to the Tojos' and had asked Tojo's daughter if she had recent clippings of his hair and nails. It
was the duty of every soldier's wife to keep such things to put in a
box on the prayer shelf and worship in case her husband died.
Mrs. Koga, Tojo's daughter, bade adieu to her husband in the belief that he was about to die. With the Spartan stoicism of a good
Japanese wife she calmly told her mother at supper what Koga had
said. Her father, Tojo, at once drove in to Tokyo to find out what
was happening. He returned greatly relieved to discover that his
son-in-law had been involved in a coup d'etat plan but that it had
been suspended.

The next afternoon, however, Tojo heard further rumors and
at 6:30 P.M. on Tuesday, August 14, he was again in Tokyo talking to War Minister Anami as he took a bath during a brief Cabinet recess. Anami, whom Tojo had known for twenty years as a
junior member of Hirohito's cabal of young officers, was strangely
preoccupied and reticent. But Tojo understood enough from his
belly talk to stress vociferously that the way to deal with the
American conquerors was not to try to deceive them but to stand
up to them honestly. "After the surrender," he said, "we will all of
course be tried by a military court as war criminals. That goes
without saying. What we must do when the time comes is all
stand together. We must be forthright in stating our belief that
the Greater East Asia War was necessary. What we fought was a
defensive war." War Minister Anami agreed abstractedly, got out
of his tub, put on his clothes, and returned to the Cabinet meeting, leaving Tojo to go home despondent.

While Mori, the general in command of the Imperial Guards,
was seeing the Emperor's chief military advisor and Tojo was see-

ing the war minister, Hirohito was taking his evening stroll in the Fukiage Gardens. The junior chamberlain who walked in respectful silence behind him was alarmed to see "soldiers in the garden where they had never been seen before." Hirohito nodded to the men lounging about under the trees and returned in silence to the Imperial Library. There he found Prime Minister Suzuki waiting for him apologetically to make a report on the progress of the Cabinet. The draft of the imperial rescript of surrender, which Hirohito had approved in the middle of the afternoon, had been debated for two hours and was still not ready for Hirohito's signature. The phrase about "preservation of sacred national treasures" had been deleted because the minister of agriculture felt "it might lead to disagreeable inquiries by the Occupation forces." Hirohito impatiently approved this amendment and several other small word changes. The one remaining problem, continued Prime Minister Suzuki, was a tiny difference of opinion between War Minister Anami and Navy Minister Yonai. Anami insisted that the words "war situation has daily deteriorated" be changed to "war situation has not developed to Japan's advantage." Navy Minister Yonai branded this change an attempted evasion of Army responsibility and refused to endorse it. Could the Emperor, asked Prime Minister Suzuki, please give the Cabinet some guidance on this unfortunate little detail? Indeed Hirohito could and asked Suzuki to tell Navy Minister Yonai that there was no objection to the war minister's proposal.

Before the Cabinet meeting reconvened at 7:00 P.M. that Tuesday evening, one of Prime Minister Suzuki's secretaries communicated the Emperor's wishes to Navy Minister Yonai in the washroom of the prime minister's residence. Yonai turned without a word into one of the booths there and only sighed expressively as he urinated. At 8:30 P.M. Prime Minister Suzuki was back at the Imperial Library with a Cabinet-approved version of the surrender rescript. Hirohito made one or two tiny stylistic changes and strengthened Anami's insertion to read: "The war situation has developed not necessarily to Japan's advantage." Then Hirohito sent a copy of the historical document over to the palace office of the *Court Gazette*. At 11:00 P.M. the *Gazette* would begin running off an extra which would be circulated among the aristocracy and would give advance warning to the nation of Hirohito's radio address, scheduled for the morrow.

THE LONGEST EVENING

During the Cabinet recess between 8:30 and 9:30 P.M., War Minister Anami drove to his office to collect personal belongings from his desk. He noted with a sense of bleak poetry that the sunset that night—the setting of Japan's sun—was obscured by a heavy mist. It entirely enveloped the War Ministry, which had been housed, since the incendiary raid of May 25, in a complex of buildings around the old military academy. Anami found everything in the Ministry at sixes and sevens. During the afternoon the parade ground had blazed in the heat as men shuttled back and forth between files and bonfires burning the documents of Grand Imperial Headquarters. Now the embers of the fires still glowed but there was no one to tend them except a few soldiers who were drunk. Most of the officers had put on civilian clothes and set out for their home villages. The corridors of the War Ministry were deserted. War Minister Anami's footfalls echoed with emptiness and loneliness as he made his way to his office. His desk was littered with copies of cables he had ordered written and dispatched that afternoon to secret police units everywhere in Asia preparing for surrender. He sat down wearily and began to sort out the papers to be kept and those to be thrown away. An adjutant drifted in like a piece of the fog from outside and was ordered to summon the rest of the staff, particularly Colonel Arao, the senior member of the coup d'etat group. While waiting, Anami drafted a note of resignation to Prime Minister Suzuki and a cable to commanders overseas explaining the surrender.

Colonel Arao of the projected coup d'etat finally made his appearance at 9:30 P.M. He had been waiting by mistake to see War Minister Anami at his residence instead of the ministry. Anami dismissed the rest of his staff members who by now had gathered to help and watch him. "This war has been given up," he said. "Please leave me with what remains to be done." His secretaries and orderlies filed from the room, bowing. Arao remained to talk with him in private.

"It is the duty of you officers," Anami said, "to live and work for the rebuilding of Japan." Whatever else he may have said, this in itself was sufficient belly talk for Arao. It meant that Anami no longer numbered himself among "you officers" but among the dead. It meant that the war minister no longer hoped to fight a decisive battle against the Americans but merely to impress them with his high-level fanaticism by committing suicide.

Arao wept and promised to carry out the war minister's intentions. Anami took a bundle of cigars which he had brought back from New Guinea out of a desk drawer and began to wrap them in newspaper. Then, as if on impulse, he handed two of them to Arao. "I'd like you to have these," he said, with his kindest smile. And then gathering up a few souvenirs in a *furoshiki*, a carrying cloth, and tucking his ceremonial shortsword in its polished cherry scabbard under his arm, Anami bowed curtly in the professional manner of the Japanese officer. "I'll see you on the other side," he said and turned on his heel to return to his limousine.

By his cryptic words to Arao, War Minister Anami had sanctioned a reactivation of the suspended coup d'etat plans. Now, however, the coup was to be a fake one, staged as realistically as possible but no longer intended as a genuine effort to prolong the war. All that mattered was a gesture which would convince outside observers, especially Americans, that the sacred Emperor had been victim rather than villain of Japanese militarism. The busy conferences of the afternoon, the circumspect words of Hirohito's aide-de-camp, Hirohito's own walk in the Fukiage Gardens—all had been contrived to convey through belly talk the need for this final gesture.

The man most responsible for reviving the coup plans and converting them into fake coup plans was a certain Lieutenant Colonel X, an officer who has been regularly identified as unidentifiable by all the witnesses of that night's work. Lieutenant Colonel X was first noticed at 8:30 P.M., talking with junior officers of the Imperial Guards at the Double Bridge, the sacred entrance to the palace used only by the Emperor on state occasions. He had with him Major Hatanaka, War Minister Anami's

pet firebrand, who would be the ringleader in the high-wire acts
which followed.

Now, no military man ever presented himself at a palace gate—
least of all at the Double Bridge—without giving his name and
showing his credentials. The identity of Lieutenant Colonel X,
in short, was not genuinely unknown to the officers of the
Imperial Guards nor to the surviving members of the guards who
have written about him since. In gossipy Japan only the imperial
taboo which gives anonymity to the private acts of members of
the Emperor's immediate family could account for such an unidentifiable personage in the Inner Palace enclosure at such a crucial juncture in Japanese history. The presumption is strong that
Lieutenant Colonel X was Lieutenant Colonel Mikasa, the Emperor's youngest brother. Mikasa was a classmate of the junior
officers participating in the coup that night. Mikasa had called
on Hirohito and his chief advisor Kido twice that afternoon. The
performance of Mikasa's classmates that night was to be so grue-
somely realistic that it could not have been staged, not even as a
hopeless samurai gesture of honor, without high priestly, imperial
sanction.

A few minutes after 9:30 P.M., when War Minister Anami left
his office in his limousine, Lieutenant Colonel X and his firebrand protégé, Major Hatanaka, visited the colonel in charge of
the two battalions of Imperial Guards waiting in the Fukiage Gardens. Earlier in the day this same colonel had refused to subscribe
to Major Hatanaka's coup plans. Now, when presented to Lieutenant Colonel X, the colonel said, "It seems I have changed my
mind."

While Major Hatanaka and Lieutenant Colonel X were making
their rounds in the palace, War Minister Anami, alone in his car,
gazed out at the ruins of Tokyo on his right and the ancient, un-
changing walls of the palace on his left. He had ordered his last
young men to die. He had thrown his last dust in the eyes of the
enemy. He returned to the Cabinet meeting at the prime minister's residence to approve the wording of the note which would be
sent that night to the Allies: "His Majesty the Emperor has issued
an imperial rescript regarding Japan's acceptance. . . . His Majesty the Emperor is prepared to authorize and insure the signa-

ture by his government and the Imperial General Headquarters of the necessary terms."

Anami listened apathetically, without comment, to the main text of the note. Then Foreign Minister Togo began to read a lengthy postscript which he planned to send in a second cable, and Anami opened his eyes wide with interest. "It is earnestly solicited that . . . the number of points in Japanese territory to be designated by the Allies for occupation be limited . . . ; that . . . the Japanese forces be allowed to disarm themselves . . . ; that . . . the honor of the soldiers will be respected, permitting them, for instance, to wear swords . . . ; that reasonable time be allowed before the cessation of hostilities . . . ; that the Allies will be good enough quickly to take necessary steps or extend us facilities for the shipment of indispensable foodstuffs and medical supplies to Japanese forces in distant islands."

"If I had known you were going to deal with the matter that way," exclaimed Anami, "I would not have felt compelled to speak so zealously earlier." Foreign Minister Togo bowed stiffly in acknowledgment of the apology.

The Cabinet sat on, reminiscing as to what might have been and speculating as to the next phase of Lord Privy Seal Kido's peace plan. When the ministers finally adjourned, about 11:30 P.M., War Minister Anami tarried for a last word with Prime Minister Suzuki. "I am afraid I have caused you a great deal of trouble," Anami said—and handed the prime minister the newspaper-wrapped package of precious cigars which he had brought from his office.

"I fully appreciate your painful position," answered Suzuki. "As His Majesty is extremely punctilious in the worship of his ancestors, however, and performs the rites required of him each spring and autumn, I am sure that the gods will show us their grace. I have not lost hope for the future of Japan."

Anami smiled and bowed and turned on his heel. "He came to say good-bye," observed Suzuki to his secretary. Anami drove to his residence and prepared for his last sentimental duty. He steeped himself in a scalding Japanese wooden tub, allowed his household maid to inject in his arm a last vitamin shot, donned a comfortable kimono, poured himself a drink, and sat down beside his telephone, with paper, ink, and writing brush, to frame his final testaments. His secretary passed in and out of the room, giving him news and scraps of conversation. The maid stole in silently from time to time with a freshly warmed pitcher of saké.

Earlier that Tuesday evening, at 10:00 P.M., U.S. B-29's had returned to Tokyo after a four-day bombing pause. When the air raid alert sounded, Emperor Hirohito decided not to wait for the adjournment of his Cabinet but instructed his chamberlains to make preparations at once for the promulgation of the surrender rescript. At 11:25 P.M., wearing the uniform of an Army field marshal, he drove across the palace park, through the blackout, to the Imperial Household Administration Building. There, in the audience hall on the second floor, a team of technicians from Japan National Broadcasting were waiting for him, and he intoned his rescript into a microphone. At the first reading, though no one presumed to remark on it, his voice trembled.

"It sounds too low and husky," he said, when he listened to the playback. "Let me try again."

On the second take his voice was clearer, more correctly high-pitched and nasal, and more nervous. He was not entirely satisfied and offered to make a third take. But the room was stifling and the technicians were awed to the point of suicide by the discomfort to which they were putting him. They assured him that a third take would not be necessary. Hirohito took them at their word and at 12:05 A.M. returned to his library.

Two records had been cut of each reading, one for playback and one for possible broadcast. After repeated hearings, the technicians judged the first reading to be far the most moving and discovered that there was a good reason to reject the second: Hirohito had left out a conjunction. All four pressings, however, were packed in cans and cotton bags and given to a chamberlain for safekeeping. After careful thought the chamberlain hid them in a safe behind the books in a room on the first floor of the Imperial Household Building belonging to one of the Empress's ladies-in-waiting.

THE FINAL GESTURE

During Hirohito's recording session and War Minister Anami's farewell to his Cabinet colleagues, the long and gingerly incubated coup d'etat was finally taking shape. At 10:00 P.M., when the air raid sirens were sounding for the first time, one of the principals in the coup, Lieutenant Colonel Ida Masataka, was lying on his bunk in the staff quarters at the War Ministry, gazing at the ceiling in romantic gloom. Ida was the member of Anami's staff whom Tsukamoto of the secret police had first contacted on his return from Taiwan. For a week Ida had been the coup's most enthusiastic booster, but since Hirohito's final decision in the bunker that morning Ida had obediently given up the scheme. He had told the young firebrand major, Hatanaka, not to count on him and had devoted himself all afternoon to a new idea: the mass suicide of the Japanese Army officer corps. If enough officers would take their lives and so demonstrate their responsibility for fighting a losing war, it would save the honor of Japan and at the same time exonerate the Emperor in American eyes. But when Ida conducted a poll of the officers at the War Ministry, he found that only 20 per cent were willing to kill themselves. Another 10 per cent thought it would be better to go underground. The remaining 70 per cent had no opinion. Ida had been so disgusted by the results of his poll that he had retired to his quarters to prepare himself for his own suicide.

When the air raid sirens shrieked out, Lieutenant Colonel Ida lay still in his bunk and hoped that a bomb would fall on him. Suddenly his friend Major Hatanaka burst into his bedchamber to give him the exciting news of Anami's commitment to suicide and of the agreement of the colonel in the Fukiage Gardens to support the coup with his two battalions of guards. Unlike Ida, Hatanaka was not troubled by subtle, palsied casts of thought. He was a man of action. Handsome, serious, slight, athletic, he had the look of a man who would make a good soldier if he ever survived his thirty-fifth birthday.

Lieutenant Colonel Ida listened to him morosely, shook his head, and told his eager young friend that the coup would never

impress Americans as much as mass hara-kiri. Major Hatanaka
swiftly explained that the two plans could be dovetailed. After the
coup the conspirators could commit suicide. Lieutenant Colonel
Ida brightened somewhat at this thought, and Major Hatanaka
pressed home his argument. Without Ida's participation, he said
flatteringly, the coup could not even begin. Ida was a kinsman of
Lieutenant General Mori who had over-all command of the Imperial Palace Guards. Without Ida's help it would be impossible to
talk to Lieutenant General Mori and persuade him to issue the
necessary orders for the coup. Ida proudly saw the logic of this argument and agreed to play his part.

The two conspirators set out on their bicycles to pedal a mile
through the sultry night from the War Ministry to the Imperial
Guards headquarters in the northernmost salient of the palace.
Ida's bicycle sprang a flat tire, and Hatanaka had to stop and help
the unmechanical colonel fix it. The two arrived at the North
Gate of the palace at 11:00 P.M. and asked to be taken at once to
Lieutenant General Mori. Mori, however, sent out word asking
them to wait a while. All evening Mori had been considering the
words about circumspection delivered to him five hours earlier
by the Emperor's chief aide-de-camp. Now he was consulting his
brother-in-law from Hiroshima and was hearing for the first time
an eyewitness account of the effects of the atomic bomb.

Lieutenant General Mori kept the conspirators waiting for an
hour and a half and did not admit them to his presence until almost 12:30 A.M. By then he knew that Hirohito had returned from
his recording session to the safety of the Imperial Library. Firebrand Hatanaka demanded that Mori call out his Imperial
Guards, seize the palace, cut off the Imperial Library, and issue instructions in the Emperor's name for the Army and Navy to continue the war. Hatanaka asserted that he spoke for War Minister
Anami. Lieutenant General Mori insisted that Hatanaka must
be mistaken. At 12:45 A.M. Hatanaka agreed to go back to Anami
and seek confirmation. He left Mori talking to his kinsman, Lieutenant Colonel Ida.

Five minutes later the courtiers at the Imperial Household
Building were informed by telephone that the Emperor and Empress had gone to bed. At that moment, at his residence to the

south of the palace, War Minister Anami was preparing for suicide. Tokyo Area Commander Tanaka was napping at his desk upstairs from Peace Faction headquarters in the Dai Ichi Insurance Building. Secret Policeman Tsukamoto from Taiwan, the watchdog of the coup, dozed in the police headquarters outside the North Gate of the palace, where he happened to have the duty that night. A stone's throw away, inside the North Gate at the guards' headquarters, Lieutenant General Mori and Lieutenant Colonel Ida were engaged in earnest conversation. At some time between 12:50 and 1:00 A.M. they were joined by the mysterious Lieutenant Colonel X.

Major Hatanaka had commandeered a staff car and set out to seek reassurance on the other side of the palace from War Minister Anami's brother-in-law, Lieutenant Colonel Takeshita. He arrived at his destination about 1:00 A.M. and implored Takeshita to see Anami and have the war minister telephone Guards Commander Mori. Takeshita promised to see what he could do, and Major Hatanaka started back for the command post of the Imperial Guards. Takeshita went off at the same time to drive down the block to his brother-in-law's. He found Anami struggling to write a poem of farewell to life. "I am thinking of committing suicide tonight according to plan," said Anami.

"Does it have to be tonight?" asked Takeshita.

"I'm glad you do not oppose the idea," replied Anami.

"Why don't you use the poem you wrote before you went to the front in China?" suggested Takeshita.

Anami laughed and ordered the maid to bring beer mugs to put the saké in. "It's all right," he said. "The revolt won't amount to anything because General Tanaka and the Tokyo Area Army will refuse to support it."

Takeshita telephoned Imperial Guards headquarters to say that Anami was going ahead with suicide according to plan. Then he and Anami settled down for a last bout of serious drinking together.

Firebrand Hatanaka returned to guards' headquarters shortly after 1:00 A.M. He found Lieutenant General Mori, Lieutenant Colonel Ida, and Lieutenant Colonel X still discussing suicide and the destiny of Japan. At Hatanaka's reappearance Lieutenant

Colonel Ida bowed himself from the room and left Hatanaka, Lieutenant Colonel X, and a newcomer, an Army Air Force captain, to finish the conversation. A few minutes later firebrand Hatanaka shot dead Mori, the commander of the Imperial Guards. The Air Force captain, Uehara Shigetaro, scion of one of the greatest military families in Japan, drew his sword and decapitated Mori's brother-in-law from Hiroshima.

In the quiet of the night and the blackout expectant ears throughout the palace area heard the gunshot. War Minister Anami heard it a mile away and realized that his colleague Lieutenant General Mori had met a meaningful end. The chamberlains at the Imperial Household Ministry also heard the shot. So did Secret Policeman Tsukamoto at his headquarters outside the North Gate.

Lieutenant Colonel X stepped from the room where the murders—the courted ceremonial self-sacrifices—had taken place and nodded to the junior officers waiting outside. He then disappeared, insofar as the records reveal, into the palace night. Firebrand Hatanaka and Air Force Captain Uehara followed him out of the murder room, glassy-eyed and spattered with blood. Tojo's son-in-law Koga and other majors entered the room, took the seals from the gory, kimono-clad general on the floor, and used them to stamp orders, which Koga had prepared earlier, for the Imperial Guards to seize the palace. As several hundred of the sleepy guardsmen were being mustered from their barracks, Lieutenant Colonel Ida told the overwrought Major Hatanaka to take charge of himself and the men while Ida went to the Dai Ichi Insurance Building and gave the signal for general uprising to the Tokyo Area Army. Ida drove to the Dai Ichi Building, reported to the Tokyo area commander, and was back at the North Gate of the palace at 2:45 A.M. The blood-stained Major Hatanaka was waiting for him. Hatanaka had successfully deployed the Imperial Guards and had seized all major checkpoints in the palace compound. He had apprehended a Cabinet minister attempting to enter the North Gate of the palace and now had him under lock and key. But Lieutenant Colonel Ida had no solace to offer. The Tokyo Area Army, Ida reported, would definitely not support the uprising.

Major Hatanaka set off, eyes glazed, to see what could be salvaged with the troops who now occupied the southern grounds of the palace. Lieutenant Colonel Ida offered to remain behind at the North Gate to preserve discipline. Hatanaka found that his rebel forces had captured the radio technicians of National Broadcasting and locked them in the keep at the southeastern gate. The technicians had lingered at the Household Ministry drinking toasts to the Voice of the Crane after their historic recording session and had been apprehended weaving an unsteady course home. Now Hatanaka's fellow officers were grilling them as to their business so late at night in the palace.

Hatanaka's men had also succeeded in cutting the main communication cables connecting the palace with the outside world. They did not know it but they had missed two secret cables: one from the chief naval aide-de-camp's office in the Imperial Household Building, the other from the chief Army aide-de-camp's office in the bunker under the Imperial Library. Over these the chamberlains of the Outer and Inner Palaces were keeping in touch with Tokyo Area Commander Tanaka in the Dai Ichi Insurance Building across the moat. At about the same moment that Hatanaka joined his men, the chamberlains learned that General Tanaka was in full command of the situation and was prepared to prevent anything serious from happening. He had just seen Lieutenant Colonel Ida and sent him back to supervise developments at the North Gate. Tsukamoto, at secret-police headquarters outside the gate, was fully informed and ready to move with his men at an instant's notice. As yet, however, Tsukamoto did not believe that secret-police intervention was warranted and feared that it might only be dangerous.

Having resolved to stage a realistic coup d'etat, the firebrand Major Hatanaka needed a military objective in the palace on which to focus the attention of his noncoms and soldiers. The logical objective was the Emperor. It would have been a simple matter to surround the Imperial Library, take the Emperor hostage, and force Japan to continue the war. Instead Hatanaka wasted two hours in meaningless comings and goings, making sure that all the guards at palace gates and checkpoints acknowledged the authority of the forged orders which had been issued.

When the soldiers began to grow restless and apprehensive, Hatanaka declared that the purpose of the coup was to seize the surrender recording which the Emperor had made and prevent it from being broadcast to the people.

At 3:00 A.M. Hatanaka's troops surrounded the Imperial Household Ministry Building and demanded that the chamberlains on night duty there surrender the recording. The chamberlains parleyed. Hatanaka's men entered the building and began to question the chamberlains individually. They all agreed that someone must have the recording but that he was "a taller man with a bigger nose" than any of the soldiers' prime suspects. All the chamberlains wore the drab blue wartime *koku-fuku* or national uniform for civilians, a Nehru jacket and unstriped pants. It was difficult to tell one chamberlain from another. All had the air of expert butlers. Hatanaka's soldiers felt that they were being made fun of. They began to look increasingly frustrated and potentially violent.

At 3:20 A.M., fearing that Hatanaka's men were about to conduct a search of the building, one of the chamberlains aroused Lord Privy Seal Kido from his pallet and advised him that the soldiers were in a vicious mood and might kill him if they found him. Kido flushed secret documents in his room down the toilet and repaired to the great steel bank vault under the building where the paper assets of the imperial fortune were stored. Together with the imperial household minister and a number of secretaries and guards, he spent the rest of the night there, locked in like some gilt-edged security. The vault opened by a staircase into a cupboard in the anteroom for ladies-in-waiting outside the audience chamber on the third floor. It was provided with peepholes and intercoms which made it possible for the two prisoners to keep in touch with much of what was happening in the rest of the building.

Once Kido was safely hidden, the chamberlain who had put away the phonograph records set out to investigate reports that the Imperial Library was surrounded and cut off. His name, Tokugawa Yoshihiro, guaranteed his safety, for the Tokugawas had supplied ancient Japan with military dictators and the scions of the family still held a place second only to the Emperor's in the esteem of soldiers.[13] Chamberlain Tokugawa negotiated the rebel guard lines with sure aristocratic poise. At the library he learned that the Emperor was fast asleep. The Emperor, according to his own later account, was not asleep but listening with amusement through the paper walls from his nearby bedroom. At the adjoining English-style country house, the Concubines' Pavilion, Chamberlain Tokugawa was told that Empress Nagako was equally oblivious. He had the iron shutters of both dwellings closed as a precaution and then walked back through the dark gardens and through a newly built tunnel under a hill celebrated for its maples.

At the Imperial Household Building, Chamberlain Tokugawa found that the rebels had begun a room-to-room search for the imperial recording. The soldiers were slashing upholstery and breaking open fine Chinese camphorwood chests. They were angry that the style of furnishing was almost entirely Western. Tokugawa followed them about scalding them with patrician sarcasms. A desperate sergeant[14] finally slapped him in the face, and a lieutenant sat him down and threatened him with a sword unless he would reveal the whereabouts of the recording. Tokugawa went to the aide-de-camps' common room to inquire indignantly what the Army was doing to restore discipline. The naval aide-de-camp took him aside and whispered that he had just spoken on his secret telephone with the Tokyo Area Army HQ and everything was well in hand. Tokyo Area Commander Tanaka had set out from his headquarters by staff car shortly after 4:00 A.M. to begin the task of suppressing the revolt. A little later he had been joined at the North Gate by secret-police Colonel Tsukamoto, the rebellion's watchdog.[15]

[13] Tokugawa Yoshihiro was the son of Tokugawa Yoshichika who will be met with later as the financier of the March Plot, an intrigue which prepared the domestic political scene in 1931 for the conquest of Manchuria.

[14] Sergeant Wakabayashi, fifteen years later, made himself known to Chamberlain Tokugawa, presenting him with an apologetic teapot made out of an ancient bronze mirror, the most cherished possession of his family.

[15] Tanaka's aide, Major Tsukamoto Kiyoshi, was also present. The two Tsukamotos have sometimes been confused in Western reporting of the record.

LIVES FOR THE EMPEROR

At 3:30 A.M., when the soldiers entered the Imperial Household Building, Lieutenant Colonel Ida deserted his post at the North Gate of the palace to report to War Minister Anami. He found Anami still drinking saké by the mugful with his secretary and his brother-in-law. He had wound his belly in a white sash and put on a white shirt given him by the Emperor. Ida reported on the gesture of rebellion being made in the palace and sat down to join in the carouse. About 4:00 A.M. Air Force Captain Uehara called to relate ecstatically his part in the murder of Guards Commander Mori. Anami remarked, "Something else to make amends for," and went on drinking. A little later his brother-in-law Takeshita asked the war minister if he might not be drinking too much. Anami discounted the idea by reminding Takeshita that saké helped the blood to flow and that a fifth-degree swordsman could hardly fail in his suicide. Nevertheless Anami shortly dismissed them all and asked to be alone.

Lieutenant Colonel Ida went outside to wait. He later said that he waited on the curb for a passing Army vehicle which would take him back to the palace. But he could have called for a car easily enough. What he meant was that he was waiting to make sure that Anami would fulfill his part of the pledge and commit suicide. Ida, after all, had stood by patriotically, outside the door, while his own kinsman, Lieutenant General Mori of the guards, was being shot.

In bold, childlike calligraphy, Anami was completing the two memorials over which he had agonized earlier. The first was the poem which he had written years ago, before going to China:

> Having received from
> His Imperial Majesty
> many great favors,
> I have no final statement
> to make to posterity.

The second was a single new sentence in prose: "In the conviction that our sacred land will never perish, I offer my life to the Emperor as an apology for the great crime." By the great crime most surviving officers believe that he meant the Army's crime in being defeated. Having completed his literary chores, he sat down with his brother-in-law for one or two more drinks. Amid the distractions of the modern world it was hard for a fifty-eight-year-old bowman to follow the ancient formulas of honor.

At 5:30 A.M. the supreme commandant of the secret police called at Anami's residence to inform him that Tokyo Area Commander Tanaka was now in the Imperial Guards compound in the northern corner of the palace, rescinding the false orders given earlier and calling the soldiers back to their barracks. The rebellion was over. Being no great friend of Anami, the commandant of the secret police was not privileged to see the war minister but delivered his report to Anami's brother-in-law.

For War Minister Anami the time had come. His death, like that of Mori's earlier, was required to show that the insurrection was not all play-acting. He walked to the veranda of his bedroom and laid out the two memorials he had written, together with a picture of his son who had died in battle the year before. He took a kneeling position, shortsword in his right hand, dagger in his left. He stared at the beams of the rising sun stealing in through the cracks of the closed blackout shutters of the porch. He listened for a moment to the tread of the guards in the garden outside. He sank the shortsword into his muscular belly below the lowest rib on the left. He wrenched the sword to the right, through his stomach and then sharply upward. Having followed the painful prescribed formula, he found himself still alive. With the dagger in his left hand he reached around to the right side of his neck and felt about for the area of the carotid artery.

His brother-in-law came back into the room, ran to kneel at his side, and assured him that the rebellion had served its purpose. "May I have the honor of assisting you?"

Anami shook his head and dug the dagger into his neck. It missed the carotid artery but cut the cervical vein. He remained kneeling, swaying from side to side, for almost an hour. Then he fainted forward and continued to bleed and writhe, unconscious on the floor. His brother-in-law sat out the long vigil waiting for

him to die. About 7:30 A.M. one of several visiting officers finally
called in a medical corpsman to dispatch him with a hypodermic.

Within the palace, half a mile to the northeast of Anami's bedroom, Tokyo Area Commander Tanaka was driving from checkpoint to checkpoint sending the soldiers back to their barracks.
His eyes flashed. His magnificent mustache, which he had first
cultivated as an undergraduate years ago at Oxford, heaved and
twisted expressively. His riding crop slapped savagely against his
riding boots as he itemized and emphasized his admonitions. It
was his noblest hour, for he too had now resolved on suicide. As
a classmate and old friend and rival of Anami he could do no less.
He would blow his brains out nine days later when he felt sure
that the Army would obey the Emperor and accept surrender in
a disciplined manner. Now, in the palace, the soldiers followed
his instructions instantly. In a matter of minutes there was no
disturbance within the sacred precincts but the dawn twitter of
birds.

Left without troops, the young rebel officers of Anami's staff
withdrew to the offices of the Japan Broadcasting Company two
blocks outside the moat. There they sought to turn on the trans-
mitters so that they could make their own last statement to the
nation. When they failed, they disbanded and went out to lose
themselves in the early morning crowds of people going to work.

Other attacks were made that night on the homes of Hirohito's
accessories in the peace plot. This was a tried and true stratagem,
a standard method of operation. In three previous sham coups
d'etat staged in the 1930's, simultaneous attacks had always been
made on the homes of the master plotters. Now, on the night of
August 14, 1945, secret policemen attacked the home of Hirohito's
chief advisor, Lord Privy Seal Kido, and had to be driven off by
other secret policemen. Groups of venal civilian patriots, seasoned
by the leadership of a few soldiers, burned the private residences
of Prime Minister Suzuki and of Baron Hiranuma, the two great
impresarios of the peace scenes in the imperial bunker. Before
both fires the victims were given adequate warning and allowed to
escape. Some of Baron Hiranuma's own stout right-wing partisans
participated in the burning of his home.

At Prime Minister Suzuki's, a comedy of fate overtook the droll old philosopher. His getaway limousine refused to start. It was loaded with family and valuables and proved too heavy for servants to push. His entire bodyguard, which was large enough to repel an army, had to be summoned from neighborhood retreats to carry the car to the top of a gradient. Everyone enjoyed the farce, including Prime Minister Suzuki. And when the car's engine finally sparked, going down the hill, the bodyguard turned back uproariously to mingle with the incendiary mob gathering at Suzuki's home. No one was later tried for the acts of arson, but Suzuki and Hiranuma both collected a little devaluated insurance. More to the point, the public was satisfied. Both men had saved face. They had established their innocence of the anti-peace coup in the palace and they had paid a little for their pro-peace coup at the counsel tables.

At 7:21 A.M., Wednesday, August 15, the Japan National Broadcasting Company, having repaired its cables cut by the rebels, went back on the air to announce: "The Emperor at noon today will graciously broadcast, in person. This is a most gracious act. All the people are requested to listen respectfully to the Emperor. Electricity will be supplied to districts not normally supplied during daylight hours." After the events of the previous weeks and the leaflets dropped the day before, few Tokyo residents had any doubt as to what the Emperor would announce. All morning long the park of the Imperial Plaza, outside the southeastern palace gate near the Household Ministry Building, filled up with relieved and sorrowful people. At noon the loudspeakers there and at every other city square in the country vibrated with the Emperor's voice:

We declared war on America and Britain out of Our sincere desire to ensure Japan's self-preservation and the stabilization of East Asia, it being far from Our thought either to infringe upon the sovereignty of other nations or to embark upon territorial aggrandizement. But now the war has lasted for nearly four years. Despite the best that has been done by everyone . . . the war situation has developed not necessarily to Japan's advantage, while the general trends of the world have all turned against her interest. Moreover, the enemy has begun to employ a new and most cruel bomb, the power of which to do dam-

age is indeed incalculable. . . . Should We continue to fight it would
. . . result in an ultimate collapse and obliteration of the Japanese
nation. . . . Such being the case, how are We to save the millions of
Our subjects; or to atone Ourselves before the hallowed spirits of Our
Imperial Ancestors? This is the reason why We have ordered the acceptance of the provisions of the Joint Declaration of the Powers. . . .

Let the entire nation continue as one family, from generation to
generation. . . . Unite your total strength to be devoted to the construction for the future. . . . Work with resolution so as ye may en-
hance the innate glory of the Imperial State and keep pace with the
progress of the world.

The throngs in the squares wept with humiliation, incredulity,
and weary relief. Men prostrated themselves and knocked their
heads on the pavements. Here and there someone drove a dagger
or bullet into himself. The crowds bowed to each corpse, muttered words of prayer for each departing spirit and dispersed in
silence to their homes. In all, 376 Army men from general to private, 113 Navy men from admiral to seaman, and 37 nurses and
civilians died by their own hands that week, a grand total of only
526.[16]

The scores who killed themselves on the precincts of the palace
in Tokyo included firebrand Hatanaka, General Tojo's son-in-law,
and one other leader of the hopeless coup the night before. A
fourth rebel, Air Force Captain Uehara who had murdered
General Mori's brother-in-law, shot himself two days later. Four
more of the rebel officers may still be found alive in Tokyo today.
One presides over the Historical Section of Japan's modern Self-
Defense Forces. A second, General Anami's brother-in-law, runs
the Self-Defense Staff College. A third, Arao, is president of an
automobile agency. A fourth, Lieutenant Colonel Ida, has
changed his name to Iwata. He has divorced his wife because she
was ashamed of him for not committing suicide. He works in an
advertising agency for Colonel Tsukamoto Makoto, the secret

16 The over-all suicide rate that year dropped dramatically from the norm
of 2.5 per ten thousand to 1.5, an all-time low even in the postwar period.
Apparently the honor of the few was more than discounted by the need to
survive of the many.

policeman from Formosa, the official witness of the coup, who in years gone by had assisted Prince Asaka at the rape of Nanking.

Through Hirohito's broadcast the Japanese became the last people in the world to learn that the war was over. Others had heard the news the previous afternoon when Domei, the Japanese news service, at 2:49 P.M. Tokyo time, had beamed a message to the American operator on Okinawa: FLASH FLASH TOKYO AUGUST 14 IT IS LEARNED THAT AN IMPERIAL MESSAGE ACCEPTING THE POTS-DAM DECLARATION IS FORTHCOMING SOON. By the time that Japanese were going home from the Emperor's broadcast to "eat stones and drink gall," as they said, London's first V-J Day celebration was spending itself in walk-up flats. In New York surging crowds of sailors, soldiers, and girls in Times Square were waiting for the magical stroke of midnight.

The Allies had laid down the terms. The bomb had enforced them. The Emperor had accepted them. The Allies had obviated an inch-by-inch conquest of Japan and postponed for a few years the communization of China. They had won a chance to cure Japan of her proud tribalism and to harness the vast powers of the Emperor for the task. Vengeance need not stand in the way of construction, for vengeance had already been taken. The 140,-000 corpses of Hiroshima and Nagasaki had paid for Nanking, and the 166,000 killed in the fire raids on Tokyo had more than paid for American, Australian, and British war prisoners who had been starved and beaten to death in Japanese concentration camps. Only ignorance and suspicion remained to be conquered. The exact arithmetic of war had to be replaced by the conversational arts of peace. Vague foreign concepts like Shinto and Emperor system, or like Christianity and democracy, had to acquire flesh-and-blood meaning. A few hundred Americans and a few thousand Japanese who spoke one another's language had to fill out the blank checks of "unconditional" surrender.

In the palace, Lord Privy Seal Kido and Emperor Hirohito waited with apprehension. They hoped that the enemy would demonstrate Christian kindness; they prayed that the enemy would fail to democratize. Unless they could preserve the Emperor system, they would not be able to answer to their ancestors.

Without aristocracy and hierarchy, the society of the living would cease to be at one with the spirit world of the dead. Up to now the peace plot had worked with the vanquished; now it must work with the victors.

3

DEFEAT

RECEPTION CABINET

The Japanese were the only people on earth who had lived in their homeland from prehistoric times and never been conquered by outsiders. Many of them, however, had studied surrender subterfuges from the greatest masters, the Chinese. And now, after surrender in 1945, Japan had two weeks in which to prepare before the first American Occupation troops would unload from their planes onto Japanese soil. Dazed and disheartened as they were, the people demonstrated extraordinary discipline and, in the words of one newspaper, "complete compliance with the imperial will." From palace on down to police box, they moved with zeal to implement the well-considered plans of the Peace Faction. Millionaires gave millions "to save the nation," and aristocratic ladies prepared to contribute even their virtue if it was required of them.

Fighting off a mood of inanition and despair, Hirohito worked early and late to set his people an example. He reviewed most of the peace preparations personally and saw a steady stream of "experts" who had ideas for handling the Americans. No rigid policy could be laid down in advance for the attitude which the people should take toward the conquerors, but tentatively one of cautious politeness and obedience was agreed upon as the best initial approach. This recommendation was transmitted to the masses by an amazingly efficient word-of-mouth system perfected during the war. Each of ten men was responsible for telling ten other men and each of them, in turn, for relaying the message to ten more. The superstructure of the pyramid was Japan's single monolithic political party, the Imperial Rule Assistance Association, which had been organized by Prince Konoye in the late 1930's in emulation of the Nazi and Communist parties of Germany and Russia. The base of the pyramid consisted of "neighborhood association" leaders who doubled as police informers and air raid wardens.

More than most people under such circumstances, the Japanese needed to be told how to behave. In their own highly structured society, they had elaborate rules of etiquette for dealing with all grades of superiors and inferiors in all types of situations. But they had no universal code of behavior to apply to human beings from outside their society. Defeat was an unthinkable situation and foreigners had no place or rank in the national family. In their bewilderment Japanese might fawn upon the Americans or might attack them with knives. Japanese soldiers who had been knocked unconscious in battle and so had fallen alive into enemy hands had almost always surprised Allied interrogators by their pliability as prisoners. Ready one day to cut out American hearts and eat them, they found themselves the next in another life, glad to be breathing but sure that they were dead to their own society. Now it was feared that the whole nation might react in the same way; that in the hunger, misery, and relief of defeat, the people might overnight forget their Japanese heritage.

To give the populace the clearest possible leadership in dealing with the conquerors, Hirohito called to office the first Cabinet in Japan's history headed by an imperial prince of the blood. Prime Minister Suzuki, the old cigar-smoking Taoist philosopher, submitted the resignation of his own Cabinet three hours after the surrender broadcast. Hirohito at once summoned his advisor, Lord Privy Seal Kido, to the library and asked him to proceed according to plan in recommending a successor.

Before making his nomination, Kido broke with all precedent and consulted only one of the elder statesmen, the canny old lawyer Baron Hiranuma. It was a symbolic gesture meant to indicate that the two greatest political camps in Japan, patrician and plebeian, had joined ranks in the hour of national crisis. Hiranuma could speak for the village mayors who controlled the peasants, for the gang leaders who ruled the urban poor, and for the majority in the Army who had wanted to fight Russia rather than the United States.

In response to Kido's summons, Hiranuma walked over immediately from the Privy Council Office where he worked to the Imperial Household Building. "My teeth got burned up with my house this morning," he mumbled as he entered Kido's office. "Now I'll have to buy another house and another set of teeth."

In less than an hour, he and Kido had agreed to recommend a slate of Cabinet ministers headed by Prince Higashikuni, the Emperor's uncle. It was Higashikuni, figuratively, who was to stand on the bridge outside the palace and shout to the Americans, "If you want to come, come." The people would understand that the imperial family was bravely accepting responsibility for defeat. And the Americans would see that Japan considered her imperial princes to be men of peace.

Emperor Hirohito accepted the nomination of Prince Higashikuni as a matter of prearrangement, but Higashikuni himself had last-minute objections. During the 1860's, after the Americans had forced their way into Japan the first time, his father, he complained, had undertaken a similar role as a peacemaker for Hirohito's great-grandfather. And for this loyal service he had later been disgraced and banished from Court. Prince Higashikuni wanted assurance that the same thing would not happen to him now. The next morning, August 16, Hirohito talked privately with Higashikuni for twenty minutes in the library and promised him a lifelong place in the imperial favor. Higashikuni later said that he was much moved by the Emperor's haggard appearance. Lord Privy Seal Kido was summoned to witness the bargain, and Higashikuni formally accepted the imperial mandate to form a government.

Higashikuni designed a Cabinet which would look like an apology to the people and a gesture of defiance to the Allies, particularly to the Chinese. He indicated the Emperor's contrition

for the disastrous adventure in the South Seas by including as
ministers several members of the Fight-Russia or Strike-North
Faction ousted in the 1930's. At the same time he took as his chief
minister of state Prince Konoye, who had led the nation into war
with China, and as war minister General Shimomura Sadamu
who had forced the plans for the rape of Nanking through the
General Staff in 1937. As special Cabinet advisor, Higashikuni
chose a retired Lieutenant General Ishiwara Kanji who had conducted the strategic planning for the conquest of Manchuria in
1929–1931.

To those in the inner circle of Japanese leadership, the most
cynical feature of Higashikuni's Peace Cabinet was Prince
Higashikuni himself. There were nine other eligible princes in
the ranks of Hirohito's immediate family who might have stood
more sincerely for peace. The bold, affable Higashikuni had
played a conspicuously active role behind the scenes in the last
twenty-five years. And if the Allies could but know it, he was better qualified than most for the label of Class A war criminal. As
a privileged Army Intelligence officer in Paris in 1921, he had
helped to recruit a private, unofficial cabal of Army officers for
Hirohito. In 1927 he had helped to persuade Hirohito to prepare
for the conquest of Manchuria. Between 1930 and 1936, as part of
the terror which silenced Japanese moderates, he had been involved in no less than eight fake coups d'etat, four assassinations,
two religious hoaxes, and countless threats of murder and blackmail. He alone among princes of the blood had taken active
measures in 1936 to help his nephew Hirohito to suppress Strike-
North or Fight-Russia insurgents. A year later Higashikuni had
assumed command of the bombing of civilian China. In 1941, after Hirohito had approved plans for the attack on Pearl Harbor,
Higashikuni had stood ready to lead Japan into the war as prime
minister. Only the caution of men like Lord Privy Seal Kido, who
considered the possibility of defeat and worried about the future
of the imperial family, induced Hirohito to nominate General
Tojo as prime minister instead.

More than any other prince of the blood, Higashikuni had always been able to work smoothly with Hirohito. The attraction
between the two men—the Emperor was only thirteen years

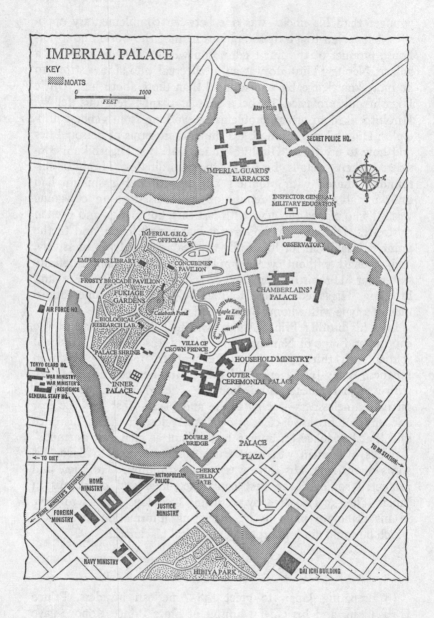

IMPERIAL PALACE

KEY

░░ MOATS

0   1000
FEET

ARMY CLUB

SECRET POLICE HQ.

IMPERIAL GUARDS'
BARRACKS

INSPECTOR GENERAL
MILITARY EDUCATION

IMPERIAL G.H.Q.
OFFICIALS

OBSERVATORY

EMPEROR'S LIBRARY

CONCUBINES'
PAVILION

FROSTY BROCADE PAVILION

CHAMBERLAINS'
PALACE

FUKIAGE
GARDENS

AIR FORCE HQ.

Calabash Pond

Maple Leaf
Hill

BIOLOGICAL
RESEARCH LAB.

PALACE SHRINE

VILLA OF
CROWN PRINCE

HOUSEHOLD MINISTRY

TOKYO GUARD HQ.

WAR MINISTRY
WAR MINISTER'S
RESIDENCE

GENERAL STAFF HQ.

INNER
PALACE

OUTER
CEREMONIAL PALACE

DOUBLE
BRIDGE

PALACE

PLAZA

TO RR STATION.

← TO DIET

HOME
MINISTRY

METROPOLITAN
POLICE

CHERRY
FIELD
GATE

PRIME MINISTER'S RESIDENCE

FOREIGN
MINISTRY

JUSTICE
MINISTRY

NAVY MINISTRY

HIBIYA PARK

DAI ICHI BUILDING

younger than his uncle—was one between complementary opposites, between a tough, unscrupulous man of the world and a hothouse product of the finest education which could be given in a palace. Nephew Hirohito was an intellectual who always strove to be more knowledgeable and rational than those about him. Uncle Higashikuni professed to be a simple, manly, religious fellow. Hirohito liked to attack problems by working from general principles; Higashikuni began all his thinking in terms of personalities and how to use them. Hirohito valued statistics; Higashikuni considered them details best left to subordinates. Hirohito surrounded himself with propriety and punctilio; Higashikuni had built up an undeserved reputation for himself as an easygoing wastrel who played the devil with fast cars, hot planes, and French mistresses. Hirohito was known for being gruff, open, and to the point, Higashikuni for his ability to speak deviously, impressively, and at length without ever committing himself to a single definite statement. Hirohito knew how to charm men of culture and breeding, Higashikuni how to manipulate violent, superstitious men of a type with whom Hirohito had no contact.

Like his brother Prince Asaka, who had had command at the capture and rape of Nanking, Higashikuni was a fully professional soldier with thirty-one years of experience, including seven in Japanese Army Intelligence in Europe. Bull-necked and flat-faced, with a high forehead and a drooping, twisted mouth, he had an air of shamelessness—totally blithe and bland—that was the fear and envy of his lower-class associates. A close friend of his once said that he looked on human beings "not as men, but as smells" —smells of human weakness which could be used to flavor his stews of intrigue. His forte was religious humbug. He knew and protected some of the best confidence men and charlatans in Japan. They reciprocated by recruiting credulous mystics to serve in his elaborate plots or by extracting information at séances which he could use for purposes of political blackmail.

GIRLS AND WEREWOLVES

In preparing Japan to greet the American invaders, Prince Higashikuni and his chief Minister of State Prince Konoye gave their first attention to the domestic problem of keeping the people's loyalty. On the day of surrender the Cabinet ordered that there should be a "disposal of government goods." Weapons themselves must be turned over to the Allies but everything else stockpiled for the "final decisive battle" could be given away. Approximately ten billion dollars' worth of cars, trucks, gasoline, rubber, tin, scrap iron, silver wire, copper, shoes, blankets, uniforms, banknotes, and blasting powder were distributed to the populace from Army warehouses. Years later the Diet—the Japanese equivalent of Congress—tried to investigate the profit-takers in the giveaway and succeeded in recovering only two million dollars. The other 9.998 billion had gone to repay old Army henchmen for services rendered or to bind them against services anticipated.

Special Cabinet Advisor Ishiwara Kanji, the retired strategist of Manchuria, was detailed to go from town to town explaining the defeat. He was a popular hero, with a rabid following of Buddhist zealots in rural areas. Special trains were laid on everywhere by the government to bring the peasants in to the provincial centers where he spoke. He seldom addressed a crowd of less than 10,000. The burden of his message was simple: former Prime Minister Tojo caused the war; no one else is responsible. Ishiwara and Tojo had worked together as bitter rivals for imperial favor in the early 1930's. Tojo had triumphed, and no one knew better than Ishiwara the details which would make Tojo seem a fit scapegoat. At his home in Tokyo, where he had been living in retirement for more than a year, Tojo accepted the vilification stoically and privately told his friends that it was his wish to take full responsibility for the war. His friends respected his desires but many of his former subordinates and servants protested. The porter at the prime minister's official residence, for instance, was widely quoted as saying that Tojo had been the most human and considerate being who had occupied the building in twenty years.

Having bribed the masses and indoctrinated them with an official explanation of war responsibility, Prince Higashikuni and his ministers turned to the external threat. In case the Occupation Forces came to wreak vengeance, there should be a *maquis* organized to make vengeance costly. Japanese officers created a web of cultural clubs, research institutes, and gymnasiums to serve as fronts for resistance work. With the connivance of the Ministry of Agriculture they founded a number of veterans' farm communes on which gunless tanks were used for tractors and the men held in tight discipline for service at a moment's notice. Pistols and grenades were cached in mountain caves. Temples became repositories for airplane engines. Uninhabited islets off the coast were heaped with camouflaged guns and ammunition. Two billion dollars' worth of gold and platinum was flown home from Korea, encased in lead and sunk in Tokyo harbor. There it remained until April 1946 when, with MacArthur's blessing, it was dredged up and returned to the economy.

Physical education instructors at middle schools were entrusted with blueprints for the resurrection of a weapons technology in case Japan's present factories were all razed. In the island of Kanawa, just offshore from the Japanese Naval Academy, a veritable time capsule of twentieth-century Japanese civilization was stored away on shelves along hundreds of subterranean tunnels. The horde included one neatly labeled example of almost every useful object known to man: bolts of cloth, Siberian furs, Chinese porcelain, and Mongolian leather; all manner of meters and motors; cameras and lenses; radio and recording gear; chemical reagents; hoes, crucibles, welding torches, and metal presses.

The romantic arrangements for werewolf resistance were expected to be useful, as a latent threat, in later bargaining with General MacArthur. More homely measures were needed to minimize the immediate ravages of American Occupation troops. Even the most sophisticated Japanese feared that the "stern justice" promised by the Potsdam Declaration would be reflected in a vindictive racist attitude on the part of the G.I.'s. A rumor made the rounds that President Roosevelt had always opened his letters with a paper knife made from the bone of a Japanese soldier. Wartime propaganda stories were recalled about secret U.S. plans "to emasculate every man and rape every woman" in Japan. Now, journalists reversed themselves and wrote reassuring essays about American civilization. But they coupled these with suggestions on the handling of G.I.'s that were sometimes less than reassuring:

"Wear old clothes and be careful not to smile; your politeness will be misunderstood."

"Be careful not to bare your breasts in public; Americans are not used to seeing the female form uncovered. They have no public baths in America and many of the women do not nurse their babies."

"When in danger of being raped, show the most dignified attitude. Do not yield. Cry for help."

Remembering the exploits of their own soldiers, town elders called mass meetings to advise that virtuous wives and daughters be evacuated to rural areas. Many municipalities offered severance pay to employees to use as escape money. Tens of thousands of women complied and fled to remote mountain villages. But thousands more refused to go and made fun of government efforts. Fifteen years of propaganda had failed to frighten them. They called the evacuation scheme "a face-saving distraction in the hour of defeat." They intimated that municipal officials were attempting to get rid of superannuated secretaries. At some town meetings cosmopolitan school teachers even had the courage to say that they would feel safer on the streets when American troops arrived than they did now when their neighborhoods teemed with half-demobilized Japanese soldiers.

While the women fled to the hills or stood defiantly by their hearths, the men sought to avoid America's "stern justice" by a wholesale reshuffling and falsification of records. Never a simple language, Japanese could be exploited as a private code. Any name written in ideographs could be read with several different pronunciations. A man could change his ideographs without changing what he was called. Then he could say, "I am not that Sato Hiroshi but this one." Or conversely, he could change the pronunciation of his name and say, "Those are my name characters but they are read Sato Makoto in my family." Other Japanese when questioned would agree that he could be telling the truth. The success of such tactics may be seen from the fact that, two years after the war was over, more than a hundred of the Japanese witnesses who testified at the Class A War Criminal trials in Tokyo were able to go down in the record under appellations by which they had never been known at home.

All the names and numbers of combat units had been changed a few weeks prior to surrender. Now many of the officers were transferred to new commands where subordinates would not know their past careers. In a move suggested to the Emperor on August 19, four days after Hirohito's broadcast to his people, and reported to him again on its completion six days later, secret policemen and thought policemen were given new credentials as civilian detectives and traffic cops. Many who had been guards at concentration camps were allowed to change their names and vanish into civilian life as if their military careers had never existed. A sadist, whose victims at Omori Prison Camp called him only by the fearful code name of Mr. Brown, was never found by Allied investigators after the war—and this despite the fact that he was well known by name and long association to Hirohito's brother's brother-in-law, Tokugawa Yoshitomo, who had served at the prison camp as an "observer" for the Japanese Red Cross. A notorious secret police major, who also escaped the Allied War Criminal Prosecution Section, caters today to an almost exclusively American clientele of tourists at his old pottery store on Kyoto's main shopping street.

"The flames of burning documents of a defeated nation preparing for the occupation of the enemy were full of sadness and sorrow," recalls one patriot. He saw them as a "glare of big fires" as he returned to Tokyo on the morning of August 16 after informing the wife of the commander of the Kamikaze Corps that her husband had just committed suicide. Every town in Japan was blazing that night with bonfires of paper. The order to destroy, from Imperial Headquarters, was itself marked "to be destroyed," and only fragments of it were later picked up in city dumps. Prefectural libraries did away with all books giving biographical information on possible war criminal suspects, including even *Who's Who*'s and their Japanese equivalents *Daijinmei Jiten*. In some libraries the books were burned; in others only their file catalogue cards were destroyed and the books themselves were taken home for safekeeping by the librarians. Few if any important documents were entirely lost. They may be found in yellowed stacks of paper surrounding former generals and statesmen interviewed today. They are still considered secret and withheld from foreign hands. But the old gentlemen who keep them are usually willing to refer to them, to answer questions about them, and to do so with specifics that have the air of authority. When Allied language officers first fanned out to look for such documents a generation ago, they found few. They were expected to look up the unequivocal truth of history in black and white, but instead they pondered a nightmare record of gray lies and half truths.

If the Occupation forces came to Japan with good intentions rather than a lust for vengeance, that too was a contingency to be prepared for. There must be facilities ready for welcoming them and for divesting them as quickly as possible of war hate. Hirohito's sixty-one-year-old mother, the handsome Empress Dowager Sadako, had been consulted on the entertainment problem by her kinsman, Prince Konoye, many months previously. Although she was a severe critic of the war and had been on strained terms with Hirohito since Pearl Harbor, she had promised that ladies of rank would do all they could to help the Peace Faction in its patriotic efforts. Now in the days immediately before and after surrender, Konoye and the police put into effect a number of the Court ladies' suggestions. Foreign embassies which had been closed for over three years were inspected and their former staffs of servants were reassembled, where possible, to re-create a semblance of convivial days gone by.[1] The plaque near Yokohama, commemorating Commodore Perry's opening of Japan at gunpoint in 1853, had been torn down by overzealous patriots during the war. Now it was put up again by the Yokohama prefectural police in the polite secrecy of a dark night.

On the day of surrender, August 15, Prince Konoye called Ban Nobuya, the superintendent of the Tokyo Metropolitan Police, and told him: "We must protect the daughters of Japan. I want you to see to it personally." The staid middle classes were hiding their women in the hills and giving them cyanide capsules to take in an emergency. In the villas of the aristocracy, where the ladies had been brought up to understand the political requirements of

[1] But the rain water which had come in through a bomb hole in the roof was pointedly left standing on the floor in the chancellery of the American Embassy.

their fathers and husbands, less dire prospects were being contemplated with equanimity if not positive pleasure. In the slums remained thousands of women who had never had the right to be virtuous nor the time to think of themselves patriotically as national assets. Now was their hour. Police Superintendent Ban convoked the leaders of the major entertainment guilds in Tokyo —the keepers of hotels, restaurants, mah-jongg parlors, geisha tea houses, hostess bars, and ordinary brothels. By August 23, these worthies had founded a Recreation and Amusement Association, the R.A.A., for Allied enlisted men. It was capitalized at $2 million through a stock issue floated among friends of the Emperor by the Hypothec Bank. In a matter of weeks the R.A.A. could offer the services of thirty-three establishments in Tokyo, five in the provinces, and two hospitals for women. Under separate management a large munitions factory in downtown Tokyo was converted into a hotel. Never was sword more profitably beaten into plowshare. Before the place was finally declared off limits, "Willow Run," as it came to be called, had a production line of 250 girls and an average quota of 3,750 G.I.'s a day.

The R.A.A. and kindred organizations were promoted and guaranteed by a group of industrialists who offered their services to the Throne as "one-yen-a-year" men. They were recruited and directed by Yamashita Taro, a chemicals and shipping magnate who had been sitting in on Peace-Faction councils and conferring frequently with Lord Privy Seal Kido for the past ten months. Yamashita and his associates put together a fund of 200 million yen, or about $14 million, and offered it to the Emperor as a contribution. Some reciprocal favors were implied by the gift because Lord Privy Seal Kido took two days to negotiate its acceptance.

Of the many tasks undertaken by Yamashita and his one-yen-a-year men, the most delicate was liaison with MacArthur and his aides. The ladies at Court advised that relations with Allied G.H.Q. would go most smoothly if the incompetent services of insular police interpreters could be dispensed with and replaced by those of cosmopolitan gentlewomen who had real ability as linguists. Accordingly, a group of princesses and marchionesses who had lived in Paris and London agreed to merge forces with a group of businessmen who had good contacts in the United States.

Money was laid aside to buy new kimonos for war widows whose conservatively invested fortunes had been wiped out by depreciation. Family villas were inspected and rated according to their chic and their entertainment facilities. Private clubs were created in imitation of those which had been observed in Occidental capitals. Some groups of wealthy blue-stockings invited famous geisha to address them on the art of entertaining men.

The nervous bustle of peace preparations was punctuated by the violence of diehards who still protested against surrender. Prince Takamatsu, the Emperor's brother, had to go down to Atsugi Air Base near Yokohama to pacify a group of dissident kamikaze pilots who were dropping leaflets on Tokyo calling for continuance of the war. Two hundred men of a provincial garrison mutinied and marched on Tokyo. Twelve extreme rightists of the Revere-the-Emperor-and-Expel-the-Barbarians Society blew themselves up with hand grenades atop a hill in Tokyo's Shiba Park.

MISSION TO MANILA

As the cult of death died and the plans to live developed at fever pace, Japan had no communication with the conquerors except by radio. The future invaders remained faceless, giving instructions and hints of their own diabolical planning by Morse code. On August 19, four days after the Emperor announced Japan's surrender and in compliance with orders from MacArthur in Manila, Army Vice Chief of Staff Kawabe Torashiro flew to Okinawa by Japanese bomber and thence by American bomber to Nichols Field southwest of Manila. After twelve hours of flying, he and his aides disembarked into a sea of American olive drab, of men who pointedly ignored hands extended for shaking, of cameras which ground ceaselessly to record every wince and twitch of shame on the impassive faces of the Japanese delegation, of crowds of Filipinos who stood beyond the police lines and screamed curses learned in years past from Japanese soldiers. The drive into town led through a corner of the Spanish citadel which had been thoroughly laid waste, looted, raped, and butchered by suicidal young Japanese aristocrats of the Imperial Marines only six months previously. The drive ended at the Rosario Apartments overlooking Manila Bay. There the accommodations were comfortable but once again the associations were not, for a group of Japanese Marines and of Filipino women seized as hostages had spent their last hours there.

After an American dinner served with frigid punctilio, the Japanese delegation went on to an eight-hour, all-night meeting at MacArthur's headquarters in the half-ruined Manila City Hall. MacArthur was represented by his chief of staff, General Richard Sutherland. Kawabe and his aides spent the night turning over to Sutherland, item by item, the maps and lists of Japanese troop dispositions in the Orient. Then the Americans submitted to the Japanese MacArthur's instructions for the reception and billeting of U.S. troops in Japan. The first American transport planes were to touch down at Atsugi Air Base on August 23, a scant eighty hours hence.

General Kawabe begged for more time: "The Japanese side would sincerely advise you not to land so quickly. At least ten days are needed to prepare." He elaborated on the unrest among the kamikaze pilots at Atsugi. He did not mention the fact that the field at Atsugi was full of holes and would require an all-out construction effort before it could be safely used.

General Sutherland agreed to a five-day postponement and told Kawabe to have the New Grand Hotel in Yokohama ready for occupancy by MacArthur and a fleet of fifty automobiles in running order for staff transportation. Kawabe agreed to do what he could but left the meeting warning that a week of preparation would be insufficient. "You are the winners," he said, "and so your decision is almighty, but to our way of thinking, there remains some uneasiness."

Back at the Rosario Apartments the members of the Japanese delegation watched the sun come up and read over some of the other American requirements. Three maids for every U.S. officer of general or admiral class, two for everyone of colonel class, one for everyone of lieutenant class—did the Americans think they were dealing with Chinese? Then there was a statement prepared in Washington which was to be issued in the Emperor's name. The Japanese text of it had the Emperor using the ordinary humble pronoun *I*. Everyone knew that the Emperor, when referring to himself, used the old Chinese imperial pronoun *Chin,* meaning moon that speaks to heaven. Before going to bed, Kawabe had his dissatisfaction with these and other small points made known to the U.S. guard unit at the Rosario Apartments. By the time he awoke four hours later, Allied translators had prepared a new packet of instructions for Tokyo in which offensive pronouns and servant requirements had been suppressed.

Kawabe took off at 1:00 P.M., highly elated by the success of his mission. Hours later as his Betty-type bomber approached Japan, it sprang a leak in a fuel line. The pilot changed course to hug the Japanese coast. About midnight the last drop of gas was gone and he brought the lumbering craft down to a crash landing a few yards from a beach in central Honshu. The buffeted members of the delegation waded ashore and found themselves looking up in the moonlight at Mount Fuji, Mount Fortunate Warrior, the volcanic symbol of Japan. It was more than a hundred miles to Tokyo, and by the time that the delegates had roused villagers, summoned a truck, and negotiated the pockmarked roads to the capital it was late in the morning.

General Kawabe reported at once to the prime minister's residence and Prince Higashikuni drove with him to the palace. Emperor Hirohito received them at 1:15 P.M. and heard a full report of Kawabe's exhausting ordeal. It closed with the assurance that "in general the enemy attitude is unexpectedly good." The next day a capable labor racketeer, who was a friend of Prince Takamatsu, the Emperor's brother, put to work his truckers and construction men to repair the Atsugi kamikaze base for the American landing. Werewolf preparations were almost abandoned. Destruction of documents and briefing of girls was pushed forward frantically to meet with the new early date of American arrival.

Lights also burned late that week at MacArthur's headquarters in Manila and at the State Department in Washington. Throughout the war the sages of American foreign policy had had mixed emotions about the war with Japan. In Roosevelt's inner councils Japan had been considered a tool and the Pacific a secondary war theater. As a result the degree of severity with which Japan should be punished had never been fully decided. Here was a nation which had shown the way in savagery to its European partners, a nation which some said was not merely sick like Germany but innately predatory. Then again, here was a society little understood, a cultural relic of an earlier, more barbaric age, a country which had developed apart and then had been forced to join the modern world by Commodore Perry and the United States.

The Japanese had succeeded beyond Roosevelt's wildest nightmares in conquering the Pacific, and the road back had been a long one. But from the beginning the American government had known it would win and had debated what it would do with its victory: reduce Japan to a pastoral state as many Australians advocated? Remake Japanese society from the bottom up and thoroughly re-educate the people as some New Deal intellectuals demanded? Trust a chastened, demilitarized Japan to carry out her own moral reformation as many old Japan hands urged? Or simply take away Japan's colonies and post observers in her ports as her former allies the British proposed?

Each of the suggestions entailed a predictable amount of expense and moral commitment. To pastoralize Japan an army would have to carry out a brutal pacification campaign and then remain in oppressive occupation for many years to come. Indeed the population would have to be decimated many times before it could be expected to subsist on agriculture alone. To remake Japanese society in the Western image might be a more humane goal, but it too would require a long occupation of several decades. To suppose that Japan had learned her lesson and could reform herself seemed foolhardy in the light of past experience. Merely to penalize Japan heavily and leave her to struggle up again out of abject poverty seemed equally shortsighted.

To choose intelligently between the various possibilities was virtually impossible because there was no information to work with. The government of Japan was a box within a box, a closed corporation within a closed and secretive society. No one knew how Japan's aggressive policy decisions had been made nor who had made them. The Emperor was said to be a ceremonial nonentity. The parliament or Diet had only limited budgetary powers. The Cabinet was always changing. During F.D.R.'s presidency Japan had had eleven different prime ministers. The bureaucracy of "militarists" in the General Staff who supposedly controlled the Japanese juggernaut shifted about so frequently that it was rare for one man to occupy the same post for more than two years. But some man or group of men surely did have hold of the helm, for Japan's aggressive policies had developed consistently. Moreover, everyone who had ever visited Japan agreed that the people themselves were gentle, courteous, and law abiding and that the domestic administration of the country was as orderly and efficient as any in the world.

Western scholars who had studied Japan and men of affairs who had lived there could cast little light on the puzzle. Only a handful were fluent in Japanese, and the rest could not speak authoritatively about any part of Japan except the white man's ghetto world where everyone knew English. Linguists who had studied Japanese institutions more closely portrayed a society which did not fit comfortably into Western frames of reference. Knights rode side by side with secret policemen. Great industrial combines were built on feudal allegiances and run like fiefs. It was not clear whether atrocities like the rape of Nanking should be thought of as Buchenwalds or Deerfield Massacres. Japan presented the sinister twentieth-century façade of a highly industrialized fascist state but was also, in MacArthur's words, "something out of the pages of mythology."

Of the various proposals for dealing with the Japanese enigma, the tolerant British plan and the vindictive Australian program were alike in that they both treated the whole Japanese people as if they were responsible for the actions of the government. Such an idea did not appeal to the idealistic American mind nor fit the known facts. It was the U.S. point of view that some element in Japanese society had misled the people and could be cut out like a cancer. The New Deal intellectuals in the State Department, led by Dean Acheson and Archibald MacLeish, believed that reform and democratization could be achieved only through overthrow of the entire Establishment, the hereditary ruling caste of imperial high priests, of professional bureaucrats and police administrators, of warriors and generals, of medieval merchant families and modern cartel owners. A less intellectual and more tolerant group of former diplomats and businessmen, who had lived in Japan, allied themselves with ex-Ambassador Grew. They argued cogently that the ruling caste were the only Japanese who knew how to govern their country or had any experience with the outside world. If a reform was contemplated, they must be the ones reformed; they must be the cornerstone for rebuilding. Otherwise Japan would become an anarchy and the United States would be forced to administer her indefinitely as an American possession.

The debate finally resolved itself into disagreement on one central question: what to do with the Emperor who ruled the ruling class. Some experts said he should be tried as a war criminal, others that he should be deposed, still others that he should be left to rule as a constitutional monarch. In the absence of any dependable information about Hirohito, the issue was argued hotly. The last two *New York Times* correspondents in Japan, drawing on the same *Times* morgue of translations and dispatches, wrote books on opposite sides of the question, Hugh Byas opting for the Emperor and Otto Tolischus against. The dispute could not be settled because the problem was logically insoluble. Could Japan be reformed without destroying her god-king? And then again, could Japan be reformed without the god-king's co-operation? The answer to both queries was patently, "No." And so Roosevelt, early in the war, decided that the best course might be to hold the Emperor as a hostage. Skillfully handled, he might be used to sponsor reform and at the same time to undercut the foundations of his own prestige and power. As early as 1942 the Office of War Information and the Office of Strategic Services spread the suggestion, through the many publicists, journalists, and authors on O.W.I.-O.S.S. payrolls, that American cartoonists should concentrate their attention on bespectacled General Tojo rather than Hirohito on his white horse.

In August of 1945 President Truman wisely decided to delegate the execution of Roosevelt's tentative policy for dealing with the Emperor to General of the Army Douglas MacArthur whose memos had helped to formulate it. MacArthur had the stature domestically to override American dissent and the experience in the Orient to carry out such a policy with flexibility and an ear tuned to changing circumstances. Truman appointed MacArthur proconsul in Japan on August 14, the day that Japan's surrender note was received. Thereafter Truman supported MacArthur in a virtuoso solo role unparalleled in American history. For five years MacArthur was to rule absolute in Japan. He was to disregard almost all suggestions from other Allied governments, and Truman was to back him up. Seldom since the days of Scipio Africanus has a proconsul had such power over a conquered people. Never has one been so popular as MacArthur was with almost 80 million Japanese.

MacArthur had been in and out of Japan since 1904 when his father, General Arthur MacArthur, had had charge of pacifying the Philippines after the Spanish-American War. MacArthur was a brilliant man: first in his class at West Point, youngest divisional commander in U.S. history, and youngest chief of staff. He had retired from the U.S. Army in 1937 to become a field marshal in the Philippine Army. He had been recalled to active duty—the defense of the Philippines in July 1941—by his close personal friend and political antagonist, Franklin Delano Roosevelt. Throughout World War II, in defeat and victory, MacArthur had commanded the American Army in the Pacific.

On August 14, 1945, as soon as MacArthur heard of his appointment to the military governorship of Japan, he instructed his staff and intelligence officers in Manila to work out the logistics of occupation and to submit ideas on the best approach to use in taming and exploiting the Emperor. MacArthur's Chief of Intelligence Charles A. Willoughby brainstormed the problem with his assistants and advised that the Emperor should be harnessed tactfully and gradually. Willoughby recommended that Hirohito should be surrounded by "liberal advisors" and made to feel that he was a "symbol" for the "regeneration of Japan." MacArthur himself had already given long thought to the problem and had his own shrewd perceptions of what would be required. He did not consider himself an expert on any Oriental country save the Philippines. He knew few of the details of modern Japanese history and did not want to know them. Bygones, he felt, should be bygones. If Americans tried to pit their detective work against Japanese deceptive cunning, he was sure that the Japanese would win and that no one would be the better for it. The solution to the problem of Japan did not exist except in some prescription—any prescription—which had the authority of a good doctor behind it. The Japanese must cure themselves.

As early as September of 1944, when he had landed at Morotai, an island in the eastern East Indies, MacArthur had expressed his considered views on the sickness and cure of Japan. He termed the disease "a type of national savagery at strange variance with many basic impulses of the Japanese people." The cure, he felt, would be automatic: "The Japanese citizen will cease his almost idolatrous worship of the military" when he discovers that "the military has failed him in this, his greatest hour of need." MacArthur either did not know or did not choose to know that a majority of the Japanese electorate had never idolized the military and as late as 1937 still had the courage to say so at the polls. Perhaps as a result of childhood association with Indians at a U.S. Army post in Arkansas, MacArthur saw the Japanese as a tribal people who would lose their proud sense of identity as soon as their false gods were broken. His view was a patronizing one, but it grew out of sincere Christian convictions and he was willing to gamble his life on its correctness. When the first surrender note arrived on August 10, he proposed that he and a small airborne detachment should be landed immediately at Tokyo airport to help the Emperor surrender. It would have been a theatrical gesture of a type which both he and the Japanese loved. More than likely no harm would have come to him if he had been allowed to try it.

The officers to whom MacArthur would delegate the execution of his policy for Japan were all with him in Manila and were all thoroughly educated in what he would expect of them. Three of the most important of them were Eichelberger, Willoughby, and Whitney. Lieutenant General Robert Eichelberger, a kindly, intelligent man, was to be MacArthur's hands. He was to have command of the Eighth Army which would manage the nonpolitical, physical half of the Occupation. It would be his men who would fan out into the Japanese countryside, his M.P.'s who would execute the raids and arrests decided on by MacArthur's inner brain trust.

MacArthur's Chief of Intelligence, Major General Charles A. Willoughby—a crude, witty, gargantuan son of a German aristocrat named Tscheppe-Weidenbach—was to be MacArthur's eyes and ears. To keep his command as autonomous as possible, MacArthur had always banned from his theater of operations the Washington-centered O.S.S. and O.W.I., and Willoughby was his sole source of background research. It was Willoughby who would teach MacArthur what he knew of the past careers of the Japanese leaders with whom he dealt, Willoughby who would be in part responsible for the United States being caught by surprise when the Chinese entered the Korean War.

Despite thirty years in the American Army, Willoughby retained a Prussian view of world affairs. In a book called *Maneuver in War*, published in 1939, he had admired almost every aspect of Japan's strike for *Lebensraum* in China except her "yellow fingers clawing at white women." "Historical judgment," he had written, "freed from the emotional haze of the moment, will credit Mussolini with wiping out a memory of defeat by re-establishing the traditional military supremacy of the white race for generations to come." He was, in brief, a straightforward military man. He admired Mussolini's exploits in Ethiopia and, grudgingly, those of other conquerors including the Japanese. His knowledge of campaigns in out-of-the-way colonial wars was encyclopedic. Having helped to form MacArthur's plan for Japan, Willoughby touted it as a "shatteringly simple formula" for resolving "the terrific tension" in Japan by "utilizing the existing Japanese government, the person of the Emperor, and the psychic force of tradition."

Brigadier General Courtney Whitney, the chief of the Occupation's Government Section, was MacArthur's mouth and writing hand. A tough, nimble-witted lawyer who had made a small fortune for himself in Manila during the 1930's, he was to conduct the political negotiations with Japanese leaders, dictate the reform of the Japanese government, and write most of MacArthur's personal utterances. In describing MacArthur's policy for Japan, he later minced no words: "We blackmailed Japan. . . . Discussion concerning the Emperor . . . was designed to encourage action toward a speed-up in essential reforms."

In the week that intervened between General Kawabe's visit to Manila and the landing of the first U.S. Occupation troops at

Atsugi kamikaze base, couriers and cables shuttled back and forth between Washington and Manila; MacArthur's ideas were integrated with those of State Department officials to become the official policy of the U.S. Government. The document that resulted was entitled "United States Initial Post-Surrender Policy for Japan." Its final text was radioed to MacArthur on August 29 after he had already started for Japan and was stopping over for a night in Okinawa. It instructed him as follows:

> The ultimate objectives of the United States in regard to Japan . . . are . . . to insure that Japan will not again become a menace . . . [and] to bring about the eventual establishment of a peaceful and responsible government which will respect the rights of other states. . . . It is not the responsibility of the Allied Powers to impose upon Japan any form of government not supported by the freely expressed will of the people. . . . In view of the present character of Japanese society and the desire of the United States to attain its objectives with a minimum commitment of its forces and resources, the Supreme Commander will exercise his authority through Japanese governmental machinery and agencies, including the Emperor. . . . The policy is to use the existing form of government in Japan, not to support it.

There followed a blueprint of the social reforms which MacArthur was to carry out: disarmament; punishment of war criminals; breakup of landlord and industrialist holdings; emancipation of religion, press, labor, and women.

U.S. TOUCHDOWN

For five days after General Kawabe's return to Tokyo from Manila, rain drummed down on the tiled roofs of the palace and branches tossed in the Fukiage Gardens. Late each afternoon Hirohito walked to the Palace Shrine, stood beneath the dripping eaves, and meditated on the ordeals ahead. Curtains of white mist enclosed the shrine, making its lustrous white-pebbled courtyard seem more private, more infinite, more close to the dead than ever before. Hirohito was not alone in his brooding; men waited in anxiety throughout the Orient. An officer at Atsugi kamikaze base, preparing to greet the Occupation troops, implored his men to kill themselves before taking offense at any action of the conquerors. Far to the south in Manila a G.I. cleaned his gun and muttered: "A people can't be turned off and on like a hot water faucet." He was one of a few hundred detailed to go into Japan with the U.S. advance party—to land in the midst of the enemy camp where 2.5 million fanatic Japanese soldiers were waiting to be disarmed.

On August 27 the weather cleared, and a single American daredevil from the carrier *Yorktown* astonished Japanese ground crews by landing at Atsugi unauthorized, a full day ahead of schedule. As General MacArthur would have predicted, he was courteously treated. Indeed he was helped to put up signs which said, "Welcome U.S. Army from the Third Fleet." As soon as he had taken off, the ground crews removed the signs lest they give offense to the serious Occupation forces due to arrive on the morrow.

At dawn the next morning a line of forty-five C-47's snaked in over the head of the giant bronze Buddha at Kamakura and landed at Atsugi in rapid succession. As an evasive precaution they came in with the wind behind them and so pulled up at the end of the airport where the Japanese least expected them. By the time that the reception committee had started a truck and raced the length of the field, the Americans were out of their planes with carbines on the ready. Greetings were exchanged stiffly and a long walk led back to the reception booth at the other end of the runway. There the Japanese had ready pitchers of freshly squeezed orange juice. It was said to be the favorite American drink, but these Americans would not so much as sip it until they had seen their hosts drink first. Into the atmosphere of tense suspicion, the Japanese commander introduced a Russian naval attaché whom he had brought with him from Tokyo expressly for the purpose. As anticipated the rival white man shamed the Americans out of their jitters. Soon Japanese and American officers were swapping cigarettes and working together smoothly. A U.S. naval group set out in Japanese vehicles to visit nearby Allied prisoner-of-war camps. Lunch, complete with fruit and wine, was served by the Japanese on white tablecloths.

After lunch the American commander, Colonel Charles Tench,

was consulted on the case of an American prisoner of war who had come down with appendicitis. The Japanese said that he was in the hands of a capable physician such as attended P.O.W.'s routinely, but added that perhaps, since the Americans were now in charge, they might wish to take over the care of their country-man or send a doctor to assist at the appendectomy. Colonel Tench replied that he had full confidence in the Japanese sur-geons who had been handling the case. He did not know the reputation of the Shinagawa P.O.W. hospital north of Yokohama to which the prisoner had been taken. It had one model wing which was used for inspections and would have been used for the appendectomy if an American observer had been sent. The rest of the hospital was a horror house of lice and excrement. The doctor in charge was later hanged for senseless experiments in sadism. Healthy men he had bled to death for their plasma. Sick men he had killed with strange injections. He had shot soy bean milk and urine into their veins. He had administered bile from dysentery patients to TB cases and serum from malaria victims to those with beriberi. Late that night the Japanese commander at Atsugi came to Colonel Tench incensed because a U.S. naval party under the command of Harold Stassen, the later presiden-tial contender, had raided Shinagawa Hospital and spirited away the appendicitis case to an American hospital ship in the harbor.

The speed with which the Americans worked astonished the Japanese. In the first four days some 5,000 ragged, emaciated, ecstatic war prisoners were evacuated from camps in the Tokyo-Yokohama area to Allied ships offshore. A new fifteen-mile oil pipeline was laid to Yokohama and was operating in a week. All through the second day, August 29, U.S. C-54's swooped down on Atsugi, landing at two-minute intervals and disgorging almost the entire 11th Airborne Division by nightfall. Japanese fliers stood by watching with rueful admiration. That same afternoon the whole of the 4th Marine Regiment came ashore in Yokohama. One of its members described it as being made up "entirely of admirals trying to get ashore before MacArthur."

On the third day MacArthur himself arrived with his retinue of staff officers and war correspondents. "Of all the amazing deeds of bravery of the war," wrote Winston Churchill a few years later,

"I regard MacArthur's personal landing at Atsugi as the greatest of the lot." MacArthur deplaned with a corncob pipe in his mouth, embraced fellow General Robert Eichelberger, and said, "This is the payoff, Bob." He climbed into a decrepit Lincoln supplied by the Japanese government and started for Yokohama fifteen miles away. Some forty cars, most of them charcoal-burners, started with him. At the head of the procession moved an old red fire engine which sometimes started and sometimes stopped. Smartly caparisoned Japanese staff officers cast down their eyes at American complaints and humbly insisted that these were the best vehicles left in Japan.

Along the entire fifteen-mile route stood armed Japanese soldiers, their backs to the roadway, watching the fields on either side for any hint of trouble. This was a security precaution normally accorded only to the Emperor. MacArthur was so delighted by it that he took the rest of the two-hour automobile burlesque in good part. Moreover, he dispensed with bodyguards throughout his remaining five years in Japan and forbade any officer walking or riding with him ever to wear a sidearm. The Japanese so justified his confidence in them that not a rock was ever thrown at him.

That night at the Edwardian New Grand Hotel in Yokohama's waterfront park, the manager provided MacArthur and his staff with an excellent steak dinner. He could not promise an egg for breakfast, however, and one of MacArthur's generals sent out a search party. In the entire ruin of Yokohama, a city the size of Baltimore, the hunt uncovered precisely one egg. MacArthur was so impressed by the people's hunger that he ordered all U.S. personnel to live entirely on their own rations, and he had his commissary contribute twenty-one truckloads of food to the Yokohama municipal government.

The American war correspondents who had landed with MacArthur proceeded by public transportation to make their way inland and occupy Tokyo. People on trams and trains looked at them curiously and then made room for them with calm civility. A Japanese Domei reporter, who had greeted them at Atsugi and warned them to be cautious, arrived back in Tokyo to find them in his office using his typewriters. Russell Brines of the Associated

Press had gone directly to the Aztec-style Imperial Hotel designed by Frank Lloyd Wright in the early 1920's. In the cool cave of the volcanic-stone lobby, the manager was standing as if waiting for him. "So glad to see you," said the manager. "Do you want a room?"

OVERTURES

On the afternoon of August 28, when the first police reports on the behavior of the Occupation troops arrived in Tokyo, they were taken at once to the palace. Hirohito was impressed and summoned Prince Higashikuni. After the audience Higashikuni rescinded previous orders to give away Army stockpiles and issued instructions to buy back any munitions which might have been distributed by mistake. The behavior of the American soldiers remained exemplary. By August 31 when there were almost 50,-000 Occupation troops in the Yokohama area, the police had reported only 216 complaints against them, and of these 167 had been lodged, over matters of jurisdiction, by the police themselves. Most of the remaining 49 cases were alleged thefts. By September 5, after nine days of Occupation, the G.I. crime rate, as reported by the Japanese police, had fallen to an average of two offenses a day and the cumulative total up to that date included only one murder and six cases of "complete and incomplete rape."

During the five-day rainstorm which had preceded the U.S. landings, Hirohito had pondered the various fates which might lie in store for him. He was not afraid of being hanged. Martyrdom would insure the loyalty of the people to his son. Nor was he afraid of being shorn of power and made a constitutional monarch. As long as the Throne survived, his heirs would have a chance to recoup. What most disturbed him was the possibility that the Allies would systematically discredit him in the eyes of his people. If they forced him to preside over their own acts of vengeance—their reparations and war crime tribunals—then the people might become disillusioned. They might turn to democratic forms of government. They might even renounce all things Japanese and allow themselves to become wholly Americanized.

Hirohito had always minimized the danger of democratic sentiments taking hold in Japan. He felt that the Anglo-American type of government was too individualistic to be compatible with Japanese society. In a democracy each voter needed a conscience of his own and an absolute scale of right and wrong. But in Japan these prerequisites did not exist. Every act, from casting a ballot to committing a murder, could be right or wrong depending on whether or not it was in the interest of the family or clan or nation. The highest justification which any Japanese ever sought for an action was *taigi meibun*, "individual share in large righteousness." And for many Japanese the largest conceivable righteousness was mere feudal loyalty—loyalty to the next man higher on the totem pole. During the early years of his reign, Hirohito had made a point of impressing on every man to whom he gave an office or assignment that *taigi meibun* meant sharing in national rather than clan or family righteousness. The idea of an individual striving to transcend the morality of his group by reference to a universal frame of reference struck Hirohito as a Western hypocrisy. Individualism, he felt, could only lead to misery and bad government.[2]

The early reports on American behavior at Atsugi made it clear that MacArthur intended to complete the conquest of Japan by kindness. Prince Konoye warned Hirohito to be wary. As Emperor he had had little experience in negotiation and compromise, but he had had the final power of decision. Now, as MacArthur's puppet, he would have no power, only a bargaining position. MacArthur would seek his seal of approval for American "reform" programs. Some of them might redound to Hirohito's credit, but most of them would undercut his authority and destroy his popularity. Konoye recommended that the safest course would be for Hirohito to abdicate. No one would hold his eleven-year-old son responsible for being manipulated by the Americans. And in due course the Americans would return to their own country.

Hirohito seized on Konoye's advice to abdicate and in the weeks ahead repeatedly offered—almost threatened—to take it. If he was to be MacArthur's puppet, he wished to make it clear at every

[2] Hirohito's convictions, as here summarized, are taken from his recorded conversations with his former chief aide-de-camp, General Honjo Shigeru.

step of the way that he was acting under duress for the sake of the nation and not for any selfish motive of his own. On August 29, after sleeping on the first reports from Atsugi, he called his special advisor, Kido, to the library in the Fukiage Gardens and told him: "To pick men responsible for the war and hand them over to the Allies hurts me more than I can bear. I am wondering if it might not go well in translation if I myself, as the one man responsible, clear the books by abdicating."

"Your magnificent sentiments do you the utmost credit," replied Kido, "but I would venture to surmise from the attitudes and preconceptions of the Allies at present that it would be rather difficult to secure agreement on a step of that sort. Then too, since foreign ways of thinking are seldom the same as our own, a proclamation of abdication would create the impression that the foundations of the Throne had been shaken. The result would be a democratic reorganization of the state structure—in short, republicanism. We should beware of arousing discussion of that type. The important point for Your Highness is to adopt a relaxed and studious façade and watch the moves of the other side with all due prudence."

Hirohito nodded noncommittally, and the next day his uncle Prince Higashikuni paid a courtesy call, as prime minister, on General MacArthur at the New Grand Hotel in Yokohama. The meeting was purely formal, but MacArthur took the opportunity to suggest that the Japanese Establishment would greatly improve its reputation in America if it would show some signs of progressive leadership. It might begin, for instance, by revising the Japanese Constitution.

Hirohito considered the Japanese Constitution a sacred document. Over the years he had used it and interpreted it freely but he was not willing to change it. It had been promulgated by his deified grandfather Meiji, and it gave the Throne a more absolute power than the Roman Senate had ever voted to Nero or Caesar Augustus. It enumerated at length the duties which devolved upon subjects and carefully restricted the rights which it conceded them: freedom of speech "within the limits of law"; freedom of religion "within limits not prejudicial to peace and order and not antagonistic to the duties of subjects." Its over-all flavor may be sampled in a deliciously Japanese clause on petitions: "Japanese subjects may present petitions, by observing the proper forms of respect, and by complying with the rules specially provided for the same."

Since Hirohito would not even consider a change in the Constitution, his courtiers cast about for other sops to throw to the American reformers. MacArthur for his part maintained a frigid reserve and made no effort to follow up Prince Higashikuni's overture. Some of his staff recommended that he summon Hirohito and tell him what would be required of him. But MacArthur assured his aides that the Emperor would make his own advances in his own good time. Meanwhile there was more than enough to do. Over 10,000 Americans were being landed in Japan each day and were fanning out to look for records and arms caches, give away chocolate bars, and make friends with children.

On both sides leaders were preparing for the official surrender ceremonies aboard the battleship *Missouri* in Tokyo Harbor on September 2. The Allies flew in General Jonathan Wainwright and General Arthur Percival, the senior American and British officers who had just been released from Japanese prison camps. Both were walking skeletons. Both had sat as losers at previous surrender tables, Wainwright in the Philippines and Percival in Malaya. The duty of meeting with them was so humiliating that it was difficult to find Japanese of suitable rank to accept it. Hirohito began the trouble himself by asking that no member of the imperial family be expected to sign the surrender documents. Several Army officers followed suit by announcing that they would commit suicide if asked to attend the ceremony. Chief of Staff Umezu was finally induced to represent the Japanese Army, but Hirohito did not give his personal approval to the text of the instrument of surrender until 1:00 A.M. of the day on which it was to be signed.

The weather was so clear that Mount Fuji, the Fortunate Warrior, could be seen sixty miles away. The sun sparkled on the white uniforms of American sailors. Tokyo Bay overflowed with Allied vessels of war—the greatest armada ever assembled. MacArthur delivered an oration and used five pens to sign the surrender instrument. The Japanese signatories walked and talked as stiffly as

mechanical dolls. As soon as possible they climbed back down to
the launch provided for them and made for shore. They went
directly to the palace and reported to the Emperor. The next
morning Hirohito and his closest advisors repaired to the Palace
Shrine to announce officially the end of the war to his ancestors
and the sun goddess.

That afternoon, September 3, negotiations began in earnest to
find out what MacArthur meant to do to Japan. Foreign Minister
Shigemitsu called on him at the New Grand Hotel in Yokohama
and informed him that the last of Japan's munitions factories had
now been shut down. MacArthur said he was delighted. If the
Japanese government continued to co-operate so well with Occupation policy, he said, it might be possible after all to work through
the local authorities rather than replace them with American officials. MacArthur had never intended to do anything else, but the
implied threat was effective and the foreign minister expressed
his gratitude. MacArthur followed up his advantage by suggesting
that if the Japanese government would also co-operate in rounding up war criminals and revising the Constitution, it should be
possible to preserve the Emperor system.

Foreign Minister Shigemitsu reported MacArthur's terms to the
palace that same evening. Hirohito heard them without recorded
comment, but the next day in a public address to an emergency
session of the Diet Hirohito obliquely reminded MacArthur that
Japan had accepted unconditional surrender on certain understand-
ings. Politely avoiding the word "defeat" and substituting for it
"termination of hostilities," he told the people that if they would
abide peacefully by the terms of the Potsdam Declaration it should
be possible for Japan to rebuild and keep her "national structure"
or Emperor system. The next morning, September 5, Foreign Minister Shigemitsu resumed his negotiations with MacArthur in
Yokohama and delicately pointed out that the Emperor's statement had an obverse: if the people were not allowed to keep their
national structure, they might abide by the Potsdam Declaration
unpeacefully. MacArthur genially ignored the suggestion and once
more sent Shigemitsu away empty handed.

The following day, September 6, Prince Konoye was sent down
to Kyoto, the ancient capital of Japan, to arrange suitable retire-

ment quarters for Hirohito in case he should decide to abdicate. In old Japan, before Perry's coming, abdication had been a routine imperial tactic. In those days the Emperor had exercised little but religious power and had delegated his political and military authority to the shogun or chief general of the nation. If the shogun failed to respect imperial wishes, however, the Emperor would set one of his children on the Throne and retire as an abbot and regent to one of Kyoto's great Buddhist monasteries. Thence he could continue to control the Throne, and free of all ceremonial duty and responsibility could devote himself full time to the plotting of intrigues which would embarrass the shogun.

It was with such a thought in mind that on September 7 Prince Konoye left the lovely old inn of his previous night's entertainment and motored west through the narrow colorful streets of the Gion, Kyoto's entertainment district, where the arts of pleasing men had been developed and handed down for a thousand years. In the northwestern suburbs at the end of a green lane he left his car and walked into the white courtyards of the great Zen temple of Ninna-ji. The chief bonze conducted him up a hillside through a park of pines and cryptomerias to the Omuro Imperial Villa. Konoye admired the fine views over Kyoto in one direction and over a little river gorge in the other. The place would be ideal for Hirohito in his old age. Konoye gave instructions for repairs and improvements and drove back to Kyoto to worship at his mother's grave.

During Konoye's trip south, MacArthur made his ceremonial entry into Tokyo. On September 6 one of his press officers had asked American reporters to leave the capital because "it is not American military policy for correspondents to spearhead the Occupation." On September 7, all Japanese troops had been withdrawn to the north, leaving only about one division of Imperial Guards who remained behind secretly, in civilian clothes, to protect the palace. MacArthur set out from Yokohama on the following morning. He had instructed the Japanese government to take no security precautions. When his car broke down on the road, however, a crowd of police and plainclothesmen materialized out of nowhere to stand about helpfully until a new car was brought up from the rear. Then MacArthur pushed on through a wasteland of war damage to the Tokyo town line. There the veteran jungle fighters of the U.S. 1st Cavalry Division were drawn up waiting, dressed for parade. At a word they rolled forward into the enemy capital, leading the way to MacArthur's future residence, the American Embassy. By nightfall they had taken up positions all around the great gray-walled palace of Hirohito. The hub of the Japanese Empire was secure. Two days later, on September 10, Lord Privy Seal Kido felt it safe to leave the palace and sleep in his own home for the first time in a month.

SEIZING TOJO

With almost 100,000 U.S. troops ashore now, MacArthur could begin, gingerly, to impose Occupation policies on the Japanese government. Politically the most pressing order of business was war criminals. Atrocity stories told by the 30,000 Allied P.O.W.'s found in Japanese concentration camps made prompt arrests mandatory. In the last week the State Department and its Australian counterpart had both supplemented the tales of the prisoners by releasing previously classified files on Japanese deeds in other theaters earlier in the war. American airmen had been cooked and eaten by Japanese generals on Pacific islands. Sixteen thousand Allied P.O.W.'s had been beaten, starved, and worked to death in the construction of a jungle railway from Thailand to Burma. The Japanese secret police had kept pens of naked Western men and women in the cellars under the torture chambers of Bridge House in Shanghai. The Japanese public knew nothing of such brutalities except what had been whispered by a few disgusted Japanese soldiers who had returned home. Now, as the horror stories were printed, public incredulity turned to fear and shame, and Japanese leaders grew nervous waiting for MacArthur to outline the terms of Western vengeance.

On September 9, two members of Prince Higashikuni's brain trust told reporters: "The Allies should announce their war criminal list soon so the Japanese people can consider it and perhaps add a few names. Prince Konoye, the deputy prime minister, and Mr. Shigemitsu, the foreign minister, should be included on it." This strange accusation, which suggested bitter hatreds within the Higashikuni cabinet, was really no more than a statement of fact. Konoye and Shigemitsu had helped to lead Japan to Pearl Harbor, and both had promised Hirohito that they would take responsibility and serve as scapegoats.

The United States had had a War Crime Subcommission making lists of Japanese suspects in Chungking since November of 1944. With Chinese help the difficult Oriental names had been sorted out but not the guilt. Sometimes it seemed that all Japanese were guilty, sometimes that no one was guilty. There was no outstanding group of leaders like the Goering-Goebbels-Himmler gang in Germany. Nor was there any clearcut party like the Nazis by which to judge affiliations. Every Western expert seemed to know a different faction which was supposed to be the keystone of Japanese fascism.

Prodded by Washington and by the anxious Japanese themselves, MacArthur approached the problem of war guilt with caution. He had his giant Germanic Intelligence chief, General Willoughby, in co-operation with General Eichelberger's M.P.'s, establish a War Crimes Board. The board worked out of Willoughby's advance headquarters in Tokyo in the old secret police building outside the North Gate of the palace. On September 10 the board issued its first tentative list of war criminal suspects who were to be arrested.

The first name on the list was that of General Tojo, the Pearl Harbor prime minister. American correspondents at once threaded their way by jeep from police box to police box, through the maze of blasted, burned-out Tokyo streets, to Tojo's suburban home. They found the bald mustachioed little man in gray knee socks, white shorts, and shirt, playing the part of a gentleman truck farmer in his garden. Unlike Konoye, Shigemitsu, or Prince Higashikuni, General Tojo was a man of conviction: straightforward, sharp, logical, and irascible. When he saw that he could not fob off the reporters, he sat down with them on a garden bench, offered them cheap wartime Hope cigarettes and told them what he thought. "I believe," he said, "that Japan's war was a just one. Although I know your country will not accept that, history will decide who was right. As for me, I accept full responsibility for the war."

A week earlier General Tojo had been summoned by War Minister Shimomura, the general who had forced the Nanking attack plans through the General Staff in 1937. On behalf of the government the war minister asked Tojo to submit to arrest if necessary and to forego suicide until he had had a chance to persuade the Allies that he, rather than the Emperor, was responsible for the war. Tojo promised to continue to do everything in his power to shield the Emperor but warned that he might feel compelled to commit suicide for the sake of honor. He would voluntarily turn himself in on request at any prison in Japan, but he would not submit to being seized like a captive on the battlefield. He was a soldier and had vowed never to be captured alive. War Minister Shimomura thanked him and intimated that whatever happened the Tojo family would be taken care of financially.

On the afternoon of September 11, when U.S. correspondents had been staked out in the Tojo front yard all day, the M.P.'s finally came to make their arrest. Tojo questioned them out his study window. What did they want? Did they have a warrant? Would the American officer in charge present his credentials? After each answer Tojo ducked back into his study to consider the next question. "It's beginning to look like the balcony scene from *Romeo and Juliet*," cracked one of the U.S. correspondents. Finally Tojo asked them to wait a moment while he opened the front door. His wife, whom he had dismissed at the approach of the jeeps, stood watching the house from a neighbor's garden. She had put on a pair of peasant-woman trousers so that she would not be noticed. It was her duty to report as many particulars as she could to the rest of the Tojo family.

Inside the house, Tojo had seated himself in his favorite red armchair and picked up a 32-caliber Colt automatic pistol taken from a downed American pilot during the war. It was the same weapon which his son-in-law Major Koga had used to kill himself after the rising in the palace on the night of the surrender. Tojo unbuttoned the top of his shirt. On his chest the outline of a heart had been drawn in charcoal a day or two earlier by the doctor who lived next door. Tojo aimed carefully at the target area and fired. The bullet went through him and buried itself in the upholstery. By an irony of anatomy it barely missed his heart, an abnormally long and slender one. Instead it punctured his lung and the two holes it had made in his skin alternately frothed and sucked as he gasped for breath. The American M.P.'s kicked in the door, found him alive and conscious, and summoned a doctor.

For two hours Tojo bled and begged to die while American correspondents photographed him from every conceivable angle and dipped souvenir handkerchiefs in his blood. "I am very sorry it is taking so much time to die," he said. "I would not like to be judged in front of a conqueror's court. I wait for the righteous judgment of history." Finally the American doctor arrived, sutured the holes in his chest and back, and administered plasma. Tojo responded well. The doctor moved him to a hospital and there, after several transfusions from G.I. donors, he recovered to stand trial and go to the gallows.

The day after Tojo's arrest, September 12, the Cabinet voted to preempt Allied justice by having war criminal suspects arrested and tried by native Japanese law agencies. Prince Higashikuni, the prime minister, hurried to the Imperial Library for Hirohito's endorsement of the subterfuge and was met with refusal. "All the so-called war criminals," said Hirohito, "wanted by the enemy, particularly those said to be responsible for causing the war, are men who spent themselves in loyal honest service to me. To judge them in my name puts me in an intolerable position. I will ask you therefore if there is not some room for reconsideration." If the Americans insisted on vengeance, Hirohito meant to let the blood be on their own hands. Lives might be saved by nominal Japanese justice, but Hirohito trusted the accused to prefer martyrdom and honor at American hands.

MacArthur had ordered twenty-four other Japanese leaders to be apprehended including all members of the 1941 Pearl Harbor Cabinet. The prickly foreign minister who had spoken for surrender in the imperial air raid shelter on August 9 was on the list. So was the ubiquitous Suzuki Tei-ichi, who had recruited most of Hirohito's cabal of young officers in the 1920's. MacArthur had his M.P.'s carry out their arrests on a leisurely, one-man-a-day schedule. Some said that he was indulging his sense of theater; some that he hoped the war criminals would commit suicide if

given enough time; some that he was waiting for Hirohito to agree
to punish the war criminals himself.

On September 12, the M.P.'s knocked at the door of Admiral
Shimada Shigetaro, Tojo's opposite number in the Navy. In the
entryway, where invited guests would have taken off their shoes,
they were greeted by Mrs. Shimada. She knelt at the edge of the
raised floor of the interior and touched her head to the matting.
Then wreathed in polite smiles, she asked to see their credentials.
She bowed again and promised that her husband would be with
them in fifteen minutes. The American M.P.'s, stamping and
chafing in the doorway, heard the sounds of a last meal being
hastily served inside. When the fifteen minutes had passed, a nisei
or second-generation American of Japanese ancestry took off his
shoes and entered the house. At the end of twenty minutes
Admiral Shimada finally appeared dressed in a new green uniform
still freshly crinkled from the tailor's box. Shimada asked to see
the M.P.'s credentials. "Tell him to get his shoes on and get going," said the American major in charge. "Tell him to quit this
nonsense." Shimada laughed and put a hand on the major's shoulder. "Be quiet," he said in broken English, "I don't suicide." As
he put on his shoes, his wife and two daughters knelt on the matting in deep obeisance. The daughters were weeping. Shimada
bid them live bravely, turned and walked away with the M.P.'s
to seven years in jail.

At about the moment that Shimada was being ushered from
his home, Field Marshal Sugiyama Hajime, the highest ranking
commoner in the Army, who had served as chief of staff from
1940 to 1944, blew his brains out. His wife took cyanide and
plunged a dagger into her throat. In an effort to save a few necks
for the hangman, MacArthur's headquarters issued an extraordinary statement claiming that the Japanese government of General
Prince Higashikuni approved of the arrests. Overlooking the six
admirals and generals in the Cabinet, MacArthur's spokesman
declared: "The government is made up principally of nonmilitary
elements which have been trembling under threats from the Black
Dragon and other supposedly secret organizations."

The name of the Black Dragon Society had caught the fancy
of Western journalists in the 1930's. It was supposed to be, and

once had been, one of the most powerful subversive tongs in the Orient. The 1911 revolution which overthrew the throne of the Manchus and brought republicanism to China had been subsidized by it. The Kuomintang party of Sun Yat-sen and Chiang Kai-shek which rules Taiwan today had held its first meeting in Black Dragon headquarters in Tokyo in 1905. Western observers had always been encouraged by their upper-class Japanese friends to think of the Black Dragon as a crime syndicate, akin to the Mafia of Sicily. But in reality the Black Dragon was first of all a revolutionary cell dedicated to Pan-Asianism and xenophobia. Its sinister name referred not to some monster of the underworld but to the Black Dragon River, the Amur, which separates Manchuria from Siberia. During the 1890's and 1900's the name had stood for Japan's determination to prevent Russia from extending her empire south of the Amur. When Japan seized control of Manchuria in 1932, the Black Dragon Society persisted in calling the main enemy Russia. It backed the Strike-North Faction in the Japanese Army and lost. After 1936 when Hirohito singlehandedly overruled the expansion plans of the Strike-North Faction, the Amur River Society ceased to be a force. It held its last public meeting in October 1935 to protest Mussolini's white invasion of black Ethiopia.

Ten years later, on September 13, 1945, MacArthur's headquarters ordered the immediate dissolution of the Black Dragon Society and the arrest of seven of its leaders. Two of the men mentioned had never belonged to the society. A third had headed the organization and had died of old age in 1938. A fourth had been forced to commit suicide by the order of Tojo in 1943. Three others had renounced their affiliations with the Black Dragon in early manhood and had since served Hirohito as responsible Cabinet ministers.

Distressed by the out-of-date intelligence in the hands of Mac-Arthur's Intelligence agents, Deputy Prime Minister Konoye sped down to Yokohama on September 13 and tried to explain matters. He phoned back that he was having difficulty in making himself understood through MacArthur's personal interpreter, Colonel Sidney Mashbir. Foreign Minister Shigemitsu at once followed Konoye to Yokohama and late that afternoon transmitted in

English a message which could cross the language barrier: if Mac-Arthur's men would consult with the Cabinet on war criminals to be arrested, the suspects would turn themselves in voluntarily at specified Allied detention points. Shaken by Tojo's suicide attempt and by the embarrassment of having tried to arrest dead men, MacArthur's War Crimes Board readily agreed. The Cabinet for its part persuaded Hirohito that it would be no treachery for him to save old retainers from the indignity of forcible arrest. General Eichelberger at once issued orders for the Japanese police to "deliver Japanese war criminals in good health."

HIROHITO'S OUTING

The five days that followed rubbed sensibilities raw on both sides. The remaining twenty-three war criminal suspects named by MacArthur's staff in its first sweep turned themselves in alive and well. The most important of them were given words of imperial comfort by Lord Privy Seal Kido's secretary before they reported for imprisonment. *New York Times* columnist Hanson Baldwin in Washington accused MacArthur of accepting the Emperor "as a sort of junior partner in the Occupation." On September 14 the glib Prime Minister Higashikuni, in answer to a questionnaire mailed him by the Associated Press, raised a storm in the United States by asking: "People of America, won't you forget Pearl Harbor? We Japanese people will forget the picture of devastation wrought by the atomic bomb and will start entirely anew as a peace-loving nation. America has won and Japan has lost. The war is ended. Let us now bury hate." General Eichelberger was criticized in Washington for telling reporters: "If the Japs continue acting as they are now, within a year this thing should be washed up." MacArthur was criticized in Washington for announcing that Allied Occupation forces would be cut from 500,000 to 200,000. State Department employees continued to publish evidence of Japanese wartime atrocities. It was leaked that the Australian and Chinese governments headed their war criminal lists with the name Hirohito. Japanese newspapers published stories of G.I. murders and rapes which were unreported by the Japanese police. MacArthur personally accused the press of "lack of good faith in handling the news." The sly old Taoist philosopher Suzuki Kantaro took his cigar from his mouth to tell U.S. reporters an outrageous lie: "The Emperor did not know that Japan had attacked Pearl Harbor until the Japanese militarists told him." Several American correspondents submitted demands to the palace that they be allowed to interview the Emperor personally.

Palace officials were frankly worried. The Emperor showed no inclination to save himself, and MacArthur's investigators now seemed intent on getting at the truth without respect for persons or rank. At the same time MacArthur himself seemed eager to believe the best of Hirohito. A dignified, idealized account of the Emperor's role in ending the war was prepared by one of the palace public relations experts and accepted gratefully by Mac-Arthur's Chief of Intelligence General Willoughby. "Based on personal confidence rather than official pressure," Willoughby later wrote, "American Intelligence in Tokyo obtained confidential notes and observations by one of the highest functionaries in the imperial entourage." Repeatedly MacArthur told visitors that he was weary of dealing through middlemen and would like to get to the point. Hirohito, too, was dissatisfied with the results brought back by his envoys from MacArthur's New Grand Hotel headquarters in Yokohama.

As a Japanese, Prime Minister Higashikuni assumed that the cause of all the unpleasantness must lie in the quality of the go-betweens being used. On September 17, he relieved Shigemitsu of his duties as foreign minister and replaced him with Yoshida Shigeru, the former Strike-South advocate who had been arrested by the secret police a few months earlier as a member of the Peace Faction. A short, scowling, cigar-chewing gnome of a man, Yoshida was an ideal emissary to use with American generals. He spoke good English and with a gruff directness most unusual in a Japanese. He needed no instruction in the inner workings of palace politics for he was the son-in-law of Hirohito's chief advisor and Lord Privy Seal from 1925 to 1935. In serving his father-in-law, Yoshida had built his career on work behind the scenes, with the result that he had held no incriminating public offices. His last public appointment, in fact, had been ambassador to the Court of St. James in the period 1936 to 1938. And although an advocate of expansion into the South Seas, he had never felt that it was absolutely necessary to attack the United States. In 1941 he had felt that attack on the United States was still to be avoided. Painstakingly groomed and trained, he now came into his own at the age of sixty-seven. MacArthur and his generals liked him so well that from 1946 to 1954 he would be five times prime minister and would be remembered as the architect of postwar Japan.

On September 18, the day of Yoshida's investiture as foreign minister, MacArthur and his staff moved up from Yokohama to Tokyo and opened for business on a more or less permanent basis. At the American Embassy which MacArthur took for his home, the entire prewar staff of servants reappeared one by one without being summoned. They stole in by the rear entrance, went up to the attic, unpacked their brown staff kimonos from trunks, and resumed service as if the four years of war had never been. For his place of work MacArthur took the white-columned, marble-and-granite Dai Ichi Insurance Building where the Peace Faction and the Tokyo Area Army had had their offices a few weeks earlier. Here were security facilities unequaled elsewhere in Japan, including shoot-the-chute tubes for personnel to use in reaching the ground floor in the event of fire. Here, from a phoneless, walnut-paneled room on the sixth floor, MacArthur would preside over Japan for five and a half years. Here he would organize an entire second government for Japan, a sprawling bureaucracy of American officers and civilians who would ultimately require a 278-page phone book and would be known collectively as SCAP, Supreme Commander Allied Powers. Here, from his sixth-floor window, MacArthur looked directly out, across a moat and plaza, onto the walls and watchtowers of Hirohito's palace. Probably never in history have two adversaries, holding such absolute power over the same land, worked so near one another.

On SCAP's first day in Tokyo, the prime minister, General Prince Higashikuni, held his first press conference for American reporters. One of them later doubted that any man "of comparable political status in any country of the world has ever been subjected to such blunt questioning by news correspondents." Rakishly dressed in a tan silk suit, Higashikuni fielded the insulting questions with bland sangfroid. Yes, he intended to broaden democratic processes. He expected soon to abolish the War and Navy Ministries and to curtail sharply the influence of the House of Peers. Yes, he would submit all his plans for approval to Mac-Arthur, but he hoped that his Cabinet would be able to keep many of the contemplated reforms in its own hands. For example, the prosecution of war criminals—it had begun long before the entry of American forces, and men were already being punished for their roughness with Allied prisoners. No, on the spur of the moment he could not give the names of those convicted nor the sentences against them, but he would make a list of them available through SCAP.

The next morning, September 20, newspapers reported that Senator Richard Russell of Georgia had asked the U.S. Senate to resolve that the Emperor be tried as a war criminal along with Tojo. With Hirohito's approval Prince Higashikuni at once paid a courtesy call on MacArthur in his new office in the Dai Ichi Building. He told MacArthur that he was prepared to resign whenever MacArthur or Hirohito requested it. He also indicated, guardedly, that the Emperor, in the interests of liberalism and democracy, would like to emerge from his cloistered life in the palace and play a more personal part in public affairs. MacArthur had the false impression, gleaned from newspapers, that the Emperor had never been interviewed, never delivered a public speech, never even used a telephone. And so he endorsed Higashikuni's suggestion with enthusiasm. He added by way of reminder, however, that Hirohito's emergence would not be accepted as a substitute for constructive steps towards reform on the part of the Japanese government.

Hirohito began his career as an extrovert on September 25, 1945. Many other Japanese remember it as the day that they were allowed to unstrap the short-wave bands on their radios and for the first time since prewar days listen again to broadcasts from overseas. Hirohito remembers it as the day that he gave ten-minute interviews to two U.S. newspaper correspondents. On being ushered into the audience chamber of the Imperial Household Building, Frank Kluckhohn of *The New York Times* strode briskly across to the dais where the Emperor was standing, reached out aggressively and shook the Emperor's hand. Hirohito showed no surprise at the unprecedented familiarity but in Kluckhohn's words "looked directly into my eyes, giving a sincere impression." He told Kluckhohn that he approved of constitutional monarchy and that he relied greatly on General MacArthur. "Once the Japanese people have been fed and clothed," he declared, "it will be comparatively easy to carry out the needed reforms within Japan." Kluckhohn also understood the Emperor to say that Tojo had acted against imperial wishes and had misused the Grand Seal of State in attacking Pearl Harbor before delivering a declaration of war.

"Hirohito in Interview Puts Blame on Tojo in Sneak Raid," headlined *The New York Times* the next day. The story drew a quick disavowal from the palace in which Hirohito pretended disingenuously that he had not known in advance the details of the Pearl Harbor attack plan. "It was usual," he declared irrelevantly, "for the High Command to handle the details of attacks. I meant Tojo to declare war in advance." In actuality both he and Tojo had meant to give the United States a few minutes' warning but had failed to do so because of a series of tragicomic accidents.

Hirohito followed his chats with American reporters by making an appointment to call on MacArthur. The historic first meeting took place at 10:00 A.M. September 27 within the clean white plaster walls of the American Embassy. Hirohito had rehearsed and discussed the role he planned to play with his favorite advisor Lord Privy Seal Kido for two hours and forty-five minutes the previous day. He was ready to take an extremely "low position," to be humble and even ludicrous if necessary, in order to win MacArthur's sympathy. He could afford to cut such a figure because, in Japan, there was an old and honorable tradition of playing the fool while waiting for revenge. It went so deep that every man in the Japanese Army had for decades cultivated a slovenly bumpkin appearance in order to seem weak and undisciplined in the eyes of potential spit-and-polish Western enemies. Japanese drill masters had taught privates to drag their heels on parade, to go unshaven, to leave buttons undone. Hirohito, who had worn Army uniforms for years, understood well this Spartan samurai mystique. And the drab disguise, the self-effacing air, became him well.

A Saladin in rags, Hirohito confronted one of the last knights to imagine himself armed in shining Christian chivalry. MacArthur came to the meeting determined to be as magnanimous as possible. He was under orders from Washington to punish Japan's war criminals, but it was a duty which he disliked, one that served no useful purpose but to satisfy vengeful voters in the United States and Great Britain. In MacArthur's view all Japanese had behaved badly, but as pagans rather than criminals. Now they needed to be enlightened, not punished. The Emperor, he believed, was a weak and ineffectual man who had the power to lead his people but no will except to be led.

Hirohito arrived at the American Embassy in one of the oldest limousines in the imperial garages, a plum-colored Daimler of World War I vintage. He had doffed his field marshal's uniform weeks ago and now, like the lowliest chamberlain in his suite, he was dressed in shabby prewar morning clothes. At the embassy steps he was met by Brigadier General Bonner Fellers. To Fellers's astonishment Hirohito held out his hand, and Fellers automatically took it and shook it. Then Hirohito and his attendants were led into the foyer and introduced to a group of MacArthur's aides. U.S. officers noticed that the Emperor seemed highstrung and trembling—almost as if he had been given an early-morning stimulant. The impression was highlighted by the fact that one of the courtiers with him was introduced as his personal physician. By prior arrangement, at Hirohito's own insistence, the meeting was to be entirely private and only Hirohito and his interpreter were ushered into MacArthur's presence.

MacArthur met Hirohito at the door of the embassy library dressed in sharply pressed khaki trousers and plain open-necked khaki shirt. He was at his most charming and genial. As he led Hirohito to a chair he recalled that in 1905, when twenty-five, he had had the privilege of being received with his father, General Arthur MacArthur, by Hirohito's deified grandfather, Emperor Meiji. He offered an American cigarette to Hirohito—ordinarily a nonsmoker—and noticed how the Emperor's "hands shook as I lighted it for him." There followed a thirty-eight-minute conversation. No minutes were kept of it but both MacArthur and Hirohito later gave accounts of what was said.

Hirohito thanked MacArthur for the excellent conduct of his troops.

MacArthur thanked Hirohito for the excellent conduct of his people. MacArthur added that he had heard of Hirohito's decisive role in ending the war and was grateful for it.

Hirohito objected modestly that he had not ended the war singlehandedly. "The public was not correctly informed," he said, and it was difficult "to bring about an end to the war without a shock to public opinion. . . . The peace party did not prevail until the bombing of Hiroshima created a situation which could be dramatized."

MacArthur said he was puzzled how it was that an Emperor powerful enough to end the war had not been powerful enough to prevent it.

"I felt my heart was breaking," replied Hirohito, "when I gave the word for war against the British royal family. They treated me with great kindness when I visited Europe as a crown prince. But the idea of gainsaying my advisors in those days never even occurred to me. Besides, it would have done no good. I would have been put in an insane asylum or even assassinated."

"A monarch must be brave enough to run such risks," said MacArthur sternly.

Hirohito replied instantly. His well-modulated nasal voice rose slightly. His eyes turned attentively on the interpreter whose English seemed suddenly hushed and hesitant: "It was not clear to me that our course was unjustified. Even now I am not sure how future historians will allocate the responsibility for the war." MacArthur was surprised. He had expected Hirohito to disassociate himself from Pearl Harbor and lay the blame for it on Tojo. Instead he heard Hirohito say: "General MacArthur, I have come to you to offer myself to the judgment of the powers you represent as the one to bear sole responsibility for every political and military decision made by my people, every action taken in the conduct of the war."

"This courageous assumption of responsibility implicit with death . . ." wrote MacArthur later, "moved me to the very marrow of my bones. He was an Emperor by inherent birth but in that instant I knew I faced the First Gentleman of Japan in his own right." Beaming paternally, MacArthur explained that the punishment of war criminals was a political necessity dictated by Washington which he, as a soldier, found distasteful. He added, however, that there could be no harm in punishing those who, for personal ambition, had given the Throne evil counsel. "I believe," he said, "that the Emperor of Japan knows best about the important men in the Japanese political world. Therefore I want to get your advice from now on on various matters."

Delighted, Hirohito promised to advise MacArthur in any way that he could. He would be ready, he said, to come to the embassy in person or send over the lord privy seal or grand chamberlain whenever he could be of assistance.

MacArthur promised to consult him often and on this cordial note their first tête-à-tête adjourned. A cameraman was summoned to record the historic moment. His photograph, showing the hulking general in fatigues towering over the tiny Emperor in striped pants, was so unflattering to Hirohito that Japanese editors did not publish it until ordered to do so by SCAP. Then it captured a curious place in the affections of the populace. The public humiliation of the little Emperor in striped pants became a symbol for the self-pity of the entire nation in defeat. Hirohito was brought close to his people as never before.

Hirohito returned to the palace and at once told Lord Privy Seal Kido of the understanding reached with MacArthur. "And this," he said, with glee, "was volunteered from MacArthur's side." Two days later, when Kido told him that the latest press clippings from America were almost all hostile to the Throne, Hirohito struck an indignant pose and threatened to go right over to his friend General MacArthur and have the criticism stopped. Kido owlishly warned him "to bottle up his resentment and keep silent." Kido's warning was reinforced by a member of MacArthur's War Crimes Board who indicated that the board had not yet decided whether or not to try the Emperor. To wile away the hours of uncertainty, Hirohito worked on a personal account of the events of his reign, a document in his defense which, unfortunately for historians, he was never called upon to produce in evidence. By October 3 he had brought his account up to the year 1929.

FIRST QUARREL

Any sense of cozy safety which Hirohito had brought away with him from his meeting with MacArthur was shattered on October 4 by a directive known as JCS 10 from the Joint Chiefs of Staff in Washington. It demanded reform of the Japanese police system; abolition of the thought police which had dealt with political crimes; amnesty for all political prisoners, including Communists; and complete freedom of the press—freedom even to criticize the Emperor. Hirohito received an intercept of the directive and Prince Konoye, a minister without portfolio in the Cabinet, at once called at the Dai Ichi Building to find out from MacArthur what it would mean. Konoye returned with the unsettling intelligence that MacArthur saw no harm in Communists, freed from jail, making speeches from soapboxes. Further, MacArthur intended to repeal the 1936 law making "thought criminals" liable to preventive arrest and the 1939 law requiring Japanese Christians to subordinate their faith to Shintoism. In addition, all commercial transactions between Japan and the outside world must now be approved by SCAP. Finally, Prime Minister Higashikuni's home minister must be dropped from the Cabinet because he had formerly been a thought policeman. That afternoon an official copy of JCS 10 was delivered to Prince Higashikuni at the prime minister's residence.

MacArthur worked late that night and emissaries shuttled back and forth between the prime minister's residence, the palace, and the Dai Ichi Building. Prince Higashikuni first suggested that he and his Cabinet should resign in protest to the directive and should then return to power with a new home minister. MacArthur, however, told a go-between: "I have the highest regard for Prince Higashikuni and I know of no one better qualified to carry out the terms of my directive, but if the Cabinet resigns *en masse* tomorrow it can only be interpreted by the Japanese people to mean that it is unable to implement my directive. Thereafter Prince Higashikuni may be acceptable to the Emperor for reappointment as prime minister, but he will not be acceptable to me."[3]

Prince Konoye then suggested that Foreign Minister Yoshida Shigeru form a Cabinet. He had, after all, been groomed for the post by his membership in the Peace Faction and by his incarceration at the hands of the secret police. Hirohito and his favorite advisor, Lord Privy Seal Kido, however, were not sure that it was time yet for a Yoshida Cabinet. The sixty-seven-year-old Yoshida had been "saved" for the prime ministership for so many years that it would be foolish to waste him now. Until the proud warriors of Japan became accustomed to American authority, until MacArthur had finished arresting war criminals, until the first hungry humiliating winter of the Occupation was over, it might be best to exploit a more expendable man. By bedtime, Hirohito and Kido had agreed that the ideal person would be Baron Shidehara Kijuro, seventy-three. In the 1920's Shidehara had been sorely used and abused as a diplomatic front man for Japan. Perennially foreign minister, perennially castigated by soldiers as "the weak-kneed diplomat," he had persuaded the world that Japan was a peaceful nation, and then, after the conquest of Manchuria, he had been put to pasture.

The next day, October 5, when the Emperor and his advisors were all agreed on what must be done, Prince Higashikuni made a great face-saving show by storming into the palace and declaring that he could not remain in office another moment after receiving such an insulting Allied directive as that of the previous evening. Foreign Minister Yoshida immediately saw MacArthur and sounded him out on the candidacy of old "weak-kneed" Baron Shidehara. "Isn't he rather old?" asked MacArthur. "Can he speak English?" Assured that he could, MacArthur nodded approvingly and said that he had no intention of interfering in domestic Japanese politics.

And so it was decided that Shidehara would be Japan's next prime minister. Persuading him to accept the post was not easy. He saw no honor in being MacArthur's lackey, and after his

[3] MacArthur in his *Reminiscences* remembers saying this of Prime Minister Shidehara during a later purge in January 1946. The story as told here follows Japanese sources.

shoddy treatment in years gone by he felt he owed Hirohito no
favors. All morning on October 6, chamberlains and Cabinet
ministers at the Imperial Household Building wooed Shidehara in
vain. At Kido's suggestion, Hirohito sent a special lunch over to
him from the imperial kitchen. After lunch Hirohito sat down
with him in private, dispensed with the usual Court formalities,
and spoke to him not as sovereign to subject but as man to man.
In an hour Shidehara was persuaded to do his disagreeable duty.

Every new prime minister of Japan always had a clearly recognized mission to perform. Hirohito and his advisors usually
formulated the mission and selected the man for it weeks and
even months in advance. Indeed, those close to the Throne could
sometimes see so far into the future as to know who would be
the prime minister after next. Prince Higashikuni's mission as
prime minister had been to see that the Japanese Armed Forces
obeyed the Imperial Will and demobilized peaceably. In addition,
by resigning, he was able to signify to the nation that the imperial family disassociated itself from the rest of MacArthur's
program. Shidehara's mission, by contrast, was to give in to Mac-
Arthur, to "bend like the young bamboo." He was to carry
out American reforms as a gesture, at the same time making it
clear that he acted without commitment and was only a figurehead. On his first day in office he promised to back MacArthur
and added sarcastically, "I hope I am not a war criminal, but if I
turn out to be one, that's all right too; we all helped to fight the
war." Three days later he attributed the war with the United
States to a "succession of minor incidents." Seven weeks later,
when petitioned by members of the Diet to appoint a board of
inquiry to fix responsibility for starting the war, he rejected the
suggestion with the words, "I would rather ask you all to continue inquiring into the causes of defeat."

The Cabinet of Prime Minister Shidehara began its truculent co-
operation with MacArthur by dissolving officially the secret police
which had retained a skeletal organization since the surrender.
Before complying with MacArthur's demand that political prisoners be released from Japanese prisons, one of Shidehara's aides
came up with the alarming information that 957,000 convicts were
about to be let loose on the Japanese population. Investigation,

however, soon showed that this figure represented the total number of arrests made in Hirohito's reign for all types of crime. Next it was said that 10,000 desperate leftists would have to be released. But this figure, too, turned out to be somewhat exaggerated. It was the number of leftists picked up in a mass arrest in April of 1929. Of the 10,000, only 1,200 had been held in jail after 1935. Of these, seven had been executed after due process, 200 had been beaten to death, and 200 had died of malnutrition and disease. A little over 700 had been released into labor battalions during the war or simply sent home on probation after American bombing began. Finally, when all the facts were in, twenty-five political agitators were released from prison, sixteen of them Communists.

The sixteen Communists celebrated their freedom by leading 500 idle citizens in a noisy hunger demonstration under MacArthur's windows on the Imperial Plaza between the Dai Ichi Building and the palace. The next morning, Columbus Day, MacArthur held his first meeting with the new prime minister, Shidehara, and urged him to press forward with other reforms: to give the people a bill of rights, to emancipate women, to allow labor to organize, to eradicate cant and mythology from textbooks. In his hereditary capacity as advisor to the Throne, the lanky Prince Konoye countered the following day with a statement to the effect that the Emperor would not object to being made a constitutional monarch but was seriously concerned over other suggested changes in the Constitution. Abdication, said Konoye, was a possibility which Hirohito had not yet ruled out. On October 14 the Cabinet voted to give women the franchise and to decrease the voting age from twenty-five to twenty. Two days later the Japanese General Staff was dissolved. On the following day the demobilization of the Japanese Army and Navy was proclaimed complete. Veterans still overseas would be mustered out as they arrived home in Japanese ports.

The reform programs of Prime Minister Shidehara had at least two happy results. Thousands of politically suspect Japanese were restored to first-class citizenship and so were enabled to clear their family escutcheons of dishonor. And in the election the following spring, thirty-eight women were elected to the Diet. Imperial ad-

visor Kido's son-in-law at once called on MacArthur to tell him
with gleeful mock horror that one of the new representatives was
a famous prostitute.

"How many votes did she get?" asked MacArthur.

"Two hundred and fifty-six thousand," sighed Kido's son-in-law.

MacArthur, who was later to give different versions of his reply
to some audiences, smiled and said, "She must be a hard-working
woman."

BLOOM OF ROMANCE

When Prime Minister Shidehara's "reform" Cabinet had been
in office a week, SCAP announced that the majority of the Occupation forces were no longer combat veterans but fresh recruits from
the United States. The Occupation was no longer a military
operation but a social experiment. MacArthur feared that it now
faced its greatest test. He had commanded the Rainbow Division
in the occupation of the Rhineland after World War I, and he
maintained that never in history had there been a successful
peacetime occupation army. Under combat conditions, he felt,
men retained discipline and respected the enemy, but in the sloth-
ful toils of peace conquerors grew overweening and veterans lost
their starch. He feared that the boys from home would soon be
subjugating women to make up for the heroics of real conquest
which they had missed.

Japan was fully prepared to take up the psychological slack
which MacArthur anticipated in his troops. The Peace Faction's
Recreation and Amusement Association had mobilized the nation's seductive powers for that very purpose. From the first when
U.S. armor began rolling into Tokyo, occupying assigned barracks
and factories and setting up checkpoints, the men were astonished by trucks of girls that were unloaded at their roadblocks
with interpreters in train to explain: "Courtesy of the Recreation
and Amusement Association." These initial advances were all rebuffed and the truckloads of presents sent home unopened. But
in a matter of weeks, when fear of Japanese treachery subsided,
the Americans began to thaw. Soon MacArthur was expressing
"grave concern and deep distress over published reports sug-

gestive of an existing widespread promiscuous relationship between members of the occupying forces and Japanese women of
immoral character."

In prewar days Japanese prostitutes had enjoyed an international reputation for their petite figures, their unabashed hedon-
ism, and the tasteful illusion they created of self-respect and
honest feeling. They lived and worked in ornate walled ghettos
on the peripheries of the major cities. The most famous of their
compounds was Tokyo's Yoshiwara, forty well-policed acres of
winking lanterns and narrow teeming streets, of gilt dragons and
red-lacquer archways, of costumed pimps and tumblers and
vendors of sweetmeats, of pools and gardens glimpsed through
lattice gates, of girls on balconies and girls in cages—of concentrated Oriental glamour and vice. MacArthur's M.P.'s knew of the
Yoshiwara by report and on their first day in Tokyo headed for
it directly to post "Off Limits" signs. They found only a ruin
gutted by incendiaries.

The girls who had survived the bombing were scattered over
the whole metropolitan and suburban area. Those who could
speak a little English had been recruited by the R.A.A. and were
waiting to serve at quaint old inns in the outskirts or in the new
cabarets and brothels which the R.A.A. was building downtown.
Eventually American demand would create such manifest hot-
spots as the Big Tits Bar in Yokohama or the Hard On Café in
Tokyo, but now, less than a month after the Occupation had commenced, the girls were being trucked about discreetly to emerge,
as if by chance, wherever it seemed that they might be welcomed.

Some of the G.I. encounters from those earliest days read like
opium dreams. A former Eighth Army sergeant, who roved the
Japanese countryside looking for caches of arms to destroy, gave
an account of a day in late October of 1945.

He and his companions parked their jeep in the dusty plaza of
a small seaside town east of Tokyo. As the men unpacked their
K-rations for lunch, a gentleman in black, wearing a top hat, came
to beg them in halting English to take their repast in the shade
of his humble roof. Standing on the back bumper of their jeep, he
directed them up a dirt road to a bluff overlooking the sea. Then
he stopped them at a bamboo grove and led them down a path

to an old inn on the edge of a cliff. In the entryway four delicate
creatures in kimono helped them off with their shoes and led
them upstairs to a room floored with mats and furnished with one
low lacquered table. Cushions were brought for them to sit upon,
and one wall was slid away to reveal a magnificent view of the
crashing surf below. Maids slipped in with bottles of beer, tubs of
steaming rice, and various hors d'oeuvres to add to the K-rations.
The girls made uproarious mistakes in English and hand-fed the
G.I.'s with chopsticks. The girls taught the G.I.'s to play parlor
games with fingers and matchsticks and beer bottles—games which
transcended language. Warm saké was brought in tiny pitchers
and drunk from tiny pottery cups. Soon food and communication
were almost exhausted and one of the girls said, "Take bath now."

Down two flights of stairs, the incredulous G.I.'s were ushered
into a grotto room in the cliff. The stone floor slanted gently to
a wall which opened on the sea. In the center of the floor was a
sunken tiled pool of steaming water. The girls disrobed and firmly
began to undress the men. Then they poured small wooden
buckets of scalding water over themselves. The performance was
repeated, with the G.I.'s the delighted victims. When everyone
was washed and rinsed, the girls slipped into the bath. Little by
little the men were induced to follow them and were taught the
trick of sitting completely still, neck deep in the 120-degree water,
until it no longer seemed to scald. As the girls mopped the G.I.'s
brows with tiny towels, they fed them small glasses of beer from
bottles brought in by the maids. In the distance the shadow of
the cliff lengthened on the Pacific swell below.

When everyone was well steeped, the maids brought clean cotton sleeping kimonos, and the men learned to knot the sashes
in front and pull them around so that the sash ends hung in back.
Then the girls led the G.I.'s upstairs to private rooms where thick
mattresses were laid out on the matting floors and more bottles
of beer were standing on the low tables. "Show me American
love," said a girl to the sergeant as she curled herself up against
him. And the sergeant, who a moment before felt stuffed,
swamped, and steeped, found himself too proud to refuse. In the
morning he awoke alone. Arousing his companions in nearby
rooms, he pooled money with them in a worried effort to find out

if they could pay for their sumptuous entertainment. The maids brought them tea and rice, and after breakfast they consulted their host in the black suit. He told them that the cost of their entertainment would be two packs of American cigarettes from each of them. In the foyer their mistresses of the night before waited with shoe horns, all smiles and bows, to see them on their way.

Memories and stories of such early liaisons made it impossible for American M.P.'s ever to begin to enforce the official Occupation policy of nonfraternization. By the time the veterans of jungle fighting had all returned "stateside," the girls knew their way around U.S. billets and around periodic clean-up campaigns. In many of the former Japanese Army barracks and converted munition factories occupied by Allied personnel, lights-out became a mysterious witching hour of tapping heels and wafted scents, sighing and creaking. At the once dignified Peers Club in Tokyo, which had been requisitioned as quarters for members of MacArthur's staff, twenty-two chambermaids and switchboard operators had to be fined for spending their nights in the officers' rooms. Before the Occupation was six months old, it was conservatively estimated that more than half the American officer corps had Japanese mistresses.

It was about the time that Prime Minister Shidehara's Cabinet took office in October that the recruits of the Recreation and Amusement Association began to distinguish between American enlisted men and officers and to urge that the entire Occupation army of 500,000 could not all be entertained in the same handsome fashion. From that date began the cheap hostess bars for noncoms and the "Willow Runs" for privates. The fine old inns were increasingly reserved for officers. By no means were all of them fully appreciated, however. Some lovely villas with exquisite gardens were fitted out with American-style bathrooms and then all but forgotten. Most popular with the American officer class turned out to be private clubs, open only by invitation, in the neon-lighted heart of Tokyo.

The most popular of the clubs was the Dai-An or Great Satiated Repose run by an effusive war profiteer, Ando Akira, who was a crony of Hirohito's second brother, Naval Captain Prince Takamatsu. A leader in the trucking and construction rackets, Ando

had recommended himself by his rapid repair work at Atsugi Air
Base before the touchdown of the first Occupation troops. At his
Dai-An club he introduced high-ranking American officers to
vivacious English-speaking noblewomen and nightly gave away
strings of Mikimoto pearls as table favors. His lavish operations
nudged him repeatedly to the verge of bankruptcy and repeatedly
he recouped through killings on the black market. After finally
serving a brief prison term, he retired to honored comfort.

Outside of the clubs, the most successful entertainments were
held at the villas of Cabinet Secretary Narahashi Wataru and of
former Prime Minister Prince Higashikuni himself. Not much has
ever been recorded of Higashikuni's parties, but Narahashi's were
such brazen seductions that they make old American generals
blush to this day. Narahashi had his villa at Atami, the beautiful,
vulgar beach resort which also houses the goddess of mercy erected
by General Matsui after the rape of Nanking. Atami's bay and
mountains and celebrated baths and hostesses needed no special
lore to be appreciated, and Narahashi was an excellent host. A
wealthy lawyer, he had spent the war years running the largest,
most lucrative listening-post hotel in Peking. One of his staff, Vis-
countess Torio, became the mistress of an officer who served under Brigadier General Courtney Whitney. Whitney ran the
Government Section of SCAP where the reform legislation for Japan was being drafted. Old hotel keeper Narahashi boasted that
he and "his princesses" would ultimately "capture" the whole of
Whitney's staff.

To the sex bribe were added many extraordinary investment
opportunities. Colonel Harold R. Ruth, MacArthur's fiscal officer,
reported that occupationaires were sending home eight million
more dollars each month than they were being paid. Many of the
objets d'art which the Japanese had looted from China, as well
as some native Japanese treasures, made their way in duffel bags
to the United States. Prince Higashikuni himself, the Emperor's uncle, went into the antique business and liked to say later that he
had bankrupted himself providing bargains for influential American officers. Years afterwards, when the Diet sought to make political profit out of alleged "jewel theft" by American officers, the in-

vestigation fell flat because it consisted of little more than a pooling of knowledge as to who had helped which American to what.

PALACE HOSTAGES

By dispensing gifts and favors, the Japanese bought little except information: gossip about personality clashes in the Dai Ichi Building, advance notice of American antitrust clampdowns, and, most important, the latest listing of war criminal suspects. Laws could be repealed after the American Occupation, business alliances could be remade and wealth returned to its rightful owners, but men hanged could not be brought back to life. Hirohito and MacArthur met at least three times during October and November of 1945 to discuss the war criminal issue in complete secrecy. MacArthur considered the punishment of a handful of discredited leaders to be of little moment in his over-all program for Japan. Hirohito, on the other hand, felt acute personal shame at the thought that others should have to suffer taking his responsibility. After first meeting Hirohito on September 27, MacArthur cabled the Joint Chiefs of Staff an account of the interview and suggested that, since the Emperor accepted all blame for the war, it might not be wise to charge others with it. The reply from Washington arrived on October 6, the day that Prime Minister Shidehara began forming his Cabinet. It was brief and explicit: "Proceed at once with the prosecution of war criminals. . . . Take no action against the Emperor without further consultation."

Saddled with a small vengeance of which he did not approve, MacArthur made the best of a bad situation and used the threat of war criminal arrests to extract concessions from Hirohito in other areas. At first he gave Hirohito the impression that Japanese co-operation might make a token punishment of war criminals sufficient. Retiring Prime Minister Higashikuni leapt at the bait and tried to swallow the fisherman: he told a farewell press conference that "Japan has already tried her war criminals and it may be assumed that their punishment has taken place." As evidence for this assertion, he submitted the names of two Japanese officers who had received prison terms, he said, for brutality during the construction of the Burma-Thailand railway.

Inasmuch as 16,000 Allied P.O.W.'s and 60,000 East Indian coolies had died as slaves along that 200-mile length of railway track, it was an unusually brazen statement even for Higashikuni.

Unmoved by Higashikuni's protestations, SCAP continued to add names to its list of Class A war criminals. These were the men to be charged not with torturing prisoners but with "conspiracy" to "plan aggressive war" and commit "crimes against peace." They were to be the principals in a showpiece trial which, it was hoped would open the eyes of the Japanese people to the evils of militarism. For American purposes the men tried did not need to be the most culpable in bringing about the war; almost any leader would serve as long as there was sufficient evidence to make a good case against him. It did not matter whether he was a righteous Japanese gentleman who had always done his best to obey the demigod on the Throne or a cynical opportunist who had sought to use the ambitions of Hirohito for his own advancement. More than enough of both sorts were put on SCAP lists, and it was left to Hirohito to rule out as many as he could. Lord Privy Seal Kido's secretary, Matsudaira Yasumasa, went over the lists, felt out the supposed criminals as to their willingness to stand trial, and indicated to Kido and the Emperor which men could be relied on and which, if possible, should be kept out of court. Neither MacArthur nor Hirohito had to keep up with every sordid detail of these transactions, but they did have to review the results and agree on them. Every few weeks SCAP published a new roster of men who should report for imprisonment.

Each list was more difficult than the one before for Hirohito to accept. The first consisted of Tojo and his Cabinet ministers. The second included former Prime Minister Hirota Koki, a whelp of the Black Dragon who, in 1936, had betrayed his tong to throw Hirohito the support of one dissident tail of it. The list of November 3 took in the 1944 Prime Minister Koiso, the 1941 Foreign Minister Matsuoka, and three important generals of the Strike-North or Fight-Russia Faction who had last enjoyed Hirohito's full confidence in 1934. One of them, General Honjo Shigeru, the conqueror of Manchuria, had served from 1933 to 1936 as Hirohito's chief aide-de-camp. Having fallen out with Hirohito in 1936 over the issue of fighting Russia to the north or the Western colonial powers to the south, General Honjo felt that he could not, in good conscience, serve the Emperor as a defendant in court. When he received the summons to present himself at Sugamo Prison, he held his tongue in the only way he knew by ripping open his belly with a shortsword.

The fourth list, published December 3, branded no less than fifty-nine individuals. It was so objectionable to Hirohito that it temporarily disrupted liaison between palace and Dai Ichi Building and had to be completed without benefit of Japanese advice. As a result it contained some curiosities. It called for the arrest of General Tada Hayao who had struggled vainly as vice chief of staff to prevent the rape of Nanking. And it left General Shimomura Sadamu, who had forced through the Nanking attack plans, at large as the Shidehara government's demobilization board director. The list also indicted the learned Dr. Okawa Shumei, a dangerous man to put on trial because, in the 1920's, he had given indoctrination lectures in the palace to Hirohito's cabal of young officers, and in the 1930's, he had served a token prison term for organizing the assassination of a financier, an industrialist, and a prime minister who opposed Hirohito's policies. A third controversial name on the list was that of Arima Yoriyasu, the "Socialist Count." Arima had recruited left-wing backing for Konoye's wartime one-party system but he was also a cousin-in-law of the Empress.

Most insupportable of all, the December list included seventy-one-year-old Prince Nashimoto Morimasa, the senior member of the imperial family. Elder brother of the Emperor's two scheming uncles, Prince Higashikuni and Prince Asaka, Nashimoto was the highest ranking of the four field marshals of the Japanese army. He was also the chief priest of Ise, Japan's cardinal shrine where dwelt the spirit of Amaterasu, the ancestral sun goddess. It was Nashimoto who had journeyed to Manchuria in June of 1937 to arrange with Tojo the outbreak of war with China. In this sense, he was the author of the whole eight years of hellish war, but whether or not SCAP's investigators knew it has never been revealed. No charges were ever pressed against Nashimoto. He was merely held in Sugamo Prison for five months until Hirohito had agreed to all of MacArthur's legislative reforms for Japan. In the eyes of the Japanese people, it was good for the image of the Throne to have a member of the imperial family bearing some share in the punishment for the war. But the indignity was monumental. Venerable prince and chief priest though he was, Nashimoto cleaned toilets at Sugamo Prison along with the rest of the Class A war criminal suspects. A heavy old man of porcine, jovial features, he went about his menial chores with a philosophical good humor that was put down to his credit.

On December 6, three days after the December list had been published, SCAP announced a codicil of two more names to be added to the roster. They were those of Lord Privy Seal Kido and Prince Konoye, Hirohito's two most intimate advisors. The decision to take them had been made in SCAP's war crimes section during early November. By the time that the public announcement was made, Hirohito had already reconciled himself to it and resumed his bitter relationship with the conqueror. Kido's diary reveals that the arrests were handled with exquisite deliberation and ceremony, making it as easy on Hirohito as possible.

Kido had advised the Emperor in October that he would be willing to serve as a war criminal. He asked only that his office of lord privy seal might be abolished with him. On October 14, he arranged to borrow a particularly beautiful suburban villa from a wealthy industrialist to live in during his last days of freedom. For the next month, however, he was too busy to occupy it and was spending from one to three hours every day in private audience with Hirohito. Finally on November 10 he submitted to a three-hour interrogation by a SCAP investigating team at the Meiji Building. He returned to the palace to accompany Hirohito to Ise Shrine and the old capital of Kyoto.

At Ise the roofs are like those of palm-thatched South Sea island huts—steeply gabled in the ancient imperial style with rafters crossing and extending outward in V's against the sky. Hirohito walked alone into the inner shrine where only he and other anointed priests and priestesses of his family are allowed. There he remained for an hour apologizing for losing the war to his supposed ancestress, Amaterasu the sun goddess. In Kyoto he repeated the apology at the shrines of his grandfather Meiji and of the supposed first Emperor Jimmu. Kido noted with great relief that the spectators along the imperial progress seemed reverent and respectful as they had been before the war. There were no great crowds of children and factory workers marshaled by the police as there had been in prewar days, but old men and women sat on mats beside the railway tracks and bowed as the train passed.

On the days that followed, members of the imperial family went on pilgrimages to the tombs of the other one hundred twenty-one Emperors who had ruled in Japan. On November 20, Kido accompanied Hirohito to Yasukuni Shrine in Tokyo, the Valhalla for the souls of warriors who had died away from home in battle. Four days later, after seeing to innumerable last-minute details, Kido went to the palace for his last day in office. He drank champagne with the Emperor and thanked him for various farewell gifts including a box of canned goods, a barrel of saké, an antique inkstone, a vase, a scroll, and two checks totaling $8,000.

On Tuesday, November 27, Kido cleaned out his safe deposit vault. On Wednesday he returned to Ise Shrine and Kyoto for his own report to the gods. The following Monday he was back in Tokyo and finally took up residence in the exquisite suburban villa he had borrowed. He devoted Tuesday and Wednesday to reading books, a pastime which he had been promising himself for twenty years. On Thursday, December 6, the radio announced that SCAP had ordered his and Konoye's arrest, effective December 16. "Having expected it," he wrote in his diary, "I heard the news with a calm heart." For the next ten days—his last days of freedom—he made an almost ostentatious display of his tranquility. He strolled in the gardens of his villa, wrote poems, played croquet, and performed a service at his household god shelf to explain to the family spirits their removal to new and temporary domiciles.

The day after the announcement that Kido would be arrested, a petty chamberlain called at his retirement villa to bring him news from the palace. The Emperor had told his grand chamberlain, "I would like to call Kido to the palace for a last visit."

The grand chamberlain, an admiral, had replied, "Kido is now a war criminal suspect so he may hesitate to come out of politeness. Possibly it is better for Your Highness not to see him at the present time."

"From the American point of view," said the Emperor, "Kido may be a war criminal, but from our nation's point of view he is a man to be acclaimed."

On hearing of this conversation from the petty chamberlain Kido felt deeply moved. "If the Emperor summons me," he declared, "I will come."

And so at 6:00 A.M. on December 10 Kido received an order to present himself at the palace that evening. He put on his old working clothes of striped pants and cutaway, stopped to worship at the tomb of his grandfather, and presented himself at his old office in the Imperial Household Ministry at 5:00 P.M. A chamberlain was there to greet him: "The Emperor is waiting for you. Please go to the Imperial Library at once."

Kido drove across the neglected gardens where the maple leaves lay unraked in windfalls. "As usual," he wrote, "I met the Emperor in his private study."

Hirohito was in a sentimental mood. "At this season I am filled with regrets," he said. "Please take care of your health. I think you understand my feelings completely, for we had talked to one another always. So please explain fully to the others in prison."

"I swear I will follow the Imperial Will," said Kido thickly. And Hirohito, in his most charming manner, at once took the conversation off into pleasant byways of reminiscence, "telling stories," as Kido wrote, "in all directions." After the tête-à-tête Empress Nagako came in and presented Kido with a precious antique table. A group of Kido's former colleagues joined the royal gathering with more presents, and wines and dinner followed. At about eight o'clock the Empress bestowed on Kido, as a last parting gift, a tray of doughnuts which she had baked with her own hand. Then, slightly tipsy, he retired from the Imperial Presence and returned to the Imperial Household Ministry to pay his farewells to the other chamberlains. He retired for the night to the home of a friend's mistress.

Before he went to bed, his son-in-law, Harvard graduate Tsuru Shigeto, a specialist in American law, called on him and told him: "It will seem to Americans that the Emperor is guilty if his privy seal tries to accept responsibility and take all blame for the war upon himself. Conversely, if the privy seal maintains his innocence, then the opposite impression will be made and the Emperor, in American eyes, will be judged not guilty. This is their way of thinking, so it is necessary to consider well the matter of lawyers for you." Kido thanked his son-in-law, asked him to get the best lawyers, and, if possible, to talk to the chief American prosecutor. Tsuru succeeded in having lunch with the prosecutor on December 15. On hearing his report Kido prepared cheerfully to present himself the next morning for incarceration at Omori, a former prison camp for Allied P.O.W.'s.

Prince Konoye, who was supposed to accompany Kido to prison, held a party that night at his luxurious suburban Hate-China Villa, which he had christened precisely eight years earlier during the rape of Nanking. The close friends and relatives who were his guests reported afterwards that he was his usual languid, cynical, witty self. When they had gone, he put on pajamas and a silken robe. On the low table beside his bed, he laid out some of his favorite books and the best of the essays he had written for the Peace Faction in exoneration of the Emperor. One of the books was a morocco-bound copy of Oscar Wilde's *De Profundis*. And one of the passages he had marked in it for posterity was this: "I must say to myself that I ruined myself and that nobody great or small can be ruined except by his own hand."

The one paper on the table which SCAP released to news reporters explained Konoye's motives for suicide: "I have been gravely concerned over the fact that I have committed certain errors in handling state affairs since the outbreak of the China Incident. I believe my real intentions are even now understood and appreciated by my friends, including not a few friends in America. The winner is too boastful and the loser too servile. World public opinion, which is at present full of overexcitement . . . will in time recover calmness and balance. Only then will a just verdict be rendered." A few hours later Prince Konoye took poison, dying as sybaritically as he had lived. He had failed to steer Hirohito from an unsuccessful war. He had proved himself a failure in the stratagems of defeat. He did not trust himself to shield the Emperor under cross-examination in court. And most important, perhaps, he was a snob and could not bear the thought of sharing a cell with a commoner like Tojo.

Half blind without his glasses, the myopic Lord Privy Seal Kido stood naked before an American doctor in the infirmary at Omori prison camp. Disinfectant was squirted over him, his clothes and possessions were catalogued by American M.P.'s, and finally he was allowed to dress and join his fellow war criminal suspects. At that moment the barons and marquises who had attended Konoye's soiree the night before were telephoning one another to transmit the intelligence that Prince Konoye had really gone through with his boast and was now dead. The last arrests had been made. More than one hundred of Hirohito's loyal retainers were in American hands. How many would be tried, how many hanged, would depend now on the alacrity with which Hirohito and the Cabinet of Prime Minister Shidehara made laws to reform Japan. MacArthur told the courtier who had had charge of negotiating the war criminal lists: "Now that the dead wood has been removed, Emperor Hirohito can be a real Emperor."

GOD IS DEAD

Land reform, disestablishment of state Shinto, women's suffrage, antitrust legislation—these were reforms which would be presented to the Diet and passed without murmur. Landlords, priests, politicians, and industrialists could be trusted to find their own loopholes in the new laws, their own ways of maintaining the status quo. The Emperor himself was willing to give away much of his personal wealth. But the fundamental charter of the land, the description of the Japanese way of government, the Constitution—that was different. To be forced to accept an imitation of the American constitution was a humiliation and danger which no one in the ruling classes could bear. While war criminal suspects languished in prison camp, the possibility of constitutional reform was tabled in committee and studied and studied again. In its place Hirohito sought to compromise and temporize by accepting a redefinition of his religious status. The suggestion came from a curious quarter, a former American Y.M.C.A. leader.

In the first week of September, when the palace was still looking for effective go-betweens to use in dealing with MacArthur, Prince Konoye had enlisted the help of Japan's most eminent native-born American, William Merrell Vories. Vories was an evangelist, an architect, and a millionaire. Kansas bred, he had come to Japan for the Y.M.C.A. in 1905 and had stayed to make a fortune selling the patent ointment Metholatum. At the same time he had designed and built many of Japan's largest modern buildings, had founded a thriving Christian sect, the Omi Brotherhood, had married the daughter of Viscount Hitotsu Yanagi, and had become a naturalized Japanese citizen. Hirohito considered Vories a friend because, shortly before the outbreak of the Pacific War, he had arranged to give Vories an "accidental" private audience. A Court chamberlain had visited Vories and suggested to him that he would find it rewarding to go to the Kyoto Palace at a specific hour on a specific day and wait there beside a specific flowering bush in the palace garden. When he did as he was told, the Emperor, down in Kyoto on a visit, chanced to pass that way on a stroll and stopped to chat with him. They talked about Japan and religion for almost an hour. Hirohito was impressed by Vories' patriotism for his adopted country and his command of the Japanese language.

On September 7, 1945, while inspecting abdication quarters for Hirohito in Kyoto, Konoye had asked Vories to visit MacArthur and sound out his intentions. Vories agreed to do what he could, but two days later, when he went to SCAP headquarters in Yokohama, he was treated like a collaborator. MacArthur refused to see him and sent word through an aide that if Konoye or Hirohito had anything to say they should say it directly without use of emissaries; also, that if they hoped for concessions, they should come bearing specific proposals for reform. Vories reported his rebuff to Konoye and was asked to stay in Tokyo and help think of a suitable reform.

On September 12 Vories awoke in the Imperial Hotel a block and a half south of the Dai Ichi Building with what he considered to be a godsent idea. Let the Emperor publicly renounce his divinity. Educated Japanese, including Hirohito himself, had never considered the Emperor a god in the omnipotent, omnipresent Western sense. Rather, he was a *kami* or immortal spirit.

All things Japanese, even rocks and trees and women, were thought to possess some share of *kami*. The Emperor had the largest and most potent share. To the Japanese mind there was nothing superhuman or moral about *kami*; it was the distilled essence of a man, his special charm and efficacy. The spirit world to which it belonged was an exact shadow of the real world. No god ruled over it. It was animated entirely by worldly spirits. Japan's social hierarchy extended into it, and the Emperor when he died joined the souls of other Emperors in presiding over it. Holding such beliefs, the Emperor would find it easy and meaningless to renounce his Western-style title to divinity.

Vories transmitted his idea to Konoye who took it to the Emperor. A dictionary revealed that the English word "God" meant "the Spirit of monotheism; the Master Craftsman of all things." Hirohito acknowledged that he was neither of these and Konoye the next day visited MacArthur. He found that SCAP welcomed Vories' suggestion with enthusiasm. During the next two months, however, the idea hung fire. It was revived in November to use as a poker chip in the final negotiations about war criminal lists. Then, in December, when Prince Nashimoto, the senior member of the imperial family, and Lord Privy Seal Kido, the Emperor's chief advisor, were safely in Allied hands, SCAP submitted a draft of a "non-divinity proclamation" such as it would like Hirohito to make. Hoping that it might serve in place of a new constitution, Hirohito had the Imperial Household Ministry draw up a counter-draft. After discussion the two drafts were dovetailed. Hirohito and MacArthur personally edited the respective Japanese and English texts, and an approved version was submitted to Prime Minister Shidehara for consideration by the Cabinet. The prime minister found the wording "too Japanese in spirit." He revised it in his best Gettysburg Address English and had it translated back into stilted Japanese.

Hirohito approved the Japanese version, MacArthur the English one, and both were issued together as the Emperor's New Year's message to his people on January 1, 1946. The key sentences were buried at the end of a long rescript in which Hirohito reiterated the charter oath made by his grandfather, Emperor Meiji, in the spring of 1868: to govern the nation through deliberative assemblies according to public opinion; to unite the land in single-minded pursuit of the national interest; to give every individual the opportunity to pursue the calling of his choice; to abolish "all base customs of former times" and follow "the laws of heaven and earth"; "to seek knowledge in every corner of the earth in order to extend the foundations of the Empire." This much was belly talk to tell the people that Japan had slipped back to the humble position of 1868 and that it might be a hundred years before Japan could rise again. Then came the crucial sentences which had gone through so much editing. Buried as they might be, couched as they might be in an alien phraseology, they were a revelation to most Japanese:

The ties between Us and Our people have always stood on mutual trust and affection. They do not depend upon mere legends and myths. They are not predicated upon the false concept that the Emperor is divine and that the Japanese people are superior to other races and fated to rule the world.

When Hirohito published his annual thirty-one-syllable *tanka* for the New Year's poetry contest a few days later, he suggested to his subjects that they must not be confused by the frosting of dissimulation forced upon them by circumstances:

> Courageous the pine
> that does not change its color
> under winter snow.
> Truly the men of Japan
> should be a forest of pines.

DICTATING DEMOCRACY

While the senior kinsman of the blood, the venerable, seventy-one-year-old Prince Nashimoto continued each night to lay his bald head on a prison pallet, Hirohito and MacArthur, through their respective intermediaries, fought a bitter battle over the Japanese Constitution. Consideration of constitutional reform had begun on October 8, 1945. Then Lord Privy Seal Kido, Prince Konoye, and Prime Minister Shidehara had agreed, first, that the old Constitution could not be improved except possibly by changing a few words in it; and, second, that SCAP would take unilateral action unless the Japanese changed far more than a few words. Prime Minister Shidehara felt it would be "easiest to surrender and keep the documents of negotiation" in order to repudiate the imposed MacArthur constitution at some later date. Hirohito had a higher view of his responsibilities and felt that he must make it clear from the beginning that he would not be an accomplice in changing a sacred document handed down to him from his grandfather. Accordingly, two committees were set up: one of courtiers, headed by Prince Konoye; the other of Cabinet ministers and scholars, headed by an expert on constitutional law, Matsumoto Joji. When the moat, figuratively speaking, froze over between the Dai Ichi Building and the palace in mid-November, Prince Konoye and his committee submitted a report to the Throne that the old Constitution needed no substantial changes and then made a great public show of resigning. Having thus washed his hands of responsibility for reform, Hirohito directed the Cabinet's committee on constitutional reform to pursue "detailed studies."

Months passed while the Cabinet committee used a thesaurus to rewrite the Constitution in new words with the same old meanings. Finally in late January, under great pressure from SCAP, the Cabinet committee submitted a "Gist" and an "Explanation" of the changes it proposed. MacArthur found the changes insufficient. He noted that the Emperor was no longer "sacred and inviolable" but "supreme and inviolable"; also that too many clauses ended with the loophole "except as otherwise provided by law." Accordingly MacArthur penciled a note on the minimal provisions which he expected to find in the new document: "The Emperor's rights and duties . . . will be exercised in accordance with the constitution and [be] responsible to the basic will of the people as provided therein. . . . War as a sovereign right of the nation is abolished . . . and no rights of belligerency will ever be conferred upon any Japanese force. . . . The feudal system of Japan will cease."

On February 3, 1946, after MacArthur assured himself that the Japanese Court and Cabinet would not be able to meet his demands without detailed coaching, he handed his scribbled notes to General Whitney and told him to have his Government Section mount a crash program and draft a sample constitution of the sort that would be acceptable. Whitney delegated the task to his right-hand man, Colonel Charles L. Kades.

Nine days later, the American constitution for Japan was ready. General Whitney laid it before the Cabinet Constitutional Reform Committee at a meeting at Foreign Minister Yoshida's residence that afternoon. "Gentlemen," he said, "the Supreme Commander has found your proposals for revising the constitution inacceptable. Your draft falls far short of the broad and liberal reorganization of the government structure . . . which the Allied Powers could regard as significant evidence that Japan has learned the lessons of war and defeat and is prepared to act as a responsible member of a peaceful community. Accordingly the Supreme Commander has had a detailed statement prepared of the principles he deems basic. We are presenting this statement to you in the form of a draft constitution. I advise you to give it your fullest consideration and I propose that you use it as a guide in renewed efforts to prepare a revised constitution. Of course there is no compulsion upon you . . . but the Supreme Commander is determined that the constitutional issue shall be brought before the people well in advance of the general elections in April. . . . If the Cabinet is unable to prepare a suitable and acceptable draft before that time, General MacArthur is prepared to lay this statement of principles directly before the people. I suggest, therefore, that you read it here and now while we wait outside."

For a moment there was no sound except a peculiarly Japanese hiss of intaken breath. The tiny, barrel-shaped Foreign Minister Yoshida, dressed in white, scowled a black Niebelung scowl. Then Shirasu Jiro, his live-in assistant and for twelve years a golfing crony of imprisoned Lord Privy Seal Kido, ushered Whitney and his aides outside into the artfully landscaped garden. He showed them to a little pavilion where they could be comfortable and left them with the sarcastic, bitter words of the vanquished, "Please bask in the atomic sunshine." Almost an hour later he returned to summon them, apologizing profusely for the long wait. "Not at all, Mr. Shirasu," said Whitney. "We have enjoyed your atomic sunshine very much." At that moment a B-29 happened to roar over, lending weight to his retort. The committee promised to use the statement of principles as the basis for a new attempt at constitutional revision.

Two days later, on February 14, Shirasu, the foreign minister's assistant, sent Whitney a letter explaining, "Your way is so American in the way that is straight and direct. Their way must be Japanese in the way that is roundabout, twisted and narrow." In the same letter Shirasu reminded Whitney, "I am afraid that I have already accelerated the paper shortage by writing this mumble but I know you will forgive me for my shortcomings for which my late father is also partly responsible."

Four days later Whitney received another letter from the committee by which he learned that "some of the roses of the West, when cultivated in Japan, lose their fragrance"; also that his brain child, the American version of the constitution, had not yet been translated into Japanese. Whitney saw MacArthur and MacArthur saw Hirohito. On Washington's Birthday, Whitney met again with the committee and ordered it to present the American draft immediately at the palace for consideration by the Emperor. Foreign Minister Yoshida did as told that same afternoon and was astonished to hear Hirohito say, albeit stiffly, "Upon these principles will truly rest the welfare of Our people and the rebuilding of Japan."

The committee obediently fussed over the translation of Whitney's constitution, made a few changes in it, and had it inscribed on fine parchment. It was submitted to MacArthur on March 4 and approved with minor qualifications. Whitney organized another crash program to edit it and reconcile the Japanese and English texts. For thirty-six hours his Government Section sat with the Japanese committee and an army of translators to thrash out the final wording. K-rations and five-gallon cans of coffee were served continuously. At 5:30 on the afternoon of March 5, 1946, MacArthur approved the completed text. The next day he announced to newsmen the "decision of the Emperor and the government of Japan to submit to the Japanese people a new and enlightened constitution."

The general election at which the people were to pass upon the

Constitution was scheduled for April 10. As the campaigning reached its noisiest, Hirohito quietly submitted to another concession which he had struggled to evade ever since it had first been suggested to him by Prince Higashikuni the previous October. It was that all members of the imperial family should give up their titles and become commoners except Hirohito and his immediate sons and brothers. Four days before the election, Prime Minister Shidehara called on Hirohito at his vacation palace at Hayama on the seashore to tell him that the first step had been taken: the Cabinet had accepted the resignation of fifteen princes of the blood from the House of Peers. The process would be completed two years later in October of 1947 when Hirohito attended a great wake in the palace at which fifty-one sisters and cousins and aunts met to drink a last bitter cup of commiseration at their downgrading to the ranks of plain citizens. With their titles went most of their emoluments. The vast imperial family fortune had been impounded and returned to the people. Imperial forests and gardens had been made national parks. Imperial treasures had been turned over to museums. Many of the imperial stocks and bonds and an unknown quantity of gold and silver had been secretly given to loyal friends of the Throne who could be trusted to handle it astutely and return it with the accrued gains at the end of Kido's suggested one-hundred-year period of quiescence. Investigators of SCAP's Economic Section traced some of these underground reserves, and the rest must have been depleted by the postwar inflation which dropped the exchange rate of the yen from 15 to 50 to 270 and finally to 360 per dollar.

On April 10, 1946, a record turnout at the polls expressed favor for the Constitution. "Oh? Has it been translated into Japanese already?" joked the voters. But they voted for it enthusiastically, and on November 3, Hirohito would declare it the law of the land. It stated in part: ". . . The Japanese people forever renounce war as a sovereign right of the nation. . . . Land, sea, and air forces, as well as other war potential, will never be maintained. The right of belligerency of the state will not be recognized." This was MacArthur's own favorite clause, put in at his insistence, but in three years he felt compelled by the Soviet menace to betray it, to give

Japan a lesson in the interpretation of constitutions, to insist that
Japan build up forces for self-defense: an Army and Air Force of
police which in twenty short years would grow to be the most
highly skilled and up-to-date military establishment in Asia. By
1970 it would have a morale-lifting tradition all its own. Instead
of answering to the traditional banzai with a great roar of "Banzai!"—May the Emperor live 10,000 years!—it would respond only
to a materialist catechism: "Do you all want color television?"

"Hai!"

"Do you all want electric rice cookers?"

"Hai!"

Sometimes in drill, when no Americans are watching, the men
of the Self-Defense Forces re-enact a scene that took place years
ago when the new American order, "Eyes right," was first screamed
at a regiment on parade. Eyes turn right, as if to ogle a passing
girl, but chins and noses remain pointing straight ahead in perfectly disciplined cynicism.

IMPERIAL BARGAIN

As soon as the Japanese people had endorsed the American constitution, old Prince Nashimoto was finally released from his four
months of unexplained detention in prison. The days of imperial insecurity were over. The Emperor had paid his ransom. He
had given up most of his wealth, all of his favorite retainers, many
of his family's privileges and titles, his claim to divinity, and now
his supreme power under the Constitution. It was an enormous
price but having made his bargain Hirohito would not renege on
it. He would tour the country making friends with the people.
He would become known to them as Mr. Ah-so-desuka, Mr. Oh-
is-that-so. Everyone would remember his visit to Hiroshima, on
an anniversary of its bombing, when he said dryly, "There seems to
have been considerable destruction here." Finally, when personal
appearances were no longer necessary, Hirohito would retire behind a façade of penitence to become the senior national consultant. He would let it be known that he was giving himself entirely
to his hobby of marine biology, and, with the help of his laboratory assistant, would publish a serious scientific book, the

beautifully illustrated *Opisthobranchia of Sagami Bay.* Domestic Japanese politics had never much interested him, and now, for several decades, Japan would have little voice in her role in international politics.

It was MacArthur's part of the bargain to keep the Emperor out of court at any cost. On May 3, twenty days after Prince Nashimoto's release from prison, the International Military Tribunal for the Far East would arraign twenty-eight of Hirohito's retainers as Class A war criminals, thereby beginning a trial of them that would last for two and a half years. It was to be a unique experiment in controlled historical research, and great effort had gone into making it a political success. While cajoling, bribing, and blackmailing the Imperial Court into co-operating with Occupation therapy for Japan, MacArthur at the same time had been fighting for the Emperor's life. More than Hirohito knew and far more than he could believe, there was a genuine desire on the part of many Americans and most of the Allied governments to treat him as a common criminal.

The various national positions on his case had been communicated to the United States at the time of surrender. Nationalist China, whose analysts had the best grasp of the historical facts and also the most reason to feel vengeful, demanded flatly that Hirohito be hanged. Communist Russia had doctrinaire theories against emperors in general but voiced surprisingly little objection to the American policy of keeping Hirohito in power as a necessary tool for renovation. Australia advised "that international law should not give immunity to sovereigns"; that Japanese "breaches of the laws of war" were "so terrible" and "so widespread that the Emperor and his ministers must have learned of them" and "abetted them if they did not take steps to prevent them"; "that it would be a travesty of justice seriously reflecting on the U.N. to punish the common Japanese or Korean guard while granting immunity to others perhaps even more guilty." The government of New Zealand concurred but in more moderate language.

MacArthur, having inherited the Emperor's absolute power in Japan, could afford to disregard the positions of the Allies but the U.S. State Department could not. It argued successfully, however, that the choice of war criminals to be tried should be made by the

U.S. intelligence agents who were "studying the evidence in Japan." Only the disgruntled Australians refused to be put off by such assurances. The files in Canberra are full of complaints from officials and journalists who visited Japan in the early months of the Occupation. They professed shock to find that MacArthur knew little about prewar Japanese history and took little interest in the fragmentary information being turned up by his War Crimes Board. They rightly guessed that the only evidence tending to exonerate the Emperor was of words rather than of deeds. They felt that MacArthur was showing a cynical disregard for historical truth and legal justice. MacArthur, on the other hand, felt that the Australians were more interested in the past than the future, more intent upon revenge than rehabilitation. He believed that the Emperor, if he had fangs at all, could be emptied of venom, rendered harmless, and used.

If MacArthur had had his way he would have extended to all Japanese leaders the same clemency that he felt obliged to show the Emperor. Politicians in both Washington and London, however, needed scapegoats to punish for the mass killings and tortures of the Japanese concentration camps. MacArthur bowed to their political necessity, but the inconsistency of punishing subordinates and pardoning superiors troubled him. As he was to write later, "The principle of holding criminally responsible the political leaders of the vanquished in war was repugnant to me."

When in October of 1945, at the insistence of the Dean Acheson group in the State Department, the Joint Chiefs of Staff ordered MacArthur to begin prosecuting war criminals, he countered with "urgent and repeated appeals" that "any criminal responsibility attached to Japanese political leaders . . . should be limited to an indictment for the attack on Pearl Harbor." His stratagem was to stage a quick trial of Tojo and the members of his 1941 Cabinet and thus avoid an investigation of wider scope that might implicate the Emperor and jeopardize the Occupation program of reform. When the Joint Chiefs insisted on a full show-piece trial, MacArthur asked to be "relieved of all responsibility having to do with the actual trial procedure." Having been assigned the formidable task of reforming Japanese society, he did not wish to impair his image as an inspirational leader in the eyes of the Japanese people.

On November 14, therefore, the trials were put in the charge of a U.S. prosecutor to be sent from Washington. And on November 25, when the palace had temporarily severed relations with the Dai Ichi Building over selection of those to be arrested, SCAP's information officers released to the Japanese press a detailed account of MacArthur's struggles with Washington on the war criminals' behalf. The press release served a double function. It cleared MacArthur with the Japanese, and it warned Hirohito that if he did not co-operate SCAP would leave him to the tender graces of the trial prosecutor. Hirohito promptly capitulated and the names of Lord Privy Seal Kido and Prince Konoye were put on the wanted list the very day that the U.S. prosecutor arrived in Tokyo.

RIGGING JUSTICE

The prosecutor who took the burden of the trials from MacArthur's conscience was a politicians' lawyer, a former assistant attorney general, Joseph Berry Keenan. In the early 1930's Keenan had made a name for himself by sending Machine Gun Kelly to the penitentiary and framing the Lindbergh Kidnapping Law. But a decade of Washington whiskey, politics, and poker had taken their toll. By the time he came to Japan he was described by one of his friends as "a florid, aggressive but not unkindly man." His enemies pointed out that in court he did not always have command of the facts at his disposal, that his language was often imprecise and full of Fourth of July oratory, that his delivery, especially in afternoon sessions, was sometimes thick and blurry.

On November 15, before leaving Washington, Keenan had discussed "his mission" with President Truman and Attorney General Tom C. Clark. On December 7, the day after his arrival in Tokyo, Keenan spent the morning with MacArthur and declared when he emerged from the Dai Ichi Building that he had found "decided harmony" in the views of the President and the Supreme Commander. Less than a week later he announced to the press that he and MacArthur "had sifted the Emperor's war record" and found nothing incriminating in it. He hoped, he said, for a speedy trial of Tojo and his clique for their guilt in the events which had transpired since July 1937, the opening of the war with China. He saw that it was a convenient date, because it marked the beginning of Tojo's rise to positions of policy-making responsibility. Three days later he conceded that he had been hasty in naming it and that SCAP had ordered the Japanese government to produce police and trial records for five prior incidents which had occurred between 1932 and 1937.

On December 15, Keenan had lunch with Lord Privy Seal Kido's son-in-law and gave him a message which cheered Kido on the eve of his imprisonment. A few days later Keenan made the acquaintance of Kido's successor in the Throne Room and former secretary, Matsudaira Yasumasa. By now Matsudaira was an expert on every phase of the war criminal issue. From the beginning he had handled all liaison on the subject between SCAP and the palace and had interviewed each of the Class A suspects before they had given themselves up. He now helped Keenan to find a suitable Japanese secretary with whom he could conduct business. The offered helper turned out to be a young aristocratic professor of German and English philosophy who had been a petty propagandist during the war—one of those denizens of the literary demimonde in Japan who arrange meetings between writers and stories. Keenan had brought with him from Washington a staff of twenty-four lawyers and fourteen assistants who were to be the nucleus of the American Prosecution Section at the tribunal. He had inherited the files of SCAP's War Crimes Board and the suspects it had arrested. Now through the good offices of his new secretary he would inherit most of the board's contacts as well. Men and women of the Peace Faction who had trooped to Yokohama in the opening days of the Occupation to renew acquaintance with old Japan hands on MacArthur's staff were obliged to repeat the performance and ask for an introduction to Keenan. The prosecutor enjoyed his popularity and welcomed the assistance given him. He needed documents to put in evidence and witnesses to testify in court. To stage any sort of trial, fair or foul, would be no mean accomplishment, he felt, in Japan's closed society.

By New Year's Day 1946, when Hirohito was proclaiming himself a common mortal and MacArthur was still waiting for the Japanese to submit an acceptable draft of a new constitution, Keenan and his lawyers had put down their roots in Tokyo and were hard at work preparing for the great trial ahead. MacArthur, through the State Department, sent out invitations to the other principal nations which had fought against Japan asking them to participate and send legal brains to preside. The panel of judges was announced in Washington on January 18. Each name on it was one of the most highly respected in the legal ranks of each of the Allied nations. There were to be eleven countries represented: the United States, Great Britain, the Netherlands, France, Canada, Australia, New Zealand, Russia, China, the Philippines, and India.

In writing stories about preparations for the trial, correspondents in Tokyo inevitably suggested to U.S. readers that MacArthur was shielding the Emperor. European lawyers and judges in transit through the United States on their way to the Tokyo trials were all asked their opinions on Hirohito's guilt. The Dean Acheson faction in the State Department renewed pressure on the Joint Chiefs of Staff, demanding that everything about the forthcoming trials be scrupulously aboveboard and fair.

MacArthur, on January 27, made a straight face of it and reassured his chiefs: "There is no specific or tangible evidence to connect the Emperor with responsibility for any decision of the Japanese government during the past ten years. The Japanese people would regard indictment of the Emperor as a grave betrayal. They understood the acceptance of the Potsdam terms as preserving the position of the Emperor. Trial of the Emperor would lead to an upheaval. There would be action by resistance groups. This could be held in check by the Occupation forces but it is not unlikely that there would be a complete breakdown of Japanese governmental machinery. The whole plan of occupation would have to be changed." MacArthur added that he would "make no recommendation concerning the Emperor," but advised strongly that, if it were decided to try him, a million troops should be stationed in Japan and it would be necessary in addition to have 20,000 or more civilian administrative personnel. "Plans should be made at once."

Two days after filing this recommendation, MacArthur was visited in the Dai Ichi Building by the Far Eastern Commission, the Allied board which sat in Washington to advise the United States on the Occupation of Japan. The commission had come to Tokyo for its first on-the-spot look at Occupation progress. The Australian members of the commission sent home a detailed report on MacArthur's reasons for holding the Emperor guiltless:

His views, he stated, were based mainly on personal talks with the Emperor himself. MacArthur gave a description of the Emperor's personality in which such phrases as "good blood," "wears his clothes easily," "cultured man," "gentleman" occurred. . . . He summed up the Emperor's position as that of a stooge who had never had a positive thought in his life. The Emperor's sense of duty was high. If held responsible for Japan's aggression, he would accept his fate. Nothing in his life would become him like the leaving of it. . . . His execution would have the effect of making him a martyr with incalculable effect on the Japanese attitude.

The Far Eastern Commission went on its way grumbling, newspapermen turned to other stories, and MacArthur and Keenan faced the next hurdle: the arrival of the Allied judges. To guide eleven sharp legal minds from eleven different national backgrounds through a millrace of half-hidden Japanese history and bring them out in a serene pond of unanimity was a challenge of an order which Keenan had never faced before—not even in Al Capone's Chicago. It was agreed that the men whom Keenan would place on trial should be charged with "conspiracy to wage aggressive war" and with responsibility for "organized crimes against humanity," that is, atrocities. That the deeds had been done was beyond question. That they were crimes, however, was not felt by more than a tiny minority of Japanese. And that the selection of men in the dock were particularly responsible for them—more than any other group of leaders who had advised Hirohito in the last twenty years—was a doubtful proposition that would be exceedingly difficult to prove. The most that could be said by thoughtful Japanese was that Tojo had assumed responsibility for advising the Emperor to take the losing gamble against the United States in 1941. The Japanese soldiers who had committed the atrocities did not usually blame their superiors in the German fashion. Nor did they seem, for the most part, to have found any sadistic satisfaction in their crimes. Rather, they said that they had done what their society expected them to do.

For any jurist the Japanese attitude posed disquieting questions —social and philosophical as well as legal. Not a single one of the twenty-eight defendants, with the possible exception of Hashimoto Kingoro who had sunk the *Panay* in 1937, was a small bourgeois gangster of Hitler's caliber. Nor was there any ideological common denominator between them except their lifelong loyalty to Hirohito. They had all served obediently under the very best families, the most polite, wealthy, English-speaking people in all Japan.

Fortunately for Keenan, Japanese atrocities had been committed on the persons of citizens of every one of the nations which would be represented by the judges. By parading witnesses to horrors, he could at least distract the judges' attention from the unsettling questions, why the Japanese felt no Germanic guilt and why they did not blame their superiors. Japan's proven atrocities had begun at the outset of Hirohito's reign in a massacre at the Chinese town of Tsinan in 1928. At that time none of the accused had been in a position to take leadership responsibility but at least most of them had been colonels. Tojo, awkwardly enough, had led an outwardly blameless life as an Army bureaucrat until 1935 when he had assumed charge of the secret police in Manchuria. To establish leadership responsibility for the policy of terror which Japan had pursued since 1928 would require, rightly speaking, an intensive investigation of Japanese history since at least 1910 when the leaders of 1928 were young. Keenan could foresee a trial interminably mired in complexity if he went back that far. He felt that he must assert his authority at once to establish boundaries and ground rules for the investigation.

With the backing of Washington, Keenan had it understood by all judges when they accepted their appointments that his Prosecution Section would have the exclusive right to choose the men to be put on trial and the evidence to be presented against them. This was a right of the prosecution in most civilized countries and was accepted without demur. Having established it and having "sifted the evidence," Keenan proceeded arbitrarily to restrict testimony about "the criminal conspiracy" charged against "Tojo's military clique" to the period of atrocities since 1928. Whether Keenan knew it or not, he was thus excluding from consideration the most truly conspiratorial years. Before 1928, as will be particularized later in this book, Tojo and other members of the imperial cabal had appeared to be harmless junior officers who went freely in and out of the Imperial Palace. After 1928, when they became busy bureaucrats and important colonels and generals—when they began to organize military adventures abroad—they severed open connections with the palace and maintained a seemly distance from Hirohito.

To Keenan's 1928-and-after restriction on behalf of the prosecution, a further obfuscation was added by the defense. Every one of the accused was represented by one American lawyer and at least one Japanese lawyer. The American defenders were mostly able, if somewhat quixotic, volunteer lawyers from the ranks of the American Army. Because of their knowledge of English and of Anglo-American legal procedure, they were to do most of the speaking for the defense in court. They depended, however, on Japanese defense lawyers for the substance of their briefs. All the Japanese members of the defense were graduates of Tokyo or Kyoto Imperial University Law Schools and thus classmates and cousins of the leaders in Hirohito's bureaucracy. Most of them had assisted at rigged trials during the 1930's to defend the assassins and plotters of coups d'etat who had terrorized the Japanese nation into accepting the overlordship of Hirohito's militaristic cabal.

In early 1946, before the war criminal trials began, these Japanese lawyers for the defense met in secret to draw up rules which might guide them in presenting evidence on behalf of Tojo, Kido, and their other clients. They considered two propositions: whether or not to use evidence favorable to their clients but "disturbing" to the Emperor; whether or not to use evidence favorable to their clients but "prejudicial to the honor of the Japanese nation." They agreed to exclude all evidence which they judged to be unfavorable to the Emperor, but they voted down the second proposition on the grounds that it would be a "breach of human rights" to sacrifice their clients for the reputation of the country as a whole. They pledged instead "not to forget the importance of saving the nation." The American lawyers for the defense were not told of these resolutions by their colleagues nor given other reason to question the selection of information fed to them.

While Keenan restricted the evidence which could be presented for the prosecution and Japanese lawyers restricted evidence which could be presented for the defense, both parties worked with a common aim to find men willing to testify in court. The clearing ground for all evidence was the palace. The office of the former lord privy seal approved all defense witnesses and steered most prosecution witnesses into Keenan's hands. Because Japanese soldiers considered it treason to reveal information to the former enemy and because they might be easily trapped into telling the truth by their combined hostility and sense of samurai honor, it was no easy matter to provide witnesses who would serve. Men were needed who could reveal as much Japanese history as it had been decided to reveal, who could do so with accurate convincing detail, and who were smart, knowledgeable, and even-tempered enough to avoid being caught in contradictions. General Eichelberger of the Eighth Army, on landing in Yokohama, had told one of his first visitors, an old retired Japanese lieutenant general whom he had known in Siberia in 1920, that he feared it would be difficult to find witnesses for the inevitable war criminal trials. And so the word had gone out through the ranks of Peace Faction courtiers to find the best man in Japan for the job.

The ideal was discovered in retired Major General Tanaka Takayoshi—Tanaka Top-luck, as his name may be translated. Tanaka was a shambling, Rabelaisian giant of a man with a ribald sense of humor and an enormous, shaven, egg-shaped head four times the size of most men's. He kept in it a voluminous, almost comprehensive file of Japanese Army intrigues between 1921 and 1945. As a former operative in Army Intelligence, he had played a role in many of them personally. In 1923 he had attended special indoctrination classes inside the sacred walls of the palace. In 1928 he had helped plan the assassination of the ruler of Manchuria. In 1931 he had become the lover of Japan's leading girl spy, a Manchu princess, and with her had created the provocations for a small smokescreen war in Shanghai in 1932. Later, in 1938, he had helped Hirohito stop an unauthorized Army probe into Russia, the Lake Khassan Incident. "Monster Tanaka," as his messmates called him, had instant access to his vast memory and an intelligence quick enough to use and sift the information it provided according to the needs of the occasion. Most of all, Tanaka was brave; Tanaka was loyal to the Emperor; Tanaka hated Tojo. In 1942 he had fallen out with Tojo over the attack on America and had lived out the war years in retirement.

With the approval of Lord Privy Seal Matsudaira Yasumasa, the new imperial advisor, Tanaka was turned over to Keenan's interrogators in February of 1946. As soon as he overcame his hate for the conquerors, he became Keenan's most valuable asset, a loyal retainer of MacArthur and the Emperor, who would testify indifferently for the prosecution or the defense and could maintain his accuracy and affability even when produced as a hostile witness. In two years of service, under merciless attack from all quarters, asked to remember details of events ten and twenty years past, he made only one mistake and that of a single day in citing a date. Small wonder that, in 1970, Monster Tanaka was still considered by Japanese to enjoy the protection of the American Embassy in Tokyo as well as of the palace.

The hulking Tanaka soon became a familiar and bodyguard of Chief Prosecutor Keenan. The two shared a common language, French, and Tanaka learned to enjoy bourbon almost as much as if it were "Super-Express," the best saké. According to Tanaka's published reminiscences, which are nothing compared to the voluminous notes which he has written but not published, Keenan used Tanaka as his guide to Japanese life. If Keenan wanted feminine companionship, he had only to insert the remark, "*Je suis fort*," into a conversation and Tanaka would be on the phone making arrangements. Tanaka, in fact, was so knowledgeable that he could arrange places of entertainment where Keenan could stride in over the delicate *tatami* (matting) floors without going to the trouble, which he hated, of taking off his shoes. Keenan disapproved of the liaisons between American officers and Japanese noblewomen. "I like a little fun, too," he used to say, "but I don't mess around with amateurs. It's no good."

While the script was being written, while the actors were learning their lines, while Director Keenan and Producer MacArthur were sedulously humored by the Japanese playwrights and prompters, a set was designed to impress all with the seriousness and high purpose of the trial. The tribunal's two-and-a-half-year run was mounted in the old Japanese Military Academy auditorium on Ichigaya Heights next door to the building where War Minister Anami had spent his last days. The witness box occupied the center of the darkly paneled auditorium and was surrounded by tables for Japanese and American lawyers. At the right of the witness box, as one entered the room, stood a stepped, three-tiered dock for the defendants. At the left, in dark solemnity, towered an unusually high polished bench for the judges. Rimming the walls were balcony seats for spectators and glass-fronted boxes for correspondents and translators. Miles of wire gave everyone headphones over which the proceedings could be heard in simultaneous translation in a language of choice: French, Russian, Chinese, English, or Japanese. Sixty floodlights made the floor brighter than day. Hundreds of translators and lawyers were to put almost 200,000 pages of testimony, debate, correction, and collateral exhibits into the murky record before Tojo, Matsui, and five others were to be hanged. The case for the prosecution was to begin on June 13, 1946. The case for the defense was to run from February 1947 until April of 1948. The judges were to pronounce sentence on November 12, 1948. And the sentences were to be executed on December 23, 1948.

SOUR VERDICT

Of the eleven tribunal judges only one could be allowed to speak in court. Otherwise the trial would have become a babel. The others would have to pass their questions and suggestions in notes along the bench. By prior political arrangement the speaking role of tribunal president was awarded, on February 14, 1946, to the Australian judge, Sir William Webb, chief justice of Australia's vast northern state of Queensland. He had had almost two years of experience trying Japanese war criminals in New Guinea and Rabaul, and he already knew so much about Japanese atrocities in those areas that American lawyers for the defense unsuccessfully moved that he should disqualify himself as prejudiced.

Tribunal President Webb was a large, indefatigable, implacably keen man. His blue eyes stung from beneath his heavy dark brows. Deep lines bracketed his mouth. His nose was massive and his command of English Churchillian. He had a high sense of the dignity, integrity, and independence of his profession. If his secretary was not picked up by the jeep on time to come to work or if Webb's own driver was given a questionable traffic ticket by the American M.P.'s, then SCAP had to reckon with a trenchant legal memo. If the air conditioning or earphone system broke down in court, that too would be the subject of a Webb brief. There was hardly room for two prose styles the size of Webb's and Mac-Arthur's in all Tokyo.

Webb was convinced that the Emperor—the man MacArthur was trying to build up as a "fine liberal gentleman"—was in actuality the first war criminal of Japan. In early 1945, responding to a request from his government, Webb had cabled the Australian foreign minister, Dr. H. V. Evatt: "Although there is a *prima facie* case against the Emperor, his case should be dealt with at the highest political and diplomatic level." For having so advised, before any trial took place, Webb also informed his government that he would feel obliged to disqualify himself from judgment at any trial of the Emperor. When he did preside at a trial from which the highest political and diplomatic levels had excluded the Emperor, he found himself champing at a bit he had put in his own mouth.

Webb's views towards the proceedings were partly shared by the most articulate of the lawyers present, Mr. Arthur Strettell Comyns Carr. Comyns Carr was the head of the British section for the prosecution. He was a bencher at Gray's Inn, a renowned London barrister of forty years' experience. Tall and thin, with a lined face full of intelligence and kindly humor, he had great courtroom charm: a lock of brown hair that kept falling over his forehead, a mellow voice, a wit that seemed gentle until it had sat a while and begun to etch. Comyns Carr had drawn up the original indictment of the twenty-eight accused. Like President Webb, he was thoroughly familiar with the known historical facts. Like

Webb he was used to the Anglican style of court business. Unlike the American lawyers, who worked for Keenan to prosecute, or for the accused to defend, he had no special interest in shielding the Emperor. He and President Webb indulged in a game of gentle mockery concerning Hirohito. Comyns Carr would touch on incriminating circumstances, spin them out with fine irony, and then, when he went too far, would be called good-naturedly to order by Webb. At one point he went so far as to suggest that SCAP had suppressed a captured copy of the minutes of Hirohito's wartime Imperial Headquarters meetings. Such a document, had it still existed, would have proved beyond question the Emperor's war guilt or innocence. Yet no attempt was made in court to deny its existence. Comyns Carr merely dropped his suggestion and passed on to other matters when he was ruled out of order. His remarks were later stricken from the proceedings and can only be found in early unedited versions of the trial transcript.

Tribunal President Webb and British Prosecutor Comyns Carr early took a dislike to Chief Prosecutor Keenan of the United States, and to his style of law, his style of oratory, and most of all to the self-righteousness with which he went about his task of saving the Emperor. Soon the "Keenan-Webb feud" as it was dubbed by the American press began to break through professional decorum into open exchanges in court. Keenan had the worst of the stiff legal repartee, but he plunged through the chill winds of Webb's sarcasm and remained doggedly buoyant. Every month or two he called a news conference and announced once more that there was no evidence against the Emperor.

With a united Japan behind him and no opposition except the well-disciplined kidding of Webb and Comyns Carr, Keenan survived the first months of the trial unscathed. But as the trial went on and evidence mounted, U.S. journalists renewed old criticisms and asked increasingly difficult questions. To quiet them Keenan tried, on September 25, 1946, to elicit from witness Okada, a retired Japanese admiral and former prime minister, some evidence that the Emperor had had no foreknowledge of Pearl Harbor plans late in 1941. He succeeded in drawing from Okada a statement that the Emperor "disliked war," was unable to avoid it, and "was not concerned with winning or losing" it.

"I fail to see the relevance of that in this trial," interjected Tribunal President Webb.

KEENAN: Mr. President . . . the relevancy is the contention that these accused were engaged in the conspiracy and that they seized the power of Japan. They defrauded the people of Japan into believing that the Emperor was behind the war with the rescript that he issued a few days after or instantly—a few hours after—the attack that constituted lawlessness in Japan as well as a part of the breach of international law, too.

WEBB: This is the first time in this lengthy trial that that has been suggested and it is contrary to the prosecution's evidence.

KEENAN: Mr. President, I respectfully call this Tribunal's attention, as chief prosecutor appointed under this charter, to the fact that the accused who are in dock, are the people we believe are really responsible for the war. If there had been anyone else, they would have been in the dock, too.

Webb snorted and made no reply. As he had often pointed out in chambers, Lord Privy Seal Kido's diary showed that eight days before Pearl Harbor, Hirohito had rejected a last-minute plea from his brother, Prince Takamatsu, to reconsider the attack plans. He had done so after seeking reassurance from the chiefs of the General Staff that Japan had a good chance of winning or at least of negotiating an advantageous peace. From a variety of evidence Webb knew that Hirohito had reviewed the attack plan on Pearl Harbor in detail, had approved it, and of his own volition had signed the necessary declaration of war well in advance of the attack. Webb also knew that his government in Canberra had conceded to the American prosecution section the right to choose the men who would stand trial. Keenan, for his part, had staked the honor of the United States on the implausible proposition that no one in Japan had had any serious responsibility for the war except the handful of defendants in the dock. Thousands of Japanese who knew better and had done worse went about their free and gainful pursuits sniffing politely.

The next day, out of court, Keenan told the press for the hundredth time, "A thorough investigation has convinced the prosecution that there is no evidence available to support a charge that the Emperor participated in the conspiracy."

Webb responded by leaking to his own newsmen the statement: "Quite early when decisions were being made as to who should be indicted and who not, it was decided not to bring the Emperor to justice. It must always be a matter of opinion as to whether this was justified for if the doctrine is to be maintained that the head of state is responsible for the acts of his ministers then at the very least he should have been made to stand trial."

As the trial drew to a close and the incidental matter of sentencing the men in the dock to hanging, imprisonment, or freedom became pressing, Keenan found his position increasingly difficult. In December of 1947 wartime Prime Minister Tojo himself took the stand in his own defense. Willing scapegoat though he was, he had been abused almost beyond endurance since the surrender. The Emperor himself had been reported in the newspapers accusing Tojo falsely of disobedience. Japanese editorial writers had called Tojo a coward for using a pistol instead of a sword and then failing in his suicide attempt. Tojo's family were being treated like lepers by their Japanese neighbors and were short of money. His brother had been arrested two months earlier for stealing a bag of rice on the elevated railway.

Tojo, in short, had a grievance and could be expected to voice it. He had an awkwardly logical, almost Western way of thinking. He might well dash his accepted cup of hemlock on the courtroom floor and spatter everyone. American prosecution lawyer John W. Fihelly had conducted the interrogations of Tojo in prison and knew the complex ins and outs of his case. Since there was much political glory to be gained in examining Tojo in court and leading him correctly, Keenan decided to displace Fihelly and conduct Tojo's cross-examination personally. To be precise, he requested that he be allowed to open the cross-examination and let Fihelly pursue it in detail, but the court, Justice Webb dissenting, ruled that it was most fair to have only one cross-examiner for each accused. Keenan accepted the full responsibility for himself, and Fihelly resigned from the prosecution in protest.

On the last day of 1947, lawyer Logan for the defense, in

direct examination of Tojo, asked the following question: "Do you know of any instance whatsoever where Marquis Kido acted or gave any advice contrary to the Emperor's wishes for peace?"

Tojo: In so far as I know there was no such instance whatsoever and I further wish to add that there is no Japanese subject who could go against the will of His Majesty, more particularly among high officials of the Japanese government or of Japan.

Logan: That concludes the examination on behalf of Marquis Kido.

The president (Webb): Well, you know the implications from that reply.

Indeed everybody did know. Keenan called his star witness Top-luck Tanaka back from vacation at his home by Lake Yamanaka near Mount Fuji and had him go at once to see Tojo in Sugamo Prison. Tojo would not yield, so Tanaka went to the palace and explained the situation to Matsudaira Yasumasa, Kido's former secretary and his successor as imperial advisor. Matsudaira, in turn, consulted with his fellow chamberlains and obtained permission from Hirohito to send a message to former Lord Privy Seal Kido in prison. Kido, who shared a cell next to Tojo's, began a negotiation. He spoke at length to Tojo around the M.P.-guarded partition. He talked to Tojo directly as they jogged through their courtyard exercises. Kido promised betterment in the position of the Tojo family, and Tojo had to listen because the myopic little Kido, even in prison fatigues, was Hirohito's representative. After two days of conversations, Tojo gave in. He returned to the courtroom and under continued cross-examination by Keenan was brought to admit that he had persuaded the Emperor to go to war and that, in so doing, he might have forced Hirohito to act against his personal inclinations.

Thereafter, on January 8, 1948, Keenan was given a truly Oriental night out. The place was a millionaire's villa in the seaside pleasure resort of Atami. General Matsui's goddess of mercy looked down from the hillside over the bay, shimmering with moonbeams. Two former prime ministers, a former war minister, and the mayor of Atami were on hand to entertain Keenan. "Je suis très fort," said Keenan. The mayor called for girls after the banquet and the old men who had been statesmen of Japan gave

Keenan first choice. "The host always pays on such occasions," said Keenan to Tanaka later that night. And on the way home to Tokyo, in the first gray of dawn, he gave his chauffeur $100 for racing a train and beating it to a crossing. Tanaka, too, was rewarded. He was invited to dinner by Imperial Advisor Matsudaira inside the palace. His double role at the War Crimes Tribunal was explained to the Emperor. "*Ah sore wa kekko desu,*" said Hirohito—"Oh well, that's all right then."

Three months later the defense rested its case, and Webb and the other ten judges retired to ponder the evidence, draft a judgment, and agree on sentences. The more Webb reviewed the facts, the more worried he became that only half the truth had been brought out in court. On February 11, 1948, in answer to a *Life* magazine allegation of a "Keenan-Webb feud," he explained in a letter to MacArthur:

My Dear Supreme Commander,
. . . I told the Chief of Counsel [Keenan] on one or two occasions that the question whether the Emperor was guilty or not was irrelevant as he was not on trial. I also pointed out to him that the Prosecution's evidence implicated the Emperor.

As spring passed into summer, Webb's doubts multiplied and he began to wonder whether it would be just to exact the death penalty of men who were clearly obsessed with loyalty and would tell lies against themselves in order to protect their lord. He conceived the idea of treating them instead like Napoleons and of remanding them to the Allied powers for exile on distant islands. He so recommended in his own first draft of a judgment, adding that death sentences, under the circumstances, would seem "vindictive" and that the defendants themselves would prefer "swift spectacular death to banishment to some remote part of the earth."

Webb amplified on his position in his second draft of a judgment, circulated among the other members of the tribunal on September 17, 1948:

. . . The great authority of the Emperor was proved beyond question when he ended the war. The outstanding part played by him in starting as well as ending it was the subject of unimpeachable evidence led by the Prosecution and of necessary findings in the general conclusions as to Japan's war guilt. But the Prosecution also made it clear that the Emperor would not be indicted. This immunity of the Emperor, as contrasted with the part he played in launching the war in the Pacific, is something which this Tribunal must take into consideration in imposing sentences on the accused. It is, of course, for the Prosecution to say who will be indicted; but a British Court in passing sentence would I believe, take into account, if it could, that the leader in the crime, though available for trial, had been granted immunity. If, as in cases of murder, the court must by law impose capital punishment, the prerogative of mercy would probably be exercised to save the lives of the condemned. . . .

The suggestion that the Emperor was bound to act on advice is contrary to evidence. He was not a limited monarch. If he acted on advice it was because he saw fit to do so. That did not limit his responsibility. . . .

I do not suggest the Emperor should have been prosecuted. His case was, no doubt, decided at the highest level in the best interests of all the Allied Powers.

Justice requires me to take into consideration the Emperor's immunity when determining the punishment of the accused found guilty; that is all.

A majority of Webb's colleagues felt that these scrupulous paragraphs would only be misinterpreted by Japanese apologists on the one hand and by Communists on the other. After being repeatedly outvoted, Webb gracefully capitulated, and on November 4, 1948, he began reading in court a majority judgment which did not contain his cherished escape clause concerning the role of the Emperor. He concurred in the judgment because, as president of the tribunal, he felt he must set an example of compromise to discourage his colleagues from each handing down a separate opinion. Even as it was, only four of the eleven judges concurred wholeheartedly and, of the seven who did not, four wrote their own independent judgments. The justices of Russia and Nationalist China, like Webb, signed the "majority" document cynically, suppressing their misgivings because they saw no other choice. Justices Jaranilla of the Philippines and Boling of the Netherlands, whose national territories had been occupied by the

Japanese during the war, wrote concurring opinions in which they spoke for heavier sentences to most of the accused. Justice Pal of India, whose land had not been overrun and who shared in the Buddhist religious heritage of the Japanese, dissented entirely because he could not see his way clear to condemning Japan for having waged war on the West. Justice Bernard of France dissented for the same reasons which had given President Webb such pause.

"It cannot be denied," he wrote, that the war "had a principal author who escaped all prosecution and of whom, in any case, the present defendants could only be considered as accomplices."

Keenan, when he heard the sentences which he had rhetorically asked for, went out for an evening of drinking with his star witness, Top-luck Tanaka. "Stupid," he said in his cups, "the sentences are stupid." The penalty to which he most objected was death for Matsui, the pathetic little general whose command had been abused at the rape of Nanking.

So it was that seven of the Emperor's most "loyal retainers" were hanged, eighteen others imprisoned for the duration of the Occupation, and the Emperor himself left on the Throne and called a "fine liberal gentleman." At midnight on December 22, 1948, before mounting the scaffold, Tojo, Matsui, and the other five men to be hanged all joined in a banzai for the Emperor, a last wish that Hirohito's dynasty might remain on the Throne eternally. Allied diplomats who were obliged, in line of duty, to witness the executions were all impressed by the stoic good humor with which the condemned went to their deaths.

In the lonely years that followed the trials, MacArthur's policy of letting bygones be bygones took hold with astonishing thoroughness. When the Occupation came to an end in 1952, the unhanged "war criminals" were first given home visiting privileges, then one by one released permanently from prison. By 1956 all were free again and most were already back in back-room politics. The dead had been brought home from the islands of the Pacific and put to rest in Arlington National Cemetery or in Tokyo's Yasukuni Shrine. The U.S. imagination occupied itself with the terrors of creeping communism and of domestic Hiroshimas. Japan rose from her ashes to become, in 1968, the third most power-

ful nation in the world, boasting a gross national product second
only to those of the United States and Soviet Russia. The majority of Japanese came to think of themselves, however unwillingly, as allies of their former American enemies. The ruling
minority of Japanese watched Communist China grow to become
a menace and took sardonic satisfaction in the fact that the
United States bore the bulk of expense for defending Japan.

Only Hirohito lived on and remembered. He was protected at
home by the reverence which the elder generation still felt for
him. No longer was his name, Hirohito, a taboo that could not be
spoken aloud, but the occasional rudeness of a Socialist Dietman
was not condoned by the populace and did not have to be taken
seriously. At first the role of retiring constitutional monarch
amused Hirohito. For four years after the war he insisted upon
sharing in the misery of his people by wearing only threadbare
prewar suits. Then in 1949, at the insistence of chamberlains who
said that American newspapers reported him walking about in
rags, he condescended to have a new suit made for his twenty-
fifth wedding anniversary. A few years later when a lady novelist,
Koyama Itoko, wrote a book about Empress Nagako, she ended
it with an account of the new suit. The Emperor was fond of
Aesop and Andersen, and she knew that he would be pleased by
her allusion to the *Emperor's New Clothes*.

Hirohito's new clothes, in a figurative sense, were embroidered
throughout the 1950's. The crass suspicions of Western jurists and
journalists in the 1940's were forgotten. For lack of records, the
handful of American historians interested in Japanese history depended heavily for their viewpoint upon the verbal information
of a small, accessible coterie of elder Japanese statesmen. The same
informants were interviewed again and again and their stories
became more charming, circumstantial, and convincing with each
telling. Schooled by centuries of experience in a frugal, authoritarian, densely populated society, all Japanese are masters at
creating pleasant illusions and at believing them to be reality. One
carefully tended shrub and one carefully selected rock in every
tiny urban front yard suggest to their proud owner all the beauty
of a forest and a mountain. A fragile paper screen drawn between
one room and another gives its occupant privacy and prohibits

the occupants of adjoining rooms from taking note of what is said behind it.

About 1960, however, Japanese historians and journalists, writing in their own language, began discreetly to suggest certain transparencies in the Emperor's new clothes. They began to draw on "lost" records: on courtiers' diaries, on admirals' logs and generals' daybooks, on the minutes and transactions of various political societies, on law court transcripts, and even on resurrected secret police files. Men who had previously held their peace began guardedly to reminisce. For the sake of the sacred ancestors and of the sacred children of the future, the proud truth of Japan's attempt—Hirohito's attempt—to conquer the world had to be set down in writing. It has been coming out in snatches, much of it in small editions by small publishing houses, much of it in private printings or in manuscripts circulated from hand to hand. From this new material, this new truthfulness of the Japanese, emerges a story to which Western historians have as yet paid little attention. It is a bizarre tale of Oriental *Realpolitik*, intrigue, and murder. Perhaps never has there been a detective story of such monumental proportions nor a hoax so rooted in antiquity. To trace its origins we go back no less than two thousand years.

PART TWO

❧

LAND OF THE
SUN GODDESS

4

IMPERIAL HERITAGE

(A.D. 50–1642)

VIKING EMPERORS

The stained and crooked carpet of imperial purple that was trod by Hirohito in the twentieth century had been unrolled for him in centuries gone by. His was an ancient house, governed by precedents and aspirations as hoary as the hills. It was literally at about the time of the coming of the first Emperor, two thousand years ago, that the sacred volcano of Mount Fuji arose out of the Eastern Plain in a single fiery night of earthquake. Ever since then the Emperor's relationship with his people and his method of government had been developing in picturesque isolation from the rest of the world. Part figurehead and chief executive, part war chief and king, part high priest and pope for his people, he was invested in heavy seals of state, heavier coats of mail, and still heavier religious robes. In the Western world there had been nothing like him, as a political institution, since the time of the pharaohs.

The first people came to Japan about 100,000 years ago. They were pre-Mongolian Asiatics, similar to the aborigines of Australia today—wandering hunters with pale complexions and heavy beards of varying color and curliness. For the next 90,000 years, during the last of the ice ages, Japan was usually linked to the

Asiatic mainland by land bridges and island chains. Hokkaido, the northernmost island, was accessible to Siberia. Kyushu, the southernmost island, was accessible to Taiwan and Southeast Asia. Then, about 10,000 years ago, the oceans were swelled by the melting of the glaciers, and Japan was cut off from the Continent by straits twice as wide as those at Dover. She became a land beyond land's end, out of sight of the mainland even on a clear day.

In her isolation Japan developed the unique qualities which set her apart from other nations of Asia or of the world. There were two cultures each with its own language, a Siberian one in the north and a Southeast Asian one in the south. The northern language survives today in Hokkaido as Ainu, a distant relative of some of the tongues of the Siberian tundra. The southern language has developed into modern Japanese. In its most homely and presumably ancient words—words for *mother, father, oyster,* or *belly* —it bears slight resemblances to the dialects of some Polynesians and of some hill tribes in the Malayan area. It is probably a branch of the family of languages spoken by ancient Southeast Asians before they were overrun by advanced Mongolian Stone-Agers out of Central Asia.

During the last 8,000 years before Christ, the aggressive, pale-faced, black-bearded bear hunters of the northern Ainu culture of Japan maintained their racial integrity and extended their hunting domains down into the central Japanese island of Honshu. By contrast, the southern aborigines—speaking a form of Japanese and leading rather sedentary lives as shellfish eaters—began to be replaced gradually, from about 500 B.C., by the Mongolian type of people associated with modern Japan. Traces of the aborigines' curly hair, gray eyes, brown or even red beards may still be found in upland valleys away from the Japanese coast, but their principal contribution to modern Japan seems to have been their language.

No archaeological evidence exists to suggest that the Mongolian race invaded southern Japan. Apparently they trickled in, raft by raft, canoe by canoe, and wreck by wreck. Each new boatload learned to speak the existing native dialects. Each new boatload brought with it new techniques from the Continent which made living easier—improved stone implements, thatched roofs, potters' wheels, elementary ideas of agriculture. Such arts, known to all

fisherfolk on the outskirts of Chinese civilization, enabled the
Mongolian newcomers to thrive in Japan—to have large families
and gradually to push back the aborigines into the hills.

About 300 B.C. traders began to arrive in southern Japan, introducing bronze, iron, and the rice plant. The colonies of castaways assimilated the innovations easily and profited by them. In
the last century B.C. a relatively small Mongolian castaway population in the southern island of Kyushu multiplied so rapidly as
agriculturists that they took over all the arable land in Kyushu.
Some of the pre-Mongolian hunters became serfs of the agriculturists and swiftly died out. Others retired to the hills whence they
continued to trouble the farmers for centuries with their warlike
outbursts. The new Kyushu agricultural community was organized as a loose confederacy of villages, each ruled by its
matriarch or fertility mother. The matriarch of the most powerful
town was called the sun goddess. The accounts of the earliest
Chinese travelers called her Pime-ko, a Chinese pronunciation of
Hime-ko, Sunshine Child.[1]

At about the time of Christ, the Kyushu sun goddess, being
sorely pressed by one of the hill tribes, the Kumaso, allied herself
with a marauding pirate-trader from Korea. This was the grandfather of Japan's first Emperor and the direct ancestor, seventy-one
generations removed, of Emperor Hirohito. Legends, archaeology,
and old Chinese and Korean annals combine to suggest that Hirohito's forebear was the Oriental equivalent of a Viking. His home
port was a buccaneers' enclave called Karak at the tip of the
Korean peninsula where Pusan stands today. The records of nearby
Korean kingdoms show that Karak, or Mimana as the Japanese
later called it, was recognized as an independent Japanese city
state from A.D. 42 until 562. Like the Normandy of England's
William the Conqueror, it was itself only a way station. The
original Scandinavia from which Japan's imperial Vikings had come
was probably far to the south in the Malayan area. That was the
vicinity which, a century or two earlier, had launched the great
Polynesian seafarers who discovered and populated the islands of
the Pacific. Some historians think that the navigational enterprise

[1] In modern Japanese *hime* has come to have two meanings: sunshine and
princess.

of the region had been stimulated by the breakup of the great fleet which Alexander the Great had assembled in the Persian Gulf for the conquest of India at the time of his sudden death in 323 B.C.

In an episode reminiscent of Dido and Aeneas, Hirohito's forebear had a son by a granddaughter of the Kyushu sun goddess. The son was allowed to grow up with the pirates and assist in their campaigns against the unregenerate Stone-Age Kumaso. He and his son, Jimmu, the first Emperor, ranged widely up the Inland Sea, exploring and provisioning along the southern Honshu coast.

As soon as he came of age, Jimmu, Hirohito's ancestor sixty-nine generations removed, resolved to carve out his own kingdom in Japan. The Kumaso had been beaten back into the Kyushu hills, and there was no longer any room for a male military leader in the matriarchal Kyushu society. Jimmu moved his entire pirate fleet—ships, warriors, women, and utensils—across the Inland Sea from Kyushu to Honshu. He anchored in what is now Osaka harbor in central Japan, 260 miles west-southwest of modern Tokyo. There a fertile plain, extending forty miles inland, lay waiting to be planted with rice. There the shellfishing aborigines needed help against the hairy Ainu-speaking hunters of the interior. Perhaps most important, Jimmu's warriors found in the hills around Osaka an iron ore which contained the right impurities for making steel. Within a few generations his swordsmiths would pass directly from the bronze age into the steel age and would turn out blades unsurpassed elsewhere in the world for centuries to come.[2]

After three years of campaigning, about A.D. 50,[3] Jimmu proclaimed himself Emperor of the fertile plain around Osaka Bay, together with its approaches in the surrounding mountains. His

[2] Precious metals, by contrast, were not discovered in Japan for centuries. Native silver began to be mined A.D. 674 and native gold A.D. 701. The first copper coins were minted A.D. 708.

[3] Official Japanese dating, adopted for ideological purposes in the nineteenth century, places Emperor Jimmu's ascension to the Throne at 660 B.C. Most scholars agree that this is six hundred to eight hundred years too early. Until after A.D. 200 the Japanese employed a lunar calendar which made Methuselahs of the first nine Emperors. The chronology used here follows that of the archaeologist J. Edward Kidder.

kingdom included the sites of modern Osaka, Kobe, and Kyoto. He called it Yamato, which is still the chauvinists' name for Japan.

Emperor Jimmu charged his three ablest lieutenants—Nakatomi, Inner Companion; Mononobe, Swordsmith; and Otomo, Mighty Friend—to govern wisely for him and to push on against the pale, hirsute hunters of the interior. He designated Nakatomi and his seed as the ceremonialists of his realm who would execute state business. He assigned to the Mononobe family the care and provision of weapons and the responsibility of enforcing state decisions. To the Otomo he gave the privilege of guarding his palace and person. Today most Japanese of any affluence claim descent either from Jimmu's progeny or from one of these three lieutenant families. Prince Konoye, for instance, who led Japan to war in 1937, considered himself the senior Konoye of the senior Fujiwara branch of the Nakatomi family.

At first Emperor Jimmu's kingdom of Yamato was only one of a hundred similar settlements reported by traders to contemporary Chinese chroniclers. Jimmu and his son, however, soon made it the most powerful. Jimmu brought to the natives a military leadership and discipline more Spartan than Sparta's. He and his kinsmen practiced a savage puritanism which equated godliness with cleanliness and required them to perform countless ceremonies of ritual purification. Like the Greeks at Thermopylae they bathed and combed their hair before battle. They also bathed after battle, after eating, after sexual intercourse, after slaying a stag—after any act which they felt to be unclean. To this day the Emperor's bath is one of the most sacred pieces of furniture in the palace, and total immersion in water at 110–130 degrees Fahrenheit is a daily ritual in the life of every Japanese.

Once having settled in Yamato, Jimmu and his men were terrified of succumbing to the pollution of death and the sloth of a sedentary life. When a man died, his home was burned. When a monarch passed away, the entire capital was moved to a new site. Nor was this a passing fancy. For more than six hundred years, the capital was studiously looked upon as a field headquarters and was moved at the end of every reign. Only A.D. 710, when the bureaucracy had become so large that a sizable city had to be destroyed and rebuilt every generation, did the Court finally settle down and accept a permanent capital city. To this day behind the great outer walls of the various imperial palaces, most of the buildings are simple wooden structures of one or two stories. Other Japanese have followed the Court example and most of them still live traditionally in flimsy homes of paper and wood. Until the advent of modern construction, it was a practical style well geared to easy moves and small losses in Japan's recurrent earthquakes.

On the animism, the local spirit worship of the natives, Jimmu built the basis for later Shintoism. He added the Continental worship of ancestral ghosts—and most particularly of the ghosts of his own ancestors who had been born, he said, by the sun goddess. He showed the shellfishers a bronze mirror, a bright sword, and a string of semiprecious stones, rubbed smooth in the fetal shape of cashew nuts, and warned them that these were the talismans of his divinity, bestowed on him in person by the sun goddess.

Jimmu gave purpose to their placid lives by making them all doughty foot soldiers and by telling them that his mission was "to encompass the eight corners of the earth under one roof." His phrase, "eight corners, one canopy," would become a slogan nineteen hundred years later for Hirohito's propagandists. Decade by decade Emperor Jimmu and his descendants led out his adopted people to conquer adjoining villages and kingdoms and drive back the Ainu.

Like the fertility cultists of the sun goddess in Kyushu, Jimmu and his retainers were careful not to mix their blood with that of the aborigines. They sought instead to replace the aborigines by having enormous families of their own. For five generations they imported women of their own race—whom they called Sacred Ones —from the home fief in Korea. Each prince and vassal, according to his wealth and power, had as many wives as he could afford. The old records tell of families with a hundred children. Such proliferation soon converted Jimmu's few boatloads of retainers into a population of thousands. After five generations, Jimmu's Court progeny began to marry their own cousins, the Great Children. The inbreeding was great, but the original stock had been healthy. A large percentage, probably a majority, of modern Japanese are descended from it.[4]

In the reign of the tenth Emperor, between 200 and 250, Jimmu's mirror of knowledge and sword of power were enshrined outside the palace for all to see and admire. Emperor Sujin felt secure in retaining only the jewels of divinity in his own keeping. The sword of power found its way to Atsuta Shrine in Nagoya, in an area newly wrested from the hairy barbarians of the north. The mirror of knowledge was housed closer to Yamato, at a shrine called Ise, overlooking the sea. Today Ise Shrine is the cardinal holy place of Japan to which every Cabinet minister reports before assuming office.

The twelfth Emperor, Keiko, who probably reigned from 280 to 316, and who sired no less than seventy-two sons, felt so sure of his power that he left Yamato in the care of his ministers and returned for six years to the kingdom of the sun goddess in the southern island of Kyushu. There he and one of his sons rid the Kyushu queens of a savage tribe of aborigines which had been molesting them and succeeded in negotiating a permanent merger between Yamato and Kyushu.

By about 400, the descendants of Jimmu and the sun goddess had subjugated most of southern Japan and their captains were fighting the hairy men of the north in the vicinity of Tokyo. The earliest state document out of Yamato, a report delivered by the Yamato ambassador to the Chinese Imperial Court in 478, asserted: "From of old our forebears have clad themselves in armor and helmet and gone across the hills and waters, sparing no time for rest. In the east they conquered fifty-five countries of hairy men and in the west they gained the homage of sixty-six countries of assorted barbarians."

While so boasting, the Japanese emissaries to China also told their hosts that Yamato, the name of their homeland, meant Great Peace. It was thus inscribed in the Chinese chronicles, and when Japan officially adopted the Chinese method of writing a

[4] If the Japanese ever cease to consider their excellent genealogical records as sacred and private and begin to use them in conjunction with blood-type and chromosome analysis, Japan should prove to be the perfect laboratory for human genetic studies.

few decades later, *Dai Wa* or Great Peace became the name of the country. In Japan, however, the Chinese characters for *Dai Wa* were given an exceptional double reading which flouted all rules. As every literate Japanese knew, the characters spelled *d-a-i w-a* when pronounced in front of a Chinese and *y-a-m-a t-o* when pronounced domestically. The truth was that Yamato really meant "mountainroad" or path to new conquests—but it would have been undiplomatic to suggest as much to the emperor of China.

THE GRAVEDIGGERS

As Yamato grew and the Emperors waxed all-powerful, they began to construct vast mausolea which attest not only to the slave labor which they could recruit but also to the fact that their Shintoism, their belief in the ghostly presence of their ancestors, had become a cult of death. Their divine descent "in a line unbroken for ages eternal" from Amaterasu, the sun goddess, took a terrible toll of their adherents.

The eighth Emperor, Kogen, who lived about 200, had a small artificial hill built to memorialize his sarcophagus. It was only 180 feet long and only a few score of his retainers were laid to rest along its slopes, but it signified the beginning of a burial madness which possessed the Emperors for the next three hundred years. Each successive ruler demanded a bigger tumulus and a larger company of victim vassals to accompany him to the spirit world. Legend has it that Suinin, the eleventh Emperor, was troubled by the wailing of retainers who were being buried alive during the obsequies for his brother, a mere prince. He therefore decreed that at his own interment clay figurines should be substituted for live victims. His humanitarian impulse wrought no lasting change, however, and the practice of retainer sacrifice continued by force up to the sixth century and sporadically by choice of the retainers themselves up to the death of Emperor Meiji in 1912.

The imperial tombs still play an important role in Japanese government. Even now in 1970 the aged Hirohito continues to send Court messengers to them to report important events like the signing of treaties. The earliest of the tombs, following the style of Emperor Kogen, are keyhole-shaped mounds, like great gourds or butternut squashes half buried in the ground. They are said by some savants to be related to a cult of gourd worship, then popular in Korea, and to represent enormous beached boats reminiscent of the ship mounds being thrown up by Norse adventurers in England at about the same time. The imperial mausolea or *misasagi*, however, are far larger than any of the Viking monuments. Indeed some of them, in sheer amount of earth moved, rival the pyramids.

That of Nintoku, the sixteenth Emperor, who probably reigned A.D. 395–427, is a moat-girt artificial mountain, 80 acres in area, more than half a mile long and, after fifteen hundred years of weathering, still over 100 feet high. As built, it is reputed to have had twin peaks and to have been planted and terraced and set about at its approaches with graceful archways in the shape of the Greek letter *pi*. Twenty years in construction, it was built by conscripted labor. As the Court chronicles point out, obliquely, of another of Nintoku's architectural efforts, "the people, without superintendence, supporting the aged and leading by the hand the young, transported timber, carried baskets [of earth] on their backs, and worked their hardest without distinction of night or day."[5]

The most ferocious of the tomb-building Emperors was Nintoku's grandson, Yuryaku, who reigned from 457 to 479. He is reported by the later chroniclers to have been a particularly monstrous sadist who executed every male member of the imperial family that he could lay hands on. It pleased him to put courtiers up in high trees and practice archery on them until they eventually slipped or were shot down. Pregnant peasant women

---

[5] Perhaps the most amazing feature of Nintoku's tomb is the fact that modern Japanese refrain from noticing it. It sprawls like New York's Central Park across the valuable real estate of Osaka's suburbs but no guide books mention it, and none but Court ceremonialists ever cross its three concentric moats to climb its wooded slopes. The skeleton of Emperor Nintoku is still supposed to lie in a stone vault inside, surrounded by his favorite possessions. Hungry antiquarians from the West have noted from afar that the sides of the mound are strewn with bones. For more than forty years they have eyed a fine stone sarcophagus peeping out from the rubble left by a landslide. But whenever they suggest an official scientific investigation to their Japanese colleagues, they are met evasively with a sudden change of subject. Nintoku's tomb is the private, sacred property of Hirohito's family.

were supposedly brought to him so that he could enjoy the sensation of tearing them open with his bare hands. After Yuryaku's death, Court advisors saw to it that Emperors did not mate with their aunts and half-sisters, or if they did, that crown princes be chosen from the broods of concubines only distantly related to the mainstream of the imperial family.

LIGHT FROM CHINA

The fourth-century union of the Yamato patriarchy of the Emperors with the Kyushu matriarchy of the sun goddesses led to three hundred years of cultural strife at Court. The Kyushu women espoused the advanced, ancient civilization of China, closer ties with the Continent, and an all-out effort to extend the Yamato empire into northern Korea. The Yamato male retainers—especially the old lieutenant clans of the Nakatomi, Mononobe, and Otomo—spoke for war against the Ainu and extension of Yamato into northern Honshu. About 400, the Chinese system of ideographic writing began to interest Court intellectuals. And Chinese Buddhism began to sap conviction in Shinto.

The Buddhism brought to Japan was an agnostic, almost atheistic creed, full of ceremony, mysticism, and homilies. It undermined the morbid superstition and sublime family confidence of the early Emperors and sowed in their minds the Confucian ideal of good government. According to Buddhist doctrine, a man's high birth could not be used as a passport to paradise. No matter how aristocratic his family, his spirit after death might pass into a peasant or a dog if he did not live wisely according to the teachings of the Hindu prophets. Only by submerging individualism in meditation and by achieving gentle unimpassioned enlightenment could a soul finally break out of the weary round of transmigration and escape into the oneness of the universe, the blessed nonexistence of Nirvana.

The Chinese system of ideographs—of characters or *kanji*—was almost equally pernicious to imperial pretensions because it made written laws and records a fact to be reckoned with. Fortunately for the Emperors, however, it was not an alphabet, and its idea pictures, which had been developed for the monosyllabic uninflected utterances of Chinese, were not easily adapted to the polysyllabic, highly inflected words of Japan.[6] Phonetic symbols had to be invented to express Japanese word endings, and long experimentation was required before general agreement could be reached on the correct matching of the Chinese idea symbols with spoken Japanese words. More than two hundred years passed before the Chinese writing system became a dangerous vehicle for Japanese thought. In those two hundred years Court scribes would have adequate time to develop an acceptable account of the past, pleasing to their masters.

It was the ladies who finally won the cultural battle. The imperial family, in 562, lost its ancient Korean fief of Karak to neighboring Korean kingdoms sponsored by China. The prestige of Chinese civilization soared. In 587 Emperor Bidatsu, the thirty-first sovereign, embraced Buddhism on his deathbed. The clan of Court armorers, the Mononobe, rebelled. The Kyushu ladies' faction at Court exterminated the Mononobes, and then, in a typical Japanese compromise, brought to power the son of a Mononobe mother, Prince Shotoku Taishi. Shotoku agreed to cooperate in a Chineseifying program for the reform and strengthening of the nation.

Prince Shotoku was a child prodigy who had mastered the difficult Chinese system of writing by the age of seven. He instituted an ambitious research into Chinese laws and letters with a view to adopting them in Japan. The scholars of his study groups wrote the first histories, geographies, grammars, and legal codes of Japan and drew up the first orderly plans for census taking, land surveys, and equitable conscription and taxation. Most important, Shotoku worked out the first accommodation between his family's cult of Shintoism and the new religion of Buddha. Buddhist monks came to accept the Shinto pantheon of ancestors and nature spirits as manifestations—*bodhisattva*—of Buddha himself. It was understood that Emperors would be spared the

[6] The spoken languages of China and Japan are totally unrelated and mutually unintelligible. Modern Chinese and Japanese, however, can communicate through writing because their word pictures have meaning independent of sound.

humiliation of transmigration and given an automatic dispensa-
tion when they died to go straight to Nirvana.

While most of his plans for reform were still on paper, Shotoku
Taishi died in 621, at the age of forty-nine. Without his leadership the Shinto princes allied with the imperial family and the
Buddhist princes allied with the Kyushu sun goddesses quickly
fell out. A small war in the streets of the capital made the Soga
family of the Kyushu ladies' faction the dictators of the country.
Twenty-four years later, in 645, a crown prince and one of the
last of the Nakatomi family, the Inner Companions, carried out
a carefully planned countercoup. They slew some Soga princes
in the Throne room in the very presence of the Empress and
drove the rest out of the Capital. The leader of the Soga clan
retired to his walled villa, set a fire, and burned himself to death.
He took with him most of his retainers and most of the research
papers and records which had been compiled by Shotoku Taishi.

VEILING THE THRONE

Crown Prince Tenji and Nakatomi Kametari of the Inner
Companions followed up their victory by reconstructing from
memory the lost programs of Shotoku Taishi and inaugurating a
thorough overhaul of Japanese government. In the great Taika
Reforms of 645–655, the country was given a bureaucracy on the
Chinese model and with it provincial governors, a census, a land
survey, and the right of petition to the Throne. Arms were collected forcibly into armories, for use only in time of war. Now,
at last, after centuries of strife, a man could walk a day's journey
without fear of being set upon by brigands.

In 670 the wise old reformer Nakatomi lay dying. To honor him,
Emperor Tenji, his patron and disciple, presented him with an
imperial concubine who was already full with child. "If it's only
a girl," said the Emperor, "then of course I will take the responsibility for her sustenance, but if it's a boy, you will want to keep
him yourself." It *was* a boy, and Emperor Tenji, before he died
a year later, bestowed on the child the name of Fujiwara. It was
this bastard imperial clan, the Fujiwaras, who were to take the
place of the Nakatomis as Inner Companions and serve as the

Emperors' most intimate counselors for the next 1,275 years. When the Fujiwara Prince Konoye, who led Japan to war in 1937, took poison in 1945, he was the last of a kind.

During the eighth and ninth centuries, as ministers on the left, ministers on the right, and ministers on the inside, the Fujiwaras turned Court life into a pageant of ceremonies and costumes. Everywhere in the courtyards of the palace walked fat old men, stiffly. The cut and color of their robes, the depth of their bows, were all prescribed. On their heads they wore shallow skull caps of stiff black silk, rather like academic mortarboards but topped with various shapes and sizes of black lacquered phallic symbols denoting their rank. In the big square Throne room, on a floor of white mats, the Emperor took on increasingly the appearance of a rouged and gilded doll, squatting motionless in the center of a gravely comic surrealist ballet. His person became so taboo and awe-inspiring that he was no longer called Emperor but identified by euphemisms such as Dawn in the Palace, Forbidden Closet, Steps to Heaven, or The Great Great. One of his names was Worshipful Gateway, the "Mikado" of Gilbert and Sullivan.

As the Fujiwaras institutionalized the Emperor, they gradually assumed responsibility for all advice given to him. Theirs was the first veil in what is known to Japanese as the Emperor's "government from behind the curtains." The Emperor lurked somewhere behind the last veil but, except on those rare occasions when he spoke with the Voice of the Crane, he did nothing overt. He accepted the advice of his ministers or asked them to reconsider it. He presided and sanctioned but never—officially—did he initiate. Thus, if state policies turned out badly, the Fujiwaras took all the blame and the imperial family was exempted from criticism or threat of violence. In a land of volatile honor and pride this responsibility was a dangerous one. The Fujiwaras accepted it partly for influence and wealth and partly out of a genuine religious conviction that the Throne must be shielded.

Through the masterful, illusion-creating stage management of the Fujiwaras, the people of Japan came gradually to believe in a head of state who was a paradox: a mortal god, a zero infinity, an impotent omnipotence. By long tradition Japanese government had always been a family matter, and the Fujiwaras simply persuaded the nation that the Emperor was the head of the national family. Everyone had a voice in family councils according to the weight of his position in the social hierarchy. The Emperor, as father, had the most weight—so much, in fact, that everyone must try to spare him from ever being proved wrong. To be born into his national family was to incur an "unlimited obligation" to him: to obey him and take responsibility for him with the fierce, unquestioning family pride of a child. His desires were binding, but under Fujiwara tutelage he cultivated a dark, oracular style of speech which was always open to interpretation. It was the duty of the subject to act in the interests of the national family according to the unexpressed will of the Emperor. No need always to ask explicit instructions; need only to take all the blame if the imperial wishes turned out to have been misunderstood.

The Fujiwaras occupied the most important positions at Court, advising or manipulating Emperors from 670 to 1945. Until 1165 they actively headed the administration of the nation's government. Over the centuries, they imparted to Japanese politics a special quality of subtlety which reflected their own temperament—their own family tradition and genetic make-up—rather than an inherent trait of the Japanese public. Almost without exception, the Fujiwaras, like their close kin the Emperors, never showed much taste for supervising civil servants or for constructing a body of workable laws. To rule, in their way of thinking, was less a science than an art—a game of skill to be played with living pieces, as if each move was a unique aesthetic experience. They unrolled history as if it were a moving tapestry which they themselves were weaving. They loved ceremony and intrigue. Ungloved might appalled them; they preferred deft assassinations. Sensitive, refined, amorous, and highly literate, also superstitious, cynical, and unscrupulous, they ran Japan to preserve the godhood of their imperial cousins and to indulge their own patrician tastes.

The bedrock on which the Fujiwaras' influence rested was not so much their own statesmanship as it was the hereditary good looks and carefully inculcated seductiveness of their sisters and daughters. For thirteen hundred years, more than three quarters of the wives and concubines who minced their way in and out of the palace were Fujiwaras. Many of them learned the arts of love before they were ten and bore princes before they were fifteen. Over the centuries they were to set an astonishing genetic record by bearing no less than fifty-four of the seventy-six Emperors between 724 and Hirohito's birth in 1900. In a Court where there were usually a score of noblewomen enjoying the imperial favor at any one time and where epidemics decimated the ranks of retainers every decade, the hygiene, charm, sensuality, intelligence, and genuine devotion of the Fujiwara ladies must be counted nothing less than heroic.

From 670 to 950 the Fujiwaras ran Japan skillfully, gradually strengthening the government, extending it into northern Japan and holding civil strife at a minimum. Under the professional management of Fujiwara ministers and mistresses, the Emperors lost their splendid barbarism and cultivated the arts. They wrote poetry and studied the mysteries of Buddhism. They accepted a permanent capital for their sacerdotal administration—first, in 710, the town of Nara in the center of the original Yamato kingdom, and then, in 794, when Nara became too infested with Buddhist priests, Kyoto, eighteen miles north of Nara.[7] Under the patronage of their brilliant Court grew up most of the handcrafts for which Japan is still celebrated: the lovely subdued silks, the fragrant unvarnished woodwork, the delicate porcelains, the gaudy lacquers, and the painted paper screens.

The very cookery of Japan was largely a product of the Kyoto Court. In those days such modern staples as rice, pork, beef, and fowl were caviar to the general. The peasants subsisted mostly on barley, millet, fish, oysters, seaweed, beans, radishes, wild herbs, and ferns. Only the Court noblewomen had the ingredients with which to experiment and create variety. Their wealth allowed them to waste vats of rice, radish, fish, and flour and to invent an unsurpassed variety of salt and rice-vinegar pickles and of soya-bean yogurts and cheeses. Their warrior husbands kept bow and sword hand in practice by daily hunts in the hills. They brought back wild boar and venison and pheasant, and many uncultivated vegetables such as bamboo shoots, mushrooms, and

[7] Kyoto means Capital Capital. Tokyo, the modern administrative center of Japan, means Eastern Capital. In the early days Kyoto was called Heian, Unruffled Peace, and Tokyo was called Edo, Navvies' Doorway.

lotus roots. From these the Court ladies created the characteristic meat cookery of Japan such as survives in the popular sukiyaki of modern restaurants. The masses did not know even that it existed. Buddhism proscribed the eating of meat and courtiers encouraged the people to be pious. For a thousand years imperial princes served as high priests at all the great Buddhist temples but privately patronized clandestine Kyoto guilds of butchers and meat cooks. When carnivorous customs resurfaced in the nineteenth century and began to be practiced on prime Western steers in the stockyards of Kobe, most Japanese beef-eaters thought that the novel Japanese recipes they followed had been freshly invented.[8]

Although the Emperors at first took a cynical view of the new Buddhist religion and studied it only to control its converts, many courtiers and Court ladies fell prey to its permissive mysticism. At length the Emperors themselves became engrossed in its theological fine points and began to rely excessively on the advice of Buddhist confessors. Empress Koken, who reigned from 749 to 758, grew so intimate with her priest that she is said to have made him her lover and plotted to put him on the Throne. This may be a canard, however, invented to justify the action of her Fujiwara ministers when they finally prevailed upon her to abdicate. In their eyes she had more foolish offenses to her discredit: she had issued a decree against the killing of any animals, and she had interested herself in yet another new religion—the teachings of a group of Nestorian Christians who visited the capital from China. With her deposition, Christian influence disappeared from Japan for eight hundred years.

The curtain which the Fujiwaras hung around the Throne was meant only to protect it, not to stifle its occupant. If an Emperor showed a talent for politics and the real exercise of power, he was not supposed to indulge it while he remained Emperor, but if he abdicated and put his infant son on the Throne, it was deemed proper that he give full autocratic play to his abilities from behind the scenes. It became standard practice for every strong Emperor to retire young to a monastery, set up his own

---

[8] Then, and only then, did imports from Southeast Asia make rice the staple of the nation, driving millet and barley from the plebeian menu.

Court and administrative offices there, and run the Fujiwaras who ran the nation. Sometimes he would outlive his successor and manipulate a whole series of reigns. Sometimes, too, his successor would abdicate and compete with him in the arts of stage management. In 1301 there were to be no less than five retired Emperors, each doing his best to govern Japan from the temple of his choice.

The city of Kyoto, which was the capital from 794 to 1868, soon grew to be even more priest-ridden than Nara before it. More than a thousand Buddhist temples were built atop the steep, pine-clad, natural fortress of Mount Hiei—Mountain of Wisdom to be Compared with the Emperor's—and from it belligerent monks regularly descended in incendiary raids on government offices which offended them. The imperial family's cult of Shinto fell into disuse. After 946 the Emperors gave up the regular practice of sending messengers to announce important events at the tombs of their ancestors. When they themselves died, they no longer built huge burial mounds but allowed themselves to be cremated and interred in little white boxes under tidy stone slabs in neat rectangular Kyoto parks. Their learned skepticism, however, was not fully shared by the common people, and periodically folk superstitions would reinfect the Court and produce a brief Shinto revival.

The days and years and centuries slipped by in an afternoon doze of sexual intrigue, poems, paintings, new concubines, and occasional duels. The people responded well to Fujiwara direction. They wore cotton pants and wide conical straw hats, tilled their paddies, and paid their tithes in much the same way that they do in rural Japan today. Little by little the valleys of Honshu, the large, central Japanese island, succumbed to cultivation, and only in crossing the mountain ranges might an agriculturist still meet with his savage Stone-Age brethren who persisted in living by the hunt. The Cains of the land, however, were coming into the possession of good steel swords and these, added to their fleet arrows, made them formidable. Outlaws banished from the strict hierarchy of society provided them with leadership.

A growing caste of nobles found use for hardy cutthroats. The Emperors and the Fujiwaras had many children, and second sons had to be provided for. They were granted provincial fiefs and lived in discontent because of their rustication from the capital. They gradually took over all the ancient clans until hardly a region in Japan did not have a member of the imperial family in its manor house. But giving second sons tax-free estates and allowing them to own the aboriginal citizens as serfs had certain inevitable drawbacks. The Ainu people of the northern culture repeatedly rebelled and had to be almost exterminated. The nobles themselves grew overproud of their provincial prowess and wanted to meddle in Kyoto affairs. Worst of all, land to give away to talented second sons grew scarce and tax-free estates kept the growing income of the nation from meeting the growing expenses of government.

The Emperors, shortsightedly, had always considered the whole land their own fief and had set aside no special crown lands for income but only a few scenic estates for pleasure. By about 950 they began to find themselves dependent upon the Fujiwaras for money to make up Court deficits which could not be covered by the dwindling tax take. The nation was falling apart into baronial estates. The barons were members of the imperial family who could not be dealt with like the old clan lords because they were relatives and had their own Iron-Age companies of soldiers. Even the Kyoto branches of the Fujiwara family, who had seen to it that they did own some estates, found themselves dangerously dependent on professional soldiers and policemen to keep the peace. No longer did a few hired braves suffice to preserve and equalize political balances; allegiances had to be made with provincial kinsmen who could provide whole armies led by skilled generals.

THE SHOGUNS

In 1192, after a war with a group of southern princes who sought to supersede the Fujiwaras as manipulators of the Throne, the princes of the north converted a makeshift council which they had established in Kamakura near Tokyo into a permanent headquarters or "tent government" for the administration of the northern half of the nation. Upon their chief, Emperor Go-Toba conferred the title *Sei-i Dai Shogun,* Great Barbarian-suppressing General. The title would be abbreviated in later years to shogun and would come to mean in Western dictionaries, "military governor ruling Japan." In reality the shoguns never did entirely rule Japan, for they remained subjects of the Throne, ostensibly loyal and often obedient. They did, however, rule northern Japan and for the next seven hundred years they usually controlled the armies which held the military balance of power in the nation.

Thus came into being the third layer of government from behind the curtain: someone to take responsibility for the Fujiwara chief minister at Court, and for the Emperor behind him. With the third veil descended also the fourth. The shoguns were rusticated imperial princelings, and the real power in their "tent government" lay with tough practical bureaucrats: either chiefs of staff or military police chiefs. Most of these soldier administrators at the fourth level of government were also distant kinsmen of the Emperor. They enriched themselves, they killed their own brothers for power, but none of them ever tried to seize the Throne or depose the godlike senior kinsman who sat on it.

Outside the immediate environs of Kyoto, where the Court ruled supreme, the military administration of the shogun or field marshal, and of his chiefs of staff, secret agents, and soldiers, policed the clan lords and collected the taxes. They soon monopolized the temporal power of Japan and left the Emperors nothing but the spiritual power. As high priests, however, the Emperors always retained the authority to confer and bless all high-level appointments. They successfully insisted that they were the overseers of the nation's welfare and that they must be consulted on all matters of national importance. In particular, they claimed absolute authority over Japan's foot soldiers. Though tenuous, their claims were never denied.

In the new fourfold system of government, all offices on the ladder swiftly became hereditary. The Kamakura chiefs of staff would resign in favor of their sons or brothers in the event of a lost battle; the Kamakura shoguns would resign under the same terms for a lost war; a Fujiwara minister of state in Kyoto would resign for a losing policy; and the Emperor would abdicate only

for personal reasons or as a gesture of national ceremonial purification after a particularly severe earthquake.

In 1221, Go-Toba, who was now the retired Emperor, grew
jealous of the growing power of the shogun, whom he had rusticated to Kamakura, and plotted to outlaw him. While laying his
plans and collecting his recruits, Go-Toba resorted to a traditional
Japanese ruse: he pretended to be a voluptuary, not worthy of
surveillance. At his strategy sessions, watered saké was served
copiously by Court beauties in transparent kimonos. The shogun's
spies admired what they saw but were not deceived. The shogun
marched on Kyoto, forced Go-Toba's juvenile puppet Emperor to
abdicate, and replaced him with another juvenile puppet Emperor, Go-Toba's nephew. From that day Kyoto ceased to be the
main center of power in the nation and the Tokyo area, in the
north, took its place. The imperial family, however, was treated
handsomely and was preserved in its Kyoto sinecure as the
national high priesthood.

KUBLAI KHAN

During the supremacy of the first shogun family, the Genji,
the neighboring land of China was overrun by Mongol horsemen
from the Russian steppes. In 1268 envoys from Kublai Khan,
the new ruler in Peking, whose grandfather Genghis had swallowed most of Asia, arrived in Japan with a letter ordering "the
king of your little country" to submit to Mongol suzerainty or
suffer invasion. The letter was carried posthaste to the shogun in
Kamakura. He deemed it so important that he decided to disturb
the celestial peace of the Court and refer the letter to the Emperor.

In Kyoto a careful note was drafted, rejecting Kublai Khan's
demands. This reply was forwarded to Kamakura for the shogun
to consider and transmit if he saw fit. He was incidentally reminded that he was responsible for the defense of the nation. The
shogun decided that the Emperor's note was unrealistic—both too
proud and too humble—and sent the Chinese envoys back to
Kublai Khan without a reply or even an acknowledgment. Kublai
Khan indignantly ordered his vassal kings in Korea to construct

a great fleet. The Koreans diplomatically kept the Japanese informed of Kublai's intentions.

For six years both nations made preparations. Finally, in 1274, 15,000 Mongols and 8,000 Koreans embarked from Korean ports and made sail for southern Japan. They first assaulted two little islands off the Kyushu coast. The Japanese garrisons on the islands established a heroic precedent by dying to the last man.

Next the Mongol fleet landed at Hikata, southeast of Kokura, the lucky primary target which would narrowly escape atomic destruction 671 years later. The Japanese fought a savage holding action at the beaches while the warriors waiting in central Kyushu were called to join in the fray.[9] That night a storm blew up and the Korean captains of the invasion ships urged a withdrawal. The Mongol generals of the landing force were nothing loath to seize the excuse. Their losses had been enormous. By the time they had regained the mainland and taken stock, they found that they had lost 13,000 of their 23,000 men.

Kublai Khan accepted the excuse of weather but not the rebuff to his pride. He coolly sent more envoys to Japan the next year, ordering the Japanese to surrender before he began to fight in earnest. The shogun had the envoys' heads cut off and secured imperial approval for an all-out national defense effort. Kublai Khan was preoccupied with wars in southern China and it would be six more years before he would launch his thrust.

The Japanese prepared for it feverishly. They built a "vast cloud of firefly boats," with which to harass the Chinese war junks, and a stone wall more than a hundred miles long, with which to contain the most likely beachheads. Every man, woman, and child contributed money or labor toward the national armory.

Kublai descended in his full wrath in 1281. He impressed all the junks of Canton and Korea into his service and floated an army of 140,000 troops—some 40,000 of them his own redoubtable northern warriors. They were landed all along the perimeter of the stone wall which the Japanese had constructed and in great-

[9] The heroic commander was Shimazu Hisatsune, a scion of the imperial family and of the local matriarchy of sun goddesses. His descendants and the descendants of his powerful Satsuma clansmen would staff the "Kyushu clique" which plotted Japan's aggressive Strike-South policy in the 1920's.

est strength at the two ends where it seemed most possible to turn the Japanese flanks. For fifty-three days desperate hand-to-hand combat continued without letup, particularly at the two ends of the long wall. Then at last came the divine wind—the kamikaze—which ravaged the Mongol fleet for forty-eight hours, August 15 and 16 in the year 1281.[10] When the skies cleared, less than half of the great Chinese host of 140,000 men survived to touch foot again on the mainland.

SCHISM

After their great victory the warriors of Japan relaxed and fought aimlessly with one another. The rule of the shoguns in Kamakura deterioriated, and the imperial family in Kyoto split into two factions. From 1339 to 1392, there were two Imperial Courts, a southern one in the mountains south of Kyoto where an Emperor wished to rule in his own right and a northern one in Kyoto itself where an Emperor was willing to delegate all but religious power to the military strongmen, the shoguns.[11] Confirmed Shintoists considered the true Court to be the southern one because it had possession of the imperial regalia—the mirror, sword, and necklace. The northern Court in Kyoto, the capital, was said to be occupied by traitorous pretenders, not anointed with the holy oil. In point of fact the northern Emperors had a better right under the rules of primogeniture to occupy the Throne, but since they lacked the talismans of divine power, they never felt sure of themselves and were to live down their usurpation for centuries to come. Hirohito himself was to be sorely vexed in the 1930's by detractors who pointed out that he came of the northern dynasty.

To substantiate their claims during the schism, the southern Emperors revived Shintoism at Court and cleansed it of many of its accumulated Buddhist trappings. Thereafter—down to Hiro-

[10] Those same August days in which, 664 years later in 1945, many devout Japanese waited expectantly and accusingly at their family shrines, asking when the kamikaze would blow again.

[11] Coincidentally there were two popes during the same period in Europe, one in Rome and the other in Avignon.

hito's time—it became a rule of thumb that Emperors who emphasized Shinto and ancestor worship in their priestly functions were restorationists who wished to exercise power in their own right, and that Emperors who preached ethics and devoutly chanted Buddhist sutra were ceremonialists, satisfied with being figureheads.

In 1392 the princes of the southern dynasty accepted a handsome financial settlement and returned to Kyoto as a branch house of the imperial family. Their capitulation, however, brought no lasting peace. From 1467 to 1600 civil war raged incessantly. Clans and clan lords struggled like Scottish sheep thieves to extend or hold their fiefs. The hereditary warrior caste of the samurai, who were descended from Emperor Jimmu and his pirate lieutenants and who were allowed, therefore, to bear arms, wear mail, and ride horses, oppressed the peasants sorely. They observed a Spartan knightly ethic which prevented them from touching money and therefore from selling their services. But their extreme loyalty advantaged only their lords. Since it was taboo for them to touch gold or silver—in the nineteenth century Japanese Army officers still accepted their pay on an outstretched fan and passed it to their adjutants—the samurai were entitled to live off the land and expect free hospitality wherever they lodged. They had the right to kill any serf or farmer without having to answer for their crime except to the samurai or clan lord who protected that commoner. They also had the right to kill one another in duels, subject only to the laws of vendetta between samurai families.

When the entire family of a clan lord was exterminated in one of the wars, his fighting retainers became masterless samurai or *ronin*—literally, wave men—who rode the billows of fortune and sold their services wherever they could. The same term, wave men, had been used to describe masterless warriors in Anglo-Saxon England eight hundred years earlier. In England wave men became mercenary brigands and pirates of the salt sea. So they also did in Japan. In the early sixteenth century Japanese wave men terrorized the coast of China and plied the seas as far away as Bangkok Bight and Manila Bay. By 1550 the kings of Burma, Siam, and Cambodia all employed stalwart Japanese cutthroats for their personal bodyguards.

Although the common folk suffered by the interminable marching of armies in Japan, it was the warriors who died, the clan lords who were bankrupted and dispossessed. Such statistics as there are show that the nation as a whole prospered in the civil war. The population rose from an estimated 15 to 25 million, making Japan almost twice as populous as France at the same time, almost four times as populous as Spain, and fully five times as populous as England. The artisan and merchant class, though considered materialists, beneath contempt by the samurai, had grown fat on war profits. Japanese lacquer and steel ware were the best in the world. Japanese traders did a thriving business in them as far away as Batavia and Calcutta. Japan was the leading exporter of arms in the Far East. Her sword blades were known and envied by Moorish craftsmen in Toledo.

The Kyoto region was hardest hit by the civil war because most of the great lords maintained their own private troops in the capital. Each lord hoped to gain imperial sanction for a campaign of extermination against his neighbors. The imperial family, however, could offer little leadership because it remained riven between princes of restorationist tendencies and princes who preferred to wield only ceremonial and religious power. The family arguments were at best academic because in that evil era the Emperors could not be sure of commanding square meals for their noble retainers much less the square miles of their domain. For years at a time they received no allowance from the office of shogun, and the country around Kyoto was so unsettled that they had difficulty collecting rents from their few crown parks and forests. Many of the lesser Court nobles, who were not closely related to the Emperor of the moment or to his Fujiwara minister of state, had to return to their home fiefs to be sure of a decent living.

Emperor Go-Tsuchi-Mikado, in 1500, lay unburied for forty-four days while the Court was shaming the shogun into putting up enough money for the traditional obsequies. His successor, Go-Kashiwabara, claimed to be so poor that, for financial reasons, he postponed his official coronation for twenty-two years. The next Emperor, Go-Nara, who reigned from 1526 to 1557, made a pitiful show of penury by having samples of his calligraphy peddled on the Kyoto streets. By such protestations he raised enough money from loyalists to build a fine new palace and bring back from the provinces many of his poverty-stricken courtiers.

BARBARIAN

It was at this juncture, when imperial fortunes had reached their lowest ebb, that the first Europeans came to Japan. They were not accustomed to associating poverty with power—not even with spiritual power. They therefore gained and reported a poor first impression of the Throne—one that was not corrected later because the Emperors soon came to fear Christians and made all knowledge of themselves increasingly inaccessible to outsiders. To most Japanese, foreigners were not human beings from another land but creatures in human form who might as well have come from another planet. They were called *ebisu* which meant, in the original murderous, insular Greek sense of the word, barbarian. By the priestly rulers in Kyoto, they were regarded as unclean vermin who would pollute the sacred soil and anger the spirits interred in it.

The existence of human creatures across the seas, more distant than the Koreans or the Chinese, had been realized in Japan since the sixth century and reported at first hand by pirates since the twelfth century. For at least a century before 1521, when circumnavigator Magellan laid claim to the Philippines for Spain, Japanese seafarers had been serving and colonizing in the Sulu sultanate of Mindanao in the southern Philippines. After 1510 Japanese adventurers were rubbing shoulders with Portuguese at Goa on the west coast of India. In 1529 Japanese buccaneers sent home some Indians to be inspected and interrogated by the Court officials in Kyoto. Pirate news of the world was regularly sent to Prince Shimazu of the Satsuma clan in southern Kyushu—the descendant of the hero of the Mongol repulse of 1274—and he relayed it, for analysis, to the shogun and Emperor in Kyoto.

In 1542 the first Portuguese ships began to call at ports in Kyushu, the southern island. Japanese officialdom, which had long expected their coming, arranged for them to be treated hospitably and given no offense. For six years intercourse with the West was sporadic, friendly, and safe. Then, in 1549, the first Christian missionaries arrived in Nagasaki. They were led by the illustrious Jesuit, Francis Xavier, later to be declared a saint. The authorities followed Saint Francis's movements closely. By full-time application he quickly acquired a working knowledge of the Japanese language, which he described, because of its difficulty, as "a contrivance of a conciliabulum of devils."

After two years of study, he extracted the taboo intelligence that there was an Emperor in Japan above the shogun. He made a painful journey to Kyoto, mostly on foot, and asked for an audience with Emperor Go-Nara. He was told that his request could not be referred through channels because the shogun was out of town and that, in any case, the Emperor—the one who sold his penmanship—was living in retreat. The streets of Kyoto were so full of dueling samurai that Saint Francis saw no hope for a useful mission there, and after a few days, set out to return to southern Japan. He never did see the Emperor and referred to him in letters as a powerless spiritual leader "called Emperor" who maintained his establishment in Kyoto. No other Westerner saw the Emperor for more than three hundred years thereafter and his very existence was forgotten in the West.

The carefully watched Europeans brought to war-torn Japan two powerful pacifiers: fear of invasion and knowledge of firearms. When three Portuguese adventurers arrived on a Chinese cargo ship in 1543 at Tanega, an island off the southern tip of Kyushu, the lord of the island promptly hired them to teach him the use of their weapon, the gun. After a month of lessons, he was so impressed that he bought the two matchlocks they had with them for the staggering sum of 2,000 taels—approximately the wages that a Japanese working man could expect to earn in thirty years, or roughly $180,000 by modern American standards.[12] The lord gave the guns to his master swordsmith to copy. The latter, having trouble with the spring in the breech, gave his daughter to the captain of the next Portuguese vessel that called

12 Only about $65,000 by modern Japanese standards, but the Japanese working man's salary is far lower today in relation to the world at large than it was in 1545.

in Tanega a few months later and received lessons in return from the ship's gunsmith.

Once the knack of gunmaking was learned, it spread quickly. The Japanese craftsmen, who already made the best sword steel in the world, were soon able to widen the bore and breech of the matchlock so that it would carry farther and kill more certainly. To quantity buyers, they suggested use of a serial firing technique. They packaged their wares in handsome waterproof lacquer boxes that protected them from powder's greatest enemy, the rain. In Europe at that time firearms were still special equipment, used to supplement the standard tools of war. In Japan they were so swiftly improved and employed that some military historians say the first modern infantry and infantry tactics were developed there. Within a decade every Japanese clan lord's armorer was making guns and cannon, and the samurai wars of the previous two centuries were to end in a clap of gunpowder.

THE GREAT MUSKETEER

One of the first to whose ears the crackle of musket fire sounded musically was a fifteen-year-old boy who had been prematurely elevated to the leadership of his sub-clan by the death of his father. In 1535, when the palace had been half destroyed by one of Kyoto's periodic fires, the father had contributed handsomely to a palace repair subscription. For this reason the son, at an early age, was blessed with Court favor and information. His fief was only a small one in the province of Owari, between Kyoto and Tokyo, but it included the port of Nagoya which housed the shrine of Atsuta, containing the sacred sword of Japan, the third item in the imperial regalia.

Oda Nobunaga, as the boy was called, came of both imperial and Fujiwara forebears. He had been a wild youth and had spent all his time with his father's soldiers instead of his books. When his father died, leaving the Oda castle to him, his tutor committed suicide and bequeathed to him a note advising him to mend his ways. Young Oda had listened to the boastful stories of foot soldiers who had wielded the earliest matchlocks in battle, and his first act on succeeding his father was to put in an order for no less than five hundred of the new weapons to the gunsmith on Tanega. This was in 1549 when the Tanega gunsmith had been in business for less than six years.

Young Oda turned out to be a military genius. Other lords had gunbearing foot soldiers but only Oda seemed able to employ them successfully. By 1559, when he was twenty-five, he had taken over his entire home province of Owari. In 1562, when he was twenty-eight, Emperor Ogimachi sent him a secret message bidding him come and rid Kyoto of its brawling samurai. Not until 1568, when Oda had defeated all the major clan lords between Tokyo and Kyoto, was he able to comply. Then, however, he entered the capital with perfectly disciplined troops, deposed the shogun, put a puppet shogun in his place, and began to build Emperor Ogimachi a magnificent new palace. It became a familiar sight for the workmen to see Oda walking proudly at the Emperor's side, giving advice on the placement of a shrub, rock, or moon-pool. A disarmingly vain man, he wore a cloak made of Chinese tiger skins and preened a twisted, upturned hairline mustache.

With the Emperor's sanction, Oda set out to destroy Japan's feuding barons and unify the country. He coolly ordered entire families of noblemen to commit suicide. Politically-minded Buddhist priests, whom he abhorred, he implacably roasted on spits. He razed all the armed monasteries of Kyoto and Osaka except one sacred mountain out in the country. That one he spared, after laying seige to it, because he received a request to do so from the Emperor.

With Christians, however, he remained lenient, and lived to see 15,000 converts and 200 churches in the Kyoto area. The pure logic and pure living of the Portuguese Jesuits fitted his conception of the holy man, and the Jesuitical view of killing as God's business, not a sport, tallied exactly with his own feelings. He found the Christian teaching as straight and practical as a bullet. It fired the hearts of some of his most Spartan warriors. They went into battle with Christian crosses and emblems hanging at their necks, and Oda found them more dependably fanatic at their posts than the best Shintoists.

In 1575, at the age of forty-one, Oda met the lords of the north coast in the biggest battle of his career. By this time he commanded an army of over 100,000 men, including many cannon and 10,000 matchlocks. His opponents had more men, far more samurai on horseback, and almost as many guns. But Oda had been perfecting the tactical use of firearms for twenty-six years. He picked out his 3,000 most disciplined musketeers—all men of low caste—and placed them in three ranks behind a zigzag palisade in the center of battle where he expected to meet the most heroic cavalry charges. He had trained the men to fire successively in three cadres of a thousand each, one pulling their triggers while the next was lighting their tinder and the third was stuffing powder and shot down their muzzles. It had been doctrine previously that a cavalry charge could always break a cluster of missile launchers. But at the battle of Narashino, Oda's three ranks of plebeian musketeers knelt and aimed and fired so rapidly, one after another, that no samurai on horseback ever came in sword's length of them. Almost 16,000 riders, the flower of northern chivalry, died on the field in front of the palisades. There was to be no battle to compare with it in Europe for almost a hundred years.

In 1582, seven years after the battle of Narashino, Oda was forty-eight and had reached the zenith of his power. He began to move his men south to conquer the southern island of Kyushu, the kingdom of the sun goddess. On his last night in Kyoto one of his most trusted generals, for unknown motives, with unknown instigation, assassinated him. The general was hunted down a few days later and died without betraying his patrons. To the mind of someone in a position of power, Oda's pride and cruelty had grown excessive. He had served his purpose. During his meteoric career the population of Kyoto, the capital, had climbed back from a low of 20,000 in 1550 to almost 500,000.

JAPAN'S NAPOLEON

Oda's place was immediately taken by the most talented of his staff chiefs, Hideyoshi. Unlike Oda or the shoguns before him, Hideyoshi was a commoner, the son of a peasant foot soldier. He had risen in Oda's army by his ability, in many campaigns, to win battles. He had a genius for engineering and had found ways to sap or flood the most impregnable strongholds. Like Oda, he gave the Emperor reverent allegiance. His administration of sixteen years, from 1582 to 1598, was to be the one period of Japanese history up to 1945 in which the real rule of the nation would be delegated to a man outside the wide pool of imperial blood.[13]

Hideyoshi completed the unification of Japan. He forced all the clan lords to come to Kyoto and renew their vows of allegiance to the Throne. He took hostages from families of dubious loyalty and held them in the capital as privileged guests. He remapped the fiefs of Japan for tax purposes and in the process gerrymandered them to break up old rebellious alliances. In a totally fraudulent gush of religious emotion, he requisitioned most of the non-government sword steel in Japan to build the largest statue of Buddha in the world. Finally, to provide employment for idle sword hands, he resolved on a course of overseas conquest. He spoke grandly of seizing Korea, the Philippines, Malaya, Siam, Burma, and India. He decided to begin modestly with Korea.

Transported to Europe, Hideyoshi's hordes of well-trained, well-equipped fighting men would have been more than a match for any army in Christendom. In crossing to Korea, however, he was challenging China, the wealthiest and most populous nation in the world at that time. The kingdom of Korea was a tributary of China, and Hideyoshi knew that, if he attacked it, the Chinese would not stand idly by. In 1591, therefore, he went straight to the point and demanded that the Korean king give Japanese troops uncontested lines of march to the Chinese border so that he could move directly on Peking. The king of Korea decided that 150 million Chinese were a more lasting menace than 25 million Japanese and refused Hideyoshi's proposal.

In the spring of 1592, after elaborate preparations, Hideyoshi dispatched an expeditionary force of 205,000 men to Pusan, the lost Japanese fief of Karak. Most of the Japanese force landed without mishap but Hideyoshi, being a dry-land general, had overlooked the importance of sea power and had relied overmuch on

---

[13] Years later many Japanese were to say that Hirohito could abide General MacArthur because he saw in him another Hideyoshi, another military genius from outside the family circle, to whom revolutionary changes could be entrusted without commitment. The comparison was to be fortified by the similarity in the experiences of Hideyoshi and of MacArthur in Korea.

Japanese buccaneers and traders to keep open his supply lines. The Japanese pirate craft were basically coastal vessels designed for conditions in the calm Inland Sea between Kyushu and Honshu. The Koreans, by comparison, had large ships, armed with cannon, and a brilliant admiral, named Yi, who made driftwood out of Japanese supply convoys.

Despite severed lines of communication, the Japanese army, once it was ashore in Korea, advanced from Pusan to the Yalu River in less than six months. Then, as anticipated, China launched a massive counterattack. At the height of her effort, she was to put more than a million troops in the field, the equivalent of at least four million in the more tightly populated world of today. Letters sent home to estate managers by samurai who had previously scorned the use of firearms are notable because they sound one refrain: "Send us more guns." Japanese garrisons, outnumbered five to one, no longer cared for sport or honor but only for efficient killing.

After a three-year stalemate, Hideyoshi, in 1594, unleashed a second expeditionary force on Korea which again swept the southern half of the peninsula. Having suffered almost half a million casualties, China put into the field fully twice as many reinforcements. In danger of losing control of the sea, the canny Korean Admiral Yi, two hundred fifty years before the *Monitor* and *Merrimac*, devised the world's first ironclad. Designed in elegant Oriental baroque to look like a fierce turtle, it glided majestically under oar power through the wooden fleets of the Japanese—and cannonaded and rammed with impunity. Once again Hideyoshi's soldiers found their supply lines severed and their backs to the sea. Garrisons of Japanese Christians and Buddhists vied with each other to see which could hold out the longest. The Chinese suffered terrible losses and once again conceded a draw.

In 1598, as negotiations toward a peace were resumed, Hideyoshi died. In his last hours he tried to make an old comrade in arms, Tokugawa Ieyasu, the guardian and regent for his five-year-old son. Tokugawa promised to see that Hideyoshi's child grew up but refused to play regent. Instead he agreed to rule the realm as one of a council of five of Hideyoshi's generals. In anticipation of a power struggle at home, the five generals accepted an immediate and barely face-saving peace treaty with China and withdrew their armies from Korea. The war was over. For sheer carnage it had surpassed anything that Europe would see until the campaigns of Napoleon more than two hundred years later.

TOKUGAWA TYRANTS

Tokugawa Ieyasu was an icy, unlovable man with the heavy face and bloodshot eyes of a bulldog, but he had a gift for administration, a prodigious patience, and, unlike Hideyoshi, royal blood flowing in his veins. Fourteen months after Hideyoshi's death, Tokugawa fought a decisive battle with his rival generals on a plain sixty miles west of Kyoto. Through the machinations of Fujiwara allies at Court, several of his enemies changed sides at the last minute, enabling him to win an easy victory. He went on to make himself and his heirs the new shoguns of Japan.

He spared the lives of his enemies, judiciously sliced provinces from their fiefs, and gave the parings to his own henchmen. He repaired the road and established new stage houses and garrisons along the great south coast trade route between Kyoto and Tokyo. He brought order to Japan's chaotic finances by creating a dependable currency of freshly minted gold coins. He provided employment for masterless samurai in a new national police network. In two years he had imposed peace on the countryside and made Japan into a beneficently efficient police state. A British merchant who ran a trading post in Nagasaki compared Tokugawa's autocracy with that of James I in England and concluded that Japan had "the greatest and most puissant tyranny that the world has ever known."

In 1603 Tokugawa Ieyasu met with young Emperor Go-Yozei and conferred on him a decent share of the tax take. It was Tokugawa's aim to put the Emperor in a gilded cage where he would live well, would be treated with respectful reverence, and would avoid embroiling himself in intrigues against Tokugawa's heirs. Except in military theory, he could no more have deposed the Emperor and seized the Throne for himself than the king of France could have declared himself Pope. Instead, Tokugawa pressed Emperor Go-Yozei to accept a Tokugawa granddaughter as a daughter-in-law.

Emperor Go-Yozei contended that such a base alliance would be impossible for a member of the imperial family unless Tokugawa could find some way to resume the offensive and drive the twin threats of white supremacy and Christianity from Japan's door. Tokugawa did not feel strong enough domestically to lead Japan in a foreign crusade and so Emperor Go-Yozei, in 1611, abdicated in protest. Then in 1614, after further negotiation, ex-Emperor Go-Yozei consented to the Tokugawa-imperial marriage, and Tokugawa Ieyasu, for his part, issued an edict ordering the deportation of foreign priests, the demolition of churches, and the renunciation of faith by all those Christians who seek "to change the government of the country and obtain possession of the land."

In making this concession to the xenophobia of the high-priestly Emperor, Tokugawa was influenced by the views of a practical Protestant layman who had no love for Portuguese Jesuits and Spanish friars. This was Will Adams, an Englishman from Kent, who had arrived in Japan in 1600 as a virtual castaway—the pilot of a Dutch vessel which had lost three quarters of her crew through storm, hunger, thirst, and beriberi. As Tokugawa's prisoner, Adams had built two European-style ships for the Japanese and had been elevated to the rank of samurai and given an estate. Though prohibited from leaving Japan, he regularly sent money home to his family in England and found his Japanese household much to his liking. "It is like unto a lordship in England," he wrote, "with 80 or 90 husbandmen that be as my slaves."

Adams eventually died in 1620 in the arms of his Japanese wife, but his spirit is still worshipped by Japanese Shinto pilgrims who visit the shrine built for him on the hill above his former estate. During his lifetime Adams enjoyed the right of informal access to Shogun Tokugawa and, as a Protestant, constantly warned him against the territorial ambitions of Spain and of her advance agents, "the Papists." As a result, Tokugawa tended to look upon all Spanish missionaries and most of the Portuguese Jesuits as fifth columnists bent on subversion.

Antagonistic as he was to the minions of Rome, Adams had no desire to see all Christian missionaries deported from Japan. Nor was Tokugawa so eager to please the Emperor that he wanted to stop the profitable flow of Western trade and knowledge which came in the wake of the missionaries. And so, on Adams's advice, Tokugawa encouraged Protestant merchants from Holland and England and used his edict against Christianity merely as an unenforced warning to the friars and Jesuits.

Tokugawa Ieyasu died in 1616—the same year as William Shakespeare. Behind him he left a dynastic system of administration centered in Tokyo, or Edo as it was then called, which would keep his heirs in office for 252 years. They would be called the "emperors" or "kings" of Japan in most foreign lands and only taboo-struck native sons would know that there were true Emperors above the shoguns. Tokugawa's thirty-seven-year-old son had been titular shogun for a decade and his fifteen-year-old grandson was already groomed to succeed his father.

In 1617 Emperor Go-Mizu-no-O succeeded to real power in the Kyoto Court. Go-Mizu-no-O was a vigorous, scholarly young man of twenty-two who would direct the highest affairs of state until his death as an octogenarian ex-Emperor sixty-three years later in 1680. At long last, in 1620, with great pomp and ceremony, Go-Mizu-no-O married the young shogun's sister. The shogun reciprocated by instituting a vigorous persecution of Christians. Hideyoshi, in the last wrathful year before his death, 1597, had set the precedent by ordering an experiment in what he understood to be the Christian form of execution. He had had six Spanish friars from the Philippines and twenty of their Japanese converts nailed to crosses and exhibited while they died. Now, between 1620 and 1635, some 6,000 Christians were crucified, many of them upside down like Saint Peter.

The menace which the Emperor saw in the Christians was, from his point of view, a real one. In seventy years, by 1620, the new religion had captured the minds of one out of every fifty Japanese.[14] The majority of the converts were peasants and many of them were foot soldiers who knew how to use guns. They had learned in the wars how to shoot down their betters at a distance, and they now had the leadership of half a dozen Christian clan

[14] In 1970 less than one out of every 300 Japanese professes Christianity.

lords. They set little store by the society of ghosts and spirits which surrounded other Japanese. They were ready to die for inhuman abstractions which they said were above the Emperor.

After the Tokugawa take-over in 1600, many Christians who had fought on the losing side refused to commit suicide, as Tokugawa magnanimously suggested, and insisted, instead, on being ignominiously beheaded in public execution. The defiant honesty of these martyrs appealed to all Japanese, and the shogun found eradication of Christianity a politically difficult duty. After promising the Emperor in 1620 to perform it, the young shogun continued to move cautiously. He spent thousands on anti-Christian propaganda and pennies on headsmen and police work. He sought to get at the root of the evil by rigorously curtailing and supervising foreign trade. He kept new foreign priests from being smuggled into the country, and those old missionaries, whom he allowed to remain under the protection of powerful native converts, he rendered ineffective by constant police harassment. Nevertheless, by the clandestine efforts of Japanese priests, the runaway, subversive creed continued to spread.

In addition to Christians, there were anti-Tokugawa partisans aplenty left over from the wars. The system of police and informers designed by Tokugawa Ieyasu functioned smoothly, but more than enough discontent simmered beneath the surface of his totalitarian state for another civil war. To quash it, the Tokugawas needed the support, however token, of the imperial family. And the Emperor and his kin continued to sulk because the Tokugawas had not yet reinstated them at the top of an unthreatened, unchristian nation of peaceful reverence. To gain imperial sanction for a realistic gradual policy of pacification, the shogun at first tried to bend the Emperor by force. An officer of the shogun's government was stationed in Kyoto and the Emperor was not supposed to leave the palace without his consent.

Emperor Go-Mizu-no-O, despite his Tokugawa wife, rebelled. In 1629, after many protests, he abdicated and put a seven-year-old girl on the Throne, the first Empress since 769. It was a sign to the nation that the Tokugawas were infringing on the imperial power and were fit to manage no one but little girls. Shogun Tokugawa Iemitsu decided to call the imperial bluff, graciously accepted the girl puppet, and settled a meager income of a million pounds of rice a year on the abdicating Go-Mizu-no-O. The latter resolved to make it do and retired to a temple to plot. For the next five years the Tokugawas led the perilous lives of tyrants.

SECLUSION

In 1634 Shogun Tokugawa Iemitsu came from Tokyo to Kyoto to parley. He came in peace, but with a tremendous show of pomp and power. No less than 307,000 retainers escorted him down the 300 miles of the great stage route, the East Sea Road, to Kyoto. Their officers overflowed the inns for miles around and their encampments filled the Kyoto plain up to the horizon. Never had the courtesans and jugglers from the city's pleasure district, the minstrels and sweetmeat makers and rollers of dice, done such business as they did around the nightly campfires. In the capital the shogun entertained the adolescent Empress, her father the retired Emperor, and all their courtiers at Nijo Castle, built by Oda Nobunaga.

During great feasting and the giving of magnificent gifts, Shogun Iemitsu and retired Emperor Go-Mizu-no-O withdrew from time to time for serious conversation in a back room. Go-Mizu-no-O called for *burei*, suspension of usual etiquette, and the two squatted as equals on straw mats across a low table from one another. The shogun had with him the globe on which Will Adams had formerly given lessons in geography to Ieyasu, the shogun's grandfather. After many hours of belly talk, of careful, noncommittal, exhaustive indirection, they had examined Japan's position in the world from every angle and reached a meeting of minds. It was to determine Japan's highest state policy for the next 233 years. Its specifics were unwritten and secret but its general tenor may be judged from its results.

On returning to Tokyo, the shogun adopted a course of stringent conservatism such as has never been matched in the history of any other nation. In 1635 he required all clan lords to live in Tokyo one year out of every two and to leave their wives and children there as hostages when they were absent. He made rebellion virtually impossible. The next year he ordered all merchants to trade only within Japan; he forbade Japanese dockyards to construct oceangoing vessels; he divested all Japanese living abroad of their citizenship and promised death to any of them who ever returned to the homeland; finally he proscribed all practice of the alien Christian religion on pain of death. Thus he found a substitute for Hideyoshi's policy of overseas expansion; thus he satisfied the imperial wish to keep Japan safe for Shintoism; thus he sealed Japan off from the rest of the world.

When the law against Christianity was enforced and half a million converts were ordered to renounce their faith, many Japanese built their own crosses and waited to be nailed to them. Thousands were imprisoned to think things over while hundreds were being crucified as examples. Jesuit fathers who lived in hiding had to warn their parishioners against the pride of suicidal martyrdom. Tens of thousands of parishioners nevertheless died. One Christian community of 37,000, which withdrew to the headland and castle of Shimabara in Kyushu, was butchered to the last man, woman, and child. Tens of thousands of other Christians went underground, and several congregations were to resurface in Kyushu and on the north coast of Honshu 235 years later.

In 1638 the shogun's police rounded up the last Portuguese priests and deported them. Thereafter one or two Catholic priests were smuggled in, hunted down, and executed, and all ships from Catholic countries were turned away at gunpoint. A Portuguese vessel, which called in 1640 to plead the cause of commerce, was sent home bearing as message to the outside world the corpses of sixty-one of its crewmen who had been decapitated. Toward the Protestant Dutch and English, Ieyasu's advisor Will Adams had given the authorities a somewhat more lenient attitude. As late as 1673 a British ship which called to trade was received civilly. The shogun was even inclined to let it discharge its cargo—or was until he learned that Charles II of England was married to Catherine of Braganza and that Catherine was Portuguese. After that all deals were off and the British East Indiaman was sent away with threats.

Only a small Dutch trading post was allowed to remain in Japan, and its staff had to pay a high price for their profits. To prove their religious neutrality they had had to provide the ships and cannon-fire which reduced the Christian fortress of Shimabara in 1638. After 1641 they were cooped up on the tiny island of De-shima in Nagasaki harbor. To comply strictly with the Emperor's feelings about the sanctity of Japanese soil, it was an artificial is-land only 300 paces long. Annually the Dutch traders had to walk to Tokyo, kiss the feet of the shogun, perform scientific tricks and buffoonery for him, and give him a written résumé of historical events in the world outside. Periodically they also had to perform a ritual trampling of the crucifix.

In 1642, the year Isaac Newton was born, the last Japanese priest had been crucified and Japan had closed like an oyster. She would not relax enough to be opened again for 211 years. She took the step deliberately after a debate which had lasted for 90 years. Hideyoshi's attempt to conquer a buffer zone to put be-tween Japan and the outside world had failed, and now Japan, in isolation, planned to improve her inner world and make it spiritually impregnable. At a time when she might still have run roughshod over Southeast Asia, it was a philosopher's decision, a decision for peace. The scholarly ex-Emperor Go-Mizu-no-O, who was largely responsible for making it, could hardly foresee that the Great Outside would undergo an industrial revolution while Japa-nese craftsmen were making better sword blades and fans. He could hardly guess that Japan, which went into seclusion as one of the two or three strongest nations on the globe, would emerge from it, centuries later, as a distinctly second-class power.

5

THE COMING OF PERRY

(1642–1900)

THE EMPTY YEARS

In closing Japan, the Emperor and shogun needed one another and shared a common aim: to keep the Japanese social hierarchy safe and reverent for their heirs. They believed that by study and contemplation Japan could rediscover the special quality that made her "the country of the gods." Under the joint sponsorship of the Tokugawas and the Imperial Court, the scholars of Japan from 1657 to 1715 conducted an exhaustive research into the fountainheads of Japanese culture and into all things peculiarly Japanese such as gardens of raked pebbles, floors of straw matting, tea ceremonies, and prayer shelves of planed, unvarnished wood. The result of these efforts was a twenty-six-volume opus entitled *Dai Nihonshi, The Great History of Japan.* The word for Japan used in the title was the Shinto one, *Nihon* or *Nippon*, which meant sun-begot land. Throughout the pages of the book the authors stressed the divine descent of the Emperors from the sun goddess and the unique verity of the ancient spirit worship, Shinto, meaning the way of the ghosts. The authors condemned as usurpers all those shoguns who had exceeded their imperial mandate and tyrannized the Throne.

Lest the hoi polloi misunderstand such potentially inflammatory ideas, the *Great History*, on its completion, was kept out of print and circulated only in manuscript form among the aristo-

cratic few. To imperial princes, fluttering their wings against the
bars of their gilded cage, the book represented a Tokugawa
promise of ultimate freedom. To Tokugawas it represented a commitment to force Japan into a perfect Japanese mold. To disgruntled warrior lords, who worried about the creeping military
weakness of Japan, the book offered a prescription: arm again
when the Emperors have been restored to full direct power.

Under the Tokugawas, the day-to-day government of Japan was
delegated to a senate of wizened elders who were no more than
half privy to the long-range national policy. All of them came of
prestigious pedigrees, representing the best interests of vast
tracts of Japanese soil. Too old for personal ambition, they were
allowed in their wisdom to draft the routine laws which governed
the state and to nominate most of its officers. The headstrong
young man who happened to be shogun at any one time sometimes overruled their appointments. The headstrong young man
who happened to be Emperor sometimes tabled their recommendations. Except for appointments, they asked for authority from
the shogun only in high policy decisions and from the Emperor
only in momentous policy decisions affecting the fate of the
nation.

Between 1638 and 1853, the Tokugawa wise men—taken like a
page from Plato's *Republic*—managed Japan with sterile autocratic
efficiency. The deep freeze into which they put the energetic
Japanese people may be measured on the tablets of life in birth
and death statistics. In over two hundred years the population increased only from 26 million to 33 million. The farmers were so
well taxed and policed that they exposed and abandoned all infants who could not be fitted into the national budget. At the
same time the authority of the clan lords dwindled, and in most
regions the villages developed a democratic independence, a
town-meeting form of self-government, which enabled them to
cope with the shogun's tax collectors and policemen.

For two centuries little happened. The arts became more
specialized and minor. The national etiquette grew more punctilious. Everything that had been peculiarly Japanese became more
so, and Japan was unified in its practice. The arts of peace were
cultivated so sedulously that the arts of war were relegated to the

status of antiquarian sports. After 1640 the shogun's government gradually licensed all gunsmiths and reduced the national annual output of firearms from about 5,000 to less than 200. Finally the guns that were being made were mostly art objects that went unfired into the collections of wealthy samurai. The shogun's coastal defense forces kept their shore batteries well oiled and polished but fired them only once every seven years. Then, since the cannon were all pre-1640 antiques and apt to burst, the gunners handled them gingerly, touching them off with matches on the ends of long bamboo poles.

KNOCKS ON THE DOOR

Many young noblemen who were privileged to read the Dutch newsbriefs from the trading post on the tiny artificial island of Deshima complained about the nation's growing backwardness and military weakness. They received reports on the spread of English colonies in the New World, of the American Revolution, and of the rapid expansion of the United States. They noted the appearance of Yankee vessels in the China Sea during the 1780's. Merchants from China reported the disintegration of Chinese influence in Siam and the Indies. Someday, muttered the young samurai, Japan would have to fight, and when she did, it might be too late.

The great center of samurai unrest was old southwestern Japan, the land of the sun goddess. There the clans had paid dearly for their opposition to Tokugawa rule in 1600. Two clans in particular had forfeited much land to the Tokugawas without losing any of their hereditary samurai families. Satsuma in Kyushu, with 27,000 hereditary warrior lords, and Choshu, in southwestern Honshu, with 11,000, had denser populations of unemployed swordsmen than any other region in Japan. Both clans had invested heavily in Hideyoshi's Korean campaigns and had fought strenuously against the Tokugawa policy of replacing external aggression with internal consolidation. Both clans were to play major political roles in the unleashed Japan of 1853–1945.

The Satsuma clan was governed by the branch of the imperial family named Shimazu or Island Port. Satsuma was the seagoing principality of Japan, in southern Kyushu. It had borne the brunt

of the Mongol invasion in 1274. It had provided most of the ships
for Hideyoshi's Korean invasion fleet in 1592. It had conquered
Okinawa and the Ryukyus for the nation in 1609. It would supply more than its share of officers to the Japanese Navy in 1941.
During the 1930's it would lead the fight for a Strike South against
the colonies of the West in southeast Asia.

Its fellow clan, Choshu, on the main island of Honshu, was governed by another ancient branch of the imperial family, the Mori,
whose name means Those Who Took Advantage of the Hairy
Ones. It was a land-based power which prided itself on its provin-
cialism and its big-handed, big-hearted family form of self-
government. It despised money, cherished land, idolized the
dynamic sons of the land, and held to a creed of revolutionary
puritan conservatism that was strictly martial. Choshu had provided a disproportionate share of the foot soldiers who had fought
with Hideyoshi in Korea and against the Tokugawas in 1600. From
1868 to 1924 its brightest spirits would control the Japanese Army
and threaten to control the Japanese state. In the 1930's its
partisans would lead the losing political fight for a Strike-North
policy against Russia.

Being ardent loyalists, the Choshu and Satsuma swordsmen
would have risen in rebellion, at any time, if they had received
a word of encouragement from Kyoto. Their readiness to defy
death enabled the Emperors to keep Tokugawa pride in bounds
during the first century of seclusion. As Western ships and cannon
became more formidable, however, Tokugawa government became
more rigid, astringent, and unrealistic. The pampered Kyoto
Court grew more effeminately sure of itself. In 1779 the main line
of the imperial family ended without male issue and a collateral
house of more vigorous cousins, the Kanins, took its place. The
Kanins instituted a revival of Shinto and a more careful supervision of Tokugawa government.

About 1820 the ex-Emperor Kokaku established a school for
noblemen between the ages of fifteen and forty which was to become the famous *Gaku-shu-in* or Peers' School. At the Peers'
School Hirohito would learn his ABC's; at the Peers' School his
son Akihito would study Western ways under Elizabeth Gray
Vining, the gracious Quaker tutor recommended for him by Gen-

eral MacArthur. When founded, the school was meant to prepare young courtiers, who already knew how to turn a pretty verse or finger a lute, for the realities of Japanese history and government. Its noble graduates were to take over policy making in the troubled years ahead.

Year after year foreign ships poked their bowsprits vainly into Japanese harbors. Some were mere merchantmen, off course and looking for a way station in a long voyage. Many were official government vessels commissioned to open trade with Japan and put an end to her fear of foreign contamination. Russian ships began calling at Japanese fishing villages in 1739. The Tokugawa government responded by refurbishing the shore batteries along Japan's northern coasts. The first U.S. vessel came to demand trade in 1791. The shogun's government had the cannon polished on Japan's southern coasts. Illicit commerce with the West began to thrive. In 1808 the crew of a British merchantman, visiting the brothels of Nagasaki, started a brawl and called attention to the fact that it had been allowed ashore without authorization. On orders from the shogun, the mayor of Nagasaki committed suicide.

In 1837 the American brig *Morrison* approached the Kyushu coast on a carefully planned mission. In token of peaceful intent her guns had been removed. Her hold bulged with presents and trading samples of the best New England textiles. On her deck stood seven Japanese fisherman-castaways ready to be repatriated. The shogun's government had received advance warning of her mission, and the antiquated Japanese shore batteries were actually fired to drive her off before she could discharge her passengers or cargo.

The *Morrison*'s bootless voyage came at a time of growing internal crisis. The progressives of the nation had reached the end of their patience and the traditionalists on the shogun's council faced problems which they could not solve. Chinese and Dutch boats had brought a virulent form of smallpox into the country over the previous centuries and by now its ravages were endemic. Poor harvests, for several unusual years, had reduced the peasantry to starvation, stealing, and even murder. The perfect Tokugawa despotism, after two hundred years of trial, found itself bankrupt. There was a rebellion in Osaka which had to be crushed ruthlessly, and Shogun Tokugawa Ienari resigned in favor of Shogun Tokugawa Ieyoshi. The new shogun tightened purse strings and cut administrative expenses to the last ragged edge of red tape. But the depression continued. Men had to be executed as public examples for espousing free trade and an opening of the country. The Tokugawas, in their debility and desperation, had promised that soon, very soon, would come the time of paradise and imperial restoration. Young men at Court were ready to take over the responsibility.

FEAR WITHIN

The crisis of 1838–1840 broke on the nation when the first graduates of the Peers' School were approaching their mature forties. It was apparent that the Tokugawas had been lying to save face and that the millennium was not around the corner. For the first time since retired Emperor Go-Mizu-no-O's compact with the shogun in 1634, imperial princes began to plot with samurai and threaten civil war unless the Tokugawas could make good on their pledge. All the most important Buddhist temples and Shinto shrines in Kyoto were run by princely priests who were first or second cousins of the Emperor. Each temple had branches in the provinces and through these the Emperor sent secret commissions to several of the most loyal clan lords, instructing them to put pressure on the shogun and make him strengthen shore defenses. In particular the Court wooed the shogun's cousin, Lord Tokugawa Nariaki of Mito.

The loyalist Lord of Mito responded by melting down all the temple bells in his fief as cannon metal. Lord Shimazu of Satsuma in the southern island of Kyushu did likewise and soon had the most up-to-date cannon factory in Japan. The officials of the shogun became alarmed that the unauthorized preparations for war might be turned against the central government. The Lords of Satsuma and Mito were ordered to stop casting cannon, and the Tokugawa police moved in against the center of the conspiracy, the defenseless Kyoto Court. They clapped the Emperor's son-in-law, Prince Akira, into house arrest at his temple and trumped up a charge against Prince Kuniye, Akira's father, forcing him to "close his doors in disgrace."

Prince Kuniye was not a person to be trifled with in this fashion. Majestically pious, corpulent, and concupiscent, he had innumerable connections and immense influence. Neither Buddhism nor Shinto attached any stigma to bawdy, burly, worldly priests, and Priest Kuniye was as much all man as he was all aristocrat. Harlots and harlequins, hangmen and holy men jumped at his nod as quickly as the most haughty courtiers. Kuniye headed the largest of the four "imperial houses" which were entitled to provide heirs to the Throne. For generations the other houses had taxed their genes to raise one adult male per generation. At least one of their princes perished whenever the Court caught a sniffle.

Prince Kuniye's house of Fushimi, by contrast, had had at least three healthy sons in every generation for centuries. Kuniye personally had two brothers and five sons. By the time he was sixty-five he would have twelve living sons by as many mistresses. From his loins would spring the whole firmament of some fifty princelings who surrounded Hirohito in the 1930's. His son, Prince Kanin, would head the Army General Staff from 1931 to 1940. And of his grandsons, Prince Fushimi would run the Naval General Staff from 1932 to 1941; Prince Kuni would father Hirohito's wife, Empress Nagako; Prince Asaka would rape Nanking in 1937; Prince Higashikuni would hand over Japan to the Americans as prime minister in 1945; and Prince Nashimoto would be held hostage by MacArthur until the acceptance of the new Japanese Constitution in 1946.

Prince Kuniye needed no prescience to appreciate the future blackguard vigor of his family. It had always been thus. His house of Fushimi was the oldest of the collateral houses and had twigged from the main stem of the imperial family in 1372. Ever since then it had kept its place in the family and avoided demotion to commoner status by providing husbands for old-maid daughters of the Emperors. The vitality of its brood stallions matched that of the Fujiwara clan's brood mares. Fushimi princes were traditionally active men, privy to back-room policy and employed by the Throne as agents in intrigues. The very name, Fushimi, means Hidden from Sight.

The moment that Prince Kuniye and his son Prince Akira were rusticated by the Tokugawa police, two centuries of Emperor-shogun co-operation dissolved into bitter political warfare. Kuniye's uncles, brothers, and sons were all abbots at the head of the Japanese theocracy. By their preaching and purple robes they had the hearts of men and women whom the Tokugawa police could control only as bodies. From their temples they spread the insidious sermon that the Tokugawas had become disloyal subjects and impious tyrants. The Tokugawas squirmed under the attack and began to delegate their responsibilities more irresponsibly than ever. They passed about the office of shogun as if it were too hot to handle. In the next twenty years four different shoguns would occupy it and each would be a greater failure than the last.

When Japan's internal political atmosphere had become implosive as a vacuum, it happened to be the Americans, the latest intruders, who most vigorously pursued the application of external pressure. In 1844 the Yankee whaler *Manhattan* sought to win over the shogun by bringing to Tokyo a group of Japanese fishermen which it had picked up adrift in mid-Pacific. Captain Mercator Cooper was allowed to put ashore his hostages and then was turned aside by a letter from the shogun. "He thanks me for picking up their men," Cooper wrote, "and sends me word that I must not come again."

As soon as the *Manhattan* had departed, Tokugawa Nariaki of Mito resumed his manufacture of cannon in defiance of his cousin, the shogun. The shogun's army invaded Mito, put Nariaki under house arrest in his favorite temple, and had him turn over the administration of his fief to his seventeen-year-old son. Not a man to fritter away his time, Nariaki had the priests of the temple install a printing press in his apartments and began to set in type the dangerously imperial *Great History of Japan* which had circulated only in manuscript since its completion in 1715. With the help of shaven-pated assistants, the loyalist Lord of Mito was to finish setting the twenty-sixth volume in 1852, the last of his nine years of templed house arrest.

In 1846 U.S. Commodore James Biddle forced his way into Tokyo harbor with two men-of-war and demanded that the shogun

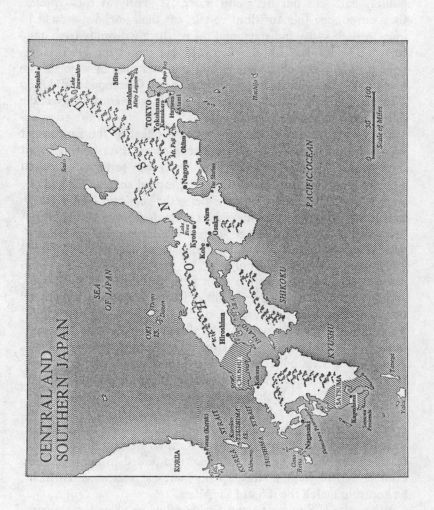

CENTRAL AND
SOUTHERN JAPAN

sign a treaty promising American castaways good treatment and consular representation. The shogun rejected the American note politely and sent out his guard boats. As gently as they could, they surrounded the American vessels, cut their anchors, attached lines to their sprits and stays, and towed them willy-nilly back out to sea. The Yankee tars set their sails but found the breeze too light to match the oar power of two hundred men in wide straw hats pulling for dear life in their war sampans. Commodore Biddle, who was a kindly man, accepted the rebuff with equanimity and sailed home for further instructions.

Only weeks before Biddle's intrusion, the first of the Emperors who had grown up under the influence of the Peers' School ascended the Throne. Emperor Komei, as he was to be called, was a powerful, robust, handsome, haughty youth of sixteen. He had as large and high-bridged a nose, as perfectly long and oval a face, as the first Emperor, Jimmu, eighteen hundred years earlier. Emboldened by a century of neoclassical scholarship, he was an ardent Shintoist who believed in the inherent war talents of his long tamed and dormant family.

He opened his reign with a stern note to the shogun in Tokyo asking for a full report on Japan's defenses, reminding him that they must be impregnable, advising him that the policy of excluding foreigners must be upheld, and demanding that the Throne, from now on, be consulted fully on every detail of foreign policy. The shogun responded with polite meaningless promises, and young Emperor Komei was only half satisfied. He communicated frequently and secretly with Prince Kuniye, under house arrest in Nara, with the Lord of Mito, Tokugawa Nariaki, in his temple prison north of Tokyo, and with Lord Shimazu of Satsuma who was still at liberty far to the south in Kyushu. Beyond the effective reach of the shogun's police, Shimazu continued to manufacture cannon, and he built several experimental war vessels with which he hoped to match the ships of the West.

When the U.S. Navy's sloop *Preble* called in 1849, the shogun tried to keep its visit a secret and swiftly handed over to it the members of U.S. whaling crews held in Japan. Some of them had been kept and interrogated at Christian House in Tokyo, an institution which had been maintained by the police since 1640 for the de-conversion of disciples of Western philosophy.

In the summer of 1851 a gifted young Japanese fisherman named Manjiro was lowered from the Baltimore clipper *Sarah Boyd* in a small boat off the coast of Okinawa. He was returning to Japan, bent on seeing his mother before she died. By a run of incredible luck, he alone of all Japanese knew the United States. Indeed Manjiro had lived there for seven years. In 1842 he had been a poor fisher lad of sixteen caught in a terrible storm on the banks in the Japan Sea. Driven ever northeast into a world of ice, he and his four companions had been wrecked finally on one of the Aleutians. For five months they had subsisted on rain water, fish, and seaweed, and then had been miraculously rescued by the *John Howland*, a whaler out of New Bedford. Taken home to Fairhaven, Massachusetts, by the captain, Manjiro had learned English, mathematics, and basic navigation. He had signed on for a four-year whaling cruise to the South Seas and had been elected second officer by his shipmates. With his share of earnings from the cruise, he had outfitted himself as a forty-niner, had worked his way around the Horn, and had promptly stumbled on a nugget as big as an egg in the goldfields outside San Francisco. Cashing in his winnings, he had traveled as an honored passenger on the *Sarah Boyd*, and now the boat in which he cast off from her was his own, purchased in the French-held Hawaiian port of Honolulu.

Manjiro rowed for the palm-girt coast of subtropical Okinawa with trepidation. One of the Tokugawa seclusion laws stipulated a punishment of death for any Japanese trying to return to Japan from the old Japanese settlements abroad. Manjiro relied on his tongue, his acquired wealth, and the value of his knowledge about the outside to get an exception made in his case. His shrewd judgment was rewarded. The police in Okinawa shipped him to Nagasaki, and there, after eighteen exhaustive interrogations, he performed the ritual trampling of the crucifix and was sent on to Tokyo. The shogun at once made him a government official, in charge of American intelligence. From December 1851 until July 1853, working with artists and writers, he recorded all that he had seen and heard in the lands of the barbarians. One product of his debriefing was a remarkably accurate drawing of Boston's Old North Church.

In early 1853 the head of the Dutch trading station on the artificial island of Deshima in Nagasaki harbor brought word to the shogun that an American naval officer named Perry was assembling a squadron on the coast of China in order to force his way into Japan. Manjiro urged that the American threat of force be used as a pretext for the Tokugawas to abandon the increasingly unpopular seclusion policy. The shogun's administrators listened to his advice carefully and kept him under close guard. Many of them agreed with him but felt that the Emperor must be persuaded to inaugurate any change of national policy from the summit of the state.

The issue was a delicate one, for though the Westerners were powerful and were much to be admired in some ways, they were also pernicious to the civilization of the Orient. As both Tokyo and Kyoto well knew, the British, in 1842–43, had fought and won a war on the China coast for their traders' right to sell opium to the Chinese masses. The Chinese emperor's prestige had been so damaged by the British victory that now a rebellion to end all rebellions was in progress in China. The Taiping insurgents were a minority group of half-Christianized peasants under the command of a self-styled Chinese messiah, Hung Hsiu-ch'uan. He had set out to create a utopia of pastoral, puritanical communism in Central China. But now he and his zealots were merely killing. Before the rebellion would be suppressed in 1864 it would take five to ten million lives. Statistically—Chinese statistics always beggar the world—it would rank as the greatest war in history until World War II.

Perry's fleet was detained in 1852, doing guard duty for American trading posts on the China coast during the upheaval sweeping the Chinese hinterland. In Japan, Tokugawa Nariaki, who had just sent his first prison-printed copies of the inflammatory *Great History of Japan* to the Emperor and the shogun, was abruptly released from nine years of house arrest. So was Prince Kuniye and two of his sons in Kyoto. The officers of the shogun hoped that Emperor Komei might be persuaded by a little kindness to open Japan to foreign trade and make it unnecessary to try to resist Perry by force. Emperor Komei, however, remained as xenophobic as ever. Out of spite for the Tokugawas, he promptly appointed one of Kuniye's released sons, Prince Asahiko, as his chief advisor.

Asahiko, who was to be the father of Hirohito's two murderous uncles, Asaka and Higashikuni, was twenty-nine at the time of his appointment, just six years older than Emperor Komei himself. Through his mother's kin—all Court ladies of charm and experience—Asahiko was a near relative of Komei, some say a half brother. He resembled Komei closely except that, if anything, he was even more handsome and haughty. Unlike Komei, who was obliged to remain ceremonially closeted in the palace, Asahiko could go where he pleased. Being abbot and chief priest of the prestigious Buddhist-Shinto monastery-shrine of Shoren-In, he had business which took him all over Kyoto.

THE BLACK SHIPS

Matthew Calbraith Perry was the younger brother of the late Oliver Hazard Perry renowned for his report—"We have met the enemy and they are ours"—made after the Battle of Lake Erie in 1813. Commodore Matthew Perry had supervised the design and construction of the U.S. Navy's first steam frigate, the *Mississippi*, and had used it as his flagship in the taking of Veracruz during the war with Mexico. He was known throughout the Navy as "Old Matt," a taciturn disciplinarian with a gift for getting things done. Portly and somewhat vain about his appearance, he dressed immaculately. His double chin always puffed out over as stiff a collar and as much gold braid as the occasion would permit. He believed that America's manifest destiny—now that California in 1848 had been ceded by Mexico—extended across the Pacific. He felt that his ships, the "black ships" as they would soon be known in Japan, were "carrying the gospel of God to the heathen."

Perry's fleet consisted of two warships under sail and two side-wheelers under steam. It was calculated that the "steamers" could win a tug of war, regardless of weather conditions, against any number of guard boats that could lay a tow line on them. Perry put in first at Okinawa, a tributary island of the seagoing Sat-

suma clan in Kyushu. There he made a great show of discipline
and firepower. His marines forced their way up the crushed-coral
main street of Naha, the capital city, into the local "palace" where
ruled a boy, reputed to be descended from the imperial family,
under the charge of a bureaucratic "regent." After giving gifts
and expressing some civilities, Perry and his men sailed on for
Tokyo harbor. Perry noted with pleasure that several of the fast
high-sided courier junks of the Satsuma clan's navy preceded him
out of Naha harbor bearing before him the evil tidings of his
coming.

On July 8, 1853, his lookouts sighted Mount Fuji rising above
the horizon and soon Japanese fishing boats were seen dropping
their sails in the offshore breeze, putting out their oars, and "fleeing like wild birds" for the distant coastline. At five o'clock that
afternoon, when the Yankee vessels cast anchor a mile off the
town of Uraga in Outer Tokyo Bay, temple bells were already
ringing a tocsin throughout central Japan. In Uraga old women
clapped their hands to summon the spirits at the shrines and
prayed for a divine tempest to come and disperse the Yankee
fleet.

In Tokyo, according to a contemporary Japanese account, "the
tramp of war-horses, the clatter of armed warriors, the noise of
carts, the parades of firemen, the incessant tolling of bells, the
shrieks of women, the cries of children dinning all the streets of
a city of more than a million souls made confusion worse confounded." Pawnbrokers and moneylenders reaped fortunes that
night supplying ready cash to well-born families who wished to
flee to the countryside. In his cozy private quarters behind the
big draughty four-square palace in Kyoto, 300 miles to the west,
Emperor Komei received news of the Americans' coming by carrier pigeon shortly after midnight.

As his ships lazed at anchor in the balmy evening breeze, Perry's
first contact with the Japanese was anything but friendly. Guard
boats flocked around the four Yankee vessels, and excited Japanese swarmed up lines and anchor chains to be dumped into the
water by shakes, prods, and bayonet jabs. In the gathering dusk,
a large official-looking junk, flying a black-and-white striped pen-
nant, approached Perry's flagship, the side-wheeler *Susquehanna*.

"I can speak Dutch," cried a voice in faltering English.

Perry's Dutch interpreter was summoned to the rail and shouted back that Perry was prepared to see no one except the highest authority in Uraga. If the delegation was prepared to deal with Perry's subordinates, it might come aboard. Uraga's assistant police chief climbed up to the deck accompanied by an interpreter who introduced him as the vice-governor of Uraga. They were led below to the chartroom adjoining Perry's personal cabin. While Perry listened and sometimes coached from the wings, it was explained to the Japanese that the commodore was the highest officer in the U.S. Navy and could be expected to see no Japanese of lesser rank. The Japanese thenceforward referred to him always as admiral, which he found slightly embarrassing.

Perry carried with him a note from President Millard Fillmore, penned by Daniel Webster and based on a first draft scribbled by Perry himself. It demanded the opening of Japan to normal civilized intercourse and was addressed to "the Emperor." By "Emperor" the American envoys quickly made it clear that they meant "shogun." The Japanese negotiators, who were all sub-sub-officials of the Tokugawa government in Tokyo, did not disabuse the Americans but introduced all those who were to deal with Perry thereafter as "princes." Privately the Japanese compared the American ignorance unfavorably with their own knowledge of the United States which had fattened on Dutch newsbriefs since 1745. But they kept the existence of the Emperor a secret and never did reveal what he meant to them as a religious figure. When the first American consul to Japan, Townsend Harris, finally did learn of the Emperor's existence a few years later, he described it, in his journal, as "a *tabu* concealed as carefully as the *tabu* of Polynesian witchcraft."

President Fillmore's letter to the "Emperor" pointed out:

Our steamships can go from California to Japan in eighteen days. . . . If your Imperial Majesty were so far to change the ancient laws as to allow a free trade between the two countries, it would be extremely beneficial to both. . . . It sometimes happens in stormy weather that one of our ships is wrecked on your Imperial Majesty's shores. In all such cases we ask and expect, that our unfortunate people should be treated with kindness, and that their property should be protected, till we can send a vessel and bring them away. We are very much in earnest in this. . . . We understand there is a great abundance of coal and provisions in the empire of Japan. . . . We wish that our steam-ships and other vessels should be allowed to stop in Japan and supply themselves with coal, provisions and water. They will pay for them, in money, or anything else your Imperial Majesty's subjects may prefer. . . . We are very desirous of this.

The letter was written on fine vellum, sealed with the Great Seal of the United States in gold, and housed in an elegant rosewood box. The Uraga assistant chief of police was allowed to look at it. He protested that such a letter could, by law, be presented only through the authorized channel of the Dutch in Nagasaki. The unseen presence of Perry in the next room boomed that such a letter from his own emperor must be presented directly, nation to nation, at the Japanese capital—or not at all. He would give it, here in Outer Tokyo Bay, to a potentiary of his own rank and he hoped that, while he waited to do so, the Japanese would disperse the swarm of guard-boat gnats that molested his fleet. Otherwise he might shoot them out of the water.

The assistant police chief asked for time to seek further instructions and withdrew, taking most of the guard boats with him. The few that remained rowed off immediately when the *Susquehanna* launched a cutter. Night fell. As the American sailors stood watch in their nests and beside their open gun ports, the shore flickered with bonfires and signal rockets. Knights wearing shoulder-length wigs of horsehair and demon-faced helmets were riding in from all over the province, accompanied by troops of mailed swordsmen. What seemed to be great forts overlooked the harbor. Their cannon were all antiques or dummies of wood; some of their parapets were painted stage sets. Perry, peering through his telescope earlier in the evening, had pronounced them "a false show." But his men did not all share his confidence. For many it was a restless night.

At daybreak the next morning squads of samurai could be seen in split skirts, jacket-length kimonos, over-cloaks, and top-knotted hairdos practicing their exercises on the shore. They rushed at one another with staves, fenced skillfully, and uttered loud nasal grunts. Periodically they broke off their sword drill, sauntered in single file along the beach, and then, as if by common consent, suddenly set to again with their quarterstaffs. As the day brightened, several sampans approached and anchored as close as they dared to the American fleet. The Yankee sailors were astonished to see that they were full of quick-sketch artists, recording every detail of the American planking and rigging. In a week all of their drawings were being studied by the shogun's military experts and some of them were being hawked on the news-hungry, fashion-loving streets of Tokyo.

At 7:00 A.M. two large junks backed oars off the *Susquehanna* and the Uraga chief of police, presented as the governor, boarded Perry's flagship. The dialogue of the night before was repeated and confirmed and the Japanese asked for four days to send to Tokyo for instructions. They meant, of course, to Kyoto. The shogun's castle in Tokyo was only 30 miles away, or two hours by stage rider. The Kyoto Palace, on the other hand, was nearly 300 miles away—a full twenty-four-hour ride even for the fleetest couriers and horses in the government's stables. And in the present crisis the shogun would wish to send an official to Kyoto, to explain matters fully, rather than an unofficial note by carrier pigeon.

Perry, who did not know about the Emperor in Kyoto, magnanimously offered the Japanese three days in which to give him an answer. While he waited for it, he had his longboats move ahead and map Tokyo's inner harbor. Throughout their survey they were shadowed by guard boats which might easily have annihilated them.

By the appointed day, Tuesday, July 12, 1853, the shogun had received only a brief noncommittal note from the Emperor, reminding him of his duty to preserve the sanctity of Japanese soil. That morning the Uraga police chief called in his barge on Perry. He offered politely to accept President Fillmore's letter in Uraga now, provided that Perry would submit it later in Nagasaki. This was the official port for dealings with foreigners, chosen because it was a full 600 miles from Tokyo. Perry brusquely rejected the proposal and was promised that a duly accredited representative of the "Emperor" would be on hand to accept the letter on shore on Thursday, July 14.

For the next two days Japanese artisans were busy hanging drapes which would screen the huts of Uraga—and the inadequacy of the shore defenses—from the evil eye of the intruder. Miles of figured curtains bearing subtle challenges in ideographs from the samurai of the various clans were stretched between bamboo poles along the beach. At the head of the central jetty a fine ceremonial shed was constructed behind a tidy quadrangular drill ground.

On Thursday morning when Uraga's assistant police chief called at the *Susquehanna* to escort Perry ashore, he was dressed in golden trousers, wide-sleeved brocade jacket, and bright lacquer clogs. According to the official log of Perry's voyage, he had "very much the appearance of an unusually brilliant knave of trumps." Perry had ready 300 picked men who were coached in putting on a show of pomp and circumstance for the American side. As they approached the shore, it was lined with foot soldiers in ribbed armor of leather and iron, shaking clan banners of green, blue, and orange. Behind the front ranks bobbed the horned helmets of restless cavalrymen. Their jeweled hilts and inlaid scabbards flashed in the sun and their long crimson pennons dangled fluttering to the ground.

As the first marines set foot on the sacred Japanese soil, hundreds of the watching samurai grunted in anger. Perry's men relied on the cannon, run out and ready, on the ships behind them and were careful not to flinch. With a blare of silver trumpets and a clash of cymbals, the marine band struck up "Hail, Columbia" and in close order followed their vanguard ashore. Then came Perry's standard-bearer and two young ensigns carrying Fillmore's message. Behind it walked Perry, "the high and mighty mysteriousness," as the Japanese had dubbed him. He alone of all his officers was in hot dress blues, plume, and cocked hat. He was flanked by American Negroes—in the words of the log, "two of the best looking fellers of their color that the squadron could furnish." Behind him paced more marines with guns and bayonets on the ready.

The inside of the pavilion where the presentation of the letter was to be made was lined with violet silk hangings and tasseled ropes of rose, white, and blue. The Japanese emissaries, impassive as sculptured Buddhas, knelt on a dais covered with red felt. At the other end of the hall chairs were arrayed for the Americans. As far as the Japanese were concerned, chairs were Chinese artifacts, unused in Japan except by a few Buddhist priests. Since the Americans were known to sit in nothing else, however, these chairs had been collected for the occasion from Buddhist temples in the area.

As soon as Perry and his officers had sat down, the two ensigns who were serving as page boys carried the rosewood box to the edge of the dais, whence it was handed on to two dignitaries, presented as princes. They were in reality the governors of the town and of the province. The chief of police arose and read the official government acknowledgment. Its straightforward lucidity showed clearly that the Japanese, for all their Dutch intelligence, still knew nothing of the diplomatic niceties:

The letter of the President of the United States of North America, and copy, are hereby received, and will be delivered to the Emperor.

It has been suggested many times that business relating to foreign countries cannot be done here in Uraga but only at Nagasaki. However, since we have noticed that the Admiral, in his capacity as the President's ambassador, would feel insulted by a refusal to receive the letter at this place—the justice of which has been acknowledged—we hereby receive the aforesaid letter in opposition to Japanese laws.

As this is no place to negotiate with foreigners, so too we can offer you no entertainment nor hold any conference with you. The letter has been received, therefore you are able to depart.

Through his interpreters, Perry and his officers attempted to engage in some post-ceremony conversation. The Japanese dignitaries, however, responded in one-word sentences, the silences grew more long and impassive, and finally Perry had it announced that he would be back "next spring" to receive the "Emperor's answer." So saying, he turned on his heel and led his marines back through the glowering ranks of samurai to the longboats at the jetty. The phrase, "you are able to depart," rankled. Before sailing away, Perry again sent his cutters into Inner Tokyo Harbor to sound and survey. When asked by the agitated "knave of trumps" why he did not depart, he replied that he was only seeking a big enough anchorage for the large fleet he intended to bring back with him in the spring. Finally on Sunday, July 17, he sailed away, to come again eight months later.

PERRY'S RETURN

During that eight-month interval, Japan seethed inwardly. The sixty-year-old shogun took the opportunity to die of "anxiety." He was replaced by a twenty-nine-year-old nonentity. The real power passed to the new shogun's chief administrator, young Abe Masahiro, thirty-four. Abe's name meant Flattery-Department Legal-Latitude, and he lived up to it with all the statesmanly cunning at his disposal. He had been appointed with an eye to his excellent connections in the Kyoto Court. Now he sent gifts and sugary letters to Prince Asahiko, Emperor Komei's chief advisor. He appointed Asahiko's friend, Prince Shimazu Nariakira of the seagoing Satsuma clan, to the shogun's inner council. He put the loyalist Lord of Mito, newly released from his temple prison and print shop, in charge of the nation's cannon foundries.

Most important, Flattery-Department admitted that the shogun's government was baffled by the immensity of the foreign threat and needed help and counsel from the whole nation. He polled fifty-nine of the greatest of the clan lords for their advice. Almost to a man they expressed themselves, in written replies, as being opposed to the opening of the country and ready to fight if necessary. Only nineteen of them, however, favored outright rejection of Perry's demands and immediate war. Eighteen of them timorously counseled a policy of appeasement and of protracted noncommittal negotiations. The remaining twenty-two suggested that a period of foreign trade might enable Japan to acquire the arts of the West and prepare for revenge. It would be time enough, they argued, to face down the barbarians when Japan had learned the military techniques which made the barbarians so bold. This moderate position was backed by most Japanese outside the warrior caste, in particular by the despised but powerful moneylenders and merchants. The seclusion policy was now universally unpopular, for Perry's contemptuous boldness had demonstrated how far Japan, in isolation, had withered on the vine.

Fortified by the opinions of the clan lords, Flattery-Department urged the moderate position on Emperor Komei. Now twenty-two, the muscular, saturnine young Emperor was not convinced by it. Rusty as they might be after two hundred years of peace, the million samurai of Japan, in their coats of mail, on their fine Mongol ponies, with their expert swords and antique matchlocks, must still count for something. And of course Emperor Komei was right. They could have made the Yankee dream of opening Japan far too costly for any Yankee to pursue. On the other hand, Flattery-Department had broad political backing. And therefore, at the suggestion of Prince Asahiko, his chief advisor, Emperor Komei compromised. He would give no official sanction to the shogun's policy of appeasement, but unofficially, while Japan was strengthening her defenses, he would agree to give Perry courteous, noncommittal treatment.

Accordingly, when Perry returned with nine "black ships," three of them under steam, on February 11, 1854, he was met in far friendlier fashion than before. Within the violet drapes of the parley pavilion, he found men who would talk and even drink with him. Flattery-Department himself and some minor courtiers from Kyoto were there in disguise, masquerading as small officials of the shogun's government. During the six weeks of negotiations which followed, Perry presented gifts to the Japanese which he had ordered from his own country more than a year previously. They included a mile-long telegraph line over which messages could be encoded, flashed, decoded, and explained to a Japanese umpire at the receiving station long before the fastest courier could bring the same intelligence on horseback.

Still more entertaining was the black horse brought by the black ships: a miniature steam engine, about the size of a small donkey, which ran on an 18-inch track. Perry had a carnival circle of the track laid out in a field by the jetty where he and his marines were negotiating. During recesses in the talks, the Japanese delegates delighted in mounting the runt locomotive as if it were a pony. Laughing bravely and hysterically, their ceremonial skirts flowing

about them, they rode the unsaddled steam monster as fast as
Perry's chief fireman could run it, which was about 30 miles an
hour. A Japanese student of Dutch engineering texts stood by
making notes on every move of the American toy railroadman.
Later, when the gift had been delivered, this studious onlooker,
much to the surprise of Perry's engineering staff, succeeded in
setting up and operating the locomotive merry-go-round in a
Tokyo park outside the shogun's castle.[1]

When the train rides were over, Flattery-Department Legal-
Latitude acceded to Perry's demands and the witnesses from Court
retired to Kyoto to nurse their saddle sores and write their reports to the Emperor. While the Court reflected, the shogun's
government went ahead on its own and provisionally approved
the draft text of a treaty with the United States. In the months
that followed, similar treaties presented by Russia and Great Britain were also accepted. Two provincial ports were to be opened
to foreign intercourse; Western consular officials were to be allowed to reside in them; Western visitors who broke Japanese laws
were to be tried in the treaty ports by their own consuls. This
last provision, which is known as the extraterritorial-rights clause,
offended Japanese officials because it implied that their own
courts and police were unjust and uncivilized. If there was one
institution on which Japan prided herself under Tokugawa despotism, it was the national police force.

IMPERIAL WRATH

Emperor Komei refused to approve the treaties with the West
and opened a political war against the Tokugawa regime which
was not to end until thirteen years had passed and a dozen of
the ablest aristocrats in Japan had been assassinated or prompted

[1] This was the beginning of a Japanese passion for railroading which has
never slackened. Wherever the Japanese Army went in the first half of the
twentieth century, it based its strategy on existing rail lines and built new
ones. It would be for their demonic driving of slave labor in the construction
of jungle railroads in Thailand, Burma, and Sumatra that many Japanese officers would be hanged as war criminals in 1946. Today the "bullet train" that
routinely streaks in four hours down the 300-mile track between Tokyo and
Osaka continues to testify to the thoroughness with which Japan learned
its first lesson in technology from the West.

to commit suicide. The final victim would be Emperor Komei himself.

Flattery-Department Legal-Latitude continued to negotiate with Kyoto and hoped vainly that the West would not take advantage too quickly of the concessions it had won. Commodore Perry, however, went directly from the bargaining pavilion on Tokyo Bay to spend the spring of 1854 inspecting the pretty little treaty port of Shimoda. He was disturbed to find that Shimoda, out on rugged Izu Peninsula, 80 miles from Tokyo, was entirely cut off by mountains from the rest of Japan. His seamen were shadowed and chaperoned wherever they went—even in the local brothels—by polite, inconspicuous police escorts. Japanese observers and quick-sketch artists were everywhere, looking down the muzzles of his cannon and drawing diagrams of his rigging, his dinner service, his very underwear. They even painted pictures of his own artists out painting what little they could see of the Japanese countryside.

When Perry finally sailed for home on June 28, 1854, a horde of Tokugawa officials left Shimoda at the same time to return to Tokyo. The citizens of the town breathed an anticlimactic sigh and returned to their old dull pastoral pursuits. Then in August 1856 arrived the first American consul, Townsend Harris. The local inhabitants were totally unprepared for him. It was inconceivable that he should insist on coming so soon when Perry had already been shown that he was not welcome. The villagers pointed out to Harris that no accommodations were ready for him; that the harvest had been a poor one; that there had been an earthquake; that the peasants were poorer than usual. Why not return in a few years when conditions were more settled? Consul Harris stayed. He established his consulate in an abandoned temple infested with rats, bats, and spiders, ran up the Stars and Stripes on a flagstaff, and wrote in his journal: "Grim reflections —ominous of change—undoubted beginning of the end. Query: if for the real good of Japan?"[2]

[2] In later years the Japanese inscribed this journal entry on a stone monument near Harris's temple—a hint to native sightseers that the Yankees had hoped to end Japan, and had felt uneasy in conscience about it, from the start.

For the next three years Harris, abetted by pressure from the American, British, and Russian navies, negotiated with the Tokugawa government for a commercial treaty opening Japan fully to free trade. Flattery-Department equivocated, pressed ahead with halfhearted military preparations, and gave his main effort to negotiations with the Imperial Court. Before he opened Japan further, he needed imperial sanction for what had already been done. Emperor Komei not only refused to give it, he branded the shogun's armament efforts as spurious and questioned the shogun's reverence for the gods of the Japanese soil. Consul Harris's secretary, a young Dutch translator, noted sadly in his journal that when his Japanese counterparts said, "We may not be able to meet again in such a pleasant manner," they sometimes meant that they had been ordered to commit hara-kiri.

Emperor Komei's advisor, Prince Asahiko, organized a subversive cell of young courtiers and clan lords. It met at Asahiko's temple, Shoren-In, which remains to this day one of the most aristocratic and inaccessible of Kyoto's holy places.[3] There, on the second floor, the acolytes built a special secret chamber for the cell meetings. No doors that looked like doors gave entrance to the room, and for exit, in the event of a police raid, there was a blind stairway, a trap door, and a tunnel leading out into the azalea garden. From this hideaway, Prince Asahiko's robed and hooded recruits disseminated a slogan that is still famous in Japan today: "Venerate the Emperor and expel the barbarians." After the clandestine meetings, Asahiko, according to one of his grandsons, often went on to the palace for further discussion. Putting the colorful canal boats and lantern-lit alleys of the Gion pleasure district at his back, he presented himself at a small postern in the southeastern wall of the palace compound and was ushered directly into the garden of Emperor Komei's private apartments. There, in his priestly robes of midnight violet,[4] he

[3] Unfortunately, the ninth century building in which Asahiko plotted burned down in 1893, and the present temple, what can be seen of it, is a structure of little interest, dating from 1895.

[4] At Court, as a general rule, the Emperor wore white, the color of the departed ancestors; the princes of the blood, black or deep violet, the color of secret action; the Fujiwara courtiers, crimson, the color of sex and intrigue;

had complete freedom of access, "entering and withdrawing from the Imperial Presence even in the dead of night."

After three years of talk, intrigue, and stalemate, Flattery-Department, in 1857 found himself in an impossible position; he was caught between his promises to Emperor Komei on the one hand and on the other to internationally-minded merchants who had helped him financially. After months of negotiation with Consul Harris, his subordinates had drawn up a trade treaty with the United States which they urged him to submit to the Emperor. In vain he sent a spokesman to Kyoto to explain the advantages of world commerce. When Emperor Komei denounced the spokesman's arguments as irreligious, the thirty-eight-year-old Flattery-Department suddenly died "after a brief illness." His patron, the thirty-four-year-old shogun, fell sick and followed him to the spirit world less than eight months later.

Emperor Komei had been promised that the next shogun would be a member of the loyalist Mito branch of the Tokugawa family. The late shogun and his chief minister, Flattery-Department, had both agreed to the arrangement. But now that these two had succumbed to the overwhelming religious pressure from Kyoto, the elders of the Tokugawa council felt rebellious. In meeting to nominate a new shogun, they passed by the loyalist Lord of Mito and voted, in defiance of the Emperor, to appoint the twelve-year-old scion of another Tokugawa branch family, an unfortunate boy who will be known in these pages as Shogun Aquarius.[5]

The new chief minister who had replaced Flattery-Department and who had steered the council toward its decision was Lord I-i of Hikone, a tough, practical executive of forty-three. He proceeded at once to sign a trade treaty with Consul Harris, opening five Japanese ports to Western commerce. Emperor Komei refused to ratify the new treaty and sent it back to Tokyo with a pettish note, framed by Prince Asahiko, abdicating all responsibility for foreign relations to the government of the shogun.

A nobleman in the Kyoto Court, the thirty-three-year-old Iwa-

---

and lesser nobles, green, the color of the land. On some occasions the upper Court ranks could also wear yellow, the color of thought.

[5] Tokugawa Iemochi. Iemochi is an astrological given name meaning House of the Dog, or by the Western zodiac, Aquarius.

kura Tomomi, who would later be called the "architect of modern Japan," promptly submitted a memorandum of protest to the Throne, advising Emperor Komei that he could not delegate his sacred authority in this fashion but must order the shogun to do his bidding. Emperor Komei was struck by the attitude of the young nobleman and elevated Iwakura to the board of imperial advisors. Iwakura was allowed to leak the news that the Emperor had abdicated his power over foreign affairs under duress and was waiting for the twelve-year-old Shogun Aquarius to reconsider. At the same time Prince Asahiko, the Emperor's principal advisor, sent north to Mito a secret commission under Emperor Komei's signature, ordering the cannon-building, *History*-publishing loyalist Lord of Mito to get rid of the shogun's objectionable new strongman. Lord I-i, the strongman, heard of the move and staged a massive counter-coup. The efficient Tokugawa police moved in on Kyoto and politely but firmly arrested more than a hundred noblemen, clan lords, and samurai who belonged to Emperor Komei's coterie of loyalists. Prince Asahiko, the chief imperial advisor, was rusticated to a little "wild" temple in the countryside outside of Kyoto, and several of his lower-ranking samurai cronies were executed. In his place, Emperor Komei took as chief advisor the idealistic young nobleman, Iwakura.

Never before had the shogun's government resorted to such a gloveless display of power. Emperor Komei warned Lord I-i that it would be civil war if he opened the ports of Kobe and Osaka —both within a day's journey of Kyoto. He coldly, flatly advised I-i: "We must assuredly keep aloof from foreigners and revert to the sound rule of seclusion." Lord I-i paid no attention. He had the young Shogun Aquarius sign the treaty in the name of Japan and in 1860 dispatched a delegation of eighteen lords and fifty-three servants to the United States to convey the instruments of ratification.

The ambassadors traveled on the U.S. *Powhatan* and took with them a Japanese escort vessel and fifty tons of baggage, including cattle, sheep, pigs, poultry, and many gifts and works of art. Their translation problems were bridged for them by Manjiro, the fisher waif who had been picked up on an Aleutian island eighteen years earlier. Wearing the traditional two swords and robes of samurai, they made a deep impression wherever they stopped—in Honolulu, Panama, Washington, Baltimore, Philadelphia, and New York. In Washington, when they went in parade to see President James Buchanan, they were cheered by a crowd estimated at 20,000. In New York they were accorded "the finest public entertainment ever given in this country"—a ball and banquet at which there were 10,000 dinner guests and five bands instructed to play all night if necessary.

The Spartan samurai were not impressed by the noise of their welcome. "There is no end to speakers," wrote one of them, "some speaking quietly, some wildly brandishing their arms." On their visit to Congress they were surprised to find a senator "making a speech at the top of his voice." They were more impressed by iced drinks and by bare-shouldered "geisha," who "hopped about" at public dances with their own husbands. But what most struck them were the massive preparations under way for the Civil War and the railroads snaking out across the huge continent toward California. In their reports later they urged emulation of Western technology but not of Western culture or religion. They found the culture "too showy" and the religion full of "good principles which are not well observed in the morality of the people."

While the shogun's scouts were reconnoitering the strength of the enemy abroad, the secluded Emperor at home plotted implacably against the minister in Tokyo who had defied him. Komei's private apartments in the Kyoto Palace became a midnight headquarters for noble recruits to the loyalist cause. There the saké cups and candles of pure wax were tended by his favorite concubine, Nakayama Yoshiko—literally Child of Joy. She was the daughter of a noble family which had suffered repeatedly at Tokugawa hands. In 1852 she had borne Komei his only healthy son, the future Emperor Meiji. Her father and brothers were all ardent believers in restoring the imperial house to direct rule. With her encouragement, Emperor Komei ordered his Chief Advisor Iwakura to recruit samurai and clan lords in western Japan for a showdown with the government in Tokyo. At her urging,

Komei finally directed the loyalist Lord of Mito to do away with Strongman I-i.

Lord I-i lived in a rambling gray-tiled villa across the moat from the great palace in Tokyo. In those days the Tokyo palace was the home and fortress of the shogun. Every morning Lord I-i was carried in a sedan chair from his doorway, across the palace moat, to deliver his daily report to the adolescent Shogun Aquarius. On the morning of March 24, 1860, he began his routine as usual. An early spring had brought the cherries into bloom prematurely, and now, in an unseasonal cold wave, snow and sleet were falling with the graying petals. As Lord I-i approached the Cherry Field Gate at the southeastern corner of the palace, his bearers and bodyguards, in wide conical lacquer hats and raincoats of oiled paper, leaned against the wind as they walked. On the other side of the bridge the rear guard of Lord Shimazu of Satsuma was seen disappearing into the palace.

Lord I-i called to his bearers to make haste; he wished to be present to hear what Lord Shimazu was about to say to the young shogun. I-i's guardsmen shouldered aside a group of nondescript sightseers in cloaks who were admiring the palace keep. When his palanquin reached the throat of the bridge, seventeen of the bystanders suddenly threw off their rain capes and revealed by their crests that they were samurai of the slighted Lord of Mito.

Drawing their swords, advancing at a crouch, wheeling and leaping, they slashed their way through I-i's litter-bearers and laid them red on the snow. The shogun's guard dashed from the palace and scattered the assassins. But too late. Lord I-i of Hikone was found crumpled in his sedan chair, a headless torso. Lord I-i's head was delivered, by an assassin who escaped, to the Lord of Mito, Tokugawa Nariaki, who had ordered the deed done.[6] Nariaki spat upon the head and sent it on to Emperor Komei in Kyoto. There it was displayed for weeks on the public execution ground above a placard which stated: "This is the head of a traitor who violated the most sacred law of Japan—that which forbids the admission of foreigners into our country."

[6] The shogun's forces claimed that this was a fake head and that Lord I-i's had been recovered after the battle at the bridge.

PROGRAM FOR UNITY

In the weeks that followed, handbills denouncing the shogun as a traitor were posted by night in Tokyo's main thoroughfares. Arcane scrolls of supposed great antiquity, foretelling the doom of the Tokugawa shoguns, were turned up in many parts of Japan at temples controlled by the princely high priests in Kyoto. Several notorious brigands and gamblers in the Tokugawa domains of the north were approached by noble emissaries who came in secret from Kyoto to buy their swords. Masked bands waylaid the mail on the post roads, intercepted shipments of merchant gold and distributed it to the poor. A gang of patriotic cutthroats broke into the Ashikaga mausoleum and decapitated the statues of all thirteen of the former shoguns who had ruled Japan from 1338 to 1573.

Released by their liege lords, samurai from all over the country flocked to Kyoto to offer their services to Emperor Komei. The coterie of restorationists around Komei's favorite concubine, Child of Joy, urged the Emperor to declare the shogun a usurper and to order a general uprising against the Tokugawa bureaucracy. Had Komei listened, the "restoration" would probably have taken place immediately. But Emperor Komei, influenced by conservative Fujiwara ministers, did not primarily wish to be restored—did not desire to resume direct responsibility for all civil affairs. He simply wanted the shogun to perform his office and drive out the barbarians.

Having done his duty and killed a retainer of his own Tokugawa clan, the Lord of Mito, a few months later, was found mysteriously stabbed to death in his own bathroom—a victim either of suicide or assassination. A spirit of thoughtful calm now descended on the nation. Civil war seemed hardly a sensible response to the threat of foreign invasion. For a year the country ran itself, smoothly and bureaucratically, in a political vacuum. Iwakura Tomomi, the Emperor's idealistic young advisor, spoke for reconciliation and negotiated a marriage between Emperor Komei's sister and the fifteen-year-old Shogun Aquarius. In return the shogun's bureaucracy wrung permission from Consul

Harris to delay the opening of Kobe and Osaka until 1868. At the wedding the boy shogun solemnly promised the Emperor's emissaries that all foreigners would be expelled from the country by 1876.

With his sister in Tokyo Castle, Emperor Komei now felt that the Tokugawas would be respectful allies and would proceed apace with the crusade against the infidels. However Iwakura, the Emperor's advisor, knew that the problem was not so easily solved. He foresaw a long period of internal reorganization and modernization before the country would be strong enough to expel the barbarians. He was not impressed with what he had seen of the shogun's government during the marriage negotiations in Tokyo. He felt that the country needed a new form of government which would make use of all clans and factions and would rally everyone around the Throne in this time of crisis. He persuaded Emperor Komei to circularize forty-nine "outer clans" of the southwest— clans which had been excluded from any voice in the government since 1600—and ask them what programs they would recommend for Japan in her hour of need.

Most of the clans responded by pledging their loyalty to any course of action which the Emperor decided upon. But the great Choshu clan, on the southwestern tip of the main island, sent back a detailed prospectus for national unification under the Emperor and for long-range strategic planning against the barbarian enemy. First unite, modernize, and strengthen; then carry the war to the enemy by "expanding across the seas" and creating buffer zones between Japan and the West. In essence the Choshu program was that of Hideyoshi in the sixteenth century —a policy to which the Choshu clan had remained loyal throughout their two hundred and sixty-two years of banishment. With Emperor Komei's sanction, advisor Iwakura persuaded the shogun to adopt it as the long-range plan for Japan. It was to remain Japan's basic policy until 1945.

The first stage in the Choshu program, unification, was the most difficult. The decadent Court in Kyoto and bureaucracy in Tokyo were not ready for the sweeping changes which it entailed. Up to this point—early 1862—the noisiest patriots in Kyoto had been swashbuckling samurai from the seagoing Satsuma clan in

Kyushu who had been given leave by their lord to go to the capital and pledge their loyalty to the imperial cause. When the program of the rival clan of Choshu was adopted by Emperor Komei, Choshu samurai also began to pour into Kyoto. In the gay streets of the geisha district, the Guion, the Satsuma men picked nightly quarrels with the newcomers. Their bloody brawls caused fires which threatened the whole city.

At Emperor Komei's order, Lord Shimazu of Satsuma came to Kyoto to suppress his troublemaking former retainers. One group of them, which had grown fond of their swaggering, masterless life, resented Shimazu's interference and plotted to assassinate their former lord. They gathered at the Teradaya Inn. It was once again the roistering season of the cherry blossoms, the spring of 1862. Lord Shimazu heard of their scheme, visited the inn in force, and in a famous melee fought entirely in darkness, killed seven of them. Sick of heart at shedding his own clansmen's blood, he resolved to rid the unification program of its Choshu leadership and the Court of its dynamic young advisor, Iwakura.

Lord Shimazu had many friends both in Tokyo and Kyoto. He was an in-law of the shogun and had sisters among the concubines at Court. He had worked with the late Lord Tokugawa of Mito in building up coastal defenses and was therefore *persona grata* to Emperor Komei. He had worked with the bureaucracy to prevent a complete rupture between Tokyo and Kyoto and was therefore *persona grata* to the Tokugawa family. After the unpleasant incident at Teradaya Inn, his first move was to have the shogun's police release Prince Asahiko, the Emperor's former first counselor —the father of Hirohito's activist uncles—from the little "wild" temple in the Kyoto suburbs where he had spent the last three years under house arrest. Then he and Asahiko had no difficulty agreeing that the first order of business was to free Emperor Komei of his upstart advisor, Iwakura, and of Iwakura's recruits, the upstart clan of Choshu.

It is a simplification but no exaggeration to say that the lines of modern Japanese history were drawn at that moment. The Army supporters of the Strike North, who wanted to turn Japanese aggression against Russia in the 1930's, were factional descendants of Iwakura and Choshu. The apostles of the Strike

South, who wished to move against the West in Singapore and Manila, were to be naval admirals of Shimazu's Satsuma clan and princely sons and grandsons of Asahiko.

As the nation's highest Shinto priest, Emperor Komei was obsessed by the idea that the few foreigners on sacred soil must be driven out. Then it would be time enough to consider the problems of national fortification and reform. The charming Prince Asahiko, whose rank as a prince of the blood gave him access at all times even to Komei's bedchamber, humored the Emperor in his fixed idea and, indeed, agreed with him. For Asahiko the old order was good enough. Reform and modernization, in themselves, were not desirable.

Very different were the views of Komei's other advisor, Iwakura. He felt that the old order was stifling Japan and that the threat of suffocation from within was greater than that of desecration from without. But Iwakura, though a skillful courtier, was only one of the "New House Noblemen" and as such he was at a disadvantage—he could not see Emperor Komei without an appointment. His one bond with the Emperor was dedication. The Emperor as a religious recluse was dedicated to the preservation of his ancestral Shintoism. Iwakura, as a brilliant visionary, was dedicated to the future he saw for Japan.

In the spring of 1862, Lord Shimazu and Prince Asahiko, plotting together, finally convinced Emperor Komei that he should order the shogun to give up many of his powers and at the same time begin a terrorization of the small foreign community, thereby forcing its withdrawal from Japanese soil. On delivering this message in Tokyo, Lord Shimazu advised the ministers of sixteen-year-old Shogun Aquarius not to pay too much attention to all clauses in the Emperor's note. The important item, he said, was the intimidation of the foreign settlement. Lord Shimazu assured the shogun's faint-hearted officials that the Emperor would compromise on matters of domestic management. And the West, too, would seek terms when its bluff was called. Thousands of miles from home, without any superiority except in cannon with which to shell the fringes of the coast, what could the barbarians do?

Lord Shimazu's swordsmen, abetted by samurai from Mito, proceeded to harass the nascent foreign colony in Yokohama and to pick duels with the strongest of the shogun's administrators. They won over the shogun's advisors one by one. They slapped the faces of Frenchmen, Russians, and Americans. They set fire to the British Legation and mortally wounded two of the British consular guards.[7] Finally, when they believed that the puerile shogun understood the wishes of his brother-in-law, the Emperor, they set out once again under Lord Shimazu to return to Kyoto.

On September 14, 1862, when Lord Shimazu and his men started back down the Eastern Sea Road toward Kyoto, they encountered three Englishmen and an Englishwoman out for an early morning canter from the foreign settlement in Yokohama. The foreign sightseers blundered into Lord Shimazu's vanguard, ignorant of the fact that every Japanese, by law, was obliged to clear the road before a clan lord's progress. One of Shimazu's samurai swaggered forward and challenged the leading Englishman, a visiting merchant from Shanghai, Charles Lenox Richardson, to a duel. When Richardson failed to respond, the samurai laid him on his horse's neck with one bloody stroke. The horse of the English lady behind Richardson bolted straight into the samurai phalanx. One of the Japanese swordsmen deftly lifted his razor-sharp blade to cut off the lady's pigtails as a trophy. She galloped on, terror-stricken, to warn the English colony in Yokohama while the two untouched Englishmen behind her backed their horses, amid taunts, out of Shimazu's way.

Richardson slipped to the ground and lay bleeding at the edge of the road. When Lord Shimazu's bodyguard had ridden past, he crawled to a hut and was nursed for a few hours by a peasant. Lord Shimazu heard of what had happened and sent back a retainer to dispatch him and dispose of the body. The swordsman dismembered Richardson and ordered the peasant to bury the pieces.

What was done was done, but Lord Shimazu was not happy with his last piece of work. When he returned to Kyoto, he found that his swordsmen there had done their butchery no more artistically than their comrades in Tokyo. They had attempted and

[7] They singled out the British as special objects of their spite because they understood that Britain was the great naval power of the West and therefore the one honorably dangerous opponent for Shimazu's seagoing Satsuma clan.

failed to exterminate the Choshu samurai from the Kyoto streets, and the old capital had become a dangerous place for him.[8] Worried about British reprisals against his provincial capital of Kagoshima, Lord Shimazu paid his respects to the Emperor and then rode hard for his home fief in Kyushu.

In his brief audience with the Emperor, Lord Shimazu complained that the sealed orders which he had taken to Shogun Aquarius in Tokyo had been less explicit about expelling barbarians than he had understood they would be. Emperor Komei, aided by his jealous advisor, Prince Asahiko, had an investigation made and discovered that unauthorized softening phrases had been written in to the final presentation copy of the orders. The Court nobleman who had physically carried them to the shogun's castle was sent in disgrace to a monastery, and advisor Iwakura, who had penned the original missive, fell under a cloud. In October, Iwakura was placed under guard in the palace, and in November, Emperor Komei issued a decree stripping him of his Court rank and offices and exiling him from Kyoto. That night, before the sentence could be executed by force, Iwakura obtained a disguise from his sister, who was a lady-in-waiting in the Imperial Wardrobe, and succeeded in stealing out of Kyoto. He established a hide-out in the countryside nearby, where he remained in contact with a handful of trusty Choshu samurai in the city and progressive young noblemen at Court. Emperor Komei dispatched a new emissary to Tokyo to tell Shogun Aquarius explicitly that the barbarians must be expelled forthwith.

In January 1863, the triumphant Prince Asahiko, alone now in the affections of his monarch, celebrated his thirty-ninth birthday. He had a small party at which the guests of honor were Konoye Tadahiro, the grandfather of the prime minister who would launch war on China in 1937, and Shimazu Tadayoshi, the twenty-three-year-old ward in whose name Lord Shimazu ruled over Satsuma. During the party, Prince Asahiko and the young

[8] During the fighting a certain Kido Koin, the adoptive grandfather of Kido Koichi, Emperor Hirohito's lord privy seal, had made a romantic name for himself by being saved from ambush by the warning of a geisha who loved him. A Choshu man by birth, he took the Satsuma side in the swordplay. He subsequently married the geisha and adopted Kido's father as his legitimate son.

Lord Shimazu met beside the gaunt winter skeleton of a particularly fine and sacred maple in the grounds of Asahiko's villa, and in the presence of Konoye pledged eternal friendship between their two families. This bond between the imperial house of Fushimi and the naval house of Satsuma was to remain the most dependable of the romantic feudal allegiances which would still be operative during the kaleidoscopic politics of the 1930's.

BARBARIANS UNBUDGED

During Asahiko's birthday party, the big, melancholic thirty-three-year-old Emperor was preoccupied with the scholarly problems associated with ancient imperial tombs. When the second emissary had returned from Tokyo in December, he had brought no assurance that the shogun would expel all barbarians immediately, but instead a promise that Shogun Aquarius would come to Kyoto in March to discuss the matter. With the promise was delivered a peace offering of money for the repair of the tombs of Emperor Komei's ancestors.

A Court committee had had charge of rediscovering and maintaining the old tombs ever since the beginning of the Tokugawa era in 1658, but there had never been sufficient funds for a comprehensive assault on the delicate scholarly questions of correct identification and restoration. Now the shogun's unexpected generosity, at a time when his own finances were precarious, gave the avid Shintoist Emperor a full-time diversion. The most gossipy barbarian-haters at Court, the oldest and most pettifogging Shinto neoclassicists, were set to work drawing up a list of the hundred most important mausolea and an estimate of cost for providing each with a *torii* archway, a stone lantern, a paved pathway, and a suitably inscribed marker. The day the work began a messenger was sent to announce the great event at the supposed tumulus of Jimmu, the first Emperor.

In March, the seventeen-year-old Shogun Aquarius arrived in Kyoto as promised. He planned to stay for ten days, but Emperor Komei had called a national congress of clan lords to meet with Aquarius in the Imperial Presence. As a result Aquarius's visit was to be prolonged by more than two months. In his suite of 300 retainers—a sad falling off from the 307,000 employed by the shogun under similar circumstances in 1634—he brought with him most of the men who had negotiated with Commodore Perry and Consul Harris or had firsthand knowledge of the United States. In vain they explained to the clan congress the immensity of the industrial revolution which had swept the West and the futility of barring the barbarians until Japan had undergone the same process.

The spiritualistic Emperor Komei was not impressed. Komei was at the height of his funerary enthusiasms and was living with ghosts. He persuaded a majority of the dubious clan lords to agree that a holy war should be opened against the West on June 25, 1863. Then, after much feasting and drinking of tea and saké, he accompanied the bemused adolescent shogun in a great midnight parade to the shrine of Hachiman, the god of war, atop Kyoto's Mount Otoko. There, in the flickering light of pine torches, he performed a brief, severe Shinto evocation of the shades and presented Shogun Aquarius with an ancient sword from one of the imperial troves. In bestowing it, he repeated the divine commission: rid Japan of infidels by June 25.

Early in May rumors of the song being sung by the Voice of the Crane leaked out to the peasant grapevine. The coasts of Japan were evacuated by tens of thousands of women and children. On May 5, the foreign settlers in Yokohama noted with dismay the overnight disappearance of all their Japanese servants. They attributed it to the stiffness of the indemnity—£100,000 sterling—which the British were demanding for the murder of the young Englishman, Richardson, eight months earlier.

Not long after the panic on the coasts, Shogun Aquarius and his retinue returned from Kyoto to Tokyo, outraged but outvoted. They came, not by the great Eastern Sea Road, but by ship, which somewhat restored public confidence in the possibility of peace. The shogun's ministers proceeded to negotiate with the West in a conciliatory fashion. On June 24, the day before Emperor Komei's war deadline, Shogun Aquarius—in a gesture of defiance to the Throne—acceded to British demands and paid the £100,000. All morning long, crates of Mexican silver were carried from

·

the Tokugawa treasure house to the British dock and counted and weighed in front of witnesses.

The news spread by carrier pigeon that the Tokugawas, the most powerful of the clans, did not intend to participate in the holy war. The other lords, reverent as they were of the Emperor as the cornerstone of their aristocratic system, did not share in his Shinto mania. The next day, when the war was to have begun, every clan remained at home except that of Choshu.

Because of its rowdy samurai in the Kyoto streets, Choshu was in disfavor at Court. Its leading noble protagonist, the former Imperial Advisor Iwakura, was in hiding. It was in order to make amends and recommend itself once more to imperial favor that Choshu now took action alone. An American ship, passing through the narrow straits of Shimonoseki, which separated Honshu from Kyushu and Choshu from Satsuma, was shelled without warning by the Choshu forts on the north bank. The American vessel barely survived the barrage and limped home to Yokohama with bloody scuppers and broken rigging.

Much excited, the consuls and attachés in Yokohama demanded that Shogun Aquarius bring the clans into line. Without ever mentioning Emperor Komei, Aquarius's ministers pleaded naval weakness and internal dissension and invited the foreign powers to seek their own satisfaction. A joint Anglo-French fleet duly sailed south in July and shelled the seventy-four cannon on the Choshu coast into silence. Then the marines of the task force went ashore and helped to put out the fires they had started. They found the natives surprisingly friendly. Choshu had made its gesture and saved face. Only about fifty of its warriors had been killed.

In early August, again with encouragement from Aquarius's ministers, a British fleet hove to off the Satsuma clan capital of Kagoshima in Kyushu to demand the surrender of Richardson's murderer to Western justice. Satsuma's Lord Shimazu refused and had his shore batteries open fire. The British flagship was, for an hour, unable to return the fire because she had the £100,-ooo indemnity silver stacked in cases over the hatch to her magazine. The Satsuma gunners worked with better cannon than their Choshu counterparts and succeeded in killing and wounding no less than sixty-three English sailors. Finally the British squadron began to pump incendiary rockets into Kagoshima. When half the flammable town was burning, the Satsuma marksmen deserted their posts for higher duty as fire fighters. This time the marines did not land to help. The British fleet sailed away without accomplishing its purpose. The deft swordsman who had cut Richardson down remained behind in the bosom of his people where he was to live to an honored old age.

Emperor Komei was elated by the news of heroism brought from Choshu and Satsuma and disgusted with his brother-in-law the shogun for conciliating the foreigners. Clearly the Tokugawas were no longer fit to wear the title of *Sei-i Dai Shogun,* Great Barbarian-suppressing General. And so Emperor Komei called on his loyalist samurai in Kyoto to revolt and overthrow the Tokugawa government. Three years earlier, such a rising would probably have swept the country. Now the clan lords had begun to doubt the wisdom of the Emperor's xenophobia, and Komei had to entrust his revolution to the rabid Shinto scholars at Court and to their rabble of samurai followers.

Being pedants and ceremonialists, the insurgents laid their plans with a keener sense of symbolism than of realism. They started by giving their plot the name of *Tenchu,* Heavenly Retribution. Then they decided that the signal for the uprising should be a state visit by Emperor Komei to the ancient capital of Yoshino where the schismatic restorationist Emperors of the southern dynasty had dined on pride in the fourteenth century. The brother of Child of Joy, Komei's favorite concubine, was to be ready in Yoshino with a small force of loyalists. They would proclaim "the restoration," attack the local Tokugawa police garrison, and then, because of Yoshino's historical associations, they could expect the whole countryside to rally to the imperial cause.

Optimistic as the plot was, the populace might have responded to it if Choshu and Satsuma had had any luck against the fleets sent to bombard them. In their first reports to Kyoto both clans glossed over their losses and exaggerated the damage they had inflicted. The populace, which had its grapevine, knew better, but the secluded Emperor Komei went ahead with his plans undaunted. Then, in late September 1863, on the eve of the uprising,

Lord Shimazu and his retinue of Satsuma samurai galloped into Kyoto on lathered horses. Hasting to the villa of Prince Asahiko, Emperor Komei's advisor, Shimazu confessed that reports of victory over the barbarians had been grossly exaggerated. Shimazu was prepared to go before the Emperor and admit the truth. Prince Asahiko, however, proposed a way of softening the blow— of saving both his friend's face and the Emperor's.

That night a group of loyalist courtiers were closeted with Emperor Komei in his private apartments, fussing over last-minute details of their coup. The Emperor in a kimono of white silk sat cross-legged before a golden screen. His fellow conspirators knelt at the other end of the room, touching their heads to the matting as preface whenever they spoke. From time to time ladies-in-waiting brought freshly warmed saké to the door of the room. There they would kneel and press their foreheads to the floor. Also kneeling and bowing, Child of Joy, the favorite concubine, would accept the pitchers and, without ever rising from her knees, would move about the room refilling the tiny cups of her lord and his guests. The sliding doors to the veranda and garden were closed to an early nip of autumn and the room glowed in the subdued light of an aromatic oil lantern.

Suddenly the veranda doors were thrown open and Prince Asahiko burst in, prostrating himself and wearing the old priestly garments which he had not had on for two years. In a hushed voice of awe he declared that he had just had a religious vision; that he had been commanded to resume the cloth; that he had been sent to warn the Emperor against any bloodshed while the stars hung in their present configuration. It had been revealed to him, he said, that natural disasters would temporarily rob the imperial cause of its victories. His forebodings were confirmed a few hours later when Lord Shimazu unexpectedly arrived from Satsuma and told Emperor Komei of the great fire which had swept his provincial capital after the repulse of the British fleet.

Against the will of the spirits, nothing could be done. Emperor Komei abruptly canceled his rising against the Tokugawas and exiled seven of his most firebrand restorationist nobles. His concubine's brother in Yoshino—the uncle of the ten-year-old crown prince, the future Emperor Meiji—did not hear of the cancellation in time and went ahead according to plan. He seized local government offices and set out to attack the Tokugawa police barracks. After a brief beating, the shogun's troops regrouped, summoned reinforcements, hunted down the rebels, and executed Child of Joy's brother. In Kyoto Lord Shimazu's men rounded up many troublemaking Choshu and Satsuma samurai and packed them off to the clan capitals with Emperor Komei's seven banished noblemen.

CIVIL WAR

In March 1864 at a national council of reconciliation in Kyoto, the new loyalist Lord of Mito, a Tokugawa, and the equally loyalist Lord of Choshu fell into a drunken quarrel before the Emperor. As a result a Choshu contingent marched north on Kyoto with a bill of grievances and a petition imploring the Emperor to broaden his circle of advisors. The Choshu men were driven off by the Tokugawa police, and Emperor Komei agreed halfheartedly to a Tokugawa expedition against Choshu.

Shogun Aquarius marched south with an army of 150,000 samurai. The young progressive leaders of Choshu prepared to meet him with cadres of riflemen which they had trained in the European style of warfare. At the last moment hostilities were averted by intermediaries from the neutral seagoing clan of Satsuma. The Choshu young bloods were not satisfied with the truce. They no longer believed it possible to compromise with Japanese traditionalists. Only a thoroughgoing reform and Westernization of the nation, they felt, would suffice to meet the challenge of the West. Kido Koin, the adoptive grandfather of Hirohito's lord privy seal, led a coup within the provincial Choshu government and unseated the clan elders who had agreed to accept peace.

In 1865 while the young samurai leaders of Choshu continued to prepare for civil war, a joint Anglo-French fleet stationed itself off the unopened treaty port of Kobe, in the Kyoto area, and requested menacingly that Japan hurry up in fulfilling her treaty commitments. Shogun Aquarius, still scarcely nineteen, moved his headquarters in June to Osaka to be near the Emperor in the hour of emergency. Horrified at the dissension that had settled on the nation, Emperor Komei was induced by Prince Asahiko and Lord Shimazu to give his sanction, at long last, to the treaties which had been negotiated eleven years earlier with the Western powers.

Having postponed the barbarian threat, young Shogun Aquarius took the government into his own hands and mounted a fresh expedition against Choshu to dispose of the domestic threat. Emperor Komei frowned, and none but the Tokugawa fiefs of the north would contribute troops to the expedition. Nevertheless the headstrong young shogun moved ahead into Choshu territory. His big army won ground but suffered staggering losses to Choshu riflemen who took their toll and vanished. The Choshu captains of the rifle companies were the future generals who would run the Japanese Army until the 1920's. The military advisors of Shogun Aquarius warned that the big army would be decimated before it ever met the main body of the Choshu forces. In September 1866 Shogun Aquarius, a twenty-year-old failure, abruptly died of an "abdominal disorder," presumably self-inflicted.

REGICIDE

The nation had come to a standstill. The Tokugawas, the Court nobles, and the lords of Choshu and Satsuma had all made their loyal efforts, but imperial wishes remained as unrealistic and insatiable as ever. Emperor Komei appointed the young loyalist Lord of Mito to be the next shogun and called on him to settle internal dissension and proceed with the expulsion of the barbarians. In December 1866, Emperor Komei and the new shogun called another council of the nation's clan lords. Of twenty-four lords invited to participate, only five came.

On January 15, 1867, Emperor Komei had a cold and his doctors prescribed a potion for him. One of the elder ladies-in-waiting, who performed menial palace housework, later said: "He was given smallpox poison." Japanese physicians, who were conversant with Dutch medical texts, had been experimenting with smallpox vaccines since about 1840. It may be that what the old woman called "poison" was an oral vaccine which Emperor Komei took in hopes that it would protect him from the recurrent epidemics which swept Kyoto. The next morning Emperor Komei felt "unpleasant," and against his doctors' advice insisted on performing his customary rituals at the palace shrine. By January 18 he was confined to bed, was running a high fever, could not eat or sleep, and babbled deliriously. The next day his chief physician diagnosed a case of "either smallpox or melancholy fever."

"A man full of blood and muscles, who never suffers so much as a sniffle," noted one of the courtiers in his diary. "This is indeed surprising and regrettable."

In the days that followed the vigorous young Emperor went through a typical case of smallpox. The pustules appeared on January 20. On the twenty-first he tossed with fever and from time to time vomited. On the twenty-second his doctors diagnosed smallpox definitely and gave orders that "prayers be said for him at the seven temples." By the twenty-third he was covered with oily pustules and his throat was too sore to eat anything but chilled liquids. On the twenty-fourth the pox turned purple, he ate some rice gruel and passed wastes from the "honorable eighth and ninth holes."[9] By January 26 he was so far recovered that Shogun Tokugawa Yoshinobu, Lord of Mito, visited his bedside. The doctors called the twenty-seventh and twenty-eighth the "key days of the crisis." The pus stopped oozing and the pox began to dry. On the twenty-ninth he seemed fully convalescent and ate heartily.

That night his handmaidens gave him a bath and a thimble or two of his favorite saké. The next day, January 30, 1867, he awoke in misery. The great draughty palace was unusually quiet and cold. No one was about but ladies-in-waiting. He asked that his half score of doctors be summoned and was given the chilling intelligence that every single one of them had been called from the palace that day on other business. Too weak to move, he dozed and waited. Somewhere in the distance a female attendant told one of his sisters that she could not be admitted to his sick chamber. He vomited repeatedly, "breathed like an insect," and "passed blood from the honorable ninth hole." Late in the afternoon he fell into a coma. During the evening his doctors reap-

[9] The first seven were eyes, ears, nostrils, and mouth.

peared in force, examined him, found his pulse growing weaker and his limbs colder. At 11:00 P.M. he died.

The death was not announced for four days, the funeral not held for thirty-two days. To courtiers whose diaries have been preserved, it appeared that Emperor Komei had survived a classic case of smallpox only to fall prey to a classic case of poisoning.

Iwakura Tomomi, the nobleman who had once been Emperor Komei's chief advisor and had been living for four years in exile and hiding outside the Kyoto city walls, returned to Court immediately. One week after Komei's death, when he was still locked in struggle with Komei's other advisor, Prince Asahiko, Iwakura sent a letter to one of the progressive samurai of Satsuma, one of the future leaders of Japan, with whom he had corresponded throughout the years of his rustication and plotting. In it, he wrote: "I wish to release you and the others from any responsibility or punishment. I alone am responsible." His correspondent wrote back: "Silence is the best course."

It was no light matter to do away with an Emperor. Whatever their foibles, the Emperors were gods and none of them had been assassinated since Emperor Sushun in 592. Others as well as nobleman Iwakura were surely implicated in the strange death of Emperor Komei in 1867. Possibly the devout Shintoist Emperor himself, believing that he was doomed to failure, trapped between the demands of his ancestors and the wishes of his people, had even agreed to die as an extreme form of abdication—a withdrawal to power behind the curtain in the spirit world.

The honorable Iwakura took all the royal blood on his own head and dedicated the rest of his life to the selfless service of Emperor Meiji, Komei's son and Hirohito's grandfather.

Iwakura returned to Court with adequate backing from young Choshu and Satsuma warriors and with a large following among the Fujiwara officials in the palace. The position of his rival advisor was parlous. Prince Asahiko tendered his resignation immediately to the new Emperor, the fourteen-year-old Emperor Meiji, and had it accepted.

As a gesture of deference to the old regime, Iwakura, who was now firmly in command, organized a fine funeral for Emperor Komei and had him buried, uncremated, in the pure Shinto fashion of the earliest "Viking" Emperors. A spur on the slopes of the pine-covered mountains east of Kyoto was cut away in a large mound 148 feet in diameter. Three terraces supported by retaining walls of cut stone led up to the grave beside which waited an immense rock of great beauty, brought from afar, to be rolled in over the coffin. Komei's body was borne to the site at eleven in the morning and placed in a stone sarcophagus. For the next five hours it inched its way up the burial mound, through countless ceremonies and symbolic barriers. At each stop priests and favorite noblemen were left behind until finally, at the top, only four pallbearers, Komei's most cherished retainers, were left to move the heavy sarcophagus into its pit and lever the great stone over the gaping hole. At four in the afternoon the last prayer was said and the loyal courtiers retired in the dusk.

A few hours later Iwakura Tomomi climbed the mound alone and knelt by the grave in the darkness. All night he remained there kneeling, praying, listening to the sighing of pine needles in the wind, explaining himself and trying to propitiate the angry imperial spirit he imagined hovering before him.

RESTORATION

Even as he prayed, Iwakura was reviewing the plans he had for a new Japan. Writing letters and receiving only night visitors at his cottage outside the city during his five years of exile, he had had much time to think. As with many other great men, a long period of enforced quiet had allowed him to solidify his ideas and accumulate a realistic program for the future. Even before the funeral he had set committees to work drafting plans for a new currency, a new capital, a new landholding system, a new way of government.

In January 1868, the juvenile Emperor Meiji issued a rescript, penned by Iwakura, abolishing the thousand-year-old system of "curtain government" and announcing reinstitution of direct rule by the imperial family. The well-administered clans of the Tokugawa in the north were dismayed at the prospect of being managed by priests from Kyoto and begged the shogun to bring the

Emperor to his senses. Shogun Tokugawa Yoshinobu led a small military retinue of 30,000 toward Kyoto for a parley.

Iwakura advised the adolescent Emperor to take military action against this attempt at intimidation. Let the people see that the Tokugawas were powerless on the battlefield and that the Emperor meant to make a complete break with the past. Emperor Meiji and his family council accepted Iwakura's advice and put two princes of the blood in charge of a large army of samurai from the "outer clans" recruited by Iwakura. The imperial forces fell upon Tokugawa Yoshinobu's 30,000 retainers in the outskirts of Kyoto and routed them utterly.

With little bloodshed, against token resistance, the imperial armies drove north on Tokyo. The former shogun ceded to the Emperor his great fortress of Edo Castle, the future Imperial Palace, and retired to his home fief of Mito, which every Japanese knew to have been a center of loyalty to the Emperor for over two hundred years. There the last shogun disbanded his troops and waited. The new imperial regime in Tokyo first sentenced him to death, then to lifelong rustication, and finally invited him back to free converse in the councils of state. A few diehard retainers of other branches of the Tokugawa family continued to resist in north Japan, but after a year of ritual suicides and little real military action, the whole nation was in the hands of Iwakura and his samurai henchmen from Choshu.

With the help of another Court noble, Sanjo Sanetomi, Iwakura ran his radical young samurai as an oligarchy of comrades under strict revolutionary discipline. Each oligarch was assigned some task of reform such as breakdown of class distinctions or abolition of clan autonomy and was told to draw up a program for his project. Then, if the Emperor and the imperial family council approved it, Iwakura made the oligarch publicly responsible for putting his plan into effect. The people were encouraged to think that the Emperor signed whatever Iwakura laid before him. Thus the advantages of the old system of government were not abandoned: the oligarchy of young reformers were used in traditional fashion as a curtain, hanging like a new shogunate between the Court and the populace.

Behind the curtain stood the fifteen-year-old boy, Emperor

Meiji.[10] The first and only Westerner to have a glimpse of him in his traditional Kyoto surroundings was Sir Harry Parkes, the British ambassador to Tokyo. When it was announced that henceforth the Emperor would be head of state and would sign all treaties, Parkes journeyed to Kyoto in March 1868 and requested an audience in which to present his credentials. On his way to the palace, he and his retinue were set upon by two expert swordsmen, one of them a warrior monk from a temple presided over by one of Prince Asahiko's priestly brothers. Before the two crouching, leaping, slashing assassins could be stopped they had wounded eleven of Parkes's Japanese guards, one of his English infantry escort, his groom, one of the Japanese officials accompanying him, and four of the party's horses.

Nothing deterred, Parkes made a fresh appointment at the palace and a few days later was ushered into one of the long bleak audience chambers there. At the far end was a dais flanked by a carved lion in black lacquer and another in gold lacquer. Over it hung a canopy of pure white silk on a frame of slender black lacquered pillars. The white drapes were tied back with bright red sashes. Before the dais, on a lawn of green silk, knelt two princes of the blood, one a general, the other a priest. The clan lords of Choshu and Satsuma knelt in deep obeisance at one side, utterly immobile and impassive in glistening robes stamped with their clan crests. Courtiers jostled outside the doorway wearing belted, thigh-length kimonos, divided skirts, and high black-lacquered hats that looked like loaves of bread tied to their heads.

As Parkes entered, Emperor Meiji on the dais arose in a white brocade, full-sleeved, tunic-length kimono and a pair of flowing crimson culottes, cut so that the leg ends trailed in little trains behind his high black-and-gold lacquered clogs. On his head was tied a mortarboard from which towered an oblong two-foot fertility symbol of stiff black lacquered silk, stamped with a suitable inscription in red. His face was powdered mask white. His cheeks were rouged. His lips were painted red and gold. His teeth were lacquered black. In a high singsong voice, he read a scroll accept-

[10] Strictly speaking, Emperor Meiji in his lifetime should be called by his personal name, Mutsuhito. Meiji, Enlightened Rule, is the name he gave his reign and the name he is supposed to bear after death in the spirit world.

ing Ambassador Parkes's credentials and the audience was over.

Behind the doll face of this pampered boy worked a strong will and a keen intelligence. Meiji had been born during the early winter of 1852 in an unpretentious cottage nestled beside the carved wooden gables of minor courtiers and courtesans under the high white wall along the north edge of the outer palace compound in Kyoto. His mother was not the official Empress, a regal Fujiwara girl, but the vivacious, dedicated Child of Joy, the favorite of Emperor Komei's score of Court-lady concubines. Because of his birth to a second-class noblewoman, Meiji had the privilege of being brought up until the age of eight by his natural mother and by her rabidly loyalist father instead of by a committee of aged chamberlains as was the wont with crown princes. On the death of the last of his half brothers in 1860, Meiji was declared heir apparent and put into normal ceremonial harness. In 1863, when the shogun visited Kyoto in state and gave money for the rehabilitation of imperial tombs, Meiji and Komei officiated together at an elaborate Shinto ceremony in the palace garden known as "worship at a distance."

Throughout the next three years, until his father's death, Meiji remained beside the Throne at all occasions of state. He came to revere the Shinto pantheon of his ancestors, to admire the free samurai spirits who swaggered in and out of the west gate of the palace, to detest the heavy robes and ceremony of state occasions, and to feel fired by the dreams of a reborn Japan, the stories of Western material progress and power, which were told him in confidence by some of the more cosmopolitan clan lords who paid homage to his father. Although not a robust child, he was sensitive and quick and had a way of endearing himself to all the strident conflicting personalities who came and went from the palace during those final tumultuous years of Emperor Komei's reign.

When Emperor Komei was killed and Iwakura returned from exile, Emperor Meiji was protected from knowledge of the sordid intrigue at Court and was soon a devoted admirer of Iwakura, the new strongman. It is likely that he had already met Iwakura, for during the final year of his banishment the revolutionary young nobleman had frequently visited the palace in secret at night. It is even said that he sometimes met with Emperor Komei, his banisher, and under flag of truce, by imperial request, aired his views on the state of the nation.

Sheltered child though he was, Emperor Meiji, even in the first year of his reign, was never a cipher. He disapproved of his father's handling of the Court, he considered many of the princely priests who were his cousins to be dangerous "madmen," and he responded to the magnetism of Iwakura. From the beginning he showed powers of decision, compromise, and realism that contrasted sharply with the sulky, conservative standing on principle of his father. Emperor Komei had been sacrificed because his words, in favor of a foolish, impossible policy, carried so much weight that there was no other way to get around them. Emperor Meiji, though he did not hear until years later of the suspicious circumstances surrounding his father's death, was careful from the first not to take upon himself too much godliness. He insisted on his right to be wrong in informal discussions, and in formal capacities he never spoke until he was sure he was right. Iwakura helped to train him in this stance and was always careful to discuss and explain all matters of state with him in great detail.

Having announced that he would rule Japan in person, young Emperor Meiji's first act was to transfer his capital from the tradition-laden city of Kyoto, where the Throne had remained since A.D. 794, and from the Western Plain of Yamato, where his "Viking" progenitors had come ashore, to the Eastern Plain and its bustling port city of Tokyo or Edo, where the shoguns had ruled for seven hundred years. Here was Japan's true center of gravity, and Iwakura, the chief of the new samurai oligarchy, was determined that Emperor Meiji should sit in it.

In November 1868, in the longest state progress of Japanese history, the entire Imperial Court wended its way, by easy stages, up the 300-mile length of the Eastern Sea Road. At every mile peasants lay prostrate along the shoulders of the highway to be present when the Being from above the Clouds passed. On November 26, 1868, twenty-three days after Meiji's sixteenth birthday, the imperial palanquin entered Tokyo. Three Westerners were on hand to watch. Meiji rode in a black lacquered sedan chair surmounted by a phoenix of gold, its head and body like a peacock's, its tail like a copper pheasant's fanned out forward over its eyes. Sixty bearers and guardsmen of the imperial blood, robed in yellow silk and wearing tiny chrysanthemum-shaped earrings of feathers, walked beside him. In front paced three aged lictors shaking fans at the assembled multitudes to warn them of the imperial approach. The crowds knelt in waves on either side of the imperial retinue, gluing foreheads to the dust until it passed.

In January 1869, from the former palace of the shoguns, Emperor Meiji decreed that commoners must no longer prostrate themselves in this fashion except before official imperial progresses. Then he ventured forth, unofficially, to inspect the first Western-style vessel built in Japan for a proposed national navy. At the same time he declared Tokyo open to foreigners and advised that henceforth foreigners should be addressed in the noncommittal polite second person which was reserved in Japanese verb forms for the occasional awkward situation in which the speaker did not know the rank of the person he was talking to. Psychologically the new form of address was a great advance over the bellicose, "Hey, you, barbarian inferior," or the obsequious "Hail, outside eminence," which had been in use previously. And since Westerners, learning Japanese, tended to speak as they were spoken to, the new form led to a great improvement in Western-Japanese relations.

The original program for dealing with the Western menace still stood as submitted to the Emperor by the Choshu clan in 1862. First Japan must grow strong; then she must expand overseas to establish a defense perimeter outside the sacred soil; then and only then should she expel the barbarians. But Emperor Meiji's edicts told every Japanese of sensitivity that the program was to be put into effect cautiously, with patience. Emperor Komei's frontal attacks had been rebuffed. The time had come to approach the cherished goal obliquely.

THE MIRACLE

Fresh edicts issued almost daily from the new palace in Tokyo. The incongruous pair, the assassin and his victim's son, worked together with astonishing wisdom and harmony. And still more extraordinary, Japan's ancient, almost fossilized tribal society responded.

Not only the common people but also the most entrenched vested interests of Japan answered to the challenge. The refined sensibilities of every member of the race—perhaps the most aesthetic, ascetic, romantic, disciplined, highly educated people on earth at that time—had been rubbed raw. It was as if everyone felt a personal responsibility for the state of affairs which had led to the killing of Emperor Komei. In two years, between 1869 and 1871, a miracle of idealism and self-sacrifice took place. While token civil war with Tokugawa partisans was still a-dying, all the feudal clan lords voluntarily relinquished the fiefs which they had ruled for centuries and gave back their patrimonies to the Emperor. The samurai, who constituted 5 or 6 per cent of the population, gave up their special rights to kill to preserve the peace and to be fed without touching money or doing work and accepted a status under law equal to that of other citizens. The people themselves promised to give up their own class distinctions and behave as equals.

There was an outcast class, the Eta or Many Filthy Ones, which was descended from the aboriginal Japanese population, augmented by "nonmen" outlaws from the criminal ranks of the rest of society. Decree gave to the Eta—approximately 5 per cent of the population—equal rights under the law with other citizens. And though prejudice against them persisted—and does to this day—Emperor Meiji's edict on their behalf was enforced with remarkable fairness.

The most leveling of all the revolutionary imperial decrees called for the establishment of a national army and navy conscripted from the whole population without regard for birth in or outside of the traditional warrior caste. True, the officers were all former samurai, but in the ranks commoners and samurai mixed. Peasants and untouchables felt positively proud to be conscripted.

As soon as the new laws had been promulgated and before they had worked themselves out in terms of enforcement, the idealistic Iwakura confidently turned over his Emperor and his oligarchy to the care of his lieutenant noble, Sanjo Sanetomi, and went on a scouting trip abroad. Officially his mission was diplomatic: to renegotiate the treaties with the West so that Westerners, residing in Japan, would be subject to Japanese laws and could not fall back on the tender mercies of their own consular courts. In this official purpose Iwakura failed, for no Western nation was ready to relegate its nationals to the inscrutable mental processes of Japanese judges and police interpreters. In the real, unofficial purpose of his mission, Iwakura was more successful: he saw for himself what Japan had to contend with. For two years he reconnoitered the capitals of Europe and America as an honored visitor. In his guarded letters home he expressed dismay at the way power was used in the West, unchecked by any of the family feeling and cohesiveness which gloved fists in Japan. He was impressed by the dispassionate scientific quest for logic which made possible, always, the manufacture of bigger cannon. In a later report to Emperor Meiji he dwelt in particular on an off-the-cuff lesson in *Realpolitik* which he had received from the old master, Bismarck. "The only way," said Bismarck, "for a country like Japan is to strengthen and protect herself with all her own might and set no reliance in other nations. . . . When international law is not to a nation's advantage, it is ignored and resort is made to war."

Iwakura's eyes were still opening when, in 1872, he was called home by rumors of a breakup in his oligarchy. The king of Korea was refusing to open ports to Japanese commerce. He was doing so as rudely and stubbornly as Japan had done earlier in the face of Western trade demands. During Iwakura's absence, his deputy, the nobleman Sanjo Sanetomi, had sided with the Emperor and a group of young Satsuma oligarchs in advocating a military expedition to teach Korea a lesson. Iwakura hastened home, his head swimming with the immensity of the task of modernization confronting Japan. He demonstrated to the twenty-year-old Emperor Meiji, in economic black and red, that the game was not yet worth playing; that Korea was too small and intractable, and Japan too poor, to make the prize worth the effort.

Iwakura found his reborn nation slipping back into the abyss. The economy was a chaos and the would-be conquistadors of Korea were ready for rebellion. For five years Iwakura wrestled with the situation masterfully. He gradually forced Korea, by gunboat diplomacy, to open her ports, and at the same time he checked Japan's runaway inflation. In return for promises of preferential treatment in the future—government pledges which later became the cornerstones of Japan's cartel system and the grubstake of most modern Japanese fortunes—he drew on the gold hoarded by wealthy merchants and established public confidence in his currency and bonds.

Finally, in 1877, Iwakura felt strong enough to challenge the rebels of the Conquer-Korea faction whose threat had brought him home in 1872. The rebels had withdrawn to Kyushu and had enlisted most of the samurai of the seagoing Satsuma clan. They were led by Satsuma oligarch Saigo Takamori. Iwakura set against them Satsuma oligarch Okubo Toshimichi who had grown up on the same street with Saigo but had also accompanied Iwakura to Europe and there shared with Iwakura a look at the realities of the modern world.[11] Under Okubo the nascent national army of Japan, recruited from all classes, crushed the proud samurai of Satsuma and left rebel leader Saigo to commit suicide on a mountaintop with his last 400 supporters.

THE WORKING YEARS

Now that the foreign putsch had been postponed, now that the clan lords had returned their fiefs to the Throne, now that inflation had been checked and all eager spirits taught to be patient awhile in harness, the nation for fifteen years germinated in the soil of hard work and money-making. The Japanese home craftsman became the light industrialist. The Japanese merchant became the shipping magnate. The Japanese moneylender became the financier. Tokyo, Osaka, Hiroshima, Nagasaki, and Kokura grew into industrial centers where armies of peasants from the countryside learned a new urban way of life working in mills and banks and railroad yards.

The patriotic duty of absorbing the spiritual strength of the

11 Okubo was the father of Count Makino Nobuaki who would be Hirohito's chief advisor and lord privy seal from 1922 to 1935. On Iwakura's European tour Okubo had been the Satsuma clan's representative. The Choshu clan representative had been Kido Koin, the adoptive grandfather of Kido Koichi who would be Hirohito's chief advisor and lord privy seal from 1940 to 1945.

West was practiced religiously by everyone—by tailors and musicians and dramatists as well as by technologists. As a result wave after wave of Western imitation swept over the surface of Japanese culture. Clan lords bustled about Tokyo wearing two swords, top hats, and plus fours. More than 30,000 Western "classics" were roughly translated into the Japanese language and given to the literate public to puzzle over. Painters deserted their own refined native style and took to copying the robust realism of Western masters. Audiences attuned to the dulcet harmonic vagaries of the Japanese guitar and lute, the *samisen* and *biwa*, allowed their senses to be assaulted and swamped by Beethoven and Wagner. New schools of Japanese writers threw over their classical conventions and began to tell stories in the contemporary vernacular. University students fed on Bacon, Hume, Kant, and Hegel and espoused ill-digested new systems of thought and government. Action groups began to call themselves anarchists and socialists and were relentlessly persecuted by the police.

In 1883, when Japan, in her great leap forward into modernity, had still scarcely left the ground, Iwakura Tomomi, the strongman of the oligarchy of young samurai, died of stomach cancer at forty-eight. He was attended in his last hours by Emperor Meiji's personal physician. Meiji, who had grown up to be a strikingly handsome and intelligent monarch of thirty-one, proceeded to take the reigns of the oligarchy into his own hands. His touch was light and sure. He remained always "behind the curtain," and handled his oligarchs with an easygoing sense of humor. On those rare occasions when a piece of paper came to his desk that displeased him, he would ignore it. Each morning he would carefully move it to the bottom of the pile of state business and would continue to do so until it was discreetly withdrawn and redrafted.

Under his keen eyes, not only the national family but the imperial family prospered. He gave monopolistic development rights in the new industrial Japan to merchant friends of his Court and received a share of the profits in return. Control of the nation's economy fell into the hands of three great cartel families, the Mitsuis of the Mitsui Company, the Iwasakis of the Mitsubishi Company, and the Sumitomos of the Sumitomo Company. Between them they ruled Japan's foreign trade, her heavy industry, and her banking. Because of their loyalty and indebtedness to the Throne, they acted as unofficial members of the government, co-ordinating their industrialization plans with long-range imperial policy. Past dependence upon doles from shoguns had taught the lesson that high-priestly power could no more be exercised without money than without arms. And so Emperor Meiji amassed the fourth largest concentration of capital for himself and his family. Through gifts, investments, and outright expropriations, he increased the imperial fortune from a paltry $51,000 in 1867 to approximately $40 million by the end of his reign in 1912.

To consolidate further the position of the imperial family, Emperor Meiji sent all but two of the fifteen sons and nephews of Emperor Komei's advisor, Prince Asahiko, away to Europe to study the Western arts of war. At Sandhurst and St. Cyr, Brest and Dartmouth, the Polytechnique and Göttingen, they learned military physics and gathered around them cadres of poorer Japanese students who would serve them gratefully, as familiars, later in Japan. Future field marshals and chiefs of staff shared intimately in the homesickness and bounty of the lonely princes in a way that would never have been possible inside the rank-and-etiquette-conscious structure of domestic Japanese society.

When the half-Westernized princes returned home, they joined Meiji's family council, his kitchen cabinet. Hidden from the public eye, this body advised Meiji on policy making; administration it left to the samurai cabinet of oligarchs. Unknown to the public, the cabinet also met regularly with Emperor Meiji—in an atmosphere not much more formal than that in the back rooms of the White House at the same period. Thus, in 1896, young oligarch Saionji Kinmochi got up in Emperor Meiji's presence to recommend an official Japanese representative to send to the coronation of Czar Nicholas II. He delivered the following preposterous encomium on behalf of his fellow oligarch Yamagata Aritomo, the most sly, tough, unreconstructed samurai in the room: "Instead of sending a man of prominent position or of thorough knowledge of conditions, or of great ability, it would be better to send a person whose words are not only trusted by foreign countries but who commands the implicit faith of our own land, too, as an indubitable national representative." When Meiji had recovered from his guffaws, Yamagata, scowling, was nominated by acclamation.

Saionji and Yamagata represented opposite poles of opinion in Emperor Meiji's oligarchy—two factions which were to haunt Emperor Hirohito decades later. Ramrod-stiff and straight, his shaggy mustache bristling, Yamagata was a Choshu-clan samurai, every inch the military man. At the restoration, he had been put in charge of national conscription and had built up the Army from a few ragged regiments to a formidable establishment of 250,000 men. A firm believer in Asia for the Asiatics, he saw the Choshu program of 1862 as strictly limited in its goals. If only Japan could create a buffer zone in Korea and North China, she would be able to draw in on herself once more and go back to her pursuit of disciplined one-family happiness. Yamagata believed the main obstacle to be the Russians for whom he had a deep hatred. In spirit, and by actual ties of blood and allegiance, he was the father of the Strike-North group which would try to force Hirohito in the 1930's to attack Russia instead of the United States.

Yamagata's tormentor in Emperor Meiji's councils, Saionji Kinmochi, was a blithe, graceful courtier of thirty-seven. He was no samurai but a prince, a prince of the Fujiwara family, which was second only to being a prince of the imperial blood. His faction was that of many Westernized Japanese who saw in the barbarians no threat and hoped that the Choshu program of 1862 would be abandoned. As a member of the Fujiwara clan, Saionji believed it his duty, bequeathed him by his ancestors, to preserve the institution of the imperial family and its pantheon of spirits. He hoped to do so, however, by making the Japanese god-king a powerless constitutional monarch. He meant every quip he flung at Yamagata to be a chip from the tree of tradition he hoped one day to fell. He was to be tragically disillusioned. Outliving the rest of Emperor Meiji's oligarchs, he would become, in the 1930's, Hirohito's senior advisor. He would be scorned by his monarch and used as a loyal tool. Remaining loyal nonetheless, he would do his utmost to steer Hirohito away from the disaster he saw ahead. Finally in 1940, he would die at the age of ninety-one, recognizing that all his dreams had been blasted.

In 1868, at the age of eighteen, Saionji had made a name for himself as the leader of a cavalry troop in the civil war with the Tokugawas. He had stood out then as a bright young knight, wearing a green plume and green silk over his corselet of wood and metal ribs. Being only three years older than Emperor Meiji and a nobleman of the highest hereditary Court rank, he enjoyed an intimacy with his monarch far closer than that of General Yamagata or of any of the other oligarchs. Although he was not allowed, by birth, to sit on the imperial family council, he was privileged to know more than the other oligarchs about the deliberations in that other, higher kitchen cabinet.

Saionji had gone abroad with Iwakura in 1871 as a member of the delegation sent to study Western customs. He had remained there, studying in Paris, for nine years. Unlike many of his fellow aristocrats, who felt themselves slighted in Western capitals, Saionji enjoyed himself enormously. By family tradition, he was a ladies' man. The first Saionji, in the twelfth century, had made a vow that he and his successors would never take wives but only mistresses. His excuse was that he played the lute in a way pleasing to the Emperor and that the muse of lute players was insanely jealous of wives. Ever since that time every Saionji had played the lute, had enjoyed many mistresses, and had adopted an heir from another family—often from the family of a man who had been cuckolded by a Saionji.[12]

[12] The aristocratic families of Kyoto have many such traditions, invented as conversation pieces in courtly years gone by but now maintained as treasures of the national heritage. Many families keep temples, supported by ancient endowments, where their first sons preside as priests. One family maintains a shrine for the spirits of broken sewing needles. I know a wealthy gentleman of fifty-five, known locally as "Prince of the Night," who obeys a vow, taken at about the time of the Battle of Hastings, that every heir to the family must do proletarian work. His father spent sixteen years at French, English, and Australian universities and came home to be a farmer. The son, Prince of the Night, put in a dozen years as an Army officer on the frontiers of Manchuria, and came home to hawk noodles from a bucket on the Kyoto streets. When his day is over, he takes off the sweatband from his forehead, and the tunic and baggy cotton pants of the laborer, dons a custom-tailored sports shirt and trousers, steps into his chauffeur-driven limousine, and drives off each night to visit the score or more of bars, night clubs, and tea houses built on his property. I had the pleasure once of accompanying him on his evening rounds. We started at a modest bar at seven and went on to twelve other establishments, each more Japanese and exclusive than the last. On the

Oligarch Saionji Kinmochi was no exception to his family tradition. He was a Tokudaiji by birth, one of the highest ranking Fujiwara families at Court. His elder brother was for many years Emperor Meiji's first Fujiwara advisor. His younger brother was adopted heir to the great cartel family of Sumitomo, the third wealthiest in Japan. Because of his excellent connections, young expatriate Saionji lacked not for money or introductions in Paris. He ingratiated himself at the finest dinner tables. He played the lute passing well. He liked the French girls and they liked him. After less than a month in Paris he had his own chic French mistress. In one of his first letters home he declared that it was far easier for him to master the difficult barbarian books he was reading with a native barbarian girl at his side than all alone.

In 1880 Saionji had returned to Japan for a year, had moved into a geisha tea house, and then had been sent abroad again to help an elder oligarch, Ito Hirobumi, draft a constitution for Japan. Ito and the young Saionji returned in 1883 with a blueprint that was 90 per cent Japanese and 10 per cent French and German in inspiration. Constitutional scholars say that its prime Western model was Bismarck's constitution for Germany. The ideas and purposes of the Constitution were debated within the oligarchy for six years.

Before considering the Constitution closely, the oligarchy hired Western jurists and interpreters to find an acceptable Western model for a legal code which would fit established Japanese police practices. Then in 1885, to test the applicability of the Constitution to the Japanese scene, Emperor Meiji appointed a national

---

way Prince of the Night acquired half a dozen new male acquaintances, three bar hostesses, and four apprentice geisha. Our last stop was an exquisite tea house, remodeled as a club, which had stayed open waiting for us from its usual closing hour of ten until our arrival at one in the morning. We left it in five rented Cadillacs which all escorted me home. A wife is a taboo item on such occasions, and mine was asleep upstairs in our Japanese-style house when the cavalcade pulled up at the curb. Prince of the Night took a package from his chauffeur and came in with me to present it as solace to the stay-at-home. When I awakened her from a sound sleep, my noble wife did me great credit in Japanese eyes by coming downstairs without a murmur to accept the gift: three teacups and saucers designed and commissioned from a local porcelain works by Prince of the Night himself. The next morning he was back on the streets in peddler's garb, crying, "Noodles, fresh noodles, all fresh, a-fresh-O."

deliberative body of wise men, the Diet or Congress. Conserva-
tives feared that the new debating society would reveal aristocratic secrets to the masses. Its powers, however, were carefully
restricted in advance to legislation pertaining to increases in the
annual national budget. Much to the disappointment of many
gossips, the appointed delegates did not stray far from this one
topic. Policy, as represented by the budgets inherited from previous years, remained beyond debate. Only the reasons for increases could be scrutinized. The Diet caused so little trouble that
it was continued and the restriction on its powers was written
into the contemplated Constitution.

In April 1888 Meiji ordered the senior members of his oligarchy
to form a new advisory body to the Throne, the Privy Council, in
order to thrash out the final text of the Constitution. For the next
nine months the Privy Councillors met weekly with Emperor
Meiji in the palace to argue and edit Saionji's masterpiece. Finally,
on February 11, 1889, the Constitution was promulgated as a gift
of the Emperor to the people. It explicitly conferred on the Emperor an unqualified, all-encompassing power that would have
warmed the heart of a Catherine or Caligula:

The Empire of Japan shall be reigned over and governed by a line of
Emperors unbroken for ages eternal. . . . The Emperor is sacred and
inviolable. . . . The Emperor exercises the legislative power with the
consent of the Imperial Diet. . . . The Emperor convokes the Imperial Diet, opens, closes and prorogues it, and dissolves the House of
Representatives. . . . The Emperor gives sanction to laws, and orders
them to be promulgated and executed. . . . The Emperor, in consequence of urgent necessity . . . issues . . . when the Imperial Diet is
not sitting, Imperial Ordinances in the place of law. . . . The Emperor determines the organization of the different branches of the administration, and salaries of all civil and military officers, and appoints
and dismisses the same. . . . The Emperor has the supreme command
of the Army and Navy. . . . The Emperor determines the organization and peace standing of the Army and Navy. . . . The Emperor
declares war, makes peace, and concludes treaties. . . . The Emperor
confers titles of nobility, rank, orders and other marks of honor. . . .
The Emperor orders amnesty, pardon, commutation of punishments
and rehabilitation.

Complex feelings and disagreements had caused the long delay in issuing this extraordinary document. Its secret purpose was to persuade Western nations that Japan had an explicit social compact which could be relied upon as legally binding. Once the West was so convinced, it would be possible to renegotiate the humiliating treaties which allowed foreigners to be tried for crimes in their own courts. Once Western business interests in Japan came under Japanese jurisdiction, it would be possible to make Western statesmen accept Japan as an equal in international power politics.

Prince Akira, the elder brother of Komei's counselor and the chief advisor on foreign policy to Emperor Meiji, hoped that by treaties and alliances it would be possible to play the Great Power game and share in the anticipated dismemberment of China. In the ranks of ordinary conservative samurai, the feeling prevailed that this was a dishonorable tradesman's approach to national goals. Yamagata, the boss of the Army, encouraged such feeling. He saw no purpose in taking on Western state trappings and advocated a simple policy of armament, followed by straightforward conquest of the required buffer zone. Saionji and a few other genuine liberals espoused the Constitution enthusiastically as an opening wedge for their plan to rationalize the mystical relationship between people and Throne and make the Emperor a being under law.

Two of the oligarchs who advocated the liberal position too openly in public were silenced by mysterious acts of violence. The day that the Constitution was promulgated, Minister of Education Mori Arinori was knifed and killed by a young Shinto fanatic. The assassin had been told that Mori, on a visit to the shrine of the sun goddess at Ise, had impiously raised a bamboo curtain with the tip of his cane in order to have a look at the relics behind the curtain.

Eight months later, on October 18, 1889, Minister of Foreign Affairs Okuma Shigenobu lost a leg when a bomb was hurled into his carriage. The public was surprised to learn that Okuma had been returning to his ministry early in the morning from a heated debate about treaty revision which had been going on more or less continuously in the palace for four days—Emperor Meiji pre-

siding over it in person. Okuma had concluded the first egali-
tarian treaty—with Mexico—the year before, and was in process of
negotiating successfully with the United States and Great Britain.
His assailant claimed to have thrown the bomb at him for the
upside-down reason that the treaty inequalities which Okuma was
trying to eliminate still existed.

LORD HIGH ASSASSIN

Behind both of the would-be assassins stood the dark figure of a
man named Toyama, who would be known as the intermediary
for important assassinations of state throughout the rest of his
long life. To Western onlookers he seemed a gangster. To the
great mass of Japanese he seemed a patriot—the conscience of the
nation, a man of the people. He took money from ward heelers in
order to fix local grievances. He took money from Army sources
controlled by Oligarch Yamagata. He accepted money even from
imperial princes. When the Great Powers had signed new treaties
and it came time for taking the first step in Japan's expansion, he
was to be entrusted with creating provocation for the step. After
the imperial family, the Army, and the genuine liberals like
Saionji, he was the fourth force in Japan, representing the people,
especially the people of the new city slums. A singularly Japanese
character, he would figure large in Western writings about Japan
for the next fifty years. It would be leaders of his foster organization, the Black Dragon Society, who would be arrested first by
General MacArthur's M.P.'s in 1945.

Toyama Mitsuru began his career at the time of the restoration in 1868 as a shrewd thirteen-year-old urchin peddling yams on
the streets of Fukuoka in the southern island of Kyushu. Barred
by his lowly birth from ever participating directly in government,
he made himself a leader of labor bosses in the new industrial
cities. Most of his henchmen were masterless samurai who had
gravitated to the city slums and embarked on wastrel careers as
poets or cutthroats. Still scornful of money, still dedicated to a
strict barbaric code of honor, they were hopelessly incompetent at
earning a living by peaceful arts. They still wore two swords, however, and still knew how to lead men. Toyama was the most

successful of several criminal geniuses who saw that these master-less samurai, the *ronin*, had a role to play in the new order. Be-cause of their former high rank in society, they could organize the new suburbs and shape up the new gangs of factory hands.

Toyama instinctively knew all the right whistles for making the fierce wolves of the slums his obedient sheepdogs. He represented whatever he did, no matter how shabby or savage, as a piece of patriotism in the service of the Throne. If a ward boss had to be murdered, it was because he had slurred the name of the imperial family; if a businessman had to be blackmailed, it was because some society dedicated to the imperial cause needed the funds. Having once gained the admiration of a masterless samurai by his profes-sions of a simple warlike loyalism, Toyama could, if necessary, ce-ment his relationship with the man by an exhibition of personal prowess as a wrestler or swordsman. He was an excellent athlete.

One of Toyama's most devoted disciples, a future Cabinet minister, explained his idol as "an example of a man who refrains from displaying his mental and physical faculties." That is, he gave an impression of unused secret strength. His antagonists of-ten capitulated to him without investigating the weaknesses of his position.

But Toyama was nothing if not an exhibitionist. He larded his conversation with vaguely threatening parables and anecdotes. In his storytelling he was a master of the *ma*, the grunt that ex-presses what is inexpressible and the long, seemingly significant pause that follows it. In his facial expressions he cultivated *bo*, an absolutely blank look of sleepy indifference which might cover a genuine doze or a hand on the dagger in the sleeve of his kimono.

In his first years of success as a gang leader, Toyama sometimes made a show of standing on a street corner passing out unopened packages of bank notes to his henchmen. He would walk weeping with gifts to the home of one of his men who had been killed in a brawl. He thought nothing of striding into the office of a rival or politician with a scroll of signatures advising his host to do hara-kiri. On one occasion, after many procrastinations and pleas of business, he finally vouchsafed an interview to a Japanese news-paper reporter who had been trying to see him for days. Shown in by a maid, the reporter found Toyama atop one of his many mistresses. "Excuse me for being on my horse," he said casually—and continued his erotic exercise throughout the interview.

In Toyama's hands, the art of silent intimidation was raised to a level which is much admired in Japan to this day. Without any show of force, without breaking any of the fragile, smiling conventions of Japanese etiquette, he could come unarmed to a man's home—to the home of a Dietman or even a prime minister—and make that man tremble for his life. As a matter of face, those whom he had successfully cowed and bluffed always touted his powers thereafter. Because he seldom needed to shed blood, his services as a bully were sought and bought by the heaviest moneybags in the land. The poor recognized him as a Robin Hood and the rich as a valuable, if costly, arranger. With aristocratic backing he founded many patriotic tongs, only one of which was the famous Amur River Society or Black Dragon. It became the most powerful of his organizations largely because of its awesomesounding name. In the minds of Japanese and Europeans alike, it evoked exotic visions of opium dens and of Chinese mandarins tugging new ecstasies of sadism out of their sparse beards.

FIRST AGGRESSION

Toyama had just established himself as a national underworld figure, just withdrawn from the hurly-burly of the streets, just begun to run the lower classes of the nation from the back garden of his home, when Japan had advanced far enough to take the first step in her program of overseas expansion. In 1893 a dramatic increase in the national military budget was debated noisily in the Diet. The debate was abruptly stilled by a special message from Emperor Meiji, explaining in grand indirections that the present state of the world required a strengthening of the nation. The message came at a time when the state of the world had been unprecedentedly peaceful—without even a minor war, anywhere, for almost twenty years. The Diet, however, passed the special military budget without further murmur. And it was then, in 1894, that Toyama was given his first big foreign assignment.

Minister of War Kawakami Soroku of the Satsuma clan, a minion of Imperial Princes Arisugawa and Yoshihisa, the two senior

generals of the Army at that time, gave an interview to a delegation of Toyama's masterless samurai. They had come to see War
Minister Kawakami for a trivial favor for their constituents. After
granting it, he held them in his office by musing expansively on
Japan in the world of 1894. The Cabinet, he said, was not officially
prepared to seize Korea at that time, but if someone were to "start
a fire" in Korea, the Ministry of the Army would be called in to
put it out, and he, Kawakami, was prepared to play "fireman."

Toyama's men "understood his meaning" and duly reported
Kawakami's remarks to Toyama. Seeing his duty at once, Toyama
hand-picked a band of fifteen self-styled "fire-setters." They went
to Korea, established relations with a group of ultraconservative
Koreans, the Tonghaks, who were militating for closure of the
country to Japanese intercourse, and helped them to start a
revolution.

The Chinese Imperial Court in Peking had countered earlier
Japanese infiltration of masterless samurai into Korea by the dispatch in 1883 of Yuan Shih-kai, one of China's most promising
young military minds, to serve as resident general in Seoul. Yuan
was to become the ruler of all China twenty years later and was
to be remembered, according to the slant of the commentator, as
a Japanese puppet or as a cunning subverter of Japanese plans.
In 1894, when he discovered that the Japanese "fire-setters" were
backing the diehard Tonghak rebellion, he made the mistake of
persuading the corrupt and ineffective Korean emperor to summon the aid of Chinese troops. This was all the fire that Meiji
and his oligarchs needed. When the Korean government had already suppressed the Tonghak rebellion, when the Chinese were
still mobilizing their intervention, when Czar Nicholas had massed
troops on the northern Korean border but had not yet sent them
across, Japanese divisions suddenly arrived by sea and occupied
Seoul and other strategic cites in a brilliantly executed nineteenth
century blitzkrieg. The Chinese Navy sought to prevent the Japanese from sending reinforcements, and so the Chinese Navy was
sunk by the Japanese Navy.

Emperor Meiji put himself in personal charge of all military
operations. To escape from the distractions of routine government
and be within a day's flight, by carrier pigeon, of the front, he

moved himself and the General Staff to the fated town of Hiroshima in southwestern Honshu and there set up a strictly celibate
headquarters, no more luxurious than those of his generals in the
field. His preoccupation with the war was so intense and his discipline so Spartan that courtiers worried for his health and arranged "a chance meeting" for him with a favorite concubine who
had come down from Tokyo—a 500-mile journey—to give him
solace.

Almost before the first Sino-Japanese war had started, China
was suing for peace. In the settlement, she gave Japan not only
the right to "protect" Korea, but also a substantial indemnity,
the balmy island of Taiwan or Formosa, and the southern seaside
appendix of Manchuria known as the Kwantung Peninsula.
Alarmed by the extent of Japan's unexpected victory, France, Russia, and Germany, in a triple intervention, at once illustrated Bismarck's earlier candid lesson to Iwakura by warning Japan that
she was taking too much. Japan resentfully relinquished her rights
to the Kwantung Peninsula only to see it leased for a song by
Russia three years later. In acquiring Taiwan, Japan had increased
her area by 10 per cent. Nevertheless, the mass of Japanese felt
balked and bilked by the triple intervention, and they were not at
all mollified by U.S. acquisition of the Philippines, three years
later, in 1898.

Not knowing the high level at which the war had been plotted,
the Japanese Cabinet approved the occupation of Korea on the
understanding that it would be only temporary. In the first year
of the protectorship, two enlightened Japanese administrators did
their best to steer Korea into a progressive policy of Westernized
nationalism and reform such as Japan had followed. They were
stubbornly resisted by reactionaries ready to die for the cause of
the old order.

Accordingly, the third of the Japanese ministers in Korea, General Miura Goro, a Choshu samurai who had run the Peers'
School for noblemen and had many intimate connections at
Court, plotted with a group of Black Dragon Toyama's men to
snuff out the one vital ruling spark in the effete Korean Court,
Crown Princess Bin. On October 8, 1895, while Miura's soldiers
restrained the Korean Imperial Guards outside the palace, Toy-

ama's thugs chased the princess and her ladies down corridors inside and lopped them limb from limb. The bodies were doused with oil and burned in the courtyard. Miura was haled home to stand trial for permitting the crime but was acquitted by his Japanese judges "for lack of definitive evidence." He remained an honored oracle behind the curtains of Japanese politics, and his advice was sought on most Cabinet appointments for the next thirty years.

The nonentity who was the emperor of Korea sought asylum in the Russian Embassy and called on Czar Nicholas II to protect him. Nicholas, the last of the czars, then thirty-three years old, was offended by the Japanese attempt to make Korea a colony on the borders of Russia, and ordered his subordinates to give refuge as requested by the Korean king and to mass troops once more on the Siberian-Korean border. Encouraged by Russia, Korean ultra-nationalists went on a rampage of assassination against the Japanese military police. With cruel efficiency the police suppressed them. The handful of liberal statesmen who advocated an enlightened administration for Korea were discredited in Emperor Meiji's councils.

The surviving brothers of Emperor Komei's advisor, Prince Asahiko,[13] recommended that the next Japanese crusade be directed against the czar of all the Russias. The emperor of China had been put down. He could be dethroned if the emperor of Russia could be held in check. Finally both emperors might be overthrown. Then, outside of Japan, there would be no monarch claiming to rule a great empire, with imperial prerogatives, except the old lady, Victoria, who sat on the throne of England. At the turn of the century in 1900, Emperor Meiji had no advice to fall back on but that of his cousins.

At that juncture entered the protagonist of the twentieth cen-

[13] Asahiko had died at sixty-seven in 1891. His elder brother Akira, after thirty years as the Throne's chief advisor on foreign policy, died in 1898. His younger brother, Prince Yoshihisa, had succumbed to dysentery as commander in chief of pacification forces in Taiwan in 1895. Out of the brood of twelve sons fathered by Asahiko's lusty father, Prince Kuniye, there remained alive only Prince Akihito, a priest turned Chief of Staff; Prince Sadanaru, an admiral; Count Kiyosu, a provincial governor; Prince Kanin, a colonel with a long future ahead of him; and Prince Yorihito, a Navy captain.

HOUSE OF

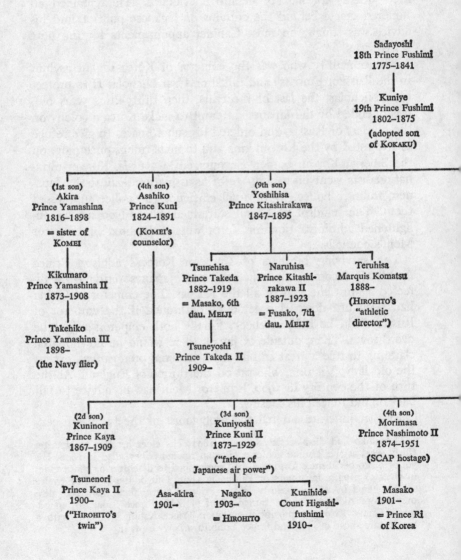

Sadayoshi
18th Prince Fushimi
1775–1841

Kuniye
19th Prince Fushimi
1802–1875

(adopted son
of KOKAKU)

(1st son)
Akira
Prince Yamashina
1816–1898

= sister of
KOMEI

(4th son)
Asahiko
Prince Kuni
1824–1891

(KOMEI's
counselor)

(9th son)
Yoshihisa
Prince Kitashirakawa
1847–1895

Kikumaro
Prince Yamashina II
1873–1908

Takehiko
Prince Yamashina III
1898–

(the Navy flier)

Tsunehisa
Prince Takeda
1882–1919

= Masako, 6th
dau. MEIJI

Tsuneyoshi
Prince Takeda II
1909–

Naruhisa
Prince Kitashi-
rakawa II
1887–1923

= Fusako, 7th
dau. MEIJI

Teruhisa
Marquis Komatsu
1888–

(HIROHITO's
"athletic
director")

(2d son)
Kuninori
Prince Kaya
1867–1909

Tsunenori
Prince Kaya II
1900–

("HIROHITO's
twin")

(3d son)
Kuniyoshi
Prince Kuni II
1873–1929

("father of
Japanese air power")

Asa-akira
1901–

Nagako
1903–

= HIROHITO

Kunihide
Count Higashi-
fushimi
1910–

(4th son)
Morimasa
Prince Nashimoto II
1874–1951

(SCAP hostage)

Masako
1901–

= Prince Ri
of Korea

FUSHIMI

(14th son)
Sadanaru
21st Prince Fushimi
1858–1923

(TAISHO's advisor)

(16th son)
Kotohito
Prince Kanin
1865–1945

(Army Chief of
Staff, 1931–40)

Hiroyasu
22d Prince Fushimi
1875–1947

(Navy Chief of
Staff, 1932–41)

(8th son)
Yasuhiko
Prince Asaka
1887–

(Commander
at Nanking)

= Nobuko, 8th
dau. MEIJI

(9th son)
Naruhiko
Prince Higashikuni
1887–

(Prime Minister,
Aug.–Sept., 1945)

= Toshiko, 9th
dau. MEIJI

IMPERIAL LINE AFTER 1779

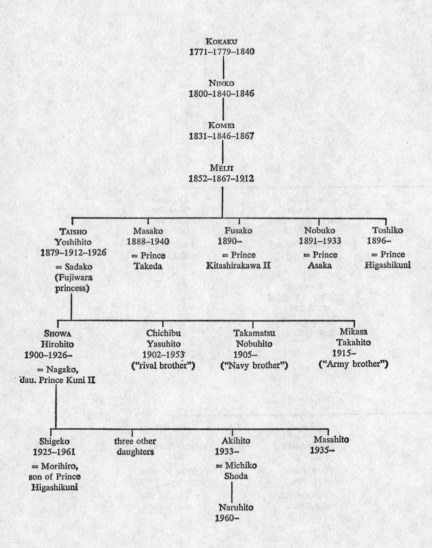

KOKAKU
1771–1779–1840

NINKO
1800–1840–1846

KOMEI
1831–1846–1867

MEIJI
1852–1867–1912

TAISHO
Yoshihito
1879–1912–1926

= Sadako
(Fujiwara
princess)

Masako
1888–1940

= Prince
Takeda

Fusako
1890–

= Prince
Kitashirakawa II

Nobuko
1891–1933

= Prince
Asaka

Toshiko
1896–

= Prince
Higashikuni

SHOWA
Hirohito
1900–1926–

= Nagako,
dau. Prince Kuni II

Chichibu
Yasuhito
1902–1953
("rival brother")

Takamatsu
Nobuhito
1905–
("Navy brother")

Mikasa
Takahito
1915–
("Army brother")

Shigeko
1925–1961

= Morihiro,
son of Prince
Higashikuni

three other
daughters

Akihito
1933–

= Michiko
Shoda

Masahito
1935–

Naruhito
1960–

tury, Hirohito. It would be his attempt to enforce restoration of his family's rule over the nation, his attempt to expel barbarians and carry out the Choshu plan of 1862 which would lead to Nanking in 1937, Pearl Harbor in 1941, and Hiroshima in 1945. Emperor Komei had died for the cause of expelling the barbarians. Emperor Hirohito would live for it. It was a holy mission bequeathed by the imperial ancestors.

PART THREE

YOUNG CAESAR

6

HIROHITO'S BOYHOOD

(1900–1912)

EARLY BABY

In the walled gardens of the Aoyama Palace in Tokyo, the cherry blossoms, which Japanese compare with warriors because they fall in the full pride of their bloom, had drifted from the boughs and lay scattered on the ground. Each morning, surrounded by ladies in waiting, a fifteen-year-old princess named Sadako walked the fragrant carpets of fading pink, around the moon-mirror pools, between the painstakingly stunted and gnarled pine trees, and across the rainbow bridges. She glowed with good health, for she had lived most of her life on a farm, following a regimen prescribed by Court physicians to make her a fertile mother. Now the fact that she was in the last stages of pregnancy enhanced her beauty, bringing a special quality of color and transparency to her white skin. Her high-bridged imperial nose, long neck, and slanting shoulders stamped her a Fujiwara, one of the family whose daughters had traditionally knelt beside the Emperors for over eighty reigns.

In carrying her child Sadako faced a challenge unknown to her Fujiwara forebears. Since Emperor Go-Momozono's birth in 1758, all the Emperors had been sons of imperial mistresses rather than of wives. To satisfy Western standards of propriety, Emperor Meiji had promulgated a new Imperial House Law stipulating that from now on only the official Empress could supply an heir to the Throne. As Meiji and his two most privy chamberlains[1] interpreted the new rule, it meant that only a proven heir-producer could become Empress. The future of the princess in the garden, therefore, depended on the gender of the child she carried. She was betrothed to Crown Prince Yoshihito, the future Emperor Taisho. If she gave him a boy, she would be married to him; if she had a girl, Meiji might give her a second chance, but only if none of the other noble mistresses of the crown prince delivered a boy first.

In due course, then, when the fallen cherry blossoms had turned almost gray, Princess Sadako's breathing quickened one morning and she retired a few weeks earlier than expected to labor in the pavilion assigned to her. That night, at ten minutes past ten, a wrinkled, premature Hirohito shouted his first cry. A trusted courtier inspected the tiny red body, whipped up his horses, and bowled across central Tokyo in his carriage to report the birth at the Imperial Palace. Emperor Meiji tabled his glass of port and the writing brush with which he had been composing a *tanka* and ordered champagne all around for the chamberlains of his bedchamber.

Princess Sadako was formally married to Crown Prince Yoshihito eleven days later, on May 10, 1900. The wedding was a small family affair, held at eight o'clock in the morning in the Shinto shrine in the private inner enclosure of the main palace. Western ambassadors in Tokyo were permitted to congratulate the newlyweds at a reception that afternoon in the semipublic halls of the outer Ceremonial Palace. The existence of Hirohito was kept a secret for almost a year, until the announcement of his first birthday on April 29, 1901. By the Oriental method of reckoning age, a child is one at the hour of his birth. The fact that, by Western standards, he is one a year later enabled the Imperial Household Ministry to represent Hirohito, without technically lying, as newly born in 1901. Thus Western propriety and Japanese practicality were both satisfied, and no honor was lost.[2]

[1] Prince Tokudaiji Sanenori, the elder brother of Prince Saionji, the lute-playing Constitutionalist; Count Tanaka Mitsuaki, who would live to meddle in Hirohito's own matrimonial affairs in the 1930's.

[2] The official date of Hirohito's birth, as acknowledged by the Imperial Household Ministry, is still 1901 rather than 1900. But the account given

Born in secret, Hirohito was kept out of the limelight throughout his childhood. Until 1912 he was not even declared heir apparent but shared the right of succeeding to the Throne with his younger brothers. During his first year he remained snugly hidden with his mother in the Aoyama Palace. Then, because it was an old custom, devised to protect heirs from the recurrent dysenteries and fevers of Court life, he was put out for foster care. Princess Sadako returned demurely to the gay, Westernized, Edwardian life of the crown prince in the Akasaka Palace, and Hirohito, wrapped in purple swaddling clothes, was bundled off by coach and four. It was typically muggy Tokyo summer weather. The carriage skirted the barbarian embassies outside the western walls of the palace and rolled south through the best residential district of Tokyo, past villas belonging to Tokugawas, Fujiwaras, and princes of the blood. Finally it drew up at the home of Vice Admiral Kawamura Sumiyoshi in Azabu, about a mile and a half from its starting point.

Kawamura was a Satsuma clansman, a retainer of the Shimazu family. He had been responsible thirty years earlier for importing ten British officers to train the men of Japan's nascent navy. Now he was an elder of sixty-five, renowned for his traditionalism and his simple way of life. His neat clean house stood for all that was purest in the old Japan: planed unlacquered cryptomeria, ground cypress, paulownia, and pine; sliding paper-paned doors opening on miniature gardens; *tatami* floors for stockinged feet; charcoal braziers and throw-pillows; pallets rolled out onto the floor at dusk for sleeping; piping hot baths in a deep wooden tub; an austere

above, which is based upon Court gossip, has been tacitly accepted by several knowledgeable writers since the 1920's. Thus F. S. G. Piggott, who later served as translator for conversations between Hirohito and Edward, Prince of Wales, described Hirohito as "in his twenty-second year" when he visited England in May 1921. And Hirohito's personal public relations man, Count Futara Yoshinori, wrote unequivocally in 1928 that Hirohito was born "on the night of April 29, 1900." The publisher of Count Futara's account is on record elsewhere with a list of all the typographical errors concerning the imperial family for which he was ever made to apologize by the police; he does not include Count Futara's statement as one of them. Finally, the issues of Japanese newspapers for the fortnight surrounding April 29, 1901, were removed from Japanese libraries in 1945 and have remained unavailable ever since.

alcove for prayer and meditation, where hung a single inspirational example of calligraphy.

Hirohito's foster home was an island of conservatism and taste in a sea of change. Outside the small villa's walls, shanties of plain pine crowded against one another as far south and west as the eye could see. The ancient fort town of Edo, now known as Tokyo, had become one of the largest cities in the world. Where the moon after dark had once stood over a few straight, empty, well-policed thoroughfares—illuminated fitfully by the glimmer of a geisha's lantern or the bumptious roar of a samurai's torch—there now twisted countless alleyways, draped with telegraph wires and busy under gaslight. It was a shark's ocean. No longer did the people ask favors of portly government officials in starched robes but of pimps, racketeers, and slum landlords.

In the eyes of Hirohito's foster father, even the great 240-acre palace, two miles to the northeast, had begun to suffer the modern defilement. Several of the grim battlements and moats had been leveled, pierced, or bridged in a manner which made them militarily unsound. A new ceremonial complex of buildings, completed in 1889, contained a Throne Room, audience chambers, and a banqueting hall, all designed to satisfy European ideas of magnificence.[3] Writhing roofs of glinting green copper overhung eaves and gables painted with green and blue floral patterns. In the steam-heated interior, coffered ceilings were set with intricately carved panels, depicting birds and beasts and landscapes, lacquered in gold. On the floors of orange-wood and cedar, covered with rich carpets rather than *tatami*, stood heavy Chinese chests, Victorian sideboards, and Empire sofas. Sliding doors of the most exquisite native joinery still communicated between the rooms, but the paper panes in them were now a leathery parchment embossed with ivory and gold. In its own way every detail was a work of art, but for a Japanese of taste the beauties were too thickly encrusted for appreciative thought. In addition, the

[3] Emperor Meiji began to use his $2 million Ceremonial Palace twenty-two years after Emperor Komei's death. After it was destroyed in 1945, Emperor Hirohito waited exactly twenty-two years before dedicating a $36 million replacement for it.

Western furniture seemed to leave little room for proper ceremonial—for ritual kneeling, backing, bowing, and prostration.

On all significant diplomatic occasions Emperor Meiji—with
mustache, goatee, and deep flashing eyes—cut an imposing figure
in Western uniform or evening dress in these roomfuls of evident
richness. But for members of his oligarchy or family, he also had a
maze of Japanese-style apartments, floored with straw mats, where
he presided either in the official robes of the old Kyoto court or
in loose, informal kimonos of white silk. When the palace burned
down on May 26, 1945, it was said that some of its rooms had
never been seen except by princes, princesses, and titled servants
of high Court rank. In such rooms Meiji wrote several thousand
classically Japanese poems and drank several thousand glasses of
classically French burgundy. A dozen Court ladies, whose names
used to be listed in the nineteenth century *Court Gazette,* had
the privilege of waiting on him in the evening and of picking up
the silk handkerchief which he dropped in front of his choice for
the night. Though he sometimes inveighed against enervating
Western customs, it was noted that he always retired, not to a
draughty sleeping floor of mats, but to a heated room with a good
Western bed in it.

The future Emperor Taisho, in his separate Akasaka Palace,
had been even more contaminated by Western sartorial, architectural, and philosophical ideas than his father. He wore Prussian
uniforms, larded his conversation with Parisian argot, cultivated
the mustache of his contemporary, Wilhelm II, the German
kaiser, and consorted by preference with imperial cousins of the
Fushimi house who had had the opportunity denied him to go
abroad and study the wonders of the Colosseum, Buckingham
Palace, and the Folies Bergère. Original paintings by Monet,
Manet, and Degas hung in his study and bedroom. On his banqueting table, huge candelabra in the shape of cranes illuminated
the masterpieces of a French chef. In 1904 he commissioned an
architect trained in Paris to rebuild his Akasaka Palace as a miniature Versailles, complete with chairs and sofas upholstered in pale
rose brocade. Emperor Meiji took one look at the plans and
vowed that he would never set foot in "Yoshihito's French house."

While his father idolized Western ways and his easygoing grandfather enjoyed and scoffed at them, Hirohito grew from baby to small boy in the pure Spartan Japan of Vice Admiral Kawamura's household. He was slow to walk because he inherited from his grandfather Meiji a slight motor malfunction of the legs which gave him a peculiar gait, known by irreverent Japanese as "the imperial shuffle." Lest his disability create in him an inferiority complex, Vice Admiral Kawamura kept him from associating with any other children until he was almost two years old. Then junior playmates were introduced into his world, one by one: first four toddling princes of the Fushimi house, and then a younger brother, Prince Chichibu, born in June 1902. Through his planned seniority, Hirohito learned to wear the mantle of leadership before he was three. Whenever he and his companions poked holes in the *shoji*, the paper-paned sliding doors in which all normal Japanese children poke holes, Hirohito always remained calmly on the scene of the crime and gravely accepted full responsibility. He and his friends early realized that he could not be punished and that others who set him a bad example might be punished severely. He learned to shield them under a look of puzzled innocence—and to expect favors of them in return.

Going on four, Hirohito was psychologically orphaned by the death of his naval foster father and was brought back to the semi-Westernized world of palaces where he had been born. He was installed in the Aoyama-Akasaka Palace compound, near his mother and father, in a small, especially constructed Japanese-style home called the Imperial Grandson's Abode. There he was taken care of mostly by titled servants. He saw his mother once or twice a week, his father more or less monthly, and his grandfather quarterly for a pat on the head. In moments of paternal feeling, brought on by wine, his father, Crown Prince Yoshihito, sometimes had him brought over to the Akasaka Palace at night to be dandled by merry-making sycophants. On one occasion they plied the little boy with so much saké that they made him drunk, sick, and a teetotaler for life.

The Court official in charge of Hirohito's new ménage was Kido Takamasa, the son of a samurai who had died in Emperor Komei's service in 1862. Takamasa had been adopted by one of Emperor Meiji's most popular oligarchs and sent to the United States for his education. There he had lived for a decade, studying mining techniques and cultivating his native prejudice against Commodore Perry's countrymen. A few years after his return to Japan, Kido Takamasa adopted the son, it is said, of an imperial princess. This was Kido Koichi who would become Hirohito's most trusted counselor and finally, in 1945, Hirohito's representative among the Japanese war criminals in Sugamo Prison.

At the time Hirohito moved in under the elder Kido's wing, Kido Koichi was fifteen. The owlish young man played big brother to the regal boy and introduced him early to several other teenage "Big Brothers" who would later become the nucleus for Hirohito's cabal. All these fledgling aristocrats had been born between 1887 and 1891 and had attended the Peers' School together: Prince Asaka, sixteen, who would rape Nanking in 1937; his half brother and near twin, Prince Higashikuni, who would become prime minister in 1945; another sixteen-year-old imperial "uncle," Prince Kitashirakawa, who would die in the course of an intelligence mission in France in 1923; Kitashirakawa's half brother, Marquis Komatsu Teruhisa, fifteen, who would oversee Naval Staff studies for the attack on Pearl Harbor; and finally a twelve-year-old hanger-on of the bigger boys, the precocious, sensitive, much teased Fujiwara prince, Konoye Fumimaro, who would lead Japan to war as prime minister in 1937.

Being typical young aristocrats of their time, the Big Brothers played soldier with Hirohito and told him war stories. They spoke constantly of Japan's mission to lead Asia out of Western bondage. They belonged to the East Asia All-One-Culture Society, a movement launched in both Japan and China by Prince Konoye Atsumaro, the father of the youngest of the Big Brothers. At the society the Big Brothers came to know and patronize a motley assortment of idealists who believed in Asia for the Asiatics and of tough adventurers who believed in Asia for the Japanese. Some were dispossessed samurai of the Black Dragon Society who scratched out a living in China as white slavers, dope importers, or common cutthroats. Others were burly undercover agents in monks' clothing who had accompanied the high priests of Hongan Temple—the temple of Hirohito's mother's family—on a 1900 pilgrimage to Thailand to bring back the ashes of the true Buddha and on a 1902 expedition to Samarkand "to explore vestiges of ancient Buddhist culture" in Central Asia. Still others were non-Japanese Asian nationalists who had taken refuge in Tokyo from troubles at home—the most notable being the revolutionary Sun Yat-sen, later known as the George Washington of China.

Sun Yat-sen had led an abortive rebellion against the Manchu throne in South China and was a fugitive from the Chinese police. He was protected in Japan by the elder Prince Konoye and by Lord High Assassin Toyama of the Black Dragon Society. In 1905, at Black Dragon headquarters in Tokyo, Sun Yat-sen met with a group of fellow Chinese exiles to form a revolutionary party which was later to become the Kuomintang or KMT. The young Chiang Kai-shek, who leads the KMT in Taiwan today, joined the party in 1907 when he came to Tokyo for postgraduate work at the Japanese Military Academy.

FELLING GOLIATH

In 1904 and 1905 Hirohito's Big Brothers of the East Asia All-One-Culture Society had one enthusiasm which excited them more than Pan-Asianism, and this was the imminent prospect of war with Russia. In the conflict of 1894–95, Emperor Meiji had bested the Dragon Throne of the Manchus. Now it was common knowledge in the palace that he was preparing to put down the czars of Muscovy.

Planning for the new war had started before Hirohito's birth in 1900. At that time the lute-playing Prince Saionji and his mentor, Ito Hirobumi, the two oligarchs who had championed codified Western-style laws for Japan, were in favor of a straightforward agreement with Russia, acknowledging her supremacy in northern Manchuria in return for unopposed Japanese control of Korea. Army Chief Yamagata insisted that the whole of Manchuria up to the Amur River must be conquered before Japan would feel safe.[4] Emperor Meiji and the surviving brothers of Emperor Komei's advisor, Prince Asahiko, listened noncommittally and de-

---

[4] Toyama, the lord high assassin of the underworld, founded the Black Dragon Society in 1901 to support Yamagata's position. The society took as its own the Chinese name for the Amur, Black Dragon River.

clined to set any limit to Japan's ultimate goals. Army Chief Yamagata assured them that Japan would have a sporting chance against Russia unless the French and Germans intervened to keep Japan in her place as they had done in 1896 after the war with China. Emperor Meiji decided, therefore, to seek an alliance with Great Britain which would neutralize France and Germany and enable Japan to challenge Russia hand to hand, one nation against one nation.

As a part of his campaign to prevent the Emperor from going to war, the Westernized oligarch Ito Hirobumi, in the fall of 1900, tried to enlist the voice of the people by founding Japan's first important political party, the Constitutionalists.[5] There had been other political parties before, no less than fourteen of them since 1882, but Ito had the popular support to create a lasting organization that would have the mandate of the majority of the people. For the next thirty-five years it would regularly command 45 to 60 per cent of the national vote. But it would struggle in vain against the overriding imperial powers written into the very Constitution it championed—in particular the power to appoint all officials. By contesting Army budget increases in the Diet, Ito dreamt that his party might be able to keep Japan at peace.

In the summer of 1901 Emperor Meiji sent a delegation of professional diplomats to London to negotiate the required treaty with England. Oligarch Ito at once resigned as prime minister in favor of his fun-loving protégé, Prince Saionji, and threw all his energies into selling the people on his idea of direct negotiations with Russia. At the outset of his campaign, he was visited one day by Toyama, the Lord of the Black Dragon and "Darkside Emperor" of the slums. Somewhat hard of hearing, the sixty-one-year-old Ito craned his neck, cocked his head, and professed to be unable to hear any of the gang lord's quiet threats.

"Let me sit closer to you, so that you can hear better," quoth Toyama.

"You are too close already," piped Ito, and dismissed Toyama under a cloak of indifference and senility.

A few days later Ito asked permission of Emperor Meiji to take

[5] In full, *Rikken Seiyukai*, Constitution Political Comrades party.

a vacation and accept an honorary law degree from Yale University in the United States. Emperor Meiji was all too happy to be rid of him, and Ito promptly took ship for San Francisco. Then, after a quick call on President Roosevelt, Ito rewrote his itinerary and boarded the fastest available packet for Europe. Via Paris and Berlin, he went express to St. Petersburg. Czar Nicholas welcomed him, even as a private citizen, and wined and dined him magnificently. The czar's ministers were less accommodating, however, and would not give Ito all the diplomatic concessions that he had hoped for.

Ito's efforts in St. Petersburg merely hastened the drafting of an Anglo-Japanese agreement in London. The British could not endure the possibility of an alliance between Russia and Japan at the northern approaches to Shanghai and Hong Kong. Ito vainly cabled Tokyo the results of his own conversations in Moscow. The Japanese cabinet on December 9, 1901, decided that the arrangements with Great Britain were the more satisfactory. Emperor Meiji, after consulting his Privy Council, cabled his approval to London, and Ito decided to accept defeat gracefully. He hurried to England and gave his blessing to the negotiations there. The historic Anglo-Japanese pact was duly signed on January 30, 1902.

Before launching her first blow against a Western nation, Japan, at Emperor Meiji's insistence, made one other preparation. The British, by the treaty, were committed to attack any third powers which allied themselves to an adversary of Japan. There was, however, a strong possibility that Russia might trounce Japan unassisted. Therefore Emperor Meiji, through his ambassador in Washington, sought and received verbal assurances from President Theodore Roosevelt that the United States, in the event, would do everything in its power to prevent Russia from occupying and annihilating Japan.

So armed, Japan readied herself for war, and Japanese envoys in Moscow pressed belligerently for withdrawal of Russian forces from the Russian rail lines and railheads in Manchuria. The czar had already agreed several years earlier that he would remove his legions in due time, but he was now of mixed mind, and he vastly underrated Japan as a threat. British leaders, too, began to have second thoughts about their new ally and cautioned Japan that she was not strong enough to win the war.

Ignoring all warnings, the Japanese government severed relations with Russia on February 6, 1904. Thirty-six hours later the taut young Japanese Navy, manned by men of the Satsuma clan and commanded by officers trained in England, stole up on the Russian Asiatic fleet in the middle of the night and scattered it by a surprise attack with torpedo boats. The Russian ships which remained afloat took refuge in the harbor of Port Arthur at the tip of the Kwantung Peninsula leasehold in southern Manchuria. There they were kept bottled up by Japanese battleships which waited broadside outside the harbor's mouth.

On February 10, two days after the naval engagement, Emperor Meiji issued a rescript declaring war. As he had done ten years previously during the war with China, he moved from Tokyo to Hiroshima and there presided personally at staff headquarters. The strategy of the conflict developed around two particularly tense situations. On the one hand the citadel of Port Arthur, defended according to the best Prussian science of the day by Russia's General Stössel, held out stubbornly against attack from the landward side by Japan's expeditionary force. On the other hand, Russia's large Baltic fleet was on its way around the world to avenge the havoc wrought by the Japanese torpedo boats. Unless Port Arthur could be taken in time, the Japanese would have to turn to meet the Baltic fleet, leaving the remnants of the Asiatic fleet free to emerge from their battle and attack the Japanese rear.

Great Britain helpfully denied the Baltic fleet passage through the Suez Canal and forced it to steam from the Kattegat, the strait between Sweden and Denmark, all the way around Africa. On the way it was further delayed by having to refuel only at the widely scattered ports controlled by the French. Nevertheless it did make daily progress and Port Arthur did not fall. When the Baltic fleet entered the Indian Ocean, General Nogi Maresuke, in charge of the Japanese army outside Port Arthur, was sent a personal command from Emperor Meiji in Hiroshima to take the citadel quickly, no matter what the cost. Wave after wave of Japanese advanced into withering fire and bewildering mine fields.

The no man's land before the fortress writhed with wounded who could not be helped. The stench of corpses hung so heavy on the air that the Russian defenders on the ramparts wore handkerchiefs soaked in camphor.

Finally the agents of Army Chief Yamagata Aritomo, who was assisting Emperor Meiji in Hiroshima, attempted to bribe three of Stössel's officers with a promissory note for $65 million payable eleven years later and signed by Yamagata. For this enormous sum, it is said that the three officers gave their Japanese contacts a plan of the Russian mine fields. Whether or not the plan reached General Nogi outside Port Arthur and whether or not it helped him capture the fortress are debatable. The fact is that on December 6, 1904, when the war had been in progress for over nine months and the Baltic fleet was approaching the China Sea, General Nogi launched his third all-out assault on 203-Meter Hill outside Port Arthur. In previous charges he had seen both his own sons mowed down before his field glasses. Now at last he saw the Japanese flag raised on the summit of the hill and knew that the battle for Port Arthur was over. The crest commanded a fine sweep of the harbor and an easy run up a ridge to the feet of the walls of Port Arthur citadel. Trapped between the pounding of Japanese field artillery from the ridge and of Japanese battleships waiting outside the bay, the Russian fleet was sunk to a vessel.

On New Year's Day 1905, Stössel decided that the position he held was no longer either strategically useful or tactically tenable and he surrendered the 25,000 men and 500 guns remaining under his command. He was later court-martialed by the Russians and sentenced to death, but the sentence was commuted to life because he successfully maintained in court that he had been betrayed.

The bizarre aftermath of the bribe has since been recounted by an American diplomat, Post Wheeler, who knew one of the traitors and investigated the whole matter personally. In 1915, eleven years after the fact, Army strongman Yamagata was not about to ask the Emperor to pay $65 million for a fortress that had cost 20,000 Japanese lives. And so when the first of the Russian officers showed up in Nagasaki in 1915, Yamagata had him shot in the back. The death of a foreign tramp was accorded one three-line obituary in a single edition of one Nagasaki newspaper. The second Russian traitor was believed by Post Wheeler to have been killed by Japanese agents somewhere in Russia. The third put his note of hand into the trust of a British syndicate which negotiated for years with the Japanese government for a settlement of payment. Yamagata's brushwork signature on the document appeared, under the glasses of experts, to be authentic and elicited from the Japanese government contradictory explanations of why it was a forgery. In 1921, when relations between Japan and England began to deteriorate as a result of postwar peace conferences, the syndicate began to press its claim in earnest. Then, abruptly, the third Russian traitor, the one material witness, vanished without a trace in Switzerland.

After the capture of Port Arthur in 1904 and the annihilation of Russia's Asiatic fleet, Japan's Admiral Togo Heihachiro was able to turn and redeploy, with little time to spare, for the reception of the Baltic fleet. Fueling problems forced the czar's ships to make a straight dash from the friendly French port of Camranh Bay in Indochina toward the depots of Vladivostok. Togo lay in wait for them at Tsushima Strait which divides two islets in the channel between Japan and Korea. As the Russian battle wagons emerged single file from the narrow waters, Togo's ships "crossed the T" of their column, booming broadsides. When the action was over, Russia had lost almost all her fleet, including twenty capital ships sunk, five captured, and some 12,000 out of 18,000 Russian sailors drowned. Japan had lost only three torpedo boats and 116 men. When news of the catastrophe reached Russia, it helped to touch off Trotsky's abortive revolution of 1905.

PRICE OF PEACE

Once Russia had tasted the bitter fruits of disaster and overconfidence, Theodore Roosevelt offered to mediate the war. Meiji accepted the offer with alacrity. For all her outward show of success, Japan faced an internal crisis. She had lost 20,000 men at Port Arthur and almost an equal number at Mukden, the capital of Manchuria, two months later. More important, her stripling economy was strained to breaking under foreign and domestic war debts. An honorable peace had to be sought, and when President Roosevelt first entertained the emissaries of the two belligerents at Portsmouth, New Hampshire, it looked as if Japan would gain enough to have made the war worthwhile. But Count Sergei Witte, the Russian negotiator, soon sensed that the Japanese were more eager to make immediate peace than he was. Little by little, he hardened his attitude, and by the time that the negotiations were concluded, the Japanese gave up what they most needed, a hard cash indemnity, and accepted instead unquestioned supremacy in Korea, Port Arthur, and the Kwantung Peninsula, and Russian railroads and rights of way in southern Manchuria.

Emperor Meiji reluctantly approved the terms of the treaty after a long and stormy conference in the palace on August 28, 1905. But the Japanese public, which had been fed on reports of unmitigated victory and had been sweated economically to make the war possible, resented the lack of indemnity and rioted obstreperously in every major city. The violence reached such a pitch that the government proclaimed martial law and the war Cabinet of General Katsura Taro had to resign. The new government was headed by Prince Saionji, the lute-playing Constitutionalist. Having been known as an opponent of the war, he successfully soothed the angry people, but he also shouldered for his Constitutionalist party the grievous financial problems and unpopular austerity created by the war.

In retrospect only young aristocrats like Hirohito's teen-age Big Brothers exulted in the great victory Japan had won. Army Chief Yamagata warned that the war had been too much of a gamble ever to be repeated. Oligarch Ito, the founder of the popular Constitutionalist party, spread the idea that Korea could have been won by negotiation. Now that it had been won by force, he said, it was all the buffer zone Japan needed. He opposed outright annexation of it because annexation would only give the Army a new border to patrol; better, he insisted, to make Korea a friendly ally and protectorate of Japan. With this aim in view he advocated a lenient civilian colonial policy toward Korea. Emperor Meiji, with characteristic good humor and poetic justice, let him practice what he preached by making him resident governor. At the same time masterless samurai of the Black

Dragon Society were encouraged to enlist in Ito's service and help him in enlightening the natives. They uncovered and savagely suppressed almost weekly insurrections, riots, and anti-Japanese murmuring campaigns, and so turned all Ito's good intentions to hate and terror.

After three and a half years of frustration the sixty-nine-year-old Ito was recalled to Japan in the summer of 1909. He was angry and ready to use his Constitutionalist party's power at the polls to change the direction of imperial policy. Three months later, he was dispatched to Manchuria on a peculiarly inconsequential diplomatic mission. There, in the city of Harbin, he was shot and killed by a Korean. Japanese Constitutionalists murmured in vain for a full investigation of the assassination. It was strange, they said, that Ito's assassin had outwitted the Japanese police, had acquired a gun, slipped out of Korea, traveled all the way to Harbin, and known where to be waiting for Ito. But the police killed the assassin during interrogation and announced that he was a fanatic, working alone. Seven months after the assassination, in May 1910, Japan formally annexed Korea.

PRINCELY ABC'S

In the triumphant years after the war with Russia, when Japan took her place as an equal beside the nations of the West, the fascist princes of the 1930's were still getting their educations. In April 1908, Hirohito began to go to the famous Peers' School. He set out each morning, usually on foot, with a chamberlain trailing along behind him. Most mornings he had for company two junior princes. It was only a ten-minute walk to the school from Hirohito's Aoyama Palace, but when the three little princes went together, they usually managed to provide a full half-hour's exercise for the nagging chamberlain who accompanied them.

Hirohito's new school was the lineal descendant of the academy for noblemen, established in Kyoto during the late eighteenth century, which had instilled in the Court the courage and independence to agitate for the restoration. In 1908 its headmaster—always a distinguished patriot—was General Nogi Maresuke, the commander who had piled up corpses outside Port Arthur and watched both of his own sons slain there. Entrusted with the planning of Hirohito's curriculum, he took an intense interest in the quiet young Emperor-to-be, and Hirohito responded by addressing him in the forms ordinarily reserved for a father.

Nogi had been born in 1849 to the traditional Spartan code of the samurai. As a child, if he complained of the cold, he was made to stand naked in the snow while his father poured buckets of well water over him. As a sixteen-year-old adolescent, learning fencing, he lost an eye. As a twenty-eight-year-old, commanding his first troops in battle, he was surrounded during the Satsuma clan's samurai uprising of 1877, crippled in one arm and one leg, and disgraced in his own mind by the capture of the imperial colors under his charge. Limping and looking out on the world through a single eye, he was probably saved from defeat in the Russian war—despite the sacrifice of his sons—only by Yamagata and Stössel's three traitors. After the war, he is said to have asked Emperor Meiji's permission to commit ritual suicide, and to have been answered with the words, "Not while I am still alive, Nogi. That is an order."

Nogi believed implicitly in the traditional samurai mystique of killing with honor, of magnanimity toward the chastened and defeated, of utter ruthlessness toward the base and mercantile, of appreciation mainly for the contrived artistic beauty of poems and paintings in life, and for the moonlight reality of the spirit world in death. This was Bushido, the way of the warrior. Out of it had come the only masculine selflessness and dedication which Japan had ever known.

While Nogi lived by command, he did all in his ken to make a good samurai out of Hirohito. He promulgated twelve rules to guide the prince and the other aristocrats under his charge. Among them:

"(4) Inquire of your parents about your ancestors, your crest and lineage, and keep them well in mind.

"(9) Be ashamed of torn clothes, but never of patched ones.

"(12) When you order your Western-style clothing, boots, and shoes, have them made larger than your present size, regardless of fashion. You will outgrow them."

On one occasion Nogi had Hirohito stand naked under a glacial waterfall. When the boy proved that he could stand still there without shivering, Nogi beckoned him out and wrapped him in a commoner's coarse winter house kimono. Nogi liked to boast that neither he nor his ward had ever known the feel of silk undergarments next to the skin.

Under Nogi's tutelage, Hirohito tackled the forbidding complexities of written Japanese. He first learned the two Japanese syllabaries of fifty-five symbols apiece and the English or *romanji* alphabet of twenty-six letters so that he could read phonetically. In Japanese, however, phonetic reading does not suffice to impart understanding, because there are too many ordinary words used in writing which all have the same ambiguous sound. When used in intellectual conversation, they have to be identified either by a lengthy explanation or by a Chinese character traced on the palm with a finger. Like other Japanese, therefore, Hirohito next embarked on the learning of Chinese characters or *kanji*. Through movement of hand and writing brush he memorized the primary and variant forms, meanings, and pronunciations of from three to four thousand characters, each consisting of one to forty-eight brush strokes. By constant drill and reading, he came to recognize 20,000 to 30,000 combinations of the characters which represented whole words. In a nation where everyone gives the best years of his life in an attempt to make the archaic system of hieroglyphs work, Hirohito learned to read and write with exceptional ease. By the age of twelve he was already trying his hand at delicate, disciplined *tanka* which, after editing, would express his mind on ceremonial occasions and would be read aloud at the national poetry contests held in the palace each New Year.

Because of the imperial shuffle, Hirohito was far less gifted athletically than he was intellectually, a fact of genetics to which he reconciled himself only with the greatest difficulty. Living in a samurai's world, he set great store on strength, agility, and endurance. By arduous effort he ultimately became a powerful swimmer, good horseman, and avid golfer, but each sporting accomplishment cost him great pain. As a small boy he had had little opportunity to learn ways of compensating for his defect because

anxious chamberlains had forever curbed in him the normal abandon of a child, encouraging him to walk, not run, down corridors
and step, not leap, down staircases. His tutor, Nogi, warned him
repeatedly against developing a hunchback's psychology.

In spite of himself, Nogi showed a spontaneous partiality for
Hirohito's graceful, open-natured younger brother, Prince Chichibu. Chichibu was free of the imperial affliction. Chichibu ex-
celled at sports. Chichibu had been publicly cuddled and
privately cuffed by Hirohito ever since his birth. Hirohito was to
make Chichibu the family scapegoat for the abortive Strike-North
Army rebellion of 1936. Chichibu was to die of another imperial
weakness, tuberculosis, in 1953.

Hirohito's physical disability, together with the other peculiar-
ities of his childhood, left him with a defensive shyness and poise
chiseled out of ice, and an almost masochistic need to prove himself by living more simply and working harder than anyone else.
He schooled himself to become a lucid, well-paced, and even dramatic speaker at official gatherings but he never learned to seem
completely at ease on the rostrum. He was steadfastly loyal to all
who served him but warm and vivacious with only a few of his
oldest intimates. His idea of humor was to give a pumpkin that
looked like a melon to one of his in-laws who was excessively fond
of melons. By exercise of an encyclopedic memory, he was able
to appear perceptive and even maliciously witty on occasion. But
few chamberlains ever felt sure how to take his sallies, because
they came so rarely. Both he and his brothers had been carefully
trained from infancy to listen rather than speak, to encourage
rather than command, to censor from their voiced thoughts every
direct expression of bias or desire, to seek and weigh the opinions
of others, and to make such advisors responsible for promoting
suggestions that seemed good.

On his way to the Peers' School each day, Hirohito often led
his entourage across the northern grounds of the main palace so
that he could watch the Imperial Guards at their morning drill.
Frequently he would see one of his Big Brothers on the parade
ground and stop gravely to salute him. Prince Higashikuni, Prince
Asaka, and Prince Kitashirakawa had graduated from military

academy and had been posted as sub-lieutenants to the Imperial Guards Division in 1908 at the same time that Hirohito had entered the Peers' School. There, in the north corner of the palace, from 1908 until 1912, they were billeted with all the young lieutenants and captains who would later be known as the great fascist generals of Japan. Prince Higashikuni, for instance, has stated that in those years he came to know well the later famous Tojo who would act as shogun for Japan in the fateful years, 1941–1944. At that time Higashikuni found Tojo "a run-of-the-mill officer," who was "ambitious for advancement."

Emperor Meiji made no secret of the fact that Hirohito's Big Brothers were his own favorites, too, and were being groomed by him for missions of national importance. He was especially partial to the four of them who were grandsons of Prince Kuniye, the father of Emperor Komei's advisor Asahiko. In token of his favor he betrothed them to his daughters with an uncanny numerological precision: Kuniye's sixth grandson, Takeda, to his sixth daughter, Masako; Kuniye's seventh grandson, Kitashirakawa, to his seventh daughter, Fusako; Kuniye's eighth grandson, Asaka, to his eighth daughter, Nobuko; and Kuniye's ninth grandson, Higashikuni, to his ninth daughter, Toshiko. To make crystal clear his high hopes for these young men, Emperor Meiji put in a personal appearance at the first three of the weddings—in 1905, 1909, and 1910. He cared so little for the daughters he thus gave away that he met all three of them, for the first time in their lives, at the nuptials.

The fourth wedding, that of Meiji's ninth daughter, was delayed because Kuniye's ninth grandson, the trouble-making Higashikuni, became involved in a palace spat which caused him to be put on probation. It was Emperor Meiji's custom, whenever he had an evening free of state business, to invite a pair of the four favorite princes to eat dinner with him. Higashikuni was invariably teamed with Prince Kitashirakawa, an enthusiastic, athletic young man who always said what was expected of him and never tired of hearing Emperor Meiji, over his port, expatiate on the future greatness of Japan. Prince Higashikuni, who in those days had not yet learned to be devious, sometimes showed boredom in the after-dinner conversations.

One day in 1911, when his stomach was upset and he was studying for the entrance examinations to Staff College, Prince Higashikuni refused one of Emperor Meiji's summonses. A palace coach called for him anyway and he caused a scandal by sending it away empty. Chamberlains came to his villa to lecture him on filial piety. Higashikuni told them rebelliously that he wished he could emigrate to the West where filial piety was left to Confucius. There the matter might have rested except that Hirohito's father, the future Emperor Taisho, who was Higashikuni's elder by only eight years, took it upon himself to tell Higashikuni that he was not worthy of being a member of the imperial family. With great wounded pride, the twenty-three-year-old Higashikuni at once submitted a formal request to the Imperial Household Ministry asking leave to resign his rank as a prince and go away to live in a foreign country. Emperor Meiji had the request ignored and asked Field Marshal Yamagata, the old man of the Army, to talk some sense into the young soldier's head. Higashikuni maintained, however, that he would resign from the imperial family unless Yamagata would agree to owe him a posting abroad, payable on demand. Yamagata promised that he would, and finally Emperor Meiji called Higashikuni in for a private audience in the Imperial Study. In his genial way, he told Higashikuni not to be so prickly; there would be foreign adventures enough when Higashikuni had finished his training and was ready for them. Then, more sternly, Meiji reminded the headstrong young prince that old chamberlains were loyal retainers and must not be alienated by childish lowerclass outbursts of pride.

REBELLION IN CHINA

Four hundred million strong, the Chinese, in less than a century, had fallen in their own eyes from one of the mightiest to one of the most miserable nations on earth. At least 20 million Chinese had become addicts of opium, heroin, or morphine, most of which was imported by Western traders. The China coast had become a necklace of foreign enclaves. Whole Chinese armies had been routed repeatedly by landing parties of European and American marines. Japan's victory over Russia in 1905 and annexation of Korea in 1910 only added to China's humiliation. The "Eastern pigmies," as the Japanese had long been called in China, were succeeding against the West where the Chinese had failed.

In 1911 peasant rebellions against the corrupt and bankrupt regime of the ruling Manchu emperors—the Ching dynasty—broke out in almost every province of China. For lack of any other national leadership the dissidents gave their allegiance to the Kuomintang or KMT cell of intellectual Cantonese republicans headed by Sun Yat-sen. Sun and his disciples—of whom Chiang Kai-shek was one—were all protégés of the elder Prince Konoye's East Asia All-One-Culture Society, of Hirohito's Big Brotherhood, and of Toyama's Black Dragon tong. With combined Japanese and American assistance Sun Yat-sen was able to help the peasant revolutionaries pay their armies until they had secured control of the southern half of China.

The Manchu throne was occupied at that time by a five-year-old boy, Henry Pu-Yi, later Japan's puppet emperor of Manchuria. The real power in the Manchu Court was held by the general in charge of the Manchu armies, Yuan Shih-kai. Like Japan's Army strongman, his good friend Yamagata, General Yuan believed that China must remain unified under a military dictatorship. Yuan therefore promised to betray the Manchu throne and throw the weight of his armies into the republican cause if he could become China's first president. Faced with the alternative of civil war, Sun Yat-sen agreed. So it was that in February 1912 the five-year-old Manchu Emperor Pu-Yi was forced to abdicate, and the Chinese Republic was born.

For the first time since Genghis Khan, China had her own native government; the Mongol-Manchu conquerors from the wastelands north of the Great Wall had been finally expelled. But the peasants who had started the rebellion gained nothing. The same soldiers and tax collectors oppressed them, and the façade of democratic government—of a congress and elections—which Yuan Shih-kai gave to his regime inspired only bitter jokes. From the day he became president Yuan began to plot against China's leading parliamentarians. In two years he would have the bravest of them assassinated. In four years he would try to make himself emperor and found a new dynasty.

7

CROWN PRINCE HIROHITO

(1912–1921)

DEATH OF MEIJI

Hirohito's thirty-two-year-old father, Crown Prince Yoshihito, saw in the Chinese Revolution a heaven-sent opportunity going to waste. Had he been Emperor he would have capitalized on it to take over one or the other of the two halves of China. Instead, while Yuan in Peking was consolidating his power, Army strongman Yamagata and the surviving members of Emperor Meiji's oligarchy ruled in Japan. Emperor Meiji, that spring of 1912, had delegated to the oligarchs all his authority—for he himself lay dying of stomach cancer.

Japanese flocked by the tens of thousands to pray in the plaza outside the palace for the Emperor's recovery. They burned hundreds of thousands of symbolic paper offerings at the most important national shrines. Nevertheless, on July 29, the great Emperor Meiji died. He had had more than a dozen sons, but only one survived him, the child of a concubine, the father of Hirohito, Crown Prince Yoshihito. Yoshihito at once assumed possession of the sacred mirror, necklace, and sword and took the reign-name of Taisho, Great Correctness.

Up to this time the boy Hirohito had been merely the eldest of the imperial grandsons. Now, while the nation mourned, a new crown prince had to be nominated. Hirohito was the obvious but not the only choice. The fact that he had been born before his parents' marriage provided an excuse to pass him by, in favor of his younger brother, if his physical disability seemed to warrant it. A rump caucus of princes and chamberlains met in the palace to discuss the matter.

Emperor Taisho and most of his courtiers wished to accept Hirohito in order to avoid any outward suggestion of irregularities. To their surprise, Hirohito's own beloved tutor, General Nogi, organized a minority which favored the election of Prince Chichibu, Hirohito's brother. Nogi had no convincing reason to urge for his stand, only a vague presentiment, a sense of something dark. He was, accordingly, outvoted and Hirohito was elected heir apparent.

In six weeks of deep mourning, wearing old-fashioned Court clothes, participating in numerous family rites of purification, the twelve-year-old Hirohito was made deeply conscious of his impending responsibilities, his coming of age. On September 9, 1912, as the progress of his grandfather's shade into the spirit world drew to a close, he was duly proclaimed heir and simultaneously appointed to the rank of lieutenant in the Army and ensign in the Navy.

Three days later, on the eve of Meiji's state funeral, General Nogi, the outvoted tutor, paid a last visit to Hirohito and to his two brothers, Chichibu, ten, and Takamatsu, seven. They received him in their private apartments at the temporary Akasaka Palace where they lived while the new one—Taisho's Versailles— was nearing completion. Nogi had recently returned from George V's coronation in London and apologized for his long absence. He apologized further that he must go out of town again, immediately, as guide to Arthur, Duke of Connaught, the emissary sent by Great Britain to Emperor Meiji's funeral. Then, earnestly, he scolded the three boys for neglecting their lessons while he had been away and reminded them that they must learn to police their own work habits if they were ever to fit themselves for the lonely task of rule.

Turning to Hirohito, Nogi discussed a recent specimen of the boy's calligraphy and said: "I ask you to study harder. You are now the crown prince, the youngest of the officers in the Army

and Navy, and the future commander of the nation. I beg you to
attend to your military duties. I beg you to take daily care of your
health, no matter how busy you are. Remember, I shall be watching. Work well for yourself and Japan." He handed Hirohito a
book of Confucian moral precepts, bowed low, and backed out of
the room.

In the next hour Emperor Meiji's funeral cortege rolled out
across the palace moat on the Double Bridge reserved for imperial
progresses. The cannon of Tokyo harbor thundered rhythmically
in the distance. Silent, prostrate Japanese lined the route which
the cortege would take to Tokyo Station. There a railway car
waited, paneled in new unfinished wood of ghostly whiteness,
unblemished by knotholes. The next day it would arrive in the
old capital of Kyoto where a heroic tumulus was being thrown up,
beside the graves of the ancestors, to receive the coffin.

General Nogi watched the cortege start from the palace and
then walked home to his villa in Azabu, not far from the house
where Hirohito had learned to toddle. Countess Nogi was quietly
waiting for him in the tiny entry hall. To the insistent tolling of
the cannon the two took a bath together, put on new white kimonos, and knelt before an autographed picture of Emperor Meiji
which hung in their prayer alcove.

Six centuries earlier a retainer of the southern dynasty, after
surrendering his army to a general of the northern dynasty, had
asked his captors to bear witness to the fact that he had surrendered for the sake of his men and not out of fear of death.
Kneeling in front of them, he had deliberately cut open his belly
and pulled out his entrails, explaining the while that he was dying
by the most prolonged and agonizing method that he knew. Since
his time the painful ceremony of *hara-kiri* or belly cutting—of
seppuku or intestinal incision as it was called by the fastidious—
had been ritualized and observed by every man of honor who
wished to "prove his sincerity" before passing over into the spirit
world. Women who wished to make a similar "meaningful gesture" were not supposed to do hara-kiri but might die slowly by
another method, the severing of the carotid artery.

Following the prescribed formulas, Countess Nogi now drove
a dagger into her neck and bled to death. When she had lost con-

sciousness, General Nogi thrust a shortsword into his bowels, gave it a pull crosswise and a final jerk upward. On the *tatami* at his side he left a note, deploring the self-indulgence of the younger generation and begging every patriotic Japanese to abide more sternly by the ancient warrior virtues. When the new crown prince, Hirohito, heard of the tragedy, he stiffened in a bow, and without any other sign of emotion said, "Japan has suffered a regrettable loss."

The story was put out for foreigners that General Nogi and his wife had committed double suicide in order to follow their liege lord, Meiji, to a new Throne beyond the grave. For the mass of Japanese, who knew that Nogi had not enough rank to consider himself an indispensable retainer, it was said that the Nogis had fulfilled a sacred pledge made to themselves and to the bereaved parents of other slaughtered sons after the costly storming of Port Arthur. It was well known that Nogi's wife had indeed taken the death of her sons much to heart. But General Nogi, according to knowledgeable aristocrats, felt most driven to suicide by pride. He had advised against the selection of Hirohito as crown prince and his advice had been spurned. He could not live to see himself rejected by his own student.

TAISHO'S COUP

On ascending the Throne at the end of July 1912, Hirohito's father, the young Emperor Taisho, sought to be an absolute monarch and an empire builder. He aspired to give Japan a "progressive" Occidental administration, patterned on that of Alexander the Great, Caesar, Louis XIV, and the German kaiser. The Japanese, he felt, were too parochial. He believed that in turning outward and making themselves a force in the world his people would require specific autocratic instruction at every step. But he did not know Japan. He understood in theory but not in feeling the web of loyalties which made the people work as one. Spoiled by diversions with polite wines and women and Western ideas, Taisho thought that he had only to issue orders. He could not imagine that the Throne would ever be disobeyed. He did not see the need for the easygoing charm and careful subterfuge practiced by Emperor Meiji. Highly intelligent but neurotically arrogant, he took no care of his public image. It was widely known that he dressed like a German hussar, waxed his mustache, and sometimes lashed out at delinquent servants on the palace grounds with his riding crop.

For all his faults, Emperor Taisho had wit and charm enough to command the allegiance of the most cosmopolitan Japanese. His immediate followers and intermediaries were six worldly-wise princes of the blood who had played uncles to him in his growing up. All but one of them had seen action in the war with Russia. Two of them were graduates of St. Cyr, the French West Point, one of Brest, the French Annapolis. Two more were graduates of Japan's own West Point. The sixth was a Shinto priest who would run the nation's religious establishment until 1937. The chief of the six was Prince Sadanaru, fifty-five, Prince Asahiko's eighth brother and Emperor Taisho's most intimate advisor. He had studied long in France, visited often in England, and attended the St. Louis World's Fair in the United States in 1904.

In traditional Japanese fashion, Taisho and his six princely advisors at once called on a loyal henchman, General Katsura Taro, to stand before them and take responsibility for their plans. General Katsura had been prime minister from 1901 to 1906 and from 1908 to 1911. He had represented the Emperor and the Army against the Constitutionalists in every election since 1900. While he was governor general of Taiwan in 1900, he had drawn up an elaborate plan for Japanese expansion southward into Malaya, Indonesia, and the Philippines. He had presented the plan to Emperor Meiji and his oligarchy and had been told that its execution would have to be postponed until the northern borders of the Empire had been secured against Russia. Now, August 1912, the war with Russia had been won, and it seemed that the time had come.

Katsura was in Russia on reconnaissance when the news of Emperor Meiji's death and the summons from Taisho reached him. He hastened home and was at once appointed by Emperor Taisho to both the chief offices in the palace: that of grand chamberlain and, concurrently, that of lord privy seal. In the one he had the duty of making appointments for all audiences with the

Emperor and in the other the privilege of being in attendance, ready to answer questions, at all audiences.

The cardinal plank in Taisho's imperial program was "perfection of national defense": a major buildup of the armed forces in anticipation of trans-Korean empire building. At Emperor Taisho's and Prince Sadanaru's suggestion, the Army General Staff began to agitate for an increase of two divisions in the strength of the Army occupying Korea. The Constitutionalists, headed by Prime Minister Saionji, the lute-playing prince of the old Court clan of Fujiwaras, opposed the increase on financial grounds. The nation was still struggling with the deficit financing left over from the war with Russia eight years before. Since Saionji and the Constitutionalists had the majority at the polls, in the Diet, and in the Cabinet, they voted down the Army expansion plan handily. As a result, in early December 1912, the war minister resigned and Emperor Taisho's palace factotum, General Katsura, saw to it that no Army officer would accept the war ministership in his place.

Prime Minister Saionji had no choice but to resign, too. In the protracted government crisis which ensued, Emperor Taisho ordered no less than five statesmen to form cabinets. Each of them in turn failed, for the civilians under Saionji's command were determined to show that they could be as disciplined about refusing Cabinet portfolios as could the military men under Katsura. Finally, on December 21, 1912, Emperor Taisho exercised his full constitutional powers and simply declared that Grand Chamberlain-Lord Privy Seal Katsura was to be the new prime minister. Katsura impressed an unimposing slate of old henchmen to serve as his ministers. The Navy at first refused to supply him with a Navy minister but was brought around when the money for new Army divisions was reallocated for a naval shipbuilding program.

Emperor Taisho's coup d'etat blew up a typhoon of popular protest. His minion, General Katsura, was accused in the Diet of "hiding behind the sleeve of the dragon," which was a Japanese way of saying that the Emperor was using him in an abuse of the imperial power. In Meiji's time when prime ministers had been assailed with this charge, Dragon Meiji had always belched softly and the accusations had been withdrawn. Now, however, Emperor Taisho issued a direct order commanding the Diet to recess for three days. When, after two more recesses, the Diet remained as openly critical as before, Emperor Taisho summoned Prince Saionji and commanded him to have his Constitutionalist party cease their opposition to the imperial will. Saionji obediently called a party caucus and delivered the Emperor's request. After two days' debate, it was voted down. Never before in the history of Japan had an express imperial order been rejected outright. Liberal though he was, Prince Saionji knew his place as a Fujiwara courtier: he immediately resigned his presidency of the Constitutionalist party.

Mobs rioted in Tokyo, Kobe, and Osaka, burning newspaper offices, waging pitched battles with the police, and threatening civil war. Finally, on February 11, 1913, when the Katsura administration had lasted just fifty-three days, Emperor Taisho accepted Prime Minister Katsura's resignation. By his obedience to the Emperor's wishes, Katsura had utterly destroyed his reputation as a deft politician. He died eight months later. Army boss Yamagata and his old rival in the oligarchy, Prince Saionji, prevailed upon Emperor Taisho to save face by accepting a military Cabinet of a different, nonpartisan sort, one headed by an admiral.

To the satisfaction of Prince Saionji and of his banker brother Sumitomo, the new Japanese prime minister, Admiral Yamamoto Gombei, cut government spending by 13 per cent and canceled most of the fat naval expansion program for which keels had already been laid during the "Army administration" of General Katsura. Emperor Taisho affixed his seal to Yamamoto's measures with a surly show of indifference. He talked of abdicating. Courtiers noted that his fits of savage temper now gave way to long moods of morose dejection and silence.

In March 1914, on the eve of World War I, the surviving elders of Emperor Meiji's oligarchy, in particular the sixty-four-year-old Saionji, persuaded Emperor Taisho to take heart and try a new approach to the realization of his imperial aspirations. Prime Minister Admiral Yamamoto was ousted from office by disclosure of a scandal involving naval procurement officers in Europe and kickbacks from Siemens Electric in Germany and Vickers Aircraft in England. Then, by prearrangement, Saionji proceeded to the palace with one of the smartest, coolest diplomats in the Japanese Foreign Service, the monocle-wearing Kato Taka-aki.[1]

Taisho, Saionji, and Kato sat down and smoked and talked together with unprecedented informality. Years later Saionji would recall that Taisho, in the bargaining, showed himself as intelligent as any of the four Emperors whom Saionji served between 1865 and 1940. At the end of the negotiations, Taisho agreed to give up, for the time being, Katsura's dream of military conquest in Malaya and Indonesia and accept in its place a shrewd mixture of economic salesmanship, watchful waiting, and diplomatic opportunism. In particular he agreed that, in the event of world war, he would throw in Japan's lot with the Western nations which had power in the Pacific: England which held Malaya, France which governed Indochina, and the United States which controlled the Philippines. It was a difficult decision for Taisho to make because he had always admired Germany most of the Western nations and had modeled himself on what he knew of the German kaiser.

Kato Taka-aki, the diplomat who sat beside Saionji in the informal smoke with Emperor Taisho, was given the key post of foreign minister in the new government. The prime ministership itself was allotted to a professorial figurehead, Okuma Shigenobu. Once a courageous liberal in the lower echelons of Emperor Meiji's oligarchy, Okuma had lost a leg to a bomb thrown by one of Toyama's underworld assassins in 1889. Now seventy-six, he was not prepared to lose another. As the "Sage of Waseda"—the president of a university which he had founded—he was popular for his easygoing fund-raising manners and for his reassuring prescription of book learning for all ills. He had acquired a respectable following in one of the minority parties but did not belong to the disloyal Constitutionalists. The people accepted him as

[1] Kato was a partisan of the late humiliated Prime Minister Katsura. He had served as foreign minister in the Cabinets of 1900 and 1906, had been created baron for his services in concluding the Anglo-Japanese Alliance, and had taken over Katsura's minority party, the Constitutional Fellow Spirits, at Katsura's death in October 1913.

their champion, and for two and a half years, in a time of war prosperity and full employment, he gave them a stable government.

FINISHING SCHOOL

While the Okuma Cabinet was planning Japan's new policy of smart opportunism, the embattled imperial household made peace with the nation. Prince Sadanaru, the eldest of Taisho's six family advisors, resigned the key palace post of lord privy seal, which he had taken when Katsura became prime minister, and turned it over to a commoner. Junior princes of the blood were transferred from the Imperial Guards Division in the palace to other, more plebeian units stationed in the provinces. Crown Prince Hirohito was withdrawn from the exclusive Peers' School and put in the hands of private tutors under the charge of popular war heros. A simple classroom was constructed for his studies on the grounds of the Akasaka Palace and its Spartan furnishings were publicized in the press.

Hirohito's chief tutor, entrusted with the planning of his studies, was Togo Heihachiro, the admiral who had turned in time to sink the Baltic fleet in the war with Russia. Unlike General Nogi, he was a prosaic, peace-loving man who believed in war only as a meticulously planned exercise in self-defense. He sensed that Hirohito was antagonistic to him and he left the boy's curriculum largely to two old Prussian-oriented generals. They were assisted by a preoccupied scientist who was a graduate of Yale and by a rear admiral who was a prolific propagandist for samurai ideals.

Under the planning of these staff officers, Hirohito's tutoring was conducted with strict formality and clockwork. Lessons were monitored in silence, from a kneeling position on the *tatami*, by a spritely old court gentleman who listened only for thoughts that might be disturbing or un-Japanese. The lecturers who gave the lessons came in from Tokyo University or from Army or Navy Staff headquarters; they knelt with bowed heads on a mat facing Hirohito and duly delivered themselves. The gap between crown prince and professor was so great that many of the pedagogues strove to say only what they imagined Hirohito should hear. If they became too trite, however, Hirohito himself let it be known that they were "bland as *jagaimo*"—bland as the white potatoes introduced from the West.

Army and Navy lecturers were the most interesting because they spoke boldly, as a matter of honor, and because they felt sure that any child surrounded by French- and German-speaking civilians must be out of contact with the people, the stark realities of a billet, and the verities of samurai ethics. They kept Hirohito well informed about the battles of World War I and about strategic implications for the Orient. He contracted a fascination for tactics and logistics which never left him. And he remained in touch with several of his military mentors throughout the rest of their lives.

One of Hirohito's more academic instructors, a viscount, succeeded in making him reasonably proficient in arithmetic. Another viscount, for lack of courage to ask him questions and correct his mistakes, left him with a knowledge of French inferior to that of his brother, Prince Chichibu. In history, a baron, who specialized in studies of Manchuria, taught him at length the importance of that land to Japan and sometimes bored him with mythology about the gods begetting the Japanese islands—tales which Hirohito questioned as historically unsound and biologically distasteful. Wada Isaburo, who held degrees from Johns Hopkins, M.I.T., and the University of Berlin, gave him an enthusiasm for airplanes and a firm grasp of mechanics and elementary chemistry.

Only two of the palace professors made personal friendships with Hirohito. One was Hattori Hirotaro, an effeminate little man who taught him natural history, Darwinism, and, perhaps most important, Herbert Spencer's apocrypha to Darwin. This was reduced by Hattori to two ideas: there are fit and unfit societies; the former must destroy the latter in the interests of the race as a whole. At the same time Hattori greatly enhanced Hirohito's enjoyment of life by training him to notice the smallest details of nature in the world about him. When Hirohito complained that nature was disturbed by the column of chamberlains who accompanied him on natural history walks in the countryside, Hattori arranged fishing and diving trips for him in boats too small to hold much of a Court. From these excursions on the water, Hirohito garnered the most pleasant memories of his childhood and a lifelong interest in the worms and shellfish of Japanese bays—an interest that was eventually to win him genuine international recognition as a marine biologist.

Hirohito's other favorite tutor was Sugiura Jugo, a professional jingoist who for thirty-odd years had lashed about with his writing brush in defense of Japanese culture against Western adulteration. Though a chemist by training, with a degree from the University of London, he was detailed to teach Hirohito ethics. And if Hattori distorted biology with his Spencerian asides on survival among nations, what Sugiura did to "ethics" was still more strange and flammable. He lectured at length on the three sacred treasures—the mirror, the sword, and the necklace—and also on the inner virtues of the flag, the nation, rice, shrines, guns, watches, water, and Mount Fuji. From the lecture notes of his beloved tutor, here are some samples:

In Europe there is little rice produced. In some Asian countries much rice is produced but of poor quality, incomparable with our own. Therefore, I feel sorry for the rest of the world, especially the Europeans.

Nowadays, although there are many nations on the earth, only two are strong: England and Russia. In the Western Hemisphere, the United States follows a close third. We do not yet know the outcome of the World War, of course, but it is plain that all the strong nations belong to the same Aryan clan, which comprises one nation. By contrast in Asia the large country, China, is degenerate. Therefore, China cannot be our partner and cannot stand with us against the nations of the West. Our Empire must decide to match arms with the Aryan clan all alone.

The ideas being entertained by the Russians are essentially American-European individualism. We must beware of them. Because of our growing closeness to Europe, esteem for the ancient sacred swords of Japan is declining.

Though we speak of 8,000,000 gods in Japan we really pray only to the excellent souls among the Rulers and the Ruled. Our religion is unique. In foreign lands there are fixed gods. The religion there is based on mere hypothesis.

At his *Genbuku* or coming of age in 1915, Hirohito donned the two swords of the samurai and presented himself at the palace shrine to be anointed a warrior. His father celebrated the event by sending the boy a young concubine to instruct him in the ways of love. Hirohito was shy but the girl was infinitely patient and tactful. Eventually—so Court gossips say—he satisfied his scientific curiosity. Courtiers at the time regretted that he did not seem to be a ladies' man to compare with his hearty grandfather Meiji.

WORLD WAR

In August 1914 the expected war in Europe broke out. Foreign Minister Kato Taka-aki promptly threw in Japan's lot with France and England. His object was not to help Britain but, as he frankly told his colleagues, to silence in advance any British objections to Japanese moves on China. For the next two years Japan undertook to protect British interests in Hong Kong and Shanghai. She sent troops to Singapore to quash trouble there with "the natives." Her Navy convoyed merchantmen through the Indian Ocean into the Mediterranean. She refused repeatedly, however, to contribute any troops to the bloody battlefields of Europe.

For her pittance of co-operation Japan expected a mountain of reciprocity. Foreign Minister Kato Taka-aki wanted the British government to run diplomatic interference for Japanese seizure and permanent possession of all German mandates and leaseholds in the Pacific. Hard pressed though she was, Great Britain refused to give Japan such a carte blanche. In October 1914, two months after the war started, Japan went ahead on her own. Imperial marines poured ashore on nominally German islands all across the western Pacific, while Japanese Army divisions landed on the Shantung Peninsula, jutting out toward Korea from the north China coast, to begin a drive on the German-leased port of Tsingtao. After three months of campaigning, mostly on the sovereign territory of China, the Japanese forces not only took the

German city but occupied the entire peninsula, a region roughly equivalent in area and population to the combined states of Connecticut and Massachusetts.

British diplomats talked for time. American diplomats frowned. And Yuan Shih-kai, the president of the new Republic of China, protested mildly. He knew that Western friends could not help him while the war lasted, and he hoped that divided councils in Japan herself might protect his regime until the war was over. At the end of 1914, Yuan politely told Tokyo that, since the Tsingtao campaign had ended, it was time for Japan to stop parading troops across Chinese territory and restrict them to police administration in the German leasehold. Japanese Foreign Minister Kato expressed indignation at Yuan's snide imputations and on January 18, 1915, delivered a note to China "to clarify the situation."

The note, which was amplified by a number of reference documents, has been remembered as the Twenty-One Demands. It explained fully—all too fully—what was required of China. The demands broke down into five groups, each making a separate point:

(1) As to Tsingtao: China must accept whatever settlement Japan might make with Germany and must let Japan build and operate a 200-mile railroad inland from Tsingtao to Tsinan on the Yellow River, thereby cutting China strategically into two halves.

(2) As to Manchuria: China must extend Japanese leases there to ninety-nine years and give Japan veto and first option rights in all future economic development of that region.

(3) As to financing: China must come first to Japan for all future loans and must here and now deliver, as collateral for past loans, supervisory control of the Chinese iron industry.

(4) As to the West: China must cede no more harbors, islands, or bays to the barbarians.

(5) As to the future: China must employ Japanese advisors for all important political, financial, and military development programs; must buy over 50 per cent of her army and navy supplies in Japan; must let Japan build a network of railroads in central China.

Foreign Minister Kato presented the Twenty-One Demands

not to the foreign minister of China but directly to President Yuan Shih-kai, enjoining him to keep all of them, particularly the fifth group, secret. Yuan naturally leaked them as soon as possible to the American ambassador in Peking, and Kato was embarrassed by diplomatic inquiries from all over the world. Kato replied to the Western Powers with a summary of the first four points and a denial of the existence of the fifth. To China he replied with the dispatch of 30,000 reinforcements for Japan's continental garrisons. When Yuan continued to resist all the demands, Foreign Minister Kato told him on May 7, 1915, that the fifth set could be reserved for future discussion but that he had only forty-eight hours to consider the first four sets, after which China would be invaded. Yuan promptly gave in and let it be known in the West that he was acting under duress. Years later, when the peace settlements were made after World War I, Chinese diplomats regained a substantial part of the ground which Yuan had temporarily conceded.

In Tokyo old Army Chief Yamagata saw clearly from the tenor of Chinese newspapers that Foreign Minister Kato had won a Pyrrhic victory. The Chinese felt that Yuan Shih-kai had actually put up a brave stand against Japan's hated cutthroats and carpetbaggers. At seventy-seven, Yamagata still had enough political influence to force the Cabinet to resign. Prime Minister Okuma obediently formed a new Cabinet which did not contain the controversial foreign minister, Kato.

In December 1915, four months after Kato's ouster, China's President Yuan Shih-kai announced that, by popular request, he planned to crown himself emperor. It was a fatal miscalculation. The war lords who commanded Yuan's armies might not be republican idealists but neither did they want to serve under a new imperial dynasty. Rebellion spread and on June 6, 1916, Yuan died of uremia brought on by nervous prostration. He was succeeded by a nonentity who preserved the central Republican government only as a façade for many separate provincial regimes, each run by one of Yuan's former generals.

Emperor Meiji's old Army Chief Yamagata was dismayed. With Yuan went all hope of a strong Japan-China to face the West. Yamagata exerted all his influence to find a new, non-republican autocrat to govern China and a new, un-Westernized Cabinet to govern Japan. He pointed out to his pro-German Emperor, Taisho, that Japan's allies were not winning the war; that the kaiser's armies were fighting the battle of the Somme and pressing on toward Verdun; that the buffer state of Russia, which separated Germany from her lost leasehold of Tsingtao, seemed dangerously weak. After a complex political parley and, for an old man, a tremendous display of energy and influence, Yamagata succeeded, in September 1916, in toppling the Okuma government. He persuaded Emperor Taisho to appoint in its place a Cabinet headed by an Army man, General Terauchi.

Through Terauchi, Yamagata backed the war lord of Manchuria, Chang Tso-lin, as the next strongman in northern China. A peasant boy, Chang had grown up hunting hares on the Manchurian prairies to help feed himself and his ailing seamstress mother. One day, as a teen-ager, he had hid behind a clump of bushes at the sound of horses' hooves. Seeing a bandit band fleeing from the imperial Manchu constabulary, he raised his gun and shot one of the fugitives. When the chase had passed, he took possession of the dead bandit's horse. With this small grubstake he went on to become a bandit himself, the most successful in all Manchuria. During the Russo-Japanese War he and his men had served the Japanese as irregulars behind the Russian lines. After the war his troops had been accepted into the imperial Chinese Army and he had made a name for himself as a capable general. Now that Yuan was dead, Chang Tso-lin planned to fill the vacuum and make himself master of China. He took to striking Napoleonic poses and wearing a Russian greatcoat lined with otter skins.

The Six Princes of Emperor Taisho's kitchen cabinet conceived an immediate dislike for Chang Tso-lin. They did not look favorably on his plans for unifying China or on his friendship with the old Choshu clan's Army chief, Yamagata. Through their contacts with the remnants of the former Chinese imperial family, they arranged to have Chang Tso-lin's ambitions nipped in the bud. In 1916 Manchu Prince Babojab of Mongolia invaded western Manchuria with a horde of Tartar roughriders, officered by Japanese "advisors" who were all protégés of Emperor Taisho's princes. The

horsemen from the steppes harassed the railroad between Peking
and the Manchurian capital of Mukden. Their presence on Chang
Tso-lin's flank made it impossible for Chang to prepare his contemplated invasion of China.

At the height of the Mongol invasion on October 15, 1916—six
days after the formation of the Yamagata-backed Army Cabinet
of General Terauchi—the youngest of Emperor Taisho's Six
Princes arrived in Mukden to preside in person over an intrigue
that was expected to end Chang Tso-lin's career. The prince was
Kanin, the tenth brother of Emperor Komei's advisor, Asahiko,
and the future Army Chief of Staff for Hirohito in the years 1932–
1940. He was on his way home by rail from a state visit to Petro-
grad—the then capital of Russia, now Leningrad—where he had
gone to assess the weakness of the czarist regime and of the crum-
bling Russian front against Germany. At Mukden station Prince
Kanin was met by a crowd of Japanese bureaucrats and Army officers employed by the Japanese governments of the Kwantung
Peninsula Leasehold and the South Manchuria Railroad Zone.
The reception committee was headed by the governor of Port
Arthur, a general whom Kanin had known intimately for years.
The general brought with him to the station, as host, Chang Tso-
lin, the war lord of Manchuria.

After the platform welcomes, the groups of dignitaries climbed
into carriages and bowled off together down the dusty unpaved
roads of Mukden to an Oriental feast. As they neared their restaurant in the Japanese quarter, a bystander lobbed a bomb at
Chang Tso-lin's carriage, which led the cavalcade. The bomb fell
short and burst amid his mounted bodyguard, killing five of them.
Chang leapt swift as an alley cat from his coach, seized a cap and
a horse from one of his surviving henchmen, and made off down
a side street, unnoticed in the confusion. The bomb thrower was
shot at once, before his affiliations could be determined, and
Chang's coachman covered his master's flight by moving on
gravely with the rest of the procession. Undaunted, a second bomb
thrower came forward to blow the empty carriage to splinters.

The next day a horde of Babojab's Mongol horsemen, accompanied by their Japanese advisors, poured into the country west
of Mukden and drove on the city. To the surprise of the Japa-

nese, a very angry and alive Chang Tso-lin marshaled his defense forces, met the Mongolians, and routed them. When the Japanese realized that they had failed, a number of nettled officers proposed to seize Mukden anyway with regular Japanese railway guard units. The acting Japanese consul general in Mukden cabled news of the plan to Tokyo, and Prime Minister Terauchi cabled back orders that no one do anything more without authorization. Prince Kanin and his cronies were bitterly frustrated. They solaced themselves in later years by describing with relish the spectacle of Chang Tso-lin fleeing on horseback in common soldier's garb down a back alley. At length, after Hirohito came to power, Prince Kanin's minions, in 1928, would inaugurate the aggressions of Hirohito's reign by assassinating Chang Tso-lin successfully. Imperial policy might change direction but it did not forget or forgive.

SIBERIA

Shortly after Emperor Taisho's ill-conceived effort to add Manchuria to the Empire, Germany turned east from stalemate at Verdun and overran Rumania. The Russian front collapsed and with it the rule of the Romanovs. During March 1917, Czar Nicholas relinquished his crown, and the whole long underbelly of Russia became a military emptiness, preoccupied with internal rumbling. To many Japanese it appeared that any day Kaiser Wilhelm might come knocking at the door, demanding payment for the seized German leasehold of Tsingtao.

In the early months of 1917 old Army Chief Yamagata was able to align most responsible Japanese behind him against further ill-considered essays in gunboat diplomacy. Taisho retired petulantly under the face-saving cover of sickness. Then, on April 7, Tokyo time, the United States joined the Allies against Germany and Emperor Taisho felt better. The Six Princes of his kitchen cabinet began at once to tout the possibility of adding eastern Siberia to the Empire. The revolutionary regime in western Russia had not the men or money to defend Vladivostok. The Germans now would need all their strength for the western front. And what was more, the British and French governments had invited Japan several times since 1915 to move troops west from

Vladivostok in order to shore up the eastern front. By accepting the invitation at this belated date Japan might not be able to annex Siberia permanently but she would at least ingratiate herself with the victors and have counters with which to bargain at the postwar peace conferences.

On June 5, 1917, Emperor Taisho appointed a Special Advisory Council on Foreign Affairs to help him consider the possibilities. At the same time he ordered the Army General Staff to prepare a detailed study of the strategic situation. The Army study, submitted in October 1917, showed that a thrust all the way to the eastern front, as requested by France and England, would overextend the Army's logistical resources, but that a simple occupation of the railheads and lines of track as far west as Lake Baikal in mid-Siberia would be completely feasible.

Army strongman Yamagata and his old oligarch rival, Prince Saionji, mustered the elders of the nation in opposition to the Siberian venture. Army agents, said Yamagata, had discovered that there were approximately 300,000 Austrian, German, Turkish, and Bulgarian prisoners of war in Siberia who would fight for the Bolsheviks in return for their freedom. Under the circumstances, a Japanese expeditionary force of less than 100,000 men would be a rash venture, courting disaster.

In late December 1917, the Central Soviet opened an administrative office in Vladivostok, and Great Britain at once announced that she was dispatching H.M.S. *Suffolk* to the port to look after British interests there and stand by to evacuate British nationals if it became necessary. Yamagata agreed that Japan would be justified in doing whatever the British did. And so on January 12, 1918, Japan sent a naval squadron to Vladivostok to make sure that the municipal government there would remain in White Russian hands.

All through the spring of 1918 Japan kept open the Vladivostok beachhead, and an intense political battle raged in Tokyo about whether or not to extend it. Almost singlehandedly the eighty-year-old Yamagata held out against unilateral Japanese action.

"We must inquire the views of the various countries," he told Emperor Taisho. "There must be a consensus and we must be fully justified."

On April 23, 1918, Emperor Taisho finally bowed to his arguments. The Japanese marines went back to their ships and on April 25 Vladivostok formed its own soviet and entered the Lenin-Trotsky fold.

Just when Yamagata had won his battle, the whole situation was changed by an about-face on the part of the United States. Fifty thousand Czech soldiers, who had earlier surrendered to the Russians in the hopes of being able to liberate their native land from the yoke of the Austro-Hungarian Empire, were now unemployed mercenaries in Russia, struggling to go home. The Allies had agreed to use them on the western front if they could find any way of getting there. They organized themselves into sixty trainloads of from 700 to 1000 men each and set off from western Russia in April 1918 to stage their way east along the Trans-Siberian railroad. At the other end in Vladivostok they hoped they would find Allied transports ready to take them to France. As they began their journey, the British landed marines in northern Russia at Murmansk, and the German government demanded that the Bolsheviks disarm the Czechs before they could gather at this potential second front. When the Reds tried to comply, the Czech rear guard, which was still west of the Volga, rebuffed the attempt with bullets. In a matter of weeks the strung-out Czech column had seized every major railhead from the Volga to Vladivostok and their peaceful exodus had become a fighting anabasis. Seasoned soldiers, they drove off every force, Red or White, that sought to stay their passage.

The thought of 50,000 Czech patriots fighting their way across 5,000 miles of steppe and tundra was not difficult to dramatize in newspapers, and the sympathy of the American public was profoundly stirred. The romantic feeling for the Czechs was used by American interests which feared the Red plague of Bolshevism, and on July 8, 1918, the United States abruptly suggested to Japan that the two nations mount a joint intervention in Siberia. Its objectives should be limited to help for the Czechs, satisfactory disposition of the 300,000-odd prisoners of war in Siberian stockades, and retrieval of Allied war supplies stockpiled in Vladivostok.

Old Army man Yamagata chuckled cynically when he heard the news. Overnight all his opinions changed, and he became, in the days that followed, an ardent champion of intervention. By July 12 he was saying, "Since the present expedition is not to fight with Germany there is no need for our inadequacy to give anxiety." On August 3 the Japanese government announced that it would participate in the Allied expedition, and three weeks later, by arrangement with China, 30,000 Japanese troops were already marching north to the Russian border through Manchuria.

The intervention was not popular anywhere. All through August, after the decision for it was made, Japanese housewives staged riots in the major cities, burning warehouses in protest against the high price of rice. Soldiers complained that no one would come to see them off when they left for the front, and many of them wore civilian clothes so that they would not be recognized as Army men. As a result of the popular protest, the Terauchi government resigned in late September, and Emperor Taisho mollified the mobs by appointing in its place Japan's first true party government, presided over by a commoner, the president of the Constitutionalists, Hara Takashi.

American observers were no more pleased by Japan's speedy co-operation than were the mass of Japanese themselves. In American eyes, too many Japanese troops had moved too quickly. Yamagata, however, smiled innocently. The Army, he said, was always kept ready to move swiftly and with a safe margin of force. What right, he demanded brazenly, had anyone to question the Emperor's constitutional prerogative of supreme command? As quickly as possible, President Woodrow Wilson shipped 7,000 U.S. troops to Siberia to keep an eye on the Japanese. Each side separately supported a succession of ill-conceived White Russian puppet regimes, all of which were blackened from their inception by the sundry tortures, rapes, and murders of their Cossack hangers-on. The Japanese soldiers themselves won a name for savagery by carrying out, under orders, several village massacres in reprisal for Russian terrorism.

None of the White Russian governments set up by the "Allies" won any degree of popular backing from the Siberian peasantry, and all collapsed in 1919 when Red Armies finally emerged out of the west and began to apply military pressure. Anglo-American troops developed a revulsion for the duty they were called upon to perform. In late 1919 the British withdrew their tiny contingent, and with them went a force of Canadians who were reported on the verge of mutiny. In April 1920 the last U.S. troops followed them, leaving the Japanese to their own devices. In the months that followed, over large areas of Siberia, all pretence of native government was dropped and the Japanese Army ruled by its own law.

The Czechs, who had never needed any help in the first place, except ships to carry them home, now began to be repatriated. They sailed from Vladivostok, regiment by regiment, all year long. While they waited they clashed frequently with the Japanese and sold the last and best of the White Russian puppets, Alexander Kolchak, to a Bolshevik firing squad.

The 300,000 German, Austrian, Turkish, and Bulgarian war prisoners—men who might have been repatriated in 1917 if it had not been for the intervention—were left forgotten in their stockades. Scandinavian, American, and German Red Cross teams began to take notice of their sorry plight late in 1919, but before anything effective was done for them, 100,000 had died of starvation, typhus, and smallpox. Of the survivors many were shipped home insane. The Japanese forces lingered on in Siberia until 1922. Only when the postwar peace conferences were over and their presence could no longer be represented as a force of leverage in international politics were they finally withdrawn.

PEACE AND MADNESS

The Versailles peace conference opened in January 1919. The Japanese delegation to it was headed by the once debonair lute-playing Fujiwara Prince Saionji. Saionji was now seventy years old, and he captivated the world's press by arriving in Paris with a great deal of baggage, including a pretty young apprentice geisha named Flower Child whom he unabashedly called his mistress. Whenever negotiations went badly for his delegation, he moved the baggage and Flower Child out to the lobby of the Hotel Bristol where he was staying as a sign that Japan might withdraw from the conference. Then he would take a stroll in the Bois de

Boulogne and await developments. As soon as his subordinates had worked out a suitable compromise, he would re-register at the Bristol and call for his effects. French hostesses, dying to see Flower Child, invited him to all their parties, but he accepted invitations judiciously and usually left the girl back in his hotel suite.[2] He attended no sessions of the peace conference but met everyone he needed to meet at the soirees. All the Western statesmen at the conference developed a liking for him as an urbane conversationalist, a shrewd bargainer, and a convincing liberal.

Saionji's objectives at the conference were to keep the territories which Japan had taken from Germany during the war and to gain recognition for Japan as a first-class power. He succeeded in keeping the leasehold of Tsingtao and the German mandated islands in the Pacific, and he relinquished in return Japan's occupied areas in Siberia and the Shantung Peninsula. He succeeded in having Japan included, after France and Italy, in the Big Five but failed to win agreement on a resolution calling for legal equality among nations without "distinction . . . on account of their race."

In the summer of 1919, while Saionji was still in Paris, the forty-year-old Emperor Taisho suffered the first in a succession of cerebral hemorrhages or thromboses which were to incapacitate him increasingly for the rest of his life. Although the attack was kept secret and indeed has never been precisely defined by the doctors who attended him, news of it spread quickly through aristocratic circles. It was difficult for Taisho to walk now, even with a shuffle. His hands trembled. His memory of recent events was blurred. His judgment and sense of propriety were dimmed. At the annual autumn maneuvers for the Army and Navy he descended unexpectedly from the reviewing stand and with his own hands unpacked a soldier's kit to see what was in it. At the opening of the Diet two months later he rolled the message he was to read into a spyglass and peered quizzically through it at legislators who had offended him in the past. Though he seemed rational, he expressed himself with a heightened sense of whimsy and sarcasm

2 He made an exception for President Wilson, who acknowledged the honor by giving Flower Child a necklace which Japanese appraisers valued at over $1,000.

which caused his retainers great pain. They called him mad, a diagnosis which young Hirohito never accepted.

Emperor Taisho's lapse removed the vortex from the hurricane of Japanese political life. The spry old Army spirit, Yamagata, stepped in to fill the void. Taisho's Six Princes consulted with their sworn allies of the Satsuma clan and decided that, now or never, they must launch an underground campaign to break the tightening stranglehold of Yamagata and his Choshu clan. Anti-Choshu cells must be established in the traditional Choshu strong-holds of the bureaucracy, in the Home Ministry which controlled the police, in the Agriculture and Commerce Ministry which con-trolled long-range industrial planning, and most important, in the Army. The nineteen-year-old Crown Prince Hirohito probably gave his consent to the scheme, for it was his favorites in the younger generation of princes and noblemen—his childhood Big Brothers—who became the most active executioners of the plot.

One of the conspirators' anti-Choshu cells, one which would cast a long shadow over Hirohito's reign, was established in the ranks of Army Intelligence. Far from the prying eyes of Yamagata's agents, it was headquartered in France and staffed by young noble-men who had arranged postings for themselves as military at-tachés in the various capitals of Europe. The task of recruiting this Parisian imperial cell fell to thirty-two-year-old Prince Higa-shikuni, the sixth and youngest of the surviving sons of Emperor Komei's advisor Asahiko and the future prime minister who would hand Japan over to General MacArthur.

By 1919 Higashikuni was far less plain-spoken than he had been eight years earlier when he had refused Emperor Meiji's din-ner invitation. In 1914 he had graduated from the Army's exclu-sive Staff College or War College where officers had to prove their intellectual capacity in original strategic planning. In 1915 he had been finally restored to his family's good graces and allowed to marry Emperor Meiji's ninth daughter, Toshiko. Since then he had served with the 2d Division in the northern city of Sendai, taken a special course in armored cars and tanks at the Chiba Infantry School, and everywhere widened his circle of henchmen. By 1919 he was a thoroughly professional intelligence officer.

In December 1919 the Satsuma clan's senior general suggested to Choshu Army Chief Yamagata that perhaps Prince Higashi-kuni should be allowed to fulfill his long-cherished ambition to study at the famous military schools of Napoleon in France. The Satsuma chieftain pointed out that most of Higashikuni's best Army friends were already in Europe and that a good spy ring was needed there if Japan was to catch up on the technological secrets developed during World War I. The bright young analysts attached to the embassies would work more closely and secretly together if an imperial prince joined them in their mission and impressed them with its importance. Army Chief Yamagata, un-suspecting, called in Higashikuni for a man-to-man chat, was im-pressed by his patriotism, and forthwith approved the orders which posted him to France.

Higashikuni took ship with another, more peripheral member of the imperial family, the husband of his eldest niece, Army Captain Viscount Machijiri Kazumoto. Within a week of their ar-rival at Marseilles, Machijiri was in touch with Captain Tojo Hi-deki in Switzerland, the later World War II "dictator." Tojo was already a thoroughly trustworthy conspirator, for in addition to being an old friend of Higashikuni, he had served for three years as a personal aide to the war minister who had helped Prince Kanin in the abortive 1916 Manchuria coup.[3] Using Tojo as an intermediary, Prince Higashikuni had soon established contact with a galaxy of ambitious young non-Choshu attachés and ob-servers all over Europe: in Berlin with Major Umezu Yoshijiro, the future chief of staff who would surrender in Hirohito's bunker in 1945; in Bern with Captain Yamashita Tomoyuki, the later general who would capture Singapore; in Moscow with Lieutenant Murakami Keisaku, the son-in-law of Prime Minister Katsura's war minister; in Copenhagen with Lieutenant Colonel Nakamura Kotaro, a later war minister; in Paris with Major Nakajima Kesago, the sadist who would bring special body-burning oils to Nanking in 1937; in Cologne with Captain Shimomura Sadamu who would force the Nanking plans through the General Staff. To these in

3 War Minister Oshima Kenichi, the father of Lieutenant General Oshima Hiroshi who, as acting Japanese ambassador in Berlin in 1940, would bring Hirohito into the Tripartite Pact with Hitler and Mussolini.

the early months of 1920 were added other notorious fascist generals of years to come.

COLOR-BLIND BRIDE

Vague rumors of an Emperor-Satsuma plot reached Yamagata's ears through his private agents in the spring of 1920. He understood, he said delicately, that young Crown Prince Hirohito's name was being used and abused by the plotters to give their machinations a semblance of sanction. Such impiety, as Yamagata saw it, stemmed from the marriage alliance which Hirohito had arranged for himself. Two years earlier, on January 17, 1918, when the Navy had just sent ships to Vladivostok, the Imperial Household Ministry had announced the betrothal of Hirohito to Princess Nagako, the daughter of Prince Kuni Kuniyoshi. Prince Kuni was the second of the surviving sons of Emperor Komei's advisor Asahiko and one of Taisho's Six Princes. His wife Chikako was the daughter of the Satsuma clan lord, Shimazu, who had sworn eternal friendship with Asahiko and his heirs in 1863. For Hirohito to marry Princess Nagako was to bring the Throne itself into the Shimazu-Asahiko alliance.

As a Choshu man and a hereditary foe of the Satsuma clan, old Army martinet Yamagata had not liked the marriage plans when he first heard of them in 1917 but had said nothing because he understood that Nagako was young Crown Prince Hirohito's own choice. Chamberlains in charge of genealogies, rituals, and other imperial mysteries had scoured the land in early 1917 to compile a complete list of eligible fiancées for Hirohito. Empress Sadako, the pretty young woman who had waited with the cherry blossoms in the garden in 1900, had insisted that her son make his selection personally. In midsummer, 1917, she had stationed the seventeen-year-old boy in hiding behind a sliding door in her suite in the Concubines' Pavilion of the palace, enabling him to observe the eligibles through a peephole while she entertained each of them in turn at a tea ceremony. He had had time beforehand to study their photographs and their curricula vitae. Many of them he had played with in years past on the beach outside the Summer Palace at Hayama or in the bamboo groves of the mountain resort of Karuizawa. Now almost a score of girls were paraded in front of him, kneeling to drink a ceremonial cup of tea and exchange a few words with his mother. They ranged in age from Hirohito's own lofty seventeen down to a gawky eleven. Half of them, the prettiest half, were Fujiwara princesses, schooled to be charming, seductive, and obedient. The other half were princesses of the blood, culled from a smaller reservoir of eligibility, and for the most part semi-Westernized, proud, and uncertain of their rights.

Chamberlains had expected Hirohito to pick one of the faun-eyed daughters of Fujiwara Prince Ichijo or the pert fifteen-year-old princess of the blood, Masako, with whom he had once spent a pleasant summer in the mountains. Masako then had been a good rough-and-tumble tomboy of a companion; Masako now, in the chamberlains' eyes, had filled out ravishingly. What teasing trick she had played on Hirohito they could never find out, but he passed her over and three years later sanctioned a purely political match for her with a foreigner; the only match which has been contracted by the imperial family with a foreigner to this day, a match, moreover, with a Korean prince, a leader of Japan's most persecuted immigrant minority.[4]

In selecting Nagako over all the rest, Hirohito took a bright, serious, placid, chubby fourteen-year-old who could not be compared, as a woman, with most of the other candidates he saw. He made the choice out of loyalty to her uncles, his Big Brothers Prince Higashikuni and Prince Asaka, and to her fifteen-year-old brother Kuni Kunihisa who had been his companion since nursery days. She was, in short, the girl-brat who had often tagged along. He was at home with her and all her family. Even her father struck a responsive chord in him, for Prince Kuni shared Hirohito's interest in science. He was an intellectual and a visionary. He ridiculed the notion that Japan would ever make a military dent in the world by sheer force of samurai ardor and gave

[4] After World War II, when the puppet princes of Korea became an unpleasant reminder of past glory, Masako found the condescending politeness of Japanese high society intolerable. In 1963, she took her ailing husband back to his homeland where they founded an orphanage for Japanese-Korean half-breeds.

his enthusiasms instead to the development of the weapons of the future: the airplane, the tank, and bacteriological warfare.

In 1920 when eighty-two-year-old strongman Yamagata became suspicious of the intentions of Hirohito's fiancée's family, he struck back with pseudoscientific arguments. He planted a learned article in a Tokyo periodical tracing the hereditary course of color-blindness down through the generations of the Satsuma clan's Shimazu family. Since Nagako had a Shimazu mother the blemish might well enter the imperial blood stream if Hirohito went through with his marriage plans.

Yamagata's family physician convoked a medical congress to discuss the problems of the color-blind. A former inspector general of Army medicine devoted a lecture he had been asked to give at the "Imperial Study"—the imperial family's standing adult self-education program—entirely to color-blindness. Empress Sadako, whose Fujiwara nieces and cousins had been rejected by her son, publicly stood by Nagako and scoffed at Yamagata's allegations. Privately, however, she consulted her kinsman, the old lute-player Prince Saionji, and asked him if there were really any genetic danger. Saionji let Yamagata understand that he would not stand in the way if an attempt were made to break up the engagement of Hirohito and Nagako.

Neither Yamagata nor Saionji knew their opponent. In years past both of them had often worked out compromises with princes of the blood. But Prince Kuni Kuniyoshi, the father of the fiancée, was a man of conscience. He believed in his daughter as he believed in military air power. When his uncle, Prince Sadanaru, the senior of Taisho's Six Princes, came to him and begged him to humor Yamagata—to withdraw his Shimazu daughter Nagako in favor of his non-clan, non-controversial niece Masako—Prince Kuni stood on principle and refused. He announced that Nagako had been chosen through no machinations of his own, and therefore he would take it as a point of personal honor if she should now be put aside. It was an extremely European stand to take, but it meant, in plain Japanese, that he was prepared to kill both himself and Nagako if she were now jilted.

Yamagata next got in touch with Sugiura Jugo, Hirohito's favorite tutor, to see if he could persuade the boy to annul the engagement by his own motion. Hirohito did not absolutely rebuff the feeler but mildly reiterated that Nagako was still his preference. Sugiura then justified all the trust Hirohito had ever placed in him by announcing that if the crown prince were not given his way, he, Sugiura, a mere school teacher, would also commit hara-kiri.

While Yamagata hesitated, Prince Kuni hired the powers of persuasion of a band of Black Dragon thugs. From mid-Meiji times, Yamagata and the Black Dragon's "Darkside Emperor" Toyama had been the upper and lower spiders in Japan's "web society." They had often co-operated in the past, and each owed part of his power to the other's help. But now that Toyama, who had started life as a street urchin, found himself directly solicited by the imperial family, he knew that his kingdom had come. No longer need he cultivate Yamagata, who was after all a mere clan samurai. Besides, the romantic gangsters and slum dwellers whom Toyama controlled and represented would always favor a prince in white armor over a sly old fox of an aristocrat like Yamagata. When Prince Kuni's bribes began to percolate down through Toyama's adept hands, an aging buck in the Diet, Otake Kanichi, sprang up to challenge Yamagata to a duel: "For old times' sake, let's assassinate each other with swords." More to the point, a Toyama henchman visited Yamagata and bowed himself out with the courteous threat: "I would be humbly honored to accept the life of Your Excellency's wife."

Yamagata had heard all these dramatic declarations before and had an old warrior's contempt for them. The police, however, who in Japan consider their function as mainly preventive intelligence rather than detective or punitive work, automatically set pickets around Yamagata's villa in the Tokyo suburb of Odawara. Yamagata was so incensed by the suggestion that he might need protection—he, a samurai who could once have routed single-handedly a dozen ruffians with his swordplay—that he drove off the police with his cane. Thereafter, a group of his fellow Choshu clansmen took it upon themselves to guard his home, standing shifts tactfully in plainclothes.

Yamagata's personal agent at Court, Imperial Household Minister Nakamura Yujiro, who had seen to it that the trumped-up issue of color-blindness was the burning question in Court gossip, now sought an audience with Emperor Taisho and Empress Sadako. Kneeling rigidly on the *tatami*, head to the floor, he said: "I must beg miserably for Your favor after the failure of my Imperial Household Agency to discover the color-blindness in the Shimazu family of Princess Nagako's mother. Now that the defect is well known, what is your Imperial Highness's pleasure?" Emperor Taisho looked straight ahead, unspeaking, and Empress Sadako, too, was strangely silent. Nakamura looked up several times from the *tatami* and saw a bitter ghost of a smile playing around her mouth. When the tension had become extreme, the Emperor suddenly spoke in the high-pitched chanting voice which he reserved for oracular priestly occasions: "I am told that scientists, too, often make mistakes." Nakamura glanced at the Empress and saw her motioning with her eyes for him to withdraw. The audience was over.

On February 10, 1921, the Home Ministry, in charge of prefectural governments and police, announced: "Although there are rumors about Princess Nagako's marriage, no changes of plan are presently contemplated. Of this the government is absolutely certain. Also Household Minister Nakamura Yujiro has determined to tender his resignation." Previously the newspapers had carried no explicit stories about the marriage controversy but had only alluded to "a delicate situation in the imperial household." Suddenly to announce Household Minister Nakamura as the culprit of the situation, when everyone knew that Nakamura was Yamagata's protégé, was rude in the extreme. Yamagata offered ostentatiously to resign all his titles and the Throne just as ostentatiously begged him to keep them. The Emperor, it was declared, had full confidence in Yamagata as a loyal elder of the nation.

BON VOYAGE

No sooner had Yamagata retired to his corner to stanch his wounds and plan the next round than a new issue was injected into the controversy, an issue which temporarily embarrassed Hirohito and permanently discredited Yamagata in the eyes of the public. For many months Hirohito had been planning to round out his education with a trip to Europe. Tentative arrangements had been made with the British and French governments and Yamagata had expressed his approval of the plan. Responsible officials of the government all agreed that the trip might improve relations with Great Britain and make it possible to renew the advantageous Anglo-Japanese alliance. Yamagata's old friend and rival, the lute-playing Prince Saionji, however, saw deeper. He had some inkling of Prince Higashikuni's mission to the young attachés at the Japanese embassies in Europe. He had seen how Taisho's Six Princes had come back from Europe in the 1880's with their private cabals of henchmen. He could imagine the magic which Hirohito's presence in France would work on Higashikuni's efforts.

Through his son-in-law and adopted son—Saionji Hachiro, a chamberlain—Saionji leaked to the press a highly distorted account of the reasons for Hirohito's trip abroad. According to the planted story, Yamagata was sending Hirohito away to cool his ardor for Nagako and break up the engagement. Overnight Toyama's thugs, the newspapers, and the romantic Japanese masses joined in indignant opposition to the European tour. Editorialists suggested that Yamagata might have Nagako assassinated in Hirohito's absence, that Westerners would ridicule Hirohito's noisy Japanese way of drinking soup, that Korean assassins would be able to cut Hirohito down in Trafalgar Square, that Hirohito would catch cold because of "the disgusting European habit of blowing noses." Knowing nothing of the West but distrust and nothing of Hirohito but reverence, the people could not appreciate the fact that their future Emperor was better equipped by training to feel at home in Western clothes, eating frogs' legs on the Champs-Elysées, than to squat in kimono, sipping noodles on the Ginza.

Toyama Mitsuru, the elder statesman of gangland, hardly needed to be told that Hirohito genuinely looked forward to his visit abroad and would come to no harm by it. His enthusiastic underlings, however, invested much face in the struggle to stop the voyage. Before Toyama was fully aware of all the niceties of the situation, some of them had vowed to strap themselves to the railroad tracks in front of the train taking Hirohito to his port of departure. And so, when visited by a chamberlain, Toyama sighed and asked for time. The impatient young Hirohito was not prepared to give it and sent to him Count Futara, one of the Big Brothers of Hirohito's childhood and the husband of one of the nieces of Emperor Komei's advisor Asahiko. Count Futara was to become Hirohito's public relations man. He would supply an image of Hirohito to satisfy the demands of Western newsmen— the one image on which Western accounts of Hirohito's character as a young man are all based. He had a flair for words and drama. "We have gone with you this far," he told Toyama, "but now we are all resolved to go with Hirohito even to the gates of death." Toyama nodded approvingly and asked only for some little diversionary act of bravado which would make it easier for his men to back down.

A few days later, on February 27, 1920, a group of toughs forced their way into the home of Saionji's son, Hachiro. They belonged to a cell of young intellectuals within the Black Dragon Society which was patronized by Hirohito's Big Brothers and used by the Throne for private civilian intelligence work in China. They were led by Dr. Okawa Shumei, who would later win a reputation as the "Goebbels of Japan" and as the ideologist for the Strike-South faction which espoused war against Western colonies in Southeast Asia rather than war against Communist Russia.

In a nod to popular chauvinistic sentiment, the intruders first accused young Saionji, wrongfully, of advocating Hirohito's trip abroad. Then they leveled their real charges. They told Hachiro that he was suspected of having connived with Yamagata's discredited Imperial Household Minister Nakamura and of having opposed Hirohito's betrothal to Nagako. Finally they upbraided him, as a palace chamberlain, for having gossiped too much to the men of the press about Hirohito's proposed trip. For these derelictions of duty they demanded that young Saionji stand up and be chastised. Hachiro realized at once that he was about to be punished sacramentally as a scapegoat for his father, the elder statesman. In defense of the Saionji family honor, he drew his sword. Dr. Okawa's toughs seized cleat bolts from the sliding screens and held their ground. Meanwhile some of them dashed outside to fetch wooden swords which they had cached at the front entrance. Flailing the air, Hachiro retreated through a doorway at the rear of the house, turned and sought to escape through his back garden. The street bullies caught him, weaving through the trees, and thrashed him thoroughly with their mock swords. When they departed they left beside his bruised body a two-foot scroll that declared him a traitor.

Saionji Hachiro did not commit suicide, and his father and Toyama duly apologized both to one another and to the Throne. All the great nobles and princes at Court agreed with Hirohito that Yamagata must be firmly ignored. Accordingly, they decided to minimize further trouble by starting for Europe as quickly as possible. In London equerries of the British royal family scurried about rearranging schedules which had been thrown askew by the announced arrival of "that bloody little prince" a whole week earlier than anticipated.

SALT AIR

Hirohito and his fifteen-man suite of chamberlains and Army and Navy officers proceeded in state through the streets of Tokyo on the morning of March 3, 1921, boarded the battleship *Katori* off Yokohama, and steamed for the open sea with the battleship *Kajima* in escort. Before moving out of sight of the Japanese coast, the squadron hove to briefly three miles off the village of Hayama where Empress Sadako and her sick Taisho lived in seclusion on the beach at their villa known as the Summer Palace. Standing at the stern of the *Katori*, above the suddenly silenced propellors, the twenty-year-old Hirohito bowed in the direction of his father and for a few moments meditated. Then he turned on his heel, the engines throbbed again, and the two warships made for the open sea trailing ribbons of soot from their tall slender smokestacks.

Hirohito sensed that this outing across the sea would be both his last childhood adventure and his first test as a ruler. For a year now he had stood in for his father at receptions for foreign ambassadors. The doctors said that Emperor Taisho's condition was irreversible, and so when Hirohito returned from abroad he would probably have to assume the fulltime leadership of his country.

As yet he had not had time to formulate a program for his reign. The long voyage through the Indian Ocean and Mediterranean would give him a chance to think.

Hirohito began all considerations with a sad awareness that his father's reign had been a failure. The dream of the ancestors to rule theocratically and keep Japan sacred for the sun goddess remained unfulfilled. Hirohito had reservations about the dream. It was too insular, too mystical and unscientific. Because of his training in geography and economics, Hirohito could not think of Japan in isolation but only as a part—the leading part—of Asia. Because of his scientific training he could not accept the legend of the sun goddess at face value. He was a devout Shinto priest and believed in the ghosts of his ancestors, but not in a simple superstitious way like most of his countrymen. He would eventually rationalize his creed by grafting onto it the semiscientific spiritualism of such Western thinkers as the astrophysicist Sir James Jeans and the physiologist J. S. Haldane. Hirohito believed that the spirits were always present and even available for consultation but only as psychic wave forms permeating the ether. He doubted that they could provide physical assistance to men in battle, as many Japanese believed. No, if his country was to realize her imperial ambitions, she would have to count on armies of living men equipped with modern weapons and deployed with coolheaded statesmanship. He was inclined to agree with his father that the most natural growth for Japan would be as a sea power into the islands of Southeast Asia.[5]

To help him formulate his plans, Hirohito had with him aboard the *Katori* the four men on whom he would continue to rely most throughout the first decade of his rule: Count Makino, Count Chinda, General Nara, and Prince Kanin.

Count Makino Nobuaki would be Hirohito's lord privy seal, principal civilian advisor, and plot-maker-in-chief until the end of 1935. He was a tall, slim, nervous, thin-lipped gentleman of fifty-nine, renowned for his mercurial wit, his courtly manners, and his

[5] This capsule of Hirohito's ideas is drawn from many accounts, put together by many men who knew him, at different times over the next forty-five years. Possibly he did not yet entertain them all in 1921 but it is likely that he did, for in other respects his thinking, character, and even turns of speech changed little from decade to decade.

velvety softness of voice. He spoke excellent English, having spent
eight unhappy years as a boy and teen-ager studying in the United
States. From 1917 to 1919 he had served as the secretary of Emperor Taisho's Advisory Council on Foreign Policy during the debate over the Siberian intervention. In 1919 he had gone to the
Versailles peace conference as Japan's active representative who
attended sessions and spoke for the coyly aloof chief delegate,
Prince Saionji. Makino was the son of Emperor Meiji's oligarch
Okubo Toshimichi of Satsuma who had led the imperial forces
against his own clansmen when they revolted in 1877.

Count Chinda Sutemi also came of a non-Choshu clan, was
also American-educated, had also served under Saionji in the Japanese delegation at Versailles. Vice foreign minister in Emperor
Taisho's disastrous Katsura Cabinet of 1912 and then ambassador
to England from 1916 to 1920, he was supposed to help Hirohito
now in renewing the Anglo-Japanese alliance. A genial sixty-five,
he would remain at Hirohito's side as grand chamberlain until his
death at seventy-three in 1929.

General Nara Takeji, fifty-three, a non-Choshu officer from the
northern province of Tochigi, was fatherly, taciturn, and efficient.
He would be Hirohito's chief aide-de-camp, in charge of all liaison
between the Throne and the Army, until completion of the conquest of Manchuria in 1933.

Before the war with the United States Hirohito would have
other chief aides-de-camp, other grand chamberlains, other lord
privy seals, but Prince Kanin, the fourth important member of the
suite aboard the *Katori*, would be with Hirohito as the senior
member of the Supreme War Council until his death of severe
hemorrhoids in May 1945. In 1921 Kanin was already a living
anachronism. He was one of the last three remaining brothers of
Emperor Komei's advisor, Prince Asahiko, and by 1924 he would
be the only remaining brother. As a baby he had been adopted by
Emperor Komei, which made him, by the abacus of royal adoption, the grand-uncle of Hirohito and the brother of the deified
Emperor Meiji. Yet Kanin was still only fifty-six years old and
would live to see Tokyo burning under American incendiaries.
Full of vitality, he was the most active of Taisho's Six Princes and
the youngest field marshal in the Japanese Army, equal in rank and

superior in social position to Yamagata himself. It was Kanin who had engineered the Mukden coup of 1916, Kanin who would head the Army General Staff from 1931 to 1940 during the conquest of Manchuria, the invasion of China, the 1939 Nomonhan war with Russia, and the preparation of war with the United States. Kanin looked even younger than his age: strikingly handsome, magnificently mustached, fit and muscular, always well tailored and in spit-and-polish press. His appearance was so un-Japanese that in France he sometimes passed successfully as a Frenchman.

In addition to Makino, Chinda, Nara, and Kanin—advisors respectively on politics, diplomacy, tactics, and strategy—Hirohito had in his retinue aboard the *Katori* three of his favorite Big Brothers: his fiancée's cousin, Marquis Komatsu, who had charge of his physical education program; Komatsu's brother-in-law, Count Futara, who handled imperial publicity; and a naval aide, Commander Oikawa Koshiro, who would be Navy minister in 1941 during the preparation of the attack on Pearl Harbor. The other eight members of Hirohito's personal entourage were Saionji Hachiro, the welted but wiser son of the old lute player; Big Brother Prince Konoye's cousin, Marquis Maeda Toshinari, a major who would later direct the attack on Bataan in the Philippines in early 1942; and six other commanders and majors of noble birth with bloody futures ahead of them.

Lounging in deck chairs or playing croquet, Hirohito and his suite discussed the future of Japan. They were predominantly members or relatives of the great naval clan of Satsuma, favorable toward maritime expansion in the South Seas and antagonistic toward the Choshu clan which had provided Emperor Meiji with most of his oligarchs. In Europe they were to be joined by representatives of other non-Choshu interests. Hardly anyone outside of Choshu who prided himself on his inside information had not hurried down to the ticket office to buy a passage to Europe when Hirohito's tour had been announced. The *Mishima Maru*, which the *Katori* would overhaul off the coast of Ceylon, was booked solid. Among these spectators were in-laws and debtors through whom Hirohito could construct any conceivable alliance of interests that he wanted. He must only beware of making his father's

mistake—of coming out too autocratically in front of the brocade
curtain hung for him by his ancestors.

The squadron of the crown prince plunged its way through
choppy seas to the southernmost point of Japan. Though many
on board were seasick, Hirohito kept the deck. When the radio
officer informed him that hundreds of school children lined the
shores waving in his direction, he dutifully gazed back toward
them through a spyglass, but, as Count Futara put it, "the distance being too great, to his regret he was unable to see the people on the coast." Two days later the battleships made port at
Okinawa, and the people of the island bowed low in silence along
his route—once Perry's route—while he walked into the center of
Naha, the Okinawan capital, and back again. Two more days and
the squadron had skimmed the last point of Taiwan and left the
Japanese Empire behind. Hirohito joined Marquis Komatsu,
chamberlain of the imperial exercise, in prayers for Komatsu's father, General Prince Kitashirakawa Yoshihisa, who had died of
malaria during the subjugation of the island in 1895.

After another two days, the squadron was in Hong Kong for a
long weekend of banquets. During the festivities, Hirohito made
a special point of inspecting the reservoir on Victoria Island,
which, as it turned out, in 1941 was to be the crown colony's tactical Achilles' heel. On March 13, 1921, the channel leading out
of the harbor was edged by fourteen steam launches bearing fourteen huge ideograms on placards, reading "Royal send-off by the
Japanese Association of Hong Kong. Banzai."

In five more days the squadron entered the bastion of Singapore where Hirohito had to stand on deck for almost an hour returning the salutes of patriotic overseas Japanese who had come
out to greet him and guide him in. The schedule for the next four
days was again crowded with state functions, and again Hirohito
requested the insertion of a few items which interested him personally. He took in the Museum of Natural History and famous
Botanical Gardens where Alfred Russel Wallace in 1857 had
penned the learned paper on natural selection which forced Darwin to publish his own theories on evolution. He stopped the
official clock one morning while he turned toward Japan and celebrated the vernal Shinto feast of the dead. He borrowed a yacht

and circumnavigated Singapore Island, of which Count Futara noted only that it "is separated from Johore by a narrow strait."

The long twenty-five-day voyage from Singapore to Suez was broken only once by a stop at Colombo in Ceylon where Hirohito was awed and amused by native dances and a down-on-the-knees salute from forty elephants trumpeting in unison. During the days at sea he played deck golf, swam in the pool, polished up his French, and imbibed lore and gossip from the in-laws and powers of Japan who traveled with him. In the battleship's makeshift cinema he demonstrated his progressive inclinations by ordering crewmen who huddled in the back of the room to come forward and take seats immediately behind his own entourage.

WAR FRONT TOURISM

Four days in Egypt, where he had the rare raw luck to see a genuine desert sandstorm whirl through the Cairo streets; two days in Malta, where he prayed for the seventy-seven Japanese who had become spirits on World War I convoy duty; three days at Gibraltar, inspecting the cisterns and tunnels of the Rock[6]—and on May 8, Hirohito docked in Portsmouth, England. In the weeks of banquets, receptions, and parades that followed, he stood for the first and only time of his life out in front of the chrysanthemum curtain, under the full scrutiny of Western cameramen and reporters. The British press were almost universally struck by his modesty, composure, and intelligence. In the adjectives of Lord Riddell, he seemed "pleasant," "unassuming," "courteous," "appreciative," "with remarkable development above the eyes, showing, I believe, great powers of observation."

Hirohito found time in his crowded schedule to memorize the toasts and shorter set speeches he had to deliver without seeming difficulty. He learned in advance and did not forget the names

[6] There Count Futara notes that Mr. Yoshida Shigeru, first secretary to the Japanese Embassy in London, came aboard "to consult us about various arrangements then being made in England for welcoming our Prince." This was the same Yoshida who would launch the political movement for a Strike South in 1933; who would be given a new face when arrested by the secret police as a member of the Peace Faction in 1945; and who would be Japan's leading postwar prime minister.

and careers of the scores of officers and diplomats—Japanese and
European—whom he met at receptions. On one occasion he caught
up a British officer on a fine point of British Army organization:
"I thought at the beginning of the Great War, England had
division organization only and no army corps." He impressed
everyone with the economy and directness of his speech and his
absolute correctness, fairness, and good manners in dealing with
subordinates. He was up every morning at six, in bed at the latest
by midnight, and seemed able to react like clockwork, without any
visible tension, to the minute-by-minute timing of his schedule.

Facing a large audience for the first time in his life at his reception by the Lord Mayor of London, Hirohito "calmly glanced at
the whole assembly"—in Count Futara's words—"and, after
lightly saluting, put his military plumed hat under his left arm,
and began to unroll the written reply to the address. As the scroll
was thick and stiff, it seemed difficult for him to straighten it sufficiently for reading, but without showing the slightest embarrassment, he straightened the paper calmly and continued his
speech in a loud, sonorous voice, with eloquent intonation. . . .
The faces of the Japanese group glowed . . . at this triumphant
performance of a delicate and trying task."

As the days passed, the members of Hirohito's entourage sometimes found that their paragon had more aplomb and sophistication than they had. On May 10 in Buckingham Palace, when they
were helping him dress for the evening's banquet after a day's
sightseeing at Windsor Castle, there was a knock on the door and
in walked George of England, unannounced and as half-dressed
as Hirohito himself: in slippers, shirt, and braces. The retainers
were flustered. Even the noblest of them was unsure of imperial
family mores in the privacy of the back palace, and they feared that
Hirohito might react with hostility to this unprecedented informality by one not of the blood. But Hirohito's eyes scarcely widened. King George put an arm around his shoulder, sat down on
the bed with him, told him what a pleasure it had been having him
in Buckingham Palace, and chatted with him, partly in French
and partly through a nervous naval aide-interpreter, about the
subject that interested Hirohito most: the recent war.

In the course of the conversation, King George mentioned that the British had lost 150,000 men at Ypres and voiced the thought that the crown prince might like to have a look at that battlefield if he found time during his stay in Belgium. Hirohito later made time and cabled the British king his impressions: "The scene before me is impressive and edifying in the extreme, reminding me vividly of the words in which Your Majesty explained to me the sanquinary character of struggle on this field of honour at Ypres."

Three days in Buckingham Palace as a guest of the king, and eight days in Chesterfield House as a guest of the British government, saw Hirohito, after a swirl of sights and ceremonies, on his way to Scotland for a week of hunting, shooting, and fishing with the Duke of Atholl at Blair Castle. He was much impressed by the system of clan democracy which brought a staff of volunteer servants to the castle to meet the taxing demands of his visit and at the same time allowed the "servants" to dance the fling one evening with the duke himself.

After his first night in a Pullman and two days inspecting aircraft and shipping companies, Hirohito was back in London on May 27 for a final four days in England as his own guest at the Japanese Embassy. There he gave a series of receptions and feasts for all the promising young commanders and captains of the Japanese Navy who had contrived to be in London to meet him.

The British phase of his trip was over. He had attended a marchpast or review. He had had his picture taken in the uniform of a British general. He had carefully watched the deportment of his frequent companion, Edward, Prince of Wales, and had admired greatly—sometimes in envy, sometimes with hurt feelings—that young man's polished, carefree airs. Hirohito could understand a good deal of spoken English, and later in his trip he came to the point of carrying on conversations with some ease in French, but at this stage he and Edward relied on Japanese equerries and British intendants to translate for them. The amount of communication that took place may be gauged from a conversation reported in the memoirs of one of the British interpreters. Toward the end of a long reception Prince Edward dutifully looked in on Prince Hirohito's corner of the reception line and said, "Tell the prince that when I was on the staff of the 14th Corps, under

Lord Cavan, you [the interpreter] were in the 20th Division in
the same corps, and that you lent me your horse one day." Hirohito, gravely attentive as always, asked particulars. The Prince of
Wales said, "Splendid! One of the star turns of the evening!"—
and drifted off.

With the *bonhomie* of King George and the *air dégagé* of
Prince Edward both working in his mind, Hirohito moved on to
Paris. After initial formalities, he ascended the Eiffel Tower. The
next day, June 3, he took in the Louvre and the Venus de Milo
"on the run," as staid *Le Temps* somewhat tartly reported,
and then repaired to the tomb of Napoleon at the Hôtel des
Invalides, where he gazed long and fixedly at the sword of Auster-
litz. Having spent three times as long at the tomb as at the
Louvre, he emerged so moved that he gave over $400 to the up-
keep of Napoleon's memory—an amount which, by the normal
standards of imperial family largesse, would have recompensed a
village for twenty summers of hospitality to a prince or princess
in Japan.

On June 4 Hirohito inspected the French Artillery School with
Prince Kanin and one of Kanin's former instructors at St. Cyr,
Maréchal Pétain. At the time Pétain was the hero—*ils ne
passeront pas*—of Verdun. Already an admirer of D'Annunzio's
Italian Black Shirts, he was to wither his garlands later as a
Nazi quisling. Throughout the rest of Hirohito's stay, he acted as
the young prince's guide to the military tourist attractions of
France.

On June 5, Hirohito canceled a scheduled visit to Versailles and
went to the races instead. The press in Japan studiously ignored
this wild debauch and padded out its trip reportage the following
day with general remarks as to the prince's keen interest in French
culture. In point of fact, the cultural phase of Hirohito's stay in
France, which lasted from May 31 to June 9, was perfunctory at
best. He made token appearances at most of the routine tourist
sights and reserved as much time as he could for personal matters.

On June 7, Hirohito had a long intimate lunch with Prince
Higashikuni, the Big Brother of Army Intelligence who was in
Paris organizing a spy ring for Yamagata and an anti-Yamagata cell
for Hirohito. On that June morning, Count Futara, the imperial

family publicity man, described Higashikuni simply as "studying
under the incognito of Count Higashi."

Two days later, on June 9, Hirohito himself assumed incognito
and for the first and only time in his life walked alone on a city
street and passed money with his own hand. He stopped at several
shops and bought presents for his family and fiancée back home.
For himself, too, he made one purchase of a lifetime: a bust of
Napoleon. It was to stand in his study thereafter, being joined
in the 1920's by a head of Darwin and in 1945 by one of Lincoln.
Conquer, evolve, liberate: this was to be the program imposed
on his reign by fate.

On June 10, Hirohito left Paris for Brussels, and for the next ten
days he was back in official harness, visiting Waterloo, Ypres, and
other battlefields of the Low Countries, and attending functions
with the Dutch and Belgian royal families. When he returned to
Paris on June 20, battlefields had become, it seemed, an obsession
with him. He paid a brief call on the Chambre des Députés, went
to the races again, inspected at his own personal request the
international meter stick of platinum at the Bureau of International Weights at Saint-Cloud, and had another long lunch with
Prince Higashikuni. All the rest of his time—nine tenths of it—he
spent in the company of Prince Kanin and Maréchal Pétain, trek-
king through the shell-scarred woods and meadows, inspecting
military schools, and watching tank and aircraft displays. One
tank maneuver that he studied was made so realistic that its commanding officer broke his pelvis when his horse bolted and threw
him.

Hirohito devoted two days to Gravelotte, Saint-Privat, and Fort
Saint Quentin near Metz, a day to Verdun, a day to the Somme,
and a day to the fields around Reims. In the interstices of his
schedule, he fitted in the old military school of French sappers
and geometers, the Polytechnique, the cavalry school of Saumur,
and the Military Academy of St. Cyr. On July 5 he saw Prince
Higashikuni again for a morning of golf at La Boulie.

The next night, July 6, he gave his last of several parties for Japanese attachés and observers in Europe. Never before had there
been so many young Japanese officers on the Continent—so many,
indeed, that American, British, and French security agents had

begun to watch them closely. They worked primarily in the triangle of three cities, Paris, Zurich, and Frankfurt, for here, in the
factories of the Ruhr, the Saar, and Switzerland, many new industrial techniques had been worked out during the secrecy of the
war years and it behooved Japan to copy them if she could. What
was remarkable about these industrial spies was not their spying
but the fact that in an army heavily dominated by men of the
Choshu clan, none of them were from Choshu. Still more remarkable, their roster included about half of the later famous fascist
Japanese generals of the 1930's and 1940's. Hirohito met all of
them and honored many of them with a moment of knowledgeable conversation and exhortation.

On July 7 Hirohito boarded a special train for Toulon in the
south of France where he would catch his battleships and start
for home. From July 10 to 18 he visited Naples and Rome, giving
cursory attention to the Colosseum and the Sistine Chapel and
spending time, once again, at tank and gun demonstrations and
in talk with local Japanese officials. One object caught his eye in
the Vatican: a piece of calligraphy brushed by an early Japanese
convert to Christianity who had journeyed to Rome and had an
audience with Pope Paul V in 1613.

Perhaps Hirohito was sated with foreign exposure. As soon as
he was back on his battleship his first athletic diversion was not
golf or swimming but Japanese wrestling. He practiced a few falls
with thirty-three-year-old Marquis Komatsu, his athletics director, and then opened the ring to any other member of his immediate suite who cared to tussle with him. Count Futara wrote:
"Time and time again His Highness struggled with his opponents,
even when troubled by nose-bleeding. The *tsukidashi* or sudden
thrust appeared to be his favorite trick." When Hirohito's ships
stopped again at Ceylon on August 9, a British colonial matron
remarked on his great increase in ease and poise since his previous
visit four and a half months earlier.

HIROHITO'S TAKE-OVER

Hirohito arrived home on September 3, 1921. Old Army
strongman Yamagata was sick and had only a few months to live.

Prime Minister Hara of the Constitutionalists, however, had taken over Yamagata's authority behind the scenes and was loudly promising the people democracy. Known as the "Great Commoner," he ran an administration which was thoroughly venal in regard to money but was considered honest in regard to ideas. Then, two months after Hirohito's return, on November 4, 1921, at Tokyo railroad station, Prime Minister Hara was knifed to death. The assassin, Nakaoka Konichi, was a young employee of the railroad. A few weeks earlier he had bragged to his fellow workers that he intended to commit hara-kiri or belly cutting in protest against the pleasure-loving laxity and creeping Westernization of the times.

"Many talk of cutting open their *hara*," jibed one of his listeners, "but few have belly enough to carry it out."

"Ha!" screamed Nakaoka. "See if I do not cut *hara*." And so, after days of brooding, he fulfilled his pledge by cutting down Hara, the prime minister.

The murder was passed off in the press as the act of an unhappy halfwit and was quickly forgotten. Hirohito's Big Brother Prince Konoye, the future 1937 prime minister, however, told his friends that he had known of the assassination in advance; that, in fact, a member of Japan's spy service in China, a henchman of his father and of Prince Kanin, one Iogi Yoshimitsu, had come to him on the eve of the knifing with the promise that it would be done. The assassin Nakaoka was given an unusually light sentence of twelve years. On his release from Sendai Penitentiary in 1934, Iogi and other right wing "patriots" met him with a hero's welcome and provided him with a living for life.

After Prime Minister Hara's murder, the other potentates of Japan—particularly those who had been along on the European tour—agreed that Hirohito was a truly Oriental leader, worth following and if possible guiding. On November 25, 1921, they gave their support to an imperial household announcement declaring Hirohito regent for the ailing Taisho and subject only to the advice of the imperial family council composed of Kanin and the other princes of the blood.

While Hirohito was taking power in Tokyo, Prince Higashikuni in Paris was proceeding apace with the organization of his imperial cabal in the ranks of Army Intelligence. The cabal held its first historic meeting—a meeting which would determine the destiny of Japan, a meeting, moreover, which has never been described before in any Western language—on October 27, 1921, at the German spa of Baden-Baden. In obedience to the imperial taboo, the participants have refused to state whether or not Prince Higashikuni was present in person, but if not present, he was at least nearby. He was a regular member of Maréchal Pétain's entourage, and that week the maréchal was making an inspection tour of the French occupation zone of the Saar which took him through Baden-Baden on the day in question. October was out of season at Baden-Baden and prices were low. The Chinese pagoda in front of the *Konversationhaus* and the many public baths made the town as homelike for Japanese visitors as any place in Europe. The Black Forest on the heights above the Rhine and the forbidding castle of the margraves against the bleak October sky lent a suitable air of somber purpose to the proceedings. The conspirators rendezvoused in one of the private chambers at the vapor baths behind the Roman Catholic cathedral.

The three principal operatives at the meeting—Nagata Tetsuzan from Bern, Obata Toshiro from Moscow, and Okamura Yasuji, attaché-at-large—came to be known throughout the Japanese Army as the Three Crows. It was they who would make the Army a modern fighting force, they who would rid it of the samurai leadership of Yamagata's Choshu clan, they who would launch Hirohito on his dreams of glory by engineering the conquest of Manchuria. All three were non-Choshu men. All three were majors, inferior in Army rank to Prince Higashikuni who was a lieutenant colonel. They were accompanied by several less senior majors who had all served in the Imperial Guards with Prince Higashikuni in the last years of Emperor Meiji's reign. One of them, the "observer" in Leipzig, a member of the "stand-by faculty of the Staff College," was the future World War II prime minister, Tojo Hideki.

The leader of the Three Crows was Major Nagata Tetsuzan, whose ghost would later be painted into the surrender deliberations in Hirohito's air raid shelter. He was the son of a doctor who ran a Red Cross hospital in a small resort town near Lake Suwa in the Japanese Alps. In those days the Japanese Red Cross served unofficially as a branch of the Army Medical Corps, and his father's patients were able to recommend him for an appointment to the military academy. There Nagata applied himself well and graduated second in his class. He went on to Staff College in 1911 and graduated with highest honors. He served with such distinction at the embassy in Copenhagen during World War I that from June 1920 he was given a carte blanche leave of absence "to travel in Europe."

No matter how complex the intrigues surrounding him, Nagata always looked as if he knew what he was doing and what others were doing as well. On him—perhaps alone in the Japanese Army —the utterly utilitarian, perfectly circular iron frames of general-issue spectacles sat well, giving him an air of detached scholarly competence. He wore his hair closely cropped, Prussian style, and his mustache trimmed down to the silhouette of an oncoming seagull. His full lips moved easily from a slight twist, denoting amusement or friendliness, to a fine grim line of utmost sarcasm and contempt. His ears were well shaped but large. It was Nagata who carried out the early phases of the imperial program decided upon at Baden-Baden, and it would have been Nagata who commanded the nation as Hirohito's shogun in 1941, if he had not been assassinated, for opposing war with China, by a minion of Prince Higashikuni in 1935.

Major Tojo Hideki, who did become the Emperor's shogun in 1941, was Nagata's protégé, best friend, and loyal servant. When Nagata died, Tojo would step obediently into his shoes. In 1921 at Baden-Baden Tojo said little, for he was one whole military academy class behind the Three Crows. To have been too forward, according to the seniority code of the time, would have been to invite a face slapping. And so Tojo lit Nagata's cigarettes for him and periodically checked the door of the steam room to make sure that no one was listening outside.

The most voluble of the conspirators was the second of the Three Crows, Obata Toshiro, an aristocrat. In the words of his colleagues he was "skinny," "nervous," and "almost too brilliant." He paced the steam-filled room naked while the others steeped in a hot pool of Baden-Baden's famous ill-smelling waters. Fifth in

the 1904 class at military academy—just behind the steady Nagata
—and first in the 1911 class at Staff College—just ahead of Nagata
—he was a brilliant strategist, and his mind brimmed over
with possibilities at the thought of invading Manchuria. He had
been stationed in Russia throughout the revolution and was convinced that Bolshevism was the number-one threat to Japan and
the Throne. So intensely had he studied Marxism, however, that
he developed a belief as the years passed that Japan must have her
own tribal communism under which all men would share alike in
mystical communion with the Emperor. These views made him a
leader of the Strike-North or Fight-Russia faction in the 1930's
and ultimately estranged him from the Emperor. After the Army
mutiny of 1936 he would be dropped from Hirohito's inner
circle. His genius as strategist and tactician, however, could not
be dispensed with, and when the war broke out with China in
1937, he would be called back to handle the logistics for Japan's
crack mobile blitzkrieg division, the 14th. Throughout the war
years he would hover on the fringes of politics, and in 1945 would
become one of the many ministers without portfolio who would
organize a welcome for MacArthur in the surrender Cabinet of
Prince Higashikuni.

The third of the Three Crows, Okamura Yasuji, a scion of the
samurai clan which for centuries had provided the Tokugawa shoguns with their bodyguards, sat stolidly in the scalding tub and
got out only to douse himself occasionally with a bucket of cold
water. Without his glasses he was half blind. When he wore them,
they gave him the typical look of a bespectacled Japanese officer
—that of a fierce owl dazzled by the beam of a flashlight. He
was unshaven as usual, for he affected the unkempt, carelessly
pressed air of a field officer rather than a staff officer. The theory
was that a fighting soldier, if he eschewed spit and polish, would
develop in himself a laudable contempt for earthly possessions
and would cause enemies to underrate his fighting trim. Behind
Okamura's stubble-cheeked look of bemusement worked a keen
mind. He had come in third behind Nagata and Obata in the
military academy class of 1904 and, when sent belatedly to Staff
College in 1913, he had worked hard, taken top honors, and
been awarded a prize by Emperor Taisho. After spending World

War I in Tokyo on the General Staff as an information officer, he had had the connections to be assigned for Crown Prince Hirohito's European trip to the entourage of Tokugawa Iyemasa, the ranking heir of the former shoguns' family.

When Hirohito returned to Japan, Okamura stayed on in Paris. He was often overshadowed in the years that followed by the other Crows, Nagata and Obata, but in the late 1930's when one of them had been murdered and the other disgraced, Okamura became the principal commander for the long, unrewarding war with China. In 1945, he saw to it that his forces did not simply throw down their arms where they stood but waited and sometimes fought until competent representatives of the Chiang Kai-shek government appeared on the scene to disband and replace them. As a consequence, he was held only briefly as a war criminal in a Shanghai prison and then, abruptly, elevated to serve as Chiang Kai-shek's military advisor in the struggle with the Chinese Communists. When the struggle was lost and Chiang Kai-shek had moved to Taiwan, Okamura Yasuji returned to Tokyo where he played an important part behind the scenes in organizing Japan's present American-supported Self-Defense Forces. In March 1963, nearing the age of seventy-nine, he retired as head of the Japanese Veterans Association and became an advisor to the Self-Defense Forces' "historical" or contingency planning section.

In the hot mineral water and later at the *Konversationhaus*, drinking kirsch, the Three Crows and their subordinates resolved to dedicate their lives to the fulfillment of a two-point program for Japan: make "a big window where Choshu sits today," and "renew the national strength along French lines" so that Japan, too, can fight "a total war." The plan, in other words, was to purge the Army of Yamagata and the rest of its Choshu leadership; reorganize the Army to be on a par with the triumphant French; in particular, train the Army to fight with modern weapons such as tanks and airplanes. During the Siberian intervention, Japanese soldiers had observed that they were altogether outclassed in equipment and even tactics by the Czech veterans whom they were supposed to be rescuing. It was for this reason that Hirohito, on his tour, had been so assiduous in attending military reviews.

A third point decided at Baden-Baden was personnel. The Three Crows selected "eleven reliable men," to carry out their program. Only two were present; the other nine were then in China, Siberia, or Japan. All were members of the military academy classes of 1904 and 1905 which had graduated during the war with Russia. All were non-Choshu. All were mere majors, though talented. Several were already specialists in aviation. Three of them, Tojo, Itagaki Seishiro, and Doihara Kenji, won fame enough to be hanged as Class A war criminals in 1948. Another, Komoto Daisaku, was to finish Prince Kanin's bloody business of 1916 by assassinating the Manchurian war lord Chang Tso-lin in 1928. Isogai Rensuke, after amassing a brilliant record for himself as a lieutenant general in China, took responsibility for defeat in the Nomonhan border war with Russia in 1939, sat out World War II as the governor general of Hong Kong, and was still alive in 1970. Three others were to die betimes in China.[7] The final three were to prove not so reliable after all and were to be cashiered following the Army Mutiny of 1936.[8]

A FUNNY HAPPENING

The first order of business in realizing the Baden-Baden program was the accumulation of technical information on modern weapons' manufacture. A few weeks after the attachés had returned to their various posts in the cities of Europe, Hirohito dispatched two more of his Big Brothers from Tokyo to encourage the plotters and help Prince Higashikuni in opening doors for them into the drafting rooms of the great European munitions works. Hirohito's new envoys were Prince Kitashirakawa, who had married Emperor Meiji's seventh daughter, and Prince Asaka, the later scourge of Nanking, who had married Emperor Meiji's eighth daughter. Princes Kitashirakawa and Asaka were both trained intelligence officers. They arrived in Paris early in 1922 and all that year the spy ring grew. By 1923 it had thirty members stra-

[7] Watari Hisao as a lieutenant general in 1939; Ogasawara Kazuo as an Air Force lieutenant general in 1938; Italian specialist Ogawa Tsunesaburo, who was the attaché in Rome in 1921, in an airplane crash.

[8] Kudo Yoshio, Matsumura Masakasu, and Yamaoka Shigeatsu.

tegically placed in the various capitals and all pledged to the anti-Choshu plan of Army reorganization. American intelligence officers who were in Paris at the time say that their Japanese counterparts, working in the Paris-Zurich-Frankfurt triangle, were effective in purchasing up-to-date plans for diesel engines and tanks.

Abruptly, in the summer of 1923, the spy ring shrank to normal peace-time proportions. The shrinkage was triggered by a curious automobile accident—curious because the circumstances surrounding it were later falsified by the Japanese press. At the end of March 1923, Prince Higashikuni flew to London on a piece of "urgent business" that forced him to cancel previous social engagements in Paris. On April 1, Prince Asaka and Prince Kitashirakawa, together with Kitashirakawa's wife and two French servants, left their residence beside the Bois de Boulogne for a "picnic" in their high-powered touring car. That afternoon at four-thirty, at Perriers-la-Campagne, on the Cherbourg road near Bernay, 88 miles from Paris, as they were heading toward the English Channel at a speed which the police later estimated at 90 miles an hour, the picnickers struck a tree. Prince Kitashirakawa, who had checked out in small planes, was at the wheel, and the official French chauffeur was sitting beside him on the right in the traditional death seat. The chauffeur was killed instantly, and Kitashirakawa "horriblement défiguré"—in fact, without legs or much of a head, died twenty minutes later. In the back seat, Prince Asaka suffered compound and complex fractures in one leg, fractures from which he would still limp on the heights above Nanking in 1937. The maid who sat beside him was "gravely wounded." Kitashirakawa's wife, Emperor Meiji's daughter Fusako, in the rear right-hand seat, had two broken legs and so many other injuries that she remained in hospital for over a year.

The French government prepared elaborate obsequies, but Prince Higashikuni caught the first boat train back from London and, with the help of the Japanese ambassador in Paris, canceled all the French plans. He paid off the families of the chauffeur and the maid and exercised influence to quiet the Parisian press. Prince Kitashirakawa lay in embalmed state for three weeks in a room lined with white silk at the home of the Japanese ambassador. On April 22 the corpse was shipped aboard the *Kitano Maru* in Marseilles for transport to the homeland.

Subsequently the *Japan Year Book* in its annual rundown of important events regularly reported the automobile accident— but as having taken place in the "suburbs of Paris," 80 miles off the mark. This error, and Prince Higashikuni's efforts to quash the investigations of French newsmen, suggest that Prince Kitashira-kawa, when he died, was driving to the English Channel on a mission connected with the intelligence network of which he was a leader. Surviving Japanese officers point out that Prince Higashikuni was in England, on the other side of the Channel. Then they grunt mysteriously. Whatever the mission that killed him, Kitashirakawa's death spelled the end of the spy ring. The number of Japanese Army officers on special assignment "to travel" or "to study" in Europe suffered such a dramatic decline that the writer of this book first noticed the decline, statistically, in Japanese personnel records and only then, in the belief that something of note had happened, turned to French newspapers and discovered the occurrence of the car crash. Hirohito himself was much affected by the death of his Big Brother, Prince Kit-ashirakawa. He fell out of love with espionage and never again subscribed to it with enthusiastic expectations. Most important, he canceled his plans for a trip to Taiwan and refused ever after-ward to leave the main islands of Japan.

8

REGENT HIROHITO

(1921–1926)

HIROHITO'S RECRUITING

It was December 1921 and Crown Prince Hirohito, now Regent of Japan, was celebrating his return from Europe and his assumption of power. Light poured from the windows of the miniature Versailles built by Emperor Taisho. The snow flakes falling on the grounds of the Akasaka Palace compound danced in the darkness to the rhythms of the latest Parisian dance records. Inside, between the pink-brocaded chairs and sofas, tripped geisha in brilliant kimonos, carrying drinks and sometimes agreeing, with a giggle, to serve as dance partners in a fox trot, a tango, or a hesitation waltz. The guests were all young men in tails—either former schoolmates of Hirohito in their twenties or intimates of his Big Brothers in their thirties. Their invitations had stipulated that the order of the evening would be *burei*, suspension of the usual laws of etiquette and precedent. Outside Hirohito's study was set up a keg of Scotch whisky given him in Scotland by the Duke of Atholl.

As the night progressed and the keg emptied, Hirohito's wish for informality was gratified. Most of the guests were typical Japanese in that they suffered from an inbred intolerance of alcohol.[1]

[1] The distinction between those who do and do not have the genetic weakness is marked. The majority become flushed after a single thimble of saké or

The first sip of Scotch darkened their cheeks, loosened their tongues, and lightened their brains. Before long men were coming and going freely from the study where Hirohito sat. Voices were raised in boasting for Japan and in scoffing against the West. Plans were laid and promises made in a spirit of hilarity which many guests later regretted. Hirohito drank tea-tinted water, put up good-naturedly with many familiarities to his person, flirted with one of the geisha, and awoke the next morning clear-headed and pleased with his performance. It had been a precedent-shattering party.

On the second day after the party, the old lute player Saionji, who had galloped in green armor through the wars of the restoration fifty-three years earlier, took the two-hour train journey from his winter villa on the coast at Okitsu and paid one of his infrequent visits to Tokyo. As soon as he had moved into the town mansion kept for him by his millionaire brother, he phoned the Akasaka Palace for an audience with Crown Prince Hirohito. He had been delegated by the other chamberlains of his family—the Fujiwaras who had the hereditary duty of keeping Emperors free from incriminating responsibilities—to speak to Hirohito about his behavior. The role of moralist and censor hardly suited the pleasure-loving old statesman. Time and again he had advised Hirohito to unbend a little and take a woman or a glass of good wine. Although he dutifully scolded Hirohito for the "looseness" and "appalling familiarity" of the recent party, he was not concerned by either one. He had seen gayer bacchanals in the Akasaka Palace during Taisho's youth. Rather, what alarmed Saionji about the party was the open recruiting of stalwarts—the explicit discussion of future plans which were now the post-party gossip of Tokyo high society.

Regent Hirohito met Saionji with an innocent face, heard his remonstrances, and apologized disingenuously for sowing wild

---

even after a rum baba. The minority can tope with the best drinkers of any nation and are much prized as negotiators for dealing with Westerners. Many and perhaps all of the minority are descended from families which immigrated from the Continent in historic times. For the majority Japanese make special allowances. Prime ministers are not held responsible for speeches made in drunkenness to the Diet, and crimes of passion are regularly excused in the law courts if intoxication can be proved in mitigation.

oats. Then Hirohito made a bargain with Saionji which the old man would live to rue. If Saionji would take the place of Army Elder Yamagata, who was then mortally ill, as senior advisor to the Throne, Hirohito would promise to give up overt leadership of his cabal and respect all the conventions of a constitutional monarch. Saionji took the measure of the intense young ruler before him and stared silently for a few moments at the carpet. He believed that the people of Japan had changed in the last decade and had come to accept the philosophy of constitutionalism and legalism propounded by Ito Hirobumi before his assassination in Manchuria in 1909. If the people expressed themselves clearly, Saionji thought that Hirohito would bow to majority opinion.

Hirohito, as he watched the old man turning over the proposition, waited impatiently. If the seventy-two-year-old Saionji accepted, he would make an invaluable ally and figurehead. Forty years of experience in Emperor Meiji's councils had taught him how to give a semblance of moderation and regularity to government. His peers respected him for his incisive realism. In the company of others, he had a talent for tangled, discreet utterances, even that rare gift of complete silence when it was needed. He had a sharp, subtle mind, an upright character, and only one foolish mental quirk: an absolute, overriding loyalty to the Throne.

Saionji looked up from the carpet and admitted sadly that it was his duty to accept Hirohito's proposal. He had hoped, he said, to spend the rest of his days in quiet at his little villa on the shore in the fishing village of Okitsu, reading French and Chinese novels, practicing on the lute, carving canes for himself, and walking up to Seiken Temple to watch the sunrise when he couldn't sleep. But if the nation demanded it, he must accept the responsibility. Hirohito promptly confirmed him in the status of *Genro*, a descriptive title that had long been used to designate the surviving members of Emperor Meiji's oligarchy. Literally it meant Founding Elder, but as applied to Saionji, who would soon become the one and only *Genro*, it meant Prime-Minister-Maker. It carried with it the formal duty of appearing in Tokyo whenever a Cabinet fell, of sounding out the political situation, and of taking responsibility for recommending to Hirohito the men he should appoint for the next Cabinet. Saionji would retain the title and the responsibility until his death, in bitter disillusionment, at the age of ninety-one, in 1940.

PALACE PLOT SCHOOL

Having promised Saionji to assume the discreet guise of a constitutional ruler, Hirohito immediately established an undercover organization through which to direct his widening circle of henchmen. At the eastern edge of the palace grounds, where a salient in the old fortifications had left a sequestered bulge of walls and moats, sprawled a low, weather-beaten, wooden building, the Palace Meteorological Observatory. On his way home from the Peers' School as a child, Hirohito had sometimes wandered through its rooms, inspecting the sextants, the astrological charts, the rain gauges, and the little, eighteenth century Dutch telescope.

The week after the party, Hirohito had the old observatory converted into a security-shrouded indoctrination center for young men who wished to play a part in his dreams for Japan. Here, in the precincts of the palace, were made the first rough plans for Japan's attempt to conquer half the world. Here were struck up the friendships and working relationships which governed Japan until 1945. Here studied every one of the Class A war criminals tried by Allied judges in 1946 and 1947. Here, if anywhere, was hatched the "criminal conspiracy" of which Japan's war leaders, with the exception of Hirohito, were judged guilty. Here only were all Japan's "criminals" together in one place at one time to "conspire." Yet the indoctrination center in the old observatory has never until now been mentioned in writing in English except passingly in an unpublished 1946 U.S. Army Intelligence report. This report was circulated among the Allied judges at the war crimes trials, but information regarding the indoctrination center was not introduced in evidence, presumably because it implicated the Emperor.

The center was first called the Social Problems Research Institute and later given the less suggestive code name of *Daigaku Ryo*, or University Lodging House. It was, of course, a tremendous honor for junior officers and fledgling bureaucrats to attend lectures and discussions within the sacred walls of the palace, and few who participated ever failed the Emperor in years to come. In founding the Lodging House, however, Hirohito has looking not only for loyal henchmen but also for ideas. The plot conceived at Baden-Baden had given him a cadre of Army shock troopers to work with, at a time when Adolf Schicklgruber was still struggling for control of an obscure band of brown-shirted racists in Bavaria. But Hirohito needed more: he needed skillful economic and political planners, a long-term plan, and a national ideology.

In assuming the regency in 1921, Hirohito had taken over a nation of 56 million people. It had increased 25 per cent in population and more than 100 per cent in gross national product since his birth in 1900. Though still backward in comparison with France or England, its economy was growing faster than any other in the world. It was bursting with surplus talent, energy, and ideas and demanded carefully co-ordinated direction.

Hirohito entrusted the organization of the Lodging House in the old observatory to his chief advisor, the tall, high-strung, charming Count Makino who had headed the imperial suite during the European tour. Makino, in turn, delegated the headmastership of the Lodging House to Dr. Okawa, the intellectual tough who had devised the thrashing of Prince Saionji's adopted son during the controversy before the tour. A keen-looking young man of thirty-seven, with close-cropped black hair and a sharp black mustache, Dr. Okawa enjoyed a filial intimacy with Count Makino. Some Japanese suggest that he was Makino's illegitimate son. Through Makino's patronage, Okawa had acquired eminent qualifications for the task at hand. He had worked closely for years with Hirohito's future chief of staff, Prince Kanin, and with the father of Hirohito's fiancée, Prince Kuni. He was a trusted lieutenant of gang lord Toyama and a leader of the younger generation of Pan-Asianists in Toyama's Black Dragon Society. He had had a decade of experience as a spy in China. And not least, he was a genuine scholar. He had graduated in Oriental philosophy from Tokyo Imperial University in 1911 and could read Chinese, Sanskrit, Arabic, Greek, German, French, and English.

Until he became headmaster of the Lodging House, Dr. Okawa had represented the assorted ideas of all the Pan-Asianists, spies, and nationalists with whom he had consorted for a decade. They had been joined together by a common enthusiasm for the future of Japan—a vague sense of mission which they had expressed in a collective credo published in the magazine *War Cry* in July 1920:

The Japanese people must become the vortex of a whirlwind which will liberate mankind. The Japanese nation is destined to accomplish the revolutionization of the world. The fulfillment of this ideal and the military reorganization of Japan are the work of the spirits. We believe that our duty will not end with the revolution or reform of Japan alone, but we must be content to begin with the reform of our nation because we have faith in the Japanese mission to free the universe.

When Dr. Okawa became headmaster of the Lodging House, many of his former comrades felt that he had sold out to the Establishment and betrayed the cause of revolution. In splitting with him, they chose to follow another erudite spy and political philosopher, Kita Ikki, the later ideologist of the Strike-North or Fight-Russia faction which would plague Hirohito in the 1930's. Dr. Okawa had discovered Kita in 1918 in a Shanghai garret where, on a diet of rice balls and water, he was just completing the eighth volume of a magnum opus, *The Fundamental Principles for the Reconstruction of the Nation*. In this lucid but radical tome, Kita poured Marxist wine into old saké pitchers and brewed a heady polemic which Hirohito found unpalatable and his brother, Prince Chichibu, found exciting. Kita called for a thoroughgoing reconstruction and purification of Japan: suspension of the Constitution under martial law; convocation of a national family council chosen by universal suffrage; restriction of individual capital to $500,000 and of corporate capital to $5,000,000; equal profit sharing between employers and employees; maintenance of friendship with the United States in order to develop China; hostility toward Russia and Great Britain which, in Kita's view, controlled an unfair share of the world's living space.

Kita's eight-volume work, circulated in a mimeographed edition run off by one of Prince Chichibu's best friends, made a tremendous impression on many young Japanese in search of a vision. Crown Prince Hirohito, however, looked on it with a narrow eye because, among its other reforms, it called for the surrender to the nation of all property held by the imperial household.

In January 1922, when Dr. Okawa received his invitation to become headmaster at the Lodging House in the palace, he and his friend Kita spent one last vociferous saké-steeped evening together and then went their separate ways as sworn enemies. In fear of police arrest, Kita hid at a Buddhist monastery where he compiled a special set of cautionary Buddhist sutra which he sent to Hirohito. Dr. Okawa moved into the palace and organized the faculty for the Lodging House.

Under Dr. Okawa's direction, the curriculum at the Lodging House was spiced with a little of every *ism* he knew. The young bureaucrats and military officers who were privileged to attend heard lectures on Confucian ethics, weapons development, contingency planning, Army reorganization, and the geopolitical theories—carefully excerpted—of Kita Ikki. Hirohito's chief advisor, Count Makino, gave a course on the place of the Throne, explaining the offices of the imperial household; their function in intermediating with loyal henchmen; the need, always, to keep the Emperor beyond the tarbrush of popular criticism. When they came home from France in January and February 1923, the Three Crows all lectured at the Lodging House. So did several of the Eleven Reliables they had chosen at Baden-Baden. So did assorted secret policemen, commercial spies, narcotics experts, pimps, terrorists, and interrogation specialists from Japan's complex web of paramilitary apparatuses on the Continent.

At Lodging House seminars the smartest junior members of the General Staff and of the faculties of the Army and Navy Staff Colleges came to know intimately the Big Brothers of Hirohito who had gone into the bureaucracy, the Diet, or the influential pool of literary handymen which supplied male private secretaries to Cabinet ministers. After classes they all went out sometimes to tea houses to drink and wench together. In later years one of Hirohito's Big Brothers recalled that Colonel Sugiyama, Japan's World War II Chief of Staff, did an excellent comic dance of the seven veils with napkin-sized towels. Commander Yamamoto, the later admiral who would plan and lead the attack on Pearl Harbor, did conjuring tricks and stood on his head.

In these after-school drinking sessions the chief topic of discussion was Japan's position in the postwar world. At the Washington Conference, begun in late 1921 when the Lodging House opened, Japan had been forced to agree to limit her Navy according to the formula 10:6:3.5—that is, for every 10 tons of U.S. or British warship and for every 3.5 French or Italian tons, Japan would maintain no more than 6 tons. Fortunately the naval ratio did not apply to submarines and torpedo boats; therefore the money saved on battleships could be applied to non-conventional modern weapons in which the fleet was deficient. A top-secret naval development plan, taking advantage of such treaty loopholes, was worked out in the Lodging House and in the Navy General Staff and was formally approved by Hirohito in late 1922.

Any compunction which had been felt by some naval officers about arming in secret against the United States and Great Britain was overcome by resentment at anti-Japanese legislation in the West. Great Britain, in 1921, refused to renew the Anglo-Japanese Alliance. The U.S. Supreme Court in November 1922 declared, in effect, that Japanese were ineligible for naturalization as U.S. citizens. The U.S. Congress in May 1924 made total exclusion of Orientals an official part of U.S. immigration policy.

QUAKE

Funds had just been appropriated and building begun for the secret naval development plan, and young Regent Hirohito was just turning his attention toward the Army reorganization scheme proposed at Baden-Baden, when his national imperial program suffered a setback of such cataclysmic proportions that it would take years to recoup the loss. At exactly noon on Saturday, September 1, 1923, as charcoal braziers in almost every house were being lit under the midday meal, tremors began to register on the seismographs at Tokyo Imperial University. The first were no larger than those which rocked the needles three hundred times a year in volcanic Japan. But they kept coming, stronger and more frequent with each passing second. In a matter of minutes they merged into a great swell that inundated the instruments. The whole of the Great Eastern Plain around Tokyo was in fact billowing as if it were the surface of the Pacific. Thousands of homes pancaked. The proud new twelve-story Tokyo Tower tumbled from the sky. The colossal thirteenth century bronze figure of Buddha in Kamakura—50 feet in stature and 100 in girth— pitched from its pedestal. On the seacoast southwest of Tokyo, near the epicenter of the quake, entire villages of debris were swept away by tidal waves.

The main shock was over in five minutes, but in the splintered woodpile that remained, the buried cookstoves still burned and soon the whole of the Tokyo-Yokohama megalopolis was aflame. Fire storms or "dragon tails" swept the ruins. At the naval base of Yokosuka near Yokohama, 100,000 tons of stock-piled oil had spilled into the sea and drifted in huge puddles along the coast. Now it too caught fire and immolated countless survivors who had taken to the water to escape the infernos ashore. In the end two thirds of Tokyo and four fifths of Yokohama were destroyed, and approximately 140,000 human beings—as many as at Hiroshima and Nagasaki combined—were burned to death.

When the shock struck, the twenty-three-year-old Hirohito was at a state luncheon in the *petit* Versailles built by Taisho on the Akasaka Palace compound. It had been Japan's first large two-story structure designed specifically to withstand seismic upheavals.[2] As a result it rode out the earth waves with hardly a crack in its plaster. Hirohito and his guests ran outside into the open in obedience to the earthquake drill which every Japanese learns as a child. There they watched the rest of the city shaking apart and saw the first plumes of the great fires.

Regent Hirohito was then in direct personal charge of the government as at almost no other time in his life. The prime minister had died the week before and Hirohito had not yet appointed a successor for him. During the interregnum Hirohito elevated General Fukuda Masataro to impose martial law and take charge of relief work. Throughout the next fortnight Hirohito and Fukuda conferred twice a day. The great problem was to assign re-

[2] A Chicago firm, E. C. and R. M. Shankland, had developed the necessary engineering concepts back in 1900. The building, 270 feet wide and 400 feet long, rested on continuous footings of concrete to which was bolted a massive steel skeleton. Every piece of masonry in the building was anchored by rods and plates to this rigid frame.

sponsibility for the holocaust. Many Japanese still believed that a monstrous catfish lay on the ocean bottom under Japan and stirred only when the sun goddess was angry with her son on the Throne. In ancient times the Emperor had often abdicated in token of penance after major earthquakes. In 1923 the destruction had been so great that the abdication of the ailing, impotent Emperor Taisho would have seemed insufficient.

Accordingly, a new way of assigning responsibility was introduced to the people: General Fukuda, the martial law commandant, gave them a scapegoat. His military secret police spread the rumor that Koreans and Socialists had offended the spirits before the earthquake and now, afterward, were taking advantage of the disaster by setting fires and pillaging shops. Fukuda's soldiers, aided by young vigilantes of the palace-sponsored Military Sports Clubs and by thugs of the Black Dragon Society, began to hunt down every Oriental they could find who spoke Japanese with an accent. Four thousand despised Koreans from the slums were given mock trials or simple linguistic tests and were then beheaded in the streets. Nine Socialists were dragged off to Tokyo's Kameido Jail by the military police, and when they persisted in singing labor songs from their cells, were, according to the report of the officer in charge, "stabbed . . . to death in accordance with Article 12 of Garrison Regulations."

At the height of the fire, a mob of frightened people sought entry to the cool moat-girt lawns of the Imperial Palace. Turned aside by the police and again turned by the fire, they began to surge in against the police lines. They were cheered on by a firebrand Socialist, Osugi Sakae, who shouted, "Remember Russia, and never lay down your arms!" The police had their way and the flames spared the crowd. But two weeks later when the embers no longer smouldered, Captain Amakasu of the secret police tracked down Osugi and escorted him, his wife, and seven-year-old nephew to the fearsome secret police headquarters in Tokyo's Kojimachi ward. There, on September 16, Captain Amakasu received a visit from Yuasa Kurahei, a chamberlain intimate with Hirohito, who would later become lord privy seal, the Emperor's chief advisor. That night after dark Captain Amakasu entered the cell occupied by Socialist Osugi, surprised him from the rear, and soundlessly strangled him.

Amakasu proceeded with two noncoms to the cell of Osugi's wife. Less trusting than her idealistic husband, she turned in time to face her murderer and utter a few gurgled screams before she died. The seven-year-old in the next cell heard her and began to shout in terror. And so, when Mrs. Osugi finally lay quiet, the boy too was strangled.

Because the Japanese loved children and because rumors had spread of direct imperial involvement in the Osugi case, Captain Amakasu's infanticide was the one crime committed in the ashen twilight of the earthquake which had to be punished.[3] After a showpiece trial, Amakasu was sentenced to ten years in prison which Hirohito inconspicuously commuted later to three years. On release Amakasu was given money by a self-styled "friend of the Throne" to "study in Europe." He did so with the remnants of the spy ring in Paris from 1927 to 1929. Thereafter he enjoyed various sinecures in Manchuria until August 20, 1945, when he took potassium cyanide and left a note saying, "We lost our big gamble; this is the end."

REGICIDE

Fourteen weeks after the earthquake, on December 27, 1923, Crown Prince Regent Hirohito rode through the resurrected shanty town which was then Tokyo to deliver an opening address to the new Diet. In the Toranomon district, a few blocks southwest of the palace, a young man darted from the kneeling crowd, shouldered through the bowing police cordon, leveled a gun three to five inches from the side window of Hirohito's Daimler limousine, brought the regent's head into the sights, and pulled the trigger. The bullet, according to the official story, miraculously missed Hirohito, ricocheted no less than five times from the reinforced panelwork of the plush interior, and knicked one of Hirohito's chamberlains. Knowledgeable Japanese quietly point out

---

[3] General Fukuda relinquished his command under criticism but his son-in-law, Lieutenant Colonel Yasuda Tetsunosuke, was singled out for honor by being appointed equerry to Prince Higashikuni in Paris.

that three months later, Kacho Hirotada, a minor member of the imperial family who resembled Hirohito and had understudied him as a security decoy, was announced to have died suddenly of "heart attack" at the age of twenty-two.

Namba Daisaku, the man who tried to shoot Hirohito, prevented the police from immediately gunning him down by raising his hands and running along quietly behind the imperial limousine until he was arrested. The police interrogated and tortured him for eleven months but finally announced that he would give no explanation of his crime except general political dissatisfaction and sympathy for the murdered Socialist Osugi and for Osugi's seven-year-old nephew. Before his execution, according to the police, Namba shouted, "Banzai for the proletariat." It was apparent to the great majority of Japanese that he was nothing but a Bolshevik traitor.

In fact, assassin Namba was not a Communist. All the few hundred members of Japan's Communist party had been clapped in prison the previous May. Rather, Namba was a knowledgeable, well-connected dissident of the late Army strongman Yamagata's Choshu clan, which Hirohito was planning to purge from its position of influence. Namba's father was a noted liberal in the lower chamber of the Diet. He was returning by train to the protection of his clan and his constituency when he heard of his son's failure. He retired to his home, barred his front gate with slats of young "blue bamboo" to keep out callers, and remained permanently in his room upstairs. Six months after the announcement of his son's execution, he left the room in a coffin.

For many Japanese the most symbolic feature of young Namba's case was the gun which he had used. It was a pistol, encased in a cane, which Choshu clansman Ito Hirobumi, the founder of the Constitutionalist party and mentor of Prime-Minister-Maker Saionji, had brought home from London before his assassination in Harbin in 1909. Ito had given the gun for safekeeping to one of his relations, Hayashi Fumitaro.[4] Hayashi had loaned it to his

4 The Ito-Hayashi-Namba family, hailing from the southern Choshu fishing hamlet of Kumage-gun, represented the samurai element in Choshu. The ancient Choshu nobility, the Katsura-Kido-Moris of the towns of Yamaguchi and Hagi farther north, were intertwined with the imperial lineage and exempted from Hirohito's purge plans. Their scions included Emperor Taisho's prime

own kinsman Namba for the assassination attempt. When it failed to kill Hirohito, Ito's spirit was presumed to have lost face among the dead and the Ito-Saionji cause of constitutionalism lost a little in prestige among the living.

WAR MINISTER UGAKI

Hirohito used young Namba's attempted regicide as an excuse for appointing a new Cabinet, one which would take the political risk of pushing ahead with the Baden-Baden program, of modernizing the Army, and of smashing the influence of assassin Namba's Choshu clan. Prime Minister Admiral Yamamoto Gombei, who had formed the second government of his career only three months earlier, after the earthquake, offered his Cabinet's resignation as a purely formal gesture of apology for Namba's attack. But Hirohito unexpectedly accepted it. In Yamamoto's place Hirohito had Prime-Minister-Maker Saionji, who was unusually tractable after the bungled regicide attempt, submit the name of Viscount Kiyoura, a pliant legal hack left over from Emperor Meiji's days. Kiyoura had little to recommend him except his venerable seventy-four years of age and his experience as a minister of justice at the turn of the century.

The portfolios of the new Kiyoura Cabinet were held mostly by aged undistinguished aristocrats who seemed to emerge like lizards from cracks in the palace walls. There was, however, one exception, the minister of war, the first since 1912 who was not a samurai of Choshu. Ugaki Kazushige was his name, a man of the people from Okayama on the Inland Sea. He was a lieutenant general, fifty-four years old, ambitious and bullnecked, with a face as honest and stodgy as bean-curd paste. When Ugaki went visiting on a political errand, he always carried his own lunch with him—rice balls packed in an ordinary *furoshiki* or carrying cloth. He was not a clever man but the cleverest non-Choshu officer who had been deemed safe by Choshu elders to leave in the ladder of command. Hirohito knew him as a supplementary tutor who had delivered a few lectures in "The Study of the Crown Prince" dur-

minister, Katsura Taro, and Hirohito's original Big Brother, the later World War II privy seal, Marquis Kido Koichi.

ing Hirohito's adolescence. Now Hirohito would use him and abuse
him until he would become one of the greatest loyal dupes in
Japan—second only to Saionji.

On being elevated to the post of war minister, Ugaki found
that a staff plan for his term of office had been carefully prepared
in advance by the Three Crows of Baden-Baden who had returned
to Japan from Paris in early 1923. The plan called first of all for a
cutback in the Army's sheer force of samurai numbers, a cutback
which could be represented as money-saving and demilitarizing.
In the course of it Ugaki was to purge the Army of its Choshu
leadership and of all other henchmen of Hirohito's late antagonist, strongman Yamagata. Finally Ugaki was to strengthen the
Army for war by equipping it with modern tank and air forces.
Ugaki realized that such a program could be carried out only in
the face of powerful opposition from Choshu clansmen in the
bureaucracy and also from any Constitutionalists in the Diet who
saw through the lamb's-wool wrappings. Nevertheless Ugaki accepted his assignment and wrote in his diary: "I will advance
bravely and carry this sublime responsibility with high purpose.
I will rush forward with a progressive attitude, intestinal fortitude,
and greatness of spirit."

NUPTIALS

With carefully considered timing, on the eve of his struggle
with Choshu, Crown Prince Hirohito consolidated his position
in the hearts of his people by getting married. Princess Nagako,
the granddaughter of Emperor Komei's advisor Asahiko, had been
waiting for him, studying under special tutors at her father's villa
ever since her choice as fiancée in 1917 more than six years earlier.
The wedding was solemnized on January 26, 1924, a fortnight
after Ugaki's appointment, a month after Namba's assassination
attempt, and almost five months after the earthquake.

During the wedding a gathering of seven hundred invited
guests—all of them Japanese, one of them the gang lord Black
Dragon Toyama—stood attendance outside the Imperial Family
Shrine in the forested area of the palace garden. In ancient Court
regalia, Nagako carrying a fan, Hirohito a scepter, the couple met

before the assembled witnesses at the shrine entrance. The gates swung open and Hirohito, all alone, entered the courtyard leading toward the Inner Shrine. The chamberlain of rituals chanted Shinto prayers in a high singsong. The doors of the Inner Shrine sprang open and Hirohito disappeared into his ancestors' Holy of Holies. Having done brief homage and declared his intentions to the spirits, he returned to the outer gate where Nagako was waiting. The two drank alternately, three times, from a goblet of sanctified rice wine and the ceremony was over. The ships of the fleet in Tokyo harbor crashed out a 101-gun salute, more than twice as prolonged as that accorded any other ruler on earth.

For the wedding, Hirohito's public relations expert, Count Futara, dinned home the image which he had been creating of his master since 1921. Hirohito was represented as a young liberal, full of Western ideas, playing golf in a tweed hat and plus fours with Edward, Prince of Wales, who had visited Japan in 1922. In an eagerness to learn to beat the West at its own games, Hirohito had built a nine-hole golf course on the grounds of the Akasaka Palace. In an effort to get to know his people, Hirohito had appeared on the beach to swim in public. The leading British editor in Japan described this press campaign as "sedulous care . . . to promote the idea of personal loyalty to him." But the people warmed to the campaign because they were fed up with centuries of stiff Spartan courtesy and military discipline.

PURGE

Behind the promotional stage drops, in early 1924, the Choshu samurai were making their last desperate stand. The leader of the Choshu clan, General Tanaka Gi-ichi—a simple fellow to wear the shoes of his Machiavellian predecessor, strongman Yamagata —called a meeting of Army elders at his home. "We face a Satsuma clan conspiracy. Let's break them utterly," he announced. Six months later the Choshu generals, and a few Constitutionalist allies, succeeded only in gaining a public save of face. They were allowed to topple the reptilian, dinosaurian Kiyoura Cabinet and in return they accepted the Army reorganization scheme.

In June 1924, a new cabinet, headed by the monocle-wearing

diplomat Kato Taka-aki, who had served the Twenty-One Demands on China a decade earlier, made light of the Army purge
as a routine economy measure and diverted public attention to a
fresh issue: universal suffrage. Since 1902 all Japanese liberals
had militated for abolition of the three-yen poll tax. Now Prime
Minister Kato and Hirohito came out in favor of abolition and
of an increase in the electorate from 3,300,000 to 14,000,000
voters, that is, to all males of twenty-five or over. The loyalist
press manufactured mossbacked commentators who opposed the
increase in suffrage and a great fake debate occupied the front
pages.

While the nation was distracted, War Minister Ugaki stood in
a small spotlight to one side, ostensibly "demilitarizing" the Army.
In reality he was carrying out a complicated horse trade within
the officer corps by which all the most important Choshu generals
and a compensatory selection of Satsuma and other clan generals
voluntarily resigned their commissions. In all some 2,000 officers
were cashiered and with them, it seemed at first, some 80,000
men. Four divisions, the 13th, 15th, 17th, and 18th, were declared
dissolved, but many of the companies and battalions in them were
preserved intact, awaiting orders. By the time the Choshu officers
had been mustered out, many of their units had been reassigned
to swell the divisions which remained or to staff new auxiliary
forces. The entire reorganization was juggled with the deftness
of a master bookkeeper. When the ink had dried, only 33,894
men and 6,089 horses had been discharged from the Army and
the other 46,000-odd men, who had seemed to be on their way
out, had been reabsorbed. There were new mechanized transport
groups, machine-gun squads for every infantry company, research
teams to study modern weapons, fresh branches of intelligence,
two new air regiments, an antiaircraft regiment, a 5,500-man tank
corps, and several new specialized military schools such as the
Signal Academy in Kanagawa and the Narashino School in Chiba
for chemical and bacteriological warfare.

In addition, the period of compulsory military training was
shortened to six weeks so that the government could afford to
give every young male some foundation to fall back on in the
event of national mobilization. To compensate for the brevity

of the training, a new Army educational corps of 1200 drill masters was organized and posted at leading high schools and prep schools. These physical education officers made sure that every adolescent, before his service, was already inculcated with the principles of martial spirit, parading, and sword and rifle drill. By intimidating fellow faculty members, they would gradually gain a tight hold on the curriculum in years ahead and would succeed in making Japanese education a bland exercise in indoctrinational cant.

As the Army reorganization scheme was unfolded step by step and battalion by battalion, cashiered Choshu officers grumbled privately, but publicly there was an uncanny lack of protest. Part of the silence did credit simply to the Japanese soldier's discipline in obeying orders; the other part reflected the excellent staff planning of the Three Crows. They had begun the reorganization by posting members of Hirohito's cabal of young officers in all the most sensitive posts. The chief of the Three Crows, Lieutenant Colonel Nagata Tetsuzan himself, spent four months of 1924 as an officer in one of the regiments which was to be abolished, a regiment stationed in Choshu territory and staffed by Choshu officers. By deft politicking he prevented its men from staging a mutiny. Students of the indoctrination school in the palace, the University Lodging House, were so widely dispersed on similar missions that the school was closed in late 1924, and its building, the old palace observatory, was condemned because of structural damage done by the earthquake.

By March 1925 when the elimination of four divisions—of four sacred battle standards around which ancestors had died—was finally announced to the public, Crown Prince Hirohito's position was so strong that his minions in the House of Peers were able to attach a rider to the Universal Suffrage Bill. When the latter was passed on May 5, 1925, its supporters had been pledged to vote also for a Maintenance of Public Peace Bill. This was largely the work of Hirohito's Big Brother, the gangling, effete Fujiwara Prince Konoye who would preside over Japan as prime minister a decade later during the rape of Nanking. Known by its detractors as the "Dangerous Thoughts Bill," it gave the police almost unlimited power to suppress political dissidents. It was passed

by the Diet, without much protest, on May 12, 1925, a week after
the Universal Suffrage Bill. Fifteen years later it would enable
Prince Konoye to transform universal suffrage into universal agreement—a single mass party of reverent imperialists.

NEW STAR IN CHINA

During the enactment of the Baden-Baden program, one member of Hirohito's cabal of young officers, one graduate of the
University Lodging House, was absent: the ubiquitous Suzuki
Tei-ichi. He was away in China observing the early struggles and
rise to power of a new Chinese strongman, a friend from cadet
days at the Japanese Military Academy, Chiang Kai-shek. Since
1920, when he had first made his way into the inner counsels of
Hirohito's Big Brotherhood,[5] Captain Suzuki had been detailed
by General Staff Intelligence to remain constantly near Chiang
Kai-shek as an advisor. To outsiders it seemed a strange assignment because, when it began in 1920, Chiang Kai-shek was a little
known commodity and currency broker in Shanghai.

The gray-eyed Chiang[6] had amassed a small fortune speculating in futures during World War I and had made the acquaintance
of China's greatest banking families. They respected him as a
handsome, taciturn, direct, forceful, shrewd dealer. He kept a
wife and a stable of mistresses but had not then met the later
Madame Chiang or become a convert to Christianity. He was
still fond of his adopted land, Japan, where he had attended military academy after graduation from China's own military school,
Paoting. He still kept in touch with dozens of Japanese friends
including Prince Asaka, who would rape Nanking; Prince Higashikuni, who would bomb Nanking; Matsui Iwane, the later general

---

[5] His patron was an artillery major, Big Brother Marquis Inoue Saburo, the
illegitimate son of Emperor Taisho's favorite, Prime Minister Katsura Taro.
Suzuki had become intimate with Marquis Inoue when the two served a one-
year stint together in special economic training at the Finance Ministry in
1919.
[6] In the coastal village of Fenghua, 100 miles south of Shanghai, where
Chiang had been born to a prosperous wine merchant in 1887, gossips attributed the unusual color of his eyes to a Portuguese or Dutch seaman en-
twined in his ancestral tree.

who would be hanged as the "Butcher of Nanking"; and in addition Lord of the Black Dragon Toyama, who had given refuge to Chiang's mentor, Sun Yat-sen. Indeed Chiang had met an entire generation of Asian nationalists and conquerors in Japan, a military elite to which he felt he belonged but with which he was destined to spend his life in mortal combat.

Chiang had led a Japanese-financed regiment in the Chinese Revolution of 1911 and since then had regularly attended the congresses of Sun Yat-sen's Kuomintang or KMT party. He had seen the Revolution turn sour, Yuan Shih-kai and his war lords take power in North China, and Sun Yat-sen grow old as a testy visionary among his most faithful supporters in the southern Chinese port of Canton. Having made sure of his future financially, Chiang, in 1923, gave up his brokerage in Shanghai and at the age of thirty-five retired to dedicate himself full time to the cause of Sun Yat-sen in Canton. The ubiquitous Suzuki Tei-ichi was detached by the Japanese General Staff to follow Chiang south.

Chiang found Sun Yat-sen, the "George Washington" of the original 1911 Republican Movement, bitter against the war lord regime in Peking and dying of liver cancer. He had surrounded himself with young Communists like Mao Tse-tung and Chou En-lai. He was under the influence of two Russian advisors: General Vasili Blücher, the strategic magician who had whipped together raw Red recruits to defeat the Cossacks in Siberia in 1921, and Michael Borodin, the product of a Vitebsk ghetto, best known to some Americans as Mike Berg, a soapbox orator on the corner of Division and Halstead streets in Chicago during the years before World War I. Chiang Kai-shek took brief stock of his old hero's entourage and in the fall of 1923 paid a two-month visit to Moscow to study communism at its source. In that brief visit he won the admiration and support of Joseph Stalin who was then locked in his own leadership struggle with Leon Trotsky.

On returning to Canton in December of 1923, Chiang enlisted the help of his Japanese friend and observer, the ubiquitous Suzuki Tei-ichi, to found an indoctrination center, modeled on the University Lodging House and known as Whampoa Academy. By 1925, when Lodging House graduates were foisting their program on Japan, Whampoa graduates were infiltrating the officer corps of the war lords' private armies in northern China. In March 1925, when the Baden-Baden program was passing the Diet in Tokyo, Sun Yat-sen was finally killed by his cancer and Chiang Kai-shek emerged as his successor. Chiang consolidated his position for a year. Then in March 1926, in a theatrical show of strength, he had his military police arrest all the Chinese Communists in Canton and make them agree to a military campaign against the nominally Republican warlord regime in Peking. Chiang's armies started north and swept everything before them.

Suzuki, the ubiquitous observer, was impressed by the support given Chiang's troops everywhere by the Chinese peasants. In his dispatches home to Tokyo he assessed Chiang as a genuine popular leader, capable of making China a force to reckon with. Japanese Prime Minister Kato Taka-aki, the server of the Twenty-One Demands on China in 1915, had shuffled off the coils of his cool, calculating, monocled existence on January 28, 1926, but there were other "China experts" in high places who appreciated the import of Suzuki's dispatches and brought them to the attention of Hirohito.

Accordingly, in the spring of 1926, Hirohito dispatched a pride of his lion cubs, including both officers and civilians, to join Suzuki in China and study the situation at first hand.[7] They agreed that Chiang Kai-shek was worth backing. He might not be entirely trustworthy, because he had dreams of unifying China, but at the moment he was willing to make Manchuria, Mongolia, and North China safe for Japan by allowing autonomous puppet governments to be established in those regions.

DEATH OF TAISHO

Early on Christmas morning 1926, as the waves of the Pacific lapped at the fringe of ice crystals on the beach at Hayama, the forty-seven-year-old Emperor Taisho, in the seclusion of his Summer Palace, a few yards up the strand, suffered his final stroke. The twenty-six-year-old Crown Prince Hirohito, who was sleep-

---

[7] One of them was diplomat Matsuoka Yosuke who would later win notoriety as Japan's chief operator in dealings with Hitler and Stalin.

ing nearby, was informed instantly over a telephone line which had been kept open ever since Taisho had lapsed unconscious a few weeks earlier. Hirohito's voice broke as he told the chamberlain at the other end of the wire how much he regretted being absent from his father's side in the last moments.

Less than two hours later a motorcade with sirens screaming arrived at the main Imperial Palace in Tokyo, the gates swung open, and Crown Prince Hirohito was rushed on through parks along malls to the entrance of the Imperial Family Shrine in the palace forest. Leaving his retinue at their limousines, he walked on with two princes of the blood and two witnesses from the nobility across the frosty white pebbles of the shrine courtyard. Entering alone into the Holy of Holies, he faced the three imperial regalia and began the solemn private ceremony of declaring himself to the spirits as the new Emperor of Japan. He touched first the fragile brocade bag which was supposed to hold the sacred green jewels, representing the verdant isles of Japan. He knew that inside the bag was supposed to be coiled a necklace of amethyst and turquoise, cut irregularly in comma-shaped beads, interspersed with oblong beads. He knew that the original almost certainly lay at the bottom of the Inland Sea, having gone down with Emperor Antoku at the naval engagement of Dan-no-ura A.D. 1185. Officially the beads had been found after the battle, floating safely in their box. He did not open the bag to admire them. Next he lifted a replica of the sacred sword of power, the *Excalibur* plucked from the tail of a dragon by the son of the sun goddess. He knew that the original of the sword was genuine, safely housed in the Atsuta Shrine in Nagoya. He could not guess that it would be destroyed by a bomb from a B-29 before his reign was over.

Finally he held aloft a replica of the most mighty of the regalia, the bronze mirror of knowledge. The original, dating from the first century, lay in the vaults of Ise Shrine on a peninsula overlooking the sea from which the first Emperor had come. If one could gaze into the mirror, one could see the face of the sun goddess and commune with her as through a glass darkly. But palace fires A.D. 960, 1005, and 1040 had reduced the original to a few droplets of bright metal. Hirohito held in his hands an imitation, almost a thousand years old, but still an imitation.

On emerging from the shrine, having perfunctorily touched the regalia and fervently declared his intentions to the hovering spirits, Hirohito was considered anointed by the holy oil. He would be publicly crowned Emperor for Western observers in an elaborate ceremony more than a year later in Kyoto, the old capital, but he was already crowned spiritually for all devout Japanese.

That night back at his study in the little Akasaka Versailles, from which he would have to move now that he was Emperor, Hirohito glanced through a list of names suggested for his reign and chose that of Showa, Peace Made Manifest. Its ideographs carried something of the force of "millennium in which men shall speak with tongues."[8] Then he took writing brush in hand and personally wrote the first draft of an edict describing the aspirations of his reign: "Simplicity instead of vain display, originality instead of blind imitation, progress in view of this period of evolution, improvement to keep pace with the advancement of civilization, national harmony in purpose and in action."

As Hirohito sat before the fire in his *petit* Versailles, composing his visions of the future, a group of young officers who had graduated from the University Lodging House before its demolition two years earlier were brought word of Emperor Taisho's passing by one of Hirohito's aides-de-camp. The messenger was Major Anami Korechika, the later general who would preside over the fake coup d'etat in the palace and prepare to do hara-kiri during the long night of August 14, 1945. Anami brought a purse of money with him and took all the young officers out for a spree in the student quarter of Kanda east of the palace. The headmaster of the University Lodging House, Dr. Okawa, opened the celebration with a toast to Japan's future conquest of Manchuria.

Lieutenant Colonel Tojo, the later World War II prime minis-

---

[8] This choice of reign-name meant that 1926, the year of his accession, would be styled in the Japanese calendar as Showa One; 1936 as Showa Eleven; 1945 as Showa Twenty. It also meant that Hirohito, at his death, would be known as Emperor Showa. The names of Emperors used in previous pages are all posthumous reign-names. Thus Komei's unspoken personal name while he lived was Osahito, Meiji's was Mutsuhito, and Taisho's was Yoshihito.

ter, reminded him, "But we can never move troops unless the Emperor says so."

"Oh, well," boasted Okawa, "I will have my friend Lord Privy Seal Makino persuade the Emperor."

Tojo was indignant at Okawa's disrespect, and the suave Lieutenant Colonel Itagaki, the member of the Baden-Baden Eleven Reliables who would later organize the conquest of Manchuria, had to inject a pleasantry to prevent a fight.

Tojo's mentor, Lieutenant Colonel Nagata, the first of the Three Crows, quietly stated the final word: "I agree that independence for Manchuria is desirable, but not complete, perfect independence. That might bring eternal enmity between China and Japan and disrupt the future peace of the Far East. So let China keep her official sovereignty."

The young officers of the cabal went on to discuss the deplorable ebb in the nation's fighting spirit. Boarding a public conveyance, a man in uniform was likely to be greeted by such remarks as, "What use are spurs on a tram car?" or "Big swords certainly do get in the way of fellow passengers." After gloomily dwelling on such signs of the times, the conspirators broke up and, at Aide-de-Camp Anami's generous insistence, took taxicabs home to their billets. One group dropped Anami off in the plaza outside the main gates of the palace. There they saw country folk kneeling in the moonlight to pray for the new Emperor. In the words of one of them, "We felt relieved by the sight, as if the independence of Manchuria was already assured."

9

HIROHITO AS EMPEROR

(1926–1929)

IMPERIAL REGIMEN

A day or two after his father's death, Hirohito left his elegantly appointed Versailles in the separate Akasaka compound just west of the main palace and moved his manifold sources of influence and affluence into the high-walled confinement of the central battlements. Thereafter he would venture forth only a score or more times a year: for garden parties, convocations of the Diet, graduation days at the military and naval academies, fleet reviews, and Army maneuvers. Within the old picturesque fortifications, his dwelling was a prim, traditional Japanese house of sliding paper doors and straw matting floors. It was uncomfortable by Western standards, and Hirohito felt uncomfortable in it. He at once selected a large room about twenty feet square, with a low, handsomely coffered ceiling, to serve as his study and place of work. He had the room furnished in Western style, putting in a carpet, a table, some chairs, and a sofa on which he might spend the night. From the walls he stripped a number of Western masters, left by Meiji and Taisho, and substituted photographs of himself in Europe with Maréchal Pétain, the Prince of Wales, and Belgium's Crown Prince Leopold. Beside the prayer alcove he ensconced his busts of Napoleon and Darwin. At one end of the room the screens slid open onto a veranda overlooking his private park. There workmen were already breaking ground to build for him a new golf course, a roofed riding ring for rainy days, and the bomb-resistant concrete working quarters, the Imperial Library, under which he would surrender at the end of World War II.

No sooner had Hirohito occupied his new quarters as Emperor than his nose was assaulted by the stench of fish. It was an old custom for the members of the imperial family to felicitate one another on happy occasions with delicacies from the sea, but on this occasion the corridors of the palace were lined with panniers that reeked. Hirohito threw one of the few tantrums of his reign. "It is no congratulation to me," he shouted, "to receive a present of fresh fish. I find it more congratulating when I see one of them swimming free around me in the sea. This nonsensical, dirty custom must be abolished." And so it was, except that Hirohito continued to send fresh fish to his mother on festival days and princes of the blood found that they could please Hirohito by sending him occasionally live fish of rare varieties with which to stock his palace ponds.

Having corrected his kinsmen's misapprehensions about the interests of a marine biologist, Hirohito made one other change in palace customs. Formerly Emperors had worn clothes once or twice and then handed them down to their retainers. "Following the teaching of my tutor Nogi," declared Hirohito, "I feel that clothes are the product of my people's industry and should be worn for a long time. Therefore the vassals of the Throne may expect a third as many presents as formerly."

These two crotchets about fish and finery out of the way, Hirohito quickly settled down in his new surroundings to be a model master. He established for himself a punctual pattern of life which delighted his attendants and has changed little to this day. He customarily arose at six o'clock, shaved and dressed himself, prayed to his ancestors, and then, if he had time before breakfast, went outside for an exhilarating canter or a thoughtful stroll. At his summer villa on the beach at Hayama he would regularly rouse the neighborhood by vigorously chopping wood. At seven he would come in, full of gruff martinet good spirits, to sit down with Empress Nagako, not to the traditional Japanese breakfast of salt plums, fish, seaweed, soya-bean soup, rice, and tea, but to oat-meal, eggs, bacon, toast, and coffee.

Having breakfasted heartily, Hirohito would retire to his study to muse over the Tokyo dailies, *Asahi* and *Mainichi*, and over the English-language *Japan Advertiser*. This homework completed, the Emperor would receive Lord Privy Seal Makino, his closest advisor, who would look in at the door of the study to pronounce the traditional noncommittal Japanese good morning salutation: "It is early." If any special plot was afoot, Makino would remind Hirohito of it in a sentence.

Then Hirohito would begin his official day by calling in his chief aide-de-camp, General Nara Takeji, to discuss the latest Army and Navy news, the list of military men seeking an audience in the near future, and the points to be stressed or avoided in the military audiences already scheduled for the day at hand. Next Hirohito would call in Count Chinda Sutemi, his grand chamberlain, who, like Nara and Makino, had been with him ever since the beginning of the trip to Europe. Chinda was a man of cosmopolitan charm and polish, with an American education and experience as an ambassador in half the capitals of the West. With him Hirohito would discuss the civilian audiences of the day. Finally, if one of the chiefs of staff had exercised his right to demand "direct access" to the Throne, Hirohito would see him on some item of urgent Navy or Army business before the start of the day's scheduled interviews.

From about ten until two o'clock, with a break for a light lunch at twelve-thirty, Hirohito would see a steady stream of ministers and officials. Many of the audiences, especially the formal ones held in the official Throne Room, the Phoenix Hall, were perfunctory affairs with relative strangers. Hirohito would merely greet his guest, hear him deliver a formal report, and then dismiss him. Other meetings with trusted or familiar ministers also began with a formal report, but after it was delivered, the Emperor frequently asked questions and drew out his informant to learn his personal opinions and concerns. During formal reports from military men, Chief Aide-de-Camp Nara was required to be present. However, by a curious custom instituted in Emperor Meiji's time, the aide-de-camp was obliged to withdraw immediately if any matter regarding personnel was brought up.[1] Thus, an officer who wished to share secrets with the Emperor could always talk of personnel shifts to secure a private audience, though with some risk of rebuff and imperial displeasure. Moreover, Hirohito, at any time after the formal report had been delivered, could direct Nara to withdraw out of earshot by a simple wave of his hand.

A similar procedure was followed with the grand chamberlain during audiences with nonmilitary petitioners. Hirohito, however, did not trust himself with civilians. He had found in the past that many of them used devious political approaches in talking to him, or else gossiped afterwards about what had been said. Therefore, when he dismissed Grand Chamberlain Chinda and gave a private hearing to a civilian, he usually had Lord Privy Seal Makino eavesdrop on the proceedings. In the old palace there were special listening closets provided for this purpose; in the new concrete library there were to be intercom devices as well. After 1930, when an official of the Railway Ministry abused a private audience to discuss a proposed government-wide salary cut, which was one of Hirohito's own pet economy measures, no more private audiences with civilians were granted except with officials of Court or ministerial rank, that is, with princes and noblemen or with Cabinet members and specially designated honorary ministers.

If state business permitted, Hirohito gave over the hours from two to four each afternoon to exercise, chiefly golf. Between strokes on the little nine-hole links, he discussed over-all situations and planning with his closest confidants. No day-to-day record of the people he played with is available, but some of his favorite partners were Fujiwara Prince Konoye, the Big Brother in charge of steering the House of Peers; Imperial Prince Asaka, the limping uncle who watched over Army Intelligence while the other uncle, Prince Higashikuni, remained in Paris; Marquis Inoue Saburo, the patron of Chiang Kai-shek's ubiquitous observer, Major Suzuki Tei-ichi; and Marquis Kido Koichi, the original Big Brother who was making plans to "rationalize" Japan's economy in the Agriculture and Commerce Ministry. Kido's published diary, which

[1] Supposedly, Emperor Meiji had heard that, during the Russo-Japanese War, the military aides of Czar Nicholas II made a practice of selling Russian officers promotions which the czar had already freely granted.

begins in 1930, suggests that some proficiency with a putting iron later became a requisite for Court advancement.

At four o'clock Hirohito took his *ofuro*, his "honorable wind on the backbone"—his bath. The Imperial Residence in the palace had been equipped in Meiji's time with shallow porcelain European tubs for tepid bathing as well as deep wooden Japanese tubs for tingling hot soaks. Hirohito favored the Japanese style of immersion, but in water at a precise, conservative 110 degrees Fahrenheit—ten to twenty degrees cooler than that of most Japanese baths. Warmed through and wrapped in the comfort of a kimono, he returned to his study to put his seal or brush his signature on a score or more state papers submitted by Lord Privy Seal Makino. About six he would try to call it a day. He would remind the chamberlain and aide-de-camp on night duty that they must disturb him if anything important came up. Then he would retire to his private apartments to dine and devote the rest of the evening to Empress Nagako, a good book, his diary,[2] or his hobby of biology. He drank not, neither did he smoke.

The punctilious round of Hirohito's domestic routine was varied on Wednesdays when the Privy Council sat. This body consisted of twenty-four distinguished aristocrats appointed by the Emperor for their meritorious service to the Empire, plus Cabinet ministers and princes of the blood. Its duty was to deliberate on treaties, on imperial ordinances issued when the Diet was out of session, and on any question submitted to it for an opinion by the Emperor. Hirohito invariably attended its plenary sessions on Wednesdays and kept informed on all its committee and preparatory meetings. This was the one occasion of the week in which he heard a semblance of discussion and observed conflicts of opinion and personality. Consequently, he always tried to keep his schedule for the next day as open as possible in order to consider and act upon the thoughts suggested to him by the Privy Council meeting. On Friday he cleared his mind for the weekend by meet-

[2] Hirohito's own day-by-day record has been kept studiously since his adolescence. It was not subpoenaed by the war crimes investigators of the American Occupation and has not been read even by Hirohito's intimates. It has, however, been seen by some of them, and a part of it now fills a sizable safe in the bombproof vaults of the new Ceremonial Palace buildings completed in 1968.

ing mainly with award-winning students, athletic heroes, and foreign ambassadors.

On Saturday mornings, Hirohito indulged in his hobby of biology, an expression of his personality which has been much misrepresented and misunderstood. He was not, as some have thought, a scientific dilettante building an undeserved reputation for himself through the effort of hired assistants. The diaries of his courtiers and his own published work demonstrate clearly that he was a good naturalist, genuinely observant, interested, and knowledgeable. Nor was he, as some others have thought, a preoccupied collector of obscure marine organisms who pursued science for its own sake. The institutes which he subsidized over the years and the comments which he made to intimates show that he believed in science as a practical tool, a necessary tool of warfare, a tool in which he knew Japan to be deficient.

Thus he prided himself that his marine biological knowledge of tides and currents was of use in naval planning. Thus, too, in 1927, at a time when the very concept of biological warfare was novel in the West, a number of biologists and physicians who were his former tutors had been encouraged to devote themselves full time to war research. By 1939 tissue cultures at the Imperial University would be producing the most virulent agents of yaws, encephalitis, botulism, and bubonic plague known to medicine. After 1940 plague bombs containing bacilli, or bacilli in fleas, or bacilli in rat food would be dropped repeatedly in China in unavailing experiments to find effective germ-delivery systems. In 1945 Occupation search teams would find large stockpiles of unused viruses, spirochetes, and fungus spores in decentralized laboratories in Japanese rural areas.

Hirohito in 1927 was personally engrossed in a study of disease-causing fungi. Some of the unclassified portions of his work were later published in 1936 by Hattori, the faithful tutor who had contrived to take him out skin diving as a child. Hattori had become Hirohito's assistant. A commodious laboratory was being built for him in the palace gardens but at this moment, in 1927, he was cataloguing fungus specimens—many of them picked by Hirohito's own hand—in a converted palace potting shed. There on Saturday mornings Hirohito visited him, dressed in a Western-style business suit and carrying a brief-case of culture charts and sketches given him by Hattori the previous weekend. For two hours he would look over Hattori's work of the past week, asking questions and giving words of praise. Then he would pick up a new brief-case of homework and start back for the palace. Empress Nagako made a special point of waiting to greet him at the end of one of the garden paths when he returned. She was a practical political woman who did not fully understand the fascinations of his hobby, but her aged father, Prince Kuni, was also an enthusiast for biological warfare and she was glad of the relaxation which it gave her husband.

On the daily framework of Hirohito's life were imposed a number of set calendar obligations. Once a fortnight he saw the vice chiefs of his own personal departments of government, the Army and Navy General Staffs. The Cabinet Ministries of War and Navy, which administered the recruitment, pay, and peacetime organization of the armed forces, belonged to the elected government of the prime minister; the staffs, which directed military operations in the field and states of martial law at home and of occupation government abroad, answered directly to Hirohito and to him alone.

On the first, eleventh, and twenty-first of each month and on twenty-four annual holidays, the Emperor also had to break his diurnal scheme to officiate at religious rites: at folk festivals similar to May Day and Thanksgiving, at ceremonies for the sun goddess, at anniversaries for the worship of the most illustrious of the imperial ancestors. On these solemn occasions the courtyard of the Palace Shrine was filled with imperial and Fujiwara princes. Court musicians, kneeling on the ground in scarlet cloaks and pointed headdresses, made doleful music on archaic flutes, drums, and viols. The chamberlain of rituals chanted Shinto prayers almost as old and obscure as the fountainheads of the Japanese language itself. At the end of the explanatory or introductory part of the service, Hirohito, clad in robes of heavy white silk, would rise from an ancient lacquered throne, intone an invocation in a stylized high-pitched monotone, and then hold high an offering or heirloom to the spirits of his family or the spirits of the land. At some of the services, the entire Court of princes, each in his turn, according to his rank, would follow him to the altar and perform an individual act of reverence. Although punctilious in all these high-priestly duties, Hirohito confessed in later years that the folk festivals stirred less devout, more objective feelings in him than the prayers to his ancestors. He did find, however, that the November offering of harvest rice and saké to the earth spirits was often "an uplifting experience."

CHIANG CLEANS HOUSE

No sooner had Hirohito become Emperor than his cabal launched an aggressive campaign of secret diplomacy to take Manchuria from China without having to fight for it. The campaign ultimately failed but it had momentous side effects. It encouraged Chiang Kai-shek to break irrevocably with the Communist wing of his KMT party, thereby planting the seeds of China's future. It set Hirohito at odds with many of the elders of his nation. And finally, when it ended in disappointment, Hirohito allowed himself to become a party to his first clear-cut international crime: the vindictive assassination of Manchuria's war lord, Chang Tsolin.

One of the masterminds of this ill-conceived effort in private diplomacy was Prince Higashikuni, the leader of the Japanese spy ring in Europe. As soon as he got word of Emperor Taisho's death, he posted home by ship from Paris. He and Emperor Taisho had never been friends, but with Hirohito, his niece's husband and his wife's nephew, Higashikuni hoped for a better relationship. He arrived in Tokyo incognito, called at the palace, and then went on to the Asiatic continent to take up new intelligence duties as an agent at large, working under an alias out of Peking.[3] It was his new secret mission to co-ordinate with palace policy the efforts of other members of the cabal in China—efforts to turn to Japan's advantage the northward march of the armies of Chiang Kai-shek.

The witches' brew that Higashikuni and his minions had to

[3] His return was not officially reported by the Japanese press until January of the following year, but his presence at Taisho's funeral was noted without comment.

work with was a rich broth even by Chinese standards. Peking, the capital of China, was controlled by the Manchurian war lord Chang Tso-lin. Following his escape in 1916 from the dynamite thrown at him by Prince Kanin's cronies, he had given his nominal public support to Sun Yat-sen's Republic. Behind the scenes, however, he had worked for a restoration of the Manchu dynasty. He was backed in his conservatism by the deposed Manchu court, by many of the old bureaucratic class of mandarins, by elders of the discomfited Choshu clan in Tokyo, and by most Western business interests in China.

Arrayed against Chang Tso-lin were the leaders of the KMT, who now controlled all of southern China from Burma to the Yangtze. They were a motley assortment of unlettered peasant revolutionaries, of tough Comintern agents,[4] and of moderates like Chiang Kai-shek. Their common aim was to "liberate" Peking and "realize" the Republican government there which Chang Tso-lin said he was protecting.

After consultation with Chiang Kai-shek himself, Hirohito's cabal agreed, first, to a purge of Communists from the KMT, then to the establishment of Chiang Kai-shek as the one ruler in the whole of classical China, south of the Great Wall. In exchange, the Chinese provinces north of the Wall—the big, empty, potentially wealthy ones of Manchuria and Mongolia—were to be controlled by Japan. Once established, Chiang was also expected to ease out Western business interests from Shanghai and to look in future to Japan for all technical and economic assistance.

When Prince Higashikuni arrived secretly in Peking, the campaign to rid the KMT of its Communists was going well. Chiang was co-operating in it for personal reasons. He wished to persuade the wealthiest of the Shanghai bankers, C. J. Soong, to abandon the cause of his daughter, Ching-ling, and espouse that of another daughter, May-ling. Ching-ling had married Sun Yat-sen and was being used as a figurehead by the Communists in the KMT. May-ling, by contrast, was a Wellesley graduate, a Christian, an anti-Communist, and an ardent admirer of Chiang Kai-shek.

[4] The dedicated Communists in the KMT movement, like Mao Tse-tung, Chou En-lai, and Chu Teh, were a minority, but they enjoyed the assistance of technical advisors from Moscow.

As they drove down the Yangtze River from the hinterlands toward Shanghai, Chiang's troops rode a crest of mass chauvinism and xenophobia. At Hankow and Kiukiang they terrorized the Western settlements. Chiang blamed their excesses entirely on Bolshevik agitators, a charge which Western businessmen were predisposed to believe. C. J. Soong, the pink banker, saw that the Reds in the KMT were spoiling his reputation and impairing his interests.

In late March 1927, when Chiang's soldiers occupied Nanking, less than 200 miles from the China coast, they burned several of the foreign consulates, killed six Westerners, and manhandled a number of consular wives and secretaries. British and American gunboats in the Yangtze laid down a semicircle of protective fire around Socony Hill while Westerners, who had congregated there as refugees, were lowered on ropes from the city wall to evacuation launches. Two Japanese gunboats steamed 50 miles downriver to help but managed to arrive too late. In the days that followed, representatives of the Western nations discussed the possibility of sending an international expeditionary force to Nanking to restore order. The foreign minister of Japan, by prearrangement, aborted the expedition by refusing to participate in it.

In the KMT advance, Western colonials saw a Red spectre marching with a flail into all they considered near and dear. Over their glasses of Scotch in Shanghai clubs they grumbled that the West had invested more than $2 billion in China. These foreign holdings were represented by the "concessions" and "legation quarters," the little enclaves of Paris, London, Tokyo, and St. Petersburg which dominated the downtown areas of all the largest Chinese cities including Shanghai, Tientsin, Hankow, Nanking, and Peking. Most were leaseholds of a few thousand acres. Several of them, notably those of Shanghai and Hankow, had been marshes or mudflats originally and had become valuable only because foreigners had developed them. By the 1920's, however, native Chinese urban areas had grown up around all of them. In septic seas of tiled roofs, narrow alleyways, intrigue, violence, and disease, they stood out as blessed isles of peace, police, and cleanliness, of Western architecture and broad, arbored boulevards. In a French concession, one could always eat snails in hailing distance of an Annamese gendarme. In a British concession, there was always a tea shop or two, a busy banking district, and a Sikh bobby on every corner. The old Russian and German concessions, which had been taken over by carefully selected Chinese administrators after World War I, still had their borscht and bakeries and Wiener schnitzel. The Japanese concessions, being less Occidental, were naturally less congenial to Westerners. They teemed with people and closely set small buildings. But to a Japanese they were pure Osaka, and the policework, neighborhood organization, geisha, and suki-yaki were of the best.

After the capture of Nanking, Chiang Kai-shek used Western threats of intervention as an excuse to summon a full-dress conference of all KMT leaders in the town of Nanchang, halfway up the Yangtze between his own field headquarters downriver and the government of the KMT Left upriver in Hankow. On March 22, 1927, after interminable sessions of fruitless talk, Chiang abruptly stalked from the bargaining table and disappeared into the countryside, submerging among his own personal troops. During his disappearance a cadre of disciplined Communists under the leadership of the later famous Chinese Communist foreign minister, Chou En-lai, staged a municipal coup d'etat in the Chinese quarter of Shanghai and put the bulk of the city in Red hands, greatly alarming the Western residents in the concessions downtown.

Far to the north, on April 6, a fortnight later, Chang Tso-lin acted on a tip from one of Hirohito's Eleven Baden-Baden Reliables and ordered his police to break into the Russian Embassy in Peking. In their raid the police seized documents which showed that the left-wing government of the KMT in Hankow was being run as a front organization according to instructions from Moscow. Chang Tso-lin hoped that this revelation, added to Chiang Kai-shek's experience in Russia and friendship with Stalin, would destroy Chiang's credit with bankers and undermine his popularity with the xenophobic rank and file. Instead, as the Japanese had understood all too well, the revelations gave Chiang precisely the justification he needed to purge the Reds from the KMT without losing the support, which he also needed, of the KMT pinks.

As soon as the news of Russian subversion in the KMT made the headlines, Chiang Kai-shek resurfaced at the head of a strong force outside Shanghai. The new Communist mayor, Chou En-lai, went into hiding. Chiang seized the municipal government of the Chinese city, and on April 12, 1927—Black Tuesday as it is now remembered in mainland China—his troops hunted down all Red officials. That afternoon he had 5,000 of them beheaded in the public squares. Chou En-lai slipped through the dragnet and escaped. But he and the other Communists never forgot or forgave. The Chinese revolutionary front of the KMT was split irreparably. From then on, whenever they were not fighting Japanese, the armies of Chiang and of the Communists engaged in civil warfare. It was a struggle deeper and more bitter than the rivalries of war lords, a struggle in which brother fought against brother and father against son, a struggle which would not end until two decades later when Chiang and over a million of his partisans were forced into exile on the island of Taiwan.

Chiang Kai-shek followed up Black Tuesday by further purges of Reds in all the towns of the lower Yangtze. Then, on April 18, 1927, he set up his own government of KMT moderates in Nanking. KMT leftists maintained their separate regime in Hankow, 300 miles upriver, but cleansed it of outright Communists. Blücher and Borodin, the KMT's two Russian advisors, returned to Moscow. Mao Tse-tung and Chou En-lai withdrew into the provinces. Ching-ling, the Communist widow of Sun Yat-sen, betook her dainty self into exile in Europe.

JAPAN CHANGES HORSES

Phase One of the cabal's plan for China was now complete. Phase Two required that Chang Tso-lin be kept from interfering while Chiang Kai-shek consolidated his position south of the Great Wall and Japan made off with the provinces north of the Wall. Up to now the Japanese Cabinet had stood for nonintervention in China. Now a Cabinet was needed which would be willing to intervene if necessary. Accordingly, on April 20, 1927, two days after the founding of the Chiang government in Nanking, Hirohito followed by appointing a new government in Tokyo. The fall of the old Cabinet was engineered by exposure of a financial scandal at a Privy Council meeting presided over by Hirohito in person.

On Saionji's recommendation, Hirohito accepted as the next prime minister Tanaka Gi-ichi, the successor to the late strong-man Yamagata as chieftain of the Choshu clan. To all appearances Tanaka was the perfect dupe to take responsibility for what was planned next. He was a big, bluff, hard-living sabre of a man, a tough-talking dandy infatuated with braid and dress uniforms, who had capitulated gracefully when voted down over the Army reorganization scheme by the Board of Field Marshals in 1925. Since then he had resigned voluntarily from the Army and had shown a desire to continue his career by accepting the presidency of the majority political party, the Constitutionalists. To Court analysts, he seemed to be an opportunist, ready to lead both Choshu and the Constitutionalists anywhere if it served his am-bition. But the analysts were mistaken. Tanaka had become a Constitutionalist mainly to resist Hirohito and restore Choshu leadership of the nation. He would pursue his plans with an apologetic bluster and suavity which were to thwart Hirohito's cabal at every turn for the next two years.

As a condition for taking office Prime Minister Tanaka agreed to delegate the detailed administration of foreign affairs to a par-liamentary vice minister recommended by Big Brother Konoye of the House of Peers.[5] In effect Tanaka agreed to take responsi-bility for foreign policy while giving over the making of it to others. It seemed incredible to Prime Minister Tanaka that a pack of young majors and ministry section chiefs—even though they might have the ear of the young Emperor—could pose any threat to the elders of the nation. He called a series of conferences with his friends in the upper echelons of the bureaucracy and agreed with them that a show of big get-tough-with-China talk would be enough to satisfy Hirohito. He summoned home the chief of Chang Tso-lin's Japanese military advisors and asked him to negotiate with Chang Tso-lin for the construction of five new Japanese railroads in Manchuria which might help in silencing

[5] Mori Kaku, a brash young man of forty, who had ridden on Prince Ko-noye's coattails for a decade.

Hirohito's young hawks. "I promise to co-operate with Chang Tso-lin in the administration of the railroads," Tanaka said. "If these plans are carried out, I can maintain order at home."

That same month, May 1927, the ubiquitous Major Suzuki left his post at the side of Chiang Kai-shek and was reassigned to Japan to help Konoye and the parliamentary vice minister of foreign affairs in implementing the second phase of the cabal's plan: the neutralization of Chang Tso-lin and the Japanese acquisition of Manchuria and Mongolia. Suzuki at once reconvoked the young Army officers who were graduates of the Lodging House and asked them to form a "study group" on the China problem.[6] The task of the Suzuki Study Group was to prepare position papers in defense of the cabal's planning—arguments which were to be laid before a full-dress conclave of Japanese elders, administrators, and colonials which the new parliamentary vice minister of foreign affairs had scheduled for late June.

While the cabal was mustering its arguments for the great debate, Prime Minister Tanaka advised Chang Tso-lin to withdraw his forces from China proper into Manchuria and make sure of his home province before it became too late. Chang Tso-lin replied indignantly:

I myself have advanced to Peking and am waging war on Communist influences. My war is Japan's war. What am I to make of Japan's good faith when, in spite of this fact, Japan is assisting Chiang Kai-shek, who has gone Red, and is advising me to return to Manchuria?

[6] In retrospect its roster would read like a who's who of Japanese fascism. It included one of Hirohito's aides-de-camp, Viscount Machijiri, who had been with Higashikuni in Paris; aide-de-camp Anami, the quiet young major who would live to kill himself as Japan's last war minister; Hashimoto Gun, who would organize the Marco Polo Bridge Incident which opened the 1937 war with China; Ishiwara Kanji, who would plan the occupation of Manchuria in 1931–32; Kusaba Tatsumi, who would commit suicide in a Russian plane in 1945 while en route to stand trial for atrocities done during his command of the Twenty-fifth Army in Malaya in 1942; Muto Akira, who would be chief of staff in the Philippines at the time of the rape of Manila in 1945; Suzuki Yorimichi of the General Staff's Operations Squad, who would command the Army Air Force on Pearl Harbor day; Tanaka Shinichi who would be chief of staff in Burma during the completion of the infamous Burma-Thailand railroad in 1944; Yokoyama Isamu who would be executed in 1946 for beheading downed U.S. pilots. Most of the study group had been introduced personally to Hirohito in Paris in 1921.

Chang followed his words, on June 18, by inaugurating a new policy with two objectives: on the one hand, politically, to reach a compromise with Chiang Kai-shek and woo him away from the KMT; on the other hand, militarily, to smash the KMT armies in one all-out offensive.

FAR EASTERN CONFERENCE

As Chang began to move troops south for a drive on Nanking, the great debate of the elders was opened in Tokyo at the foreign minister's residence in the same garden of atomic sunshine where Japanese leaders in 1946 would accept an American-made constitution. The debate lasted from June 27 to July 7, 1929, and was attended by all Japan's proconsuls—the generals and "experts" from Korea, Manchuria, and the legation listening posts in China proper. The meetings, which are collectively known to scholars as the Far Eastern Conference, were chairmanned and keynoted by the ubiquitous Major Suzuki Tei-ichi. Only Suzuki's own recollections of his opening address to the conference have emerged from the white water of subsequent history:

It was my aim to unify their ideas about the course that Japan should follow on the Continent. Most of us felt that Manchuria should be cut off from China proper and brought under Japan's political control. This required that Japan's whole policy—domestic, foreign, and military—should be concentrated on the achievement of this one goal. . . .

Unless Japan waged war, she would find it difficult to solve her Continental problems. . . . We knew . . . no minister in Tanaka's government would support such a plan.

Prime Minister Tanaka countered the schemes of Suzuki and the cabal by laying before the conference a comprehensive long-range program for the economic infiltration and exploitation of China, a program which, though frankly rapacious, would have been merely a continuation of classical Choshu clan policies. In an effort to please Hirohito, Tanaka presented his program in the most belligerent terms possible. When he had finished, one of his old comrades in arms, General Muto Nobuyoshi, arose. Muto was commander in chief of Japan's leasehold garrison in Manchuria, the tough Kwantung Army, and was known as "Muto the Silent." He had once ridden for ten hours on a train beside his chief of staff without uttering a single word. Now, however, he spoke at some length, objecting strenuously to Tanaka's program:

"Japan must be prepared to face a world war if such a drastic program is to be carried out. To begin with, America will not tolerate it. If America will not acquiesce, neither will England nor the rest of the Powers. Are you prepared to cope with America and the eventuality of a world war?"

"I am prepared to face the consequences," Tanaka replied.

"You are sure you will not waver later on, are you?" asked Muto.

"I am all set to face the worst," answered Tanaka.

"If the government is so determined," declared Muto, "I have nothing else to add. We shall wait for the order to come and simply carry it out."

Throughout the remaining days of the conference, Muto voiced not so much as another syllable. His timely opposition to Tanaka's program of economic aggression, however, made the alternative of armed aggression unthinkable. In vain the young staff officers of the Suzuki Study Group presented their own more ambitious plans. General Muto, on behalf of the Kwantung Army, looked on silently shaking his head. Finally, when the young men had completed their presentation, the other proconsuls voted overwhelmingly to accept Tanaka's proposal as the lesser of two evils. In the final analysis they agreed only to demand of Chang Tso-lin in northern China a number of specific rights similar to those stipulated in the Twenty-One Demands of a dozen years earlier.[7]

---

[7] The right to renew all present Japanese leases in China and to supply all future loans to China; the right to provide all arms for Manchurian-Mongolian wars and all ships for Manchurian-Mongolian commerce; the unrestricted right of Japanese to travel and trade on the Continent without being subject to Chinese criminal jurisdiction; the right to build and manage a dozen new railroads which would be useful in the event of war for carrying Japanese troops to the strategic garrison towns of North China.

TANAKA MEMORIAL

After the conference, on July 25, 1927, Tanaka presented a report to the Throne on the decision which had been made. Chinese intelligence agents tried to reconstruct this report by piecing together fragments which they had obtained of Tanaka's plan and of the position papers which had been delivered by members of the Suzuki Study Group. In their reconstruction the Chinese got the two points of view all mixed up. The result, which they published, became one of the most famous documents in Japanese history—a pastiche of truths adding up to a gigantic forgery. Under the title, *The Tanaka Memorial*, it was widely reprinted in the West, a few years later, as evidence of Japan's piratical aspirations. It permanently confused Western intelligence analysts, leading them to identify Tanaka and his Choshu-Constitutionalist faction with Japanese militarism.

According to the Chinese version of Tanaka's memorial to the Throne, Tanaka advised Emperor Hirohito that "the plan left to us by Emperor Meiji" was first to conquer Manchuria and Mongolia, then to occupy China, then to "crush the United States," and finally to subjugate all Asia "in order to conquer the world." In reality, according to knowledgeable courtiers, Tanaka warned Hirohito that military conquest of Manchuria, Mongolia, and China would lead inevitably to war with the United States and that Japan could not win such a war unless she had already gained economic control of Asia's raw materials and factories.

CHIANG GOES A-WOOING

Hirohito tabled the decision of the Far Eastern Conference at the bottom of his in-basket, and Chiang Kai-shek, closely questioned by colleagues about his ties with Japan, dramatically resigned his presidency of the KMT and retired to his villa to sulk. Chang Tso-lin, the northern war lord, descended on Chiang's capital of Nanking with a huge army and was fought to a standstill, in an epic engagement, by the noncommunist forces remaining in the KMT. Chang fell back toward Peking and the KMT armies

pursued him north. Hirohito's cabal in the Army demanded that
Japan abandon Chang Tso-lin to his fate and seize his home base,
Manchuria. Prime Minister Tanaka stolidly insisted: "Our government is taking the position that we negotiate with Chang Tso-lin
so long as he prevails in the north and likewise with Chiang Kai-
shek so long as he is in control of the south."

Emperor Hirohito called in for rebriefing the Japanese consul
general from the Manchurian capital of Mukden. This was the son-
in-law of Lord Privy Seal Count Makino and the future Peace-
Faction leader and American-Occupation-era prime minister,
Yoshida Shigeru. On instructions from the palace, Yoshida returned
to Mukden and approached the commander of the Kwantung
Army, Muto the Silent, with a proposition: why not deploy the
Kwantung Army to cut the Peking-Mukden railroad, making it
impossible for Chang Tso-lin to receive supplies from his home
base or to retreat to it? Muto bluntly refused to have any part in
the scheme without official orders, passed on by Prime Minister
Tanaka. A week later Hirohito stamped orders recalling Silent
Muto to a titular position of honor in Tokyo.

At this juncture Chiang Kai-shek, the temporarily retired president of the KMT, arrived in Japan, seeking clarification. Ostensibly he came for a personal reason: to court and marry Soong May-
ling, the noncommunist Wellesley daughter of the pink banker,
C. J. Soong. May-ling was summering with her family in Nagasaki
and it was thither that Chiang Kai-shek traveled first. He told the
Soong parents that he had divorced his former wife, given up his
stable of concubines, and was prepared to lead the irreproachable
life of a Western-style head of state. His future mother-in-law,
Madame Soong, asked him if he would now become a Christian
like the rest of her family. He replied that, no, he had no immediate conversion plans because Christianity was not a pill that a
man should take at a swallow. Madame Soong was struck by his
frankness.

While father and mother Soong were thinking over his proposal, Chiang left May-ling to plead his cause for him and went
up to Tokyo for three months. There he negotiated a clarification
of the future with the ubiquitous Major Suzuki, with the Emperor's
Big Brothers, and at second hand with Hirohito himself. There,

too, he visited with such old Pan-Asianist acquaintances as Chief of Army Intelligence Matsui Iwane, the general who would later be hanged unjustly as the "Butcher of Nanking." There, a photograph was taken of him squatting cross-legged on a *tatami* floor with Black Dragon Lord Toyama. Toyama, in kimono, with long white beard, was staring sagely off to his right, as if at some transcendental geometric proposition; Chiang, in Western business suit, with loud tie, was gazing directly at the camera with a smug, pucker-lipped half-smile.

At the meetings Chiang had with members of Hirohito's cabal no photographs were taken, but Chiang reconfirmed the bargain which both he and Sun Yat-sen before him had made with the Japanese: China's outer provinces of Manchuria and Mongolia in exchange for Japanese help and friendship during the unification of the Chinese heartland south of the Great Wall. Specifically, Chiang promised to make no more than token protests against Japanese actions north of the Wall if Japan would remain a friendly neutral during the civil war which he foresaw with the Communist leaders of the KMT who had survived Black Tuesday. Satisfied with the hedged manner in which he had made this compact, Chiang returned to Nagasaki to marry May-ling on December 27, 1927. In January 1928 he went back to Nanking, his new bride on his arm, and was at once re-elected to the leadership of the KMT.

Hirohito's cabal did not wait for the wedding or for Chiang's return to China to begin acting on their understanding with him. In November 1927 Big Brother Prince Konoye resigned from the Research Society in the Diet, which he had helped to found in 1921 and which had become the ruling circle in the House of Peers, and founded his own clique of twenty-one young imperialist noblemen, all close to Hirohito, which he dubbed the Tuesday Club. The Research Society, he said, had come to be dominated by reactionary old men who believed in war lords like Chang Tso-lin. It was one of the charter tenets of the Tuesday Club that alliance with Chiang Kai-shek might ultimately lead to a united Asia under Japanese leadership.

In early December 1927, Colonel Komoto Daisaku of the staff of the Kwantung Army—a member of the Suzuki Study Group and

also of the Eleven Reliables chosen at Baden-Baden—superintended the dynamiting of a small railroad bridge on a branch
line in Manchuria. He meant no special harm by the explosion. It
was simply a dry run. He wanted to make sure that the noise and
damage could be attributed to Chinese bandits. He was gratified
to discover that it could be—that Russian, Japanese, and even
Chinese newspapers all accepted the obvious explanation. He repeated the experiment several times on several different bridges
in the months that followed. The reaction was always the same:
bandits. The stage was set.

CHANG AT BAY

During Diet elections, in February 1928, agrarian reformers,
labor unionists, Communists, anarchists, and shockingly emanci-
pated *mobos* and *mogas*—"modern boys" and "modern girls"—
demonstrated vociferously against militarism and authoritarianism
in Japan. In March, the police arrested 5,000 of the troublemakers
and held them indefinitely without trial or bail. Hirohito forthwith approved a strengthening of the Peace Preservation Law, enabling the courts to exact the death penalty of political unde-
sirables. Even with this imperial easement the police, four years
later, in July 1932, were forced to let 4,520 of the so-called radicals
go free. Of the remaining 480, kept in jail, only 190 could ultimately be proved deserving of execution or prison sentences.

Shortly after the arrests, in May 1928, the Northern Expedition
of Chiang Kai-shek's KMT "Army of Liberation" reached the Shantung Peninsula where some 2,000 Japanese nationals lived in and
around the old German leasehold of Tsingtao. To help his old
friend Chang Tso-lin, Prime Minister Tanaka reinforced the
Japanese garrison in the area and thereby interposed a force which
would delay Chiang Kai-shek's advance. Hirohito puzzled his intimates by sanctioning the plan. To take charge of the expedition,
he appointed Lieutenant General Fukuda Hikosuke, a kinsman of
General Fukuda who had massacred Koreans after the 1923 earthquake. When Fukuda's officers met to parley with Chiang Kai-
shek's vanguard at the railhead of Tsinan in China a few days

later, a Japanese Special Service Organ agent,[8] working under the command of one of the Eleven Baden-Baden Reliables, fired a pistol from one of the nearby rooftops. Fukuda's men assumed that they were being attacked and promptly massacred 7,000 of the Chinese within easiest reach. In a nine-day reign of terror, Fukuda thoroughly discredited Prime Minister Tanaka's "intervention."

Chiang Kai-shek had his government protest the massacre in the usual polite terms of diplomacy. Then, knowing that it was a maneuver of domestic Japanese politics, he had his men bypass Tsinan and press on against Peking. On May 18, 1928, Field Marshal Prince Kanin, the elder of the imperial family, had an order sent to the Kwantung Army in Manchuria, asking it to be ready, on twenty-four-hour alert, to seize the Manchurian rail system and disarm Chang Tso-lin's soldiers if they attempted to retreat to Mukden. On the same day the Japanese diplomatic representative in Peking handed Chang his last ultimatum: either withdraw at once or be caught between Chiang Kai-shek and a hostile Kwantung Army. The old war-lord fox was trapped. He began to move his men secretly back to Mukden, laid elaborate cover plans for his own personal retreat, and at the same time shouted public defiance toward Chiang Kai-shek.

INTERNATIONAL MURDER

Assassination of another nation's political leader is a relatively simple tactic of statecraft but one which is rarely used because it invites reprisal in kind. Hirohito turned to it in 1928 out of frustration and spite. In so doing he rounded a corner and gave Japan the name of a killer nation in the West.

On May 21, 1928, taking full advantage of Japan's ownership of

[8] The Special Service Organs were branches of Army and Navy Intelligence, specializing in political intrigue. They were attached to all Japanese garrisons overseas and were usually housed blatantly in substantial concrete buildings of their own. As will be described later in more detail, they worked closely with all agencies of Japanese subversion including the Opium Board, the Secret Police, Military Intelligence, and Japan's shadowy, supragovernmental Civilian Spy Service.

the South Manchuria railroad, the headquarters of the Kwantung Army and a few crack Japanese regiments moved 250 miles north from Port Arthur into Mukden, Manchuria's capital city. There the Japanese forces, surrounded by an ocean of Chinese, waited tensely to carry out the disarming of Chang Tso-lin.

Through intermediaries, Prime Minister Tanaka informed the American Embassy in Tokyo that a flammable situation existed, and suddenly from across the Pacific, the U.S. government spoke up, warning Japan not to take unilateral action without first consulting the Powers. Prime Minister Tanaka's de facto foreign minister, the parliamentary vice minister for foreign affairs, stormed from ministry to ministry in Tokyo trying to prevent influential bureaucrats from paying heed to the American warning. The disarming of Chang Tso-lin's forces, he argued, was "a predetermined plan" and therefore could not be shelved without great sacrifice of national prestige. Many were prepared to agree with him, but that evening a general and a diplomat who were disciples of the old lute player Prince Saionji visited Prime Minister Tanaka at his villa in the suburb of Kamakura. Walking on the beach with him, they persuaded him to do his utmost to restrain the young bloods who had Hirohito's ear. The next morning, May 26, without consulting anyone, Tanaka cabled the Kwantung Army chief of staff to cancel the scheduled disarming.

Once again the Throne had suffered a rebuff. Short of a public confrontation with Prime Minister Tanaka and the elders of Japan, Hirohito could do nothing. The members of his cabal vented their collective spleen on Chang Tso-lin. Chang's son, Chang Hsueh-liang, was reputed to be an admirer of Chiang Kai-shek. Possibly, if Chang Tso-lin were dead, the son might understand Chiang Kai-shek's bargain with Japan and agree to serve as Japan's puppet.

The planning of Chang Tso-lin's murder was entrusted to Major General Tatekawa Yoshiji, a protégé of Field Marshal Prince Kanin, the imperial family elder who had presided over the previous attempt on Chang's life in 1916. Suave, chubby, inscrutable, Tatekawa was known to his friends as the "Man Snatcher" or the "Peerless Pimp." He was a charter member of the imperial cabal. During the war with Russia he had organized a group of irregulars, the Tatekawa Volunteers, to work with Chang Tso-lin and other Chinese bandits behind Russian lines. After the war he had been decorated by Emperor Meiji and had become a favorite at the palace. In March 1928 he had been transferred from the important post of European and American intelligence chief in the General Staff to that of attaché at the Japanese Embassy in Peking. In that lowly capacity he had been visiting and watching Chang Tso-lin for two months.

In May 1928 Tatekawa dispatched a fellow attaché to Mukden to advise the new commander of the Kwantung Army in Manchuria of the cabal's latest plan. Leaving the commander's office, the attaché encountered Reliable Komoto, the experimental dynamiter, who had now blown up a dozen of Manchuria's sturdiest bridges. The attaché told Komoto that Chang Tso-lin was to be assassinated by a hired cutthroat in Peking. Komoto begged leave to handle the assignment himself. It would be so much more poetic if Chang, who had escaped dynamiting in 1916, should fall by it now. The attaché promptly wired Tatekawa in Peking that Komoto had accepted the assignment.

On June 2, Chang Tso-lin circularized his commanders by telegram to let them know that he had finally decided to withdraw into his Manchurian homeland beyond the Great Wall. Major General Tatekawa, the Peerless Pimp, had a man ready in the Peking rail yards, studying the composition and routing of all trains moving north. The man was Captain Tanaka Takayoshi, later American Prosecutor Keenan's star witness at the Tokyo war crimes trials. On May 30, 1928, three days before Chang Tso-lin announced his decision to return home, the elephant-memoried Tanaka wired Komoto in Mukden a provisional report on train scheduling in Peking.

In Mukden, Komoto was prepared for any train which might pass. Outside Mukden, where the Chinese-owned Peking-Mukden rail line ran under the Japanese-owned Dairen-Mukden line, Komoto had had his men bury three bags of blasting powder, wired to a plunger on a nearby hill. Three Manchurian soldiers with a grudge against Chang Tso-lin were hired to stand sentry duty over the section of Chinese track where the charges had been planted.

After Chang Tso-lin's beaten soldiers had been pouring into Mukden for days, Chang finally boarded a train to follow them. Having heard rumors of a Japanese plot against him, he sent his "number-five wife" and other dispensable members of his suite ahead of him in a yellow train of seven coaches exactly like his own. When it had been on its way for six or seven hours, his own train left its siding in the Peking yards, at 1:15 A.M. on June 3. Three of its passengers were Japanese officers who had long been his military advisors. Two of the three got off the train when it stopped in Tientsin at daybreak. The third, Major Giga Nobuya, remained aboard. Chang knew Major Giga to be a henchman of Prince Kanin and therefore felt safe from dynamite as long as Giga was close at hand to share fate with him.

About five the following afternoon a Japanese spotter, posted by Major General Tatekawa, confirmed the passage of Chang's train through the Great Wall of China at the border town of Shanhai-kwan. The men of Reliable Komoto reported it rolling through Chinchow station in Manchuria during the night. Sightings further along the line of a similar train led to momentary confusion in Mukden, and Komoto's assistants were all set to blow up the decoy. Fortunately for Chang's number-five wife, the distinction between the two trains was sorted out in time from the rising drift of intelligence telegrams, and the pretty young creature was allowed to pass unmolested into Mukden about midnight.

As Chang's train bowled through the dark across the flat Manchurian plains, he and his suite, including the Japanese Major Giga, sat up playing mah-jongg. In Mukden, where it was clear now that the train would not arrive until five or six A.M., some of the conspirators napped in town and some at their posts near the railroad overpass half a mile outside of town. By the time that the sky had begun to lighten with a promise of dawn, all of them had rendezvoused by bicycle at the bridge. On the theory that dead men tell no tales, Komoto's men stole up on the three Manchurian soldiers who had been bribed to stand sentry duty and rushed them with fixed bayonets. One escaped in the darkness. The corpses of the other two were laid by the railroad track and tricked out with forged orders from one of Chang's tributary bandit lords. In their stiffening hands were planted Russian-made bombs bought at a secondhand store in Tokyo and donated to the cause by the general in charge of the Tokyo secret police.

On the onrushing train, when it was a few miles from Mukden, the gambling game broke up and the players hurried back to their respective cars to assemble their gear for arrival. Chang Tso-lin and Governor Wu of the province of Hailar nodded over the scattered mah-jongg tiles and spent bottles of beer. Japanese Major Giga snatched a blanket from his berth, ran to the caboose, wrapped himself up, and lay down on the rear platform. On a convenient knoll nearby, Komoto's chief assistant, Captain Tomiya Tetsuo, watched tensely as the train entered the underpass, and at the precise moment that Chang's own car passed over the explosive, he pushed the plunger. There was a dramatic puff of fire and black smoke, and the car jumped shattered from the track. Chang and Governor Wu were both dead along with seventeen of their retainers. Giga, merely shaken, leapt from the caboose as the train dragged to a halt, rushed forward to the remains of Chang's carriage, and is reported to have exclaimed with great feeling, "Ah, how dreadful!"

The other conspirators, appearing at the site of the wreck, announced that they had just bayoneted the criminals responsible. It was a flimsy story at best, and the third Manchurian sentry, who had escaped in the dark, knew the truth. He found his way to Chang Tso-lin's son, Chang Hsueh-liang, and told his story. But the young Chang feared that he might push Japan into war if he caused her to lose face. Therefore he had his officials gravely bear his father's body to hospital and did not announce the success of the assassination until it seemed sure, almost two weeks later, that war could be avoided. In the meantime Peking attaché Major General Tatekawa, the Peerless Pimp, professed to be so "shocked" at what had taken place that he burned all relevant telegrams in his possession.

IMPERIAL IMPENITENCE

Hirohito, after Chang Tso-lin's murder, was in a mood of defiant self-confidence. He had been trained from childhood to be above ordinary Japanese feelings of pride in face. He exulted in the downfall of old bandit Chang Tso-lin and expected Prime Minister Tanaka to take responsibility for it. If Tanaka was sensible he would conduct a token investigation of the assassination and mete out nominal punishment to a handful of loyal Army officers. If Tanaka was not sensible he would be condemned by the reverent, taboo-conscious Japanese electorate for trying to hide behind the sleeve of the dragon and foist off his responsibilities on the sacred Throne.

Nine days after Chang Tso-lin's assassination Hirohito gave public indication of his mood by having a banquet of celebration in the palace. The occasion was a routine one: the Feast of the Five Families, held annually to honor the five branches of the Fujiwara clan which served as the innermost veil in Hirohito's government from behind the curtain. Without precedent, however, Japanese newsmen were allowed to look in on the proceedings, to note that they were merry, and to publish the names of the six notables who sat at Hirohito's table. All six were personal acquaintances of Chang Tso-lin's assassin, the Baden-Baden Reliable, Colonel Komoto Daisaku.

Prime Minister Tanaka at once paid a call on old Prime-Minister-Maker Saionji at his seaside villa in the fishing village of Okitsu. Guardedly he told Saionji that "the Chang Tso-lin affair" must be disposed of and that some of Hirohito's most trusted Army familiars were almost certainly involved in it. How was he, the humble prime minister and front man of imperial government, to handle the matter?

The seventy-eight-year-old Saionji considered the question well before replying. As the elder of the Fujiwara family, he had the duty always of being a friend to the Throne and an apologist for it. As a pro-Western liberal who had helped to frame the Constitution, he must also disapprove of Hirohito's recent policies. All the best and brightest of Japan's heredity aristocrats looked up to him for leadership.

Prime Minister Tanaka waited patiently for an answer. Saionji had aged greatly in recent years and had suffered a succession of personal tragedies. One by one all his boon companions had died, including his younger brother, the millionaire. Moreover, Flower Child, the mistress he had taken to Versailles, had had a child by a young lover and Saionji had felt compelled to banish her from his bed and board. Now he was all alone.

Choosing his words carefully, Saionji finally replied: "Wrong-doing is wrongdoing and must be punished accordingly. It would be bad for military discipline if we did less." With this preface Saionji exhorted Prime Minister Tanaka to probe the assassination of Chang Tso-lin "to the bottom" and "do it bravely."

Tanaka asked warily if it would be proper to sound out Hiro-hito in person and make sure that this was also the Emperor's view. Saionji assured Tanaka that it would be "extraordinarily proper." So Tanaka did go to Hirohito, and Hirohito coolly assured him that he wanted no semblance of impropriety or of Army insubordination in his government.

At Hirohito's suggestion, Prime Minister Tanaka sent the chief of the Tokyo Secret Police, Major General Mine Komatsu, to Manchuria to make an on-the-spot investigation. Mine was an apt choice for he was already an expert on the affair, having supplied the Russian-made bombs found in the hands of the dead sentries beside the railroad track. In mid-August 1928 he submitted his preliminary findings. They were burdened with details of track measurements, train schedules, and bomb techniques but delicately vague as to the names of the assassins. Mine suggested, however, that certain officers around Colonel Komoto, the perennial bridge blower, had been remiss in seeing to the security of Chang Tso-lin's train and should perhaps be transferred and reprimanded.

Hirohito urged Prime Minister Tanaka to take the disciplinary action suggested and close the case as quickly as possible. Tanaka, however, knew the Mine report to be a whitewash and was encouraged by old lute-player Saionji to keep the case open as long as possible.

When Tanaka failed to lay Chang's ghost, Hirohito took a step which would increase his secret power to undercut the prime minister's authority. On August 21, 1928, he had a phone installed in his study. It was a precedent-shattering innovation, with a set of push buttons, which gave him instant access to all his aides on the palace grounds. Previously he had had to delegate his communication with the outside world entirely to slow, gossipy intermediaries. Now he could phone one of the ministers of the vast imperial family fortune and exercise his influence immediately on the financial world. His various political chamberlains could be summoned individually to his study without the chamberlain on duty knowing why they had been called. Most important, the Army and Navy aides-de-camp could put him through on their own private tie lines direct to the War Ministry and General Staff offices outside the palace walls. In using his new phone, Hirohito exposed himself not at all, for he never identified himself on the phone but trusted that his respondent on the other end of the line would recognize his voice.[9]

On August 27, 1928, a few days after the installation of the phone, Prime Minister Tanaka's relationship with the Throne deteriorated further when his subordinates in the Foreign Ministry signed the Kellogg-Briand Pact in Paris, outlawing war as a legitimate instrument of statecraft. It was a triumph for Saionji, Tanaka, and the Constitutionalists because they knew that Hirohito, as national high priest, could never come out openly against the idea of peace. The Tokyo press and public greeted the treaty with applause. Hirohito, however, referred it to the Privy Council over which he presided, asking that a thorough study be made of the wording of the treaty before he signed it. The loyal privy councillors quickly found a fault and attacked Prime Minister Tanaka for having allowed the pact to be signed "in the names of the respective peoples." This wording, said the councillors, violated the Japanese Constitution by enthroning the people in the Emperor's place and by denying the Emperor his explicit constitutional right to declare war in defense of the nation. Before Hirohito would sign the treaty, Tanaka was forced to notify other signatory nations that the pact was understood not to compromise Japan's right of self-defense and that the objectionable phrase "in the names of the respective peoples" did not apply to Japan.

On September 9, 1928, when Prime Minister Tanaka found himself at odds with Hirohito over the Kellogg-Briand Pact, he

[9] Several American historians have used the phrase "without even a phone" to describe Hirohito's supposed isolation in the palace. The installation of the phone was reported by *Mainichi*, the great Tokyo daily, on August 22, 1928. Hirohito's use of it is described several times in the diaries of Big Brother Harada, the political secretary to Saionji.

harkened to the pleas of old Saionji and ordered Secret Police Chief Mine back to Manchuria to conduct a more thorough investigation of Chang Tso-lin's murder. On September 22, Tanaka followed by convoking a committee of Diet Constitutionalists to deliberate on the Chang Tso-lin affair under the eyes of newspaper reporters. On October 8, while the committee was still sitting, Secret Police Chief Mine submitted his second report, "top secret." Tanaka at once recessed his political investigators and reassessed his political position. Mine's second report implicated not only Hirohito but many of Prime Minister Tanaka's own oldest and closest Army friends. Tanaka had never before appreciated fully the breadth of Hirohito's Army backing and the depth of its planning.

In the days that followed, Tanaka was given further evidence to make him hesitate and to convince him that Hirohito was in earnest. On October 10, he learned that the Army Engineering Corps at Tumen, on the northern border between Korea and Manchuria, had just completed a railroad bridge which led nowhere at the moment but which stood ready to be connected with a northern terminus of the Manchurian railroad system in the event that the Army should need a second strategic entryway into Manchuria. A few days later he heard that Lieutenant Colonel Ishiwara Kanji, the most brilliant strategist in the ubiquitous Major Suzuki's Study Group, had been posted to the Kwantung Army to begin staff planning for the conquest of Manchuria.[10]

Once more Tanaka consulted Prime-Minister-Maker Saionji. Once more Saionji encouraged Tanaka to pursue his investigation of the Chang Tso-lin affair, to let the chips fall where they might, and to keep Hirohito fully informed of all implications as the case developed.

Prime Minister Tanaka returned from Saionji's villa on the beach, without making any promises. Basically a somewhat honest, simple man, never sure of himself in his role of antagonist to the Throne, he became frightened by the subtlety of the situation in which he found himself. Finally, after a week of anguish, he decided to forget the Chang Tso-lin case and smother

---

[10] Strategist Ishiwara later testified at the war crimes trials that he had orders from the Emperor "to use force if necessary."

it with inaction. He conceded warily to Hirohito that a suitable show of discipline might have to be meted out to certain Japanese Army officers. And he protested noncommittally to Saionji that nothing could be done at present because everyone in official Tokyo was preparing for the imminent ceremony of Hirohito's official enthronement in the old capital of Kyoto.

On November 10, 1928, Western correspondents followed Hirohito's progress from the Kyoto railroad station to the palace where Emperor Meiji had been born. There a few select Japanese saw him mount the antique lacquered throne of his ancestors and stood by as witnesses when he withdrew into a cluster of specially constructed ceremonial huts on the palace grounds for an all-night solitary vigil with the presence of the sun goddess. Throughout the next month, Hirohito's popularity ran high and he seemed unusually dedicated and preoccupied. Prime Minister Tanaka ignored representations from Saionji and let the Chang Tso-lin matter slumber.

THE BANDIT'S SON

Chang Hsueh-liang, the thirty-year-old son of the murdered Chang Tso-lin, was a dope addict. During a bout of influenza, a Japanese doctor had dosed him with opium and he had caught the habit. The Japanese assumed he was debilitated. He seemed to them a war-lord's spoiled child, who had traveled abroad and acquired the manners of a Western gentleman. But Chang Hsueh-liang had kept a firm grasp on the realities of politics in his homeland.

Beneath his silken exterior, Chang had the same courage, cunning, and ruthlessness as his father. In addition he had a streak of idealism in him which made him devoted to the cause of Republicanism in China, the cause ostensibly of Chiang Kai-shek. Over the years he was to become Chiang Kai-shek's conscience, a constant reminder of the ideals which Chiang Kai-shek often lost sight of in pursuit of means. A David-and-Jonathan relationship would grow up between the two. It still exists to this day, 1970, when Chang Hseuh-liang, now seventy-one, remains a pampered prisoner, under house arrest, in the Taiwan of Chiang Kai-shek, who is now eighty-two.

The strange firm friendship between these two politicians—both renowned for their harems, their evident heterosexuality—began in the fall of 1928 when Chiang Kai-shek, at the behest of the Japanese, recognized Chang Hseuh-liang as the new ruler of Manchuria. On December 29, 1928, Chang Hsueh-liang responded by raising the KMT flag on every government building around Mukden. In the early stages of opium addiction, burning his candle fervidly at both ends, Chang felt that Chiang must be reminded of Manchuria's organic place in the body of China. He realized, too, that the Japanese would consider his gesture a hostile act, violating the spirit of their unwritten agreement with Chiang Kai-shek.

He was right. In the first week of January 1929, Japanese agents began to post anti-Chang handbills on walls throughout the three Manchurian provinces. The text of one of them—totally at variance with the facts—stated in part:

Since Chang Tso-lin captured the Three Eastern Provinces . . . good people have suffered from his evil government, causing the neighboring powers to interfere in our domestic affairs. For this reason heavenly punishment was inflicted upon him and he fell under a bomb. The son, Chang Hsueh-liang, who succeeded him is worse than his father to such an extent that the land has been turned red and the sufferings of the people are beyond description.

To this challenge the thirty-year-old Chang Hsueh-liang responded with a bravado that caught up Chiang Kai-shek and carried him in its political rip tide. Chang and Chiang both knew that the only hope for preserving the integrity of Manchuria, short of defeating a Japanese attempt at conquest, lay in making Manchuria seem an exploitable puppet state, in effect playing for time. Old hands in the Japanese Army had hoped to manipulate the young Manchurian leader through a general named Yang Yu-tang and through the chief of the Chinese railroads in Manchuria. But on January 10, 1929, young, idealistic Chang Hsueh-liang, suffering from withdrawal during one of his earliest attempts to kick the opium habit, confounded everyone by inviting these two worthies to an evening of mah-jongg in his Mukden palace and having them both shot as they entered the game room. He announced that Yang had conspired with Tokyo to become the chief executive of a Japanese-managed Manchurian Republic. At the same time he sent 100,000 Manchurian dollars—some 40,000 U.S. ones—to Yang's widow. Every Chinese patriot applauded his merciful dispatch and liberal generosity.

FACE WASHING

Chiang Kai-shek was impressed by the popular support which Chang Hsueh-liang had uncovered and refused to disassociate himself from it. For the first time Hirohito's Big Brothers began to talk of Chiang Kai-shek as an enemy. Bitter "re-evaluation of the Manchuria problem" filled the front pages of Tokyo newspapers. The American manager of United Press in the Orient, Miles W. Vaughn, reported home that the only question was whether Japan's Kwantung Army would seize Manchuria at once or wait, "believing that an opportunity will soon present itself to take not only Manchuria but most of North China as well."

Colonel Komoto Daisaku, the unpunished Reliable who had murdered Chang Tso-lin, cabled a memo to Hirohito and the General Staff, stating: "Any rational and thorough disposition of outstanding issues in Manchuria and Mongolia must start with the elimination of the Nanking government [of Chiang Kai-shek], to which end a war with China must be expected, and one with the U.S., too, must be considered."

Hirohito was not yet prepared to abandon his hopes for Chiang Kai-shek or to alienate the rest of the world. Field Marshal Prince Kanin, the senior member of the imperial family, warned that Manchuria was a huge country and could not be occupied without careful military planning. Young Prince Konoye, Hirohito's chosen familiar from the Fujiwara family, warned that domestic opinion was not yet prepared for a war of conquest. Prime-Minister-Maker Saionji, the Fujiwara elder, inferior to Konoye in hereditary rank but vastly superior to him in seniority and influence, showed every inclination to cause real trouble if an attempt were made to seize

Manchuria now. All through February and March of 1929 Saionji's friends spread rumors in Constitutionalist circles that, if the investigation of Chang Tso-lin's murder were pursued, Hirohito's "august face would be muddy."

Hirohito refused to be embarrassed but saw that he must proceed with caution. He let the members of the cabal know that they must plan the conquest of Manchuria thoroughly, down to the last rifle bullet. While preparations were in progress, he asked that the imperial face be cleared of all taint. Through Lord Privy Seal Count Makino, he arranged for two of the most loyal members of the cabal to shoulder some of the responsibility for the failure of the cabal's China policy. The ubiquitous Major Suzuki Tei-ichi was sent on a ten-month leave to Europe, and Big Brother Kido Koichi, at work on industrial mobilization plans in the Agriculture and Commerce Ministry, was persuaded to take a year's sabbatical in the United States. The two rustications were meant to indicate to the informed public that events in China had displeased Hirohito and that he had privately punished two of the men responsible for them. Having made these gestures, Hirohito went ahead undaunted with his secret military planning and insistently pressed Prime Minister Tanaka for a satisfactory burial of the Chang Tso-lin scandal.

In April 1929 Hirohito summoned the commanders of Japan's seventeen standing divisions for their annual individual audiences with him. This year they were known to have two worries which Hirohito sought to allay. They feared that Chang Tso-lin's murder would set a precedent of action without official imperial orders that might undermine Army discipline. And they were excited by rumors of secret General Staff planning for a full-scale invasion of Manchuria. It was Hirohito's task to tell the division chiefs that Komoto would be punished for Chang Tso-lin's murder and to make clear to them that the General Staff's blueprints for Manchuria were contingency plans which would be used or modified according to events. As the division chiefs entered and withdrew from Hirohito's presence, Hirohito learned from an aide that he was making the right impression and that the division chiefs would support him fully.

Prime Minister Tanaka discovered that, after Hirohito had applied his magic touch, the murder of Chang Tso-lin was no longer an issue worth mentioning. Nevertheless, at Saionji's bidding, Tanaka refused to settle the dust by staging a nominal show of disciplinary action. On June 28, 1929, Hirohito finally called Tanaka to the Throne Room and asked him, disingenuously, if the Chang Tso-lin case were yet solved. Tanaka replied that, after all, despite his previous reports, no Army staff officers were implicated but only policemen and the like who could be disciplined by administrative action at a low level. In effect Tanaka was refusing to stage the mock trials which Hirohito had requested and was trying to tell the public that his investigations had led to the taboo gates of the palace.

In great displeasure Hirohito dismissed Tanaka with a wave of the hand and one icy statement of fact: "What you say now differs from your previous explanations." As soon as Tanaka had bowed himself from the audience chamber, Hirohito summoned Grand Chamberlain Suzuki Kantaro, the clever old cigar-smoking Taoist who would stand beside the Throne as prime minister during the last desperate, plot-filled months of World War II. "I cannot understand what Tanaka says," complained Hirohito to Suzuki. "I do not ever wish to see him again."

When the sentence of banishment from the Imperial Presence was repeated to Tanaka, he wept. He asked several times thereafter for an audience but was always refused. And so, three days later, without notifying his Cabinet or the Constitutionalist party whip beforehand, he abruptly had his resignation delivered to the Throne. It was accepted immediately, and no future prime minister of Japan would ever again venture to oppose Hirohito so openly.

Three months later, in the early morning hours of September 29, 1929, Tanaka died. It was widely rumored that he had committed suicide as a gesture of patriotic protest against national policy. According to a more explicit account, however, which was circulated with relish by members of the Court, he attended a political rally, got drunk, and later expired in the arms of his geisha mistress.

In May 1929, a few days after Hirohito's audiences with the Army division chiefs, War Minister Shirakawa had complied with imperial wishes and reposted Colonel Komoto, the bridge blower, to a stand-by position with the 9th Division in Kanazawa on the Japanese north coast. In July, when Tanaka resigned as prime minister, Komoto had been officially stripped of command and given a year to find himself before being mustered out into the first reserve. Token amends were thus made for Chang Tso-lin's murder, and both Hirohito and Chang Hsueh-liang pretended to be satisfied that the incident was closed. In fact Komoto had been rewarded, for he would remain in Manchuria enjoying various sinecures in the business world and amassing a small fortune. Today his son, Komoto Toshio, is a prominent industrialist, a Diet man, and an inner member of Japan's ruling Liberal Democratic party.

The other conspirators in Chang's assassination went unpunished. In August 1929, Major General Tatekawa, the Peerless Pimp, was promoted chief of the key Second Department of the General Staff: Army Intelligence.

There was one conspirator, however, whom the Chinese were not disposed to let off so easily. Giga Nobuya, the man wrapped in a blanket on the caboose of the murder train, was promoted after the killing to lieutenant colonel. Since he had been one of Chang Tso-lin's closest advisors for many years, partisans of the dead war lord felt that he had played Judas. They hunted him from Mukden in Manchuria to Hiroshima in southern Japan, to Sendai in northern Japan, to Tsitsihar on the Manchurian-Siberian frontier. In 1937 Prince Kanin's son turned over to him a walled villa in Tientsin as a secure place of hiding. But to no avail; there on January 24, 1938, after a decade's stalking, a Manchurian assassin finally reached him with a bullet. Thus young Chang made at least a token revenge to dispel the curse which, according to the Chinese Book of Rites, falls "on him who suffers his father's murderer to exist on the same earth with him."

JAPAN'S PREWAR GOVERNMENT

EMPEROR   NOBILITY   PEOPLE

People — Diet

Function: to approve or veto *increases* in national budget and to discuss legislation presented by prime minister to Emperor

House of Representatives (Lower House)
466 politicians elected by some 14 million eligible male voters (out of population of 70 million, 1940)

House of Peers
to guide House of Representatives; included:
66 rich men elected by the 6,000 highest taxpayers in Japan
150 of lesser nobility elected by the 1,000-odd adult male members of same
all princes and marquises
125 imperial nominees selected for eruditon or meritorious service

Emperor — Cabinet

Prime Minister: appointed by Emperor on advice of Prince Saionji and elder statesmen; until 1932, often the head of a political party
Foreign Minister
  Foreign Ministry
  Ambassadors
Home Minister
  Thought Police
  Tokyo (Metropolitan) Police
  Prefectural governors and prefectural police
Finance
  Board of the Budget
  Bank of Japan
  Yokohama Specie Bank
War
  Military Affairs Bureau
  Military Affairs Section
  Aviation Headquarters
  Personnel Bureau
    Appointments Section
  Soldiers' Affairs Bureau
  Army Investigation Committee
  Press Relations Squad
  Secret Police: semi-autonomous, responsible to commanders overseas and expected to work with Home and Justice
  Prisoner of War Administration (founded 1942)
Navy: administered naval affairs through bureaucracy similar to War Minister's
Justice
  Courts
  Judges

Emperor — General Staffs

Army Chief of Staff
General Affairs Bureau
  Organization and Mobilization Section
  First Department: Operations
  Second Department: Intelligence
    Russia Desk
    Europe-America Desk
    China Desk
  Special Service Organs: political counterintelligence overseas
  Third Department: Transport and Communications
Kwantung Army
Korean Army
North China Army
Taiwan Army
Tokyo Guard
War College
Navy Chief of Staff
  First Department: Operations
  Second Department: Intelligence
Commander-in-Chief, Combined Fleet
  First Fleet
  Second Fleet
  etc.
Naval Staff College

Inspectorships

Inspector General of Military Education
  Military Academy
  Tank, Signal, Infantry, other specialized schools

Palace Institutions

Imperial Family Councillors: all adult male members of the imperial family down to fifth generation in descent from an Emperor; through most of Hirohito's reign, 25 princes: to advise Emperor on matters affecting family, e.g., property, marriages, princely peccadillos, major decisions of state

Privy Councillors: 26 elder statesmen appointed by Emperor on advice of prime minister: to advise Emperor on any question he refers to it for opinion

Lord Privy Seal: to give Emperor day-to-day political advice
Secretary and staff: to keep track of imperial seals and all documents of state to which they are affixed
Imperial tombs and shrines
Imperial archives
Peerage and Heraldry Bureau: to keep track of all noble houses
Peers' and Peeresses' Schools
Code Research Institute
Spy Service Directorship, to co-ordinate and keep track of all Japanese espionage; roughly equivalent to C.I.A.

Grand Chamberlain: to advise Emperor on matters of his personal health and recreation and, in practice, on matters of international diplomacy
Board of Chamberlains: stewards, butlers, grooms, etc.

Board of Ceremonials
Court Physicians' Bureau
Bureau of Imperial Cuisine
Imperial Stables Bureau
Imperial Poetry Bureau
Imperial Recreations Board
Households of Crown Prince, Empress, Empress Dowager

Imperial Household Minister: to supervise and manage imperial fortune; investments, rents from 3.2 million acres of crown lands, upkeep of 23 secondary palaces
Imperial Treasury
Maintenance and Works Bureau
Board of Imperial Auditors

Chief Imperial Aide-de-Camp: to advise Emperor on military matters
Imperial Naval Aide-de-Camp
Other aides-de-camp

Supreme War Council: High-ranking Army and Navy officers appointed by Emperor—the military counterpart of the Privy Council
Board of Field Marshals and Fleet Admirals

Imperial Headquarters: Founded 1937 to centralize Emperor's command functions in palace; top ministers and bureau chiefs from General Staff and War and Navy ministries plus permanent palace staff to co-ordinate all war plans and maps for Emperor's reference

Military preparatory schools
Inspector General of Military Aviation
Air schools, research institutes, cartel liaison committees

Prosecutors
Education
Schools
Government publications and propaganda
Commerce and Industry
Agriculture and Forestry
Communications
Railways
Colonization
Prosperous Asia Institute: semi-autonomous, to administer occupied areas in China
South Sea Development Board: semi-autonomous, to administer conquests in Southeast Asia
Welfare
National health
Food rationing
Cabinet Planning Board; to write all legislation discussed by Diet (began as inspection board, 1935; became planning board, 1941, and took charge of all domestic legislation and mobilization for the war

PART FOUR

※

RUBICON MANCHURIA

10

SEA POWER

(1929–1930)

CHOICE OF A LION

On the evening of July 3, 1929, the seventy-nine-year-old Prime-Minister-Maker Saionji had his chauffeur drive up past Ueno Park in Tokyo so that he could get out for a short walk among the people and the plum trees.[1] It was dusk and the plainclothesmen assigned to him hovered behind at a respectful distance. A group of office workers were picnicking under the trees, dancing tangos and Charlestons to the records of a wind-up Victrola. Two of the men, over their bottles of beer, were talking with vociferous pride about Tokyo's growing subway system, opened in 1927. Two others were acclaiming a levelheaded editorial in *Mainichi* which came out for nonintervention in China and reduction in armaments. Their girl friends, flirting and frolicking in the summer heat, seemed altogether unself-conscious in their chic Western cloche hats, silk stockings, and gauzy, high-hemmed dresses. Never had the smiling people of Tokyo appeared more peaceable, pleasure-loving, and modern.

Saionji was gratified by what he saw. "The trend of the times,"

[1] This and the two succeeding vignettes of men's minds that night are based on the recollections and assumptions of friends who met the principals during the weeks following. I have added some explanatory background information to make the thoughts intelligible.

as he told a friend a few days later, was running against "palace imperialism." There would be no place soon for police despotism and militarism in Japan. In the end Hirohito would have to bow to the sentiments of his people and relinquish the warlike ambitions of his youth.

Saionji had come up to Tokyo to recommend to Hirohito a successor for General Tanaka, the prime minister who had been made the villain of the Chang Tso-lin killing. Tanaka was the president of the Constitutionalist party. Hirohito was accustomed to thinking of the other party, the anti-Constitutionalists, as pliant instruments of the Throne. And so, when Saionji had nominated the president of the anti-Constitutionalists as the next prime minister, Hirohito had accepted with alacrity.

Saionji, however, had high hopes that the new government would show a mind of its own. Its prime minister, Hamaguchi Osachi, was a tiny man of humble parentage. His stubborn convictions and fiery indignation had won him the nickname of "the Lion." He had been responsible, in 1927, for uniting all the various anti-Constitutionalist tongs founded by friends of the Throne in the past and for proclaiming them a new mass party, responsive to the needs of constituents and capable of presenting the Constitutionalists with their first professionally managed political opposition.[2] Saionji had backed and had arranged cartel financing for the new party from its inception. He saw promise in its existence of a mature, two-party system which might become increasingly difficult for anyone to manipulate from the back rooms of the palace.

The foreign minister in Lion Hamaguchi's new cabinet was Baron Shidehara Kijuro.[3] Like most diplomats he was inclined to say what was expected of him but Saionji considered him basically a well-meaning man. His statement on assuming office called for "co-existence and co-prosperity" with China. Saionji had looked over the text that very afternoon and had approved it. He could not know that the term co-prosperity, as later used in Japan's

[2] Trading on the magic of the Constitutionalists' own name, Hamaguchi had named the new party the *Rikken Minseito* or Democratic Constitutionalists.

[3] Later the "moderate of the Peace Faction" who would become prime minister under MacArthur in October 1945.

World War II "Co-Prosperity Sphere," would acquire an infamous place in history as a byword of hypocritical propaganda.

Saionji returned the next morning to his home, Sit-and-Fish Villa, on the seashore at Okitsu. He was pleased with the new government he had arranged for Japan and settled back complacently into the pastimes of his retired life: the reading of risqué French novels and the carving of signature-seals and cane handles for old friends.

YOUNG ARMY GENIUS

The same evening that Saionji took his stroll in Ueno Park to look at the people, a group of Japanese Army officers, a thousand miles to the west, crossed the border between Japan's leasehold on the Kwantung Peninsula and Manchuria proper. Their papers declared them "tourists on a sightseeing trip." But as their train bowled north through flat fields of millet and soya bean they turned their cameras and field glasses on every passing hamlet and pointed out to one another features of the landscape on which they took written notes.

"It is like an ocean," breathed one of the captains in awe.

"Yes," mused the lieutenant colonel in charge, "on such a terrain we may have to adopt naval tactics."

No one asked the lieutenant colonel what he meant by this remark—something fluid, they assumed, something brilliant and dynamic—for this was Lieutenant Colonel Ishiwara Kanji, the most original young strategist in the Japanese Army, the member of the ubiquitous Suzuki's Study Group whom Emperor Hirohito had hand-picked for the planning of the Manchurian venture in late 1928. During the eight months since his arrival in Port Arthur, the leasehold capital, Ishiwara had spent all his time reading books, studying maps, and talking to old hands in the Kwantung Army officer corps. Now he was out for twelve days of personal reconnaissance into Manchurian topography. When the twelve days were up, he and his staff must begin to develop their ideas on paper for the scrutiny of the Emperor.

The light of sunset warmed the drab colors in the railroad coach and softened the perpetual scowl on Lieutenant Colonel

Ishiwara's boyish face. The members of his staff did not dream
of disturbing his reverie. They adored him personally, treasured
him as a military genius of the nation, and also revered him as a
religious leader and prophet. At forty, Ishiwara had made a name
for himself as the *enfant terrible* of the Army. Few other commanders could be so gentle with subordinates, so acidly blunt
with senior officers. He invented pet names for all his superiors
which he did not hesitate to use to their faces. He addressed
the commander of the Army in Taiwan as "Daddy Raccoon." Colonel Tojo, the later World War II prime minister, he called "Dear
Dunderhead." From his father, a spellbinding Buddhist priest,
Ishiwara had inherited a huge following in the militant, gong-
beating, knight-templar sect of Buddhism, the Nichiren. Returning home in 1925, after three years of service with the cabal's
European spy ring in Berlin, Ishiwara had been met at every station platform by welcoming committees of his father's Nichiren
devotees. He had ingratiated himself with them by delivering a
set platform speech, telling them how he had always worn traditional samurai dress to Reichstag banquets, how he had always
kept chopsticks tucked up his kimono sleeve with which to delight his hostesses.

Now, as the young prophet stared out the train window at
the rich, unconquered farmlands of southern Manchuria, he was
acutely conscious of the trust placed in him. It was his bold idea
that Japan might take Manchuria from the inside out, by an action more resembling a coup d'etat than an invasion. Japan's right
of way in the South Manchuria Railroad would provide the necessary access and privileges. And infiltration and subversion would
be far less expensive and dangerous than outright conquest. Chang
Tso-lin's son, Chang Hsueh-liang, had a tremendous numerical superiority in troops. But if the timing were perfect; if privates, officers, diplomats, and politicians were all properly coached;
if a Manchurian government of puppets were ready in the wings
to present a fair face at once to the League of Nations; then Ishiwara would be able to take Manchuria for Hirohito like a magician
in a flash of powder.

If Ishiwara could do all this—and he felt that he could—he
would be in a position to advise the Emperor on the policies

which the Empire should pursue in years to come. The righteous course for the nation was a theme close to Ishiwara's heart, one on which he was writing a book.[4] In his almost completed manuscript, he foresaw harmony, alliance, and ultimately unification for Japan, Manchuria, and China. This unification of Asia would be followed, perhaps in thirty years, by a "total war" between yellows and whites. If Japan could supply moral leadership, she would gain the support of Asia's masses and the total war would end inevitably in the annihilation of the West.

Lieutenant Colonel Ishiwara knew that his dreams were shared in general terms by most of the young officers in Hirohito's cabal. All of them agreed that the first order of business was military seizure of Manchuria. Beyond that horizon, however, loomed fundamental moral differences of opinion. The visionaries, of whom Lieutenant Colonel Ishiwara was one, felt that with the addition of Manchuria, Japan should perfect herself as a self-sufficient theocratic state. There should be a thoroughgoing domestic reform to make Japan a classless, co-operative, single-family society inspired by filial obedience to the Emperor, the father. Once this uniquely Japanese form of communistic utopia was realized, it would serve as a model for the other nations of Asia. And when the racial Armageddon came, the other nations of Asia would voluntarily side with Japan and trust themselves to Japanese leadership. It was axiomatic that the Armageddon would begin against the largest Western colony in the Orient, belonging to "the natural enemy of the Imperial Throne," namely, the Siberia of Bolshevik Russia.

The pragmatists of the cabal—and Ishiwara was afraid that Hirohito might be one of them—scoffed at the idea of idealism in other Asiatic countries. They foresaw no way to unify the Continent except through conquest. They counted on the raw materials of Southeast Asia as prerequisites for Armageddon. They anticipated that the collective Russian society might be persuaded to remain on the sidelines. They believed that the first enemy would be the "individualistic societies," the democracies with colonies in Southeast Asia: France, Great Britain, the Netherlands,

[4] *Sekai Saishu Senso*, The Ultimate World War.

and the United States. Lieutenant Colonel Ishiwara feared that this pragmatist view would lead Japan into a war which would be unjustified from a moral standpoint and would be dangerously premature from a practical one.

Last week Kita Ikki, the ideologist of the visionaries, had accused Lord Privy Seal Count Makino, the patron of the pragmatists, of accepting kickbacks in the handling of imperial estates in the northern Japanese island of Hokkaido. If such accusations were made in the cabal of officers closest to the Emperor, the rift between visionaries and pragmatists might ultimately spread to the ranks and the national program might be jeopardized. As the light went out over the Manchurian plains and as Lieutenant Colonel Ishiwara unbuttoned his Army tunic for a nap before his train arrived in Mukden, he conceded to one of the young officers in his suite that the military problems of the future were minor in comparison to the political ones.

YOUNG NAVY GENIUS

That same evening of July 3, 1929, when Saionji walked in Ueno Park and Lieutenant Colonel Ishiwara began spying out the land of Manchuria, the naval officer who would later plan and execute the 1941 raid on Pearl Harbor emerged from the Tokyo villa of his patron and protégé, the Empress's brother, Prince Asa-akira. Captain Yamamoto Isoroku of the Naval General Staff was a friend of Lieutenant Colonel Ishiwara in Manchuria. Indeed the forty-five-year-old Yamamoto was considered to be Ishiwara's naval counterpart: the most brilliant of the younger generation of naval strategists. But Yamamoto was no pale, irascible prophet. He was a calm, diffident professional, a muscular athlete, a clown and storyteller. The son of a humble schoolteacher, he had no following except his shipmates, no conviction except his self-confidence.

Captain Yamamoto had called at the villa of Prince Asa-akira in order to sign the guest register in the foyer as a token of condolence for the illness of the Empress's father, Prince Kuni. Old Prince Kuni had severe ulcers and little hope of living out the year. He had championed the development of air power in Japan since before World War I, and Captain Yamamoto had been the brightest of his disciples.

After graduating first in his class at Naval Staff College, Yamamoto had gone on, under Prince Kuni's sponsorship, to two years at Harvard. Already appreciating the problems of the future, he had specialized there in the manufacture of petroleum and aviation gas. He had hitchhiked to Mexico during one of his vacations and spent a summer slumming in the Mexican oil fields. Back in Japan in 1921, he had put in two years as an instructor at the Naval Staff College and at the University Lodging House in the palace. In 1923 he had taken over planning for air development in the Naval General Staff. And in 1924 he had assumed charge of the Navy's top-secret Air Development Station on the banks of Kasumigo-Ura, the Misty Lagoon, a lake the size of Lake George some 30 miles northeast of Tokyo. There he had worked with Empress Nagako's cousin, young test pilot Prince Yamashina, to develop naval torpedo-bombing techniques superior to any in the West. There, in the mists, preparing for the day when Japan would have task forces of aircraft carriers, Yamamoto had taught a generation of Navy pilots to land on the simulated flight decks of wharves and barges. After brief stints of duty as an attaché in Washington and as a skipper in the fleet, he had returned to the Navy General Staff in 1928 as a full-time planner and proponent of non-conventional weapons.

Now, as he had just confirmed in his brief call on Empress Nagako's brother, Yamamoto was to be offered a new assignment as chief technical advisor to the Japanese delegation at the forthcoming naval disarmament conference in London. If he accepted the appointment, he would be expected to trade on former friendships in the West in order to deceive the other naval powers as much as possible. On the other hand he would have the opportunity to help work out the international diplomatic bargain on which would depend the building of a powerful naval air force.

Outside Prince Asa-akira's villa, Captain Yamamoto broke his usual rules of frugality by hailing a taxicab instead of a ricksha. He gave the driver the address of a teahouse—the equivalent of a nightclub—in Tsukiji near Tokyo's big Western hospital, St. Luke's. There he knew he would find a convivial hostess and a group of fellow officers with whom he could waste the evening while he sorted out his thoughts.

The naval disarmament question was politically complicated. The shipbuilding ratios agreed on in Washington in 1922 were unpopular with many Japanese because they acknowledged in legal form Japan's position of naval inferiority to the United States and Great Britain. At the same time the ratio system had released funds from capital-ship construction and had made possible the secret naval development plan which Japan had pursued since 1922. No one could deny that the secret plan had vastly enhanced the strength of the Japanese fleet relative to the American and British fleets. Japan now had four of those new experimental ships, aircraft carriers, in which Yamamoto saw the future of naval warfare. She was building destroyers superior in speed and armament to anything which Western nations had on their drawing boards. Her new cruisers were in fact the precursors of pocket battleships. Her submarine fleet was the world's third largest. Every year since 1923 the Diet had approved without once demurring the unearmarked "supplementary naval funds" which had made these new weapons possible. And while Japan had been developing novel ships to the limit of her capacity, the United States had not yet even launched her allotted quota of conventional battleships and cruisers.

Japan would soon be equipped, Yamamoto felt, to defend the western Pacific against U.S. fleet attack in any hypothetical war. Continued development of unorthodox weapons, in particular of aircraft, would make it possible, if necessary, for Japan to fight an offensive war. Perhaps Japan must have this threatening capability to gain equality among nations. If so, she must continue to avoid an expensive competition with the United States in the building of battleships. The unpopular ratio system would have to be kept and Yamamoto, at the disarmament conference, would have to take the responsibility for seeing that it was kept.

Yamamoto's taxicab rounded the southernmost salient of the palace walls and sped on southeast towards the fashionable stews of Tsukiji ward. Yamamoto tried to imagine the welcome he would receive at the teahouse to which he was going if he did not have the right introductions. The very thought made him squirm with

humiliation. It was not the best of the teahouses but it was on
the same block with them. Someday he would graduate to the
Sign of the Carp, down the alley, where Emperor Taisho's prime
minister, Katsura Taro, and Hirohito's Prime-Minister-Maker Saionji had found their mistresses in years past.

An hour later, in a private room at the teahouse, Captain Yamamoto was drinking saké and gambling money against favors in a
card-guessing game with a popular apprentice geisha. As he
touched the backs of the cards, he did his best to conceal the fact
that two fingers were missing from his left hand. They had been
blown off by a Russian shell in one of the naval engagements of
the war of 1904–05. It was the challenge of hiding them when
they were most exposed which had first drawn him to card games.
And now card games were an essential part of his philosophy:
bluff or be bluffed; peek as little as necessary; study routine combinations with the utmost care for they were the ones which concealed the greatest opportunities for subtlety and surprise. For
Yamamoto card games were a social occasion in which he could
gauge the mentality of potential adversaries or quarry. He had
learned to play poker while assessing his classmates at Harvard.
He had become an enthusiastic bridge player among his fellow
naval attachés in Washington.

Having lost money gracefully to his entertainer, he returned
with her to the outer room of the teahouse, traded jokes with a
carousing circle of fellow naval officers, and had a word with the
proprietress. Someday, he promised her, when he became a famous
admiral, he would make her hostel famous and bring to it half
the officers of the fleet. At the moment, he said apologetically,
he could offer her nothing but a Havana sent to him by a friend
in America. As predicted by the young geisha, the proprietress
admitted that she was inordinately fond of cigars and gave permission for the girl to leave with him. Yamamoto made a triumphant exit with his conquest at his heels. A recently promoted
captain from Yamamoto's last fleet command, the aircraft
carrier *Akagi*, led the other captains and rear admirals in the room
in a rousing banzai to cheer him on his way.

In those days in Japan, a trained entertainer, attached to one
of the good teahouses, did not give her favors lightly. To have

one for a night was to have her for many nights. And this was possible only for a man with money or with powerful friends to put in the right words for him with the leaders of the entertainment guild in the Black Dragon Society. In his own right Yamamoto had no way to keep such a mistress. It was hard enough for him on his captain's salary to support his wife and his little home. Then again, a mistress was a recognized sign of success, bringing glamor and prestige to a man in his career.

The girl took Yamamoto to an inn where they were expected. She found—so she liked to say in later years—that beneath his façade of rough-and-tumble boyish charm he was shy and serious. A few hours later, in great pleasure, Yamamoto decided that she was indispensable to him. He would accept the assignment offered to him by Prince Asa-akira. He would go to London, play bridge and poker, and negotiate a continuation of the ratio system which would give the Japanese Navy time.

HIROHITO IMPATIENT

The coming negotiations in London caused Hirohito to turn his attention to the Navy and to the long-range objectives of his reign. The Army might conquer Manchuria, but it was the Navy on which he must ultimately rely in the dimly envisaged war with the West.

Hirohito's great-grandfather Emperor Komei had vowed to rid the sacred homeland of infidels and to safeguard it by surrounding it with a buffer zone. The discredited samurai of Choshu had created a small buffer zone by adding Korea to the Empire. The modern Army thought only in terms of deepening this zone by acquiring more miles of dry land on the Continent in which to maneuver regiments and dig trenches.

Since about 1900, the imperial family had taken a more sophisticated view of the national program, based on a growing appreciation of trade and technology. In order to face down any challenge by the barbarians, the Empire had to be a self-sufficient military bloc, including within its borders not only the buffer zones on which to fight invasion but also the raw materials with which to maintain a war machine that would be a standing deterrent. In terms of the physical geography of Asia, this meant that Japan must control the oil of Borneo, the rubber of Malaya, and the rice and metals of Java and Sumatra.

To extend the Empire to the islands off the coasts of Southeast Asia and also to create a buffer zone on the open Pacific side of Japan, a navy was needed capable of meeting the U.S. and British fleets. The Army need be strong enough to handle only the relatively crude and ill-equipped land forces to be found in China and Siberia. The Navy by comparison must meet the most demanding technological standards of the times.

For all Japan's amazing industrial growth during the last seventy years, she was still an underdeveloped nation. If her Navy was to rival the world's finest, it must be given a disproportionate share of the national budget for at least a decade to come. Hirohito had known for years that it would take a long time to build up the Navy to required strength, and also that the nation must be perfectly disciplined in patience and silence while the build-up proceeded. The Army must not become jealous. The Navy must not grow proud. Foreign nations must not be alarmed.

In considering the arduous task ahead, Hirohito in the summer of 1929 felt impatience. He did not see in the widening rift in the cabal, or in the emergence of a second intractable political party, or in the continuing fashion-following, peace-loving, pleasure-seeking frivolity of the masses, any sign of the national dedication which was called for.

"I have always tried to leave domestic politics to my advisors," he told an old school friend, "but I sometimes wonder if they are necessary, or at least if they need be so complicated."

All summer long Hirohito continued to worry his chief vassals with such complaints. Unless domestic politics could show some progress, he said, it would become necessary to tear down the chrysanthemum curtain, step forward onto the apron of the stage, and take personal charge of the state. This was the sort of self-destructive threat which Hirohito had been making to chamberlains ever since he had first thrown a tantrum as a child. But the chamberlains were still impressed. Lord Privy Seal Makino

begged him repeatedly to be prudent. Prime-Minister-Maker Saionji, from his seaside villa, sent him a cautionary message:

> Bismarck firmly believed that Germany would expand in the future
> and although he was strongly determined to realize this belief he was
> also aware of the fact that it could not be done immediately for lack
> of power. Therefore Bismarck paid his respects to a seemingly unnec-
> essary extent to Disraeli in London and Napoleon the Third in Paris.

A WIN WITHOUT TRUMPS

Count Makino and other subtle minds at Court advised Hirohito to make the most of the worrisome naval negotiations pending in London by turning them into a noisy national debate which
would arouse the martial spirit of the people and might serve also
to confuse and soften Western attitudes toward Japan.

On October 10, 1929, Hirohito called together in his presence
the Cabinet and his own Navy General Staff and had them agree
privately that, if better terms were not negotiable, Japan should
accept continuance of the 10:10:6 ratio set at Washington in
1922, which gave Japan 60 per cent of the fleet strength allowed
the United States or Great Britain. It being only good statecraft,
however, to go to the London Naval Conference asking as much
as possible, Prime Minister Hamaguchi emerged from the meeting
announcing to reporters that his government wanted a semblance
of parity with Western nations and would insist on 10:10:7 or
fight.

The venal Japanese press immediately mounted a campaign to
show that naval limitations were unpopular in Japan. Out of a
drowsy autumn sky readers were given reasons to think that limitations would impose personal hardships on them. Dockyard workers would be idle. There would be no room for young sailors in
the Navy. The influential periodical *Nihon oyobi Nihonjin,* Japan
and the Japanese—a publication founded by Hirohito's favorite
tutor, Sugiura Jugo, and now staffed by Sugiura's disciples—devoted an entire issue to the question of national defense. Some
of the most trusted members of Hirohito's cabal contributed articles on "National Mobilization, the Basis for the National De-

fense," on "Japan and the Air Defense of Her Cities," and on "The Coming War and Our Navy."

On October 24, 1929, the New York stock market collapsed in a heap of ticker tape, and the free economics of the world were plunged into a decade of financial night. Japan had already survived a small depression of her own, and the co-operative measures of control worked out between the government and Japan's handful of banking families now proved adequate to prevent the world panic from affecting the domestic economy.

The Wall Street crash greatly improved Japan's bargaining position at the naval conference because it stripped Western delegates of attentive home audiences. Hirohito personally instructed Japan's delegation, before it left for London in November, to hold out for the 10:10:7 ratio until it received his instructions to accept less. On the eve of its departure Saionji summoned the chief delegates to his home on the seashore to give them his own instructions. He exhorted them to reach an amicable arrangement with the West at all costs.

One of the delegates, Navy Minister Takarabe Takeshi, asked Saionji whether it would not be better to take a straightforward approach to the Emperor, the public, and the world. "How would it be," he inquired, "if we convoked a council in the Imperial Presence in order to unify public opinion and decide, once and for all, on the claims made by the Empire." Saionji told Takarabe that he would consider the suggestion, but as soon as Takarabe had gone, Saionji sent a message to Lord Privy Seal Makino, Hirohito's chief civilian advisor, registering "absolute opposition" to the idea. Saionji still hoped to change Hirohito's expansionist ambitions, and he feared that Hirohito, if pressed to take a stand, might ask Japan to claim half the earth.

The Navy minister, Takarabe, and a former and future prime minister, Wakatsuki Reijiro, led the Japanese delegation to London. Its day-to-day decisions, however, were made by the cabal's Captain Yamamoto, the later hero-villain of Pearl Harbor. En route to London for the formal part of the conference, Yamamoto spent three weeks in Washington negotiating an informal pre-conference agreement with the United States. He dealt at a high level through an old Washington acquaintance, Captain Allen Buchanan, who was the naval aide to President Herbert Hoover.[5] He learned that the United States was prepared to declare a moratorium on the construction of battleships and aircraft carriers until 1936.

Yamamoto readily agreed that Japan would do the same. Battleships, he felt, cost far more than they were worth and aircraft carriers could be replaced in the western, Japanese half of the Pacific with runways on the permanently anchored flight decks of Japan's mandated islands. The only problem, then, was to establish a United States–Japanese ratio for cruisers, destroyers, and submarines. Japan wanted a 10:7 ratio; the United States wanted a 10:6 ratio. By dint of charm, "sincerity," and hours of bridge playing, Yamamoto wrung from his American contacts an assurance that Japan would get a ratio close to the one she wanted.

On December 18, 1929, the Japanese delegation concluded its feeler negotiations by dining with President and Mrs. Hoover at the White House. The table was laden with pink snapdragons, butterfly roses, and smilax. Captain Yamamoto, who sat far down it with Hoover's aide, Captain Buchanan, was so relaxed that, in the course of the state banquet, he showed his companions a trick with matchsticks and the White House wine goblets.

Four months later, in London, Yamamoto's expectations were fulfilled when the American and British delegations formally acknowledged Japan's right to maintain 6.9945 tons of cruisers and destroyers for every 10 U.S. and British tons. In addition the U.S. delegation agreed to delay the construction of three heavy cruisers for which appropriations had already been allocated in order to give Japan 73 per cent of naval parity with the United States until at least 1936. Best of all, from Yamamoto's point of view, no limitations whatsoever were attached to the building of naval aircraft.

In gaining this dazzling, unexpected diplomatic victory, Yamamoto had made no promises but had successfully convinced his Western counterparts that he and the Emperor and the Japa-

---

[5] Buchanan was prematurely retired in 1933 from what seemed to be a brilliant career in the Navy and was not awarded the customary retirement rank of rear admiral. He died in 1940.

nese Navy were only interested in defending Japan's home waters against Chinese pirates and Soviet fishing fleets. Twelve years later when Yamamoto crept up on Pearl Harbor and sank half the Pacific fleet, his smiling reassurances and parlor tricks were not to be forgotten or forgiven. When an opportunity arose during the war, the U.S. government, by President Roosevelt's own particular order, took an unusual personal vengeance on the Japanese naval commander.[6]

NAVAL SMOKESCREEN

Yamamoto came home from his triumph in London in 1930 with Navy Minister Takarabe, one of the two chief delegates to the "disarmament conference." They took the Trans-Siberian Railroad and, before arriving in Japan, were met secretly in Manchuria by the tall, languid Prince Konoye of the House of Peers —the youngest and most aristocratic of the Big Brothers who had taken Hirohito in hand when he was still a toddler. It was Konoye's mission to remind the delegates that they had left the artificial world of international diplomacy and were re-entering the peculiar insular reality of the Japanese ruling class. Konoye gently warned them that their success in London was "unexpected" and constituted a positive embarrassment in Tokyo. It had been assumed that the West would give Japan no more than 6 tons for every 10 tons of British or American capital ships, a ratio which Hirohito had been prepared to accept. When Yamamoto got an official 6.9945 tons for Japan on paper and U.S. word for an actual 7.3 tons afloat, it was more than Japan had demanded. Indeed, said Konoye laughing, it "transcended reality, extended credibility, and confounded sanity." Japan had half the population, a tenth the gross national product, and a twentieth the area of the United States, yet that nation had just accorded Japan the right to better than 70 per cent naval equality with her.

Having congratulated Takarabe and Yamamoto on their fantastic feat, Konoye went on to explain to them, with apologies, that much of the public recognition for their achievement would have to be smothered. Having anticipated a continuance of the

[6] The story is told in Chapter 28.

10:6 ratio, the Emperor's cabal had already made arrangements for a great public outcry to be staged, protesting Japan's treatment as an inferior power. It was now too late to cancel the arrangements without much loss of face for the cabal's loyal editors, ward heelers, and gang leaders. Besides, an issue was vitally needed with which to drum the people out of their pacifist lethargy. Technically the 6.9945 tons received were less than the 7 tons demanded, and so the public outcry would go ahead as planned. The figures after the decimal point would be ignored by the Japanese press; the Emperor would delay in ratifying the treaty; and, while he considered it, the people would be treated to a great national debate.

To oppose the treaty the cabal was exploiting a group of conservative admirals, known as the Fleet Faction, who believed in capital ships; Navy Chief of Staff Admiral Kato Kanji was among them. Konoye warned that, except for his Highness Admiral Prince Fushimi, the members of the Fleet Faction were dangerously sincere individualists. They opposed Yamamoto's treaty because they saw in it a blind behind which Japan could prepare in secret to make war with the United States and Great Britain. To impress the Emperor, they spoke like hawks, but in reality they were doves who wished to abandon the national program handed down by Emperor Meiji.

Konoye did not know it at the time but events would prove his analysis correct. The members of the Fleet Faction would all resign their commissions or go into the reserve in the years ahead. By contrast those who spoke like doves in favor of Yamamoto's "disarmament treaty" would turn out to be hawks who would help Yamamoto plan and execute the 1941 attack on Pearl Harbor.

Duly warned by Konoye of the situation at home, Captain Yamamoto and Navy Minister Takarabe disembarked in Japan on May 18, 1930. Crowds turned out, unprompted, to acclaim them as conquerors. The vast majority of the people, knowing only what they had read in the newspapers, welcomed naval limitations as a guarantee against high taxes and as a blow for peace. When the two delegates reported at the palace, Hirohito delivered to each of them his customary noncommittal words of praise, "Thank you for your pains."

The chief civilian delegate to the London Naval Conference, Wakatsuki, a former and future prime minister, arrived home by ship a month later. By then receptions were better organized. The crowds still cheered, but a professional agitator of the Black Dragon Society handed Wakatsuki a ceremonial dagger wrapped in silk—a delicate hint, it was said in the newspapers, that he should commit suicide for having endangered the national defense.

While the great fake debate filled headlines and occupied the public mind, liberals allied with Prime-Minister-Maker Saionji urged Hirohito to sign the naval limitations treaty at once and the conservative Fleet Faction urged him not to sign it at all. Hirohito insisted that, before deciding on the treaty, a co-ordinated national defense plan be prepared, one that would govern military expenditures during the coming decade. The plan was duly drawn up in great secrecy by key men in the Army and Navy bureaucracies. Its text is not extant, but an officer who worked on it recalls that "it agreed pretty well with the actual military development of Japan as far as 1939."

By July 23, 1930, the War and Navy ministers and the Board of Field Marshals and Fleet Admirals, controlled by Hirohito's cousins, accepted the plan and forwarded it to Hirohito. With the plan went a covering memorandum to the effect that the naval limitations treaty would create some "insufficiencies in the national defense" but that the offensive power provided for by the plan would offset any real danger and would assist substantially in "advancing the national program."

The next day Hirohito asked his Privy Council of elders to consider the treaty and advise him on whether or not to sign it. Under the Emperor's benign gaze and with his tacit encouragement, the Privy Councillors refused to recommend the treaty for his sanction because they were not allowed to see the co-ordinated national defense plan which Hirohito, as commander-in-chief, had sponsored, approved, and declared top secret.

The reason for this Gilbert-and-Sullivan impasse was that Hirohito had no intention of signing the naval limitations treaty until the elected government approved a long-range budget for the defense plan—in particular for the naval and naval air development programs which were the most expensive parts of it. At the behest of eighty-year-old Saionji, however, Prime Minister Hamaguchi refused, under one pretext or another, to find funds even for the first year of the plan.

EPIDEMIC OF ABSENTEEISM

In blocking the co-ordinated national defense plan, Saionji counted heavily upon an ally in the Army, one with enough influence to mire section after subsection of the plan in deep red tape on the desks of major generals. This was War Minister Ugaki Kazushige, the bull-necked officer who had served Hirohito, earlier in 1925, by purging the Choshu clan from the Army. Having given his approval in vague, reluctant terms to the defense plan, Ugaki pleaded a middle-ear infection and retired to rest in his country home for the next four months. In so doing he withdrew from Hirohito's support the Ugaki Faction—a majority of the generals and colonels in the Army. These were the military professionals who assessed with realism Japan's strength as a warrior nation. They were eager to add Manchuria to the Empire but they would not support long-term naval preparations for war with the United States and Great Britain.

During Ugaki's absence from Tokyo—his "sick-down strike" as it was called by Hirohito's clever, Oxford-educated brother, Prince Chichibu—Prime-Minister-Maker Saionji caught an extended case of the flu which made it impossible for him, too, to exercise his political influence on behalf of the Throne. From his quarantine, Saionji sent a tongue-in-cheek note to Ugaki begging him not to give in:

Although I should come to you in person [he wrote], I am, as you know, sick myself. . . . Certain individuals are passing rumors to the effect that you will resign. For the sake of the fatherland, I beg you to be prudent. Leave the cares of your ministry to someone else. Then take all the time you need to rest and recover.

On August 17, 1930, Big Brother Konoye of the House of Peers invited Marquis Kido—the first of the Big Brothers, the son of Hirohito's childhood foster father, the loyal retainer who would go to prison as Hirohito's personal representative in 1945—to a round of golf at the Hodogaya Club near Kido's villa in Yokohama.[7] It was a fine day but hot, and the tall, languid Fujiwara prince stretched himself in the rough near one of the early greens. The dapper, owlish marquis, a rabid golfer, stood over him scolding for a moment and then signaled their companion, the director of the Bank of Japan, to play through.

Marquis Kido had had few opportunities to speak privately to Prince Konoye in more than a year. In early 1929 Kido had gone abroad on an extended sightseeing trip to indicate to the public that he took partial responsibility for the killing of Chang Tso-lin. Kido had made a tour of the United States, hating every minute of it. After a day at Niagara Falls, he had written superciliously in his diary, "In this humdrum fashion, I celebrated the 1930 New Year." Returning home from exile in late January, he had plunged back into his work at the Commerce and Industry Ministry. He had been busy ever since drafting memos on industrial mobilization for perusal by the members of the Eleven Club. This was a forum which Kido had founded on the eleventh day of the eleventh month of the eleventh year of the reign of Emperor Taisho—that is, on November 11, 1922. At least once a month, usually on the eleventh, the club met for lunch or dinner in a private room at one or another of Tokyo's best restaurants.[8] Since its founding, its membership had grown from three to more than a score. Under Kido's tactful direction it had become the co-ordinating center of the Big Brotherhood, which was itself the brain of Hirohito's cabal.

Sensing that he was about to hear something which would not be said even at an Eleven Club meeting, Kido sat down in the long grass. Konoye beside him launched into one of his "résumés of the present situation"—a prelude always to some sort of important Konoye proposal. It was time, said Konoye, to break the "sick-down strike" of General Ugaki and old man Saionji. Matters had come to such a pass that Saionji was privately accusing Count

---

[7] This account is based on the reconstruction of a third party who talked to Kido and Konoye in the clubhouse that afternoon.

[8] It would continue to meet until the night of January 11, 1945, when the conspirators agreed that the shriek of air raid sirens made further talk unprofitable.

Makino, the lord privy seal, of opposing disarmament and advising
Hirohito not to sign the naval treaty. On the other hand the Fleet
Faction's Admiral Kato, since resigning in June as Navy chief of
staff, had been accusing Count Makino of exerting improper influence over the Throne on behalf of the treaty. Specifically Kato
complained that Count Makino had sidetracked his privileged reports to the Throne and kept Hirohito from hearing the facts.

In order to refute Saionji's charges against Makino and to
mollify Admiral Kato, said Konoye, Hirohito had agreed to let
Count Makino's chief secretary retire.[9] It would be noised abroad
that he was taking responsibility for certain irregularities in connection with Admiral Kato's efforts to report to the Emperor. The
public would then see that Hirohito had gone so far in the cause
of disarmament as to condone a breach of Court rules rather than
hear the conservative admiral's arguments against the naval treaty.

"It is my feeling," said Konoye, "that the Emperor is disappointed by the attitude of the public." Opinion had not turned
against Saionji or against pacifism, and Hirohito was obliged to go
on dissimulating, even before his most loyal subjects. Under the
circumstances, said Konoye, it had been decided to "strengthen
the Emperor's personal leadership of the nation." Hirohito had
just appointed Colonel Nagata Tetsuzan, the first of the Three
Crows of Baden-Baden, to the directorship of the sprawling, influential Military Affairs Section in the War Ministry. Now the
office of secretary to the lord privy seal was vacant.

"I have been thinking," said Konoye, "that His Majesty might
be pleased if you were proposed, Kido, as a candidate for the
vacancy. In fact, if you feel that you can give up your career to
serve as Count Makino's secretary, I can assure you that the position is almost certainly yours."

Kido was deeply gratified that the Emperor recognized his accomplishments in keeping the Big Brotherhood together. Up to
now the principal intermediary between the Throne and the ci-

9 Okabe Nagakage, the son-in-law of former Prime Minister Kato Taka-aki
who had served the Twenty-One Demands on China. Okabe was consoled
with the title of viscount and a seat in the House of Peers. As a faithful
member of the Eleven Club, he remained an influential figure behind the
scenes and would re-emerge into the limelight when he became minister of
education in the 1943 Cabinet of World War II Prime Minister Tojo.

vilian half of the cabal had been Prince Konoye who had the
hereditary Court rank to meet Hirohito often at social functions.
Now, if Kido moved his files into the palace as secretary to the
lord privy seal, he would be bringing papers to the Imperial Study
at all hours of the day and night. He would be the reins of the
cabal, close at hand for Hirohito whenever he wished to reach for
them.

"I accept without any reservations," said Kido, standing up.
"Let's play a few more holes."

A day or two later, the aged Field Marshal Prince Kanin, senior
member of the imperial family, summoned to his villa his old
protégé from the cavalry, Major General Tatekawa Yoshiji, the
Peerless Pimp. "The time has come," announced Prince Kanin,
"to break the deadlock with War Minister Ugaki." The suave
Tatekawa, who had so smoothly handled the Peking end of the
killing of the Manchurian war lord Chang Tso-lin, was now director
of Army Intelligence. With Prince Kanin's backing Tatekawa began at once to beg, buy, and borrow the allegiance of the officers
of the Ugaki Faction in the General Staff. He was assisted in the
War Ministry by Colonel Nagata of the Military Affairs Section.

HIROHITO HAS HIS WAY

By September 1930, War Minister Ugaki's Army slowdown
had been effectively canceled, and necessary outlines and estimates for the defense plan had begun to move across desks into
the hands of the civilians in the Finance Ministry who were
trying to draw up budgets. With the co-operation of First Crow
Nagata, Intelligence Chief Tatekawa went ahead to devise an
intimidation for the bankers, intellectuals, and politicians who
made War Minister Ugaki and Saionji formidable forces to be
reckoned with.

Tatekawa had his Intelligence experts draw up its annual "Inspection of General Circumstances" in a revolutionary new form.
In previous years this cryptic title had always graced the cover of
a report in depth on the political, economic and military conditions within a potential enemy nation such as Great Britain or
the Philippines. This year, 1930, the adversary scrutinized was Ja-

pan itself. And the conclusions were, briefly, that corrupt political parties and cartels were interposing a fogged filter between the pure executive light of the Emperor and his moths of men in the regiments and on the farms. To remove the blemish and "perfect the national structure" a *Showa Isshin* or Hirohito Restoration must be carried out which would convert Japan into a "National Defense State" that would be "mobilized for total war."

The threat implied by the 1930 "Inspection of General Circumstances" was clear: either the politicians and business magnates of Japan would find money for the co-ordinated national defense plan or they would be conscripted in a total mobilization. To make sure that this message was broadcast widely, Intelligence Chief Tatekawa sponsored the organization of a noisy debating society in the ranks of young Army staff officers—one which received so much publicity at the time that some historians have seen in it the fountainhead of Japanese fascism. It was called the *Sakurakai* or Cherry Society, a name rich in murderous historical associations, which meant by implication society of young warriors ready to die.

Veteran politician that he was, Saionji could not help but admire the marksmanship and saturation of the fire being poured upon his faction of liberals. In a self-mocking mood, over his saké cup one night, he acknowledged to his political secretary, Big Brother Baron Harada, that the only satisfaction left in life for Prime Minister Hamaguchi was "like scratching your toes with Western shoes on."

Finally on September 15, 1930, with a sigh of approval from old man Saionji, Prime Minister Hamaguchi gave in. At a meeting of Hirohito's Privy Council of elders he put himself on record promising to assume full responsibility for finding the necessary funds for future secret naval development. The Privy Councillors asked him several waspish questions and finally he replied, "We are all men of the Inner Circle. There is no room for debate." At its next meeting the Privy Council resolved that the Board of Field Marshals and Fleet Admirals could keep its secret co-ordinated national defense plan and that the naval limitations treaty might now be submitted to Hirohito for his sanction. According to the notes of Baron Harada, this abrupt *volte face* on the part of the Privy Council was brought about by one Privy Councillor telling the chairman in private that the treaty debate was beginning to "vex" Hirohito.

LION SLAYING

Trusting Prime Minister Hamaguchi's word that funds would be found, Hirohito signed the naval limitations treaty on October 2, 1930, and gratefully turned his attention from politics to military matters. Lieutenant Colonel Ishiwara, whom Hirohito had entrusted in late 1928 with the planning for the conquest of Manchuria, had now, in September 1930, submitted his detailed tactical blueprint to Hirohito and the General Staff. Hirohito saw that it was satisfactory and tabled it temporarily while he studied the more important, longer-range naval development program. This had been drawn up, in large part, by Rear Admiral Yamamoto, the future architect of the attack on Pearl Harbor. It contained one imponderable: Yamamoto's enthusiastic belief in the eventual effectiveness of naval air power.

Since the London Naval Conference, Yamamoto had been feverishly drilling his naval pilots in all-weather operations from the decks of Japan's tiny task force of four aircraft carriers. A score of pilots had crashed and died but now Yamamoto was ready to justify the trust which the imperial family had placed in him by staging a demonstration of naval air power at the annual Navy grand maneuvers. In the fourth week of October 1930, Hirohito steamed south to the Inland Sea to watch the maneuvers from the bridge of his battleship.

On October 22, while Hirohito was absent from Tokyo, Prime Minister Hamaguchi presented the national budget to his cabinet. The Navy minister was far from satisfied. Instead of the 500 million yen ($250 million) requested for the naval half of the new national defense scheme, the government was offering some 300 million. Weeks of bargaining lay ahead. Prime-Minister-Maker Saionji cautioned his political secretary, Baron Harada, not to let the Navy's budget exceed 400 million yen because it might "cause popular agitation."

"In Germany," he said threateningly, "the people on the whole possess a martial spirit and they do not engage in agitation. As a result, political control there is no great problem. In Japan, however, matters have come to such a pass that the people could easily turn Communist. My anxiety on this account would be altogether out of place in Germany, but here, unless something is done, the militarists among our leaders will see to it that my worst fears are realized."

On October 26, the Navy's grand maneuvers came to an end in a glorious triumph for Rear Admiral Yamamoto and his flyers. Carrier-borne torpedo planes of "Fleet White" had theoretically sunk the battleships of "Fleet Blue."

On October 27, a young professional hoodlum, Sagoya Tomeo, who belonged to a provincial patriotic club spawned by the Black Dragon Society, came to Tokyo by train with the express purpose of assassinating Prime Minister Hamaguchi. He understood that the prime minister, in offering 300 million yen instead of 500 million for naval development, had broken his word to the Emperor. On the train, however, Sagoya had an "encounter with an imperial prince"—so he later described it to the police—which persuaded him to postpone his deed.[10]

Instead of killing Hamaguchi immediately, cutthroat Sagoya followed the prime minister around the city, posing a silent threat during the conclusion of the budget debate. Saionji's political secretary, Baron Harada, learned from the police that "someone has been stalking the prime minister." Official Tokyo watched the hunt with fascination. Home Minister Adachi Kenzo, who had charge of the police, was himself a member of the Black Dragon who had ingratiated himself with the Throne in the 1890's by contributing to the murder of the queen of Korea. His police shadowed the shadower but made no attempt to arrest him.

Prime Minister Hamaguchi, the Lion, refused to be intimidated. On November 9, he finally persuaded the Navy minister to accept a compromise budget of 374 million yen. It appeared that Hamaguchi had won a great victory, and finding himself still alive, he began to talk bravely of making a thorough overhaul of the

[10] The prince was almost certainly Big Brother Higashikuni who took the same train back to Tokyo from the naval maneuvers.

machinery of Japanese government. It was his ambition, he said, to subordinate to the supreme authority of the Cabinet all de facto instruments of policy making, even the Emperor's own Privy Council. Prime-Minister-Maker Saionji sympathized with this goal and asked his political secretary to encourage the prime minister. Harada reported Saionji's words at Court.

One evening in the second week of November 1930, Big Brother Prince Konoye received a visit from Iogi Ryozo, the burly, sixty-year-old editor of *Japan and the Japanese,* the periodical that had touched off the naval limitations debate in 1929 with its special issue on national defense. Iogi was a charter member of the Black Dragon; it was he who, in 1921, had notified Konoye in advance of the assassination of Prime Minister Hara. Now, in 1930, he intimated to Prince Konoye that a similar mishap might soon befall Prime Minister Hamaguchi. "Things," he added, "may gradually start to happen from now on. Something big will follow in due course, about February or March."

On the evening of November 13, 1930, Big Brother Baron Harada spent an hour and a half in private with Prime Minister Hamaguchi at his residence. The Emperor was out of town again, this time attending the annual grand maneuvers of the Army. Hamaguchi explained to Harada his government reorganization scheme, the implications of the new budget, the need to curtail the powers of Hirohito's Privy Council and Army and Navy General Staffs. "Take good care of yourself," said Harada meaningfully, as he left the prime minister's residence.

"I hoped there would be no mishap," he added piously to his diary when he had returned home.

Sagoya, the assassin, spent that night in one of Tokyo's best brothels. His bill was taken care of for him by a patron whose identity the police later kept secret. The next morning, November 14, 1930, at 9:00 A.M., Saionji's secretary, Harada, and Prince Konoye were closeted together when the phone rang. An aide informed them that five minutes earlier Prime Minister Hamaguchi had been shot at Tokyo station as he was about to board a train on his way to join the Emperor at the Army grand maneuvers. Assassin Sagoya had thrust a Mauser-8 from the crowd on the Tokyo platform and sunk a bullet deep in Hamaguchi's vitals.

Two doctors who happened to be on the scene attended him in the stationmaster's office. They found him conscious but in great pain. His pulse fell to 90 and his belly swelled alarmingly. The chubby figure of Baron Harada pushed its way through the circle of bystanders, looked at the body and then withdrew, without speaking, to make some calls on the stationmaster's phone. Harada then took a train to report to Saionji in the town of Okitsu two hours away.

Hamaguchi murmured, "I feel worse." At 11:30 A.M., he was moved to the infirmary at Tokyo Imperial University. There, he was given a partial anaesthetic and X-rayed. He had lost two pints of blood and had eight perforations in his small intestine, plus several more in the adjoining valves. The University chief of surgery,[11] snipped out 20 inches of intestine and sewed together the tract that was left. Exploring from the rear, the surgeon found the bullet lodged deep in the pelvic arch where he felt he could not safely get at it. So he sewed Hamaguchi up and gave him 250 grams of whole blood. He estimated that the prime minister had a 60 to 70 per cent chance of survival but feared he would be too weak to defend his budget at the coming session of the Diet.

At the time of the shooting Hirohito was at his grand-maneuver field headquarters, 300 miles south of Tokyo. When he received word there of Hamaguchi's "mishap," he expressed his regrets and advised the Cabinet to pick an acting prime minister to handle routine administrative affairs while Hamaguchi remained incapacitated. On the afternoon of the shooting, the Cabinet duly met to carry out the Emperor's instructions. The members finally settled on Foreign Minister Shidehara, the sanctimonious moderate of Japanese diplomacy who would become prime minister in his own right under MacArthur in late 1945.

A ghost of a lion, Prime Minister Hamaguchi continued to haunt the fringes of the political forest for nine months to come. He would finally die after a succession of debilitating surgeries on August 26, 1931. His dream, which he shared with Saionji, of

11 Eighteen months later, through incompetence or design, this same surgeon, Dr. Shioda Hiroshige, would fail—under extremely suspicious circumstances—to save the life of another prime ministerial assassination victim, Inukai Tsuyoshi. (See Chapter 15.)

constitutional prime ministers who would run the nation in fact as well as name would die with him. So, too, would his hopes for peace.

The police made a lengthy investigation of the assassination and divulged no relevant details except that the assassin, Sagoya Tomeo, resented Prime Minister Hamaguchi's part in passing the naval limitations treaty. As far as the public was concerned, that ended the matter. Sagoya spent three years out of jail on the recognizance of various police chiefs during his investigation and trial. Then, on November 6, 1933, he was finally condemned to death. Three months later, on the eve of his execution, he was amnestied by Hirohito and set free. Under the name of Sagoya Yoshiaki, he continued, until the late 1960's, to live the life of a national hero, supported by unseen hands, and always ready to contribute a rabble-rousing speech at gatherings of Japanese rightists.

11

MARCH 1931

OLD MAN AT SUNUP

When Baron Harada phoned Prime-Minister-Maker Saionji with the news of Hamaguchi's shooting on the morning of November 14, 1930, the old man seemed momentarily shocked and confused. He demanded querulously that Harada come out from Tokyo immediately with full particulars.

Saionji had celebrated his eighty-first birthday the month before, and like most well-cared-for old men, he thought of his personal health as a matter of some importance. Surely it was inconceivable that anyone would dare to assassinate him. He was the elder of the Fujiwaras, the second family of the nation. He was the last of the noblemen who had brought the restoration to Japan in 1868. In the eyes of Japan's spirit worshippers, he was surrounded by an aura of divinity almost as bright as the Emperor's. And if he should fall by the hand of a political assassin, not even the Emperor would be immune from the vengeance of Saionji's partisans in the clans and in the cartels and political parties. Yet Saionji knew how easy it was to arrange assassinations through the Black Dragon Society. If the mad dogs of Hirohito's cabal would gun down a revered leader of sixty like Prime Minister Hamaguchi, where would they stop? Hamaguchi had politicked with Saionji for thirty years. In paring the naval budget he had only followed Saionji's suggestions.

By the time that Baron Harada arrived at Sit-and-Fish Villa in Okitsu that afternoon, Saionji had regained his composure and was coldly indignant. He gave Harada explicit instructions to all the Cabinet ministers that they must not be intimidated but must carry on with Hamaguchi's program as if nothing had happened. By evening Saionji was on the phone trying to make sure that the Cabinet would appoint a moderate as prime minister pro tem. The next day he was disappointed by the defeat of his own candidate, War Minister Ugaki, but half satisfied with the compromise candidate, Foreign Minister Shidehara.

On the morning of November 16, according to a banker friend who was close to him at that time, the old man could not sleep. He arose at first light, drew the screens of the room where he lived and worked, and stood on the balcony watching the fishermen launch their boats. If ever there had been a time to think, it was now.

A decade ago Saionji had seen in Hirohito's ambitions the callow innocence of youth. But Hirohito, at thirty, had not mellowed. He was unflagging in his attention to duty, always fairminded in discussion, invariably courteous and intelligent. But he remained deceptive in his openness, hard in his kindness, ruthlessly objective in matters of life and death. Even his warmest partisans acknowledged a cold, mechanical quality in him. They called it a "godlike, awe-inspiring purity," but Saionji sometimes wondered if it were not a form of madness.

All efforts to guide Hirohito had failed. The time had come to oppose him positively. The chiefs of the Army and Navy and police were under the Emperor's control. Only the people could help. But to tell the people the truth would be to make them all republicans, Communists, regicides. They must be kept in ignorance and led. The problem was to give them a leader, a twentieth century shogun to compare with Ieyasu, the first of the Tokugawas. Then Hirohito would have to back down.

Saionji called out in the silent house for someone to help him. His maid appeared, half awake, and assisted him as he put on a lined winter kimono. Since the infidelity of Flower Child in 1924, Saionji had had no regular live-in mistress, and the maid was no more than a servant. Saionji never felt more lonely than on a morning such as this when he wanted a sympathetic listener on whom to try his thoughts. As he passed through his garden gate and started up the hill, the maid roused his gatekeeper and chauffeur so that someone would follow him and be ready to help him if his walk tired him.

Above the streets of the fishing village of Okitsu where he lived, Saionji planted his cane resolutely on each flagstone step along the wooded pathway up the hill. When he reached the gate of the temple at the top he turned to rest and looked back over the bay below. Then he turned and contemplated the view inland toward Mount Fuji. A turban of mist had slipped down over the sacred mountain divorcing its perfectly conical, snow-capped summit from any visible connection with the earth. To safeguard this mountain, this land of the gods, this heritage of the difficult young Emperor—these were Saionji's tasks. And he felt inadequate to fulfill them. His sight and hearing were sound, but his diabetes troubled him. He could no longer drink enough to feel drunk. He could no longer remelt his thought processes and pour them into new molds. The art of politics had become for him a stale exercise in tricks which he had learned decades ago.

In the lee of one of the stone lanterns of the temple he struck a match and lighted one of his favorite imported cigarettes, a Pall Mall. The sun peered over Izu Peninsula, the spur of Mount Fuji running down into the sea. The pine trees turned to blood and fire, the waters of the bay to bursts of diamonds. Saionji's mind floated back to the sunrises of his childhood, which he had watched from the courtyard of the palace in Kyoto before the coming of Perry. In those days he had been Emperor Komei's favorite page boy and had felt superior to his junior, the future Emperor Meiji. Now Meiji and Meiji's son were both dead and he alone remained to remember the honorable aspirations of the country at its awakening.

Saionji dropped the butt of his Pall Mall as it began to burn his stained knuckles. His faithful private secretary Nakagawa—not a Court spy like Harada—came up the mountain behind him, breathing heavily. The priest of the temple was approaching from the other direction to offer a cup of hot green tea. In a few minutes Nakagawa would escort him down the hill to his breakfast.

Saionji abruptly made up his mind. He would break with his lifelong public advocacy of civilian government and would join forces openly with the Army faction of War Minister Ugaki. Ugaki might not have the greatness required of a shogun but he had courage and good intentions and his followers in the officer corps were known as moderates.

SAIONJI WARNS HIROHITO

That afternoon when Baron Harada, the secretary-spy assigned him by the Court, came out to Okitsu with a report on the selection of the prime minister pro tem, Saionji conveyed his purposed threat to the Throne in guarded hints. He told Harada that it was a pity War Minister Ugaki had not been made acting prime minister. Didn't the Emperor know that during Ugaki's long convalescence in the country he had been asked separately by representatives of each of the two major political parties to become their president? Didn't the Emperor know that Ugaki might create an opposition by putting together either of the political parties with disaffected elements inside Hirohito's own cabal of military officers?

"Mark my word," concluded Saionji, "if the administration does not make enough of Ugaki, he may well resign and strike out on his own. Then, believe me, the administration's loss of face will be something to see."

Secretary-Spy Harada hurried back to Tokyo and waited impatiently for Hirohito to return from the Army grand maneuvers. Hirohito, on his way home, had had his battleship heave to off the Kii Peninsula so that he could spend a day there with the scientists of a biological institute specializing in bacteriological and chemical warfare studies.[1] When he finally arrived back in the palace on November 21, Harada at once sought an emergency

[1] His suite found the scientific talk boring and Grand Chamberlain Suzuki Kantaro, the old Taoist who would be prime minister at the time of the surrender in 1945, inquired, "Are you not tired, My Liege?"

"No, whatever I hear I listen to," said Hirohito. "If you understood, you would find many useful things to be learned here."

"If he were not a god," sighed one of the chamberlains, "he could not do it."

audience with Lord Privy Seal Makino, the Emperor's chief civilian advisor. Baron Harada told Count Makino that Saionji was ready to make common cause with Strike-North visionaries in the Army and also with Baron Hiranuma, the long-faced lawyer who would itemize Hirohito's mistakes before allowing him to surrender in the bunker in 1945.

In reality, Saionji had not even considered an alliance with Hiranuma. He was one of Saionji's oldest and most bitter political enemies. He represented the clan lords of yesteryear and the Black Dragon gang lords of the modern cities. He stood—at least in Saionji's mind—for a return to the eighteenth century police state of the Tokugawas against which Saionji had fought as a young knight in green armor riding for the royalists in 1868.

Nevertheless, in Harada's imagination, War Minister Ugaki was about to be backed by a Saionji-Hiranuma-Strike-North coalition and had become a formidable threat. "General Ugaki's value as a man," he said, "may be vastly overrated, but the charisma seen in him by the public could enable him to wreak havoc. We must try to keep General Ugaki as happy as possible within the present Cabinet."

After duly weighing Harada's warning, Count Makino decided that instead of placating Ugaki it would be better to frame him for high treason and then control him by threat of exposure. Makino turned the matter over to his private political fixer, Dr. Okawa, the ideologist of the Strike-South pragmatists and former headmaster of the palace Lodging-House indoctrination center.

THE MARCH PLOT

Dr. Okawa proceeded to make Ugaki the chief gull of a fantastic scheme for an imperial coup d'etat. The coup was never executed nor was it ever meant to be. It never made the headlines nor, until years later, was it much talked of outside the ruling class. Yet within that tiny insular world the March Plot, as it came to be called, would ruin Ugaki, shackle Saionji and remain a sharp instrument of Hirohito's domestic power for the next seven years.

The March Plot had been first conceived as a way of preparing domestic politics for the conquest of Manchuria. The idea was that a threat of coup d'etat by right-wing elements could be used to persuade the masses that Manchuria would provide a safe spilling space for domestic poisons. As a member of the Black Dragon Society, Dr. Okawa had been recruiting underworld involvement in the scheme since some time in the fall of 1930.[2] Army involvement was being arranged at the same time by Field Marshal Prince Kanin, the Army elder who was also senior member of the imperial family. The combined threat of militarists and street bullies was calculated to intimidate all the many Japanese who have never handled a gun or studied karate.

As stirred by Dr. Okawa's spoon, this diversionary plot quickly thickened as if it were being improvised by a pair of joke writers in a hotel room late at night. While pretending to make General Ugaki and Black Dragon Toyama the leaders of a scheme to dynamite the Diet, why not also implicate the troublesome anti-Soviet Strike-North visionaries in the bosom of Hirohito's own cabal? Why not incriminate the cabal's First Crow, Colonel Nagata, or even the propriety-loving members of Hirohito's Big Brotherhood? From Dr. Okawa's point of view, it was good personal insurance to involve as many important people in the web as possible. So well did he succeed that he was later able to plan murders with impunity and even to slip the noose of MacArthur's justice.[3] Indeed the ghosts of blackmail and counterblackmail which he raised in March 1931 still hang over the moats like will-o'-the-wisps to haunt the palace to this day.

UGAKI'S COYNESS

During the incubation of the March Plot in late December 1930 and early January 1931, General Ugaki, the war minister, asked time to consider Saionji's secret proposal that he join in a coali-

[2] That was why Editor Iogi—also a member of the Black Dragon—had promised "something big in February or March" when he had advised Prince Konoye of the imminent assassination of Prime Minister Hamaguchi.

[3] The palace made special efforts to help him evade American trial and cross-examination—efforts which were not made for any of the other war criminals after their formal indictment. The story of his escape under guise of feigned insanity is told in the final chapter of this book.

tion against the Throne. He dined almost nightly with representatives of the two major political parties, trying to decide of which one he would accept the presidency.

In those same weeks Acting Prime Minister Shidehara was busy amending the budget forced through by his mortally wounded predecessor and trying to find in it an extra 50 million yen ($25 million) for the Navy. With Hirohito's backing he even asked the Army to curtail its own development schemes. As chief of the Military Affairs Section in the Military Affairs Bureau of the War Ministry, the first of the Three Crows of Baden-Baden, Colonel Nagata, was forced reluctantly to draft an unpopular plan to lay off manpower from every Army division in order to preserve some funds in the Army till for long scheduled increases in tank and mobile units.

In the second week of January 1931, as War Minister Ugaki was returning to his office from one of his lunches with politicians, he was accosted in the corridors of the War Ministry by Lieutenant Colonel Hashimoto Kingoro, who would go down in American history for ordering the sinking of the U.S.S. *Panay* in the Yangtze River in 1937. Hashimoto had just returned from a tour of duty as an attaché in Turkey. He had interesting theories about fascism for small nations. When he hailed Ugaki as the "Kemal Ataturk of Japan," Ugaki stopped to chat with him. By way of explaining his greeting, Hashimoto persuaded Ugaki to stop by for a moment in the office of Major General Koiso Kuniaki, the over-all chief of the War Ministry's Military Affairs Bureau. Though technically a subordinate of Ugaki, Koiso administered his bureau with great independence, born of his recognized position as an old favorite of Field Marshal Prince Kanin.[4]

With many hooded words, Major General Koiso suggested to General Ugaki that the "Center of the Army"—a euphemism for Hirohito—had a historical mission for him to perform. Koiso then took Ugaki to an unpretentious adjunct of the General Staff Headquarters and ushered him into the office of Major General Tate-

[4] Koiso had ridden with the Mongols in their drive on Mukden during Prince Kanin's abortive coup in Manchuria in 1916. It would be Koiso who would act as Japanese prime minister during the black months of the kamikaze in late 1944 and early 1945.

kawa, the Chief of the Second Department, Intelligence. The ponderous, sleepy-eyed Tatekawa—the "Peerless Pimp" who had masterminded for Prince Kanin the Peking end of Chang Tso-lin's killing in 1928—suavely suggested to Ugaki over a cup of green tea that Emperor Hirohito was tired of Japan's interminable dirty politics; that the time had come to cleanse the nation; that Hirohito was ready to accept an honest shogun like Ugaki if he would lead the Army in an imperial coup d'etat.

The first diary reaction of the enthusiastic General Ugaki was favorable to the proposal, but after a few days' thought and investigation, he grew increasingly cautious and circumspect. He told Koiso and Tatekawa that he wished to see evidence of genuine national support before he committed himself. It was arranged for him on January 29, 1931, to take lunch with members of the Eleven Club, Hirohito's inner civilian circle, presided over that day by Big Brother Marquis Kido, the secretary of Lord Privy Seal Count Makino, and by Big Brother Baron Harada, the secretary-spy of old man Saionji.

Ugaki was visibly gratified by the luncheon but remained evasive about accepting his role in the plot. During the first week of February 1931, he told Major General Koiso that he was waiting to see realistic preparations for the coup. Koiso summoned his principal section chief, First Crow Nagata.

"Nagata-san," he said, "I want you to draft an operations plan for a military coup d'etat which will bring General Ugaki to power as the Emperor's shogun. Unless we have such a plan ready to use, a plan to restore the Emperor to true imperial power, we will never be able to get the politicians to support our program in Manchuria."

"Is it to be a real or a fake plan?" asked Nagata suspiciously.

"Write it as if it were real," ordered Koiso.

"It is a bad South American way to gain power," said Nagata, shaking his head. But a few days later he obediently slapped down a sheaf of papers on Koiso's desk with the contemptuous comment: "Here is the novel you asked me to write."

Nagata's novel called for a mob of 10,000 patriots to surround the Diet on March 20 and hurl smoke bombs at it. Then the 1st Division and the Imperial Guards Division were to proceed, for the sake of public peace, to throw a cordon of troops around the administrative heart of Tokyo. Major General Tatekawa of Intelligence or Major General Koiso of Military Affairs would stride into the Diet and demand a quick vote on the Army program: realization of the National Defense State under Ugaki and dissolution of political parties. Thereafter Ugaki would present himself to the Emperor in the palace to crave sanction for what was done, and an emissary would go to old man Saionji in Okitsu to demand his formal approval of it.

When Ugaki was advised of the plan, he wondered only where the bombs and the mob of 10,000 patriots were to come from. Major General Tatekawa promised that the mobs would be provided by the Black Dragon Society under the direction of Lord Privy Seal Makino's man, Dr. Okawa. As for the bombs, Tatekawa undertook to see to them himself. He wrote a letter to the principal of the Infantry School in Chiba, asking him to deliver to bearer 300 training grenades. The bearer was Lieutenant Colonel Hashimoto, the later *Panay*-sinker. The grenades were large, paper-encased firecrackers designed to create the illusion of battle during maneuvers. Each was guaranteed by the manufacturer to produce a six-foot jet of smoke and as much noise as four simultaneous rifle reports. Lieutenant Colonel Hashimoto brought them back to General Staff Headquarters in Tokyo, stacked them in Intelligence Chief Tatekawa's offices, and there, a day or two later, delivered them to an underling of Dr. Okawa for distribution to his civilian agitators.

Seeing at last that the coup might have some solid foundation in gunpowder, Ugaki sounded out Lieutenant General Mazaki Jinzaburo, the commander of the crack 1st Division which was slated in the coup planning to seize the Diet.[5] To General Ugaki's consternation Mazaki insisted that he knew nothing of any plans to seize the Diet and had no intention of participating in

[5] Mazaki was soon to become the number-two leader of the Strike-North idealists in the Army who would fight a long losing political battle with Hirohito over his plans to conquer China. He was a thoroughly blunt and honest officer, and the father of the Mazaki, mentioned in the Foreword, who befriended the author and his fellow inmates at a concentration camp in the Philippines during World War II.

"illegal activities" without direct written orders from the Emperor.[6]

UGAKI'S SEDUCTION

War Minister Ugaki was so shaken by Mazaki's advice that the unsavory Dr. Okawa had to begin courting him all over again. On February 11, 1931, Okawa took Ugaki out for an evening of talk and play at the Golden Dragon geisha house in Tsukiji. It was one of Tokyo's most expensive pleasure restaurants, a favorite of Lord Privy Seal Count Makino. Now, however, Ugaki was not easily to be seduced. The political planning for the coup still seemed vague to him, he said, and he was not yet convinced that it had the support of the "Center of the Army." After much drinking of saké, Ugaki went home, pleased with his discretion, to await developments.

On February 13, by Dr. Okawa's arrangement, Ugaki began a social whirl calculated to turn the head of any man born, as he had been, in a farmhouse, and living, as he was, on a salary of $3,000 a year. Not a day passed in which he did not lunch or dine with someone above his own hereditary station who could claim to be close to Hirohito. He started on January 13 with Colonel Okamura Yasuji, the third of the Three Crows of Baden-Baden, who, but for Commodore Perry, would have inherited the command of the Tokyo castle guard. Ugaki went on to lunch on February 14 with Hirohito's trusted go-between to Chiang Kai-shek, the ubiquitous Lieutenant Colonel Suzuki. A few days later Ugaki dined with Suzuki's patron, Big Brother Colonel Marquis Inoue Saburo, the illegitimate son of Emperor Taisho's Prime Minister Katsura. Next it was an invitation to the villa of Prince Konoye, the leader of Hirohito's faction in the House of Peers. And finally, through Konoye, War Minister Ugaki sat down to dinner in the villa of Count Arima, an in-law of the Empress.

Count Arima stated unequivocally that it was time to complete

---

[6] By so saying, Mazaki permanently alienated himself from the Throne. He would be relentlessly persecuted by the princes of the blood for the next five years and finally disgraced by unjust imprisonment and dishonorable discharge.

the Restoration of 1868 and place the Emperor at the helm of a National Socialist state.

For further details, Count Arima referred the befuddled, bedazzled Ugaki to the "paymaster of the proposed March incident," Baron Tokugawa Yoshichika, a scion of the great family of shoguns which had governed Japan from 1600 to 1868. Baron Tokugawa was well-to-do but not truly rich. Nevertheless, for the March Plot, he had at his disposal $100,000, which, as he said himself, was a large sum to disburse in the midst of a world depression.[7] War Minister Ugaki agreed.

On February 26, 1931, after two weeks in high society, Ugaki returned to a second evening of beguilement with Dr. Okawa and the geisha of the Golden Dragon teahouse. Ugaki was far more respectful toward Dr. Okawa than he had been but he continued to ask questions. What had become of the manifesto which Dr. Okawa was drafting? What was being done to enlist the massive popular support which Dr. Okawa had promised? The glib doctor assured Ugaki that the manifesto was being written and that an underground web of conspiracy was spreading through the people like mushroom roots. In the meanwhile it would greatly facilitate preparations if Dr. Okawa could tell his recruits that the great General Ugaki had promised to head the coup d'etat government.

"I have waited to see a concrete political plan for the new government," said Ugaki, "and some evidence of popular support for it. When I see these things, then I will give you my answer."

Ugaki passed the evening drinking saké, enjoying the geisha entertainment, and talking to a group of young Army officers who came to the party late with *Panay*-sinker Lieutenant Colonel Hashimoto. Before dawn, his head in the lap of a geisha, Ugaki was

[7] Tokugawa was the brother of Hirohito's chamberlain in charge of peerage and heraldry. His hobby was natural history and he was one of a group of amateur biologists who dined regularly with Hirohito in his private quarters. Through business interests in Malaya and Sumatra and through friendship with the rajah of Johore, Tokugawa was also a leading advocate of a policy of Striking South. When the Strike South finally came in 1942, Hirohito made him curator of the Botanical Gardens and Natural History Museum of Singapore. Under his charge this cradle of the theory of evolution would become, in 1943, a front for the master intelligence organization through which Hirohito kept track of his proconsuls in the newly acquired territories of the South Seas.

heard to boast: "If our plans go awry and the Emperor refuses to give his approval, I swear to cut open my belly in the Imperial Presence." Drunk though he was, Ugaki had thoroughly incriminated himself before geisha witnesses. He had threatened to embarrass the Throne. He had committed lèse majesté. It was all that the March Plotters needed—enough to keep Ugaki out of politics, enough to blight the rest of his career.

The next day, while Ugaki was recovering from his hangover, some of the members of the cabal who were closest to Hirohito began to spread word among their minions that the plot had served its purpose and would soon be canceled. At the same time Prince Kanin's Army conspirators, who wished to create a genuine national scare in preparation for the seizure of Manchuria, urged Dr. Okawa to stage at least a small public riot before the plot was allowed to grow moribund.

For the next three days Dr. Okawa remained imperturbably drinking saké at the Golden Dragon and signing chits in the name of Baron Tokugawa. Finally, on the evening of March 2, Military Affairs Bureau Chief Koiso invaded the teahouse, dragged Okawa from the arms of Yoshimaru, his geisha mistress, had him immersed in a scalding tub, and then sat him down in a quiet room to dictate notes to Black Dragon leaders instructing them to raise a mob the following afternoon in Hibiya and Ueno parks.

The "show of force" which materialized in the parks the next day was disappointing. Three thousand laborers, vagrants, and drunks, hired at fifty cents apiece, turned out to hear some routine patriotic speeches by ward heelers and shout a few banzais.

Too late, on the morning of March 3, General Ugaki telephoned Military Affairs Chief Koiso and announced, "I see no reason to become a party to this foolish scheme." Three more days passed before Ugaki realized that "this plot was not an ordinary one" and that he had been thoroughly traduced and suborned. On March 7, he went to the palace to declare his innocence of any disloyal intent. Dr. Okawa's patron, Lord Privy Seal Makino, who saw him on behalf of the Emperor, agreed to be lenient and promised Ugaki a face-saving assignment soon, out of the way, in Korea.

DR. OKAWA'S PROFITEERING

For the purposes of state the March Plot ended here, with Ugaki's shamefaced withdrawal from the presence of Lord Privy Seal Count Makino. For the private purposes of Dr. Okawa, however, it did not end until many months had passed. The devious doctor realized that his position was precarious and that he must make the most of his blackmail materials while they were still relevant and in his hands. The lord of the Black Dragon Toyama had lost face and needed to be recompensed. Prince Kanin's minions in the Army were disgusted by Okawa's performance and disposed to be unfriendly. After communicating by letter with his patron Count Makino, Dr. Okawa determined to use the 300 training grenades in his possession to embarrass the Army and to make sure that his bills would be paid to the hustlers of both the Black and Golden Dragon establishments with which he had done his business.

Until the third week of March, Dr. Okawa maintained that he intended to go ahead with the planned bombing of the Diet on March 20. Military Affairs Chief Koiso and General Staff Intelligence Chief Tatekawa became increasingly fearful that the Army's part in supplying the bombs might be made public. Finally, through the mediation of retired Colonel Komoto Daisaku, the Baden-Baden Reliable and bridge-blower who had dynamited Manchurian war lord Chang Tso-lin, Dr. Okawa agreed to give up his attack on the Diet in return for a suitable fee—one million yen ($500,000)! Baron Tokugawa, the March Plot's financier, observed that "these details make me feel unpleasant."

By retired Reliable Komoto's arrangement, Tokugawa met with Dr. Okawa at the Totaku Building in downtown Tokyo on the afternoon of March 18 and agreed on a greatly reduced but still stiff settlement of 200,000 yen ($100,000). The deal was witnessed by the administrator of Baron Tokugawa's estates and by Dr. Okawa's chief henchman. The administrator undertook to pay the 200,000 yen in four monthly installments and the henchman, "weeping with patriotic disappointment," promised to cancel the attack on the Diet.

It was agreed that Dr. Okawa would keep the Army's bombs for security until the money had been paid. That night Dr. Okawa's henchman moved the bombs secretly from his girl friend's home to a trucker's warehouse in northwestern Tokyo. There they were kept for a year and used as a reminder to the high brass of the Army that the March Plot could be revived at any time. Baron Tokugawa paid the huge blackmail, stayed solvent, and continued to enjoy his intimacy with Hirohito. Dr. Okawa settled with the Black Dragon, paid his bill at the Golden Dragon, and remained at large to carry out many more nefarious commissions for Hirohito's chief advisor, Lord Privy Seal Count Makino.

Late on the afternoon of the settlement, the first of the Big Brothers, Count Makino's secretary, Marquis Kido, took the train out to Prime-Minister-Maker Saionji's villa on the seashore at Okitsu and told the old man about "the coup d'etat of General Ugaki" which had just been successfully "nipped in the bud." Saionji, recognizing defeat, assumed an air of noncommittal indifference. In the course of the evening, however, he allowed some of his bitterness to come out in critical reminiscences about Lord Privy Seal Makino at the Versailles Conference. Years later, writing in prison, Kido was to admire Privy Seal Makino's deftness "in conducting . . . the March Plot . . . out of darkness into darkness."

Both the Strike-North rightists in the Army and the strike-nowhere Constitutionalists around Saionji had been intimidated. General Ugaki had seized the bait and run with it far enough to spoil his chances for a political career. Many important fish knew of the fishing but hardly a bubble had broken through to the surface of Japan's deep political sea. In less than a year Hirohito was to appoint Major General Koiso, the plot-master, to the post of vice war minister.

12

SEIZURE OF MUKDEN

(1931)

CLEARING THE DECKS

Disquieting rumors of the March Plot, dissatisfaction with budget cuts, and alarm at the military's share in the planning for the future made for a stormy spring session of the Diet. At the end of it, in April 1931, the Cabinet resigned and left its prime minister, Hamaguchi, to die of his gunshot wounds in the quiet of private life. Hirohito appointed as the next prime minister Wakatsuki Reijiro, vice president of Hamaguchi's party and former chief delegate to the 1930 London Naval Conference. Ex-War Minister Ugaki, notwithstanding his past services to the Throne, his firm intention of going into politics, and his recent flirtation with high treason, meekly withdrew from the domestic scene to become the governor general in Korea.

Prime Minister Wakatsuki obediently submitted to Hirohito an ordinance requiring all government employees except judges to accept a 10 per cent decrease in salary if they made more than $50 a month. Judges' salaries, by a peculiarity of the administrative code, could not be decreased except by the judges themselves. During the formulative stages of the ordinance there had been bitter complaints from young bureaucrats of good family and even from some of the patriotic but already underpaid officers of the armed forces. Now, however, when Hirohito signed the decree on May 27, 1931, the nation's servants gave an astonishingly Japanese exhibition of self-denial by "tightening their loincloth strings" and submitting in silence. The bar association resolved that the judiciary should follow suit voluntarily and individual judges did so without known exception.

Hirohito was now ready, politically and financially, to launch his imperial program on the Asiatic continent. Throughout the summer of 1931 he devoted his attention to a detailed review of the military plans which had been made. His objectives differed from those of most of his Army advisors. He wanted to control Manchurian bases in order to establish a pattern which would enable him later to control other strategic bases all down the China coast toward Singapore. He did not set high priority on outright conquest and colonization of Manchuria. The acquisition of Korea, under his grandfather, had already demonstrated that Japan's overpopulation problem could not be solved by expansion toward the north. The mass of Japanese were simply not interested in emigrating to chilly farmlands, no matter how rich. Even Ainu Hokkaido, subjugated centuries ago, was still sparsely populated. What Japan needed were warm lands for colonists and resources for industrial development—the oil and rubber and minerals of the East Indies. Only the unsophisticated Army mind could desire Manchuria as an end in itself.

Hirohito had before him two plans. One called for a cutback in Army manpower, an increase in mechanization, more divisions stationed in Korea, and no increase in the Army budget. It would strengthen the Army for any use to which it might be put. Hirohito approved it formally on July 15, 1931.

The other plan, of greater moment, was the operational blueprint for the take-over of Manchuria which Hirohito had commissioned in 1928 from the young, corrosive-tongued military genius, Lieutenant Colonel Ishiwara Kanji. Ishiwara's completed study was exhaustive and imaginative. It anticipated all military contingencies and gracefully suggested a number of political stratagems which might be used in Japan and abroad to make the operation seem accidental. Hirohito admired all of it except for a few visionary pages toward the end in which Ishiwara expressed his hopes for making Manchuria a "paradise."

Officially, in late 1930, Hirohito had had Ishiwara's opus filed away as "contingency planning, top secret." Unofficially he had told his great-uncle, Field Marshal Prince Kanin, to see that all necessary military preparations were made so that the plan would be ready for execution by August 1931. Secretly with Count Makino, Hirohito was now gnawing over the political implications and deciding on certain options which he would reserve for himself, to exercise or not, when the time came.

As soon as Hirohito gave his unofficial nod, operatives of the cabal in Army Intelligence and in the military secret police began to find and make provocations for intervention in Manchuria. In June 1931, a Japanese intelligence agent, traveling as an "agricultural expert" in eastern Mongolia, was apprehended and shot by Chinese soldiers for being a spy. In July the Kwantung Army sent troops into a border area of Manchuria to protect the rights of Korean immigrants there who were being harassed by Chinese farmers in the digging of a drainage ditch.

CHOICE OF A COMMANDER

From July 13 to 17, the regimental commanders of the principal division which would be used in Manchuria, the 10th, met for "map exercises" and "tactical studies." Their chief was Lieutenant General Honjo Shigeru, an ideal leader for a controversial operation. At fifty-five he was respected by the rank and file as one of the most capable of the elder generation of nonpolitical Army professionals. Trained in garrison duty in China, long a friend of the murdered Manchurian war lord Chang Tso-lin, he spoke fluent Chinese and was a firm believer in ultimate Sino-Japanese partnership. Now, because of mounting tension with China he was letting his mustache grow to conceal his striking personal resemblance to Chiang Kai-shek.

On July 13, as Lieutenant General Honjo presided over the opening of his division's map exercises, General Ugaki, on his way to Korea as the new governor general, stopped by at the 10th Division base southwest of Osaka to greet Honjo and have a talk with him. Seven years of strict Japanese military seniority separated the two, but Honjo, the junior, was warmly disposed toward Ugaki.

He owed Ugaki many past favors, and he knew that Ugaki's new post was not all that the older general had hoped for.

The two men met over tea in a kiosk beside the railroad track. Ugaki circled in slowly to the point of the conversation. It was a part of his penitence to the Throne for high treason—part of the price he was paying for his position of continued honor in the hierarchy—that he persuade his protégé Honjo to lend his name and leadership to the seizure of Manchuria. Without going into details, he suggested to Honjo that a bargain had been made with Chiang Kai-shek, that Japanese occupation of Manchuria was a necessity in view of the growing military strength of Bolshevik Russia. Some day, he piously hoped, Manchuria would be a model Asiatic state which would serve as a bridge and a bond of friendship between China and Japan. Then, abruptly, he told General Honjo that he was "the choice of the Center of the Army" to be the next commander-in-chief of Japan's leasehold presence in Manchuria, the Kwantung Army. Honjo realized that he was being asked a question and replied at once that he would be greatly honored if the majority of the Army, the sensible field officers of the Ugaki Faction, should back him for such a promotion.

Ugaki grunted his appreciation and returned to his train. At the next station, he wired old Prince Kanin's man, Major General Koiso of the Military Affairs Bureau in Tokyo, that Honjo would accept. Two days later Hirohito set his great seal upon Honjo's reassignment papers, and the cabal's ubiquitous Lieutenant Colonel Suzuki Tei-ichi arrived at Honjo's headquarters to inform him, unofficially, of the great confidence which the Emperor placed in him.

Furthermore, continued Colonel Suzuki, the Emperor had approved the appointment of Colonel Doihara Kenji as chief of the Special Service Organ in Mukden, the Army's political espionage agency there. General Honjo knew Doihara well—he had worked with him in Peking in 1918. Doihara was one of the Eleven Reliables chosen at Baden-Baden. Having served in China almost continuously since 1913, he had a wide acquaintance with petty war lords, malcontent mandarins, and out-of-power Manchu princes. His understanding of transactions conducted in the irregular currencies of China—women, bombs, opium packets—had

JAPAN AND
HER NEIGHBORS

☐ JAPAN IN 1930

gained him a name as the "Lawrence of Manchuria." The Mukden branch of the Special Service Organ had hitherto been run by minor operatives; at the very least, Doihara's appointment to it meant a change in Chang Hsueh-liang's regime in Manchuria.

Finally, Suzuki reported, the Emperor had appointed Colonel Tojo Hideki, the later military strongman of World War II, to be chief of the General Staff's Organization and Mobilization Section. Honjo knew Tojo only slightly; he seemed to be a competent desk man, a stickler for details and efficiency.

Honjo sighed expressively and told Suzuki that he was ready for whatever duty lay ahead. Privately, as revealed in his diary, he had many doubts, suspicions, and second thoughts.

AN EERIE QUIET

In mid-July old Saionji confided to Prime Minister Wakatsuki that he was alarmed by rumors which he heard from many directions about plans for war in China. Wakatsuki took advantage of the recent "incidents" in Korea and China to make a special report to the Throne on the growing tension between Japan and China. Chiang Kai-shek, he said, had correctly accused the Japanese Army in a recent speech of supplying money and guns to anti-Chiang insurgents in the Canton area. A delegation from the Canton faction of the KMT or Kuomintang had now arrived in Tokyo to negotiate official Japanese recognition and support for their regime. The experts in the Foreign Ministry advised a friendly but noncommittal response on Japan's part. Nodding approvingly, Hirohito said that he deplored the deterioration in Sino-Japanese relations. He added, "I may assume, may I not, that you will keep Sino-Japanese goodwill as the cornerstone of our policy?"

Prime Minister Wakatsuki, emerging from the audience chamber, asked Baron Harada if the Emperor meant "Sino-Japanese goodwill or its opposite." Saionji, when the quip had been relayed to him, sent a note to Privy Seal Makino asking him to clarify the Emperor's ambiguity. A vice chamberlain at once arrived in Okitsu by the sea to assure old man Saionji that when the Emperor said "Sino-Japanese goodwill," he meant only that and nothing more.

"Bear in mind," sniped Saionji at his political secretary, his intermediary with the cabal, "that they sent me only an *assistant chamberlain.*" He implied that any higher chamberlain, knowing better, could not have relayed the message without shame of lying.

Everyone in the aristocracy, many in the middle-class bureaucracy, and a few in the masses of the foot soldiers knew that the conquest of Manchuria was in the making, but not a word of their suspicion was printed in the press or discussed at public gatherings. The Emperor's secret was the secret of the nation. Nowhere but in Japan could the plans of the chief be held so privily in the minds of the whole tribe. On small uncivilized islands out in the Pacific American anthropologists had encountered similar secrecy toward outsiders. But in such a large industrial nation as Japan, the thought had to be dismissed as madness. Intelligence officers at the American Embassy in Tokyo warned Washington of tension in the Far East but discounted the possibility of war.

Even the Chinese government showed no unusual signs of alarm. Chiang Kai-shek was waging one of his periodic "bandit suppression campaigns" against the peasant "rabble" of Communist Mao Tse-tung. Chiang had with him the whole of the Manchurian Army as well as its leader, his faithful disciple, young Chang Hsueh-liang. It seemed inconceivable to Western military observers that Chiang and Chang would leave Manchuria defended only by raw levies unless they thought that Japan meant nothing serious. Western observers, however, did not know that Chiang Kai-shek, and Sun Yat-sen before him, had agreed to sacrifice Manchuria with only a token face-saving fight if Japan would promise not to interfere with KMT unification of the rest of China.

By July 22, 1931, it was apparent to American reporters in Manchuria that the Kwantung Army had set up field pieces all along the right of way of the Japanese-owned South Manchuria Railroad. Chiang Kai-shek filed no protest, and Chang Hsueh-liang merely retired to the American Rockefeller Hospital in Peking for one of his recurrent treatments for opium addiction.

READY AND AIMED

On July 25 the last bolt was tightened on the iron floor of the most monstrous of Japan's unseeable war preparations: a pair of 9.5-inch cannon mounted in a shallow silo in the very heart of the

Manchurian capital of Mukden. Twenty-five years earlier the Russians had used the cannon to good effect at the siege of Port Arthur. The bold idea of trucking the weapons north and installing them in the Japanese compound in Mukden had occurred to the brash young strategist, Lieutenant Colonel Ishiwara in late 1928. During the summer of 1929, he had prepared an emplacement for them under the unlikely cover story that the Japanese community of attachés and aides in Mukden were building themselves a swimming pool.

Hired Chinese coolies dutifully sank in the earth a concrete pan 33 feet in diameter and 39 inches deep. To keep out the cold and preserve bathing officers from the ogling of Chinese passers-by, the "pool" was surrounded by a large shed covered with a flimsy pretext of a roof that would permit an easy exit for shells. At one end were hung big barnlike doors to permit an easy entrance for heavy aquatic equipment such as diving boards. Late one night in May 1931, however, the doors were opened to admit two heavily guarded vans, containing the cannon. One of the cannon was installed so that it was permanently trained on the main barracks of the Mukden constabulary; the other so that it was aimed at the airfield from which Chang Hsueh-liang flew his fledgling air force. While this incredibly brazen piece of chicanery was under construction, Chinese plainclothesmen stood daily watch across the street from the shed. When the moment to use the guns finally arrived, no countermeasures had been taken to prevent them from hailing down shot on their two targets.

COMPROMISE FOR CONQUEST

Since receiving Hirohito's go-ahead in early June 1931, Ishiwara had worked with a fanatic's zeal to prepare for his scheme of inside-out conquest. As soon as the emplacement of the big guns in Mukden had been completed, he returned to Tokyo, in the last week of July, to answer questions about his efforts from the other military members of the cabal. The young bloods of the Strike-North faction in the General Staff approved his plans enthusiastically. But from older cabalists—like First Crow Nagata and the later World War II prime minister, Tojo Hideki—he received only qualified encouragement, tempered with many political anxieties.

The thorny Isiwara, knowing his own limitations as a politician, had come to Tokyo forearmed for such objections. He had brought with him from Manchuria Colonel Itagaki Seishiro, one of the Eleven Reliables chosen at Baden-Baden. Itagaki had worked with him in Manchuria since the summer of 1929, supplementing his tactical vinegar with the oil of a consummate politician. Itagaki came of a good family, high among the retainers of the old Nambu clan which had governed the northern extremities of Japan for the Tokugawa shoguns. He had the sleek round-faced neatly mustached look of a seal, and he slapped backs like a veteran tour director. He never gave the impression of being too quick-witted. Indeed, on a later occasion, Emperor Hirohito would tell him to his face, "You are the most stupid man alive." But he had the knack of making other men's ideas socially presentable and politically acceptable. Long after Ishiwara's genius and ideals had been put prematurely to pasture, Itagaki would remain at Hirohito's side, full of bland inoffensive energy. He would lead Japan's best mobile division to the worst defeat of Japan's war with China. He would reign as war minister during Japan's disastrous Nomonhan border war with Russia in 1939. He would command the Korean Army throughout World War II. He would officiate over the humiliating surrender of Singapore to the British in 1945. Until his hanging in 1948, he would serve in prison as the most relaxed and optimistic of the defendants at the Tokyo war crimes trials. Even his American captors would admire him for his open, bloodthirsty, devil-may-care attitude.

On the morning of August 1, 1931, Lieutenant General Honjo reported at the Summer Palace in Hayama to take lunch and receive his new command officially at the hands of the Emperor. The time had come, under Honjo's aegis, to brief the field commanders of the Army on the confusing pressures which would be exerted on them in the months ahead. Hirohito, as the representative of his high priestly ancestors, could not openly take responsibility for the seizure of Manchuria. The responsibility must be shouldered by the official government of Cabinet and prime minister. The government, however, was unwilling to accept the responsibility. Hirohito and Count Makino planned to use the Army to intimidate the government. At the same time, the government's timidity would serve as an excuse to keep the Army from bulling north across Manchuria into a war with Soviet Russia. In this fashion Hirohito hoped to control both the moderates, who wished to avoid foreign entanglements, and the militarists, who wished to exhaust Japan's empire-building energies in Siberia. Hirohito's personal ambition, the Strike-South into the rich fleshpots of the South Seas, was still so futuristic in terms of national strength that mention of it would only align the militarists and moderates against Hirohito.

The commanders of Japan's seventeen standing divisions and three colonial armies met for briefing on the Manchurian operation on August 3. Hirohito gave an individual audience to each commander, dropping word that he knew and approved of the events scheduled for the near future. During the audiences with the Emperor, General Honjo of the 10th Division was put in another room of the palace to work out secret lines of liaison between the Throne and his future command in Manchuria. Closeted with him were the ubiquitous Lieutenant Colonel Suzuki, to speak for the Throne, and the affable Colonel Itagaki, to speak for strategist Ishiwara and the Kwantung Army's troops in the field.

That night at a secret meeting in the muggy offices of the General Staff just outside the palace walls, Prince Kanin's two minions, Peerless Pimp Tatekawa and March Plotter Koiso, cautioned a select gathering of field commanders not to divulge classified sections of the planning for Manchuria to War Minister General Minami Jiro. Too much knowledge, they agreed, would only compromise Minami and compound the difficulties of the role he had to play as intermediary between the Throne and the Cabinet.

The next day, August 4, General Minami delivered his scheduled address to Japan's commanders before they returned to their divisions. It was the one function of the three-day conference which was to be public and open to the press. Innocently assuming that the conquest of Manchuria was to be a blunt, straightforward, above-board military operation, General Minami added to his speech a patriotic exhortation to the troops.

"Accordingly," he concluded, "those who must render service in military affairs this fall have the obligation to pursue their training and arduous education diligently. It is to be expected that they will be completely prepared to exercise their duty."

War Minister Minami had unwittingly alerted the public to the coming Manchurian campaign, for Japanese newspaper reporters heard in his words the first official admission that Japan was going to war.[1] The big dailies at first printed Minami's remarks without comment, but two days later, *Asahi* (the equivalent of *The New York Times* in Tokyo) noted editorially: "The military seems to be openly disregarding public opinion and defying the government."

This oblique statement was the only reporting of the fact that old Saionji and his fellow liberals were waging a desperate last-ditch struggle behind the scenes to prevent the planned war. Saionji had persuaded the civilian members of the Cabinet to refuse to approve the necessary transfers of funds for the war. Hirohito, for his part, refused to give his official sanction to the war unless the Cabinet would back him by assuming fiscal responsibility. War Minister General Minami took the position that he could not begin the war without properly signed imperial orders.

Unofficially, Hirohito was encouraging the junior officers of his cabal to push forward on their own. On August 25 the spokesman for a group of concerned young men in the Naval General Staff asked Secretary-Spy Harada to warn Saionji that Hirohito was, in effect, planning to move troops in Manchuria even without first giving his sanction.

Saionji was obliged to recognize that the Cabinet's refusal to be involved in the war would avail him nothing. That same day, at his summer villa in the mountain resort of Gotemba, he received a visit from Prime Minister Wakatsuki who urged him to accept a compromise. As he watched the sun sink behind the

---

[1] That night Kido, Lord Privy Seal Makino's secretary, wrote in his diary: "A strong wind from Minami made things very damp." In one of his typically discreet private jokes with his diary, Kido was punning on the name Minami, which is also the Japanese word for south. Honjo's diary and the newspaper weather columns for the date of Minami's speech leave no doubt that it was an ordinary hot, overcast, August day without a drop of rain or a breath of wind.

towering cinder cone of Mount Fuji, Saionji said he would consider Wakatsuki's proposal.

Sometime in the following week, a month before his eighty-
second birthday, Saionji sent word to Prime Minister Wakatsuki
that he would accept the offered compromise: first a limited operation around Mukden in southern Manchuria, then "a pause for
reflection" before further advances. Through Japan's ancient, efficient, uncensorable communications system, the word-of-mouth
grapevine, the general public was informed that an adjustment
had been made and a consensus reached. During the next week
the Tokyo daily papers received several thousand calls from readers
asking, "When is the war going to start?" Westerners living in
Japan, particularly Western intelligence agents, were given hardly
a hint of the excitement in the air.

VEILED ORDERS

On September 14 Saionji summoned War Minister Minami
to his villa in Gotemba and gave him a broadly constructed version of the terms which he had accepted. The Emperor, Saionji
said, had decided that the Kwantung Army must proceed with
"prudence and caution" and must limit its operations—at least
to begin with—to the environs of Mukden and a few other railheads in south central Manchuria. Saionji did not explain how
the Army could attack and kill with prudent caution or how it
was to seize and hold an enclave without strategic boundaries,
in the midst of China.

When War Minister Minami returned to Tokyo the next morning, he summoned an emergency meeting of Army brass and relayed Saionji's strictures. At first the majority of the offices present
were in favor of shelving the conquest plans entirely rather than
court disaster by starting something that could not be finished.
The officers closest to Hirohito, however, assured the others that
no such drastic change of course was expected of them. In the
end it was agreed that Saionji's orders must be delivered verbatim
to the Kwantung Army but must also be explained lest they cause
confusion. To tell an obedient, circumspect commander like Lieutenant General Honjo that the Emperor wished him to move with

caution would be to tell him not to move at all without further instructions.

The choice of the emissary to Honjo might have been made by War Minister Minami if alert members of the cabal had not pointed out that a commander on war duty was under the jurisdiction of the General Staff and that the courier to General Honjo should be appointed by the Chief of Staff. Minami agreed and the meeting broke up.

Major General Koiso of the Military Affairs Bureau at once telephoned Major General Tatekawa, the Peerless Pimp, Chief of Operations in the General Staff, and Tatekawa quickly arranged to have himself sent to Manchuria with Saionji's message. Then Tatekawa summoned to his office the chiefs of the Russia and China Desks in Army Intelligence, who listened while Tatekawa treated them to a long, musing soliloquy. The scheduled date for the "rising" in Manchuria was September 28, was it not? In view of the mounting dissension in the Army, it would be well to move the date up to the earliest moment possible. The Emperor had taken it upon his own conscience to lead the nation in what must be done. Because of Japan's relative weakness, duplicity was required. It was up to every loyal Japanese to lighten the Emperor's burden as much as possible and prevent any tarnish from settling on the sacred Throne bequeathed by the ancestors. In this present critical period, there must always be one official plan for foreigners, a second for Japanese, and a third for the Emperor's personal retainers. It should not be necessary for the Throne to issue explicit orders for the drawing up of such covers. They should come into being automatically out of the patriotic desire of every Japanese to preserve the honor of the nation.

Having expressed his thoughts in front of his two subordinates, Tatekawa sat down and drafted an official Army cablegram to General Honjo. Tatekawa announced that he planned to visit Mukden, the Manchurian capital, three days later, arriving by train at 7:05 P.M. on the evening of September 18. The fact that he gave Honjo three days to prepare for his coming and that he wished to meet Honjo in Mukden rather than the Kwantung Army's leasehold headquarters in Port Arthur 250 miles to the south suggested broadly that Honjo should carry out the coup ahead of schedule and be ready as conqueror to receive visitors in the enemy capital by September 18. Tatekawa read the cable aloud, affixed to it his seal, and asked the two desk chiefs, who had been standing by throughout his performance, to see that it was properly encoded and dispatched.

The chief of the China Desk returned to his office and drafted a second telegram of his own to Colonel Itagaki, the politician of the Kwantung Army. In it he repeated the itinerary of Tatekawa's trip to Mukden, and added: HOSPITABLE TREATMENT WILL BE APPRECIATED; HIS MISSION IS TO PREVENT THE INCIDENT. The Russian Desk man, Lieutenant Colonel Hashimoto, who six years later was to order the sinking of the U.S.S. *Panay*, sent off a third telegram. Stamped "top secret, personal," it was addressed to a close friend who was an aide of Ishiwara, the strategist of the Kwantung Army. This telegram said succinctly and dramatically: PLOT EXPOSED. ACT BEFORE TATEKAWA'S ARRIVAL.

While Tatekawa proceeded leisurely by train through Japan and Korea, stretching a one-day journey into three, his cablegrams were causing consternation at Kwantung Army Headquarters in Port Arthur. General Honjo was away inspecting preparations in Mukden, and Itagaki and Ishiwara had been left in charge. Itagaki, the politician, took the cable to mean that the Emperor wished the seizure of Mukden to be executed immediately. Ishiwara, the strategist, was concerned lest his delicately timed plans be spoiled by last-minute haste. Both men feared that General Honjo's reaction to the cables would be to postpone everything until he heard more from Tokyo. Then the glorious enterprise for which they had both worked night and day for over two years might all come to naught. While they discussed what to do, they held up the cable to Honjo and did not forward it. Finally they resolved to ask Honjo to schedule the seizure of Mukden for the night of September 18, a few hours after the anticipated arrival of Peerless Pimp Tatekawa. In this way they would be able to hear from Tatekawa the situation in Tokyo around the Throne and would still have time, if need be, to call all units and cancel the action. While Ishiwara was drafting the necessary orders, Itagaki entrained for Mukden to present the plan to General Honjo.

On September 16, while Ishiwara and Itagaki were agonizing over the contents of the cablegrams, Honjo completed his inspection and went by rail to a place called Liaoyang or Far-from-the-Sun, a junction 40 miles south of Mukden where the Japanese railroad management had a small airfield. There Honjo met old General Suzuki Soroku who had just flown in from Tokyo. Suzuki was the near twin and for forty years the cavalry comrade of Field Marshal Prince Kanin, the gray eminence of the imperial family. He had left Tokyo at about the same time as Tatekawa's cablegrams. Over dinner he and Honjo discussed the situation at home.

Later that evening when Itagaki arrived breathless from Port Arthur, Honjo introduced him curtly to General Suzuki and told him, please, to take some responsibility and handle details himself rather than bothering old generals in their moments of relaxation. Itagaki hastily bowed his way out, consulted with Ishiwara by phone, and then issued the necessary orders for the night after next.

Cover plans were now completed. If the operation went awry, Prince Kanin was ready to take responsibility for Hirohito, Tatekawa for Prince Kanin, Honjo for Tatekawa, and Itagaki for Honjo. If all went well, each would share in the credit, according to his station. Ultimately Ishiwara and Itagaki would take the blame, and Itagaki would be hanged for it by the Allies.[2]

THE GO-AHEAD

On the morning of September 17, 1931, after spending the previous evening with Prince Kanin's emissary from Tokyo, General Honjo went to a park in Far-from-the-Sun. There he reviewed a dress rehearsal by Japanese troops of the "incident" on the railroad which was to serve as provocation for the war of conquest scheduled to start the next night. Early on D-day, September 18,

---

[2] The multiplicity of cover stories would convince Western historians that junior officers had acted on their own and later shamed senior officers into sanctioning what had been done. The reality, in which every man on the ladder, from lowest to highest, conspired to deceive, knowing exactly what was afoot, is demonstrated by Lieutenant General Honjo's diary.

Honjo canceled a scheduled visit to one of the battlefields of the Russo-Japanese War and devoted the morning and early afternoon to a detailed run-through of all plans with his field commanders. At 2:00 P.M. he boarded a Pullman car for a good sleep during the six-hour journey back to his headquarters at Port Arthur.

While his Pullman clattered away from Mukden toward the southwest, the train of Peerless Pimp Tatekawa crossed the Korean border and approached Mukden from the southeast. At 5:18 it stopped to take on water at the village station of Pen-hsi-hu, Lake-at-the-Bottom-of-the-Valley. There it was boarded by the affable politician of the Kwantung Army, Itagaki. He was ushered to the parlor car of the affable Tatekawa, and the two like-minded officers sat down to enjoy an hour and forty-seven minutes of circumspect belly talk while their train completed its run into Mukden. The opening gambits of their conversation, as reconstructed from stories they later told their friends, went like this:

Itagaki: "You are well, sir, I hope."

Tatekawa: "Well, as a matter of fact, I have not slept much on the train and I hear you boisterous youngsters need discipline, but let's leave all that until I have had a good night's rest."

Itagaki: "We young men are also tired by our recent efforts, sir. So have no doubts about us but let me take you to a good inn when we arrive in Mukden and we will discuss business in the morning."

When the train reached Mukden at 7:05 P.M., a staff car was waiting, chauffeured by a young major, the officer who had received *Panay*-sinker Hashimoto's cablegram three days earlier. He drove Tatekawa and Itagaki to the best teahouse in the Japanese quarter, the Literary Chrysanthemum. There the choicest geisha and saké had been laid on for the night. Itagaki drank one toast and then said that he was expecting a very important phone call at the Special Service Organ. With this excuse, he left Tatekawa, to have his bath and drink and eat, in the care of the young major and the geisha.

The Special Service Organ office, a two-story building of reinforced concrete, had been chosen as the communications center for the night's activities. Linesmen of the South Manchuria Railroad had equipped the switchboard with open connections to all the Japanese garrisons along the railroad right of way. A staff of lieutenants and captains stood by to man the phones, armed with maps and synchronized watches. Colonel Doihara Kenji, the "Lawrence of Manchuria," who was in command of the Special Service Organ, was out on the town politicking with Chinese friends to prepare a way for himself to become "Mayor of Mukden" in the morning. In his absence an elaborate pretence was maintained that Colonel Itagaki was merely filling in for him during a routine evening's operation.

When Itagaki arrived from the Literary Chrysanthemum, he put through a call from Doihara's private office in Mukden to a portrait painter in Dairen, the harbor town adjoining Port Arthur. It so happens that, a few moments earlier, at 8:00 P.M., General Honjo had also intruded upon the same portrait painter in Dairen. On his way to Port Arthur, after his exhausting day of reviews and travel, he had decided to stop off and inspect progress on a portrait of himself which the artist was painting. After what must have been a prolonged chat with Itagaki on the phone, Honjo left the painter's home a little after 9:00 P.M., drove to Port Arthur, and retired to restore his flagging energies in a hot Japanese tub.

In Mukden, having finished his phone call, Itagaki emerged from his office all smiles, thereby signifying to his staff that the light was green. Then he lay down ostentatiously on a couch to take a nap in preparation for a long night's work.

At the South Manchuria Railroad track north of Mukden, an operative of the Special Service Organ[3] was wiring up forty-two cubes of yellow blasting powder on the embankment, five feet to the west of the tracks running in from the northern town of Changchun or Long Spring Thaw. He buried the explosives carefully so that they would throw a lot of dirt but would cause no real damage to the strategically important Japanese-owned railroad track. Later the Japanese Foreign Ministry would maintain that Chinese soldiers had set the blast and that it had destroyed

[3] Lieutenant Komoto Suemori, a member of the same Kobe family of Komotos whose Colonel Komoto Daisaku had blown up Chang Tso-lin under similar circumstances in 1928.

over a yard of track, seriously disrupting operation of the line. While making repairs, the Japanese Army would cordon off the area so that no Chinese could go near the damage to inspect it. After an "official investigation" the Army would try to explain how the 10:40 express from Long Spring Thaw had passed over the track a few minutes after the explosion and arrived in Mukden without its passengers feeling a jolt. The Army would produce an "eyewitness" of the should-have-been derailment and quote him as saying: "When the express reached the site of the explosion, it was seen to sway and incline to one side but it recovered and passed on without stopping."

ONE-NIGHT WAR

The plunger for the mock bombing of the tracks was pushed at approximately 10:20 P.M. Japanese railroad guards who had been ready waiting in the area for a week "conducting night maneuvers"—so they had told the Chinese—at once fell upon a Chinese constabulary patrol which had been sent to watch them. Two companies of Japanese regulars from the Kwantung Army, who were billeted nearby, joined instantly in the mopping-up operations.

The Japanese dynamiter at the track phoned the Special Service Organ in Mukden. There Colonel Itagaki had just risen, glanced at his watch, yawned, put on his coat, and announced to his amazed staff that he was going home to sleep in his billet. When the phone call came, however, he calmly told the dynamiter at the other end of the line to begin at once to attack the North Barracks of the Chinese garrison, some 300 yards from the scene of the mock bombing. No sooner had he given this order than the switchboard cut him into a second line, leading to the concealed battery of 9.5-inch Russian cannon. He ordered the gunnery officer there to commence firing. One after another the staffers of the Special Service Organ connected Itagaki with duty officers at Japanese garrisons up and down the right of way of the South Manchuria Railroad. Over and over again Itagaki repeated the order: "This is Itagaki; proceed at once according to plan." Within two hours most of the small junction towns in south central Manchuria were in Japanese hands.

At 9:00 P.M., in the Literary Chrysanthemum, Major General Tatekawa from Tokyo had retired to rest with one of the geisha provided for him. "I have no intention," he told her, "of blocking our patriotic young officers." At about 10:30 when the big guns opened up on the Chinese airport and constabulary barracks, his bedmate shook him awake and said she was frightened by the explosions. He made his way to the inn lobby, dressed only in sleeping kimono, and found there a group of soldiers who politely assured him, "We have been ordered to guard you and prevent you from going out where it is dangerous."

"Very well then," said Tatekawa, "the girl and I will go back to bed and leave the hard work to you young men." Tatekawa returned to his room, slipped on his clothes, and stole out a back door to be escorted by another group of soldiers to the headquarters of one of the units engaged in the action. Later that night, while his geisha swore he was sleeping like a baby at her side, he was seen with drawn sabre leading an attack on the walled citadel of Mukden.

As the shells of the big guns fell upon the massive gate leading into the Chinese constabulary barracks, the 10,000 Chinese within the compound began an orderly withdrawal through a back gate. They left the lights on in the buildings where they had lived in order to draw Japanese fire and demonstrate to the world that they had been going about their normal evening pursuits, expecting nothing. A force of 500 Japanese soldiers, in full battle dress, occupied the vacant compound inch by inch and secured it without casualties.

At 11:00 P.M., as the "storming of the barracks" began, General Honjo was still steeping in his hot bath at Port Arthur, 250 miles to the south. His chief of staff burst in on him, exclaiming, "Itagaki is on the phone! He has activated the garrisons without your express permission!"

"So that's how it is, is it?" growled Honjo. He arose majestically from the bath water, donned a kimono, and strode into the next room where his staff officers were waiting for him around the phone. Ishiwara, the strategist, spoke for them in terms of sup-

plication. "The odds against us are staggering.⁴ The entire countryside may rise. Offense is our only defense. I hope, sir, that you
will allow Itagaki to proceed with the contingency plan that has
already been prepared."

Lieutenant General Honjo squatted dramatically on the matting by the telephone for a moment of Zen contemplation. "Very
well then," he declared, opening his eyes, "let it be done on my
own responsibility." He took the phone, loudly reproved Itagaki
for acting without authorization, and then simply listened, inter-
jecting an occasional "Hai! So be it."

Honjo approved Itagaki's plans for attacking the walled city of
downtown Mukden at 11:30 P.M. A full regiment, said Itagaki,
had already grouped for the attack. Major General Tatekawa, incognito, was assisting the colonel of the regiment in order to give
the troops "fighting spirit." By the railroad track north of the city
Japanese troops had occupied most of the constabulary barracks.
The 9.5-inch cannon trained on Chang Hsueh-liang's airport was
reported to be putting shells right on target, demolishing hangars
and planes. None of the Chinese airmen had attempted to take
off in the dark.

Honjo hung up smiling and ordered his staff to prepare for
immediate transfer of Kwantung Army Headquarters north to
Mukden. At 1:30 A.M., September 19, he phoned the commander
of Japan's Korean Army in Seoul, seeking to share a little of his
responsibility. He was assured that Japanese troops in Korea
would lend assistance as necessary. A wing of Japan's Korean-
based air force would be ready to land at the Mukden airfield as
soon as light came. Having notified Colonel Itagaki of these arrangements, Lieutenant General Honjo boarded a train for Mukden at 3:30 A.M.

Ten minutes later Mukden's walled citadel was declared secure
and Major General Tatekawa returned to the Literary Chrysanthemum to sleep. About an hour later the Hasebe Brigade oc-

---

⁴ By later Japanese reckoning 200,000 to 10,000. In reality Honjo had at his
disposal about 20,000 men—an augmented division plus five battalions of railroad guards. The 200,000 Chinese arrayed against him consisted of green
levies and irregulars, ill-equipped and undisciplined. They were under orders to
avoid confrontations and to retreat in order if fighting did erupt.

cupied the center of Long Spring Thaw, 190 miles north of Mukden. By 5:00 A.M. all the Chinese towns along the South Manchuria Railroad from Port Arthur 500 miles north were in Japanese hands. At first light Japanese bombers from Korea landed at Chang Hsueh-liang's captured airport.

By noon, when General Honjo arrived in Mukden, the war for south Manchuria was virtually over. There was still heavy fighting in Long Spring Thaw but it would be finished by nightfall. By then all Chinese troops would be in full retreat toward the Sungari River which separated south Manchuria from north Manchuria and the thoroughly Chinese business community of Mukden from the White Russian lumbermen, miners, and money-lenders of the northern provincial capital of Harbin. The plans for inside-out conquest which strategist Ishiwara had begun to lay more than two years earlier had fully justified the obsessive patience and attention to detail which he had lavished on them. Only 400 Chinese had been killed—and precisely two Japanese.

SEARCH FOR LEGITIMACY

On the evening of September 19, twenty-four hours after his arrival in Mukden, Major General Tatekawa, the Peerless Pimp, strolled down the pacified streets from his billet at the Literary Chrysanthemum. He savored the long twilight of the northern summer and issued jovial remarks at frightened Chinese shop-keepers who were being forced by the military police to open their shutters for business as usual. At the Special Service Organ he announced himself and climbed the stairs to the command post on the second floor. General Honjo was waiting for him, and now at last Tatekawa officially delivered the message from Prime-Minister-Maker Saionji that the Kwantung Army should proceed "with prudence and caution."

Honjo was impatient with the mock solemnity of Tatekawa's manner. That morning—so Honjo had learned while Tatekawa was sleeping—the Emperor had been awakened before dawn with the news from Manchuria. He had started his palace day by giving audience to Prime Minister Wakatsuki. Wakatsuki, without first feeling out the position of the Throne in the usual manner, had

declared precipitantly that it was the government's policy to curb
the Army in its unauthorized "adventure" and to insist on "non-
enlargement" of the Army's operations. Taken aback, Hirohito
had replied cautiously, "The government's position seems altogether appropriate." With this encouragement Wakatsuki had
spent the day trying to force the War Minister to ask the General
Staff to order all Japanese forces back to the Kwantung Leasehold.
The General Staff, of course, had refused and lacking any new
orders from Hirohito would continue to do so. But Honjo was
frankly worried. Japan's ambassador to the League of Nations
had promised on behalf of his government that the Kwantung
Army would be recalled to its barracks. How committed, how
dedicated was the Emperor?

"Rest easy," replied Tatekawa. "Just restrict operations to south
Manchuria for the time being and everything will be all right."
Tatekawa went on to explain that Hirohito wanted the people
and the Cabinet to support the Army in what had been done
before doing more. He wanted to assess the reaction of the
world's banks and chancelleries before swallowing the rest of Manchuria. While his political advisors were negotiating domestic and
international acceptance, it was Honjo's duty to hold what had
been gained and wait patiently. Honjo shook his head dubiously.
The present positions were difficult to defend. Hesitation now
would allow the enemy to regroup north of the Sungari River.
The morale of Japanese troops would sink rapidly if they had to
take a defensive stance without any surety that the Emperor approved of their war. In vain Tatekawa lured Honjo out of his
command post for a night of victory celebrations. At every saké
house, with every wench and geisha, Honjo kept a phone by his
side in order to keep track of military and political developments
in the field and in Tokyo.

At 6:30 P.M.—about the time that Honjo and Tatekawa had
begun their conversation—Prime Minister Wakatsuki summoned
to his Tokyo residence the political secretary of Saionji, Baron
Harada. He asked Harada to tell Saionji that the civilian members
of the Cabinet had decided to appeal directly to the Throne. They
would beg Hirohito to order the Army to obey Cabinet instruc-

tions and to refrain from enlarging the theater of operations. After dinner at 8:30 P.M.—about the time that Honjo and Tatekawa finished their conversation—Hirohito's principal advisors met in an anteroom of the new concrete Imperial Library in the palace woods to consider the Cabinet's demand. Attending were Lord Privy Seal Count Makino; his level-headed secretary, Big Brother Marquis Kido; Grand Chamberlain Admiral Suzuki Kantaro, the cigar-smoking Taoist philosopher who would preside over Japan's surrender in the bunker under the library fourteen years later; and Imperial Household Minister Ikki Kitokuro, a graduate of the bureaucracy who had been used at Court since Emperor Meiji's day for handling delicate liaison work with the Home Ministry and police forces. These four discussed Prime Minister Wakatsuki's demand until 11:00 P.M. They recognized the fact that the prime minister represented not only the civilian politicians of Japan but also Saionji, the Sumitomo cartel, and a majority of intellectuals, industrialists, and professionals. In vain the four courtiers looked for a compromise, a formula of words which would please all parties. The Army wanted imperial sanction. The Cabinet wanted imperial non-sanction. And Hirohito wanted national unity. He demanded that the Cabinet vote funds and encouragement for the men in the field.

After two and a half hours of brain teasing, Hirohito's three principal chamberlains, together with Marquis Kido, decided to tell the prime minister that it was "displeasing to the Emperor for the prime minister to depend too much on others"; that the Throne sensed "a lack of complete unity in the Cabinet"; and that, therefore, if the prime minister wished to stop unauthorized troop movements, "he must do it on his own responsibility." After Hirohito had approved the message, it was delivered to Prime Minister Wakatsuki the following morning, September 20.

Also that morning the ranking officers of the Army met at the old War Ministry outside the palace walls to consider a request from Lieutenant General Honjo in Manchuria. Honjo asked that reinforcements be sent to him from the Japanese Army in Korea. War Minister Minami pointed out that the policy of the Cabinet —a policy which Hirohito had called "appropriate"—was one of "non-aggravation of the incident."

In essence the reinforcements would make possible an enlargement of the theater of operations. It was up to the officers present,
said War Minister Minami, to decide whether or not this would
constitute an "aggravation of the incident." After debate Minami
found that the majority were against him. A group of senior generals who had been to see Emperor Hirohito's chief aide-de-camp,
General Nara, earlier that morning sided with the young members
of the cabal and spoke in favor of the reinforcements. Finally, with
great solemnity, General Minami acknowledged, "I see now that
non-aggravation of the situation does not necessarily mean non-
enlargement of the theater of operations."

Prince Kanin's man, Major General Koiso of the Military Affairs Bureau, arose with equal solemnity to add that, of course,
no reinforcements should be sent from Korea without the consent
of the war minister and the entire Cabinet. Constitutionally no
such consent was necessary. The right to move troops belonged
exclusively to the Emperor, advised by the General Staff. In a
matter of such national importance as war, however, it was well
for the Emperor to have the unanimous support of all the
branches of the government, including bureaucrats and politicians. The gathered generals agreed that such unanimity was
worth waiting for. They approved a cable to the commander of
the Japanese Army in Korea which stated: IF CONSENT FROM TOKYO
CANNOT BE OBTAINED IN TIME . . . [YOU ARE] GIVEN THE AUTHORITY
TO TAKE APPROPRIATE MEASURES.

The commander of the Japanese Army in Korea[5] had various
telephone connections in Tokyo which enabled him to understand the message. For one full day he waited, studiously avoiding
a scheduled liaison conference with General Ugaki, the governor
general. Then at noon on September 21, he cabled back to the
General Staff that his 39th Mixed Brigade had been ordered to
move and would cross the Manchurian border in about twenty-
four hours. This leisurely scheduling was meant as a politeness
to the Cabinet to allow it time to change its collective mind.
Everyone of importance knew that planes of the Japanese Army
in Korea had been in action over Manchuria for two days and

---

[5] Lieutenant General Hayashi Senjuro, a later war minister and prime
minister.

that the whole of the Korean Army was massed along the Manchurian border ready to cross it in five minutes if General Honjo really needed help.

Prime Minister Wakatsuki might maintain that troop movements were none of the Cabinet's business. Generals were normally inclined to agree. But in the present instance, generals were helping Hirohito prove that the lives of Japanese boys in the field were the business of everyone, particularly of politicians. On September 21, General Honjo sent the Peerless Pimp Tatekawa and Prince Kanin's private emissary General Suzuki both back to Tokyo to add their weight to government councils. At the same time he moved the bulk of his strength north to the Sungari River, leaving Mukden unprotected while it awaited the reinforcements.

On September 22, as popular pressure mounted on behalf of the men overseas, Hirohito offered the prime minister a face-saving compromise. Let the Cabinet vote funds for the expedition, and Hirohito would personally take responsibility for ordering in Japan's Korean Army. To old man Saionji's disgust, Prime Minister Wakatsuki capitulated. On the morning of September 23, the Cabinet voted to fund the troop movement, and Hirohito signed the orders for the Korean Army to cross the frontier into Manchuria.

Japanese Counterintelligence, as a part of its cover story for the Emperor, later made much of the fact that one battalion of the Japanese Army in Korea crossed the Manchurian border before receiving the imperial sanction. The implication was that Hirohito had bowed to the pressure of a *fait accompli*. The truth was that eager Army officers had such excellent liaison with the Throne Room that they knew when to move even before receiving their formal orders.

During this mummery the world reacted. On the advice of their ambassadors in the Orient, all the Western powers believed that the Kwantung Army had acted without orders and would be brought into line shortly. For months the ambassadors had ignored warnings by Western journalists and businessmen and had heeded reassurances from officials of the Japanese Foreign Ministry. Now the ambassadors had much face at stake and were not prepared to change their professional judgment overnight. Nelson

T. Johnson, for instance, the U.S. Minister in Peking, had received a memo from an American advisor of Chiang Kai-shek only twenty-four hours before the seizure of Mukden. The memo had bluntly stated that the Japanese Army was about to occupy Manchuria. Minister Johnson had labeled the memo "incredible, fantastic" and forwarded it to Washington in an ordinary diplomatic pouch which did not reach its destination until Mukden was already in Japanese hands.

In Tokyo, U.S. Ambassador W. Cameron Forbes, the polo-playing grandson of Ralph Waldo Emerson, had thought so little of similar warnings that he had arranged to embark for the United States for a routine rebriefing on the very day of September 19. When news of the Mukden coup broke that morning, he of course called Washington and inquired whether he should not cancel his sailing. Secretary of State Stimson—the same man who would later urge the atomic bombing of Hiroshima on President Truman—advised Ambassador Forbes to come home as planned. Stimson could not believe that all his competent observers overseas had been deceived and that Japanese diplomats, handing out reassurances everywhere, could all be whistling nervously in the dark.

Accordingly, on September 22, 1931, Stimson cabled the chief U.S. observer of the League of Nations in Switzerland: "It is apparent that the Japanese military have initiated a widely extended movement of aggression only after careful preparation. . . . The military chiefs and the Foreign Office are evidently sharply at variance as to intention and opinion. Consequently it would be advisable . . . that nationalist feeling not be aroused against the Foreign Office in support of the army." Similar instructions were sent by other Western governments to other representatives at the League. The truth was that no power was prepared, militarily, to oppose Japan. The U.S. Navy, half of it in mothballs, had never been weaker. Stimson was told that it would take five years to prepare for war with Japan.

That same afternoon the Council of the League of Nations voted to ask the "Chinese and Japanese governments to refrain from action that might aggravate" the situation. Coincidentally, a few hours earlier, Great Britain had announced that she was going off the gold standard. The whole of the sterling bloc—half the economies of the world at that time—would no longer redeem their scrip in precious metal. Clearly the West, weak and pre-occupied, would send no troops to the Orient. Not even the Soviet Union showed any readiness to intervene.

To Hirohito and his palace advisors, it seemed that Asia could belong to Japan if Japan could take it politely enough. No Japanese could deny that Hirohito had won a great victory. His men in the Kwantung Army had seized south Manchuria against great odds, with negligible casualties. The diffident Japanese public had been given a heady sniff of military glory. The elected government had shouldered a part of the responsibility. The moderates had acquiesced. Hirohito had invoked his true powers without exposing so much as a little finger from behind the sacred chrysanthemum curtain.

Only Hirohito's closest intimates knew how premature victory celebrations would be and how many balls still remained juggled aloft. The most talented members of the cabal in the Army—the visionaries who wished to conquer Russia—had been promised north as well as south Manchuria. Saionji, the business community, and the moderate Army officers of the Ugaki faction had been promised a national pause for thought before the escalation into north Manchuria began.

Abroad the League of Nations had recessed until October 13 to await developments. Then, it might yet impose economic sanctions and boycotts. Even without ships and guns the League still had the power to touch the Japanese pocketbook and weight the domestic Japanese scales against Hirohito and in favor of Saionji. Many Japanese businessmen, in their proud, indirect, belly-talking fashion, said as much to their Western colleagues, but almost no Westerners grasped the urgency of the message.

The day the League voted for "non-aggravation," Hirohito's most loyal vassals turned at once to the problems pending. Means must be found to awaken the West as gradually and painlessly as possible to reality. Face must also be saved for old Prime-Minister-Maker Saionji and the Strike-North idealists in the cabal. To meet these challenges, Prince Konoye, Count Makino, Marquis Kido,

and the others devised for the year ahead—for 1932, the unlucky
Year of the Monkey—a triple intrigue and a triple assassination.
Their efforts, never before described in English, were to be
Machiavellian masterpieces of pure witch gossamer.

13

DOLLAR SWINDLE

(1931–1932)

THE SPY SERVICE

One tangled skein of intimidation—of war and threat of war abroad, of assassination and threat of assassination at home, and of bribery and blackmail on both fronts—preoccupied Japan from late September 1931 to late May 1932. Only a few score men starred in this eight-month melodrama: a motley cast of palace advisors, patriotic street toughs, retired China experts, crack naval pilots, and Army Intelligence officers. In Japanese accounts their individual parts are recorded separately, without being fitted into any over-all script. It is always noted, however, that this actor dealt with that actor, and when all these connections are put together, it turns out that a single web was involved, of men who were all friends of friends of one another. They were associated not because they shared the same guilty aims but because they were organized—organized by a brain trust roughly comparable to that of the Central Intelligence Agency in the present United States.

Not much is known about this "Civilian Spy Service" as it is called by one informant. What few written records it kept of its transactions, it destroyed annually. Before the American Occupation in 1945, even its last official code name was successfully forgotten. However, the clues that survive indicate that it was not an authorized institution of the Japanese government but an ad hoc network which had grown up, contact by contact and friendship by friendship, around the person of the Emperor and his well-lined privy purse. All evidence suggests that Hirohito inherited the skeleton of its structure from his grandfather, Emperor Meiji.

The shadowy directors of the spy service acted as nerve center for many different semi-autonomous organs of espionage: Army and Navy Intelligence departments, market research organizations in some of the largest cartels, and civilian clearinghouses for information which were disguised as cultural or scientific foundations. One of the most important of the clearinghouses was the Everyday Meiji Biographical Research Institute in Oarai, a spa in the old loyalist region of Mito some 50 miles northeast of Tokyo. The staff of the institute sent its briefs to Hirohito's advisors through an unpublicized cover agency on the palace grounds, which was known in the 1920's as the Imperial Code Research Institute.

The director of the Everyday Meiji Biographical Research Institute in Oarai was Japan's spy emeritus, Count Tanaka Mitsuaki, sometimes known as the "Spider." This tough old conspirator was eighty-nine and stone deaf, but healthy enough to live to be ninety-six and see the conquest of China. For thirteen years, from 1898 to 1911, he had served as imperial household minister and had been one of the two most trusted chamberlains of Emperor Meiji. It was Spider Tanaka who had arranged the peculiar circumstances of Hirohito's post-mature birth. It would be Spider Tanaka who would now provide terrorists for the intrigues ahead.[1]

[1] Tanaka had been born a provincial samurai of Tosa in 1843, had gone up to the ancient capital of Kyoto in 1863, and had participated there in the complex intrigues which had preceded the restoration of 1868. At twenty-five he had been appointed chief judge in Kobe, the most important of the ports opened to foreigners. In 1871 he had been sent along as secretary-spy when Emperor Komei's murderer, Iwakura, embarked on his fact-finding tour of America and Europe. After coming home in 1874, Tanaka had been made first the auditor, then the treasurer of Japan's new national army. In 1885, when the later-to-be-assassinated Ito took office as Japan's first prime minister, Tanaka was inserted under him as chief Cabinet secretary. In 1889 he was made principal of the Peers' School and supervisor of the education of Emperor Meiji's twelve-year-old son, the future Emperor Taisho. At the end of his thirteen years' service as imperial household minister, Tanaka retired to supervise the writing of Meiji's official biography. It was for this purpose,

In the two decades since the Meiji era, Spider Tanaka had watched the spy service grow until by 1931 it had cast its net over all Asia as far south as Australia, as far west as Iran. By 1941 it would be world-wide, with operatives in every major city of North and South America as well as Europe. When the war with the West broke out, President Roosevelt would appraise its fifth column so highly that he would allow the forcible relocation of all Americans of Japanese parentage on the West Coast to detention camps inland. In the Philippines when the Japanese Army arrived in 1941, U.S. colonials would be surprised to find that Filipino carpenters and masons of Japanese birth stepped immediately into high positions of authority in the Japanese occupation governments. In Baguio (where the author and his family were captured), a chain of command within the Japanese community would spring into being or be activated even before the arrival of the first Japanese occupation forces.

A unique glimpse into the leadership of the spy service was given in a book written in 1936 by Amleto Vespa, an expatriate Italian Blackshirt who had made a career in China as a mercenary, a police chief, and an espionage expert. The Japanese were able to dismiss his revelations when they appeared in print as the spiteful fabrications of an adventurer. But Vespa was a professionally trained observer with years of relevant experience. Evidence brought out at the war crimes trials after World War II showed his dates and descriptions to be accurate. His verbatim reports of Japanese boasting and exultation seemed too melodramatic for credence when he published them, but they were later matched many times by speeches made to Allied P.O.W.'s during World War II.[2]

Vespa had worked for Manchurian war lord Chang Hsueh-liang and was impressed into Japan's spy service in February 1932, five months after the seizure of Mukden. Four years later he escaped in disgust and despair to central China and wrote his book. He

---

ostensibly, that he had founded the Everyday Meiji Biographical Research Institute.

[2] Theatricality was part of the Japanese samurai tradition. It is faithfully reflected in a Japanese movie cliché: the guttural scream, the rush of footfalls in the darkness, then the blade glistening with blood in the moonlight.

prepared it frankly and carefully as blackmail to secure the release of his wife and children who were still held hostage by the Japanese in Manchuria. A copy of the manuscript won freedom for his family but not payment of his back wages. And so he broke his blackmail agreement with the Japanese and published his book anyway. He had no other means, he said, of raising enough money to transport himself and his family home to the West.

Vespa was first introduced into the spy service by Colonel Doihara, the Baden-Baden Reliable and so-called Lawrence of Manchuria who had taken over as mayor of Mukden on the morning after its seizure. Having tested Vespa, Doihara turned him over to his "chief"—"a pleasant-looking man," wrote Vespa, "of about forty-five . . . in civilian clothes . . . of unusual intelligence." Vespa continued:

During the whole of my service under this remarkable man I never discovered his name or his true identity. Never have I met him at any function, at any party, or at anyone else's house. He always had at his disposal an aeroplane which he reached by private car when he went on his mysterious journeys. . . . His English, a rare thing among the Japanese, was almost perfect, leading me to believe that he must have lived many years abroad. . . . I remember almost every word he said.

"Mr. Vespa, . . . if Colonel Doihara has told you anything unpleasant, please pay no attention to it. . . . He delights in showing his greatness by his hectoring manner. He has worked for me for many years. . . . He has done well in many of his undertakings, but . . . he has many failures to his discredit. . . . For instance, do you think that the death of Marshal Chang Tso-lin was a master stroke? . . .

"Remember that I never appear on the scene; I am never in evidence except in matters strictly and intimately Japanese. Your main capacity is to act as my intermediary. . . . I do not give you this privilege because I trust you, but because you are a naturalized Chinese citizen, and as such I can have you shot at any time. Besides, we hold your family. . . .

"The Japanese are the only divine people on earth; that is the reason why they never try to mix with other people. Our culture is sacred. . . . The people whom we have conquered or shall conquer . . . will simply disappear. The Koreans will be eaten by vices; the Chinese will be the victims of opium and other narcotics; the Russians will be ruined by vodka. . . . Do not smile. . . . The destiny of Japan has been outlined by the gods. Nothing can stop Japan from becoming the greatest empire on earth. . . .

"No, no, do not speak Japanese, even though you know the language. . . . It sounds sacrilegious. . . . Every time I have to listen to a foreigner speaking Japanese, I feel a strong desire to strangle him. Let us speak English. . . . It is the proper language when speaking of things unpleasant and disagreeable. Whenever I have to swear at anyone I always prefer to do it in English. . . .

"These instructions which I am giving you I have given also to all the other heads of the Japanese Intelligence Service in northern Manchuria. I am the only one who can give you orders, and you have no one to report to but me. . . . Our Intelligence Service must not be anything like a chain. One link must not lead to another link. Rather it must be a succession of points which work in harmony but without any immediate contact."

The speaker of these words, if he and Vespa were telling the truth, must have been a Court noble of the highest rank. No other Japanese in his mid-forties could have spoken as he did about Doihara, a forty-nine-year-old of samurai caste. Elsewhere Vespa distinguishes carefully between his chief, belonging to the Civilian Spy Service, and the chief of the Special Service Organ, the "Military Mission" as he called it, belonging to the Intelligence Department of the Army General Staff. According to his portrayal, the two worked closely together but the military chief was always subordinate to the man in plainclothes. Vespa regularly knew the name of the military chief and correctly identified the three Special Service Organ directors in north Manchuria between 1932 and 1936. He never knew the name of his civilian chief in the same period. The second of his civilian chiefs, however—"a man in his early fifties"—he recognized as the former director of the Special Service Organ in Irkutsk whom he had met in Siberia in 1918. Available Japanese personnel records reveal that this was a young aristocrat named Takeda Nukazo. From 1918 to 1928—when he vanished into the anonymity of the spy service—Takeda had worked his way up through military intelligence in close collaboration with Hirohito's two uncles and with Hirohito's former deckboard sparring partner, Marquis Komatsu Teruhisa. The first of Vespa's "chiefs," who spoke with such impassioned paranoia about Japan's aspirations, was undoubtedly a disguised princeling from the same circle.

DINNER AT KIDO'S

At 6 P.M. on Wednesday, September 23, 1931, five days after the Japanese seizure of Mukden, Marquis Kido, the first of Hirohito's Big Brothers, received the members of the Eleven Club, his fellow Big Brothers, at his town house around the corner from the American Embassy. There he treated them to a modest supper of fried duck and saké, served without benefit of geisha. The occasion was not a social one. The guests were all high-level operatives of the spy service and had come together to consider "arguments" which might be used against Prince Saionji and his supporters, the liberals and banker-industrialists, during the "pause for reflection" which the Emperor had promised before completing the conquest of Manchuria. Specifically, a plan was needed to circumvent the League of Nations and to head off economic sanctions or boycotts that would damage Japan's international trade. Also, a way must be found to silence and control the banker-industrialists so that they would continue to provide funds for military budgets, particularly for the build-up of the Navy. In five hours of brainstorming, the members of the Eleven Club decided that three ideas were worth pursuing. These three were the germs for the three acts of the eight-month drama which followed, the Triple Intrigue.

The first idea, the Dollar Swindle, was concocted by Baron Harada, the secretary-spy from Saionji's own household. He had picked it up that afternoon from banking circles.[3] The second of the ideas, the Fake War to "save the face of the League of Nations," was relayed by Konoye, the tall, languid prince of the ancient Court family of Fujiwara. It was being proposed tentatively, he said, by officers of the Emperor's cabal in the Kwantung Army in Manchuria. The third of the ideas, Threat of Coup d'Etat, was

---

[3] Harada was nominally a banker himself. He drew his salary from a purely titular position at the great Sumitomo bank—a position created for him by the director of the bank, Sumitomo Kinzaemon, who was old Saionji's nephew and grandson-in-law.

an old one on which Big Brother Uramatsu, in touch with underworld operatives of the spy service, simply gave a progress report.

The Dollar Swindle was to be a speculative peculation of monumental proportions designed to furnish Japan's business community with a massive bribe. Two days earlier, when Great Britain had unexpectedly gone off the gold standard, the value of the pound on the free market had dropped 20 per cent. Japanese bankers calculated that collectively they had lost $22 million by the sudden depreciation of their sterling holdings. Some of them were angry that they had not been forewarned by British colleagues, but others pointed out that British bankers had themselves lost far more. The British government had failed to protect its financiers by privately spreading advance information of the move. If a similar step were contemplated in a nation like Japan, said the British apologists, the relatives of the finance minister would have profited handsomely. They would have sold their yen for foreign currencies beforehand, and afterwards they would have bought back their yen at a substantial discount. Forced to admit the truth of this argument, the disgruntled Japanese bankers said that the British must be fools.

The titled young men of the cabal were delighted by the thought that the bourgeois moneybags of the nation—Saionji's staunchest supporters—might be bribed en masse to betray their Western liberal cause. Those in the Eleven Club who understood high finance reckoned that as much as a $100 million profit might be turned if yen were sold discreetly for several months before the gold standard was renounced. Those who knew politics saw in this figure a bribe of sufficient size to rob Prime-Minister-Maker Saionji of his main support. Later it might be possible to take back most of the profits from the cartels by threatening to reveal their speculations to the public. Harada said that Saionji was counting heavily in the forthcoming "pause for reflection" on the backing of the largest of the cartels, the Mitsui combine, which traditionally made up the campaign purses of most of the candidates of the Constitutionalist party. How would it be if Mitsui were promised the appointment of a Constitutionalist Cabinet in three months and the approval of the Emperor in advance for a paper-backed Japanese currency?

When the immediate political crisis with Saionji was over, other cartels could be brought in for a share of the spoils. The government's Yokohama Specie Bank could itself buy dollars. The nation's finance would benefit over all. And Hirohito would be pleased. In July, after President Hoover had proposed a one-year moratorium on all debts payments between nations, Hirohito had had a personal translation made for him of Hoover's statement and had suggested after reading it: "We should be able to find some way of circumventing these unilateral financial pronouncements of the other powers."

The Fake War, item two in the Triple Intrigue, was touched on at the Eleven Club meeting but not discussed in depth. Prince Konoye said only that the Kwantung Army was prepared to stage a diversion in Shanghai that would provide the League of Nations with an opportunity to satisfy its peace-making propensities and so "save the League's face." As it turned out, Konoye's "diversion" became a bloody little brush-fire war, costing 30,000 lives, that would directly jeopardize a billion dollars' worth of Western investment in the Chinese port of Shanghai. In demanding that it be stopped, the nations of the West would be surprised and gratified: Japan would back down, would suppress the wounded honor and aroused passions of many samurai, and would withdraw after breaking open the very door to Nanking, the Chinese capital.

After gaining this public concession, the League's peacemakers might be inclined to ignore the conquest of north Manchuria which would take place during the diversion. To make appearances as flattering as possible for the League, Manchuria would emerge from the gunsmoke as a nominally independent nation. The former boy emperor of China, Henry Pu-Yi, would be restored to the Manchu throne of his forefathers and would rule Manchuria for Japan as a puppet. The thought of Pu-Yi, a pathetically effete and ineffectual young man, posturing as the head of a modern police state in the hands of the Kwantung Army, amused the most knowledgeable of the Big Brothers. At Kido's supper party the wits found enough material in it momentarily to break up serious discussion. Konoye drolly called for order and the meeting resumed.

The Threat of Coup d'Etat, item three on the agenda, had been suggested earlier in 1931 by the aftermath of the March Plot. At that time Lord Privy Seal Makino's henchman, Dr. Okawa, the former headmaster of the cabal's palace indoctrination center, had kept the bombs which the Army had provided for the plot. He had done so simply to make sure that the Army General Staff would help him pay his bills to the Black Dragon Society and to the Golden Dragon geisha house. But as the months had passed, his continuing possession of the bombs had proved a most useful political tool. It had helped silence the Army's moderate faction before the seizure of Mukden, and it was still being used to intimidate vested interests in the business world. With a little twisting, it had convinced Western ambassadors in Tokyo that Japan required delicate handling; that allowances should be made for the difficult domestic problems faced by Hirohito; that unless the West were understanding, the stability of the biggest market in Asia might be swept away by revolution.

According to Big Brother Uramatsu's report to the Eleven Club, Dr. Okawa's services could be used further. Through old Spider Tanaka's Everyday Meiji Biographical Research Institute in Oarai, Dr. Okawa had been put in touch with three bands of loyal activists who were eager to keep the Threat of Coup d'Etat alive—willing, on behalf of the Emperor, to plot coups and if necessary to stage them.

One group from which willing assassins might be recruited was the Native-Land-Loving Society, a commune of philosophic farmers who admired Tolstoy and worked a twelve-acre co-operative about halfway down the ten-mile spur of track connecting Oarai with the prefectural capital of Mito. In 1930, after a poor harvest, Big Brother Konoye of the House of Peers and Hirohito's uncle Prince Higashikuni had arranged an endowment for the Native-Land-Lovers so that they could start a school on their farm and teach their communal philosophy to others.

The second cell of activists was the Blood Brotherhood, a cadre of toughs selected from the ranks of student spies being trained for work in China. They were all graduates of two schools—one for self-defense, the other for spiritual indoctrination—which had been set up in Oarai as subsidiaries of the Everyday Meiji Biographical Research Institute.

A third "death-defying band" had been recruited from the officers of the Navy flying unit at the Air Development Station on the Misty Lagoon 30 miles south of Oarai. Since ordinary pilots and bombardiers in the Japanese Naval Air Force were noncoms and seamen, these lieutenants and commanders at the lagoon considered themselves an elite, ranking at least two grades above their counterparts, of equal rating, in any of the other branches of the armed forces. They were the students of the brilliant Captain Yamamoto Isoroku who would devise the 1941 attack on Pearl Harbor. They were the protégés of Empress Nagako's father, Prince Kuni, the pioneer of Japanese air power. They were the day-to-day comrades of torpedo-plane test pilot Prince Yamashina, the best of the five aviators in the immediate ranks of the imperial family.

At mention of the Misty Lagoon airmen, some members of the Eleven Club audibly sucked in breath. To expose such men in a political mission showed extreme determination on the part of the imperial family. When the Eleven Club meeting broke up at eleven o'clock that night, its participants were resolved to try to spare the Throne the necessity of a Coup, and if possible of a Fake War as well. Other, political means, such as the Dollar Swindle, must be exhausted before resorting to such extreme measures.

HENRY THE PUPPET

While his Big Brothers were preparing the Triple Intrigue, Hirohito agreed to a period of watchful waiting. It was not easy for him. When the first favorable reports came in from the League of Nations, his cabalists in Manchuria began to agitate at once for an advance across the Sungari River into northern Manchuria. In Manchuria's northern provincial capital of Harbin, the Kwantung Army's local espionage agent—the secret policeman Amakasu who had strangled Socialist Osugi, his wife, and nephew during the aftermath of the 1923 earthquake—hired Chinese toughs to hurl bricks and grenades nightly into Japanese shopfronts. By day he penned plaintive wires to Kwantung Army headquarters begging for troops to come and protect the hapless local Japanese residents. One of Empress Nagako's numerous relatives in the Tokyo General Staff had to go to Harbin and tell Amakasu to be patient. Other imperial messengers dealt equally firmly with provocateurs in other unconquered areas.

At a nod from the palace, the disappointed young officers of the cabal diverted their energies into preparations for the Triple Intrigue. On September 30, 1931, twelve days after the seizure of Mukden, a young Japanese Army interpreter, sent by Colonel Itagaki, the politician of the Kwantung Army, called at the villa of Henry Pu-Yi,[4] the former boy emperor of China. It was a modest home in the outskirts of the Japanese Concession in Tientsin, the second city of north China. The interpreter was shown into the "audience hall," a small Western-style sitting room replete with over-stuffed chairs and antimacassars. The walls were virtually papered with calligraphies, the testimonials penned by Chinese, Japanese, and Westerners who had sought to flatter the boy emperor during his twenty years as pretender to the Manchu throne.

The interpreter looked at the crowded, boastful walls with some contempt. This shabby "palace" belonged to the boy emperor only because the Japanese government had for many years paid the light and gas bills. Henry Pu-Yi could pretend to be a king only because he had allowed Japan to keep him, like an ugly concubine, for some conceivable moment of usefulness.

Pu-Yi was a great-nephew of the Chinese empress dowager, the Manchu harpy Yehonala, who from 1861 to 1908 had ruled China by a combination of whimsy, cunning, murder, and depravity. It was largely due to her dissolute methods of statecraft that imperial China had squandered its treasures, its authority and pride, to become the broken confederacy of knaves and paupers which, in Japanese eyes, was the Republican China of 1931.

From his crowning in 1908 at the age of three to his deposing in 1912 at the age of seven, Henry Pu-Yi had grown up among eunuchs and concubines who had apprenticed under the salacious tutelage of great-aunt Yehonala. Until he was seventeen, the Chi-

[4] This is the form of his name which he used in dealing with the West. In China he was known as the Emperor Hsuan-Tung. In modern Communist China, until his death in 1968, he was addressed as citizen Aisin Gioro.

nese Republican government had continued to support him and his entourage in a corner of the old palace in Peking. He had matured to be a weak, vain, bespectacled pervert. He cultivated classical literary pursuits at which he was pathetically incompetent. He found his sexual pleasure in caning the buttocks of his few remaining eunuchs. In the 1920's during Chang Tso-lin's occupancy of Peking and Chiang Kai-shek's rise to power in south China, the Republic had not always remembered to post him his pension checks. Enticed by Japanese blandishments, he had moved to the Japanese Concession in Tientsin.

Pu-Yi entered his drab little hall of state accompanied by his prime minister. The Japanese envoy snapped to attention with a great show of respect and announced to Pu-Yi that his fellow emperor of the great Japanese Empire looked favorably upon him. A messenger had come from Hirohito's army in Manchuria bearing a communication which could be delivered to Pu-Yi only in person and only at the Japanese garrison in Tientsin. If His Majesty Pu-Yi would condescend to accompany the humble interpreter in a staff car, he would hear a proposal of great interest. Pu-Yi had been expecting some such approach ever since the seizure of Mukden twelve days previously. With ill-concealed excitement, he turned to his prime minister for an opinion. Fat and impassive, the minister stated that His Majesty was disposed to accede to the highly irregular Japanese request.

Minutes later Pu-Yi was ushered into the commander's office at the Japanese Treaty Forces' barracks in Tientsin. The lieutenant general in charge introduced him to the messenger from Mukden and then excused himself. The messenger said, "If Your Majesty will come to Manchuria, Japan is prepared to restore the Manchu throne there and make you an emperor again." Pu-Yi beamed and promised to consider the proposal. The messenger, a member of the spy service, wired Colonel Itagaki, the Kwantung Army's politician, that the boy emperor could be persuaded to accept the role of Japanese puppet. Itagaki in his turn wired the director of the Special Services Organ in the Japanese Concession in Shanghai, 800 miles to the south, asking him to come to Mukden immediately for rebriefing.

EASTERN JEWEL

The director of the Shanghai Special Service Organ was Major Tanaka Takayoshi, the big man with the huge head and leviathan memory who would later become the star witness for Allied prosecutor Keenan at the Tokyo war crimes trials. When Itagaki's wire arrived, Tanaka was out dancing at Shanghai's Cathay Hotel with the girl spy who would become the provocateuse for the Fake War. She was a distant cousin of the boy emperor and a Manchu princess. Her original given name had been Eastern Jewel. Eastern Peril would have been more appropriate.

Like the boy emperor Pu-Yi, Eastern Jewel was a direct descendant of the roughriding conqueror Nurhachi who had founded the Manchu dynasty in 1616—the death year of Shakespeare and of the first of the Tokugawa shoguns. Unlike the anemic Pu-Yi, Eastern Jewel was a creature of boundless vitality, eternal itch, and catholic taste. Her father, one of the eight "Princes of the Iron Helmet" in the former imperial court in Peking, had inherited the allegiance of the tribes of Inner Mongolia. He had been a rash, extreme Manchu prince of the old school, a close friend of Empress Nagako's great-uncle Prince Kanin, and the rouser of the rabble of Mongol horsemen who had attempted to seize Mukden for Prince Kanin in 1916. Eastern Jewel was only one of his score of daughters; he had given her in 1914, when she was eight, to his Japanese blood brother, a member of the spy service, Kawashima Naniwa. Kawashima had renamed her Kawashima Yoshiko, had moved her from her fourteenth century yurt to a twentieth century home in Tokyo, and had re-educated her as a Japanese. At fifteen, according to her later boasting, she was seduced by Kawashima's septuagenarian father. At sixteen she slept with Kawashima himself. Before she was twenty she had begun to seduce in her turn.

Married off during the mid-1920's to the son of a Mongol prince, she quickly deserted her husband and returned to the Chinese student quarter in Tokyo where she was known as Yang Kuei Fei, a Chinese imperial concubine of yore who had played Helen of Troy in wrecking an empire. In late 1930, at the age of twenty-four, Eastern Jewel took a trip to Shanghai with a Japanese Diet-man who rapidly ran out of money in his attempts to support her. By luck, at a New Year's party there, she met Major Tanaka of the Shanghai Special Service Organ. She was entranced by the huge-ness of the man and astounded him by recalling a Buddhist funeral service at which she had seen him in Tokyo twelve years earlier when she herself had been only twelve. That night she tried to seduce him. He rebuffed her politely, reminding her that she was a princess and he was a commoner. The next day she dropped by his office and borrowed the equivalent of $160 (U.S.) from him. She continued to borrow smaller sums from him in the weeks that followed. Finally her insistence on being his debtor destroyed his caste humility. "You are a giant of a man," she said, "and I am small in every part."

"She was then twenty-five and still exceedingly pretty," wrote Tanaka in later years. "Our encounter was a mature one of mus-cle against muscle."

She and Tanaka shared a foot fetish. He loved to wear high black boots and she insisted that he wear them always. The boots scuffed the polish on the brightest dance floors of Shanghai and ended each evening dangling over the end of a bed. To justify the sums he withdrew from the Special Service Organ's "plot fund," Tanaka in the summer of 1931 sent her to a Chinese school to learn English so that she could be useful in the future as a Japa-nese spy. By the fall of 1931 she had learned her role so well that her relationship with Tanaka was to blossom into a rather general affair between herself and the Army officers of Hirohito's cabal. It would last almost up to her final beheading at the hands of the Chinese in 1948.

On the morning of October 1, 1931, in response to the wire from Colonel Itagaki of the Kwantung Army, Eastern Jewel's lover Tanaka boarded a train for Mukden. He expected to be dis-graced for his embezzlement of Special Service Organ funds. He spent the two-day train journey going over and over in his mind the arguments by which he hoped to represent Eastern Jewel and her extravagances as a useful investment. When he arrived in Muk-den he was surprised to find Colonel Itagaki concerned with some-thing else entirely.

"The Japanese government," said Itagaki, "is cowed by the League of Nations. As a result our plans have been disturbed. At our next push we want to take Harbin [the northern capital] and make Manchuria independent. We have detailed Colonel Doihara to go and get Pu-Yi [the boy emperor]. If we are successful, the League of Nations will make a big fuss and the government in Tokyo will be worried. I want you to start something in Shanghai, please, that will serve to distract the attention of the Powers. During your commotion, we will take Manchuria."

Nodding with relief, Major Tanaka assured Colonel Itagaki that he would be able to carry out the assignment. He had in training, he said, the perfect agent to buy Chinese agitators in Shanghai and start the Fake War.

"Yes, I know all about your mistress," interrupted Itagaki. "She is a childhood friend of Pu-Yi's number-one wife. The wife is a dope addict and a bundle of nerves. She is trying to persuade Pu-Yi not to accept our plan. If Doihara has too much trouble with her, I may want to borrow Eastern Jewel from you so that she can go to Pu-Yi's villa in Tientsin and reassure them."

Then Colonel Itagaki gave Major Tanaka the equivalent of $10,000 (U.S.) from the Kwantung Army's coffer of nonaccountable special service funds, and Tanaka returned to Shanghai. With the money he cleared Eastern Jewel of debts and began frugally to arrange provocations for the Fake War.

BALKY OLD MAN

On September 17, the day before the seizure of Mukden, Prime-Minister-Maker Saionji had abruptly decamped from his summer villa in the mountains and gone to Kyoto, the old capital in the south, to pray at the graves of his illustrious forefathers. By removing himself from the Tokyo area and from Hirohito, he silently told the nation that he had been consulted in advance about the Manchurian adventure and did not approve of it. Family unanimity is considered essential in Japan. As long as Prince Saionji absented himself from the Emperor's circle of advisors, no Japanese would feel easy in mind about the nation's new course of conquest.

Less than three days after the meeting of the Eleven Club at Big Brother Marquis Kido's residence, Saionji's private agents began to bring him gossip in Kyoto of the plots being prepared for the Triple Intrigue. Realizing that Hirohito and his advisors were not observing the promised "pause for reflection," the old man mustered his energies to open the eyes of the ruling classes to the machinations in the making.

At the Kyoto villa of his late brother Sumitomo, Saionji was in a position to wield his influence over the managers of the Sumitomo cartel and persuade them to take no part in the Dollar Swindle. Through them and through his other contacts in the nearby business community of Japan's great merchant city, Osaka, he launched a whispering campaign. It was directed not against the Emperor, of course, but against his advisors.

Still more pointedly, Saionji had one of his agents—Takuno Dempu, an artist and bohemian who belonged to the Black Dragon Society—publish a letter in the newspaper *Nippon*, accusing Lord Privy Seal Makino of malfeasance. So well prepared was Saionji to document the charge that when the Special Higher Police—the Thought Police as they were commonly called—arrested Takuno on suspicion of lèse majesté, Saionji simply had a heart-to-heart talk with his secretary-spy, Big Brother Harada. Much shaken, Harada at once went up to Tokyo, spoke to the head of the Thought Police, and had Takuno released without indictment.

Alarmed that Saionji might be reaching a breaking point at which he would betray his heritage and broadcast Court secrets to the masses, Hirohito's three chief chamberlains sent Secretary-Spy Harada back to Kyoto on October 6, 1931, to draw out Saionji further.

Saionji was delighted to have an opportunity to transmit to Hirohito the observations which he had been spreading through the business community. At the "center of the Army," he said, a communistic tendency was at work, militating for state socialism. In this tendency he saw a prelude to revolution and the overthrow of the Throne—a set of symptoms familiar to him from his experience of prerevolutionary Russia and Germany. The Black Dragon Society of the underworld, he said, was splitting into two factions:

elders who advised caution and young radicals who agitated for more conquest immediately. The nations of the West, he said, might not be willing to fight Japan or even to impose sanctions against her, but privately the Western Establishment was ready to cut off Japan from raw materials and markets.

Finally, he said, even the masses were restless and suspicious. People were saying—and Saionji was conveying a truth—that imperial princes of the blood like the Emperor's uncle Higashikuni were sponsoring terrorist societies and pricking their fingers at voodoo ceremonies in order to subscribe to the blood compacts of assassination gangs.

Secretary-Spy Harada hastened to Tokyo to report Saionji's veiled threats at the palace. Two days later, on October 8, he was back in Kyoto with a request from the Emperor that Saionji come up to Tokyo at once and preserve the appearance of national unity. In his quick trip north Harada had met with Biggest Brother Kido, with Lord Privy Seal Makino, and with old cigar-smoking Taoist Grand Chamberlain Suzuki Kantaro. He returned to Kyoto with the knowledge that the largest of the cartels, Mitsui, had succumbed to temptation and bought $100 million (U.S.) in anticipation of the Dollar Swindle. With Mitsui committed to a heavy speculation in a dollar that was sagging on the international exchange, the business community in which Saionji had banked his hopes was already subverted. Other cartels were beginning to buy in on the swindle. If they held back, Hirohito was ready to retain the gold standard, ruin Mitsui, and plunge the nation into economic chaos. If they joined in the bribe, they stood to make millions; if they supported Saionji, they stood to lose millions.

Knowing that he was cornered, Saionji nevertheless refused to come up to Tokyo. At the same time he advised the bankers of his late brother Sumitomo's cartel that a financial killing was in the making, and he released them to profit or not to profit by it as they saw fit. To their credit most of the branch directors of Sumitomo remained loyal to Saionji and sustained heavy losses two months later when the yen was devalued.

On orders from Tokyo, Secretary-Spy Harada remained in Kyoto for two days trying to persuade Saionji to return to the capital. In the course of his protracted conversation with the old man, Harada discovered that only one consideration moved Saionji at all: the Emperor's health. According to Empress Nagako, said Harada, Hirohito was suffering great strain in the prolonged crisis. He worried night and day that the League of Nations might impose economic sanctions. When no one was looking, in the private corridors of the imperial apartments, he limped and shuffled again, showing the signs of the inherited infirmity which he had successfully concealed since his boyhood. Sentimental courtier that he was, Saionji melted a little at such pleas. He refused, however, to give in completely. He promised Harada that he might come up to Tokyo on October 21, after he had "observed a little longer the trend of events."

DIVERTING THE LEAGUE

The League of Nations Council had recessed shortly after the seizure of Mukden with an admonition to both China and Japan "to refrain from action that would aggravate" the situation. Now it was to reconvene on October 13. Five days before that date Lieutenant Colonel Ishiwara, the zealous strategist of the Manchurian campaign, acted to foster the impression that the Kwantung Army was a law unto itself and might not be bound by any promises which the League could exact form Tokyo. Ishiwara personally led an eleven-plane air raid that dropped 10,-000 leaflets and 75 bombs on the southwestern Manchurian city of Chinchow. The Japanese Foreign Ministry had specifically promised the League that the Army would not attack Chinchow; now it branded the raid as unauthorized. Western newspapers played the incident on their front pages and expressed skepticism as to the good faith of Japan's foreign minister.

To further impress the League Council with the domestic problems faced by the Japanese government and with the impracticality of sanctions against Japan, the Emperor's Big Brothers decided to give the world a glimpse of the Coup d'Etat Threat which they had ready in the wings. Secretary-Spy Harada heard of their scheme as soon as he returned to Tokyo on October 10 and promptly labeled it the October Plot.

Got up on short notice, this October production was a burlesque of the earlier March Plot. "Young militarists in the Army"
would be "uncovered," prevented "in the nick of time" from effecting their horrendous plan, and full particulars would be leaked as
news to all the foreign corrrspondents in Tokyo. Dr. Okawa, the
master plotter, and the cabal's ubiquitous Lieutenant Colonel
Suzuki handled the preparations offstage. On stage were Lieutenant Colonel Hashimoto of the Russia Desk in Army Intelligence
—the same who in 1937 would sink the U.S.S. *Panay*—and Major
Cho Isamu of the North China Special Service Organ. These two
had repaired to the Golden Dragon teahouse in the first week of
October and had stayed there ever since, competing to see who
could drink the most and who could write the best operational
"novel" for the coup.

Major Cho's novel was the one chosen to be publicized. He had
a gift for dramatic writing. It was he, in 1937, outside the walls of
Nanking, who would draft the orders signed by Prince Asaka saying, "Kill all prisoners." It was he, in 1945, in the caves of Okinawa, who would pen the final command to Japanese soldiers and
civilians on the island: "Fight to the last and die." Now, however,
he showed some sense of humor. His October plan called for Dr.
Okawa, the ideologist of the Strike-South Faction, to man a barricade beside his most bitter intellectual rival, Kita Ikki, the
apostle of the Strike North. Cho designated as their support
"about ten men of the Navy's fencing unit."

Waxing serious, Cho proposed that the coup be supported by
ten infantry companies, one machine-gun company, and thirteen
planes from the Misty Lagoon Air Station.

Our objectives [he wrote] are to attack the prime minister's residence and kill Wakatsuki and his ministers during a Cabinet conference; to seize Metropolitan Police headquarters; to occupy the War
Ministry and General Staff Headquarters; to punish various good-for-
nothings in the Army and the bureaucracy; to establish a new government with Lieutenant General Araki Sadao [the senior officer of the
Strike-North Faction] as prime minister, [*Panay*-sinker] Hashimoto
as home minister, [Peerless Pimp] Tatekawa as foreign minister,
[master plotter] Okawa as finance minister, [the blood-thirsty Major]

Cho Isamu as Metropolitan Police chief, and Rear Admiral Kobayashi Shosaburo [the commander of the Misty Lagoon Air Station] as Navy minister.

Every au courant geisha, party politician, and Army bureaucrat learned of this huge joke between October 10 and October 13. The serious Colonel Tojo, later the World War II prime minister, circulated a memo in the Army Ministry criticizing it as "a foolish action." The newspapers published hints of the plot on October 13 and 14, the first two days of the League of Nations Council meeting in Switzerland.

On the evening of October 15 the most important young generals and colonels of the cabal met in the War Ministry to ring down the curtain. They decided that the senior officer of the Strike-North Faction in the cabal, Lieutenant General Araki Sadao, inspector general of military education, should be given the responsibility, as the might-have-been prime minister of the coup government, to go down to the Golden Dragon and speak to the plotters.

Court advocates of the Strike South may have hoped to gain a small blackmail hold on Araki by making him the supposed strongman of the plot, but Araki was far more sophisticated than General Ugaki, the dupe of the March Plot. Araki was a consummate politician and a golden-tongued orator. With great zest he went down to the Golden Dragon and regaled the geisha there with a sermon on the samurai sword which, he said, "should never be drawn indiscriminately from its scabbard." In conclusion he added, "It is almost inconceivable that I should have to come here in military uniform to a place where you are drinking saké in order to admonish you in this sort of matter."

Having broadcast his integrity to the entire teahouse, Lieutenant General Araki sat down with Hashimoto and Cho to toss off a few thimbles of saké and explain to the two conspirators, in reassuring terms, the disciplinary procedures which would have to be applied to them for form's sake.

More than a day later, in the early hours of October 18, the secret police descended on eleven young officers involved in the October Plot and impounded them wherever they found them.

Cho and Hashimoto languished pleasantly under protective house arrest at the Golden Dragon for twenty days. The other nine young officers were held briefly and then released after being delivered lectures. Dr. Okawa and his civilian participants were not troubled at all. Lord Privy Seal Makino told anyone who would listen that the plotters had planned to assassinate him. His protégé, Dr. Okawa, went about town bragging that the October Plot "had inflicted a mortal wound on corrupt Japanese party politics."

When the October Plot was exposed on October 18, Saionji visited an obliging medical friend in Kyoto for a physical examination. On October 20 he told Harada that, on doctor's orders, he was going straight to his seaside villa in Okitsu for a long rest. He could not come up to Tokyo on October 21 as he had hoped, and he wished Harada to convey his regrets to the palace.

On the way from Kyoto to Okitsu on October 21, Saionji's train was boarded by Military Affairs Bureau Chief Koiso Kuniaki, the cavalry crony of Prince Kanin who had arranged the Army's part in the March Plot. Hirohito had just promoted him to the rank of lieutenant general. On the train Koiso sat down beside Saionji and in polite Japanese belly talk warned him that his health would fail utterly if he did not come up soon to see the Emperor in Tokyo. Saionji listened in silence and pretended that his uninvited traveling companion did not exist. On arriving in Okitsu, he withdrew to his seaside villa and waited there, incommunicado, for the decision of the League of Nations.

The League Council disappointed Saionji and reacted to the October Plot exactly as the plot planners had intended. On October 24, after a twelve-day session in which it had taken into account the "delicate situation in Tokyo," the Council recessed without asserting any blunt censure of Japan. Instead it resolved to reconvene on November 16 by which time, it piously hoped, Japan would withdraw her forces from Manchuria. The Japanese representative on the Council deplored the impoliteness of "this ultimatum," and in voting against it, cast his first lonely nay.

ANOTHER HUMILIATION

Through his protégés in the Foreign Ministry, old Saionji had followed the debate in the League hour by hour. As soon as he saw how the vote would go, he capitulated as quickly and gracefully as possible. His surrender was announced at a cabal dinner party on October 23. Saionji neither denied nor confirmed the announcement. He waited until October 30 and then, in response to a humble note from Lord Privy Seal Makino—who said, "I feel inadequate to advise the Emperor at the present juncture"— Saionji agreed to pay his long postponed call at the palace.

Court circles politely spread the face-saving story that Hirohito's nerves were frayed by the prolonged crisis and that Saionji, as a loyal courtier, was coming up to Tokyo to encourage the Emperor and exhort him to take better care of his health. The health of the tired, intimidated, eighty-two-year-old was politely ignored, as Saionji proudly asked that it should be. Nevertheless newspaper men who saw him helped down from the train at Tokyo station on November 1, 1931, remarked on his growing feebleness and the "blue caves" which surrounded his eyes.

On the morning of November 2, 1931, Saionji was driven to the Imperial Household Ministry in the palace to meet his former protégé, his lieutenant at the Paris Peace Conference, Lord Privy Seal Count Makino. As soon as the two were alone, Saionji told Makino in many carefully chosen Japanese words that he had failed his country.

"Your father, Okubo Toshimichi," said Saionji, "was a great man. . . . At a time of crisis, when it was touch and go whether the nation would sink or survive, when the people had been worked up over Korea until they were almost in favor of war, your father turned away from his dearest friend, Saigo, his elder and fellow townsman, and by his opposition succeeded in preventing the attack on Korea. Since it is largely because of Prince Okubo's stand at that time that Japan is what she is today and that the Meiji restoration was a success, he was a minister of state, a so-called great retainer, who was literally worthy of the name. Believe me, a man who wants to accomplish anything lasting in today's world must stand equally firm. . . ."

"Yes," rejoined Count Makino quietly, "it is a fact that Father was a close friend of Saigo and that nevertheless he did what he did." Makino did not need to add that, as his father had destroyed Saigo for the Emperor, so he, Makino, might have to destroy his old mentor Saionji.

From Lord Privy Seal Makino's office Saionji went on, at 2:00 P.M., to visit the Imperial Library. He spent forty-five minutes alone with Hirohito in correctly formal conversation. Afterward he sent a message to Foreign Minister Shidehara advising him to play upon the Emperor's fear of economic sanctions.

"There is no need to exaggerate," said Saionji. "Just speak to the Emperor carefully and fully, in a leisurely, sophisticated, agreeable manner."

Saionji returned to Okitsu in a more hopeful frame of mind. The next day, however, he learned that, while the Emperor had been talking to him, Japanese troops under imperial orders had been crossing the Sungari River into the northern half of Manchuria.

FEINT IN MANCHURIA

Lieutenant General Honjo in Mukden had ordered the invasion of north Manchuria on October 30. The invasion was part of the cabal's master plan for dealing with the League of Nations. The objective was to seize the town of Tsitsihar in far northwestern Manchuria and then withdraw from it ostentatiously as a present to the League of Nations when it reconvened on November 16. Tsitsihar was chosen as the target because, of all the cities of north Manchuria, it was the farthest from Mukden and therefore the most spectacular to capture. In addition, the largest of Chang Hsueh-liang's armies was regrouping in the Tsitsihar area. If it could be smashed now, north Manchuria would remain easy to conquer later in the winter when the League's face had been saved.

To spearhead the invasion, Lieutenant General Honjo dispatched cadres of engineers to repair the railroad bridges leading north across the Sungari. They had orders to clash with the Man-

churian troops dug in on the northern bank of the frozen river.
The engineers were backed by a hastily assembled puppet army of
Manchurian mercenaries—a façade for the fiction that the Kwantung Army acted on behalf of a native Manchurian independence
movement. Behind the mercenaries trainloads of Kwantung Army
regulars rolled north to do the real fighting.

Warm in their olive-drab suits of blanket cloth, their sleeveless
goatskin jackets, their padded stormcoats, their fur-lined helmets
with earflaps, the Kwantung Army soldiers expected to break
through the ragged, hungry, provincial levies of Chang Hsueh-
liang in four days. General Ma, the Chinese commander, however,
told his men that, if they could hold Tsitsihar until the League
met on November 16, they would cause Japan a great loss of face.
With this limited objective in mind—this small revenge—the
Chinese fought like dragons and upset the Japanese timetable
by two bloodstained weeks. Not until November 18 could the
Japanese take Tsitsihar. Not until November 26 could they turn
the town over to the Manchurian puppet army which they had
hired, and withdraw as promised. By then their gesture of courtesy
to the League had become a graceless concession to angry League
demands.

HENRY'S ABDUCTION

The same day that Saionji said he would come to Tokyo and
that Lieutenant General Honjo launched the invasion of north
Manchuria, the collective leadership of Japan's spy service activated their plans to install boy emperor Henry Pu-Yi as the puppet ruler of Manchuria. That morning Colonel Doihara, mayor
of Mukden and chief of Special Service Organs in Manchuria,
called on the Pu-Yis at their villa, the "Quiet Garden," in Tientsin.
He found that the boy emperor had succumbed to the worries of
his wife and eunuchs. Pu-Yi still longed to be restored to the
throne of his ancestors, but he had been persuaded that it would
be too rash to move his court to Mukden until Japan had completed her conquest of Manchuria and settled her differences
with the League. In vain Doihara cajoled and argued. Pu-Yi was
adamant. Shortly before noon Doihara returned to the Tientsin

Special Service Organ and wired Shanghai for the services of the seductive Manchu princess, Eastern Jewel.

When the phone rang and the summons was relayed to her in her Shanghai apartment, Eastern Jewel was still in bed. She called a Japanese pilot of her acquaintance and persuaded him to fly her to Tientsin immediately. Then she got up, tucked her bobbed hair into a skullcap, and put on the loose robes of a Chinese gentleman. In this disguise, she arrived in Tientsin that same evening. She and her pilot friend checked in briefly at a hotel and before midnight she was at Doihara's headquarters in the Tientsin Special Service Organ. With an air of great mystery she told the desk sergeant that she could not reveal her name except to Doihara personally. Doihara, who did not expect her for at least another day, was putting in an evening catching up with his paper work. He kept her waiting while he finished it, then laid his service revolver on the desk before him and had the mysterious visitor ushered into his presence.

"Your name, please?" he said with a curt nod.

"My name is of no importance," she muttered in her deepest voice. "I have come to help you."

"You speak like a eunuch," observed Doihara. "Are you one of Pu-Yi's men?"

She shook her head and laughed at him.

"Very well then," said Doihara, according to the account he later gave friends, "if you will not tell me who you are, let's see what you are." He drew his sword, and with the tip of it, holding it at arm's length, he deftly cut one after another of the string fasteners down the front of her robe. She held her ground unflinching and continued to smile at him provokingly. He flicked open the robe, moved in, and seized her by the shoulder. Then with a guttural samurai yell, he suddenly severed the silk scarf with which she had bound her breasts. "I saw that she was a woman," he liked to say later, "so I conducted a thorough investigation and determined that I had not put even the smallest scratch on any part of her white skin."

The next day Eastern Jewel visited the "Quiet Garden," the villa of boy emperor Pu-Yi. Her tongue tripping with all the latest

Shanghai gossip, she spent the afternoon reviving her acquaintance with Pu-Yi's neurasthenic, opium-smoking wife, Elizabeth.
That evening Elizabeth ate her dinner without throwing a single
tantrum. "The 'Quiet Garden' is quiet again," noted one of Pu-
Yi's ministers. Pu-Yi invited Eastern Jewel to consider his home
her home as long as she remained in Tientsin.

Much as Elizabeth enjoyed Eastern Jewel's company, no
amount of coaxing would make her favor the contemplated move
to Mukden. After four days had passed, Colonel Doihara grew
impatient and decided to frighten Pu-Yi into going to Mukden
alone. He bribed a waiter at a local café to call the villa and warn
Pu-Yi that he was about to be assassinated by partisans of the
former war lord of Manchuria, Chang Hsueh-liang. Daily thereafter Doihara saw to it that the unhappy boy emperor received
a letter of warning from an old friend or a threatening phone call
from an old enemy. When Pu-Yi still hesitated, Eastern Jewel
arranged to slip two harmless but ugly-looking snakes into his
royal bed just before he retired for the night. On November 8,
a former Manchu acquaintance sent Pu-Yi a basket of fruit in
which Eastern Jewel discovered two bombs. A squad of Japanese
military policemen summoned by Eastern Jewel carried the explosives out of the house with a great show of bravado and excitement. Investigation by Japanese criminologists promptly
"proved that the two bombs had been manufactured in the arsenal
of Chang Hsueh-liang."

That night, November 8, Doihara engineered the first in a series
of nightly riots in the Chinese quarter of Tientsin. Using the
disturbances as a pretext, the Japanese garrison commander on
November 10 declared martial law in the Japanese Concession
and isolated the "Quiet Garden" with a cordon of protective
troops and armored cars. Now at last the frightened Pu-Yi agreed
to flee to Manchuria. Eastern Jewel persuaded him that he would
be safest if he went alone that very night and left his wife Elizabeth to follow later.

Pu-Yi was spirited out of the "Quiet Garden" locked in the
trunk of his convertible. The Japanese sentries and roadblocks
outside the villa made his chauffeur so nervous that he took a

wrong turning, backed up, and smashed into a telephone pole. Pu-Yi, in the trunk, received a hard blow on the head and completed his wild ride in a daze. The car pulled up at a restaurant on the darkened outskirts of the Japanese Concession. Pu-Yi was let out of the trunk and given a Japanese Army overcoat and cap. In this disguise he was whisked off in a Japanese staff car which took him to a dock in the British Concession. There a motor launch was waiting for him.

Stowed in the bilge of the launch—beside a drum of high-octane gas which was meant to incinerate him if anything went wrong— Pu-Yi was piloted down river, past Chinese coastal entrenchments, toward the China Sea. Once, the launch was challenged by Chinese sentries and ordered to put in to the bank for inspection. The helmsman obediently cut his motor and drifted in toward shore. When the sentries on the bank had relaxed and the current of the river had carried the boat a little downstream, the pilot abruptly started the motor and roared away safely to the accompaniment of scattered rifle fire.

At the mouth of the river the merchant ship *Awaji Maru* lay anchored under a full head of steam. Pu-Yi was bundled aboard in a boatswain's chair, and the *Awaji* headed out across the gulf for the Kwantung Leasehold. The following day at the Yingkow docks of Japan's South Manchuria Railroad Company, Pu-Yi was welcomed ashore by a delegation under the leadership of the infamous secret police strangler, Amakasu Masahiko. It was a foretaste of the type of Court which would surround Pu-Yi's puppet throne in the years ahead.

During the next five weeks Pu-Yi was kept a pampered prisoner. He was regally lodged, first at a spa outside Port Arthur and then in the executive suite of the Yamato Hotel in Mukden. At both places, however, he found that he was not allowed to mingle with the other guests. In mid-December, his wife Elizabeth, lulled into her pipes by Eastern Jewel, finally joined him. The two resumed their separate dream lives together in a Mukden villa which had once belonged to Eastern Jewel's father, Prince Su of the Iron Helmet. The following March Pu-Yi was to be proclaimed chief executive—not emperor—of the new puppet state of Manchukuo.

PRE-SWINDLE POLITICS

During these Army preparations to take all of Manchuria and put it under a puppet government, Hirohito's Big Brothers in Tokyo were busy devising a suitable combination of political forces to take responsibility for the Dollar Swindle. The swindle, Act One of the Triple Intrigue, was to raise funds for the Fake War, Act Two, which in turn would distract the League and save its face. The Big Brothers succeeded in putting together a coalition of Strike-North Army officers, Constitutionalist politicians, and the directors of the Mitsui cartel. The arrangements with the Strike-North Faction were handled personally by Prince Chichibu, Hirohito's younger brother.

Since the seizure of Mukden, Prime Minister Wakatsuki had tendered his resignation repeatedly to Hirohito. He and his anti-Constitutionalist party, the Democratic Constitutionalists, were eager to be out of office during the Triple Intrigue. They made no secret of the fact that they hoped to lose at the next elections. The out-of-power Constitutionalists were also reluctant to form a government, but they had no alternative because they had promised their financial backers, the magnates of Mitsui, to take Japan off the gold standard. The Mitsui directors had $100 million stagnating in U.S. banks. They were impatient for a change of government that would allow them to collect their profits and put their money back into use.

Hirohito insisted that Prime Minister Wakatsuki remain in office until the League of Nations delivered its verdict. Days of waiting turned to weeks and the bookkeepers of Mitsui grew increasingly nervous. To give them temporary relief, the president of the Constitutionalists, at a rally on November 11, 1931, promised publicly to take Japan off the gold standard. The announcement caused a drop in the value of the yen on the open market and a rise in the relative value of the dollars being hoarded by Mitsui abroad. It decreased the risk Mitsui was taking and cut the potential profits of Mitsui competitors who were latecomers to the dollar-buying swindle. When old Prime-Minister-Maker Saionji heard of the announcement, he shook his head in puzzlement. "It is like a bank," he muttered, "declaring bankruptcy before it opens its doors."

THE LEAGUE'S DECISION

After the League met in Geneva, Switzerland, on November 16, it remained in session debating the Manchurian problem for a month. In Tokyo Hirohito suffered from the prolonged tension and his courtiers feared for his health. On November 19, as he returned aboard his battleship from the annual Army grand maneuvers, he went on deck after dark and stood at the rail waving his hand at the black empty sea. A chamberlain who had been following him at a discreet distance ran to his side full of solicitude and alarm.

"It's all right," said Hirohito, laughing. "On that headland, beyond the dark, thousands of firefly bonfires have been lit by the peasants in honor of my passing tonight. I am simply acknowledging their homage."

As the League's debate turned increasingly against Japan, the professional politicians in Tokyo expected momentarily the fall of the Wakatsuki government. In speculating on the composition of the Cabinet which would take its place, most of them predicted a coalition which would divide the responsibility for the future among all factions. Black Dragon Lord Toyama opined that only a "darkside cabinet" of his own underworld leaders could be patriotic enough to shoulder the burden. Hirohito and his courtiers kept their own plans to themselves and waited for the League to deliver its verdict.

The League voted on December 10, 1932. It decided neither to condemn Japan's aggression nor to condone it. Instead, in a surrender of principle which the New York *Herald Tribune* called "handsomely staged and impressive, but virtually unconditional," the League opted to send a "commission of inquiry" to the Orient to decide on the spot the rights and wrongs of the case. Though better than a vote of censure, the League's decision to temporize hardly pleased Hirohito and his Court. To have an unsympathetic commission snooping about in the Orient, under a spotlight of publicity, violated every maxim of aristocratic Japanese government. The commission would stir up domestic political problems. It would encourage Chinese belligerence. It would extend indefinitely Japan's crisis with the League.

The day the League voted, Hirohito allowed the home minister, a hireling from the Black Dragon, to topple the Wakatsuki government by refusing for forty-eight hours to attend Cabinet meetings. Hirohito accepted the resignation of the Cabinet en bloc and sent Secretary-Spy Harada to Okitsu to fetch Prime-Minister-Maker Saionji for the ceremony of nominating a new government. Saionji sarcastically asked Harada what choice had already been made by the Eleven Club. Harada mentioned President Inukai of the Constitutionalists. "In that case," sighed Saionji, "Inukai seems inevitable."

Tiny, even by Japanese standards, and rated deep in political cunning, even by Chinese standards, Inukai qualified as a leader for the Fake War, Act Two of the Triple Intrigue, because he was a close friend of Chiang Kai-shek. Together with Black Dragon Toyama and with General Matsui, the future scapegoat Butcher of Nanking, Inukai was one of the three messiahs of Asia for the Asiatics. He had befriended Sun Yat-sen and Chiang Kai-shek many times during their years of exile in Japan. If he told Chiang now that the projected war in Shanghai was a sham, staged for the benefit of the League, Chiang might believe him. If he also told Chiang that the war was a smokescreen behind which Japan meant to prepare for a Strike North into Russia, Chiang might even be willing to co-operate with him in the staging.

At 2:23 P.M. on December 12, the day after Hirohito accepted the resignation of the Wakatsuki Cabinet, Saionji arrived at Shimbashi Station in Tokyo to fulfill his onerous ceremonial duties in selecting the next Cabinet. His Secretary-Spy Harada extricated himself from the crowd of dignitaries which had assembled on the station platform to greet Saionji and ducked into the station-master's office to use the telephone. He called Marquis Kido, the favorite Big Brother who was secretary to Lord Privy Seal Makino.

"I can say positively," he told Kido, "that Inukai's is the name which Prince Saionji will submit to the Throne."

"That's fine," said Kido in his usual guarded manner. "There will be no objection to Inukai. The lord privy seal, however, is greatly concerned about financial management—or shall we say foreign relations? Accordingly it would be most appropriate if you would just give a hint to the finance minister, telling him that it will probably be Inukai and that various matters should be taken care of before the resignation of the Cabinet is announced to the public."

CASHING IN ON $$$

That evening, a Saturday, when the bourses of New York, London, and Paris were all closed, Finance Minister Inoue Junnosuke alerted Japanese businessmen abroad to the favorable opportunities in the offing. Various loose ends of complex transactions in "short sale" of currency and "short purchase" of commodities were hastily tied up in a dozen different capitals. In Japan department store clerks worked all weekend long to retag merchandise with new inflated prices reflecting the sudden drop expected in the value of the yen. On Monday morning housewives despaired at food prices which had jumped 30 to 40 per cent since Saturday.

In September 1931, before the Dollar Swindle had been conceived, Japan had had 900 million yen of paper currency in circulation backed by 870 million yen in gold. Each paper yen had been worth half a U.S. dollar. Now the 900 million paper yen were backed by only 370 million yen's worth of gold and the paper yen would soon be quoted at a value of 32 U.S. cents apiece. No less than 500 million yen's worth of gold had been shipped abroad to cover Japan's quiet but enormous speculation in depressed Western currencies. In theory the paper money of Japan should have fallen to 43 per cent of its previous value. In fact the secret of the swindle had been so well kept that the yen fell to only 64 per cent of its pre-swindle value. Because the yen remained inflated, Japanese speculators abroad converted their dollars first to raw materials and then secondarily to yen. Mitsui textile executives, for instance, bought heavily in the bumper 1931 U.S. cotton crop. They shipped it back to Japan, wove it into yard goods on the cheap Japanese labor market, and used it to swamp the bazaars of India and the Middle East. Textile mills in England went bankrupt and Japan acquired a name as a purveyor of cheap goods. Japanese industrialists doubled their swindle money by taking full advantage of the lag between domestic inflation and domestic wages. Collectively the Japanese cartels and the government's own Yokohama Specie Bank had netted an immediate paper profit of $60 million which would be realized finally as a cash profit of almost $200 million.

14

FAKE WAR

(1932)

A PRINCE TAKES COMMAND

The curtain rose on Act Two of the Triple Intrigue with the investiture of the Inukai Cabinet on December 13, 1931. That afternoon, in a frigidly formal audience with Hirohito, Saionji formally recommended Inukai as the nation's next prime minister. The new Cabinet met immediately and voted funds for the final pacification of all Manchuria. In China an envoy of Prime Minister Inukai, who had been ready and waiting in Nanking for several weeks, called on Chiang Kai-shek. Before dusk Chiang Kai-shek had stirred up a tempest in his KMT party and threatened to resign. He carried out his threat two days later and retired to his luxurious villa in the mountains. There he would remain, observing the Fake War, until the time came for him to take credit for ending it.

On December 16, the day after Chiang Kai-shek resigned, so did General Kanaya Hanzo, the chief of the Japanese Army General Staff. For two years he had performed deeds of political heroism above and beyond the normal call of military duty and now he begged to be relieved of the onus of presiding over the Fake War ahead. The triumverate of generals who managed the Army —war minister, chief of staff, and inspector general of military education—agreed to nominate General Minami, the outgoing

war minister, as Kanaya's successor. Hirohito, however, had found
Minami somewhat obtuse during the seizure of Mukden and suggested, through intermediaries, that the three chiefs reconsider
their recommendation. After discreet inquiries the three chiefs
discovered that Hirohito's personal choice for chief of staff was
Prince Kanin, the gray eminence of the imperial family. Prime-
Minister-Maker Saionji and the Strike-North Faction in the General Staff fought the appointment for six days—to no avail. On
December 23, Hirohito overrode all objections and confirmed his
great-uncle in Japan's highest military office.

Though still only sixty-six years old, Prince Kanin was the last
surviving brother of Prince Asahiko who had counseled Emperor
Komei at the time of Commodore Perry's opening of Japan
seventy-eight years earlier. He alone knew all the secrets of imperial family policy making in the years which had intervened. He
alone outranked Prime-Minister-Maker Saionji as a father of the
nation. It was his cavalry cronies, Tatekawa and Koiso, who had
masterminded the plots leading to the seizure of Mukden. It was
his responsibility to enact the rest of the imperial program bequeathed to Hirohito by his grandfather, Emperor Meiji. For the
next nine years, until the autumn of 1940, Prince Kanin would
fulfill meticulously the trust he had inherited. He would preside
over the formulation of all Army staff plans and would present
them to Hirohito for his signature. Before his retirement he would
oversee the conquest of north Manchuria, Mongolia, China, and
northern Indochina. Before his death—of severe hemorrhoids in
May 1945—he would see Japan's Armageddon against the West
spend itself in rubble and flame.

Kanin's appointment was celebrated by a mass rally of "national
thanks" at Tokyo's Meiji Stadium. No less than 18,000 members
of veterans' associations, youth groups, women's leagues, and cultural clubs turned out to express their gratitude to the Emperor
for appointing a member of his own family to a position of public
responsibility. The proceedings were broadcast on radio and
beamed overseas to the farthest corners of the Empire. No member of the imperial family had ever before talked on the radio to
the common people. To assure them that they might listen without being struck deaf, Black Dragon Toyama, the idolized Robin

Hood of the slums, acted as master of ceremonies. After his introduction Prince Kanin arose, ramrod stiff in his field marshal's
uniform. Strikingly handsome, his waxed mustache glittering under the lights, he delivered his speech with great dignity. In a few
well-chosen words he called for national unity and selfless service
to the Throne in the heroic ordeals which Japanese would have
to face in the years ahead.

SEDUCTIONS IN SHANGHAI

Having reunited boy emperor Pu-Yi with his number-one wife,
the energetic Manchu princess Eastern Jewel returned in mid-
December, at the time of the Cabinet change in Tokyo, to the
arms of her muscular lover, Major Tanaka of the Special Service
Organ in Shanghai. Sun Fo, the son of Sun Yat-sen, was in Shanghai trying to persuade Japan to support his Cantonese faction of
the KMT against the faction of Chiang Kai-shek who had just
resigned. Major Tanaka had money to spend for arranging provocations for the Fake War. Eastern Jewel was in her element. She
seduced Sun Yat-sen's son and passed on to Major Tanaka an
exhaustive account of the rivalries and factions within the KMT
party. She slept with a British military attaché in Shanghai and
wheedled out of him a realistic estimate of the small commitment
which Western nations were willing to make in stopping Japanese
aggression in Manchuria. In her spare time she hired Chinese
thugs to stand by for street brawls, arsons, and bombings that
would serve as tinder for the Fake War. Being a Chinese princess
she could move in Chinese circles closed to any other employee
of the Shanghai Special Service Organ. Being a Manchu princess
she looked down upon the Chinese masses with a fanatic contempt beyond Chinese understanding.

On December 17, 1931, four days after Eastern Jewel's return
to Shanghai, a certain I Pong-chang of the Korean Independence
Movement in Shanghai took ship for Kobe with a suitcase of hand
grenades and a determination to throw one of them at Hirohito.
At the Kobe docks he managed mysteriously to slip past Japan's
usually efficient immigration officers. On the eight-hour train
ride up to Tokyo he somehow escaped the notice of railroad plain-

clothesmen. In Tokyo he took a room at the Owariya Inn in the lower-class pleasure district of Asakusa. There he spent his time reading newspapers, studying Tokyo street maps, and waiting for his opportunity.

HIROHITO'S EXTRAORDINARY ESCAPE

Throughout the last week of 1931 the Kwantung Army in Manchuria was preparing for a final, full-scale occupation of Manchuria's northern provinces. In the first week of January the plans were executed with an aplomb and celerity that left the League of Nations gaping. On January 5, 1932, the politician of the Kwantung Army, Colonel Itagaki, flew to Tokyo to report to Hirohito and the General Staff that the spine of Chinese resistance was broken and that nothing remained to be done except routine mopping-up operations. Itagaki stayed on in Tokyo to assist in the operational planning for the Fake War.

Japan's renewed aggression in Manchuria, at a time when the League of Nations' Commission of Inquiry had not yet started for the Orient, stung many Western statesmen like a slap in the face. Secretary of State Stimson considered recalling the American ambassador in Tokyo and curtailing U.S.-Japanese trade. He found, however, that he could not muster enough political support in Washington for either measure. He contented himself with sending to Japan the stiffest note up to that time in the history of U.S.-Japanese relations. The note promised that the U.S. government would never recognize a Japanese puppet regime in Manchuria.

If Hirohito's cabal had any lingering doubts about activating its plans for the Fake War in Shanghai, they were dispelled when Stimson's note arrived in Tokyo early on Friday morning, January 8.

That day the Emperor was to attend a military review in the north Tokyo suburb of Yoyogi. Contrary to precedent, a map of the route he would follow had been published in the newspapers five days earlier. Security precautions were unusually strict. Secret policemen from the Kwantung Army in Manchuria had been flown in to assist the various Tokyo police forces. Many teahouses, brothels, and Korean boarding-houses had been raided and searched beforehand. Nevertheless the Korean assassin from Shanghai, I Pong-chang, with a grenade in each pocket, managed to find a place for himself in the front ranks of the spectators outside the Cherry Field Gate of the palace through which Hirohito was to pass on his way home.

Ever since the attempt on Hirohito's life in 1923, the policemen along the margins of an imperial progress had stood with their backs turned to the roadway, their heads respectfully inclined and their eyes staring into the eyes of the crowd. The crowd by ancient tradition was kneeling. From this reverent posture I Pong-chang had an opportunity to study the imperial cortege as it came toward him down the street. There were several carriages in the procession but only one emblazoned with the crest of the imperial chrysanthemum. Nevertheless, according to the account given out later by the police, I Pong-chang became confused. He leapt to his feet, snatched a grenade from his pocket, and hurled it 65 feet —a fair toss even for a trained shot-putter. Under the left rear wheel of the carriage of Imperial Household Minister Ikki Kitokuro, there was a small explosion. No one in the dense throng along the curbs of the roadway was harmed, but three scraps of shrapnel were later exhibited as having been dug from the underside of Household Minister Ikki's carriage. The assassin was seized at once by the police and held entirely incommunicado. Nine months later the secret police announced that he had been sentenced to death.

Big Brother Kido of the Eleven Club noted in his diary before the assassination attempt that he felt something bad would happen that day. Afterwards he characterized the bombing briefly as "a kind of political plot." Imperial Household Minister Ikki, whose coach had been struck, calmly told Secretary-Spy Harada on the phone a few minutes after the bombing that the incident was not important enough to warrant a special report to Prime-Minister-Maker Saionji. Hirohito himself, when told the identity of the assailant, chuckled and said, "He would have to be from the Korean Independence Party." Kinoshita Mikio, one of the palace chamberlains, remarked that afternoon that the attempted assassination would be useful in re-enlisting the sympathy of citizens who had grown disillusioned with Hirohito. Many patriotic Japanese felt that the home minister, who had charge of the police, should make amends for the carelessness of his subordinates by committing hara-kiri. But the home minister merely tendered his resignation to Hirohito as a formality along with the rest of the Cabinet. Without reading them, Hirohito handed the letters of resignation back to the prime minister and asked the entire Cabinet to remain in office.

That night Secretary-Spy Harada arrived in Okitsu to give Saionji a full briefing on the assassination attempt and the background for it. Harada in his diary reported none of the details of the conversation except one statement by Saionji, a statement which no other Japanese could have made without being arrested by the Thought Police.

"It is generally said," mused Saionji with bitterness, "that the Emperor transcends the Constitution, but where except in the Constitution is his existence justified?"

The day after the bombing, Saturday, January 9, 1932, a Chinese newspaper acquaintance of Eastern Jewel in Shanghai wrote tactlessly in his column that the bomb meant for Hirohito had "unfortunately missed its mark." The story was carried by the *Minkuo Daily News* in Shanghai and by a number of papers in other Chinese cities. Well-disciplined Japanese residents in China rioted in protest and demolished the offices of several Chinese newspapers. Though Chinese editors apologized for their impoliteness, Japanese Special Service Organ agents kept the insult alive and finally, after three weeks of agitation, inflated it into a cause for war.

GHOST HOUSE

No sooner had the *causa belli* been supplied for the second act of the Triple Intrigue, the Fake War, than preparations began for the third act, the Threat of Coup d'Etat.

On the evening of the day after the unsuccessful bombing of Hirohito's entourage, the children of a neighborhood in north Tokyo reported to their parents that the ghosts of "the empty house" were holding a meeting again. The families in the immediate vicinity of the empty house politely drew their rain shutters so that they would not see the eerie lights next door or seem to be prying into the affairs of the spirits.

The empty house belonged to a veteran of the spy service with long experience in China.[1] He had lived on the premises once and had written a book there on agrarian philosophy. But about a year ago he had closed the place up and gone to live elsewhere. Not long after his departure lights began to be seen in the house at night. Whenever the police were called to investigate, the lights went out and the police could find no one inside. The neighbors accepted the fact that spirits had moved in and did their courteous best to ignore the house thereafter.

What the neighbors could not guess and the local police may have been instructed to overlook was that the empty house had been taken over as the secret headquarters of the Blood Brotherhood, one of the three groups of potential terrorists with which Lord Privy Seal Makino's man, Dr. Okawa, had been put in touch through the good offices of old Spider Tanaka, the director emeritus of the spy service.

On the night in question, the empty house was the scene of an initiation ceremony. A burly Buddhist priest in white vestments stood at the end of the entry hall, limned from the rear by flickering candlelight. From time to time a tapping at the front door would stimulate him to chant a sepulchral welcome. A sturdy recruit would enter the foyer and at the priest's direction would put on a white hood from a pile beside the umbrella stand. Then the priest would usher him into the darkness of the room beyond —the "bone-cooling hall"—and tell him to meditate until everyone had arrived.

When a dozen men had assembled to contemplate the darkness of the inner room, the priest joined them with his candle. He chanted the mystic Lotus Sutra from Buddhist scripture and then delivered a solemn sermon of indoctrination. Their time of service was approaching, he said. From now until they were given their assignments, they would live with him here performing the necessary purification rites. When they had purged themselves of all

[1] Gondo Nariaki.

unclean and selfish motives, they would be ready for the final cleansing in blood, the "killing of one man by one man" which would gain them entry into paradise. After the priest's lecture, the recruits pricked their fingers with their daggers and renewed their signatures on a scroll which the priest called "the compact of blood." Then he assigned each of them a small room and a pallet for the remainder of their stay in the empty house.

Like the owner of the empty house, the priest, Friar Inoue, had once been a member of the spy service in China. He had returned to Japan in 1920 with his good friends and former colleagues Dr. Okawa, the ideologist of the Strike South, and Kita Ikki, the ideologist of the Strike North. When Okawa and Kita had fallen out, Friar Inoue had felt his loyalties torn between them. He had retired to meditate in a hermit's cave among the grotesque rock formations along the Pacific coast near the spy-service center of Oarai. One day while fasting—so he later remembered in his autobiography—he fell into a trance and saw a vision of Japan conquering the United States. The vision persuaded him to follow the star of Dr. Okawa and the Strike-South Faction. He emerged from the mountains and announced that he had changed his name from Inoue Akira, Inoue the Radiant, to Inoue Nisho, Inoue Summoned by the Sun Goddess. Along with his new name he assumed the frock of a Buddhist priest of the warrior Nichiren sect.

In the late 1920's, under the sponsorship of old Spider Tanaka of the spy service, Friar Inoue had opened a "school for the defense of the nation" in an abandoned temple in Oarai a few doors from Spider Tanaka's Everyday Meiji Biographical Research Institute. Here he gave advanced courses in espionage to the most promising graduates of Oarai's elementary school for spies, the Purple Mountain Academy.

Now, in the empty house, Friar Inoue had with him the most dedicated of his former students. In a few weeks each of them would be ready to assassinate a sacrificial victim—an industrialist or politician from the "plutocratic classes" which, in Inoue's view, were impeding the fulfillment of Hirohito's mission in life.

Before a dusty mirror Friar Inoue removed his hooded robe. A shaven pate and a hard round face emerged. Two cold humorless eyes peered out through perfectly circular spectacles. Friar Inoue snuffed out his candle and lay down for the night. The ceremony of initiation had gone well. The idea of using stage effects borrowed from Western spiritualism and African voodoo had been a good one. He was much obliged for it to the Emperor's uncle, Prince Higashikuni. In a moment Friar Inoue was asleep.

For the next two months Friar Inoue's Blood Brotherhood was to terrorize Japan's Westernized community of businessmen and politicians. By assassination and threat of assassination it would prevent Japanese liberals from talking frankly to the League of Nations' Commission of Inquiry and would force them to put up money to pay for the Fake War and the development of the new colony of Manchuria. Until the brotherhood's mission was accomplished, it would enjoy a strange immunity from police arrest, an immunity made possible by the high rank of its patrons. Friar Inoue was an intimate of Big Brother Prince Konoye and of Big Brother Prince Higashikuni. Inoue took his orders from Dr. Okawa who relayed them by special messenger directly from Hirohito's chief civilian advisor, Lord Privy Seal Makino, in the palace. In addition Friar Inoue had the support of the naval fliers of the Air Development Station on the Misty Lagoon. The fliers supplied him with guns and ammunition and had set up their own coup-threat headquarters a few blocks from the empty house. This close collaboration was hardly surprising because the fliers were all disciples of Friar Inoue's elder brother, Navy Commander Inoue Fumio. Commander Inoue was the senior flight instructor at the Misty Lagoon. He had taught the imperial family's test pilot, Prince Yamashina, how to fly, and also Captain Yamamoto who would raid Pearl Harbor.

PROVOKING WAR

On January 10, 1932, the day after the initiation ceremony in the empty house, Colonel Itagaki, the visiting political officer from the Kwantung Army, completed his arrangements with the Army General Staff in Tokyo for the Fake War. From his Tokyo hotel room he dispatched the following telegram to Shanghai Special

Service Organ Chief Tanaka, the lover of Manchu princess Eastern Jewel:

THE MANCHURIAN INCIDENT HAS DEVELOPED AS EXPECTED, BUT THE OP-
POSITION OF THE STRONG COUNTRIES IS STILL GIVING CERTAIN PERSONS
AT THE CENTER DOUBTS. SO PLEASE USE THE CURRENT TENSION BETWEEN
CHINA AND JAPAN TO BRING OFF YOUR INCIDENT AND TURN THE EYES
OF THE STRONG COUNTRIES TOWARD SHANGHAI.

The next morning Itagaki went to the palace and delivered a
full report to Hirohito on the "progress being made in establishing the new nation" of Manchukuo. According to Big Brother
Marquis Kido, who received a résumé of the audience in an anteroom afterwards, Itagaki explained to Hirohito that the new puppet state would preserve a façade of independence and self-rule.
Japanese "advisors," he said, would really run the state, but they
would be given Manchukuoan citizenship and would be called
Manchukuoans. At the same time they would keep their Japanese
citizenship and would remain obedient to orders from Tokyo.
Hirohito inquired whether there were any precedents for such
dual nationality, and Itagaki cited several. At this turn in the conversation, the Emperor's chief aide-de-camp, who had stood in
attendance during the first half of the audience, hastily bowed
himself out. It was a Court rule that he must never listen to discussion of personnel questions. As a result Hirohito and Itagaki
finished their meeting in complete privacy.

On receipt of Colonel Itagaki's telegram from Tokyo, Major
Tanaka of the Shanghai Special Service Organ advanced some
$6,000 from organ funds to his mistress, Eastern Jewel. Disguised
as a man, she distributed half of the money, by her own account-
ing, to some Chinese laborers at the Japanese-owned Three
Friends bath towel factory. The manager of the factory was unpopular in the local Japanese community because he was supposed
to have socialistic leanings. The other half of the money, Eastern
Jewel said, she gave to a gang of street toughs who were to assist
the towel weavers.

On the afternoon of January 18 two Nichiren priests and three
disciples of the Myoho Buddhist temple came swaggering along

Yinhsiang Creek near the towel factory, banging gongs and bellowing sutra as was their offensive wont. Tanaka later explained that he chose them as victims because most Myoho temple men "were only Koreans." The five monks and novices were set upon by the Chinese towel weavers—and by enough street toughs to justify Eastern Jewel's expense account—and were brutally beaten. One of the priests subsequently died on January 24, but long before he did, on January 19, a scant ten hours after the original skirmish, thirty-two members of the Japanese Young Men's One-Purpose Society, led by a secret policeman named Shigeto,[2] made a predawn attack on the towel factory and burned down one of its buildings. During the fire the Chinese police appeared on the scene. Two of them were killed and two wounded. Of the One-Purpose Society's goon squad, one was killed and two wounded.

Shortly after daybreak that same morning, the Japanese residents of Shanghai held a mass meeting and at the urging of Major Tanaka resolved to beg the Tokyo government for an expeditionary force to protect them. Tanaka and secret policeman Shigeto took the request to the local representative of the Mitsui cartel and forced him at pistol point to relay it by cable to his head office in Tokyo. The Mitsui management in Tokyo failed to submit the request to the prime minister, as ordered, but the telegram was later used by the cabal as evidence that the Fake War had been launched to protect Mitsui interests—a service for which Mitsui should bear part of the financial burden.

The mayor of Shanghai, Wu Tieh-ching, immediately apologized on behalf of China for the roughness of the Chinese towel weavers who had been hired by Japan. On January 21, he went so far as to promise that he would arrest and punish the towel weavers and would pay medical and consolation expenses to the kin of the termagant Nichiren priests. The Japanese had demanded that he should also make the Chinese citizens of Shanghai stop feeling hostile to Japan. Mayor Wu promised to do his best but pointed out, with polite regrets, that the private feelings of the populace were out of his hands. The Japanese consul general

[2] The brother of Colonel Shigeto Chiaki of the Tokyo General Staff who had played a prominent role in the March Plot a year earlier.

in Shanghai retorted: "In the event that such compliance is refused, we are determined to take such steps as may be necessary."
In the days that followed young Japanese bravos in Shanghai and
even small Japanese children went out of their way to pick fights
with their Chinese counterparts. The carefully manufactured tension grew by the hour.

DOMESTIC EXTORTION

In Tokyo that day Prime Minister Inukai asked Baron Dan
Takuma, the top executive of the Mitsui cartel, to contribute
22,000,000 yen—some $8 million—to the government to cover the
cost of shipping troops to Shanghai to protect Mitsui interests.
Baron Dan protested that Mitsui needed no such protection, could
ill afford such a huge sum of money, and would pay it only under
compulsion. Prime Minister Inukai reminded Baron Dan that
Mitsui had made at least $20 million when Inukai had taken Japan
off the gold standard and that one good turn deserved another.
If Mitsui would pay for the Fake War, Inukai had an arrangement
with Chiang Kai-shek by which the Manchurian problem might
be settled and constitutional government in Japan might be
preserved.

Inukai did not state his plan but Baron Dan probably knew it
already. Inukai hoped to establish Manchuria as a nation independent of both Japan and China. The conversations between
Inukai's representative in Nanking and Chiang Kai-shek indicated
that Chiang would recognize such a nation. In return Japan would
destroy the Chinese 19th Route Army in Shanghai—the army of
the dissident Cantonese faction in the KMT which contested
Chiang Kai-shek's absolute authority. Once Chiang Kai-shek recognized the independence of Manchuria, the League of Nations
would have no reason to censure Japan. For the sake of international harmony and the domestic co-operation of Japan's business
community, Hirohito might be willing to accept such a compromise. He would only have to order the Kwantung Army to return
to its garrisons in the South Manchuria Railroad zone and all the
rest could be worked out. A token of good faith on the part of the
cartels, however, was urgently needed to persuade Hirohito to
consider the plan.

Baron Dan promised to think over Prime Minister Inukai's proposal but held out no hope that he could persuade the Mitsui family or the industrialists of the other cartels to back the scheme. Baron Dan suspected that Hirohito was already too committed to military empire-building to change his plans now and that the lines of conflict between the liberal Saionji faction and the imperial faction at Court were too sharply drawn to be erased without a showdown.

That afternoon, January 21, 1932, Hirohito recessed the Diet in preparation for a general election on February 20. In the interim he would have the constitutional right to arrogate the one power which the Diet possessed—that of authorizing additional expenditures which had not been foreseen in the last national budget.

That night Lord Privy Seal Count Makino, Hirohito's chief civilian advisor, warned Saionji, through Secretary-Spy Harada, that continued non-support of the Fake War by the cartels would lead to a new imperial coup d'etat on or about February 10. What he meant, as it turned out, was that the Blood Brotherhood of Friar Inoue would then assassinate its first sacrificial victim.

COMMENCEMENT OF HOSTILITIES

Shanghai was an ideal city in which to make the nations of the West appreciate Japan's effort to save the face of the League of Nations. Here were the biggest Western enclaves and the headquarters of the main Western business interests in central China. Here the Western nations had invested more than a billion dollars. Here Japan had a garrison of 2,000 of her crack troops, the Imperial Marines.

On Saturday, January 23, 1932, a Japanese cruiser and four destroyers, all loaded with additional bluejackets, cast anchor in the mouth of the Yangtze, to be followed the next day and the day after by two aircraft carriers. On Sunday, January 24, Chinese civilians held a mass meeting to ask Nanking for military reinforcements. Chiang Kai-shek, however, was sulking in his villa, and the other KMT leaders entrusted the defense of Shanghai to the 19th Route Army of Sun Yat-sen's son, Sun Fo, who was in Shanghai negotiating with the Japanese and sleeping with Eastern Jewel. That night a group of Eastern Jewel's hirelings made an unsuccessful, almost nonexistent attempt to set fire to the Japanese consulate in the French Concession.

On Tuesday, January 26, before a shot had been fired, Hirohito's Supreme War Council, presided over by Chief of Staff Prince Kanin, instructed Admiral Shiozawa in Shanghai to "exercise the right of self-defense." That afternoon Shanghai's Mayor Wu closed the *Minkuo Daily News*, which had offended Japan by regretting the poor aim of Hirohito's Korean would-be murderer. On Wednesday, January 27, Mayor Wu ordered his police to break up all anti-Japanese societies and demonstrations. The next morning, Thursday—"about eight o'clock," according to the official Japanese account at the time—"a Chinese, seemingly of the anti-Japanese National Salvation Society," threw into the Japanese consulate "what seemed like a bomb, though it failed to explode." Eastern Jewel had successfully laid on her last pathetic straw.

That afternoon at 3:15 Mayor Wu notified the Japanese naval commander, Admiral Shiozawa, that the Chinese municipal government would comply with every Japanese request. Nevertheless at 4:00 P.M. the non-Chinese Municipal Council of the International Settlement, acting under Japanese pressure, proclaimed martial law throughout the concession area, and British, French, and Japanese guard units deployed to defend their assigned sectors against the possibility of attack by Chinese mobs.

At 5:00 P.M. *New York Times* correspondent Hallett Abend visited the Japanese flagship in the harbor for cocktails with Admiral Shiozawa. Over the second Scotch and soda, Shiozawa told Abend that Mayor Wu's acceptance of all Japanese demands was "beside the point."

"At eleven o'clock tonight," said Shiozawa, "I am sending my marines into Chapei to protect our nationals and preserve order." Chapei was the show-piece borough of Chinese Shanghai. It lay just to the north of the Japanese quarter of the International Settlement. The Japanese who lived in Chapei and supposedly needed protection had already been evacuated two days earlier.

As soon as he politely could, Abend hurried ashore and cabled his story to New York. Then he phoned all the Western diplomats of his acquaintance in Shanghai. To a man they told him that he was mongering sensationalism. But Admiral Shiozawa was as good as his word. After eleven o'clock that night, he sent Mayor Wu a note declaring his intentions and before twelve o'clock his bluejackets began crossing the northern boundary of the Japanese defense sector and moving north along the dark streets of Chinese Chapei. Behind them at the border their rear guard unrolled barbed wire and built roadblocks. Westerners in evening dress, who had come across town after their dinner and theatre parties to see if there would be any action, stood about smoking and joking. The only thing worse than a Japanese victory, said the wits, would be a Chinese one.

When the probing patrols had been gone for about half an hour, heavy firing broke out. The Japanese marines had been told not to expect much resistance. They had advanced as if to a picnic, talking and laughing and lighting their way with flaming torches. Now their outing had turned into an immense ambush. On walls and in upstairs windows between the border and the North Station for which they were headed, there had suddenly materialized riflemen and machine gunners of the 19th Route's 78th Division. The marines were caught in cross fire and several hundred of them were mowed down before they could regroup and begin to withdraw.

As the night wore on, every dispensable seaman on the Japanese ships in the harbor was given a gun and sent ashore on the double to join the battle. Despite their efforts, the men of the Chinese 19th Route Army pressed forward. By the first light of day on Friday, January 29, they were threatening to break through the barricades into the Japanese settlement. In desperation Admiral Shiozawa ordered into action the planes of his two aircraft carriers. By 7:00 A.M. they were strafing the advancing Chinese soldiers and strewing little 30-pound terror bombs all over densely populated civilian Chapei. One of their targets was the Commercial Press, the factory for all China's textbooks. It housed a priceless collection of old Chinese scrolls and manuscripts. It was reduced to a gutted shell. The Japanese were frank to explain that anti-Japanese propaganda had been printed on the premises.

Never before had the world witnessed the results of wholesale civilian bombing by airplane. Dynamite dropped from German dirigibles had cut open a few houses in London toward the end of World War I, but casualties had been neglible. Now, in Chapei, the later horrors of Hiroshima might be glimpsed as in a glass darkly. Hundreds of women and children were blown to shreds. Admiral Shiozawa became known in the West as the "baby-killer."

As the bombing and the morning progressed, the 19th Route commander, General Tsai Ting-kai, to the chagrin of his political leaders—especially of Sun Yat-sen's son, Sun Fo, who had taken refuge from the fighting in Eastern Jewel's apartment—announced that the 19th Route would "fight the Japanese to the last man if it has to dye the Whampo River red with its soldiers' blood." That afternoon when Chiang Kai-shek realized that the men of the 19th Route were making heroes of themselves instead of being wiped out, he returned immediately to Nanking and offered his leadership to the KMT "at this time of crisis." The Cantonese faction of the KMT might be his domestic rivals but they were Chinese, and he could ill afford to be out of command when they were sacrificing themselves for the nation.

For Japan's benefit, Chiang continued to negotiate in secret with Prime Minister Inukai's emissary in Nanking, Kayano Chochi. For China's benefit he announced publicly that he had ordered his own personal "guard divisions" to prepare for action. None of Chiang's men, however, arrived at the battle line until over three weeks later. Moreover, Chiang's small navy declared itself neutral and kept out of harm's way well up the Yangtze River. It had ordered a new vessel from a Japanese dockyard in Kobe. The warship was launched while the war still raged and the Chinese minister in Tokyo attended the commissioning ceremony. He drank toasts with the Japanese naval officers present and exchanged sentiments with them of Sino-Japanese friendship and good will.

In later years the valiant 19th Route Army would go over to Chiang's open enemies, the Communists of Mao Tse-tung. In

1932, however, its officers were simply idealistic agrarian reformers. They served the socialist Cantonese faction of the KMT because they believed it to be more in tune with the interests of the Chinese peasantry than were the bankers around Chiang Kai-shek. In their political innocence they felt inspired by Chiang's promise of aid. They dug into the rubble of Chapei and, to the surprise of the Japanese Imperial Marines, held their ground even under a hail of bombs and naval shells. Japanese local civilian reservists —the "mufti army" as they were known in Tokyo—took revenge behind the lines for the losses being suffered by the marines at the front. They raided Chinese shops on the fringes of Chapei, looting, raping, and beheading. The naval deck hands who now held rear posts for the marines spent their days disposing of the bodies of Chinese civilians murdered by Japanese vigilantes.

Altogether the Chinese had some 33,500 men in the Shanghai area compared to a Japanese force which at first numbered less than 5,000. Other foreign armies in the International Settlement and French Concession amounted to over 18,000 men and with their superior equipment and training were thoroughly capable of defending foreign interests against the 19th Route Army. But the Japanese Navy was not disposed to seek Western support. Instead it fought its own desperate defensive battle, bringing in the crews of all the Japanese ships it could muster in the China Sea and finally, in great humiliation, asking the Japanese Army for help. The Imperial Marines were beside themselves with rage to retrieve their laurels.

In Tokyo Hirohito was gravely worried that the wounded honor of his samurai might turn the controlled "incident" into a runaway war which Japan would not be able to afford. Repeatedly he sought assurance from those about him that reinforcements, when landed, would proceed slowly, avoid face-saving confrontations, and remain ready to withdraw at his command. His absorption with the tactical and financial details became so tiresome that Big Brother Marquis Kido of the Eleven Club waxed almost critical of him and expressed a wish that he would shed his pettifogging anxieties and "sit big as a mountain." Hirohito's nervousness was needless, as it turned out, but he was playing a dangerous game.

He was trying to deceive not only the world but also the Japanese electorate and the men who were dying.

As a precaution against uncontrollable escalation Hirohito approved the appointment of his wife's cousin, Prince Fushimi, as chief of the Navy General Staff.[3] In a breach of normal Court protocol, old Prime-Minister-Maker Saionji was not consulted about the appointment beforehand but was simply informed of it afterward when it was a *fait accompli*. Now imperial princes were in charge of the operations of both military services, and absolute, reverent obedience could be expected of the samurai in the ranks.

The Imperial Household Ministry made a special point of announcing that Prince Fushimi's appointment had nothing to do with the fighting in Shanghai. But the nation knew better. An imperial prince would not have been put at the helm unless Hirohito meant to see the Shanghai incident through to an honorable conclusion. To all those wealthy, cosmopolitan, educated Japanese who felt that Japan should not try to deceive the world or risk alienating friends abroad for the sake of Manchuria, the appointment was a clear warning that they would have to reckon with Hirohito.

On this note began Act Three of the Triple Intrigue: Threat of Coup d'Etat. No longer was the threat directed simply at the West; no longer was it intended simply to persuade sympathetic Westerners that the official Japanese government stood powerless and in danger of overthrow. Now the threat was aimed also at internal opponents of imperial policy; now it offered domestic dissenters a hard choice—co-operate or face the possibility of assassination.

[3] The previous staff chief, Admiral Taniguchi Naozane, had discovered the involvement of the Misty Lagoon Air Development Station with the killers of the Blood Brotherhood. He had pointed out that flight instructor Inoue Fumio, the brother of Friar Inoue of the assassin band, was "a strange man" to have in the Navy. When his request to discharge Commander Inoue was tabled by Hirohito, Admiral Taniguchi had resigned in protest.

15

GOVERNMENT BY ASSASSINATION

(1932)

BLESSING THE KILLERS

On Saturday, January 30, 1932, the bombs had been bursting in Shanghai for more than twenty-four hours, and the banking houses of Mitsui and the other cartels had not yet agreed either to give or lend the government enough money to pay for the action.[1] The money itself was important, but the gesture of making it available was symbolically still more important. By withholding it, the Japanese business community remained in dissent against the imperial program. The merchants, in effect, were denying the uniqueness of the Japanese race and the mission handed down from the sun goddess.

That same Saturday night, therefore, Friar Inoue, the leader for the Blood Brotherhood, conducted the final rites of purification for the assassins under his charge who were to intimidate the business community. One by one the young killers filed into the "bone-cooling hall" of the empty house and to the accompaniment of dedicatory incantations were allowed briefly to handle one or another of the ten pistols which had been provided by Dr. Okawa and Commander Inoue Fumio's naval group at the Misty Lagoon. Having blessed the weapons and their wielders, Friar Inoue returned the guns to their locker for distribution later.

[1] In Japan it was and is normal procedure for the government to consult the great banking families on policies affecting national finance.

On paper Friar Inoue assigned each of the eleven assassins eleven specific victims to kill at specific times and places. But in practice he later juggled and postponed the assignments so that only two of the victims were ever killed. On one occasion he failed to get the assassin his gun on time and on another he sent the killer to a rendezvous where the quarry was not to be expected.

In such fashion great fear was created by only two murders, and it was arranged for many leaders of the cartels and of the Constitutionalist party to be ostentatiously spared. Typically, Lord Privy Seal Makino was one of those who turned out to be not for killing. The assassin assigned to take care of him was a knowledgeable Tokyo University graduate student who had acted as the courier between the Blood Brotherhood and Makino's own man, Dr. Okawa.

STAY OF EXECUTION

The first week of February 1932 was taken up entirely with the outbreak of the Shanghai war. The restless fliers of the Misty Lagoon, who were to supply military support for the Blood Brotherhood, found themselves temporarily distracted from all else by being called to duty for raids and reconnaissance at the front. On Monday, February 1, while their precision bombing was demolishing Chinese structures a stone's throw from Western-owned docks and warehouses, the Japanese foreign minister offered Western diplomats in Tokyo the opportunity of using their good offices to mediate the Sino-Japanese "misunderstanding." That same evening the American, French, and British ambassadors responded to the suggestion informally but favorably.

On the afternoon of the next day, Tuesday, February 2, Lord Privy Seal Makino told Prime Minister Inukai that "resolution of the Manchurian problem is going unexpectedly well" and that "the results may be almost perfect because of the understanding attitude of the United States and Great Britain." Perhaps, after all, the Shanghai affair might not have to be carried through to the end.

"What's done is done, of course," said Makino, "but now we

must co-operate as much as possible with the other nations to prevent escalation."

Prime Minister Inukai had just come from a Cabinet meeting at which his ministers had approved the dispatch of regular Army troops to Shanghai. For a few hours he found himself in the awkward position of having approved a war which might not be necessary. That evening, however, it developed that U.S. Secretary of State Stimson would not co-operate in any Shanghai settlement that did not also include some provision for a Manchurian settlement. Neither the Emperor nor the Army would accept such a proviso, and for the next three days the Fake War was held in abeyance while Japan negotiated with the United States.

In the interim, on Thursday, February 4, the war minister was carefully briefed by the finance minister on the reasons why the war must be a brief gesture and nothing more. Japan could not afford a real war, not even if it could be won in six months, not even if it could be waged on a budget of $30 million. The Army, emphasized the finance minister, must be ready and disciplined to obey at any moment a truce arrangement. Army talk of breaking through to Nanking and teaching Chiang Kai-shek a lesson must be stopped.

"We have absolutely no righteous cause," said the finance minister, "to warrant hopes of being able to raise financial assistance in foreign capitals." Then he showed War Minister Araki telegrams demonstrating that Japanese credit in New York had struck rock bottom and that President Hoover had recently written financier Thomas W. Lamont that the U.S. government had now "wholly lost confidence in the Japanese government."

KILL THE BANKER

By February 5, unofficial secret negotiations had made it clear that the United States could not be cajoled out of coupling the Manchurian and Shanghai settlements. Nor would the cartels subsidize the Shanghai war as long as they could hope for a firm Western stand. Accordingly Hirohito directed Prime Minister Inukai to reject the mediation plan of the West as unsatisfactory, and all plotting lights were turned on green again.

On Saturday morning, February 6, Friar Inoue in the empty house received a visit from one of the junior officers of the Misty Lagoon, Second Lieutenant Ito Kijomi. Ito brought with him a Browning automatic which had belonged to his squadron leader, Lieutenant Commander Fujii Hitoshi, who had been shot down and killed on reconnaissance over Chapei the day before. Commander Fujii had been the prize pupil of Friar Inoue's brother, the flight instructor, and also the leader at the fliers' coup headquarters near the empty house a week earlier. Lieutenant Ito begged Friar Inoue to proceed according to plan even without the fliers' support. The Browning automatic, he said, shone with the departed spirit of Lieutenant Commander Fujii whose dying regret it had been that he could not lead the Emperor's coup in person. Friar Inoue accepted the Browning and swore to use it to satisfy the one-day ghost of its former owner. That night after suitable ceremony and dedications he turned over the Browning and forty-six bullets to one of his best assassins, a young man named Konuma Tadashi.

Konuma's assigned victim was the former finance minister, Inoue Junnosuke. He had to be killed for several reasons. He had made the initial arrangements with the Mitsui cartel to buy dollars in preparation for the Dollar Swindle. He was one of the few men in Japan who knew that the idea for the swindle had emanated from the palace. He had not co-operated later in forcing the cartels to turn back a suitable percentage of their profits to the service of the nation. And finally, someone had to be assassinated as an example to the rest of the recalcitrant business community. Assassin Konuma spent two days practicing with his Browning and waiting for final orders.

In the interim on Sunday, February 7, the Japanese Army came to the rescue of the embattled Navy by landing a mixed brigade of 10,000 men in Shanghai. On Monday, February 8, Hirohito gave his personal instructions to the Japanese Diplomat who was going to Shanghai to be ready to negotiate a truce as soon as the Fake War had served its purpose. The negotiator was Matsuoka Yosuke, a University of Oregon graduate who would later become famous for his expansive hobnobbing with Hitler and Mussolini. Since 1925 he had been one of the junior members of the cabal in the Foreign Ministry. His meeting with Hirohito that quiet Monday morning was disguised as a "lecture in the Imperial Study on noncurrent historical events." At the end of it, however, Hirohito had a few words with Matsuoka on current events.

Matsuoka expressed the opinion that the Fake War should not be stopped until the Japanese forces in Shanghai had taken the offensive and won a decisive victory. China, he said, was Japan's lazy elder brother. The industrious younger brother had the duty of chastising the elder brother when the honor of the whole family was at stake. Appealing to Hirohito's interests as a biologist, Matsuoka cited the "Darwinian principle" that competition is always most fierce between those who are closely related. Hirohito nodded, but Saionji, when he heard of the Matsuoka audience, asked that Army and Navy commanders in Shanghai be warned about Matsuoka's proclivity "for falling into paradoxes."

It followed from Matsuoka's advice that the Fake War must be well staged and that the cartels must be cowed into paying for a handsome production. Early the next afternoon, Tuesday, February 9, Emperor Hirohito invited a most unusual "lecturer" to speak to him in his study at the Imperial Library. This was Lieutenant General Banzai Rihachiro, retired. Banzai for many years had run Japan's espionage network in China and had been the immediate superior of Friar Inoue, the leader of the Blood Brotherhood. In the shadowy directorate of Japan's Civilian Spy Service, Banzai now ranked second to no one except perhaps old Spider Tanaka of the Everyday Meiji Biographical Research Institute in Oarai.

Retired General Banzai emerged from his talk with Hirohito that Tuesday afternoon at two o'clock. Two hours later the Blood Brotherhood's assassin, Konuma, received a messenger from Friar Inoue, telling him to proceed according to plan. At 7:00 P.M. assassin Konuma alighted from a streetcar on a corner a few blocks from Tokyo Imperial University. He took up a loitering vigil at the gate of the Komagome Elementary School where former Finance Minister Inoue Junnosuke was scheduled to deliver an election speech that night. Although Konuma paced back and forth and smoked countless cigarettes, the passers-by paid him no special attention. Twenty-two years old, fifth son of an Ibaraki fisherman, first in his class at junior high, later a baker's assistant and a carpenter's apprentice, he looked like any restless, impoverished university student, waiting for a girl or the results of a crucial examination.

The former finance minister's limousine pulled up to the curb at 8:02 P.M. The candidate for whom he was stumping stepped out and bowed to a political welcoming committee. The sixty-six-year-old financier followed; he advanced five or six steps and was just inclining his head to the crowd when Blood Brother Konuma burst from the ranks of spectators behind him and fired three shots into the old man's back. One bullet lodged in his left buttock, another in his right lung, and the third shattered his spine. Former Finance Minister Inoue Junnosuke died almost immediately. Assassin Konuma let himself be taken to the police station where he was treated with such unusual gentleness that he appeared in criminal court a few months later looking the rosy picture of health.

KILLERS LEFT AT LARGE

On the day of financier Inoue's murder, his namesake, Friar Inoue of the Blood Brotherhood, moved his base of operations from the empty house to the House of Heavenly Action, a student hostel maintained by the Black Dragon Society next door to the home of the Black Dragon himself, Toyama Mitsuru. The hostel was managed by Toyama's son, Hidezo, and by Toyama's secretary, another former spy of the China Service, Honma Kenichiro. Until 1930, Honma had been Friar Inoue's colleague at Oarai and had run the elementary school for spies there, the Purple Mountain Academy.[2]

In his new headquarters Friar Inoue maintained business as usual, pursuing his campaign of escalating terror as if nothing had happened. Messengers shuttled back and forth daily between his House of Heavenly Action and the nearby coup headquarters of the Misty Lagoon flight officers. The pledged assassins of the

---

[2] Black Dragon Toyama and his son Hidezo later maintained successfully in court that they had known nothing of Friar Inoue's activities and had given him lodging only at the recommendation of Honma.

Blood Brotherhood boarded in private homes nearby and kept in touch. The civil and military police compiled dossiers on the Blood Brotherhood and the Misty Lagoon fliers. The dossiers were handed up through channels to the chief of police and to the supreme commandant of the secret police, and then, after guarded inquiries had been made at the palace, were filed away for reference.

Although nothing was done to prevent further murders, everything was done to advertise their lurking danger. The very day after the assassination, Wednesday, February 10, Count Arima of the imperial family lunched with Big Brother Kido and the gossipy Secretary-Spy Harada at the excellent Known-for-Mulberries Restaurant, the Kuwana. Count Arima asked Kido and Harada to spread the news that a coup d'etat remained an imminent likelihood and that a Strike-South millionaire[3] had replaced Baron Tokugawa of the March Plot as the paymaster for cutthroats employed by the Throne.

That same day the Board of Fleet Admirals and Field Marshals met to pledge full Army-Navy co-operation in a "burst of power" to break the back of the Chinese 19th Route Army in Shanghai. Twenty thousand fresh Army troops were landed in Shanghai between February 14 and 16. The joint chiefs of staff, Prince Kanin and Prince Fushimi, hoped that these reinforcements, added to the 10,000 soldiers and 10,000 sailors already fighting, would be able to make the Chinese 19th Route Army give ground.

VOTE FOR NONVIOLENCE

The week of the troop dispatches, February 14 to February 20, was also the last week before elections—the elections which had

[3] Ishiwara Hiroichiro. Baron Tokugawa Yoshichika had introduced Ishiwara as his successor to Dr. Okawa at the Fukuya teahouse in Hamamachi—the eastern terminus of Tokyo's modern airport monorail—on Sunday, January 10, the day after the first initiation of assassins in the empty house. Along with Baron Tokugawa and with Count Ohtani Kozui, a husband of Hirohito's mother's sister, who would later play a vital role in planning the conquest of Singapore, millionaire Ishiwara had been staked by the Throne during World War I to set up a commercial arm of the spy service in the Dutch East Indies. Through his cover, a mining company in Java, Ishiwara had made a fortune of some $5 million and was now one of the most affluent proponents of the Strike South in Japan.

been called in order to muzzle the Diet at a time when the Emperor wanted to exercise his powers of fiat to authorize the Shanghai war expenses. The anti-Constitutionalist party of former Prime Minister Wakatsuki campaigned on the slogans "Inukai and Dollar-Buy," "Friends of Dollar-Buyers are Enemies of the Masses," "Rising Prices and Declining Loyalty." Prime Minister Inukai's Constitutionalists were somewhat embarrassed by posters that they had put up earlier proclaiming "Finance Minister Takahashi Brings Fortune; Former Finance Minister Inoue Brings Misfortune." Since former Finance Minister Inoue had had the misfortune of being assassinated, the posters did not seem to be in the best of taste. The people, however, understood. The Constitutionalists had inherited the Dollar Swindle and the Fake War from the previous administration and were not held responsible for them.

As election week progressed, it began to look as if the Constitutionalists would win a resounding victory. Hirohito's political advisors were disappointed. A big vote for the Constitutionalists traditionally meant dissatisfaction with imperial policy-making. For a generation the Constitutionalists had stood for economic rather than military expansion of the Empire, for long-term cooperation with China, for low taxes and cheap money, for blustering loudly and carrying a small stick.

Encouraged by the popular trend, the Japanese business community stiffened its spine and refused to be intimidated by the continuing threat of assassination. The previous October many of the cartel leaders had deserted old Prime-Minister-Maker Saionji for the profits they saw in the Dollar Swindle. Finding himself fighting alone, Saionji had withdrawn in disgust and had quietly watched developments ever since from his seaside villa. Now, however, the great merchant families began once more to court Saionji's favor. They founded a "Constitution Protection Movement" and began to recruit goon squads of their own with which they hoped to be able to meet the Blood Brotherhood on equal terms. Instead of offering to lend the government enough money to pay for the Shanghai war, they sought to bribe the Kwantung Army and so strip Hirohito of his most ardent supporters. General Honjo in Mukden refused the first of many such bribes on election-week Wednesday, February 17. A representative of the second-ranking cartel, Mitsubishi, came to Honjo's office and tried to give him a check for over $100,000 as a "contribution." Honjo refused to touch the check, told the Mitsubishi representative that the sum was far too small, and advised him, when Mitsubishi was ready to be more generous, to present its donation directly to the war minister or chief of staff in Tokyo.

On election-week Friday, February 19, the Big Brothers of the Eleven Club spent the entire day consulting with operatives of the spy service, with leaders of the underworld, and with one another. They were reassured that the cartels could never recruit a formidable following among the dispossessed samurai of the demi-monde. In the words of one of the most knowledgeable of their underworld contacts: "No movement either of the Left or the Right can ever succeed unless it is centered around the Emperor."

STAGE MANAGERS' MEETING

That same evening the dapper, owlish Big Brother Marquis Kido from the office of the lord privy seal in the palace and the lanky, languid Big Brother Prince Konoye from the House of Peers met for dinner with their Army counterparts at the elegant villa of Colonel Marquis Inoue Saburo, the son of Emperor Taisho's Prime Minister Katsura. To speak for the military half of the cabal, their host had invited his protégé, the ubiquitous Lieutenant Colonel Suzuki, and the most aristocratic of the Three Crows of Baden-Baden, Colonel Obata Toshiro.[4] The prince, the two marquises, and the two soldier-courtiers drank cocktails, Western style, on Marquis Inoue's screened porch overlooking Yokohama Bay where Commodore Perry had steamed in with his Black Ships seventy-nine years earlier.

All five men agreed that the Throne faced an acute political crisis. The self-seeking merchants of the realm had won the support of the voters and now threatened to buy the support of the Army. Prime Minister Inukai persisted in negotiating with Chiang

---

[4] Saionji's Secretary-Spy Harada had been included in Marquis Inoue's original guest list but had been finally excluded because the Army members of the cabal did not trust his wagging tongue.

Kai-shek in an effort to neutralize Manchuria and make it an autonomous region outside the Empire. He and his government had outlived their usefulness. No other political-party government would be any better. Party politicians had simply become too "corrupted" by money and Western parliamentary ideas to serve the Throne obediently.

The alternative of an imperial coup d'etat, making Hirohito open dictator, was not feasible either. The threat of coup might still be a useful political tool, but a genuine coup was opposed by all Hirohito's senior courtiers as an infringement of the Constitution and an unnecessary exposure of the imperial family.

The only possibility left, then, was a "transcendental," nonpolitical government of recognized national elders—old men who understood the imperial program and could take responsibility for it. Such governments had been tried several times during the years of Emperor Taisho's madness in the early 1920's. The people did not like them but had always put up with them because, in the past, transcendental patriarchs had tended to be cautious and not do much.

Now a transcendental Cabinet was needed that would advance the national program. It must obviously have a strong war minister, for unless the privates in the Army felt adequately represented by their minister, they could, by their letters home, cause more peasant discontent than a rise in taxes, a flood, or a famine.

Present War Minister Araki was known to be well liked in the ranks. Indeed, as Big Brother Kido acknowledged, he was "too popular to be dispensed with." Unfortunately, however, he believed that Japan's true mission was a Strike North into Bolshevik Russia. Since in this he differed with the Throne, the Big Brothers wanted to know how loyal he was. They had invited Colonel Obata to their cocktail party because Obata was himself a Strike-North leader and could speak as an intimate friend about Araki's character.

Obata gave it as his considered opinion that War Minister Araki would serve honestly to unify the nation during the build-up of military strength planned for the next four years. Araki would hope to use the new strength against the Soviet Union but he would bow to the wishes of the Emperor, the Supreme Field Marshal, if his views and the Throne's finally came into conflict. Second Crow Obata, himself, would do the same. Russia was the natural enemy of Japan, but if Hirohito could not be persuaded to lead Japan against Russia, Second Crow Obata and War Minister Araki would be willing to retire gracefully and leave the strategy of Armageddon to others.

The suave, ubiquitous Lieutenant Colonel Suzuki—impeccably tailored as always and looking like a banker costumed in military uniform for a fancy dress ball—pointed out quietly that War Minister Araki would make a difficult ally because he was a man of principle.

Recognizing this danger, Hirohito's political stage managers, when they broke up that night, had nevertheless decided to recommend to Hirohito that Prime Minister Inukai be replaced by a transcendental government built around the popularity of War Minister Araki of the Strike-North Faction. The next morning, Saturday, February 20, the people went to the polls and, as anticipated, gave Inukai's Constitutionalists in the Diet 301 seats to the anti-Constitutionalists' 147. Hirohito's kitchen cabinet of Big Brothers at once launched a campaign of rumor and innuendo by which they hoped to nullify the people's vote and overthrow Inukai.

At the urging of Big Brother Kido, Secretary-Spy Harada that night told Saionji that the Kwantung Army had become completely intractable and had laid definite plans for a coup d'etat to "suppress political parties" and safeguard Manchuria from "exploitation by political party interests." To Harada's astonishment old Saionji simply smiled and shrugged his shoulders.

"Oh well," he said, "if the plot plans are already complete, that's that."

After four months of hibernation and thought, Saionji was a jump ahead of the young men around the Throne. He knew that there would be no genuine coup d'etat. Through intermediaries, he had already reached his own understanding with War Minister Araki. He had determined that Araki was a man of integrity and brains, and in addition a golden-tongued demagogue who knew how to lead the masses. Araki undertook to embroil Hirohito by 1936 in a war with Russia. Better by far for Japan to fight Russia, if fight she must, than to attack the combined powers of America and western Europe. In the great undesirable buffer land of Siberia, Araki might be able to bury Hirohito's samurai ardor in a desert of stalemate and weariness.

INSPECTION EVE

The week following the elections was a hectic one. The League of Nations' Commission of Inquiry was expected to arrive in Japan on leap year's day, February 29. The Japanese forces in Shanghai were still attempting—as yet with little success—to drive out the Chinese 19th Route Army. On March 1, Manchuria was scheduled to be declared an independent sovereign state, Manchukuo, under Chief Executive Pu-Yi, the former boy emperor of China. If all went well, the League's investigative team would be presented on arrival with a cease-fire in Shanghai and a new nation in Manchuria—with every evidence, in short, that the "Far Eastern crisis" had blown over and that the League's investigation had become academic.

Prime Minister Inukai was exchanging flurries of cables with Chiang Kai-shek in an attempt to reach an understanding with him on what both of them would say privately to the League's commissioners. It was Inukai's idea that he and Chiang and the commissioners, acting in concert, could persuade Hirohito to give Manchukuo genuine independence and to order the Kwantung Army back to its leasehold.

Hirohito's Big Brothers were busy undercutting Prime Minister Inukai and solidifying their plans for the regime with which they hoped to replace him. They spread excited gossip about the imminence of an Army coup d'etat and told newspaper reporters that Prime Minister Inukai was negotiating treasonably with Chiang Kai-shek while Japanese boys were dying in Shanghai.

On Wednesday, February 24, Prince Konoye went down to Okitsu by the sea to try to find out why his elder kinsman, Saionji, seemed so smugly unconcerned about the possibility of a coup d'etat. He proposed to Saionji that after the coup a military man like War Minister Araki should be made prime minister and that a member of the imperial family like Prince Higashikuni or Prince

Asaka (the Emperor's two uncles in the spy service) should take the post of lord privy seal at Hirohito's side.

Saionji had nothing against Araki as a duly appointed prime minister but much against unconstitutional processes such as coups d'etat. And as for the two imperial uncles, Princes Asaka and Higashikuni, Saionji distrusted them both. At the thought of either one of them taking the position of lord privy seal—the traditional position of Minister on the Left which had been occupied for centuries by the most tried and true elders of Saionji's own Fujiwara family—Saionji blazed up.

"Before I recommend any such appointments," he spat, "I shall resign my post as senior advisor to the Throne. I shall renounce all my ranks and privileges as a prince. And I shall descend to the status of a commoner."

Konoye returned to Tokyo puzzled by Saionji's self-assurance and convinced that the old man had something up his kimono sleeve. He sent Secretary-Spy Harada back to Okitsu to keep a close watch. The old man, however, revealed nothing to Harada except more mysterious good spirits. The next evening, Thursday, February 25, over a bedtime cognac, he said to Harada: "When you youngsters have forced Prime Minister Inukai out of office through some exposure or other, I shall be interested to see how you go about forming this 'Rising Nation Cabinet' you all want."

BETWEEN TWO THREATS

While Saionji still mystified and the League inquiry drew closer, the frenetic activity of the preceding days began coming to a head. On Saturday, February 27—two days before the League commission's scheduled arrival in Tokyo—the morning papers carried a letter—one written to be leaked—from U.S. Secretary of State Stimson to William E. Borah, the chairman of the U.S. Senate's Foreign Relations Committee. The letter warned Japan that any modification or abrogation of the structure of interlocking treaties which was intended to safeguard the peace would release the United States from its obligations under any one of them. That is, if Japan, with impunity, violated the Nine-Power Treaty guaranteeing the "open door" and "territorial integrity" of China, the

United States would feel free to build capital ships beyond naval treaty limitations and to strengthen U.S. military establishments in the Philippines, Guam, and Hawaii.

Prime Minister Inukai promptly telephoned the palace and announced that he would recommend sending a special envoy to the United States to clear up Secretary Stimson's misunderstanding of Japan's intentions. The envoy proposed by Inukai was Baron Dan Takuma, head of the Mitsui cartel.

That afternoon Army Chief of Staff Prince Kanin's old cavalry minion, Koiso, the later kamikaze prime minister of 1944, called upon Baron Dan in his office at the Mitsui holding company headquarters. Lieutenant General Koiso, since his leadership of the March Plot, had been elevated by Hirohito to the office of vice war minister. He was patently a man whose patrons would back him to the hilt. He warned Baron Dan bluntly not to accept the mission of good-will ambassador to the United States. Baron Dan knew only too well that he could not protect his family from assassins nor his cartel from loss of Army contracts. At the same time he was too proud to negotiate with Koiso the exact degree of his intimidation. With many stiff smiles and bows, he told Koiso that he had no intention of leaving Japan at the moment. On the contrary, he said, he was engaged in a patriotic struggle for the nation's survival and would not leave his post of duty until he either conquered or died.

Vice Minister of War Koiso returned to the War Ministry and reported to his patron, old Prince Kanin, chief of the Army General Staff. That night Friar Inoue, operating out of the Black Dragon Society's House of Heavenly Action, sent a student messenger to one of his Blood Brotherhood assassins, instructing him to stand ready to kill Baron Dan Takuma of Mitsui. The assassin, a former professional gangster named Hisanuma Goro, began at once a thorough study of Baron Dan's daily movements and work habits.

SAIONJI SHOWS HIS HAND

On the following morning, Sunday, February 28, 1932, old Saionji awoke to a buoyantly crisp winter's day. He looked out at the fairy-story waters of Suruga Bay, dancing with fishing boats and sunbeams, and resolutely put through a call to Tokyo. The time had come to declare himself. He roused Secretary-Spy Harada from sleep and summoned him to come down at once to Okitsu by the sea. Four jolting hours later, having had to take a local express, Harada knelt on Saionji's matting floor and watched the old man stride in, wearing a new kimono, with an air of great purpose.

"I called you," said Saionji, "because the other day the grand chamberlain dropped in, concerned about the Emperor. The Emperor, he says, is not sleeping well. The other night at about eleven o'clock he sent a chamberlain to the grand chamberlain requesting an immediate consultation. Well, the Emperor is undoubtedly worrying, but this old Saionji is worrying even more. . . . So I am planning to go up to Tokyo about March fifth. . . . Tell them Saionji does not have to come out into the open this way, nor does he expect to bring peace. Tell them that he is going out of his way, right or wrong, to take this opportunity to stand up and do his duty. If you are questioned further, I want you to say, 'It is primarily to pay respects to His Majesty that he comes and because, at a time like this, he feels he should meet personally with the people who bear the responsibility.'"

Harada listened to the old man's speech with mounting, ill-suppressed horror. After pleading ill health repeatedly and refusing to pay attendance on the Emperor, Saionji was now coming up to Tokyo in order to make himself available to members of the Lytton Commission who were due to arrive in Tokyo on the morrow. It seemed almost an act of treason. Harada hurried back to Tokyo to have a tap put on Saionji's Tokyo phone and to apologize for lack of foresight to fellow Big Brother Kido.

VICTORY IN SHANGHAI

Late that night, up an estuary in the gaping, mud-yellow mouth of the Yangtze River in China, a division of Japanese soldiers—almost 20,000 men—silently waded ashore, wave after wave, from their assault boats. They, too, were under pressure because of the League commission's arrival in Tokyo the next morning. For two weeks, despite Japanese numerical equality and fire-power superiority,[5] the heroic young provincials of the Chinese 19th Route Army had refused to be driven from the native quarters of Shanghai. They had fought for the borough of Chapei street by street and ruin by ruin, and now they still occupied most of the two remaining boroughs. The Japanese frontal advance, begun nine days before, had been thrown back repeatedly by counterattacks and had gained ground only by inches. Hirohito himself had criticized the commander in Shanghai and now had replaced him.

The pressure, passed down to the men, had forced three privates on February 22 to make a suicide charge against a crucial barbed-wire entanglement, carrying on their shoulders a tube of dynamite. They had blown up themselves and the entanglement and were now immortalized by the Japanese press as the "three human bullets." A Japanese major who felt responsible for their sacrifice had himself been captured by the Chinese in their counterattack. When liberated by the Japanese a few days later, he had gone to the site of the hard-fought roadblock, knelt, and deliberately blown out his brains.

Now on the eve of the League commission's arrival, the Japanese 14th Division had just added some 20,000 fresh troops to the barricades in downtown Shanghai, and the Japanese 11th Division was disembarking under cover of night on the mud flats upriver to turn the Chinese flank. By morning there would be some 70,000 Japanese troops pressing in on three sides against the 20,000-odd survivors of the 19th Route Army.[6]

The early-morning landing of the 11th Division behind his lines took General Tsai Ting-kai of the 19th Route completely by surprise. He had entrusted watch over that particular stretch of coast line to only 100 men with three machine guns. Japanese give the

[5] At the start of the fighting, the 33,500 men of the 19th Route had only 27,500 rifles, 72 machine guns, and 64 trench mortars and light field pieces.

[6] There were also three of Chiang Kai-shek's guard divisions, numbering 40,000 men, loitering just outside Shanghai. In a spare moment on February 18 or 19, detachments of the 19th Route had turned briefly from the Japanese and had captured a substantial part of one of these guard divisions. The prisoners had been marched to the front and forced at gunpoint to fight the Japanese. Some were later captured by the Japanese, and some died honorably fighting the Japanese, but most were mowed down by their 19th Route countrymen when they panicked and fled before a Japanese advance on February 25.

credit for his shortsightedness to the deceptive wiles of Eastern
Jewel, the Manchu princess and Japanese girl spy. During the first
desperate days of the fighting, when vengeful Japanese vigilantes
roamed the streets around her, Eastern Jewel had kept Sun Yat-
sen's son safe in her apartment and had extorted from him letters
of introduction to all the most important officers of the 19th
Route Army. In return she had finally smuggled him aboard a
coastal tramp steamer of uncertain registry, which took him out
of harm's way to his home port of Canton in southern China.

Her principal lover, the huge Major Tanaka of the Shanghai
Special Service Organ, now put her in touch with some of the
Navy fliers of the Misty Lagoon Air Station who were flying reconnaissance over the Chinese lines. They took her along on several
missions as co-pilot and gave her thorough briefings on the topography of the Chinese city and the command posts of the 19th
Route Army. One of them later complained that she was a troublesome co-pilot because she pestered him to arrange some way
of making love aloft.

Fully briefed and equipped with her letters of introduction
from Sun Yat-sen's son, Eastern Jewel one night in late February
put on her favorite spy disguise of a boy and set out on foot to
visit 19th Route Commander Tsai Ting-kai. By prearrangement
Japanese sentries let her pass without question through their lines
and then followed her with a hail of bullets in the air. Hearing
her piteous cries for help, uttered in her best approximation of
Cantonese dialect, the sentries of the 19th Route let her into their
lines. There her letters of introduction passed her up the chain
of command until she came to the dugout of Tsai Ting-kai himself. She spent several hours with him and gave him more or
less reliable information about Japanese troop dispositions. She
undertook to take back to Shanghai a verbal message from him
to Sun Yat-sen's son, who she said was still in her apartment.
She told of having seen the Japanese 11th and 14th divisions unloading at the Shanghai docks that afternoon. In fact they were
still lying out to sea in their transports. Tsai Ting-kai knew from
Chinese agents in Japan that the two divisions were on their
way. He had taken men from his second line to guard the various
harbors on the river where he thought they might make a surprise

landing. Now, after Eastern Jewel's departure, he recalled the
men to the fighting line and left the possible landing points
unguarded.

So it was that on leap year's day, as the League's Commission
of Inquiry steamed into Tokyo harbor, the tired men of the 19th
Route found themselves outnumbered three to one, outgunned
twenty to one, and attacked from the rear as well as the front.
For a month they had fought stolidly and shrewdly. Now, in forty-
eight hours, their defenses collapsed on all fronts. Tsai Ting-kai
ordered them to give up the city. They fell back to the southwest and succeeded in preventing the Japanese from completing
their encirclement until most of them had withdrawn with order
into the countryside beyond. On March 3 and 4, their rear guard
broke up into pockets. The Japanese troops attempted to annihi-
late them, but many survivors submerged into the civilian populace and succeeded in slipping through the Japanese cordons to
rejoin their units upcountry.

LEAGUE'S WELCOME

The Frenchman, German, Italian, American, and Englishman
who were to write a judgment on the circumstances of the Manchurian Incident for the League of Nations were given an effusive
welcome by the crowds organized to greet them when they disembarked at the Yokohama docks on February 29. In Tokyo a swirl
of social activity had been laid on for them and their first five
days in Japan were all banquets, toasts, and speeches.

Emperor Hirohito's special envoy in Shanghai, diplomat Matsuoka Yosuke, opened negotiations with Chiang Kai-shek's representatives on March 1 and concluded them in an armistice
agreement on March 5. Less than two weeks later Japan's 70,000-
man expeditionary force began to be shipped home, leaving the
defense of the Japanese quarter in Shanghai once again to the
small garrison of Imperial Marines. Only cynics remarked on the
marvelous discipline of the Japanese troop withdrawals. The Japanese militarists who were supposed to be completely out of hand
in Manchuria had proved completely tractable in Shanghai. Having opened the door for a drive on the Chinese capital of Nanking,

having sustained heavy losses of both life and face at the hands of the 19th Route Army, they nevertheless obeyed orders perfectly in giving back to China the hard-won streets of Chapei. The League's commissioners were supposed to be favorably impressed. They were supposed at the same time to realize that Shanghai was only one half of the bargain and that the other half was the new Japanese puppet state of Manchukuo, which was proclaimed with pomp and ceremony on March 1.

On March 2, an event took place in the United States which deprived the League's commission of all front-page publicity in the West and diverted the attention of many Japanese. The infant son of U.S. aviator Charles Lindbergh was kidnapped.[7] During the partial news blackout which followed, Secretary of State Stimson found to his dismay that most of his fellow statesmen in the West were disposed to accept Pu-Yi in Manchuria for peace in Shanghai. They acknowledged that Japan's play in Shanghai had been tantamount to blackmail, but also that the West had no guns to commit to the Far East. In the public distraction created by the Lindbergh kidnapping they saw an excellent opportunity to let the Far Eastern crisis blow over.

KILL THE BARON

While the Shanghai "incident" was being settled, the state of Manchukuo founded, and the world distracted, the League's Commission of Inquiry stood by in Tokyo, beholding in mute astonishment the murder of their Japanese League colleague, Baron Dan of the Mitsui cartel.

Dan was the director of the central holding company of Mitsui. He was a member of the League's Investigation Committee, the parent body of the Commission of Inquiry. He was known as a

[7] Lindbergh had been out in the Orient on a flood relief mission to China seven months earlier. He had greatly annoyed the Japanese authorities by making a forced landing in a sensitive fortified area in Hokkaido. In Tokyo he had been entertained by Japan's leading aeronautical engineer, Wada Koroku, the brother of Marquis Kido, the Emperor's favorite Big Brother. A White Russian menial of the spy service in Harbin would later insist—in a manuscript which he smuggled out of Manchuria before his death at the hands of the Japanese—that the Lindbergh kidnapping had been arranged by Japan through payments of Dollar Swindle money to the American Mafia.

friend of DuPonts and Fords and Rockefellers and as a prominent
member of the Japan-American Society. In 1871, at the age of
thirteen, he had been one of the fifty-four Japanese children sent
to the United States to learn at first hand the ways of Commodore
Perry's homeland. Lord Privy Seal Makino, then nine, had also
been one of the fifty-four children. Makino had swallowed his
eight years in the United States as dutifully and courageously as
a pill and had regularly omitted all mention of them from the
annual entries which he had since submitted to Japanese biographical dictionaries. Baron Dan, by contrast, looked back with
pleasure on his seven years in America and always had a bed ready
in his villa for any itinerant graduate of his American alma maters
—of Miss Arland's School in Boston or of the Massachusetts Institute of Technology. As director of the holding company of
Japan's largest cartel, Baron Dan was the unquestioned leader of
Japan's business establishment.

On Wednesday, March 2, 1932, the directors of all the Mitsui
companies met as stockholders to hear the annual report of their
great cartel's nerve center, the Mitsui Bank. The manager of the
bank, elegant in his Saville Row tailoring, gravely recited a story
of hard luck. "The general banking business," he reported, had
been fairly good that year, "but because of the drop in the market
prices of securities" and "the decline of pound holdings," the bank
had suffered "a net loss for the term of 12,297,026 yen"—about
$4 million. He added that "any criticism for having carried on
speculative buying of the dollar is unjustified." He pointed out
that there were matters of arbitrage and gold movement to be
considered. His easy flow of financial jargon, however, failed to
disguise entirely the fact that the stockholders in the room had
all received unusually large dividends that year from holdings in
other branches of the Mitsui combine, some amounting to 17
and 18 per cent.

Undeterred by the Mitsui Bank's statement of losses, the Japanese Finance Ministry announced the next day, on Thursday,
March 3, that to meet debts incurred in the Shanghai fighting, it
was floating a 22-million-yen bond issue (roughly $8 million)
which it expected to be subscribed by Mitsui and the other cartels. On Baron Dan, as chief of Mitsui, devolved the dangerous

duty of replying that the great industrialists of the nation were agreed that for lack of ready cash they could not co-operate.

In the evening Friar Inoue of the Blood Brotherhood had his student go-between deliver a Browning and sixteen bullets to assassin Hisanuma Goro for Dan's killing. Dan himself, in an attempt to assess the amount of support and of publicity he could expect from the United States in the domestic struggle he saw ahead, held a dinner party for all his most influential American friends in Tokyo.

"His home was simple," recalled Wilfred Fleisher, the editor of the *Japan Chronicle,* "but the garden of the Dan mansion was famous for its beauty. The house was built on the edge of a slope which led down to a pond where storks strutted about, and the hillside was covered in spring with azaleas, and in the autumn with the red tint of the maple foliage."

On the following morning, Friday, March 4, Baron Dan was formally introduced to all his colleagues on the League's Commission of Inquiry and sat down with them for their first business meeting. Assassin Hisanuma Goro went out to Funabashi Beach on Tokyo Bay just east of the city to practice firing his Browning. Saionji's secretary-spy, Baron Harada, consulted with other Big Brothers of the Emperor before entraining for Okitsu to bring the Prime-Minister-Maker up to the capital for his announced trip of protest.

In the evening Baron Dan attended a banquet given in honor of the League's commission by the posh Industrial Club of which he and other captains of Japanese enterprise were directors. Knowing that he would be called upon to make a speech, he penciled notes for himself, as he ate, on a piece of paper which is preserved by his family. According to the notes he concluded his welcome to Lord Lytton with the sentence, "Any questions you may feel inclined to make we are pleased to answer frankly." Then in his final act of discretion and personal honor he crossed out the word "frankly" and delivered his remarks without the dubious benefit of the adverb.

At 11 A.M. on Saturday, March 5, Baron Dan had his car draw up at the inconspicuous side entrance of the Mitsui Bank Building. But Hisanuma Goro, the most sophisticated tough in the Blood

Brotherhood, had cased well the nervous habits of his victim and
was waiting on the curb. He lunged to open the door of the
limousine. Finding it locked, he allowed the chauffeur no time
to start away but fired once through the glass of the car window.
Once was enough. Baron Dan died in twenty minutes, and assassin Hisanuma calmly waited for the police to come and arrest
him.

Saionji and Secretary-Spy Harada were then on their way to
Tokyo. Their train was immediately stopped and boarded by civil
police who placed the old man under guard. In Tokyo Saionji
repaired at once to his city house and for the rest of that day
and the next refused to see anyone.[8]

SAIONJI'S SETTLEMENT

On the second day after Baron Dan's murder, Monday, March 7,
Saionji began to receive official visitors: Prime Minister Inukai
in the morning; Hirohito's personal financial advisor, the minister
of the imperial household, in the afternoon; Hirohito's personal
diplomatic advisor, the cigar-smoking Taoist philosopher, Grand
Chamberlain Suzuki, in the evening.

As a son is expected to call on his father when he returns to
his home town after a long absence, so by the rules of Court etiquette a chief vassal of the Throne like Saionji was expected to
call on the Emperor as soon as possible after his arrival in Tokyo.
The Japanese public waited with fascination, but Saionji did not
make his mandatory palace visit—not that day, and not the next,
and not for six days thereafter. From Baron Dan's killing on
March 5 until March 14, the ancient statesman snubbed Hirohito and nursed all his energies for phone calls and interviews
with others. He was trying to negotiate a bargain which would
put a stop to the assassins' reign of terror and preserve some hope
for constitutional parliamentarianism. He intimated that he was

[8] A classic photograph survives that shows him as he alighted from his car
at the porte-cochere of his Tokyo residence. His eyes blaze with indignation out
of a gaunt and wasted face. Secretary-Spy Harada stands by, having just opened
the car door for him. The photographer's lens has foreshortened Harada's body
in its bowing and scraping so that it appears hideously deformed—a gnome
of malevolent lickspittle.

in earnest and would call a press conference that would amaze the world if he was not given his way. He said that if anything happened to him the hired goon squads of the Constitution Protection Movement would cause a small civil war in Japan and certain safety deposit boxes in foreign capitals would be opened to the Western press. He accepted no personal guards for his house who had not been approved by his personal cronies in the secret police.

On Tuesday, March 8, Dr. Okawa had his chief henchman—once a bicycle repairman in Shanghai—return the smoke bombs of the March Plot of 1931 to War Minister Araki.

On Wednesday, March 9, Saionji for the first time met Araki face to face. "He has a slight utopian tendency," he said to Secretary-Spy Harada afterwards, "but, my goodness, he really knows how to talk, doesn't he?"

On Thursday, March 10, having judiciously felt out members of the Court circle for permission, the Tokyo Metropolitan Police chief began to make gingerly arrests on the fringes of the Blood Brotherhood.

Finally, on Friday, March 11, six days after Baron Dan's killing and thirty days after banker Inoue's, assassin leader Friar Inoue was deferentially escorted by the police from the Black Dragon's House of Heavenly Action to one of Tokyo's cleanest jails. Friar Inoue's colleague, Dr. Okawa, however, was left at liberty. He was so well known as the henchman of Lord Privy Seal Makino, Hirohito's chief civilian advisor, that Saionji did not insist on his arrest.

Saionji insisted only that the killing cease and that the duly appointed prime minister, Inukai, be allowed to continue in office. In return Saionji persuaded Mitsui and the other cartels to subscribe the $8-million bond issue for the Shanghai war and to advance another $7.5 million as a loan for the development of the new puppet state of Manchukuo.

Saionji spent the weekend of March 12 and 13 working out the financial details of his settlement with the cartels. Finally, on Monday, March 14, he consented to come out, under heavy guard, from his villa and pay his long postponed courtesy call on the Emperor. Contrary to custom, he did not take lunch at the palace but ate it alone before setting out for his audience. At 2 P.M.

he met the Emperor and Empress and paid them his formal respects. Then the Empress withdrew and he talked to Hirohito alone for a little over an hour. He told his secretary-spy Harada afterwards that the Emperor had said "nothing special."

Saionji spent three more days in the capital in which he attended to private business and paid a courtesy call on his Fujiwara kinswoman, Hirohito's mother, the Empress Dowager. She was his staunchest ally. At forty-seven, she was still extremely handsome. She had great charm and poise in handling people, and her years taking care of Emperor Taisho had given her a sophisticated understanding of state affairs.

As queen mother she had consultative and veto powers over most of the domestic arrangements in Hirohito's household. She had long disapproved of her son's policies and had frequently remonstrated with him, to no avail. Saionji urged that proper guidance had never been more necessary. Empress Dowager Sadako promised to do her best and to send trustworthy messengers to Saionji who would keep him informed at all times on affairs at Court.

Saionji returned to Okitsu-by-the-sea on March 18, feeling proud of the settlement he had worked out. His kinsman, Prince Konoye, personally escorted him. The younger Fujiwara prince respected the elder's political experience and patriotism, but in his view the settlement that Saionji had accomplished was an unrealistic, stopgap arrangement. For three days Konoye tried to persuade the old man to agree that the continuation of the old, corrupt political parties would only give rise to more intrigue, more assassinations, more haggling and waste of talent. Better by far to declare Japan the totalitarian state that it was, to let Hirohito lead it and to surround him with the smartest, most realistic advisors. Old Prince Saionji stubbornly refused to see any merit in this solution.

Prince Konoye returned to Tokyo convinced that the game of intrigue must continue and that means must be found to circumvent Saionji and his supporters.

On April 3, Lord Privy Seal Count Makino's disciple Dr. Okawa gave a flight lieutenant from the Misty Lagoon $500, five pistols, and 200 rounds of ammunition as a token to show that the coup d'etat was still alive and seriously considered. That night and again at breakfast and lunch on April 4, members of the Eleven Club met in great privacy to decide among themselves who would be the first non-party, all-nation, post-coup prime minister of Japan. Out of courtesy they at first nominated Prince Konoye as their ranking leader. Big Brother Kido, however, who was their effective leader, had already agreed with Prince Konoye that this must be a gesture of courtesy and nothing more. Marquis Kido pointed out that Prince Konoye had as yet no viable policy nor slate of ministers.

For the transcendental prime minister a more realistic choice must be made. After discussion the Big Brothers decided on 73-year-old Admiral Saito Makoto, once a favorite of Emperor Meiji, long a governor general of Korea, a man whom Prince Saionji, Emperor Hirohito, and they, themselves, could all accept.

Chosen by Hirohito's junior clerks on April 4, 1932, Admiral Saito would in fact become prime minister of Japan forty-two days later when all arrangements had been made, Prime Minister Inukai had been murdered, and the long-envisaged coup d'etat had taken place. Admiral Saito himself would be notified of his appointment when Hirohito called him to the palace and made it official. In the interim, Hirohito felt satisfied that his Big Brothers had a workable plan.

LORD LYTTON

The League of Nations' five-man, five-nation Commission of Inquiry was headed by its Englishman, Lord Lytton. He was the son of a viceroy to India and the grandson of the Bulwer-Lytton who wrote *The Last Days of Pompeii*. An Eton-Cambridge man, he had seen service in the Admiralty, the India Office, the governor's mansion of Bengal, and briefly in the Indian statehouse as viceroy. At fifty-six, though somewhat uncomfortable and short-tempered as a result of kidney difficulties, he prided himself both on his statesmanship and his command of lucid, stylish, author's prose. He knew little about Japan but he was a conscientious reader and clear-sighted observer.

In his first five days of banqueting in Japan Lord Lytton had received hints from some of the Japanese he met which convinced him that he must correct the tendency of his aristocratic public school alumni in the British government to excuse Japanese imperialism. After the murder of Baron Dan, his Japanese colleague, he was more than convinced; he was incensed. During old Prince Saionji's settlement-making stay in Tokyo, Lord Lytton and his fellow commissioners all tried to see Saionji. Through emissaries, Saionji excused himself repeatedly because of the delicacy of the situation in which he was involved. The emissaries, however, did their discreet best to tell Lord Lytton that Saionji wanted the League to go as far as possible in condemning Japan's actions on the Continent.

The day that Saionji finally went to the palace to pay his respects to Hirohito, Lord Lytton and his fellow commissioners took ship for Shanghai to begin hearing the Chinese side of the story. They planned to spend five weeks in China, interviewing all the various factions there, and then to proceed on April 21 to Mukden in Manchuria to inspect the source of the trouble.

During the commissioners' stay in China—the first honeymoon weeks of Saionji's settlement in Japan—the Army half of Hirohito's cabal saw to it that they would receive the most favorable possible impression of Japanese-occupied Manchuria. Hirohito assigned the former Japanese ambassador to the Soviet Union to Kwantung Army commander General Honjo to advise him on the diplomatic niceties. One of the Eleven Reliables chosen at Baden-Baden, Colonel Watari Hisao, was detached from his post as chief of the European Section of the Intelligence Department of the General Staff so that he could travel as an advance man for the Lytton Commission and see that suitable arrangements had been made for it wherever it went.

Watari was the America expert of the Eleven Reliables. A Kyoto nobleman of presence and charm, he had specialized in English, put in five years at the Japanese Embassy in Washington, and won a name for himself as a good friend to all the foreign military attachés at the Western embassies in Tokyo. According to British intelligence officer F. S. G. Piggott, he was "a sincere admirer of Anglo-American ideals . . . universally respected."

With all the resources of the Kwantung Army put at his disposal by General Honjo, Watari was determined that whatever the Lytton commissioners wished to see, whenever they wished to see it, would be shown to them in a state of fresh whitewash that would not strike them unfavorably. The political inmates of Man-chukuoan prisons and the French- and English-speaking patients in Manchukuoan hospitals were removed from their cells and sick rooms and sent for the duration of Lytton's stay to detention camps in the countryside. They were joined there by all the un-sightly beggars and derelicts which the military police could sweep from the streets and by anyone suspected of having enough cour-age and conviction to stand up and shout anti-Japanese remarks during parades. Literally thousands of potential face-spoilers were put under preventive arrest—1,361 in Harbin alone. Substan-tial rewards were offered for information leading to the appre-hension of anyone who schemed to smuggle a bill of complaints to Lytton's party.

"Petitions" in praise of Japanese rule were drawn up a month in advance at Kwantung Army Headquarters and given to promi-nent Chinese and Russian citizens who had to sign them and later submit them to Lytton. Crowds were coached in what to shout and how to dress. An enterprising official of the South Manchuria Railroad netted over $100,000 for his firm and for the Army by suggesting that the military police require every inhabitant along Lytton's itinerary to buy for one yen a small Manchukuoan flag to hang over his doorway and a cheap portrait of Pu-Yi to put in his window. Manchukuoan officials scheduled to be interviewed by the commissioners were carefully rehearsed in what they must say. Every opium den was aired out, cleaned, and hung with a new sign which proclaimed it to be either a "Cultural Center" or a "Social Club." Every Japanese uniform vanished from sight and the man inside it endured the temporary indignity of going about in a span-new Manchukuoan one.

In all the hotels where the commission would be staying, Japa-nese and White Russian agents of the Manchukuoan State Politi-cal Police were given rooms adjoining those to be occupied by the commissioners. Desk clerks, bell boys, waiters, room boys, hall boys, and chambermaids were all replaced by specially coached police agents. Spies were spotted in the staffs of leading stores, theatres, and restaurants. The drain on the police and intelligence personnel pool was heavy. When the pool ran dry, the local chief of the spy service in Harbin distributed 500 Manchukuoan Army uniforms to a native bandit band in the employ of the spy service and stationed its cutthroats as "guards of honor" at the homes of Chinese malcontents who were too prominent in society to rusticate at the detention camps.

Colonel Watari, who arranged this magnificent reception for Lord Lytton, was joined in Manchuria on April 15, a week before Lytton's arrival, by the second of the Three Crows, Obata Toshiro. Obata had attended the Big Brothers' cocktail party at Marquis Inoue's two months earlier, and now Hirohito had just promoted him to the rank of major general. Obata knew that Hirohito was planning a "transcendental government." If Lord Lytton could be persuaded to approve what he saw in Manchuria, the transcendental government might prove to be unnecessary. Obata reviewed with Colonel Watari the preparations made for Lord Lytton and discussed them several times with Kwantung Army commander Honjo. He warned Honjo that if Lytton could not be deceived, a military coup d'etat would have to be staged in Tokyo to overthrow political party government and show the League of Nations that it could achieve no constructive result by condemning Japan as an aggressor. In the event that the coup became necessary, he asked General Honjo to lend him a division and a cavalry brigade.

Second Crow Obata stayed in Mukden long enough to witness the arrival of Lord Lytton on April 21 at the Mukden railroad station. Then he took a train himself to the South Manchuria Railroad's executive airport, south of Mukden, and flew home to report to Hirohito and the Big Brothers. He judged that Lord Lytton was not favorably disposed toward Japan and that his attitude probably would not be changed by the preparations made for him in Manchuria. At the same time Lytton seemed to be approaching his task carefully, like a scholar, and would probably not deliver his judgment of Japan, good or bad, until many months had passed.

POLICY REVIEW

Prompted by Major General Obata's assessment of Lord Lytton's intentions, Hirohito's Big Brothers commissioned the ubiquitous Lieutenant Colonel Suzuki to draft a tough new foreign policy for Japan "in the light of the changed situation in the Far East" and a domestic political plan for "realization of the Hirohito restoration." The gifted Suzuki, whose years as private envoy of the Throne to Chiang Kai-shek had accustomed him to thinking in global terms, completed his assignment in thirty-six hours and presented the results, in the form of two position papers, to Big Brother Kido on Saturday evening, April 23. In the first he advocated that Japan pursue an independent course in the Orient without troubling herself about Western reactions. In the second he urged immediate suppression of political parties and a transcendental caretaker government, backed by General Araki and the Army's Strike-North Faction, which would allow Hirohito to come forth gradually as the absolute master of the Japanese nation.[9] Kido took Suzuki's two papers to the palace the next evening and discussed them with the other Big Brothers on the following Tuesday and Wednesday.

On Thursday, April 28, 1932, Hirohito's personally instructed delegate to the Shanghai truce negotiations, University of Oregon graduate Matsuoka, called at the palace to report to Hirohito on the successful completion of his mission. Hirohito asked him what he thought of the ubiquitous Suzuki's proposal to pursue a tough independent foreign policy in the Far East. Matsuoka responded with enthusiasm. Japan, he said, had nothing to fear from the League. Indeed, if Japan withdrew from the League altogether, she would gain stature and influence in the minds of the most powerful and practical Western statesmen.

After talking to Matsuoka, Hirohito had his Big Brothers discuss the Matsuoka proposal. None of them saw any harm in with-

---

[9] These summations are based on the recollections of a member of the Army bureaucracy who saw the two position papers some months later. The full texts are not now extant but may perhaps come to light after the publication of this volume.

drawing from the League, though some of the Army officers felt
that it might not be necessary. In due course old man Saionji
heard of the idea. "Wishful thinking," he called it.

"I am truly worried," he told Secretary-Spy Harada. "The Emperor may be smart and may avoid bringing the nation to catastrophe, but plans shown me recently by Lord Privy Seal Makino for
dealing with Russia do not look smart."

Nevertheless, Hirohito tentatively accepted Matsuoka's League-
withdrawal plan, and a year later he would put Matsuoka in charge
of executing it.

In his second position paper—"on the realization of Hirohito's
restoration"—Lieutenant Colonel Suzuki had dwelt in some detail
on the difficulties that might be encountered if an Army coup
d'etat were used to improve Hirohito's leadership position. Suzuki
warned that many Army officers, particularly those of the idealistic
Strike-North Faction, would expect a coup d'etat to make Hirohito overt military dictator of Japan, governing exclusively
through staff officers. The problem in establishing a transcendental government by means of a coup, therefore, would be to
prevent Army radicals from carrying the coup to extremes and
robbing Hirohito of civilian executives—of courtiers, economists,
diplomats, gang lords, politicians, and publicists.

ARRANGEMENTS WITH HONJO

On Monday, April 30, 1932, when Suzuki's position papers had
been studied for a week, an embassy set out for Manchuria to make
arrangements in the Kwantung Army for keeping firm control
over the projected coup d'etat. One of the ambassadors was Dr.
Okawa, the headmaster of the cabal, the ideologist of the Strike-
South Faction and the minion of Lord Privy Seal Count Makino.
Having worked for many years under the cover of a research employee of the South Manchuria Railroad, he had a wide acquaintance with the spy service's commercial and secret police agents in
the blossoming Japanese underworld in Manchuria. During the
next eleven days he made sure that everyone who was to be involved in the coup d'etat could be controlled through some form
of blackmail.

The other member of the embassy was Hirohito's personal emissary, Lieutenant General Segawa Akitomo.[10] He had been an intelligence officer in Switzerland in 1919, an aide-de-camp in the palace during the 1920's, and was now the scholarly noncontroversial principal of Japan's military academy. Segawa took with him to Mukden a troop of his military pupils—the cadets who were to be used as foot soldiers in the coming coup d'etat.

Segawa spent the afternoon of Sunday, May 1, in earnest conversation with his old friend General Honjo, commander of the Kwantung Army. He persuaded Honjo that the projected coup was not intended to establish a military dictatorship, that its purpose was to intimidate the cartels and the Constitutionalist party, and that the plan had the Emperor's backing. Afterward the two generals set out to show the cadets—the young men whose careers were soon to be blighted by their involvement in the coup d'etat —a big night on the town.

Late the next afternoon, Monday, when all the cadets had sufficiently recovered, Honjo personally led them on a short march to the monument erected for Japan's war dead in Manchuria. Before the monument, he delivered to them, in the words of his diary, "an elevating lecture." After the lecture he saw them off on their return to Tokyo.

When Segawa had left, Lieutenant General Honjo began to hear the details of the coup plan which he had told Segawa he would support. He met with Dr. Okawa on Saturday, May 7, and then on Tuesday, May 10, with a second team of underworld operatives from Tokyo: the equerry of Hirohito's spy-service uncle, Prince

[10] Two years later, in April 1934, Segawa became critically ill with a gall bladder inflammation. When the news arrived in the palace late one evening, the aide-de-camp on duty happened to be Colonel Machijiri Kazumoto, who had helped Prince Higashikuni set up the spy ring in Paris in 1920. Machijiri was the brother-in-law of the Empress's aunt Suzuko and also the husband of the Empress's cousin Yukiko. Presuming on his close ties with the Empress and on his intimate knowledge of the Emperor's affairs, Colonel Machijiri dared to telephone the news of Segawa's illness to the imperial bedchamber. The Emperor at once arose and came in person to the chamberlains' common room. Having heard the particulars, he ordered a present of cheer to be sent immediately to Segawa's sickbed. The civilian chamberlain on night duty with Machijiri ventured to object that there was no precedent for such unusual imperial solicitude. Hirohito said: "I used Segawa as my personal envoy so it is unnecessary to consider precedents." And with that he went back to bed.

Higashikuni, and the lawyer who had undertaken to defend Friar Inoue and the Blood Brotherhood.[11] Honjo did not like all the details he heard and sat up most of the night arguing with the lawyer and the equerry. It was one thing, he objected, to support a controlled coup d'etat in the interests of moderation and Hirohito; another thing to sanction the blackmail, deception, and physical intimidation of some of the best families in Japan. Honjo had had long experience with intrigues in China, but he was a stuffy, proper, honorable man in terms of his own Japanese society.

In the morning, convinced against his will, Honjo saw off the equerry, the lawyer, and Dr. Okawa on their departure for Tokyo. With them he dispatched retired Colonel Komoto Daisaku, the Baden-Baden Reliable who had taken responsibility for the killing of Manchurian war lord Chang Tso-lin in 1928 and who had conducted the final financial negotiations in calling off the March Plot in 1931. Having given his reluctant blessing to these four "fixers," Honjo washed his hands in his diary by labeling the projected coup "the business of [War Minister] Araki." He thereby implied that the coup, in its emasculated, controlled form was not the concern of field officers but belonged purely to the political world of the War Ministry where any right-thinking samurai should fear to tread. The next day Honjo remained so full of doubts, questions, and second thoughts that he spent three hours closeted with the Naval Special Service Organ chief in Manchuria, Rear Admiral Kobayashi Shosaburo, who until the previous December had been in command of the Misty Lagoon Air Station.

AT A COUNTRY INN

When Dr. Okawa arrived back in Tokyo on Thursday, May 12, he reported to Hirohito's chief civilian advisor, Lord Privy Seal Makino, and then turned over 2,000 yen, or about $700 to one of the Navy fliers of the Misty Lagoon. The next morning, Friday, two of the Misty Lagoon fliers met at Tokyo's Ueno Station with the ranking military academy cadet who had accompanied Hirohito's emissary, Lieutenant General Segawa, to Manchuria. The

11 Yasuda Tetsunosuke and Amano Tatsuo.

fliers and the cadet were joined shortly by the Tokyo Imperial University student—unaccountably overlooked by the police in their arrests after the murder of Baron Dan—who had served as Friar Inoue's courier in delivering Blood Brotherhood messages to Dr. Okawa for relay to the palace.

The four young men, student, cadet, and fliers, took a train out through the northeastern suburbs. It had been raining steadily for the last twenty-four hours but now the sun shown fitfully through scudding clouds. Out in the country the train ran through farm villages and paddies. The thatched roofs glistened and steamed, and the pale green shoots of young rice plants protruded from the flooded fields.

The foursome got off the train in Tsuchiura, a garrison town a few miles from the flight school on the Misty Lagoon. A car from the air station drove them out through the farmer's market and the busy district of bars and brothels to the town's best inn. It was a rambling provincial hostelry with a good kitchen and many private eating rooms. For years it had enjoyed the patronage of Chief of Staff Prince Kanin and other princes of the blood as a place where a man could spend a pleasant weekend with a geisha or meet in absolute privacy with a contact from the underworld.

The four conspirators advised the innkeeper that they would require no baths, no kimonos, and no geisha to entertain them and that they expected no one to join them except a "farmer" from the neighborhood. He arrived a few minutes later, and over a pitcher of the cheapest grade of saké the four young men from Tokyo felt out the reliability of their visitor, one Tachibana Kosaburo. Their long conversation that afternoon was eventually recorded in police interrogations and court trials years later.

Tachibana was no ordinary farmer but the leader of the Native-Land-Loving Society, the Tolstoyan farming commune which Prince Konoye and Prince Higashikuni sponsored, near the spy center at Oarai. He and his followers were genuine idealists who wanted a change of regime to improve the lot of Japan's peasants. They were needed in the coup to lend it a smudge of genuine earthy support, and the two flight officers soon found that a share of their 2,000 yen provided by Dr. Okawa was not required—Tachibana was ready to act for ideas alone.

The young men from Tokyo had been assigned the task of planning the assassination of Prime Minister Inukai, who they understood must be killed because he continued to oppose substantial budgets for the military and because he was involved in treasonable negotiations with Chiang Kai-shek and other Chinese leaders. Tachibana agreed to this objective, and toward the end of their five-hour conversation the five conspirators got down to details—to duty assignments and the synchronization of watches.

The youthful shavetail from the military academy, who had just come back from Manchuria, wanted to act at once, on the following day, Saturday. Then, he observed, the famous motion-picture comedian, Charlie Chaplin, was arriving in Yokohama. The secret police would be busy arranging security for him. And in the evening a Cabinet reception was scheduled for him at Prime Minister Inukai's residence. That, surely, would be the perfect time to strike. The murder of Charlie Chaplin along with the Japanese prime minister and the entire Japanese Cabinet could not fail to command international attention.

The two flight officers from the Misty Lagoon hastily interceded to spare the life of Charlie Chaplin. "As a matter of fact," stated the senior of the two, "we have already made sure that the police will be expecting an attack on Chaplin. They will all be out in force Saturday night exhausting themselves. That is why, on Sunday, when we really plan to attack, most of them will be off duty, catching up on their sleep."

According to the final plan agreed upon at the country inn, Tachibana's farmers, armed with sweat towels, axes, and a few grenades, would knock out Tokyo's electric power substations and throw the city into darkness. At the same time the military academy cadets, led by Misty Lagoon flight officers, would blow up several government establishments such as the Bank of Japan. The main body of flight officers would lead a raid on the prime minister's residence and assassinate Prime Minister Inukai.

When times and muster points had all been arranged and written down in notebooks, the five conspirators adjourned. Staff cars took the young men back to the railroad station for Tokyo, and Tachibana boarded a train north to Oarai to organize his farm hands.

KILL INUKAI

Came the dawn of Sunday, May 15, 1932. At 7 A.M., Hirohito's favorite Big Brother Kido, the secretary to the lord privy seal, was just dressing for a day of golf when, according to his guarded, elaborately edited diary, he received a phone call from his boss in the palace, Lord Privy Seal Makino. Never before had Count Makino called so early in the morning—and on a Sunday, too. Kido finished dressing and negotiated the quarter mile around the southern skirts of the palace between his official residence and Makino's in fifteen minutes. Makino told him—according to Kido's diary—that the Emperor had received important information the evening before from the former ambassador to the Soviet Union and that the Emperor wished the Eleven Club to arrange a meeting with the former ambassador as soon as possible in order to hear the information at first hand.[12]

This was all belly talk. The former ambassador to the Soviet Union, for the last month, had been in Manchuria as Hirohito's highest representative, advising Kwantung Army commander Honjo on the handling of Lord Lytton and incidentally watching over the coup preparations which had been made there. In his audience the evening before with Hirohito he had advised the Emperor that Manchukuo would never be a self-sufficient nation without strict Japanese supervision and that the League of Nations could never be persuaded that Manchukuo was independent as long as that strict supervision had to be exercised.

Kido left out of his diary the important news that the Emperor, acting on the former ambassador's advice, had given his final go-ahead to the coup d'etat scheme. But Kido showed by his actions that he understood perfectly that the coup would be staged that day. On leaving the palace he called on Secretary-Spy Harada. Harada phoned members of the Eleven Club to arrange a meeting with the former ambassador to the Soviet Union on the following evening. Then Harada took a train to Shizuoka, not far from

[12] The former ambassador was Tanaka Tokichi, a kinsman of Hirohito's cigar-smoking Taoist grand chamberlain, Suzuki Kantaro, Japan's final World War II prime minister.

Okitsu where old Prime-Minister-Maker Saionji had his seaside villa. He did not notify Saionji of his presence in the area. He registered at a good local inn and told the manager to listen to the radio all day and inform him if any important news was broadcast. Then he retired to his room and spent the afternoon "quietly writing letters."

Kido meanwhile went to his golf club at Hodogaya, outside Yokohama, and, instead of competing in the "Prince Kuni Cup tournament" as he had intended on awakening that morning, took a lesson from the club's golf pro. After a siesta, he played a few holes with club members of no consequence and then, with a great show of insouciance, started home just after five in the afternoon.

At about that same moment, as the sun was growing long shadows, three naval fliers of the Misty Lagoon, five cadets of the Army military academy, and one naval reserve lieutenant, ranging in age from twenty-four to twenty-eight, stepped out of two taxis at the side entrance of Tokyo's Yasukuni Shrine. Here, according to Shinto belief, lived the spirits of 126,363 heroes who had laid down their lives in the imperial cause since the Meiji restoration.[13] Here, by definition, was the Valhalla of all good soldiers who died in action. Five white stripes running horizontally around the walls, each signifying one of the five Fujiwara families who were supposed to stand around the Throne and protect it, proclaimed the special status and utter holiness of the place. In other shrines encircled by such stripes dwelt exclusively the souls of departed Emperors and princes. Only here—albeit in death—could the subject be honored as the equal of his sovereign. Within the wall, at the center of a spacious park, squatted the shrine building, its round rafters jutting out beyond the green copper roof on both sides of the ridgepole after the fashion of the earliest Japanese tent architecture.

The young officers walked a quarter circle around the park in order to enter the shrine building, which faced toward the sunrise

[13] Official Japanese casualty figures were always understated. Unless ten of the enemy died for every one Japanese, it was considered an affront to the virtue of the Emperor. At Yasukuni Shrine, however, the roll of honor was kept honestly and, on a year-to-year basis, the number of Army and Navy souls crossing the river may be found graven to a man.

and the goddess of the nation, from the east. Once inside they stood before the altar, caps tucked under their arms, and clapped their hands to invoke the 126,363 ghosts of the "never-opened chamber" within the "inner-inner room." They inclined their heads briefly for a moment of prayerful communion and then bowed profoundly in the direction of the mirror kept in the room "where the spirits of the deities are invited to descend." The mirror had been presented to the shrine by Emperor Meiji as a token, if not a replica, of the sacred one in which he communed with his ancestress.

Turning on their heels like any officers summoned to Manchuria, the assassins started out of the shrine. On the way one of them bought some charms from a priestly attendant and distributed them to his fellows for protection against police bullets. Emerging through the north exit, they passed the military museum, paused at the purifying "hand-washing place," circled around to the "hall where sacred dances are performed," and finally came out again on to the street by the south entrance where an officers' club, a men's club, and a veterans' club crowded up against the outer shrine walls. For the second time that day, they called taxis and squeezed in, four in one vehicle and five in another.

Turning their tailpipes to the gilded dome of the Russian cathedral and the Kanda quarter—the "Boul' Mich'" of students, universities, and second-hand book stores—they motored along the wide boulevard which skirts the immense moated park of the Imperial Palace. At 5:27 P.M. they reached the southern extremity of the Emperor's urban fief where stood, not far from the walls, the prime minister's official residence. Built of volcanic stone like Frank Lloyd Wright's Imperial Hotel, laid out in horizontal slabs like Wright's hotel, designed by a Japanese architect after the hotel, it was said by Western wits of the time to be an excrescence created when Wright's structure one ghostly evening took a short walk north and pupped. Disembarking from their cabs the nine young assassins entered the hotel-like lobby of the prime minister's residence.

At that moment on the other side of the city in the port area to the south, a second group of plotters consisting of one naval officer, three military academy cadets, and one civilian had just completed rites at the graves of the Forty-Seven Ronin in Sengaku Temple.[14] Now they, too, had embarked in taxis on their own mission of terror. A third group had mustered at Shinbashi Railway Station eleven blocks south of the prime minister's residence.

The first group of assassins stormed into the prime minister's residence and politely inquired of the receptionist where the Right Honorable Inukai might be on that quiet Sunday afternoon. She replied coolly that she did not know, but if they left their cards, she would give them to Inukai's secretary in the morning. The assassins turned to the policeman on guard and asked him, still politely, to lead them to Inukai's private apartments. The policeman tried to make conversation. A plainclothesman rose from a seat in the corner of the lobby and sauntered toward the front exit. One of the young officers noticed him as he broke for the door and felled him with a bullet. The policeman blanched and refused to utter another word. Leaving a guard to watch the receptionist, the policeman, and the wounded plainclothesman, the young officers set out to search the house. They captured and threatened several servants in the labyrinth of staircases and corridors but not one would point out the front door to Inukai's inner quarters.

Then one of the assassins heard the scratch of a key in a lock on the second floor. He called his comrades and broke down the door. Inukai's personal secret police bodyguard stood waiting for them in the prime minister's front parlor. They shot him and

[14] The Forty-Seven Ronin of Sengaku Temple in Shinagawa quarter are revered by Japanese for an act of heroic adherence to the code of feudal loyalty and vendetta. In 1701 a certain haughty lord, by studied insults and oversights, baited their master into drawing his sword in the shogun's anteroom. The shogun summarily ordered their master to commit suicide in expiation. Left liegeless, the forty-seven then refused all new employment and lulled the police into ill-founded contempt for them by pretending to live as vagrants and wastrels. On the night of December 14, 1702, however, they crept up on the Tokyo mansion of their master's tormentor, took him by surprise, cut off his head, and carried it to Sengaku Temple where they laid it as a peace offering on their master's grave. In recognition of their valor and popularity, the shogun allowed them to take their own lives in a solemn ceremony of collective belly-cutting and then to be buried beside their late lord. Ever since then Japanese youths and maidens have paid a steady stream of tribute at their graves and have relived their romance with death in countless prints, poems, novels, movies, and TV serials.

rushed over his wounded body to the dining room where Inukai sat smoking in an unlined summer lounging kimono such as a man might wear in the bosom of his family after his evening bath. He had been talking to his daughter-in-law and his personal physician who sat beside him. The assassins saluted him and addressed him politely. Then one of them, Second Flight Lieutenant Mikami, raised a pistol, aimed, and pulled the trigger. The gun clicked harmlessly, for it was not loaded. The seventy-six-year-old Inukai shook his long white goatee emphatically and held up both hands in an authoritative gesture to them to stop and wait a moment. One of the military academy cadets excitedly accused the old man of signing letters and checks which had been found in the safe of Manchurian war lord Chang Hsueh-liang in Mukden.

"All right, wait," said Inukai. "You will understand if you talk with me a while. Let's go over there to my work room." He stood up calmly and walked slowly to the door. Second Flight Lieutenant Mikami was surprised to see that the five-foot Inukai was as tiny as everyone said he was.

"I decided," said Mikami in his later testimony in court, "that it would be only a warrior's mercy to listen to what he had to say in his last testament."

Throwing his left hand over the prime minister's shoulder and prodding him with the pistol in his right, Mikami proceeded to escort the old man from the room. "I didn't have any personal grudge against him," he recalled later, "but I felt a tragic feeling. I tried to convince myself that we were straws in the wind of revolution. And so nothing changed my will to kill."

Mikami's colleagues turned guns on Inukai's maid, daughter-in-law, grandson, and doctor to prevent them from following the master of the household into the next room. The doctor, who had just treated Inukai for a nose condition, later told in court the strange story that he thought the young officers were merely escorting the prime minister from the room to protect him from a mob outside—this despite the shooting of Inukai's bodyguard in the next room.

Out in the corridor, Second Flight Lieutenant Mikami shouted to the lagging members of the death squad from the second taxicab who had entered the house by the back gate: "Here he is! Here he is!"

Prime Minister Inukai retorted, "Not too hasty. Not too hasty."

Mikami and Inukai entered the study, a big room of some thirty feet by thirty feet, and squatted on the *tatami* at either side of the square table at the center of it. Two of the other assassins took places, one at Inukai's side, the other standing cater-cornered from him with gun trained.

Inukai said sternly, "How about taking off your shoes."

Having invaded the sanctity of a home and already defiled the delicate matting of several rooms with their Western boots, the officers replied: "Worry about that later. You know why we are here. Do you have anything to say before you die?"

Nodding assent, Inukai leaned over the table in a bow, pressed his hands down firmly on it for emphasis, and half rose as if to speak.

"*Mondo muyo*" ("No use discussion"), cried the Misty Lagoon lieutenant beside him, and a second lieutenant on reserve—the man who had picked up the 2,000 yen from master conspirator Dr. Okawa three days earlier—dashed out of his corner and fired the first shot. Inukai folded forward onto the table, and the talkative Mikami, drawing a bead on the sinking forehead, fired carefully and let a stream of blood from the right temple.

The assassins stood up. Mikami would later have liked to have said, "Wish you a peaceful slumber." But someone cried "Out!" and they tumbled back toward their waiting taxicabs. In the corridors they met a Metropolitan policeman whom they shot twice and wounded gravely. But they got away in their cabs without having yet killed anyone. The secret police bodyguard would die ten days later. The servants and policeman whom they had wounded would all recover.

REFUSAL TO DIE

As for the prime minister, he seemed at first to be merely wounded. "Call them back," he demanded, as his family gathered around him. "I want to talk to them."

One bullet had torn into his left nostril, down through the roof of his mouth and out his right cheek. The other had pierced his right temple, furrowed his forehead, and come to rest just behind the bridge of his nose. His physician, Dr. Ono, did his best to staunch the bleeding of the two head wounds. Then he called Dr. Shioda, the chief of surgery at Tokyo Imperial University, who had operated on Prime Minister Hamaguchi after his shooting in 1930. Shioda sent over two specialists from his university staff to take charge of the case. They found the seventy-six-year-old prime minister not only conscious but still talking coherently and authoritatively. They judged it best not to aggravate the bleeding by moving him. When the amazing old man did not go into shock, they concluded that his condition was not critical.

At 7 P.M., a little more than an hour after the shooting, Inukai called a Cabinet meeting at his bedside and discussed with his ministers the measures which would have to be taken. He learned that his assassins had driven on past the Metropolitan Police Headquarters, firing bullets wildly into the air. They had continued to the Bank of Japan where they had repeated the same performance. Finally they had pulled up at the secret police station in Kojimachi, paid off their cabbies, and given themselves up.

A second death squad had driven from the tomb of the Forty-Seven Ronin to Lord Privy Seal Makino's residence where they had lobbed a grenade, wounding the policeman on guard at the entrance. They had flung a second grenade outside Metropolitan Police Headquarters, but it had failed to explode. Finally they too had surrendered to the secret police in Kojimachi.

A third death squad, driving in taxis from Shinbashi Railroad Station, had bombed the empty-Sunday-afternoon headquarters of Inukai's Constitutionalist party and had also surrendered after a noisy pass at Metropolitan Police Headquarters.

Finally, the Tolstoyan farmers of the Native-Land-Loving Society had attacked an impressive number of transformers at the city's unguarded power stations. For lack, however, of electrical know-how and of bombs that would explode, they had done no serious damage. A single sub-ward in the slums had suffered a temporary power blackout because one dauntless Land-Lover had severed a high-tension cable with a stroke of his wooden-handled knife.

Relieved that the incident had not been worse, Inukai wearily dismissed his ministers about 8 P.M. The two doctors from Tokyo Imperial University decided to build up his strength with a shot of blood. They took "150 grams" of blood from the arm of Inukai's eldest son, "mixed it with Ringer's solution"—normally a neutral medium for diluting blood—and "injected" it into Inukai. This procedure went unquestioned by the nonmedical bystanders but would have been questioned as idiotic and possibly murderous by any physician interested in preserving Inukai's life. One hundred and fifty "grams" or cubic centimeters of blood amounted to less than a third of a pint—a drop in a desert to a man with a nose-bleed like Inukai's. Such an injection could not possibly do Inukai any good and might do him harm if his son's blood did not match his own. In minutes, however—long before any mismatch effects could have shown themselves—Inukai suddenly lapsed into semi-consciousness and began to twitch and babble as if "confused in his thinking."

From his golf game, instead of going home to his wife in the suburbs as he usually did, Big Brother Marquis Kido drove to his official residence, just outside the palace, and took a bath. The phone rang and he learned from a minor chamberlain that the residence of his superior, Lord Privy Seal Makino, had been bombed. Before rushing over to inquire about the state of Count Makino's health, he phoned to the inn at Shizuoka where Secretary-Spy Harada was standing by to bring old Prime-Minister-Maker Saionji up to Tokyo.

Harada had already heard radio news of the "incident" from his inn-keeper and had already phoned Saionji's seaside villa to announce his presence in the vicinity. Saionji, too, had been listening to the broadcast bulletins and tartly observed that Prime Minister Inukai did not seem to be dead as yet. Therefore Saionji, at the moment, was making no preparations to go to Tokyo for the ceremonial chore of advising the Emperor on the selection of a new prime minister. Furthermore, Saionji had many questions in his mind and had no intention of seeing Harada until they could be answered.

Kido advised Harada to stay where he was and make the best possible use of his phone to get answers to the questions which Saionji might ask. Then Kido went to the palace where he reported to Lord Privy Seal Makino. Saionji, he said, was being his usual troublesome self and would muster other malcontents around him if the incident should be unduly protracted.

Standing by in attendance on Hirohito, Kido and Makino waited for Inukai to die and made the necessary ceremonial preparations for the investiture of a temporary prime minister who would take the reins of state until Saionji came up to Tokyo. When Inukai did not die, Hirohito dispatched his own personal physician to Inukai's residence to have a look at the case. Kido, in his diary, took pains to note that Hirohito's physician was dispatched at 8:20 P.M. and that the blood and Ringer's solution had been injected into Inukai at 8:10.

THREAT OF MUTINY

While Inukai lingered on and the palace waited impatiently, a group of young staff officers of the Strike-North Faction gathered at the war minister's residence to demand further action which would "make the coup meaningful." As section, squad, and desk chiefs in the Army bureaucracy, they demanded to know why this coup d'etat, which was to have established Hirohito finally as ruler in his own right, should have been allowed to waste itself in sham and mockery. War Minister Araki, the senior spokesman of the Strike-North Faction, had deliberately gone away to the seashore for the weekend, leaving his lieutenant, General Mazaki, vice chief of staff, to parry criticism for him. Mazaki, in a normal Japanese attempt to share responsibility, had collected a group of other senior officers to stand behind him. They included the Three Crows of Baden-Baden and Vice War Minister Koiso, the later kamikaze prime minister, a proponent of the Strike South.

Since Koiso was known to represent Army Chief of Staff Prince Kanin, the elder of the imperial family, he was allowed to speak first. He explained that the coup had been organized simply to rid the nation of the corruption of political parties. He waxed so eloquent as to the evils of party politicians that War Minister Araki's friend, General Mazaki, interrupted him brusquely. Too much oratory, said Mazaki, was not required in the Army. The pride of the Army was discipline. Every member of the officer corps was pledged to obey the Emperor, not to reason why. And with that, Mazaki stalked from the room.

Five of the young men of the Strike-North Faction ran after Mazaki and caught up with him in the lobby of the war minister's residence. They were led by a lieutenant, War Minister Araki's personal valet, who had lost much face by having helped to recruit the eleven cadets from the military academy who had sacrificed their careers to participate in the pathetic coup. General Mazaki, seeing that his pursuers were angry and carried pistols, ushered them into a waiting room off the foyer where he attempted to reason with them. They refused to sit down, but talk they did—for almost two hours.

"Our comrades," they exclaimed, "are ready all over the country. They expect action. We must rise tonight."

General Mazaki listened to the talk with unusual patience, saying little. Gradually his broad, honest face, concerned and friendly, took its effect. When the young men had talked themselves hoarse, he said simply, "The war minister will not rise, nor should we rise. That is General Araki's opinion as well as mine."

Mazaki stared shrewdly at the young men, waiting to see if any of them would offer now to shoot him. When none of them did, he rang for an aide and summoned the first two of the Three Crows, and three other senior officers waiting outside, to come in and talk to the five young rebels man to man. Second Crow Obata Toshiro, the most dedicated proponent of the Strike North in the triumvirate of the Three Crows, is recorded as having said to his young rebel, "I too feel deep regret over tonight's incident. We were steadily preparing our plans to realize the fruits of national reform with you and the rest, but suddenly everything turned to bubbles."

Even after such expressions of sympathy, the five lieutenants refused to return to their billets in peace. They insisted, instead, that they be arrested by the military police and taken to their regimental lockups. General Mazaki reluctantly humored them. He had them held for several weeks and then released without charges being filed against them. Four years later they would all participate in the military rebellion of 1936, after which two of them would die before a firing squad.

INUKAI SUCCUMBS

The chief aide-de-camp informed Hirohito of the trouble at the War Ministry about 9 P.M. At approximately the same time Lord Privy Seal Makino and the cigar-smoking Grand Chamberlain Suzuki began to hear reports that Saionji was making many phone calls from his seaside villa in Okitsu. Shortly thereafter Big Brother Kido, Makino's secretary, drove from the palace to the prime minister's residence to inquire about Inukai's condition. He had a word with Inukai's secretary, a former district director of the Thought Police, and consulted with the Court physician in attendance at Inukai's sickbed.

The remarkable old Inukai returned to full consciousness at 9:30 P.M., "threw up about 50 cc. of blood"—less than a quarter of a cupful—and said "I feel a little better." These were his last words. One of the doctors gave him a sedative. He lapsed into coma and convulsions but still did not die.

Kido returned to his residence at 11 P.M. and noted in his diary: "The reality of the [Inukai] condition is thought to be less than hopeful." Kido lay down for a nap. Shortly after midnight a chamberlain phoned him to come back to the palace and stand by during the investiture of the new temporary Cabinet. According to the chamberlain, it had been reported to the Emperor that Inukai had died at 11:20.

Having returned to the palace at 1 A.M., Kido learned that the news was premature. Secret police files opened by Allied Intelligence after the war reveal that Inukai was not declared dead by the doctors until 2:36 A.M. Once the news had been reported to the Emperor, the death was, of course, mandatory, but Hirohito, with his usual propriety, postponed the investiture ceremony until the death had become a physical reality. Kido waited about in the palace anterooms for two hours. Finally at 3:15 A.M. on that Monday morning, Finance Minister Takahashi was invested prime minister pro tem, and Hirohito went to bed. Kido remained at the palace, supervising paper work and discussing contingencies with highstrung courtiers until almost 7 A.M.

STERN REPRESSION

At about 8:30 A.M., in Kido's official residence, the phone rang —and rang. Stone-headed after less than two hours of sleep, Kido eventually rolled over on his pallet and reached for the receiver. It was Harada calling from Shizuoka. The secretary-spy had spent most of the night on the phone gathering information for Prime-Minister-Maker Saionji. At first light, when he knew the old man would be stirring, he had presented himself at the seaside villa to deliver his report. But Saionji, with unprecedented rudeness, had refused even to see him. Instead, Saionji had sent out word by a menial that he had no intention as yet of going up to Tokyo and that Harada might as well return to the capital and observe developments until the old man was ready to summon him.

At 9 A.M. Kido was back at the palace with the news that Saionji meant to stage another of his demonstrations of passive resistance. The sixty-nine-year-old Lord Privy Seal Makino, who had had only a few hours of sleep himself, inquired at the imperial bedchamber and learned that Hirohito was already up and dressed. After consulting with him, Makino instructed the cigar-smoking Grand Chamberlain Suzuki to draft a formal summons to Saionji from the Emperor and send it to Okitsu by the hand of an officially designated imperial messenger from the board of chamberlains. By tradition no Japanese nobleman could refuse such a summons except by committing suicide. It was a straightforward hint to Saionji that Hirohito meant to put up with no nonsense.

At 10 A.M., before Kido and Makino could finish their breakfasts, a second crisis broke. Temporary Prime Minister Takahashi arrived at the palace to announce that the Cabinet, after an all-night session, refused to serve under him. He was obliged, therefore, to tender the Cabinet's resignation en bloc. During the next five hours, Hirohito saw each of the Cabinet ministers personally and somehow persuaded every one of them to remain at their posts as caretakers.

In mid-afternoon, Hirohito found time to glance at the missive which had been written to send to Saionji. It struck him as meaningless and old-fashioned. He sat down and dashed off a list of points that he wished the note to make—points so blunt and specific that Count Makino and Grand Chamberlain Suzuki needed the rest of the afternoon to put them into customary veiled Court language. Kido waited about with fascination to see the result, but the text which Hirohito finally approved was considered so full of secret information by the elder courtiers that even Kido was not allowed to see it.

Chagrined and groggy, Kido returned to his residence at 5 P.M. He took a tingling hot bath in his *ofuro*—his "honorable wind on the backbone." And at 6 P.M. he went on to dine at Harada's with the former ambassador to the Soviet Union. Prince Konoye and four other haggard members of the Eleven Club were present. The ex-ambassador warned them all that Hirohito's temporary alliance with the Strike-North Faction in the Army would be an uneasy one unless something could be done about the administration of Manchukuo. Young Strike-North idealists, who had risked their lives in capturing the new colony, wanted to make it a model state. At the moment, however, influential adventurers, who could claim a semblance of Court backing, were busy milking and looting Manchuria by every shady trick known to man. The new colony could not bear such exploitation. It was undeveloped and underpopulated. Its present products were competitive with Japanese products. Its huge, cold, fertile plains would never attract large numbers of Japanese settlers. To make it a gainful colony, Japan would have to curb the influx of profiteers and send in technical men with slide rules and spirit levels. The administration would have to be put in the hands of more "great spirits like Ishiwara and Itagaki"—the Army strategist and politician whose planning had made the conquest of Manchuria possible. Unless such reforms were carried through, the Strike-North idealists would become a constant source of trouble, threatening discord at home and rebellion or secession abroad.

Kido heard the ex-ambassador's report "with surprise" and went home as soon as he politely could to think it over. Before retiring, he wrote a memo to himself on his conclusions: "Stern measures of repression are required. This is partly because the incident [the assassination of Inukai] happens outwardly, by blind chance, to resemble direct action [the action of rebellious troops acting without orders], but mostly because the incident, if unduly protracted, will shake the very foundations of the national house [the Imperial Throne]."

THE NEW REGIME

The next day, Tuesday, May 17, Hirohito's messenger arrived in Okitsu and delivered to Saionji the threatening imperial summons to come to Tokyo at once. Saionji did not refuse the summons outright, but he politely protested his ignorance of current political events and begged time to study the situation. The imperial messenger returned to Tokyo without being able to say by what train, if any, Saionji would follow.

On the heels of the abashed messenger, a second deputation arrived in Okitsu from the Army bureaucracy. It was led by Prince Kanin's henchman, the intimidating Vice War Minister Koiso of the Strike-South Faction, and by War Minister Araki's henchman, Vice Chief of Staff Mazaki of the Strike-North Faction. These two opposites were accompanied by the chief of the secret police and by Major General Obata, the second of the Three Crows of Baden-Baden. The four Army men told Saionji that the Strike-North and Strike-South leaders were prepared to cooperate in a transcendental Cabinet but would find it difficult to preserve Army harmony and discipline if Saionji should recommend another political party Cabinet.

Saionji sent the Army delegation back to Tokyo without making any firm commitments to it. Because he liked and trusted War Minister Araki, however, he was visibly mollified by the Strike-South Faction's willingness to include the Strike-North group in future policy making. Within hours, Secretary-Spy Harada was self-confidently setting up appointments with the men whom Saionji would wish to see when he came up to Tokyo. Some of the appointments needed only to be confirmed, for Harada, in an excess of efficiency, had first made them a full week earlier, three days before Prime Minister Inukai's murder.

The following morning, Wednesday, May 18, Saionji continued "to study the situation" from his retreat in Okitsu. Hirohito's two principal Big Brothers, Marquis Kido and Prince Konoye, agreed that the position of the Strike-North Faction was growing stronger by the hour and that Saionji must come to the capital at once or the planned transcendental Cabinet would become a Strike-North Cabinet. The indefatigable train rider, Harada, visited Saionji, offering that Prince Konoye himself should come to Okitsu bringing concessions from Hirohito. Saionji said, "Fine," and Harada phoned Tokyo. Less than half an hour later a palace limousine drew up outside Tokyo Station with a squeal of rubber. Konoye and Kido jumped out and respectively loped and galloped to catch the southward bound 1 P.M. express. Kido rode with Konoye as far as Yokohama, discussing what must be said to Saionji. Four hours later Konoye arrived at Saionji's seaside villa and went in at once for an audience with his venerable kinsman. He promised Saionji that Strike-North leader Araki would be held over into the new Cabinet as war minister and that some lesser portfolios would be given to party parliamentarians. An hour later he emerged with the old man's promise to come up to Tokyo the following day, Thursday, May 19. Konoye and Secretary-Spy Harada retired to the local inn to celebrate their achievement with saké and geisha.

On the morrow, Thursday, May 19, when Inukai had been dead for more than three days, Saionji climbed aboard a special train with Konoye and Harada for a wearisome journey north. Arriving in Tokyo, Saionji moved into the mansion kept for him by the Sumitomo cartel and began the round of political consultations which always preceded the appointment of a new Cabinet.

Prince Konoye reported at the palace. Hirohito agreed to the bargain which had been made, then called his cigar-smoking, philosophizing grand chamberlain, Suzuki Kantaro, and asked him to transmit to Saionji a set of guidelines to follow in picking the members of the transcendental Cabinet:

"Select men who are not real fascists; people who have a relatively mild philosophy and ideology, not too militant; also, they should not have personality problems."

Grand Chamberlain Suzuki honeyed this terse directive with much imperial solicitude for Saionji's health, much protestation of respect for the Constitution, and duly delivered the message to Saionji that same night. Tentatively Saionji had already accepted the transcendental prime minister chosen by Hirohito's Big Brothers six weeks earlier, on April 4. It was to be the biddable, seventy-four-year-old Admiral Saito Makoto, once an aide-de-camp for Emperor Meiji and long governor general of Korea. Nevertheless, Saionji took his time before recommending Admiral Saito officially to the Throne. The young modernists around Hirohito had made all the arrangements as easy for him as possible, but the old man insisted on examining the carefully wrapped package from every angle before putting his seal upon it.

On Friday, May 20, Lord Privy Seal Makino, in his interview with Saionji, asserted that young Army officers in all the main provincial cities were preparing to come up to Tokyo to agitate for an Army dictatorship. "They cannot be arrested," smirked Makino, "because, no matter what you may feel, it is not really a crime to come up to Tokyo." That same afternoon the chief of the Political Investigation Division of the Thought Police warned Saionji that the activities of Saionji's own partisans were fully known to the authorities. Pretending great concern over the possibility of civil war, the Thought Policeman said: "The so-called Constitution Protection Movement, organized by that sector of the economic community which does not yet admit to being intimidated, is mustering to come up and burn the capital."

The next morning, Saturday, May 21, the chief of the Metropolitan Police begged Saionji to see the Emperor soon because "the police are exhausted by their guard duties during the protracted crisis." That evening, when he retired to his private apartments, Saionji was surprised to find waiting for him his former geisha mistress, the mother of his two daughters. He had not seen her since she had left him out of jealousy—not since he had taken up with the wanton Flower Child during World War I. In the sentimental scene which followed, the eighty-two-year-old Saionji resolved to preserve Japan's civil peace at any cost.

On the following day, Sunday, May 22—one week after Inu-kai's murder—Saionji abruptly capitulated and went to the palace to perform his ceremonial chore. Once again he avoided the customary lunch in the palace and had only the most perfunctory of audiences with the Emperor—lasting from 2 until 2:30 P.M.—but he did what was expected of him and nominated Admiral Saito as the next prime minister.

Old Admiral Saito was summoned to the palace and said to Hirohito, "This is most unexpected. I have had no experience in this sort of thing but I will certainly do my best."

Two days later Admiral Saito was back in the palace with a list of ministers for a "transcendental rising-nation Cabinet." With a few minor exceptions the names on the list were those selected by Hirohito's Big Brothers six weeks earlier. Only one minister in the new Cabinet stood for a group in any way representative of a popular following. This was War Minister Araki, the leader of the schismatic Strike-North Faction which had grown up unwanted in the womb of Hirohito's own cabal—grown too large to be aborted for the moment.

To make sure that War Minister Araki and the Strike-North Faction would not seek to transcend the transcendental Cabinet in which they had been given a place, Hirohito took a small, nepotistic precaution. He raised his wife's cousin, Navy Chief of Staff Prince Fushimi, to the Supreme War Council with the rank of fleet admiral, the naval equivalent of field marshal or five-star general. This meant that the Board of Field Marshals and Fleet Admirals, which was the policy-making nucleus of the Supreme War Council, was now conveniently packed: three imperial princes as against only two subjects of the realm.

HIROHITO'S ACHIEVEMENT

So ended Japan's experiment in government by popular suffrage. The murder of Inukai had effectively silenced his Constitutionalist party. Throughout the next thirteen years Japanese would continue periodically to go to the polls, but their votes would be meaningless—at best quixotic expressions of opinion on publicized issues of the moment. In the months that followed, while the cartels were allowing themselves to become cogs in a national armaments machine, the only opposition to the military program bequeathed to Hirohito by his grandfather and great-grandfather would come from the "militarists" of the Army.

When the last grenade had fizzled, the last taxicab had screeched to a halt in front of the secret police building, and the last bluff had been laid down by Saionji and called by Hirohito, only four men were dead: Prime Minister Inukai, his bodyguard, Baron Dan, and financier Inoue. Hitler, in seizing power in Germany a year later, would have to assassinate fifty-one political opponents and burn down the Reichstag. Hitler's name would at once become a synonym for monster all over the world. Hirohito, after his great *Putsch*, the Triple Intrigue, would remain as unrecognized as ever—still a mysterious figure wrapped in taboo, and still, to all appearances, a paragon of propriety. It helped to be an emperor. It helped to have a thousand years of experience in intrigue to draw upon. It helped most of all to speak an Oriental language in which no Westerner had the equivalent of a Japanese college education.

Even in Hirohito's cabal, few knew as many details of the putsch as have been recorded in these pages. Even in postwar Japan the story of the plotting has never before been told in sequence. Nevertheless, many and perhaps most Japanese understood at the time that the Throne had conquered and that all the other powers of Japan had been humbled. Hirohito—as will be shown hereinafter—had to go to great lengths to reassure the public of his innocence. Cynics privately dubbed the attack on Prime Minister Inukai "the murder which had to be performed twice." Publicly the putsch was given the noncommittal name of "5–15" or "the May Fifteenth Incident."

In describing their reactions to 5–15, Japanese chose their words carefully and called it "a historic milestone." The peasants, to a man, repeated an age-old formula, *Shikata ga nai* (nothing can be done). An Osaka newspaper editor told an American correspondent, "We are accustomed in times like this to feel that the Emperor and his advisors should make the decisions." At Inukai's funeral on May 19, Western newsmen noted a profusion of expensive orchids on the simple white pine coffin and a totally inexpressive apathy on the faces of some 2,000 onlookers. Kwantung Army commander Honjo, on the day of Inukai's killing, wrote in his diary, "Military men in action under the gaze of their ruler today defied authority with a negative deed of daring."

Recognizing the mixed and apprehensive feelings of his subjects, Hirohito decided to issue a public statement explaining to the people what had been accomplished by the previous six months of concatenated terror. Two drafts of suitably vague imperial sentiments were drawn up by two separate members of the imperial circle, and both were deemed inappropriate by Hirohito. Finally Big Brother Kido, as secretary to the lord privy seal, took the delicate matter in hand himself and devised a thesis which Hirohito approved of. Kido's draft argued that the two great achievements of Emperor Meiji had been universal conscription of the people in a national army and creation of a native Japanese Constitution which explicitly gave the Emperor absolute power, overriding all other checks and balances. These two great accomplishments and ideals, wrote Kido, had been lost sight of during World War I. Now the assassination of Prime Minister Inukai had brought them once more into view. Hirohito delivered this argument in a formal speech to the new Cabinet three weeks after Inukai's murder. Not a minister, not an editorial writer, ventured to remind Hirohito that Emperor Meiji was most acclaimed for having improved the lot of the masses—for having abolished clans and castes and serfdom, for having created national public education and a measure of equal opportunity for all.

MERRY JUSTICE

After the consummation of the Triple Intrigue, the Throne took good care of all the loyal blackmailers and assassins who had helped to make it a success. A life-long protégé of the eighty-nine-year-old Spider Tanaka of the spy service became home minister in charge of police in the new transcendental regime. Under his auspices, the police moved with marvelous tact in apprehending the law-breakers. About half of Hirohito's Big Brothers were graduates of Tokyo Imperial University Law School, and through their connections they were able to enlist both the judiciary and the police apparatus in Hirohito's cause.

Dr. Okawa, the headmaster of the cabal, turned himself in to the procurator general a few days after Inukai's murder. The procurator questioned him personally on an informal conversational basis for almost a month. Then on the night of June 14, thirty days after Inukai's murder, the procurator phoned the new Cabinet's minister of justice. "There is business to do," he said. To the amazement of the justice minister, Dr. Okawa was suddenly put on the phone. Dr. Okawa was supposed to be wanted by the police, but now he chatted pleasantly with the justice minister. In the course of the phone call, Dr. Okawa revealed conversationally that he expected to be traveling tomorrow to Tsuchiura, the railroad station near the Misty Lagoon. So advised, the justice minister at once notified the home minister that the police, if they were serious in wanting to arrest Dr. Okawa, would be able to pick him up on the train to Tsuchiura.

The next morning, June 15, 1932, detectives mingled with a throng of well-wishers who had come to see Dr. Okawa off on the platform of Tokyo's Ueno Station. There were so many of the well-wishers that the detectives thought it best to postpone the arrest. They all bought tickets and boarded the train. They sat down in seats near Dr. Okawa, and when the train reached Tsuchiura they arose to arrest him without fuss as he was disembarking.

"You could have arrested me at home," he said, with an air of injured innocence.

A fortnight later, on June 30, Dr. Okawa's secretary was arrested.

On July 10, Baron Tokugawa, who had supplied funds for the preliminaries of the Triple Intrigue, was politely interrogated at the club of the Japan Legal Association.

Native-Land-Loving leader Tachibana, who had organized the inept attacks on Tokyo's power substations during the incident, escaped to Manchuria "to write a book." In the book he called upon the Japanese people to "smash the United States" and "spread the Japanese Imperial Way over the whole world." In another ceremony of exquisitely negotiated courtesy, he turned himself over to the Kwantung Army military police on July 25.

The principal of the spy service's former fencing school in Oarai, Black Dragon Toyama's secretary who had supplied the House of Heavenly Action to the Blood Brotherhood after the empty house had become too hot, negotiated his arrest late in September 1932. Hidezo, the son of Black Dragon Toyama, who had made the House of Heavenly Action available, placed himself in police custody on November 5, 1932, almost six months after the Inukai murder.

Such velvet-gloved methods were hardly characteristic of Japanese police work. On October 30, 1932, sixty policemen in bullet-proof vests stormed a hotel in the seaside resort of Atami where eleven Socialist and Communist leaders were holding a secret meeting. After a prolonged gun battle the subversives were "captured alive." Four days later one of them was announced as having "died of advanced tuberculosis, beriberi, and overexertion while resisting arrest." He was buried in potter's field and all the half-dozen mourners who turned up for his funeral were arrested, interrogated, and tortured. A few days later an aged accessory of the Blood Brotherhood died in the arms of his wife under house arrest. He was given a gangster's funeral, attended by hundreds of rightists including Big Brother Prince Konoye.

After dilatory arrests and kind questioning the killers of 5–15 enjoyed a long year in court in which they made rambling arrogant speeches and told nothing. Their trials did not begin until the second half of 1933, at which point their protestations belonged to a new era of Japanese politics, which will be described in a later chapter. Not one of the murderers, however, was severely punished. Of fifty-four killers and accomplices taken into custody, all but six were free men again by the end of 1935. These six, who had led the death squads and pulled the triggers, were released in 1939 and 1940.

Only token adjustments had to be made after 5–15 by the immediate members of Hirohito's circle. Yamashina, the "Flying Prince," who had incited the airmen of the Misty Lagoon had "a nervous breakdown" and retired from active duty. He is still secluded to this day. His mentor, Commander Inoue, the brother of Friar Inoue, retired to the reserve, where he remained until his professional services as a flight instructor were required again a few years later.

Ancient Spider Tanaka of the spy service converted his Everyday Meiji Biographical Research Institute at Oarai into the Everyday Meiji Memorial Hall, a museum open to the public. To celebrate its debut as a public institution he held a party at it. The Emperor's uncle Prince Higashikuni attended for the imperial family. On his way home to Tokyo afterward Higashikuni caused a scandal by stopping off indiscreetly at the Native-Land-Loving Society to cheer up the disciples of the jailed bombers who had failed to destroy Tokyo's power supply on the evening of May 15. The scandal was hushed up with difficulty, but Higashikuni succeeded in holding the loyalty of the Land-Lovers so that their services could be called upon again in future intrigues.

Lord Privy Seal Makino received many anonymous letters after 5–15 protesting that the bomb run made on his home had been "strange and insincere." He ignored the letters but had the police terrorize the writers of the letters, the civilian disciples of Strike-North ideologist Kita Ikki. For their part the police never interrogated Lord Privy Seal Makino; they only asked his permission, regularly, before making their gingerly arrests.

Dr. Okawa, when he submitted to arrest in June 1932, had on his person a number of useful, personal letters signed by Lord Privy Seal Makino and several other of Hirohito's intimates. When he came out of prison in 1935, Hirohito promptly had him made director of the South Manchuria Railroad's East Asia Economic Research Bureau and dean of Hosei University's "Continental Department."

Black Dragon Toyama, who had been genuinely duped by the Blood Brotherhood in the use of his facilities, turned up a trump by making public a letter in his praise which had been written by Prime Minister Inuaki shortly before his death. Toyama had the testimonial read aloud at his seventy-seventh birthday party on June 26, 1932, less than six weeks after Inukai's murder. In it Inukai had written:

I deem it my good fortune that Toyama Mitsuru is one of my most intimate and revered friends. Our friendship has endured for more than forty years, since the days when as a young man I entered the Imperial Diet.

Toyama is Japan's foremost subject. He has never held office, has no Court rank, has no official status whatsoever. But he has remained a sort of inspector and overseer of every government of Japan for half a century. He has made his influence felt whenever a national crisis has appeared. It was his magnetic leadership that caused us to risk our very existence in the wars with China and Russia.

What is the secret of his power? I believe that it stems from his immense loyalty to his Imperial Majesty the Emperor and to the Imperial House; from his complete unselfishness; from [his] patriotism . . .

Frair Inoue of the Blood Brotherhood was well treated in prison but did not emerge from custody until 1940 when he had wasted eight years of his life. Then, however, he moved into Big Brother Prince Konoye's villa in Yokohama, became a regular informant to Bigger Brother Marquis Kido, and enjoyed the lean years of World War II as a fatted prodigal on Prince Konoye's unlimited ration card.

Flight Lieutenant Mikami, who had adroitly shot Prime Minister Inukai through the nose, was also paroled in 1940 and remained comfortably unemployed for the next twenty-one years. On June 5, 1961, however, he was rearrested for plotting a coup d'etat in which he hoped to enlist the modern U.S.-trained Self-Defense Forces of Japan. His unsuccessful coup at this later date was dismissed by the Japanese press as the "Three Nothings Incident" —a quixotic attempt to bring bribery, taxes, and unemployment all to nothing. Mikami was held in jail briefly and released without publicity. By 1965, in his late sixties, he was back in circulation making speeches for patriotic clubs sponsored by Hirohito.

As for Eastern Jewel, the provocative little Manchu princess who had given her favors so unstintingly to incite the Fake War in Shanghai and to create her kinsman, Henry, a puppet emperor, she continued for many years to serve and shock the Japanese Army. After settlement of the Shanghai war, she took up with a branch manager of a Japanese cartel who gave her the use of a villa. She hired a bodyguard with the Special-Service-Organ money of her true love, Major Tanaka. Then she slept with the bodyguard. She engaged a "sing-song girl" from a Shanghai restaurant to solace Major Tanaka. Then she slept with the sing-song girl. Her behavior, observed Tanaka, years later, was "beyond common sense." Consumed by jealousy and ruined by extravagance, Tanaka had her transferred in mid-1932 to Manchuria. There she became the mistress of Major General Tada Hayao who was chief military advisor for puppet emperor Henry Pu-Yi. For a time Tada allowed her to play general over her own detachment of big handsome Manchurian soldiers.

Eastern Jewel went on to other influential lovers in the late 1930's. During World War II, beginning to look a little jaded, she became the *douane* of the Chinese community in Peking. As such, she handled the ransoming of wealthy merchants taken into custody by the Japanese secret police. On the proceeds she bought actors and waitresses for herself in the manner of her Manchu forebear, Yehonala, China's nineteenth century empress dowager. After World War II, in 1948, Eastern Jewel was beheaded by the order of one of Chiang Kai-shek's war crime tribunals. Her judge, in his remarks to the court, condemned her most of all for having ridden in Japanese airplanes and looked down in contempt—she, a woman—on the good earth of China.

16

OUTCAST NATION

(1932–1933)

THE AMERICAN AMBASSADOR

How courteous is the Japanese;
He always says, "Excuse it, please."
He climbs into his neighbor's garden,
And smiles, and says, "I beg your pardon;"
He bows and grins a friendly grin,
And calls his hungry family in;
He grins, and bows a friendly bow;
"So sorry, this my garden now."

So wrote Ogden Nash in 1932, expressing a feeling that was widespread in America at that time. The total variance between Japanese deeds and words in Manchuria made it obvious that Japan was predatory and mendacious. Westerners who knew Japan, however, considered the Ogden Nash view a popular prejudice. It was inconceivable to the experts that Japanese events must speak entirely for themselves and that Japanese words must be entirely discounted as national propaganda. No Westerners appreciated the subtle escape clauses of Japanese belly talk, the little adjectives and adverbs which enabled even the best Japanese to lie patriotically without violating their code of honor. And so the conquest of Manchuria, the Dollar Swindle, the Fake War, the assassinations of Inoue, Dan, and Inukai, and the threatened 5–15 coup were passed off in 1932, as they still are by most Western historians in 1970, as spontaneous outbursts of Japanese energy —hardly more than accidents.

On the day party government was murdered in Japan, a new American ambassador to the Court of Hirohito was just boarding the San Francisco-bound *Overland Limited* in Chicago. On the platform a reporter of Chicago's *Herald Examiner* rushed up to him with a copy of the paper's Sunday evening edition. Its headlines announced: "Japanese Premier Slain; Serious Revolt; Palace in Peril." That evening as the *Overland Limited* sped west through the corn belt toward Omaha, the new ambassador wrote in his journal: "In spite of the press reports, I can't believe the Emperor is threatened, considering the supposedly universal veneration for the throne. There must be something wrong here."

For most of the eight months since the seizure of Mukden, the United States had been represented in Tokyo largely by attachés and consuls who were not privileged to peer into the whole keyhole available to U.S. Intelligence in Japan at that time. The previous ambassador, W. Cameron Forbes, had left Japan on the morning after the Japanese seizure of Mukden, returned in time for the Fake War in Shanghai, and left again two months ago during the assassinations. He had been an outspoken man and not at all popular with the Japanese.

The new ambassador, Joseph C. Grew, was resolved to be more diplomatic than Forbes and at the same time more attentive and narrow-eyed. Like Forbes, Grew was a Harvard man. He had won the admiring patronage of Teddy Roosevelt thirty years earlier when he had shot a charging tiger between the eyes from a fallen position, on his back, in the Malay jungle. Since then he had filled a variety of important posts in Europe and the Middle East. One of his brothers-in-law was J. P. Morgan. His wife, Alice, was a granddaughter of every Japanese child's hobgoblin, Commodore Perry of the Black Ships.

Ambassador Grew was to remain the eyes and ears of the United States in Japan for the next ten years, until he was repatriated on an exchange ship in 1942 after the Japanese attack on Pearl Harbor. Later in the war years, Under Secretary Grew headed the faction in the State Department, which successfully advocated retention of the Emperor as ruler of Japan after she surrendered.

When Grew first arrived in Yokohama on June 6, 1932, the Japanese press gave him a snide reception. The *Japan Times* misquoted him as saying, "I know hardly anything about modern Japan but I hope to get down to serious study." The other great daily, *Asahi*, said, "As regards Japan, which has attained a marvelous development unprecedented the world over, his knowledge may be as imperfect as a fairy tale."

Despite Grew's resolve to remain on his guard, despite his rough reception by the Japanese press, he soon found himself charmed by Hirohito's courtiers and impressed by the skillful illusions they created. A month after his arrival in Japan, on July 13, 1932, he called on Count Makino, Hirohito's lord privy seal and master of intrigues. After the interview he wrote in his journal: "Count Makino impressed me as a really great gentleman. He is close to the Emperor but he doesn't, alas, carry much weight in these days of military domination." Within a year Grew would sometimes give way in his diary to such musings as: "The public guesses but does not *know* today who blew up the *Maine*. The public guesses but does not *know* today who engineered the incidents which led to the Japanese attack [on Mukden] of September 18, 1931."

OPERATION CONCUBINE

One day at about the time Grew arrived in Tokyo, Emperor Hirohito took an unprecedented turn in his afternoon walk through the Palace Gardens. As was his wont, he had strolled south from the Imperial Library, where he worked and lived, to the Biological Research Laboratory where he kept his poisonous fungi and his marine worms. From the lab he had continued south to the old private villa of Emperor Meiji which was used now by the princes of the blood as an occasional overnight lodging house and conference place. There Hirohito turned northeast to the white-pebble courtyard of the Palace Shrine for his brief daily hand-clap and prayer to the ancestral spirits. Continuing north, he entered the best part of the Fukiage Gardens, stopping repeatedly to appreciate the vistas of gnarled pines, rock heaps, and early summer flowers arrayed artfully along his way. Atop a knoll he came to the particularly gratifying outlook over Calabash Pond. He descended, crossed a rainbow bridge, and looked in at the pondside Pavilion of Frosty Brocade where Empress Nagako pursued her hobby of experimental sericulture. With several of her attendants, all dressed in aprons, slacks, and blouses, she was deeply immersed in sorting out the mulberry leaves to be fed to her various colonies of silkworms.

It was on leaving the Empress and the Pavilion of Frosty Brocade that Hirohito departed from his usual itinerary. Instead of following the path northwest from the sericulture laboratory to his Imperial Library, he took the path northeast past the comfortable English-style house of half-timbered brick known by the quaint old name of *Ka-in-tei* or Concubines Pavilion. There he and the Empress did their private entertaining. Beyond it, on the other side of the roadway which bordered the Inner Palace enclosure, he came to the cottage where dwelt his three daughters, aged six, two, and one.[1] Across the rustic dirt track from the Daughters Abode stood the Court Ladies Dormitory. It was not unheard of for him to stop at the Abode for a brief romp with the children, but today he walked purposefully past the Abode to the Court Ladies Dormitory and strode directly into the ladies' common room. There Empress Nagako's personal attendants were gossiping in French and sewing pearls to one of Nagako's Paris gowns.

The Court ladies did their best to conceal their panic and to entertain Hirohito with sophisticated small talk. He gruffly returned their courtesies and went about the room looking hard at each one of them. Some of the elder ladies had been beauties in their day but almost all the younger ones were at least as plump as the five-foot, one-hundred-twenty-pound Empress Nagako herself. Hirohito complimented several of them and then nodded his way out to complete his short walk back to the Imperial Library.

The next day the office of chamberlains promulgated a secret

---

[1] Another daughter, the second, had died at birth.

directive to the astonished Court ladies reminding, advising, and telling them that, first, the Empress had just passed her twenty-ninth birthday and as yet had borne the Throne no heir; second, the Emperor was considering the taking of a concubine; and third, it was every Court lady's patriotic duty to make herself as available and attractive to Hirohito as possible. The Court ladies professed horror to one another at the waywardness of the Emperor —and still only thirty-two years old!—but collectively they lost more than a thousand pounds and began to wear, as everyday, their finest dresses and perfumes. The ladies' common room, noted one chamberlain, "took on the air of a sultan's harem."

Throughout the early summer of 1932, Hirohito made the common room a regular stop in his afternoon rounds. He listened gravely to each lady's witty anecdotes but always returned to the library without giving any sign as to which lady he fancied. The ladies, for their part, were graduates of Bryn Mawr, Radcliffe, Oxford, and the Sorbonne. They deplored the bad old days of female servitude in Japan, but they began to see advantages in the straightforward customs of the past. They recalled with a certain scholarly nostalgia that, in the Court of thirty years ago, Emperor Meiji had simply dropped a handkerchief before an attendant when he wished her to go to bed with him.

Poor ladies, they were the dupes of a monstrous diversionary public relations scheme propagated by old Spider Tanaka of the spy service. The moderates of Japan were meant to hear of Hirohito's shy advances toward the Court ladies, meant to imagine him a loving husband under pressure from dirty old chamberlains, meant to think that perhaps, after all, Hirohito really was the proper, progressive young man portrayed by palace press releases in the 1920's.

The truth was that Hirohito felt no pressure at all to produce a son, for if one may believe the testimony of two of his courtiers —testimony corroborated by certain broad hints in the documents of the period—Hirohito had already had a son. After the birth of his fourth daughter, in March 1931, he had faced up squarely to the need for an heir and had agreed with his Great Vassals that the time had come for drastic measures. At the same time he did not wish, for personal reasons, to take a concubine. The affection of Empress Nagako and the support of her family—his imperial cousins, the Fushimis—were too important to him to trifle with. If he was to have a son immediately, the child must be a precautionary measure and nothing more, an heir begot impersonally and kept in the background for the time being. Later, if Empress Nagako remained barren of sons, the boy might be brought forth for adoption as crown prince and explained away, with small blemish to the imperial virtue, as the result of a youthful peccadillo. On the other hand, if Nagako should have a son, the stand-by heir would be kept a secret and handsomely provided for.

Sometime in the spring of 1931, therefore, during an afternoon visit to his Biological Research Laboratory, Hirohito had donated a test tube of seminal fluids to the care of one of his personal physicians. The sperm had been incubated, divided, and distributed to an unknown number of noble female recipients. One of them, in early 1932, had duly borne a male child.[2]

Once the succession was safe and Hirohito had proved his manly ability to sire sons, it was only a matter of time until some chamberlain in the imperial confidence would conceive a way to amuse Hirohito and turn his fertility problems to political account. The honor fell to Spider Tanaka who had helped to arrange Hirohito's post-mature birth at the turn of the century. Eighty-nine and still amorous, Spider qualified for the title of senior cupid in the Imperial retinue. After the 5–15 murder of Prime Minister Inukai, Spider had converted his Everyday Meiji Biographical Research Institute into a museum, had taken up residence at the chamberlains' dormitories and had begun to enjoy a freer run of the Inner Palace than at any time since the termination of his decade of service as imperial household minister to Emperor Meiji, twenty years earlier.

Following Hirohito's first call at the Court Ladies Dormitory, Tanaka held almost daily background briefings for reporters on the unprintable story about "the concubine question." Tanaka

[2] The informant who relayed this gossip to the author sidestepped questions as to the identity of the mother and the later life of the baby. Discreet references in Kido's diary, however, suggest that the existence of the test-tube prince was considered a problem at Court until November 1937. Then Kido ceased to worry about it—presumably because the little boy was adopted, in traditional Japanese fashion, by a noble house which lacked heirs.

complained to the reporters that Hirohito was "too staid" and "a firm believer in monogamy." What the Emperor needed was "a nice sturdy woman—a woman who can produce at the touch of the imperial hand."

So widely did the gossip spread on the grapevine that the newspapers in midsummer of 1932 began to allude, without explanation, to "the delicate situation in the palace." Spider Tanaka kept the gossip alive by visiting the ladies' common room himself and telling the Fujiwara girls there that if they could not do their duty he would find more seductive noblewomen outside of the Court.

Ostentatiously Tanaka compiled a list of eligible aristocratic young women and sent out a deputation of photographers and chamberlains "in quest of the glass slipper." A surprising number of well-born modern Cinderellas professed their willingness to serve the Throne as brood mares. Old Tanaka and a committee of aging chamberlains enjoyed a gluttony of reminiscence and boastful story-swapping in poring over the photographs. Finally they chose three candidates whom they judged to be the most blythe, bonny, lissome, eligible, and available. Tanaka personally, in his own most elegant brush strokes, inscribed the pedigree of each of the three temptresses on the back of her eight-by-ten glossy. He had the three photographs wrapped in fine rice-paper tissue and placed on top of the state papers in Hirohito's in-basket. The next morning when Hirohito sat down behind his desk in the Imperial Library, he glanced at the three photographs and moved them to the bottom of the stack of papers. He continued to do so every morning throughout the rest of the summer.

On the national grapevine, the concubine question soon overshadowed all other subjects of debate. Women sympathized with Empress Nagako. Men theorized shrewdly on the political implications. It surprised no one when, in August, Tanaka spread the rumor that he had fallen out with his old friend, Empress Nagako's uncle, Prince Higashikuni. On August 4, when Prince Higashikuni was late for a reception, calls to his villa disclosed that he was detained by a confrontation with Tanaka. The old spy supposedly accused the young princely spy of letting his jealousy for the honor of his niece, Empress Nagako, eclipse his concern for the interests of the nation. Days later old Spider Tanaka was reported to be at swords' points with another old friend, Imperial Household Minister Ikki. He accused Ikki of being too timid in pressing concubines on the Emperor.

Tanaka dueled in the gossip columns with Household Minister Ikki and with Prince Higashikuni for the next six months. Both conflicts were nominal, punctuated by hand-claps rather than by real blows. While they raged, Empress Nagako was represented in the gossip as awakening gradually to the awful possibility that her husband might be considering a replacement for her. The Court ladies discovered her several times dabbing at her eyes. She began to tease the youngest and slimmest of her attendants by making anonymous calls to her on the palace telephone and addressing her as "Fatty."

Fatty's uncle was the deputy grand chamberlain. He told Fatty of the photographs on the Emperor's desk. To escape the Empress's jealousy, Fatty passed on her information to the chief lady of the Empress's wardrobe. The chief lady relayed the information to Empress Nagako. According to her Japanese biographer Empress Nagako reacted in a way that fitted perfectly into the schemes of the palace public relation's experts. "I cannot believe you," she said hoarsely. "He would not do that to me and he could not."

A few days later Empress Nagako described to a group of her ladies a most affecting scene which she said had taken place the night before in the "room of the grated gate"—a euphemism for the imperial bedchamber, harking back to bygone days when a guard always stood outside at a peephole to make sure that the Child of Heaven was safe with his bedmate of the night. Finding Hirohito in an affectionate mood, Nagako by her own account had pointed out the sweet smell of hibiscus wafted in from the garden on the September night air. She had reminisced about their first evening together in bed, and then, beginning to weep, she had said, "I know everything. I just want you to tell me yourself. I love you, even if you don't love me anymore."

It had taken Hirohito a moment, related Nagako, to understand what she was talking about, but then he had reassured her with many tender words that he had no intention of taking a mistress.

In February 1933, five months after Nagako's description of the scene in the room of the grated gate, old Spider Tanaka and Imperial Household Minister Ikki settled their duel of hand-claps by both going into retirement. It was advertised to the grapevine that Hirohito was weary of their quarrel and no longer amused by the concubine question. Oddly enough this protestation was interpreted by Japanese with an ear for belly talk to mean that Ikki and Tanaka had compromised and agreed to share the duty of taking public responsibility for the assassinations and the abortive rebellion of 5–15.[3] Lord Privy Seal Makino, who might have assumed the responsibility with greater justice, remained at Hirohito's side for almost three more years.

In March 1933, a month after the settlement, Empress Nagako became pregnant again. The palace midwives assured her that she was going to have a boy. In April, the lady-in-waiting who had borne Hirohito a son by artificial insemination called at the common room to show off her baby to the other ladies-in-waiting. Empress Nagako looked in at the common room during her visit and enticed the toddling illegitimate heir to the Throne back to the private imperial apartments. There Nagako gave the little boy a teddy bear and assured the mother that she and her son would always be well provided for. The Court ladies said that it was a good omen that the little boy had followed the Empress and recognized the leadership of the unborn child in the Empress's womb.

LORD LYTTON INSPECTS

As Grew in his embassy accustomed himself to the subtleties of communication in Japan and Hirohito in his palace created smokescreens to cover the dark deeds of the previous spring, Lord Lytton was scrutinizing Japanese policy in Manchuria.

[3] Ikki obediently accepted this responsibility despite the fact that he had opposed the murder of Prime Minister Inukai—opposed it so strongly that Big Brother Kido, three days before 5–15, had announced to Secretary-Spy Harada: "*Ikki dja dame*" ("Ikki is no damn good").

The heroic Chinese General Ma, who had fought so effectively against the Japanese in November 1931, pretended to sell out to them in February 1932. Chang Hseuh-liang, the ousted Manchurian war lord, had sent Ma a check for almost $2 million (U.S.) with which to pay his troops. The check was drawn on a Japanese-controlled bank. The Japanese allowed Ma to cash it, and in return Ma accepted the puppet post of war minister in the new government of Manchukuo. Six weeks later, however, Ma absconded into the wastes of Manchuria's northwest with most of the $2 million and a truck convoy of Japanese guns and uniforms. By April 14, he was in Hailun, on the Russian frontier, announcing his independence and defiance of the Japanese.

A week later Lord Lytton and the League of Nations' Commission of Inquiry arrived in Mukden. Throughout the six weeks of Lord Lytton's stay, General Ma and his hastily reassembled army caused the Japanese acute embarrassment by taking the offensive in north Manchuria and demonstrating that the spontaneous popular backing which the Japanese claimed for their administration was less than unanimous. General Ma daily broadcast an invitation to Lord Lytton to come north and see for himself the last corner of a genuinely Manchu Manchuria. Lytton, of course, could not respond to the invitation, much less accept it.

But Ma's stand encouraged many Manchurians to defy the Japanese secret police in an attempt to tell Lytton the truth. Messages were sent to Lytton by every undercover contrivance known to man: wrapped in bath towels, written on menus, buried in pastries. In the northern city of Harbin, alone, hirelings of the Japanese spy service pounced on five Chinese, two Russians, and one Korean who tried to communicate with members of the League Commission directly. All eight died in police custody, most of them after prolonged torture. One young Russian student who merely wished to protest the closing of the Harbin Polytechnique, where he had been studying, was caught on the second floor of the Hotel Moderne and killed so quietly that the League's commissioners, preparing for bed and reading reports in nearby rooms, did not hear a sound.

On June 4, 1932, Lord Lytton returned to China with the scent in his nostrils of an insufficiently aired opium den. He retired to the legation quarter of Peking to pull together the material which he and his fellow commissioners had collected and organize it into a formal report to the League in Geneva. The Japanese Army officers who had chaperoned him through Manchuria suspected that they had failed to deceive him. They turned their spite on the shrewd double-dealing General Ma and hunted down his guerrilla forces, band by tattered band.

On July 27, 1932, Japanese troops on the Russian border ambushed a force of 800 Chinese cavalrymen attempting to escape into Russia. After the slaughter, General Ma's horse and saddle bags were found among the corpses on the battlefield. Emperor Hirohito was officially informed that General Ma was dead. A few days later, an irreverent Chinese editorialist in Shanghai inquired rhetorically: "Can God be misinformed?" General Ma had turned up alive and well in Russia. He proceeded to make a triumphant trip around the world, publicizing the cause of the Manchurians and finally returning to the side of his liege lord, Chang Hsueh-liang, in Peking.

LESS THAN PARADISE

Ma's escape was used by Hirohito as an excuse for recalling to Japan the conquistador of Manchuria, Kwantung Army Commander Honjo. Honjo and Hirohito were in polite disagreement as to the colonial policy which should be pursued in Manchuria. Honjo wanted to make the latest acquisition of the Empire a model state, "a paradise," which would set an example of Japanese efficiency for the whole of Asia. Being an Army man, however, Honjo was impractical about economic matters. He begged that the new colony be treated as a long-term investment and excused from showing an immediate profit. Hirohito's Big Brothers, on the other hand, felt that the new colony must pay its way from the start. If Honjo and the Strike-North idealists had their way, Japan's surplus energies might be entirely absorbed by Manchuria for a decade or more and the national program might be set back in its timetable.

From the first Honjo had found himself the dupe of hard, bright disciples of *Machtpolitik*—the young officers of Hirohito's cabal who had been placed under him as staff officers. These young men had their own channels to the palace in Tokyo. Some of them, like the religious zealot and strategic genius, Lieutenant Colonel Ishiwara, who had planned the Manchurian campaign, were idealists whom Honjo admired. But after the operational phase of the Manchurian occupation was over, Honjo found that he had other assistants whom he did not admire: operatives of the spy service, sadistic secret policemen, dispossessed samurai who had become "China experts" in their youth and had learned the trades of dope peddler and white slaver in the Japanese gay quarters of Shanghai, Hankow, and Tientsin.

The original plan for Manchuria, as Honjo had understood it, would entail development of the country's mineral and chemical resources, realization of its potential as a manufacturing nation, and settlement along its borders and in its empty areas of Japanese colonists. Following orders from old Prince Kanin, the chief of the General Staff, he had sanctioned the relocation of some 25,000 Chinese and Manchu farm families to make way for their replacement by Japanese settlers. He had had to delegate the relocation project to subordinates of the spy service and Special Service Organ which were both autonomous of his command and directed from Tokyo.

As executed, the relocation scheme turned out to be an eternal blot on Honjo's honor. Chinese bandit bands hired by the spy service rounded up villages of native farmers and set them to work building Japanese-style houses for the settlers who would take their place. The native farmers were promised new lands, new seed, and implements of their own when their building was done. And when it was done, they were turned over to regular units of the Japanese Army for escort to their new homes. The soldiers of these units were told that the native farmers were bandit families who had been sentenced to death and must be herded into stockades and machine-gunned. Some of the farmers were distributed to Japanese infantry companies to be used for bayonet practice by green privates who had arrived in Manchuria too late for the toughening experience of real combat.

A White Russian university student, who had become a minion of the spy service and who later smuggled out of Manchuria an account of his experiences, described this bayonet drill in some detail. He called it not sadistic but masochistic—a school exercise for the training of automatons. The Japanese boys, he said, seemed dazed and foolish. They smiled and laughed and handed out candy to their victims before tying them, apologetically, to stakes driven into the ground. Then the soldiers took turns charging with fixed bayonets at each bound captive until he finally slipped in gobbets out of his ropes.

Oleg Volgins, which was what the White Russian student called himself in his memoirs, had greeted the Japanese motorcycle troops as liberators when they had entered Harbin in February 1932. As refugees from revolutionary Russia in 1920, Oleg and his family considered any anti-Bolshevik an ally. At first Oleg assured his mother that the Japanese were "simple ascetic warriors." Not until he had worked as an agent of the spy service for a year and seen his mother made a hostage and his wife a prostitute did he become a Japanese slave and learn to hate his masters. His account was not published in the West until 1943, when seven years had passed since its writing and it could be assumed that he was dead.

Oleg himself underwent an indoctrination course at the hands of the Japanese secret police which he compared to the indoctrination being given to Japanese soldiers in Manchuria. His secret police instructor, a man named Kato, asked him, "Do you fish? No one is sorry for fish; you must assume the same attitude." A young Manchurian accused of being a Communist was then brought into the interrogation chamber which served as classroom and beaten up with fists. He was burned with cigarettes on cheeks, lips, and eyelids. A mixture of water and red pepper was poured down his nostrils to give him a taste of burning to death and drowning at the same time. He was hung up and whipped. Attendants burned pits in his privates with their cigarettes. He lost consciousness. A Japanese doctor of evident education and contempt for the proceedings entered the room bowing and smiling and resuscitated the victim with an injection. The young leftist's fingernails were torn out, then his toenails. Strips of flesh were cut from his body with a knife. His teeth were knocked out. Finally Instructor Kato, "using his favorite tool, the cigarette, methodically burned out his eyes."

"Then, thank God," wrote Oleg, "he died."

These methods, practiced by agencies over which he had no
control, induced Kwantung Army Commander Honjo, in June
1932, to beg Hirohito, through all the channels at his disposal,
to give Manchuria a more enlightened administration. The answer came a month later, when Hirohito approved the dispatch
to Manchuria of 166 young technocrats who were all satellites
of Big Brother Kido's Eleven Club. The young technical experts
brought efficiency to Manchuria but made the latter state of that
colony worse than the first.

A Manchukuoan Aviation Company was chartered, funded with
Japanese capital, staffed by Japanese pilots, and dedicated to
"the development of air routes into China." For the next five
years it would act brazenly as a civilian extension of the Japanese
Air Forces, conducting thousands of provocative overflights, touching down at Chinese airfields unannounced, paying no ground-
crew fees much less runway tolls, and carrying little beside
espionage agents and contraband guns, money, and dope, all calculated to catalyze the disintegration of China.

Japan's great South Manchuria Railroad Company, a quasi-
governmental institution modeled on the East India and Hud-
son's Bay companies of British colonialism, extended its tracks
over more than a thousand miles of new rights of way. Each fresh
tentacle of track had a strategic purpose: one cutting across the
Manchurian branch line of the Trans-Siberian Railway, another
opening a way into Mongolia, a third pointing a dagger at Vladivostok, a fourth communicating with a new Japanese artificial
harbor for naval vessels in North Korea.

A fine new capital, called New Capital or Hsinking, was built
to the north of Mukden, in the former Chinese town of Long
Spring Thaw. The streets had been surveyed and laid out even
before the Manchurian Incident. By the time of Lytton's visit
the new city was nearing completion and was ready for occupancy
by Henry Pu-Yi and his puppet government a month later, in
July 1932.

An oil refinery and a chemical complex for nitrates, phosphates,
and sulphates came into being across the bay from Dairen in the
old Kwantung Territory Leasehold. Beside one of the largest strip

seams in the world—a slab of coal ten miles long, two miles wide, and some 350 feet deep—the Japanese built the model company town of Fushun just east of Mukden. In it the colliers enjoyed free housing, electricity, transportation, and central heat and had nothing to buy with their wages except food and drugs at the company store. The wages were only 40 cents U.S. a day but that was more than four times the national per capita daily average. Native Manchurians supplied all the labor, 1.3 per cent of the clerical help, and none of the engineering and managerial staff.

To pay for these showpieces of material advancement Hirohito's 166 young technocrats instituted a money raising scheme as diabolical as any ever devised by a colonial power. The Italian operative of the spy service in Harbin, Amleto Vespa, called it "the greatest organized squeeze in history." It was first outlined to him one day in the summer of 1932 when his nameless but princely chief announced: "Japan is poor. The Japanese Army in Manchuria costs millions every day."

The Manchurian farmers had too much peasant cunning to make ordinary tax collecting a feasible proposition, and so Japan's spy service, secret police, and Special Service Organ agents set out to milk the country by exploiting the natives' human frailties. Monopolistic opium, heroin, gambling, and prostitution concessions were sold to guilds of vice experts from the various Japanese settlements in China. Of these the most cold-blooded sharks—sharks in a swimming pool of blood—were the dope peddlers. After they moved into Manchuria, mass graves beside the garbage dumps outside all the major cities were kept open for the daily disposal of overdose victims cleared from the streets each morning.

The Japanese themselves had always had a healthy fear of dope addiction and an enviable record in their other colonies of suppressing it. The smoking of the poppy had been introduced to China about 1650 by the Dutch. Until about 1800 it was a luxury practiced mainly by Chinese who were old and rheumatic and rich. Then competition among British, Portuguese, Dutch, and American traders drove the price down and the supply up. In eighteenth century China, aged mandarin addicts had commonly traveled about on official business accompanied by wet nurses who suckled them in their pipe dreams and kept a supply of easily digestible nourishment flowing into their withered guts. The poor who took up the opium pipe after 1800 could not afford such refinements. They used the marvelous anodyne of the pipe to go on working, without food, until they literally dropped dead in their tracks. It was still common, in twentieth century China, for ricksha coolies, who had run twenty miles on a bowl of rice and a pipe of opium, to expire in their traces without a word of complaint.

The Japanese had recognized from the first the danger of the drug which was debasing China. In 1858, before any treaties had been concluded with the outside world on other matters, the shogun's government negotiated an agreement with Great Britain to keep opium out of Japan. When Japan's abstemious samurai conquered the island of Taiwan, in 1895, they found 14 per cent of the Taiwanese natives smoking opium. Forty years later, the cold, efficient, paternalistic efforts of the Japanese police had reduced addiction to less than one half of 1 per cent of the population. The Japanese drug police licensed addicts, issued them three-day supplies of pipe poppy at prices far below the going rate on the illicit market, and saw to it by stringent detective work that no smugglers could compete with the government monopoly and no youngsters could find courage to try the habit. Eventually old addicts died and few new ones emerged to take their places.

By 1926, when Hirohito came to the Throne, Japan had as fine a record of opium control as any nation in the world. At that time approximately one out of every 3,000 Americans was an addict of opium in drug form—a hangover from the days of narcotic patent medicines. By comparison only one out of every 17,000 Japanese was an addict and only one out of every 4,000-odd inhabitants in Japan's most recent colony, Korea. In Manchuria, however, the Japanese pursued a new policy. Throughout the late 1920's Japanese dope peddlers, operating out of the Kwantung Leasehold, had sought to weaken Manchurian resistance by selling as much dope in Manchuria as possible. When Japan's take-over of Mukden occurred in September 1931, the League of Nations' statistics indicated that about one out of every

120 Manchurians was an opium addict. Seven years later one out of every 40 Manchurians was an addict.

The Japanese opium-selling campaign was simple and direct. Bonuses were paid to farmers who would rotate their soya beans with poppy crops. All opium smokers were registered and issued a weekly ration for which they were expected to pay in much the same fashion that a subscriber is expected to pay for his weekly issue of a magazine. At first, subscriptions came at introductory rates and comfortable dens were provided for those who wished to dream away from their families.

The smoking dens were supplemented by approximately three times as many booths, installed in the downtown streets of major Manchurian cities, where smokers and novices could learn the joys of the hypodermic. At these booths a man, a woman, a boy, or a girl could take a trip on morphine or cocaine, as well as heroin. Special introductory rates of less than the equivalent of a nickel a dose were offered to teen-agers and children. Officially every partaker was a registered addict on whom the opium monopoly could supply a certified medical record. In reality the booths were open to any and all comers who could plunk down a few coppers. The dispensers at the booths were so undiscriminating that they even gave shots to intrepid American newspaper reporters out for an exposé. One of the reporters wrote that he paid twenty coppers to a roustabout, rolled up his sleeve, thrust his arm through a hole in a canvas tent, and got his needle sight unseen.

Beside the opium booths sprang up brothels. No less than 70,000 Japanese and Korean prostitutes were imported into Manchukuo in its first year as a state. And in addition to the whorehouses, the licensed opium-smoking dens, and the unlicensed dope-by-needle booths, the official Japanese crime syndicate organized a dozen other rackets. Enterprising concessionaires, backed by the Japanese secret police, collected charges for the right to hold a wedding, a wake, or a simple feast; for the duty of having a clean sidewalk; for the privilege of having a new compulsory house number; for the once free right to cut ice in the river; for numberless stamps, seals, and countersignatures on every transfer of property, every business contract; for the duty of having each chimney cleaned once every two months; for the privilege of not being constantly dunned with forged IOU's. Every bank transaction ran a gauntlet of special charges which made it impossible to liquidate an asset without a loss of 30 to 40 per cent.

Breakfasting on humble pie, lunching on air, dining on opium, the Manchukuoans paid and paid again. The Japanese and Korean concessionaires who ran the rackets paid, too. They paid initially for their monopolies and then many times again in bribes to secret policemen who backed up their extortion with terror and torture. Emissaries of the Throne in Tokyo collected twice: first, from the concessionaires for their charters; and second, from the secret policemen for their appointments to positions of responsibility in which they could squeeze the concessionaires. The best of the police jobs were auctioned off in Tokyo for as much as ten times their annual worth in terms of salary. The friends of Hirohito, who used his power of appointment to squeeze the squeezers, realized a substantial part of the total profits and plowed it back into the Throne's intrigues and weapons research institutes. Hirohito remained entirely invisible, behind many veils. A single trustworthy chamberlain from his Court took up residence in Manchukuo to keep watch over the rackets as vice imperial household minister to Puppet Henry.[4]

To administer Manchukuo the Japanese set up an elaborate copy of their own system of curtain government. In front of the curtains sat a native Manchurian Cabinet of ministers, each of whom was the puppet for a Japanese vice minister and a staff of Japanese secretaries. Behind the veil sat Puppet Henry, guarded by Japanese secret policemen. Henry was titular commander-in-chief of a Manchukuoan militia which was officered by Japanese and employed as a labor force by the Kwantung Army. The commander of the Kwantung Army reported to Hirohito's great-uncle, Chief of Staff Prince Kanin. The commander of the secret police reported to the Tokyo secret police chief. Prince Kanin and the Tokyo secret police chief both reported to Emperor Hirohito.

As described by a Japanese who grew up in Manchukuo, the puppet nation was organized "like a miniature garden planted

4 Iriye Kanichi

according to the strict aesthetic of mimicry." That is, each shrub was carefully selected, pruned, stunted, and tamed to give an illusion of some natural forest beauty. Each office and institution was made to look like a functional enterprise and to hide the fact that its animus was a shadowy Japanese, a wild creature from the world of reality.

All Japanese of any moment in Manchuria were completely and cynically aware of their role as stage managers. The 166 technocrats sent from Tokyo drafted the plan of the puppet state in consultation with the staff officers of the Kwantung Army. Their plan was modified by the chief of Intelligence in the General Staff, Major General Nagata, the first of the Three Crows chosen at Baden-Baden. Prince Kanin approved Nagata's draft and Hirohito made minor editorial changes in it. The final wording was sent to Manchuria and subscribed to by the staff officers of the Kwantung Army. Mincing no words, it stated that the Manchukuoan government was to strive for "co-prosperity and co-existence with the Japanese economy." In form it was to be "nominally constitutional" but "substantially autocratic." Its "inner leader" was to be the commander of the Kwantung Army working with state ministers "of Japanese lineage."

REPORT TO THE LEAGUE

Kwantung Army Commander Honjo, when he was recalled to Tokyo in July 1932, and Lord Lytton, when he retired to Peking to write his report in June 1932, both visualized the social monster which Hirohito's planners were creating in Manchuria. Honjo went into semiretirement as a member of Hirohito's Supreme War Council and began to lobby for reform in colonial policy. Lord Lytton, whose kidney ailments had been in no way alleviated by entertainments and frequent changes of drinking water, secluded himself in the German Hospital in Peking, surrounded himself with nurses, and began to write his classic report to the League of Nations. He felt that he must criticize Japan strongly and found that he must negotiate every sentence of his criticism with his fellow commissioners.

The Italian commissioner, a count, and the German commissioner, a former colonial governor, both wished to make the report as vague as possible. General Claudel of France threatened to issue his own minority report unless Japan's position was presented in the most flattering light possible. Lord Lytton strove mightily with his pen, conscience, and temper in order to satisfy his fellow Europeans. Being a literary man he tended to write sentences which said directly and intelligibly what they meant.

The American commissioner, Frank R. McCoy, sided with Lytton on the general drift which the report must take. He had none of Lord Lytton's literary gift, but he was a master mediator.[5] He kept the other commissioners from disturbing the quiet of the sickbed where Lytton lay working. And as countless scribbled drafts and redrafts issued from the hospital, McCoy negotiated the softening phrases which were necessary to preserve the commission's unanimity.

In the last fortnight of Lytton's labors, the Japanese did their utmost to coax and distract him. Between August 21 and 25, Japanese marines in Shanghai took up "sightseeing excursions" into the Chinese areas of the city and enjoyed their outings so boisterously that they caused a panic and evacuation of Chapei. On August 27, *New York Times* correspondent Hugh Byas in Tokyo learned from a source close to Japan's foreign minister that the issue came down to this: "whether or not Japan is to be censured in terms that will compel her withdrawal from the League of Nations. . . . If Geneva merely endorses Secretary Stimson's doctrine of non-recognition of any situation brought about in contravention of treaties, Japan will not object." In other words, if the League issued a statement of theory without being so rude as to criticize Japan by name, Japan would condescend to remain in the League of Nations.

[5] McCoy had made a name for himself as a walker in troubled waters at the very outset of his career. In Cuba, during the Spanish-American War, his colonel asked him if the river ahead was fordable. McCoy waded across to the other side and called back, "It is." The colonel remarked, "I shall make that young man my aide." The colonel's general, however, was standing by and said, "Sorry, Colonel, I already made him my own aide when he was halfway across." In later years McCoy would be recalled from retirement to head the Allied Powers' Far Eastern Commission which was supposed to advise MacArthur in his authoritarian Occupation of Japan. Then, once again, McCoy would be responsible for preserving a semblance of unanimity.

The ousted Manchurian war lord, young Chang Hsueh-liang, dramatized the reality of continuing resistance to Japan's puppet regime by mounting a guerrilla attack on Mukden in the early morning hours of August 29. The guerrillas destroyed the airport, set fire to the arsenal, shot up the wireless station, and even penetrated into the walled city. When the "bandits," having made their point, vanished into the countryside before daybreak, frustrated Japanese spokesmen could only leak to Western newspapermen another threat: that any more such raids would force Japan to conquer the next adjoining province of China, the poppy-growing province of Jehol. Part of the U.S. Atlantic fleet joined the Pacific fleet for maneuvers in a move which Japanese decried as menacing. In Japanese movie houses Hollywood's *Hell Divers*, retitled *The Bombing Corps of the Pacific*, played to capacity audiences which believed that the hypothetical targets depicted in the film were the cities of Japan.

In this maelstrom of pressures, by Tuesday, August 30, the last comma of the Lytton report had been haggled, the last *i* dotted, and the 400-odd pages went into their final typing. The members and secretaries of the commission moved into the German Hospital in Peking and turned its antiseptic corridors and lounges into a publishing office. Compromises scribbled in longhand had to be unscrambled, punctuated, and typed. Not until Saturday, after three days' work, was there a clean master copy, plus carbons, of the historic document. Some secretaries and members of the commission sat up all that Saturday night proofreading it so that it would be ready for signing the next day. Minor last-minute changes were arbitrated on Sunday morning, and after lunch Lord Lytton, using a pen made in Japan, and the other commissioners using a pen made in the United States, put their signatures on it. They consigned it to the pouch of a courier who would set out via the Trans-Siberian Railway to carry it the length of Eurasia to the League in Geneva.

The commissioners at once dispersed to leave Peking that very night, some for planes, some for trains, some for steamers—all to reconvene in Geneva three weeks later. Their report was supposed to be entirely secret and was scheduled to be distributed, one copy to the representative of each nation, on September 25, three

weeks later. The very next morning, however, Japanese spokesmen in the Tokyo Foreign Office and War Ministry began to attack the Lytton Report, citing exact references by chapter and
verse. Japanese military intelligence had succeeded in buying a
true carbon of the report from one of the commission's secretaries. It arrived in Tokyo by plane the same Sunday that the
commissioners signed the master copy. There the delicate duty of
reading it quickly and writing a fair report on its salient features
for perusal by the Emperor and his chief vassals devolved upon
the chief of the War Ministry's Press Relations' Squad, Colonel
Honma Masaharu.

A close friend and perennial aide-de-camp of Hirohito's brother
Chichibu, Honma had become fluent in English with the British
army of occupation in Cologne in 1919–20, as an assistant attaché
in London in 1921–22, and as an attaché to India in 1922–25. So
thoroughly had he imbibed British ways that he was known to his
fellow officers as "the linguist with the red nose." Subsequently, in
1937, he became director of the Intelligence Department in the
Army General Staff, a post which he occupied throughout the
rape of Nanking. He was executed by the United States in 1946
as being responsible for the 1942 Bataan Death March in the
Philippines.

After an all-night effort, Honma turned the last of Lytton's
stylish pages during the gray morning hours of Monday, September 5. Looking at the sheaf of neatly hieroglyphic notes he had
taken, he felt some sense of accomplishment. The Foreign Ministry would not complete its own official résumé and rebuttal of
the Lytton Report for another four weeks. At the same time, his
labors revealed that—as feared—Japanese Army attempts to deceive, impress, and humor Lord Lytton during his tour of Manchuria had failed utterly. The testy peer complained in his report
that "the effect of the police measures adopted was to keep away
witnesses, and many Chinese were frankly afraid of even meeting
members of our staff. . . . Interviews were therefore usually arranged with considerable difficulty and in secrecy. . . . In spite of
these difficulties, we were able to arrange private interviews with
businessmen, bankers, teachers, doctors, police, tradesmen, and
others. . . . We also received over 1,500 written communications;

some delivered by hand, the majority sent by post to different addresses."

The Lytton Report went on unequivocally to deny the various claims which Japan had made to the League in her defense: that China was not an organized state; that Manchuria was not Chinese; that China had no sovereignty there; that the Kwantung Army had acted in self-defense; and that Manchukuo sprang from an indigenous independence movement. Lytton concluded: ". . . without declaration of war, a large area of what was indisputably Chinese territory has been forcibly seized and occupied by the armed forces of Japan and has in consequence of this operation been separated from and declared independent of the rest of China."

THE GREAT WALL BREACHED

On the morning after Colonel Honma's heroic translation effort, a Japanese Foreign Office spokesman announced to Western newsmen that Lord Lytton's findings were "less severe than expected." This was a Japanese way of saying that the report was disappointingly persuasive, and too moderate in tone to give Japan much excuse for righteous indignation. The spokesman added, however, that "Japanese recognition of Manchukuo may modify views at Geneva." By recognizing Manchukuo and giving it diplomatic status, the Foreign Ministry hoped to make the puppet nation legally responsible for its own genesis.

The treaty of recognition between Japan and Manchukuo had been under preparation throughout the writing of the Lytton Report. The Foreign Ministry had taken pains to announce that the treaty would contain "no secret clauses" and that its terms would be "less onerous than those . . . in the U.S. agreements with Cuba and Panama." This was a Japanese way of saying that, instead of clauses, there would be whole separate secret protocols and that they would contain all the onerous terms. The most important secret protocol, duly signed by Puppet Henry, stated flatly that Manchukuo "shall entrust the national defense and maintenance of public peace in the future to your country [Japan], all necessary expenditures for which shall be borne by our country [Manchukuo]."

Hirohito approved the Japan-Manchukuo recognition treaty, secret protocols included, at his regular Wednesday morning meeting with the Privy Council on September 7. The following Tuesday, September 13, he made his approval official at a full dress plenary session of the Privy Council held with great mock solemnity in the magnificent Eastern Hall of the Outer Ceremonial Palace. As at all such special plenary sessions, a full set of minutes was kept and Hirohito sat absolutely mute and motionless before a golden screen on a dais at one end of the room. Below him, arrayed according to their Court rank, at three long tables set vertically to his own little altar, sat the highest ranking princes of the blood,[6] the twenty-six members of the Privy Council and the thirteen ministers of the Cabinet.

The meeting had been carefully rehearsed beforehand. Lord Privy Seal Count Makino had spoken to each of the Privy Councillors and Cabinet ministers who were to "debate" the treaty. All the questions to be asked and answers to be given had been submitted in advance to Hirohito. One of the Privy Councillors asked War Minister Araki of the Strike-North Faction how long Japan would have to support Manchukuo. Araki answered that Manchukuo would be able to defray part of the cost of maintaining the Kwantung Army on its soil by 1933 and after five years of development would be able to pick up the whole of the tab. The spokesman of the Throne persisted, "Is it not possible to obtain payment before the lapse of five years?" Araki replied that the defense of Manchukuo was the defense of Japan and it was therefore "fair and reasonable that Japan bear part of the cost."

Another Privy Councillor, speaking on behalf of the Throne, inquired: "Our relations with other countries may become increasingly eventful; are our Army and Navy ready?"

6 His adult brothers, Prince Chichibu and Prince Takamatsu; the two chiefs of staff, Prince Kanin and Prince Fushimi; and the young fascistic Prince Kaya who was Hirohito's near twin. These five were considered senior princes because they headed traditionally important collateral houses of the imperial family. Later in his reign Hirohito would raise ten other members of the family to senior princely status, thereby making them eligible to sit on the Privy Council and pack it if the necessity ever arose.

"Always," responded Araki—and went on to orate at length on the fighting spirit of the men in the armed services.

Finally the foreign minister, surrounded by a half circle of sleek, reticent aides who attended Big Brother Kido's Eleven Club meetings, presented the clinching arguments. If Japan recognized Manchukuo as a sovereign state, the foreign minister said, it would be entitled to send an observer to the League of Nations and could take responsibility in its own right for having seceded from China. Moreover, said the foreign minister, he wished to put into the palace record copies of historical documents which showed that Manchuria had not been originally a province of China and that it had first come under the rule of Peking as a part of the dowry of an ancient Manchu princess, Ai Chin-lo.

The proceedings had come to an end. The Privy Council voted unanimously for recognition of Manchukuo. Hirohito was satisfied that the amenities had been observed and that others had taken the necessary responsibility. He nodded his approval and withdrew to the Inner Palace. There, in the comfort of his Imperial Library, he formally sanctioned the treaty and its attached protocols by affixing to them his Grand Seal of State.

Japan's recognition of Manchukuo was announced to the world on September 15, 1932. It was coupled with a rumor, leaked to Western embassies in Tokyo by foreign ministry spokesmen, that an Araki war-party resolution for the immediate conquest of China's next province, the poppy province of Jehol, had been narrowly voted down in Hirohito's inner circle of advisors. Although not usually considered part of Manchuria, poppy-growing Jehol was indisputably Manchu, for it was the original tribal land of the Manchu dynasty which had usurped the Dragon Throne of China in 1644. In fact, until the abdication of the Boy Emperor, Puppet Henry, in 1912, a substantial part of the province had been maintained by Henry's family as a hunting preserve to which the Princes of the Iron Helmet, when they felt themselves growing soft in the luxuries of Peking, would periodically withdraw in order to lead again their ancestors' tough life on horseback.

Japan could and would make good on its threat against Jehol, and the League could not and would not offer any effective military opposition. Yet League members, in a fashion incomprehensible to many Japanese, failed utterly to make any concessions because of the threat. The depression-plagued United States, which had bugled the world to take note of Japan's aggression, underwent a general election. On November 8, 1932, Franklin D. Roosevelt won a landslide victory and Hoover's secretary of state, Henry Stimson, who had played a major role in challenging Japan, became a lame duck.

During the American election campaign, the ubiquitous Lieutenant Colonel Suzuki conducted an embassy for Hirohito to Chiang Kai-shek. In a private house in Peking he met with one of Chiang's intimates, a former Chinese foreign minister, Huang Fu. Through Huang, Suzuki informed Chiang that Hirohito was losing patience with him. Chiang's representative in Geneva was doing his utmost to embarrass Japan before the League of Nations, and Chiang's protégé, the former Manchurian war lord, Chang Hsueh-liang, persisted in harassing the Kwantung Army by guerrilla activities. Huang Fu told Suzuki that Chiang had no political option except to put on a good show for the Chinese press at Geneva and that, as for young Chang Hsueh-liang, he was a law unto himself. Suzuki replied, "In that case, if the League vote goes against us, we will feel compelled to eliminate the threat of Chang Hsueh-liang on our flank by conquering the province of Jehol."

Former Foreign Minister Huang pointed out that Jehol lay along the northern side of the Great Wall of China and that if the Great Wall was threatened Chiang might have no political alternative to war. Suzuki knew that the Great Wall was a symbolic barrier of great importance to most Chinese—the oldest Maginot line in the world. South of it sprawled the old classical heartland of China which had spawned and nurtured an exclusively Chinese civilization until Genghis Khan had breached the Wall A.D. 1227. Begun in the third century B.C. the Wall was one of the greatest engineering feats of ancient man, handily dwarfing the pyramids of Egypt, the hanging gardens of Babylon, or the gigantic funeral barrows of the early Japanese emperors. Two stories high, two chariots wide on top, it ran 1500 miles along the ridges of available mountain ranges from the Tibetan plateau in the west to the Liaotung Gulf of the Pacific in the east. There, where it ran into the sea at Shanhaikwan, it had been perforated by a modern railway tunnel which twice daily let through the Peking-Mukden express.

Suzuki gently reminded the former Chinese foreign minister that the half-baked bricks of the Great Wall already lay in reach of Japanese cannon fire. The recognized boundaries of Manchuria included a narrow finger of coast line which crooked south from the main body of the country, nudging Jehol back from the ocean and just touching the Wall at Shanhaikwan, its seaside terminus. Manchukuo's Kwantung Army already occupied most of this corridor, said Suzuki, and could always push on to Shanhaikwan with a few hours' notice.

Nevertheless, said the Chinese former foreign minister, Japanese occupation of Jehol would expose hundreds of miles of the Wall to possible Japanese penetration and would force Chiang Kai-shek, out of honor, to adopt the undesirable course of all-out war.

"The Japanese Army does not shrink from all-out war," said Suzuki, "but no one enjoys fighting with his brother. If Chiang Kai-shek will redouble his efforts to silence anti-Japanese voices in China, exterminating the Communist bandits of Mao Tse-tung and removing the young war lord Chang Hsueh-liang from his councils, then the Emperor of Japan will undertake to prevent Japanese troops from forcing their way through the Great Wall after their conquest of Jehol. This is the Emperor's promise and I can add to it nothing except the renewed hope that Japan and China will someday share as brothers in dominion over Asia."

The former Chinese foreign minister communicated Suzuki's message to Chiang Kai-shek, and Chiang, as noncommittally as possible, conveyed his acquiescence.

After repeated recesses requested by Japan, the League's central Committee of Nineteen—a body resembling the modern United Nations Security Council—reconvened on November 21, 1932, to consider Lord Lytton's findings. By now the Lytton Report had been circulated in all the major languages, had been exploited as a best-seller by an enterprising Tokyo publisher, and had been officially rebutted as a pack of misunderstandings by the Japanese foreign minister.

The Japanese delegation at Geneva was headed by Matsuoka Yosuke, the imperial cabal's University of Oregon graduate. Earlier that year Matsuoka had handled the Shanghai ngotiations for Hirohito and had then suggested to him that Japan would have little to lose by withdrawing from the League. Now it was a foregone conclusion that Matsuoka would eventually lead Japan out of the League. As long as the other nations were willing to carry on the debate, however, Matsuoka had instructions from Hirohito to play for time. Having served as old Prime-Minister-Maker Saionji's information officer at Versailles after World War I, Matsuoka had some training in the nice diplomacy of procrastination, but he employed it crudely. In addressing the League when it reconvened, he stated categorically, "We want no more territory."

While the League deliberated, the Kwantung Army packed troops and supplies into the narrow seaside corridor along the southeastern frontier of Jehol and advanced slowly down it toward the Great Wall. On December 8, 1932, just nine years before Pearl Harbor, the Japanese vanguard entered the Manchurian half of the town of Shanhaikwan, in the shadow of the Wall. The Chinese defenders on the battlements fired a few shots and caused a few Japanese casualties. That night Secretary-Spy Harada gave a quaint glimpse into the thought processes of a courtier by noting in his diary, "the precedent for the Shanhaikwan Incident has occurred." On Christmas Day, 1932, War Minister Araki of the Strike-North Faction concurred in the threat being made to China and the League by announcing in a public speech: "Any part of Jehol which the Kwantung Army feels forced to occupy in defense of its flank, it will indubitably keep."

The heralded Shanhaikwan Incident duly occurred on January 3, 1933. A Japanese soldier was supposedly hit by a bullet fired from the top of the Great Wall. A Japanese armored train forced its way through the railway tunnel in the darkness of night. A flood of Japanese infantrymen followed, occupying the Chinese half of Shanhaikwan and butchering several thousand Chinese in their nightshirts. The breach opened in the ancient Wall put the Kwantung Army at the head of a rail line that ran straight west across flat farmland, 180 indefensible miles, into the old northern Chinese capital of Peking.

JAPAN AN OUTLAW

Having demonstrated its ability to ravage the whole of north China if necessary, the Kwantung Army withdrew all but skeletal guard units from Shanhaikwan and left Chiang Kai-shek to nurse the wound in China's pride. Later that month, as the League in Geneva neared its final vote, Hirohito approved operational orders for the conquest of Jehol and for the elimination of all Chinese forces which might threaten Japan's corridor to Shanhaikwan. Before affixing his Grand Seal to these orders, Hirohito exacted a solemn promise from Strike-North officers in the War Ministry and General Staff that they would abide by his pledge to Chiang Kai-shek, would not allow troops in the field to pursue Chang Hsueh-liang's levies south of the Great Wall, and would absolutely discourage any attacks on China proper until at least a year had passed after the conclusion of the Jehol campaign. Hirohito had heard that some of the Strike-North idealists hoped to incite the League to intervene in defense of China.

To counter the intrigues of the Strike-North Faction, Hirohito's Lord Privy Seal Count Makino, organized for the first time a semipublic alliance of politicians which held as its express ideal a policy of Strike South. The leaders of the new movement were Big Brother Prince Konoye of the House of Peers and Makino's son-in-law, Yoshida Shigeru, the later World War II Peace Faction leader and postwar prime minister. By arguments unknown, at a Mafia-style meeting on January 24, 1933, Konoye and Yoshida established a rapprochement with Baron Hiranuma, the long-faced lawyer of the monied rightist National Foundation Society and with the conservative wing of Black Dragon Toyama's underworld. Their basic sales slogan was: "First south into China, then await developments." Senior admirals pledged the Navy's support of the new movement.

Up to this time few of the men close to Hirohito had privately supported Strike-South aspirations—much less voiced them in public. The military officers of the cabal, trained in the 1922 palace indoctrination center, had pledged themselves only to break the power of clan leadership in the Army and to make the armed forces modern and formidable. The civilian courtiers and bureaucrats of the Big Brotherhood had a better appreciation of Hirohito's ultimate objectives but thought them too secret and too futuristic to require immediate discussion. Like most Japanese, they feared the possible consequences of a policy which might lead to war with the United States. In the new alliance Count Makino was, in effect, launching a trial balloon. When few politicians rushed to board it, Hirohito let it drift away into the clouds and returned to his old slow tiptoeing style of march.

On February 10, 1933, Hirohito called the philosophizing, cigar-smoking Grand Chamberlain Suzuki Kantaro to the library in the palace woods and told him that Japan was compelled to secede from the League of Nations. Hirohito said that he made the decision reluctantly but that he could see no alternative. The League was almost certain to accept the Lytton Report, asking Japan to withdraw her troops and entrust the preservation of peace in Manchuria to an international police force. Since Japan must reject this proposal, she could not remain in the League as a member in good standing. Grand Chamberlain Suzuki nodded and asked whether withdrawal from the League might not invalidate Japan's title to the islands in the Pacific which had been given her to administer under a League mandate after World War I. Hirohito had a phone call put through to the Foreign Ministry and was reassured that membership in the League was not a precondition for continued rule of the islands. Hirohito then gave his sanction for the Japanese delegation at the League to withdraw when necessary.

On Friday, February 17, in Geneva, the League of Nations' Committee of Nineteen recommended adoption of the Lytton Report to the full League Assembly and issued its own 15,000-word summary of the case against Japan. The summary was broadcast to the world at large in a ten-hour shortwave transmission in Morse code. *The New York Times* made journalistic history by transcribing the broadcast and reprinting it in its entirety the next morning.

That same day the Japanese Cabinet met to consider officially the League question. Prime Minister Saito held out against withdrawal and the Cabinet had to make one of its rare non-unanimous reports to the Throne. Hirohito instructed Prime Minister Saito to accept the majority view and to notify Matsuoka in Geneva to lead Japan out of the League as soon as the vote went against him.

On Tuesday, February 24, the full League Assembly met at the Palais des Nations on the shores of Lake Geneva to consider endorsement of the Committee of Nineteen's acceptance of Lord Lytton's judgment against Japan. The Chinese delegate delivered a rambling academic paean in praise of Lytton's objectivity. Matsuoka spoke well and forcefully on the proposition that China was not an organized nation, could not be represented by a delegate from Chiang Kai-shek's Nanking government, and deserved no more real jurisdiction in Manchuria than Egypt enjoyed in Suez or Panama in the Canal Zone.

Finally the issue was put to a vote and the clerk called the roll. The delegates of forty-five of the fifty-five member-nations were present. All were entitled by League rules to have their votes counted except for the two "disputing parties," China and Japan. As the roll proceeded, the morning mist cleared from the lake outside and the sun shone through into the windows. One by one the delegates arose and said, *Oui*—"Yes, we accept Lord Lytton's findings."

"China, disputing party," called the clerk.

"*Oui*," responded the Chinese delegate.

More ayes followed uninterruptedly until the clerk called, "Japan, disputing party."

Matsuoka arose, turned slowly, sweeping his fellow delegates with a dramatic look of hurt, and shouted, "No!"

The ayes continued to have it unanimously until the clerk called on the delegate of Siam, the only other nation in the Orient which was not in whole or in part a colony of the West. "Siam," said the Thai in a modulated voice, "has been a friend of Japan since the fifteenth century. Siam abstains." The remaining delegates, from Spain to Venezuela, all voted against Japan with a simple aye.

Since abstainers and disputants were not counted, Japan had been condemned forty-two to nothing. The Assembly president noted that Japan had chosen "to follow her own policy into isolation." Matsuoka strode to the rostrum and read a brisk brief statement of farewell. "With profound regret," he said, "the Japanese government are obliged to feel they have now reached the limits of their endeavors to co-operate with the League regarding the Sino-Japanese differences." He added loudly, "I want to thank the League members." Then he walked purposefully down the center aisle, and as he passed his seat, beckoned to his fellow Japanese delegates to follow him. Many of the Japanese in the room had hoped that he would wait for a translation break and make his exit less dramatically, but at his summons they all arose—not only from the official Japanese benches but from the galleries as well. A single member of the Japanese delegation remained in his seat; he was a hired American consultant, a former *New York Times* correspondent and future State Department advisor, Frederick Moore.

In the lobby, staring out through the trees toward the lake, Matsuoka thrust an unlighted cigar into his mouth and talked loudly to assembled newsmen until his car came for him. That afternoon, Japan being absent, the League Assembly voted to implement Lord Lytton's report by asking all member and affiliate nations to refrain from recognizing Manchukuo "*de jure* or *de facto.*"

POPPY PROVINCE

As they voted, the members of the League knew that, at that moment, the Japanese were invading Jehol, China's poppy province. The campaign had been in preparation for weeks. Four days before the vote, on Friday, February 20, an American correspondent had reported that the railway between Mukden and the Jehol border was choked with military traffic; that trainloads of motorcycles and American trucks could be seen on every siding; that he was reminded of France in 1918. The attack had been scheduled to begin after the League voted against Japan—if it did. But China's Chang Hsueh-liang and Japan's Strike-North Faction wanted to make sure that the League would not honey its words at the last moment, and so hostilities had been provoked by both sides on February 21, three days early. The Kwantung Army high command overreacted by occupying all the railheads of eastern Jehol overnight. The next morning, Sunday, the invasion made headlines throughout the world. Hirohito was furious.

On Monday, with some loss of face, War Minister Araki of the Strike-North Faction announced, "Actually Japan's campaign is not yet underway." While Japanese troops sought to guard the railway stations they had taken in eastern Jehol without seeming too conspicuous about being there at all, an ultimatum was served on China demanding instant withdrawal of Chang Hsueh-liang's forces from Jehol because they were "incompatible . . . with the sovereignty of Manchukuo." Nanking rejected the ultimatum early on Tuesday the twenty-fourth, hours before the delegates at Geneva met to cast their ballots. When Matsuoka left his seat in the council hall, Japanese soldiers had already been up for hours, fighting and dying eagerly after their two days of restraint.

Despite the farce of the false start, the Jehol campaign was no laughing matter. Western military attachés who accompanied the Japanese troops were not particularly impressed by the four-to-one numerical superiority of Chang Hsueh-liang's rabble. But they were impressed by the cold rugged terrain of the battle-ground, and they foresaw a long and arduous campaign for the Japanese invaders. In the event they were confounded and embarrassed in their professional forecasts by the almost inhuman discipline and efficiency of the Japanese in the field. To cut down on the weight they would carry, the Japanese foot soldiers advanced through the cruel February weather without greatcoats and with only nominal supply packs. They kept warm by marching without pause from town to town, twenty-four hours, thirty-six hours, even forty-eight hours at a stretch. It was a *dengeki sakusen* or lightning-strike campaign—what the Germans would later make famous as *Blitzkrieg*.

In nine days Chang Hsueh-liang's forces had been routed and all the strong points of Jehol—a province the size of Pennsylvania, or of Belgium-Holland-Denmark—had been occupied. On the tenth day, March 5—the day that Hitler won a majority in the Reichstag—Japanese waitresses were serving food in Tungliao, the Jehol capital. Most serious from Chiang Kai-shek's point of view, Shanhaikwan had been reoccupied in force and the Great Wall breached at several other points besides. The whole of north China—a million square miles, two hundred million people—lay defenseless and the samurai sword hung over it by a slender thread of restraint.

Western military attachés admired the curt brilliance of Japan's conquest of Jehol and the nations of the League did their best to ignore it. Hirohito followed it up in March by assigning the Special Service Organ's "Lawrence of Manchuria," Major General Doihara, to the task of buying Chinese leaders throughout north China and Mongolia and sponsoring them to found their own regimes autonomous of Nanking. Doihara's assistant, the huge Major Tanaka who had helped girl spy Eastern Jewel provoke the Fake War in Shanghai a year earlier, was sent to Inner Mongolia where he succeeded in establishing an independent government under the chieftainship of the Mongol Prince Teh, known in the yurts of his tribesmen as Demchukdongrub. Eastern Jewel herself was in Jehol in breeches, somewhat disappointed that she had not been allowed to participate in its conquest, but altogether in her element as the "general" of 5,000 Manchu roughriders. Her captains, all selected on the criterion of physique rather than tactical genius, accepted her embarrassing leadership and humored her indefatigable sexuality because she paid them regularly with Kwantung Army gold.

Chiang Kai-shek was left to negotiate the best peace that he could. In April and May, the Kwantung Army twice impugned Hirohito's word to Chiang by sending foraging expeditions beyond the Great Wall to ravage in the north China farmlands. Hirohito angrily dispatched the Strike North's Vice Chief of Staff Mazaki to the front to put a stop to such adventurism. Mazaki accomplished his mission and Araki apologized to the Throne, but Hirohito never forgave either of the Strike-North leaders for their insubordination.

On May 31, 1933, Chiang Kai-shek's representative and Major General Okamura, the third of Hirohito's Baden-Baden Three Crows, signed a document known as the Tangku Truce. By its provisions, Jehol was ceded de facto to Japan and, more shameful, 5,000 square miles of the densely populated triangle south of the

Great Wall, vertexed by Shanhaikwan, Peking, and Tientsin, became a "demilitarized zone." In the zone Chinese were left no rights but those of civil drudgery, and the Japanese soldiers were given all rights and no duties or responsibilities.

Hirohito announced his success to the warrior spirits of the dead by a state visit to Tokyo's Yasukuni shrine. To the living he issued a rescript explaining, with many lofty sentiments, that Japan had been forced to withdraw from the comity of nations because the West misunderstood Japan's goal of keeping peace in the Orient. He emphasized in the rescript that Japan would continue to co-operate with the League in technical matters such as international control of health and currencies. Finally, to reassure the people as to the conduct of statecraft in the future, he formed a "diplomatic general staff" in the palace.

When old Prime-Minister-Maker Saionji heard of these measures, he shook his bald head gloomily. Nothing, he said, could disguise the fact that Japan had now become an outcast among nations. The new "diplomatic general staff," he feared, would prove as dangerous as the old military general staffs. As to the hypocrisy of the imperial rescript of explanation, Saionji was scathing.

"The same old cant," he fumed. " 'Peace in the Orient, peace in the Orient!' That's what he keeps repeating, but just by wanting peace in the Orient, how will that further goals such as world peace? Better talk first of wanting things in the style of world peace and the welfare of mankind, and then peace in the East, as an attainable goal, will ultimately follow. Standing up at the start and just braying 'Peace in the East'—will it get us domestic peace or what? It's an awful funny way to talk."

PART FIVE

❧

DISCIPLINING
THE LEGIONS

17

NORTH OR SOUTH?

(1933–1934)

PSHAW!

George Bernard Shaw, a well-known seventy-seven-year-old Anglo-Irish playwright, arrived in the Orient on Sunday, February 22, 1933, at the height of the League-Jehol crisis. At his first press conference in Peking he said, "If all the thirty million Chinese in Manchuria were to become nationalists in the Irish way, the Manchurian problem would be solved." Having thus questioned the sincerity of Chinese patriotism, he turned to Japan: "There is a Japanese soldier pointing a rifle at every Chinese inhabitant, but keeping down nationalism is like sitting on a horse's head—there's no time to do anything else."

A week later G.B.S. arrived in Japan. "I detest all sports," he told a Japanese sports reporter. "They cause bad manners and ill feeling. International sports meetings sow seeds of war." Commenting on the Jehol campaign two days later, he said: "The European war was imperialistic, yet it led to the disappearance of three empires. Have you in Japan ever thought that in your imperialistic aims you may end as a republic, and that that is not at all what your rulers want? European imperialists, or what is left of them, would give their eyes for the return of 1914." He went on to urge Japan to adopt birth control. "There is no reason," he said, "why Japan should continue to expand and demand the right to overthrow other countries which naturally resent an influx of a lower civilization."

For a week Shaw cut a swathe through Japan, inveighing impartially at "the horrors of modern cities of which Japanese are so proud" and at "the futility of war, patriotism, and the League of Nations." Then, on his last day in Tokyo, March 8, Shaw met his match in a two-hour interview with the golden-tongued War Minister Araki of the Strike-North Faction. Araki seized on the occasion to lay a counterintelligence smokescreen for Japan's biological warfare research, sponsored by Hirohito and Empress Nagako's late father, Prince Kuni.

"I understand," said Araki, "that European countries are studying the use of bacteria for warfare."

"I'm not scared of bacteria, Your Excellency, but of bombs," said Shaw. "When bombs are dropped, children have to run away."

"We in Japan," observed Araki, "lack money for advanced weapons so we feel that the most economic way is to fight sixty million strong with bamboo spears."

"I'm lazy and a coward," resumed Shaw, "so lazy I wouldn't even run to a bomb shelter. I tremble at the sound of guns but find it too boring to go to the basement."

"Laziness," declared Araki, "is courage. You have the enlightenment of *Zen*. I regret that you have never seen an earthquake. No one who is not lazy can live in Japan. An earthquake is both a catastrophe and a form of religious enlightenment for the national spirit. There are no sirens blown to warn of earthquakes. We have only to think of an earthquake here in Japan and we are no longer afraid of air raids."

"If you had been born in Russia," rejoined Shaw, at the end of the conversation, "you would have become a politician greater than Stalin. . . . I would like to stay here talking to you until the Chinese land on the Japanese mainland."

THE STRIKE-NORTH LEADER

War Minister Araki was a tiny, agile man with a narrow, sensitive face and a huge handlebar mustache. During 1932 and early 1933, he had emerged as the only Japanese leader who could stand up against Hirohito. Constitutionalist party politicians, Strike-North idealists in the Army officer corps, cosmopolitan aristocrats in the circle of old Prime-Minister-Maker Saionji, and many businessmen and underworld leaders were all willing to bury their differences in support of his droll, well-meaning political genius.

Araki opposed Hirohito's increasingly explicit Strike-South ambitions because he saw in them the possibility of a suicidal war with the United States. To save Japan from this fate he prescribed a different war in which he foresaw less chance of disaster: a war with the Soviet Union. He specifically proposed to begin it in 1936. A mystical notion that 1936 would be a turning point in the history of Japan had entered the prophetic writings of Dr. Okawa and other intellectuals of the spy service as far back as 1918. By 1933 it held a secure place in the apocalyptic dogma of all true rightists. There was a '36 club and a '36 magazine for Army reservists. Araki could expatiate on the importance of '36 for hours at a stretch. His exploitation of the prophecy was not entirely tongue in cheek nor entirely madness. According to the best intelligence projections of comparative military buildup, Japan would have a better chance of defeating Russia in 1936 than in any of the years just before or after.

Araki's hostility to Russia was professional and deep. He had served as a major in Japanese Intelligence in Russia from 1909 to 1913. He had read *Das Kapital* and begun inveighing against the threat of Bolshevism years before the Russian Revolution. He was convinced that Hirohito was blind to the Marxist menace and had tried in many audiences during 1932 to open Hirohito's eyes. Hirohito, however, trusted his favorite economic advisor, Finance Minister Takahashi Korekiyo. Brilliant, unorthodox, and unscrupulous, the seventy-six-year-old Takahashi was years ahead of his times as a Keynesian economist. His suggestions had been largely responsible for bringing Japan through the world depression with money to spare for armaments. He gave it as his expert opinion that Bolshevism in Russia could not survive once Russia had developed heavy industry and a need for capitalistic complexities.

Hirohito was disposed to believe Takahashi. In Hirohito's personal view Bolshevism could not be compared to Shinto as a national religion. It had no stable leadership group like the Japanese aristocracy. It was merely an economic phase in the growth of a nation which Hirohito felt to be fundamentally flawed by racial impurity and a mixed half-Occidental, half-Oriental culture.

In opposing Hirohito, War Minister Araki relied outwardly on his charm and his ability to persuade. Inwardly, however, he relied on a file which he had been keeping on Hirohito since the early 1920's. To his death in 1967, he always kept the file at his side. He hinted that every paper in it had been photostatted and a copy sent in a sealed envelope to a trustworthy friend. In the event of his untimely death the envelopes were to be opened and their contents circulated. The unopened strongbox is still in the keeping of Araki's family. His nephews consider it a talisman which continues to bring them prosperity.

Araki had begun his file in April 1921 when he was made chief of the Europe-America Section in the Intelligence Department of the Army General Staff. In this capacity he had access to the coded cables from all the young military attachés whom Hirohito was meeting at embassies during his crown-princely tour. Araki had continued to add to his file as commandant of the secret police during Hirohito's purge of the Choshu clan from the Army in 1925. In 1928 at the time of the assassination of Manchurian war lord Chang Tso-lin, Araki had first realized that his ideals differed from Hirohito's and had first gathered his papers together in a portable strongbox.

He founded a club and an employment agency for purged Choshu clan veterans and was shunted into various sidings of honor and impotence in the Army bureaucracy. Nevertheless, his following grew. He won the admiration of disaffected Strike-Northists from Hirohito's cabal. He returned from the twilight of a military career to high noon as an Army politician. At the age of fifty-four, in December 1931, he became war minister in the Cabinet of the ill-fated Prime Minister Inukai. Still war minister in 1933—"too popular to be dispensed with," as Hirohito's Big Brothers acknowledged—he had become Hirohito's last domestic adversary.

RED SMEAR

When Araki crossed wits with G.B.S., he had just begun to feel powerful enough to challenge Hirohito in public. It had been his henchmen in the field who had embarrassed Hirohito by crossing the Great Wall during the Jehol campaign. And earlier, in January, during the debate about withdrawing from the League, Araki had mounted a domestic offensive against the Throne—one so thoroughly devious that Japanese politicians suspected in it the cunning stage direction of old Saionji and Western observers completely missed the point. The attack began when a moss-backed old baron, a friend of Araki, announced in the House of Peers that the law faculty of Kyoto Imperial University was riddled with Reds and fellow travelers.

To Westerners the accusation sounded like a typical rightist smear, violating academic freedom of conscience. To Japanese, however, who did not believe in individual conscience, it had a different ring. Kyoto University was the alma mater of Big Brother Prince Konoye, of Big Brother Marquis Kido, and of Secretary-Spy Baron Harada. In their undergraduate days, during World War I, it had been a hotbed of Marxist study and discussion. There, they had first conceived the strange synthetic form of government toward which Hirohito was leading Japan: a parliamentary Marxist theocracy; a monolithic, one-party super-tribe built on racism; a cartel of cartels held together by a gigantic police protection racket. As this misbegotten creature of the intellectual elite, combining all the worst features of East and West, began to take concrete shape, the public had every reason to hold the university responsible.

If mobs had razed the university, Araki and Saionji would have chuckled at the irony of it, for Kyoto's Big-Brother graduates had made academic freedom a mockery. They had made fear of entertaining dangerous thoughts second only to fear of committing lèse majesté. Public peace legislation sponsored by Prince Konoye in the late 1920's had already stripped most universities of their truly independent thinkers. One by one most of the Marxists, trade-unionists, and Fabian socialists, and many even of the apologists for democratic voting procedures had gone quietly into retirement where they were kept under polite police surveillance. Only the faculties of the Kyoto and Tokyo Imperial universities had survived unscathed and that largely because of the personal ties between the professors and Hirohito's courtiers.

To stop Araki's witch hunt before it gained momentum, the police immediately picked up the one subversive thinker at Kyoto University, professor emeritus Kawakami Hajime. Economist Kawakami had translated *Das Kapital* into Japanese and years ago had taught Konoye, Kido, and Harada all they knew about Marxism. Since his forced retirement in 1928, Kawakami had turned increasingly left and professed to be a Communist. Now he was charged with dangerous thoughts and clapped under house arrest. He remained virtually a prisoner until his death in 1946, thirteen years later.

The police followed on February 20, 1933, with their first wholesale roundup of leftists since March 1928. All the pinks and cranks who had been released after earlier mass arrests were reinterrogated and made to reveal the names of any new recruits to leftist movements.

The prompt action of the police convinced Araki and his allies that their attack on Court thinking would have to take a subtler twist. In March, a month after the arrests, one was devised by an Araki partisan at Keio University. The Keio professor began innocently by attacking a Kyoto law professor for holding the unorthodox Tolstoyan view that adultery should be considered a crime. The Kyoto law professor happened to be the leader of a seven-man economic brain trust of Prince Konoye, including the prince's favorite teacher and six of his former school friends.[1] Swallowing the bait, the seven at once banded together to ridicule the Keio professor for his old-fashioned anti-feminism.

When all the old-fashioned men and women of Japan were thoroughly amused and interested, the Keio professor abruptly lobbed toward Kyoto an intellectual shell of larger caliber. He charged that the seven professors in Kyoto were guilty of the her-

[1] Sasaki Soichi, Suekawa Hiroshi, Tsuneto Kyo, Miyamoto Hideo, Tamura Tokuji, Moriguchi Shigeji, and Takikawa Yukitoki.

esy of believing the Emperor an "organ or mechanical component of the state."

Whether the Emperor was a part of the state or whether he transcended the state had been argued by scholars of Constitutional law ever since Emperor Taisho's abortive attempt to be dictator in 1912. Hirohito personally had accepted the theory that he was an organ and could delegate all responsibility for his decisions to other, lesser organs. Indeed his publicists maintained that he was hardly more than an automatic rubber stamp. Theologically, however, Hirohito encouraged the idea that he was the Zeus in the Shinto pantheon of great spirits. Araki's learned friend at Keio University implied that it was sacrilege for the Emperor to hide himself as an "organ" and so shirk his true responsibility as a god. Hirohito's spirit, he insisted, was the state, and the spirit of the state was Hirohito. As the living god and the high priest of the dead gods, Hirohito must strive to *be* his nation and not merely to *lead* it.

To make his point crystal clear, the Keio professor coupled his attack on the Kyoto professors with slurs against the two spy-service faithfuls being held by the police, the owner of the Blood Brotherhood's Empty House, whom he termed "disloyal" and "communistic," and Dr. Okawa, the factotum of Hirohito's Lord Privy Seal Makino, whom he termed "impure and Darwinistic in his observance of Shinto." Whatever the other adjectives meant in the peculiar Japanese dialectic of those days, "Darwinistic" clearly referred to the beliefs of the biologist on the Throne.

The Keio professor's charges represented the sort of delicately snide dangerous thinking that all Japanese belly talkers appreciated. At Araki's urging the minister of education, Hatoyama Ichiro, was soon threatening Kyoto University with suspension of its government subsidies unless the seven "organ theorists" were discharged. For two months Hirohito and Konoye encouraged the Kyoto University administration to stand behind the professors, but ultimately, unwilling to come forth from behind their curtains, Hirohito and Konoye sanctioned an accommodation for the seven professors which gave them all new research posts at better salaries in other institutions.

INCREDULOUS EMPEROR

When Araki began his campaign against the Throne in March 1933, Hirohito was at first loath to believe that he was being opposed intentionally. The Eleven Club held a meeting to discuss how best to teach him "the realities of the existing situation." For his part Hirohito decided that he needed an intermediary to deal with Araki. Therefore, on April 6, 1933, he took into the palace a hero of the Strike-North Faction to serve as his chief aide-de-camp. This was Lieutenant General Honjo, the conqueror of Manchuria. He remained at Hirohito's side for exactly three years and sixteen days, and throughout this period he kept an intimate diary record of his conversations with Hirohito.[2] When he arrived in the palace he believed Hirohito to be an innocent young god who needed guidance through the maze of reality. When he left in 1936, he knew Hirohito to be as tough and cynical as any colonel or general of the secret police. From his diary emerges a clear picture of the struggle between Hirohito and the Strike-North Faction which occupied the next three years.

During Lieutenant General Honjo's first week in the palace, Hirohito laid down a book he had been reading on European history and mused pointedly: "The first half of Napoleon's life contributed to the welfare of France, but in the second half of his life Napoleon worked only for his own honor. The result was not good either for France or for the world." By this parable, Hirohito meant to enlist Honjo's help in persuading the Strike-North Faction to leave the direction of Japan's next strike to Hirohito and give Japan a few years of domestic political peace in which to fulfill her ambitious armaments program.

Despite Hirohito's suggestion, the Strike-North Faction continued to embarrass Japan by making raids south of the Great Wall. Hirohito sent the number-two Strike-North leader, Vice

[2] Only a carefully censored 13 per cent of the diary has yet been published in Japan. It came out in 1967, in a limited edition, through a tiny publishing house, largely, I believe, as a result of my own personal representations. The remaining 87 per cent of the diary is kept under lock and key in the Historical Section of Japan's modern Self-Defense Forces.

Chief of Staff Lieutenant General Mazaki Jinzaburo, personally to the front to restore discipline. While Mazaki was gone, the Big Brothers succeeded in explaining to Hirohito the grim reality of the Strike-North Faction's opposition to him.

As soon as Mazaki returned from the front in late April 1933, Hirohito's scheming uncle, Lieutenant General Prince Higashikuni, accused Mazaki of trying to exercise improper influence on the Throne. According to Higashikuni's own account, Mazaki came to him one day and ordered him, as a subordinate in the Army chain of command, to use his influence with Hirohito in favor of a Strike North.

Higashikuni replied, "I cannot do such a thing. The Emperor has always looked at the whole picture, sanctioning some requests and refusing others. So I cannot obey you even if you issue me orders."

A week later Prince Higashikuni charged that Mazaki was trying to subvert the servants in Higashikuni's own imperial villa. Another week later, in May 1933, Hirohito retired Vice Chief of Staff Mazaki from office, promoted him to general, and moved him up out of harm's way to the Supreme War Council.

On May 21, 1933, before the decision to repost Mazaki had been made public, Hirohito's popular younger brother, Prince Chichibu, came to the palace to plead Mazaki's cause and to ask Hirohito to reconsider his entire domestic program. He urged his elder brother to give up the pretense of being an organ of government, to tear down the veils around the Throne, to assume direct command of the nation, and if need be, to suspend the Constitution. Hirohito refused, and privileged courtiers later reported that the two brothers "had a hot argument." Afterward Hirohito told one of the courtiers: "I will reserve my absolute power in governing the nation for important matters, maintaining constantly a large view for over-all trends. As for suspending the Constitution, that would be to destroy an institution established by Emperor Meiji, which is absolutely unthinkable."

The next day Hirohito sent Big Brothers Kido and Konoye to Chichibu's villa to have a two-and-a-half hour talk with the wayward prince.

ARAKI'S BIG PLAY

In the next few days War Minister Araki made the grand gesture of his career by mounting a carefully planned political blitz calculated to commit Hirohito to war against Russia in 1936.

On Wednesday, May 24, Araki expanded the earlier Red smear by announcing that members of the imperial family were falling under the spell of the red witchcraft at Marxist study seminars held at the Peers' School. The charge was serious because it was true. For generations imperial family members had been expected to inform themselves on all shades of political opinion. The pink of the modern left was no exception, and Empress Nagako's own brother, Prince Higashi-Fushimi, was deeply tinted and tainted by his researches in it.

On Friday, May 26, War Minister Araki persuaded the minister of education to order Kyoto Imperial University to suspend the chief of the seven professors in Konoye's brain trust who subscribed to the Emperor-Organ theory.

On Saturday, May 27, the leading strategists of the Army met at 3d Division Headquarters in Nagoya, on the road between Kyoto and Tokyo, to decide what nation to recommend to Hirohito as "enemy number one."

Surprised by Araki's swift sequence of blows, Hirohito detailed Marquis Kido to study countermeasures against the expanded Red smear and his uncle Higashikuni to watch the proceedings in Nagoya. In the crisis Hirohito left the Kyoto University administration to fend for itself.

ENEMY NUMBER ONE

The meeting of Army brass in Nagoya had been billed as a table-top maneuver, a routine annual—and sometimes semiannual —exercise which did not require the Emperor's express sanction but was merely reported to him. This year it lasted for a week and Lieutenant General Prince Higashikuni sat in as the mute representative of the imperial family.

The Nagoya headquarters of the 3d Division lay a few blocks

from the shrine which housed the sacred sword, one of the three treasures in Japan's imperial regalia. The offices were as modern as any in Japan. No delicate white matting forced the attending staff officers to take off their boots and remember their heritage. They marched in, sat down at desks, and reached for telephones when they wanted detailed information from their staffs in Tokyo.

The Strike-North position was represented by War Minister Araki and an overwhelming majority of the other officers present. They pushed forward chart after chart showing that Japan would have provocation, international backing, and a reasonable chance of success if it attempted to seize Siberia in 1936. They left most of the presentation of their case to Major General Obata, the second of the Three Crows of Baden-Baden. He had long been "one of the Emperor's men" and few of the junior Army bureaucrats present knew that he and Hirohito were now at odds.

Hirohito's own wishes were represented at the exercises—somewhat half-heartedly—by First Crow Major General Nagata, who was now chief of the General Staff's Intelligence Department. Nagata spoke from memoranda which had been drawn up for him by his disciple and chief assistant at the conference, Major General Tojo, the later World War II prime minister. It was Tojo's strategy to conceal his faction's objective of a Strike South and to plead instead for a policy of "Reorganize China first, then Japan."

Nagata and Tojo argued that Japan could never attack any Western nation, even Russia, without being prepared to confront and face down all the other Western nations. Japan must, therefore, be able to call on the resources of all the yellow race and must be "mobilized for total war." This meant that China and her 500 million inhabitants must stand behind Japan's samurai as a vast work battalion and that Manchuria's resources and Japan's own factories must submit to a complete "industrial rationalization." Such a program, insisted Nagata, could not be completed by 1936. It would take years merely to infiltrate, subvert, and reorganize China. Then would follow the Herculean labor of domestic renovation. During these years of preparation, he said, Japanese should not even talk of attacking the Soviet Union. On the contrary the first order of business was to negotiate a nonaggression pact with the Soviet Union which would keep Russia on the sidelines until China and Japan were both sufficiently "rationalized."

The Strike-North Faction of Araki allowed Nagata, on behalf of the Emperor, to lead the proceedings up to a vote on this non-aggression pact with Russia. Then Araki made one short speech and the pact was voted down. Araki immediately called for a second vote resolving that the assembled staff officers of the Japanese Army should advise Hirohito that the "enemy number one" was not China but Russia. The resolution was passed by an overwhelming majority, and Nagata, Tojo, and one other general were left together talking in a corner.[3]

This juncture of the table-top exercises was reached on the seventh day, June 2. As soon as the vote was cast, the silent observer, Lieutenant General Prince Higashikuni, left the meeting and took a train to Okitsu where he paid a call at the seaside villa of old Prince Saionji who was widely believed to be backing Araki in his intransigence. Emerging from the presence of the venerable statesman, Higashikuni announced to the press that he and Saionji were perfectly agreed that war with Russia, the United States, or any other nation must be avoided at all costs. Then Higashikuni hastened home to the palace in Tokyo to report to Hirohito and prepare a counterplot against the Army's unwelcome advice.

MUD TO BURY MUD

Hirohito politely tabled the Army's recommendation that Russia be considered enemy number one. In the meantime, in hopes of turning the Red smear against Araki's own hidden patrons, Big Brother Kido, secretary to the lord privy seal, was conducting an exhaustive research into Communist influence on all members of the Japanese aristocracy. On June 3, the day after Prince Higashikuni had left the table-top maneuvers in Nagoya, Kido played a game of golf with one of his son's friends, Saionji Kinkazu, the twenty-seven-year-old grandson of the prime-minister-maker, begot by the daughter of the old man's first and favorite geisha mistress. The ambitious young Saionji was weary of his grand-

---

[3] The ubiquitous Suzuki and other leading Strike-South officers were away in China signing the Tangku Truce which concluded the seizure of Jehol.

father's liberalism, disillusioned by his grandfather's defeats, and eager to find new political creeds for Japan. He had come home from Oxford University in 1930 with a degree in politics and economics, and had associated since with a variety of aristocratic intellectuals, most of them left-wing.

Between putts on the greens and again in the club house later in the afternoon, the forty-four-year-old Kido drew out the young nobleman with casual questions. Young Saionji responded freely, taking iconoclastic delight in showing Kido how widely Marxism, individualism, and other dangerous thoughts had spread through the establishment's hereditary leadership.

In the next week, following up the leads which young Saionji had given him, Kido received a liberal education in the political left. He was made to glimpse the world of *To-a Dobun,* the East Asia All-One-Culture University founded by Prince Konoye's father, Atsumaro, in 1901 in Shanghai. There Japan's spy-service intellectuals and aspiring scholars of the Chinese classics had shared desks and lockers and enthusiasms with a motley assortment of nationalists and revolutionaries from other Asian nations—followers of Sun Yat-sen, Gandhi, U Nu, and Mao Tse-tung, the best and brightest, worst and shrewdest outcasts of Western colonialism.

The students at the East Asia All-One-Culture University learned as freshmen to recognize plainclothes operatives of the Western consular police, of the Russian Comintern, of the Japanese Spy Service, and of Chiang Kai-shek's gestapo, the Blue Shirts. Off campus, at the *Zeitgeist* Bookstore, subsidized by the donations of German and Russian Communists, the students fraternized with *apparatchiki* from all over the world who crossed paths there to swap dialectic parables and occasional packets of money and microfilm.

At the *Zeitgeist* Bookstore, the mannish, eccentric, determined Missouri-born journalist Agnes Smedley, one of the earliest apologists for Mao Tse-tung, held court with Indian intellectuals and boys from the Bronx. There a man named Johnson, alias Richard Sorge—now famous as the Russian agent whose Tokyo spy ring would play an influential part (described later in this book) during the final fateful years before Pearl Harbor—widened his journalistic acquaintance with Chinese and Japanese intellectuals. There Ozaki Hotsumi, the only important traitor Japan would ever have to acknowledge, got to know Agnes Smedley and was introduced by her to Richard Sorge of whose spy ring he would later become the main cog.

Kido—though of course he learned little of these prophetic details—sopped up the atmosphere of Shanghai's cosmopolitan spy world with fascination. At the same time, in his usual business-like fashion, he compiled a roster of aristocrats who were allies of old Saionji or the Strike-North Faction and could be tarred with Araki's own brush. He found that the House of Peers' outspokenly capitalistic Baron Inoue Kiyozumi had a niece who was a fellow traveler. Count Yoshii Isamu, a poet who wrote paeans in praise of individualism, had a wife who collected literary men of extreme opinions and entertained them not only in her salon but also in her bedroom.[4]

Most important, Secretary Kido unearthed political dirt to sling at the conservatively liberal leader of the anti-Konoye faction in the House of Peers, the eighty-year-old Prince Tokugawa Iesato, heir presumptive to the Tokugawa clan, who would have been shogun had it not been for the intervention of Commodore Perry eighty years before. On his last trip to Europe, to attend an international conference of the Red Cross, Prince Tokugawa had taken with him as cabin mate a young female interpreter, Imanishi Keiko, who had a long record of previous associations with leftists.

Months later, when Kido had fully milked his threat to Prince Tokugawa's good name, he leaked his information to the gossip columnists. Then, as he sarcastically noted in his diary, the Tokugawa advisors held "a pigeon-necked" conference—a capsulated Japanese image for a meeting of old men cocking their heads, craning their necks, and pecking all about them in a bootless effort to solve an insoluble problem.

By his researches, Kido laid the ghost of the Red smear against the imperial family. Empress Nagako's younger brother, Count Higashi-Fushimi, who had attended Marxist seminars at the Peers'

---

[4] The best-known of her lovers was Kawaguchi Matsutaro, the novelist, playwright, and movie producer.

School, was demoted from prince to count and had to retire to a professorship of literature at Kyoto University. Several old palace retainers, including the mistress of the Empress's wardrobe, had to be pensioned off out of reach of scandal. By dint of Kido's efforts, however, Red infiltration of the aristocracy had proved too widespread to be used to advantage by the Strike-North Faction. Moreover, in young Saionji, Kido had acquired a valuable contact in the left wing—one which he would later use to influence no less a maker of history than Joseph Stalin.

GO-STOP INCIDENT

On June 17, 1933, two weeks after the table-top maneuvers, an incident took place in Osaka, the big port city near Kyoto, which War Minister Araki, the Strike-North leader, played up at his news conferences as evidence of growing popular resentment against civil government. Second Class Private Nakamura disregarded the gestures of a traffic policeman in Osaka and crossed a street against a red light. The policeman stopped all traffic in order to ask the soldier slowly and distinctly, before bystanders, how a peasant such as he, from the northern provinces, had ever learned enough to pull on a pair of Imperial Army breeches. The soldier, who was not such a peasant after all, haunted the street corner and repeated his offense again and again. When he had crossed against the lights seven times, increasing his audience with each performance, the policeman naturally arrested him and had him booked and fined in septuplicate.

The Go-Stop Incident, as it came to be dubbed by the people in their persevering quest for humor, rapidly escalated in late July and August to become a major confrontation between the civil and military police. At one juncture, flying wedges of both forces, starting from opposite ends of an Osaka street, were narrowly prevented from meeting in head-on battle. The military secret police maintained that Private Nakamura should not pay his seven-fold fine because his honor as a member of the Emperor's Army had been publicly injured. The Osaka municipal police insisted that a traffic violation was a traffic violation and a fine was a fine. The metaphysics of the matter were wrangled out almost daily in the newspapers. Finally Hirohito personally advised War Minister Araki to settle the farce with a compromise. The Army paid Private Nakamura's fine, and the Osaka police sent a written apology to Nakamura's commanding officer for any discourtesy which might have been done to the Army in the manner of his arrest.

PRAYER MEETING PLOT

During its day on the front pages—a day that lasted from July to December of 1933—the Go-Stop Incident applied pressure on the Throne while another, less publicized incident, bruited about only on the grapevine, was applying pressure on Araki. This was the Prayer Meeting Plot of July 10, 1933, a warlock's brew for the universal blackmail of all Hirohito's opponents which Prince Higashikuni had been mixing ever since his return from the table-top maneuvers on June 2. Its many strands of blackmail were so intricately woven that Japanese law courts would not acquit the last of the unwary plotters implicated in it until that final hectic month of unfinished secret business, September 1945, twelve years later, when MacArthur had already landed in Japan and begun the Occupation.

Higashikuni's plot was superficially a simple one. It called for 3,600 stout rightists from the provinces to come to Tokyo disguised as pilgrims. They were to assemble for prayer at the huge park-girt shrine dedicated to Emperor Meiji in western Tokyo, and there receive a blessing as "soldiers of the gods" from the imperial priest on duty. After the prayer meeting they were to disperse and terrorize Tokyo. One death band was to assassinate War Minister Araki, another Prime Minister Saito, and another the leaders of the Constitutionalist party. Civil police headquarters were to be seized and the prisons stormed to let out Friar Inoue and the members of the Blood Brotherhood. Overhead, Commander Yamaguchi Saburo, one of the dozen highest ranking officers in the naval air force, was to be cruising, eagle-eyed, ready to drop bombs on any centers of resistance. When Tokyo had been pacified, Prince Higashikuni or Prince Chichibu was to be made prime minister.

All this grandiose planning was pure humbug. The leaders of the conspiracy were enlisted partly by bribes and partly by assurance that the plot had the backing of the Emperor. The recruiting agent was Colonel Yasuda Tetsunosuke, retired. Yasuda was the son-in-law of General Fukuda who had kept martial law for Hirohito after the 1923 earthquake. Yasuda had served for many years, both at home and in Paris, as Prince Higashikuni's equerry. Yasuda still lived in Prince Higashikuni's villa and received a regular stipend from him. When one of the dupes of the conspiracy doubted his intimacy with Higashikuni, Yasuda posted the dupe across the street, marched up to the front entrance of Higashikuni's villa, and asked the Prince to come out in person to give him an effusive welcome.

By such methods Yasuda collected for Prince Higashikuni a motley band of plot co-sponsors, all representing factions in political life which the Throne needed to blackmail. Commander Yamaguchi, the naval air leader, for instance, had been active in a cell in the Navy which agitated for reconstruction at home as a prerequisite to further conquest abroad. He was the director of the Experimental Weapons' Workshops at Yokosuka, the largest naval yard in the nation. Other co-sponsors included Amano Tatsuo, the lawyer who was representing the Blood Brotherhood assassins of 5–15 in their public trial in law court; Nakajima Katsujiro, a member of the Saionji family's clan of hereditary gatekeepers and in former years a confidential messenger and bodyguard for the old prime-minister-maker; Suzuki Zenichi, the leader of the youth movement of the Black Dragon Society; Fujita Isamu, a publisher and agent of the spy service, who in his undercover work of infiltrating leftist circles had grown too close to the Strike-North Faction; and finally a stock market plunger who represented one of the cartels, the Matsuya department store interests.

This plunger, a fellow called Naito Hikokazu, provided both the money for the plot and the comic relief. Naito had staked a borrowed fortune on Strike-North Army plans for a munitions factory to be built on a piece of property he owned in northern Tokyo. The projected factory had been cut from the national budget in the interests of naval development. Naito tottered on the verge of bankruptcy. Prince Higashikuni's equerry, Yasuda, had promised

Naito early warning of an imperial coup d'etat in exchange for financial backing. Naito had borrowed some $200,000 from creditors who hoped to keep him afloat and had raised another $400,-000 by the sale of forged stock certificates. He had contributed about $20,000 to equerry Yasuda for the coup and had invested the other $580,000 to buy $3.3 million worth of stock on margin. He sold the stock on margin for promissory cash and waited to buy the stock back at a discount when the coup d'etat had materialized and plunged the market into a panic. By this devious transaction, if the coup succeeded, he stood to gain more than a million dollars.

The coup did not succeed, nor was it ever meant to. Prince Higashikuni's factotum, Colonel Yasuda, laid in a supply of 98 swords, 10 pistols, 700 bullets, and 16 canteens of gasoline. Word spread to the 3,600 gun hands recruited by the Black Dragon Society's youth movement that they would be insufficiently supplied with arms for the seizure of Tokyo. Throughout the first week of July 1933, the young patriots journeyed to Tokyo, looked at the arsenal, and, for the most part, went home in disgust.

July 10, the day scheduled for the Prayer Meeting, dawned fine and clear. One of the morning newspaper gossip columns carried hints that a fake coup d'etat was in the air. A group of creditors called on plunger Naito that morning and found him ashen-faced and shaky. He asked them to come back in two days when he assured them that they would all get their money. They went away unconvinced and some of them instituted legal proceedings against him that afternoon.

That evening the Prayer Meeting at Meiji Shrine drew a total congregation of only thirty-three stalwart sword hands. At the urging of their sponsors—and with the blessing of a priest who was intimate with Prince Hagashikuni—they resolved to go ahead with their plan "as a gesture." That night at ten o'clock the police raided the hostel for pilgrims attached to Meiji Shrine. They surprised the thirty-three men who had attended the Prayer Meeting, plus an additional sixteen fresh strong-arm recruits, lighting lanterns and tying on their samurai swords for a midnight attack on War Minister Araki's home. Five hours later, at 3:00 A.M. on July

11, the police intercepted a busload of seventeen fanatic farm-hands approaching Tokyo from the former spy service center of Oarai. All seventeen belonged to the Native-Land-Loving Society, the Tolstoyan farming commune, subsidized by Prince Konoye and Prince Higashikuni, whose members had attacked Tokyo's power stations on the evening of 5–15 a year earlier. The police had the bus turned around and driven back whence it had come. Eleven more Native-Land-Lovers were roused from their pallets at a cheap Tokyo inn and returned to Oarai by the morning train. Before noon the police politely searched the headquarters of the Black Dragon Society's youth movement and confiscated a number of headbands, bellybands, cigarette lighters, leaflets, and banners proclaiming, "Establish Government by the Emperor," "Exterminate Communists," "Perfect the National Defense."

Offstage laughter of the gods; a fist covered with velvet, leering jesters' faces emblazoned on the knuckles—that was all the threat that was intended by the Prayer Meeting Plot. The toughs arrested at the shrine were all released on probation by the police and their cases were not even brought to trial—much less disposed of—until almost five years later. Most of the sponsors of the plot were handled with equal caution.

The police compiled a dossier on Prince Higashikuni and turned it over for adjudication to Hirohito's chamberlains. His equerry Yasuda was forced to move out of the Higashikuni villa.

The spy service's Red expert, publisher Fujita, was booked on unspecified charges and released immediately to behave better in the future. For the next three years he acted as an undercover agent for the police and the Throne in the ranks of the Strike-North Faction. In 1935 and early 1936, he provided money, food, and lodging to a fellow antagonist of the Strike-North, a man named Kawai, who became a member of Richard Sorge's Communist spy ring.

The leader of the youth movement in the Black Dragon Society, Suzuki Zenichi, was released on the understanding that he would provide full information on Black Dragon activities. His intelligence enabled the police in the next two years to destroy the Black Dragon as a political force.

Amano Tatsuo, the lawyer for the Blood Brothers who were standing trial for the murders leading up to 5–15, escaped to Manchuria and was given sanctuary there by operatives of the Strike-North Faction. The spy service made an attempt to poison him and when he survived it with nothing more than a severe stomach ache, he submitted to a negotiated arrest and extraditon home to Japan. Released on parole, he visited the prison cell of his client, Friar Inoue of the Blood Brotherhood. The trial of the Blood Brothers had begun on June 28, 1933. Now, six weeks later, it was abruptly discontinued. Friar Inoue and his twelve Blood Brethren arose in the dock, accused the presiding judge of inattention, and announced that they would take no further part in the trial. The judge called a recess and went personally to Friar Inoue's comfortable cell to learn what the trouble was. Friar Inoue explained that, as a partisan of Prince Konoye, he must decline to stand trial during the term of the present crisis. The judge, who was forty-seven years old and due for promotion to the District Court, accepted this explanation but resigned his career on the bench. He withdrew, on a comfortable pension, to permanent retirement. The trial was prorogued until March 27, 1934—at which time defense lawyer Amano, himself out on bail, conducted a nice quiet case, a model of harmless patriotic propaganda.

Naval Commander Yamaguchi Saburo, who had rashly offered to provide the Prayer Meeting with tactical air support, never took off to participate in the plot but was treated more harshly than any of the other plot sponsors. For four months he remained at liberty while the police sought to negotiate with him. He proved utterly intractable, however, refusing to abandon his belief that Japan must be reformed internally before expanding further externally. And so, in November 1933, he was arrested, in December interrogated, in January tortured and killed.

As for plunger Naito, he fled his creditors on the day after the Prayer Meeting by getting himself admitted as a patient at Tokyo University Hospital. There, under police guard, a few months later, he died "of stomach cancer"—a police euphemism for the fact that he was finally induced to take the honorable way out of his debts and forgeries by cutting open his belly.

A TRUCE IN THEIR TIME

The grapevine news that samurai with swords had set out from
Meiji Shrine to assassinate the leader of Japan's mechanized twentieth century Army touched the sentimental heart of every tradi-
tionalist count and baron in Japan. It also touched War Minister
Araki, the intended victim. In the weeks that followed, a temporary settlement was negotiated. In effect the Emperor said a *mea
culpa* and his antagonists promised to cause no more trouble. The
decision whether to Strike North or to Strike South was briefly
postponed.

On July 17, six days after the Prayer Meeting, Hirohito sent
word to old Saionji that on the one hand Empress Nagako was
pregnant again and that on the other he was thinking of abdicating. His place on the Throne, the Emperor suggested, could be
filled by the toddling bastard prince engendered by artificial insemination, and the realm could be ruled by one of Hirohito's uncles or brothers acting as regent.

At this same juncture, War Minister Araki and the rest of the
Cabinet agreed to a settlement of the Red smear. Professor
Takikawa, the leader of Prince Konoye's seven organ theorists at
Kyoto University, would resign his post. So would the principal
of the Peers' School, which was accused of sponsoring Marxist
seminars. And so would the palace chamberlain of peerage and
heraldry who was responsible for the Peers' School. The new
peerage and heraldry director would be Big Brother Marquis Kido
who would continue concurrently in his old post as secretary to
Lord Privy Seal Count Makino. Kido duly purged all Marxists
from the palace. In addition he instituted a procedure for entering on the Court rolls the mistresses of noblemen. By this device
he enlisted for the Throne the help of marchionesses and count-
esses in all future dealings with refractory marquises and counts.

For his part War Minister Araki acquiesced in a reposting of
Strike-North officers from influential positions in the Army bureaucracy to field commands. Their places were taken by officers
who were "China experts." In addition Prince Higashikuni was assigned out of Tokyo to command of the 2d Division in the north-

ern Japanese city of Sendai. First Crow Nagata and his opponent, Second Crow Obata, were both removed from the General Staff and reposted as active brigade commanders. Major General Tojo, the later World War II prime minister, organized a new body to study Army discipline and morale, the watchdog Committee for Investigations, which was attached to Araki's own War Ministry.

The settlement in Tokyo, designed to take the Army out of politics, coincided with an unexpected change of command in Manchuria—a sudden death or suicide which robbed Araki of one of the main props of his Army influence. Lieutenant General Honjo, who was now Hirohito's chief aide-de-camp, had been succeeded as commander-in-chief of the Kwantung Army by "Silent General" Muto Nobuyoshi, who had opposed Hirohito in the national policy-making of the Far Eastern Conference before the 1928 murder of Manchurian war lord Chang Tso-lin. Early in July 1933, just after the Prayer Meeting, Silent Muto, now a field marshal, wrote Hirohito a letter pleading for a policy of greater liberality and mercy toward the Manchukuoan citizens under his charge. Hirohito's answer is not on record but on July 21, after receiving it, Silent Muto mailed a thirty-one-syllable poem to his second and favorite daughter Misako in Japan:

> You here and I there—
> understand, please, that we part
> for sake of country.
> Even when we've spent our lives,
> we can meet again beyond.

The next day, July 22, Silent Muto retired to his private quarters and announced that he was ill. Five days later, on July 27, Hirohito was informed that he had died of "a general abdominal ailment." The imperial household minister submitted a formal petition to the Throne suggesting that the title of baron be conferred upon the late field marshal.

Hirohito answered, "Although it is altogether fitting and proper to reward Muto with a barony, how will it sit with his children?"

Big Brother Kido, as secretary to the lord privy seal and now, concurrently, director of peerage and heraldry, researched the question and replied to the Throne a few days later that Silent Muto's heirs would find it a financial burden to support a baron's title.

"Muto's wife," wrote Kido, without having consulted her, "has already reported herself [in her own family name] as mistress of the household. Therefore it is very clear that she would have no desire to see the title passed on."

Hirohito, accordingly, made Silent Muto, posthumously, a non-hereditary baron and with that the matter was dropped.

In Muto's place as ambassador to Manchukuo and commander-in-chief of the Kwantung Army Hirohito appointed a fire-breathing, sabre-rattling general of the Navy-oriented Satsuma clan named Hishikari Taka. There was poetic justice in the choice because the ideographs in Hishikari Taka's name meant literally "cutting back water-chestnut prosperity." Water chestnuts were known by Japanese as a gourmet's delicacy in China, a symbol of the epicurean degeneracy of China's ruling classes. On meeting the Japanese press after his appointment, Hishikari strode forward in summer kimono wearing an ancient samurai sword handed down in his family. He fanned himself energetically with an antique fan.

"If there is anyone who opposes the Imperial Army," he barked, "I will do this to him."

And with that, according to the accounts published the next day, he drew his *katana*, cut the air with it, and "laughed bois-terously."

Hishikari, on his arrival in Manchuria, legitimized and systema-tized all the malpractices which Hirohito's young experts had in-troduced the year before in their attempt to make Manchuria pay. Strike-North staff officers in the Kwantung Army prepared a book-let on conditions in Manchuria and had it smuggled home to their former commander, Lieutenant General Honjo, the chief aide-de-camp in the palace. On August 6, 1933, Honjo submitted it to Emperor Hirohito, telling him that it described "the realities of peace preservation in Manchukuo." In his diary, on August 8, Honjo wrote: "I asked the Emperor to read it, adding, 'It has been hot recently, so do it whenever you have a moment.' Today, two days later, he called me and said, 'I have read the passages you marked.'

And he gave the booklet back to me. I was surprised at how quickly he had read it—personally I spent a long time on it."

THE KASPÉ KIDNAPPING

Hishikari brought to Manchuria a new form of racket, kidnapping. Many well-to-do Chinese merchants were kidnapped two or three times before they were ascertained to be either dead or bankrupt. Westerners, too, who could claim consular assistance against other forms of extortion, found themselves helpless against the kidnapping routine. In carrying out the abductions, the secret police used agents who were invariably described as bandits: Chinese desperadoes against Chinese victims and White Russian ones against whites. The kidnappers were given the benefit of Japanese secret police protection and were rewarded with a percentage of the ransom money when and if it was paid. In scores of cases it *was* paid and the victims were returned to their homes. They seldom gave their stories to the press because they feared Japanese vengeance.

On August 24, 1933, less than a month after General Hishikari's appointment, the spy service operatives in Harbin struck at the most potentially lucrative kidnap victim in Manchuria, the son of a wealthy Russian Jew named Joseph Kaspé. The elder Kaspé had settled in Harbin after the Russo-Japanese war in 1907. A jeweler by trade, he had started out as a watch repairman and pawnbroker and ended up as one of the richest gem and silver merchants in the Orient. As well as his business, he owned Harbin's main café and Hotel Moderne, and most of the movie houses in North Manchuria. It was said by his detractors that he owed his prosperity to the gratitude of the Soviet Union for his services as a fence for jewels and art objects seized from the homes of White Russian aristocrats during the Russian Revolution. For this alleged traffic in Soviet stolen goods, Kaspé was cordially detested by the White Russians among whom he lived. But so were the rest of Harbin's Jewish community. Anti-Semitism was engrained in White Russian culture, and it had deepened in recent years because many White Russians, being by definition anti-Communists, were also admirers of Adolf Hitler.

The Japanese, too, at this time were beginning to use Jews, along with Masons and Bolsheviks, as bugbears in propaganda. It was a posture which many Westerners thought ludicrous because few Japanese could tell Jew from gentile and there were less than a dozen self-appointed converts to Judaism in all Japan. To the haunted mind of the samurai, however, unfamiliar devils could be as fearful as familiar ones. The Jews of Harbin, most of them virtually stateless and so defenseless, soon learned to their grief that Shinto persecution could be as merciless as Christian. As soon as the Kwantung Army entered Harbin in 1932, it made an agent and collaborator of the local Russian Nazi leader, a hoodlum intellectual by the name of Rodzaevsky who edited a hate sheet called *Nash Put.*

When millionaire Kaspé saw the drift of Japanese political thinking, he put all his properties in the names of his two sons who were both French citizens. From the Japanese point of view it was an insulting gesture and after the make-Manchuria-pay policy came into force in late 1932, the Japanese authorities began to work overtime on schemes for milking Kaspé somehow of his millions. Kaspé himself was not one to be caught unawares. He never left his suite in the Hotel Moderne without a substantial bodyguard.

One of Kaspé's sons, however, was less cautious. He returned to Harbin in the summer of 1933 after graduating from the French Conservatoire de Musique, a talented pianist with high hopes for a concert career. While his father arranged bookings for him in Shanghai and Tokyo he made the most of Harbin night life and often ordered the armed chauffeur, supplied him by his father, to drive down to the gay quarter on the river bank and leave him at the Tatos or Iberia Club where he could find some Chinese singsong girl, Japanese mama-san, or Russian café chantant.

On the evening of August 24, 1933, when young Semyon Kaspé was escorting home a Miss L. Shapiro, two White Russian fascists in the pay of the Japanese secret police jumped his car, disarmed his chauffeur, and drove the car to the suburbs. There they let out the chauffeur and, after arranging maildrops and phone numbers, released the girl so that she could act as go-between in the ransom negotiations. Her dedicated involvement in the later ins and outs

of the case suggest that she either loved young Kaspé deeply or
was a paid agent of the secret police. The kidnappers drove Semyon
to a hideout in the woods "some 55 versts" or about 36 miles west
of Harbin and from there delivered daily phone calls, ransom
notes, and ultimatums.

Semyon's father indignantly refused to pay the $100,000 de-
manded and offered $12,000 instead, to be paid on delivery. After
a month of negotiation he was delivered a bloody half of one of
his son's ears. Either out of obsessive frugality or stubborn courage
in the face of intimidation, he still refused to pay. He had interested the French Vice Consul Monsieur Chambon in the outrage,
and Chambon's agents were working on good leads. Moreover the
Japanese secret police commandant himself said that he had all
his men at work on the case. Agents stood by at Harbin's central
telephone exchange to trace ransom calls from the kidnappers,
but, according to the Japanese explanation, the artful abductors
always put through four calls at once to all four of the monitored
numbers, thereby making it impossible, for technical reasons, to
trace the calls.

In October the agents of energetic Vice Consul Chambon captured the youngest of the kidnappers, a teen-age hoodlum called
Komisarenko, who confessed the names of his White Russian
accomplices. Chambon went to court and pressed charges
against the members of the gang. The Japanese secret police seized
Komisarenko and took him out of town. They made the mistake
of hiding him in an area along the South Manchuria Railway's right
of way which fell under the jurisdiction of Japanese railway agents
who despised the secret police. Colonel Oi Fukashi in charge of
the railway police happened to be a fine unreformed old samurai.
Exercising his full powers, he relieved the secret police of
Komisarenko and took the young thug into his own custody. The
secret police arrested all of Vice Consul Chambon's agents on
various trumped-up charges and encouraged fascist Rodzaevsky
in his newspaper *Nash Put* to label Frenchman Chambon a Jewish
Bolshevik. Colonel Oi brought Komisarenko back to Harbin and
had him swear out a formal confession to the native Manchurian
police. Foreign newspapers began to take note of the case and
cause embarrassment.

Kidnapped concert pianist Kaspé was meanwhile dying by inches. His captors starved him, periodically beat him, and began to wrench out the nails from his soft, piano player's hands. At least once the secret police provided vehicles to move the young man and his tormentors to a new hideout. In his last detention place Kaspé lived underground in a pit dug into the half-frozen earth and covered with a lid. Finally on November 28, 1933, Colonel Oi arrested two more of the kidnappers and the gang panicked. One of them made tentative arrangements to return Semyon to his father for $3,000. That same night, in a move modestly described as a "triumphant raid," the secret police descended on the hideout, shot the double dealer, allowed the other guard on duty to escape, and either killed or merely buried the mutilated, gangrenous young pianist. In the days that followed the White Russian members of the gang gave themselves up to the Manchukuoan police.

After several months of questioning and litigation, their trial began before a native Manchukuoan court. It was conducted—with a fine Chinese flair for diplomatic mockery—as a miniature of the trials being conducted in Tokyo for the heroes of 5–15 and the Triple Intrigue. The accused were allowed to make interminable political speeches in their defense. They contended that Kaspé's fist was full of Bolshevik gold and that they had sought to extract it, out of pure selfless patriotism, in order to contribute it to the cause of White Russian partisans operating along the Soviet border.

The Chinese judges listened politely and patiently for two years and then, in 1936, sentenced six of the gang to hang "within three days" and the rest to serve long prison terms. Taken by surprise, the Japanese authorities behind the curtains of Manchukuo's puppet stage were forced to act with awkward abruptness. Two days after the sentence was passed they had both the judge and the lawyers for the prosecution picked up and held for interrogation on suspicion of being "grafters." At the same time, on the appeal of one of the wives of the kidnappers, Kwantung Army Chief of Staff Itagaki ordered a new trial under the political rather than the bandit section of the criminal code—to be conducted by a Japanese court.

In the retrial the Japanese prosecutor spoke eloquently about the extenuating difficulties and pure motives of the "fine young patriots" in the dock and asked lenient sentences for them of no more than ten to fifteen years. The court complied and the prisoners were relieved at their reprieve. Japan, however, was not about to support idle hands in prison which might be useful elsewhere. To the astonishment of the prisoners themselves they were haled back into court a week later and told that they were eligible for amnesty. Ten days later, in consideration of services rendered and promised, they were set free and given jobs with the Special Service Organ in other cities in Manchukuo.

The Harbin *Herald* and the Harbin *Observer* denounced the proceedings as a travesty. Long ailing under oppression, both papers were now closed down and their editors deported. Colonel Oi was recalled to Japan. Vice Consul Chambon was declared *persona non grata* and recalled to France.[5] As for old man Kaspé, he is said to have gone mad when he saw the exhumed corpse of the son he would not ransom. He lost interest in his financial empire and retired thereafter to oblivion with his French wife. His motion-picture houses were bought up by the Manchuria Motion Picture Association, a monopoly headed by Amakasu Masahiko, the secret police tough who had welcomed Puppet Henry Pu-Yi to Manchuria in 1931 and had strangled socialist Osugi, his wife, and nephew during the aftermath of the Tokyo Earthquake in 1923.

WAR FOOTING FOR THE NAVY

As the pianist Kaspé lost his fingernails one by one in Manchuria, Hirohito in Tokyo pushed forward with his plans, oblivious

[5] It was French policy at this time to avoid giving any offense to Japan. Ever since the breakdown of the Anglo-Japanese Alliance in the 1920's, the possibility of a Franco-Japanese alliance had seemed attractive to many French statesmen. General Claudel had done his best to emasculate the Lytton Report. And on October 17, 1933, it was a French syndicate, with government blessing, which first broke the League boycott and lent Manchukuo $60 million. The South Manchuria Railroad then spent the money mainly for the development of a port and naval base in Korea. Ultimately, of course, it would be Germany rather than France which Japan would choose as its European ally.

of oppression abroad and of opposition at home. He had never felt more buoyant. Midwives and doctors agreed that the child in Empress Nagako's womb was a boy. War Minister Araki had bowed loyally to imperial pressure and for the time being had stilled his partisans' agitation for war with Russia. Hirohito walked Empress Nagako on the beach at the Summer Palace at Hayama and quarreled amiably with chamberlains who protested that walks might not be good for her in her present delicate condition. The Eleven Club held a rousing geisha party for Prince Higashikuni to cheer him on the eve of his departure to the 2d Division in northern Japan.

On August 4, 1933, the Empress's cousin, Navy Chief of Staff Prince Fushimi, began to ask his colleagues in the Navy's bureaucracy to support a change in regulations which would put the Navy on a permanent war footing. Specifically Navy General Staff decisions and orders would no longer have to be cleared with the Navy minister who was a member of the Cabinet but only with the Emperor in the privacy of the Throne Room. The Navy minister, War Minister Araki, and Saionji all protested the change as uncalled for. Hirohito himself asked that a full set of secret position papers be drawn up for his consideration so that he could examine all the implications of the change.

To remind the people that the Army, too, was preparing for emergencies, and that Soviet air bases were not too far away, War Minister Araki had his subordinates institute air raid drills. Starting August 9, announced the military police, Tokyo and other brightly lit cities would observe strict blackout regulations. Everyone was inconvenienced, and the police found themselves both busied and embarrassed by the number of violations. Even from the palace airmen observed a few bright twinkles of defiance. And so, after two gloomy evenings, the drill was dropped without explanation.

On August 16, while still studying the proposed change in naval regulations, Hirohito boarded the battleship *Hiei* for his annual attendance at the Navy's grand maneuvers. His retainers observed his behavior closely for they knew that it would reflect his pleasure or displeasure with the proposed change in the status of the Navy. From the moment he was piped aboard, Hirohito positively beamed. His chief vassals took pains to spread anecdotal evidence of his high spirits. They reported that the next day, during a conversation with the grand chamberlain, the imperial household minister, and the chief aide-de-camp, Hirohito abruptly arose from his deck chair, fell prostrate on a hatch cover, and began to do push-ups. When his courtiers all jumped to their feet, he said "I am exercising for myself and you three are not, so why don't you continue your conversation without being disturbed?"

Returning to port on August 19, Hirohito entered wholeheartedly into a game of croquet on deck. When his team had won and he was standing by watching the late finishers, he remarked: "My side worked together as a team. We dispersed the enemy's balls. We used billiard techniques. We applied our geometry." It was Hirohito's way of saying that he had liked what he had seen of naval science and discipline. After years of preoccupation with Army matters, the sea breeze and feel of the deck had returned him momentarily to 1921 when he had set out full of youth and adventure for Europe. Plans made then for modernizing the Army and ridding it of feudal clans had been realized. The Army had gone on to put a buffer zone between Japan and the Red menace in the north. Now the time had come to look south and think again in naval terms. Hirohito returned to the grim confines of his moated battlements in Tokyo refreshed and reassured that his reign was going aright.

Hirohito's good spirits were not dampened in the least by Strike-North-Faction attacks against the Navy and against Hirohito's advisors during the weeks that followed. At a meeting with Cabinet ministers on August 30, 1933, he impressed everyone with his "penetrating questions" about the welfare of Japanese colonists in Sakhalien to the north and in Dutch New Guinea far to the south. Chief Aide-de-Camp Honjo, in his diary, expressed "awe that in a mere thirty-three years" Hirohito could have acquired "such a vast store of knowledge and relevant inquiries." What Honjo meant was that he wished Hirohoto would think less of Papua and more of his home island, Honshu.

The peasants of Japan, who formed the backbone of the Army, had suffered greatly during the last two years. Villages had lost their best workers to the Army and the munitions factories. Dollar swindle and devaluation had raised the purchase price of all manufactured goods but not the market value of rice and turnips. The depressed American public had almost given up buying Japanese silk. And worst of all, the weather had made for poor harvests for several seasons. Under such circumstances it was difficult for Army politicians like War Minister Araki to preserve discipline in the ranks, much less enthusiasm for naval development.

Day after day Honjo gently, stubbornly sought to dispel the Emperor's euphoria. He observed that Prince Takeda, twenty-four, and Prince Kitashirakawa, twenty-three, had sought honorary memberships in the Tokyo Riding Club and that their applications were being processed slowly instead of being seized upon eagerly. Big Brother Kido, the director of peerage and heraldry, confessed that the "attitude of the other club members" was "bad," and had been bad ever since Prince Higashikuni had joined the club. It was the same way in the club for training Army carrier pigeons which Prince Takeda and Prince Kitashirakawa had already entered.

One day, in his campaign of attrition, Chief Aide-de-Camp Honjo complained to Hirohito that no monument had ever been erected in the palace to commemorate the peasant soldiers who had fallen in the Manchurian campaign and that imperial afternoons away from work, collecting marine biological specimens from a boat on Sagami Bay, were widely regarded in the ranks as callous frivolity. With blithe even temper, Hirohito took Honjo out on the battered old imperial biological yacht, explained to him that there was no money, patriotically speaking, for meaningless monuments, and gave him a lecture on the tides of Sagami Bay. Honjo learned that, if the Emperor had not made his own observations, the hydrographic office of the Navy would not have corrected its charts and some day some Japanese ship would have miscalculated the depth of Sagami Bay. Honjo expressed his admiration for the Emperor's dazzling display of broadmindedness and perception.

On September 21, Hirohito suggested to Chief Aide-de-Camp Honjo that the change in naval staff regulations, which would bring all fleet movements under his exclusive control, had best be kept secret from the reading public except in broad outline. Four

days later Hirohito approved the new regulations with the one
proviso that they should be set down sharply and simply in writing. He went to some pains to explain his decision to Honjo as
follows:

Years ago when Holland was prosperous and strong, the famous
Admiral Ruiter defeated the British Navy and was on the point of
pursuing the British fleet into the Thames Estuary. But the Dutch
Army was in trouble and so, to help the Army, the Navy was called
back. Thus Ruiter was frustrated, which led to the decline of the Navy
and with it of Holland. So armaments for the Navy must not be decreased. At the same time an imbalance in national finance must not
be created by increasing the mere number of the Navy's sailors. Bal-
anced adjustment is very important.

DECISION TO GO SOUTH

The new status for the Navy was but one part of a package
which also included more money for the Navy in the forthcoming budget and official Cabinet sanction for a national Strike-
South policy. The Army's tabled recommendation that Russia
should be considered enemy number one was entirely forgotten.
War Minister Araki fought vainly, through months of subtle but
unimportant maneuvering, to have it remembered. By October
1933, however, the rest of the Cabinet had given in to Hirohito's
wishes and War Minister Araki was fighting only a delaying action.

At a meeting of the inner Cabinet, on October 11, the foreign
minister shrugged hopelessly toward the Army and Navy ministers and declared, "We will expand as far as we can by diplomacy
but after that we will have to call on you." Three days later the old
man, Prime-Minister-Maker Saionji, expressed a similar feeling of
fateful resignation to Big Brother Kido who had come to the seashore in an attempt to improve relations between Saionji and his
fellow prince of the ancient Fujiwara clan, Konoye.

"There is no middle way," said Saionji, "between complete military dictatorship and retention of the constitutional system we
have. If Konoye is flirting with the former, I shall disappear as a
person of the past."

The next day, October 15, Hirohito's Big Brothers—all in their forties now—gathered for a Chinese feast at Konoye's hilltop villa overlooking the ocean in Kamakura and talked for five hours.

Six days later, on October 20, 1933, the ministers of the Cabinet officially put their seals to Hirohito's program. They agreed: "to go as far as possible by diplomacy; . . . to build up as much military strength as possible; . . . to co-operate domestically, ministry with ministry, in order to realize our international goals."

PATRIOTS ON TRIAL

All this had been accomplished while the executioners of Prime Minister Inukai and the 5–15 plot were standing trial and talking reams of newsprint. The trials were potentially explosive because most of the defendants had been partisans of the disgruntled Strike-North Faction. Many of them now distrusted War Minister Araki, the Strike-North leader, however, because they suspected that he had persuaded them to act in the 1932 coup even after he knew it was to be a fake one. Confused by the way in which they had been used, they now allowed themselves to play a role for which they had been perfectly coached by loyal or at least venal police minions of the Throne. Araki could hardly believe it, but the defendants, in their long day in court, incriminated none of their sponsors, neither Lord Privy Seal Makino nor Araki himself. Still more incredible from Araki's point of view, they voiced at tedious length the yearning of the people for domestic reform and Hirohito paid absolutely no attention to it.

The Army court-martial of the eleven military academy cadets who had assisted at the murder of Prime Minister Inukai had opened on July 25, 1933, and closed on September 19. Given every opportunity by the judge to speak their minds, the cadets had strummed on the theme that Japan was a unique society in which the Throne did not exist for the State but the State for the Throne. As one of the shavetails put it: "We demand direct rule by the Emperor. Our focus today is on the imported egotistical notion of popular rights. That is wrong. Manhood suffrage and the grant of social and political rights to the people are a gigantic mistake."

The Navy court-martial for the ten more sophisticated flight officers of the Misty Lagoon had opened on July 24, 1933, and would come to a close on November 9. Their ringleader, Lieutenant Koga, told the court: "The condition of the country is such that it cannot be improved except by shedding blood." His assistant, Ensign Mikami, explained: "Our revolution is intended to bring about . . . harmony between ruler and ruled. . . . As we aim to establish direct imperial rule, we are neither leftists nor rightists." Another of the ensigns asserted: "My life's desire will be fulfilled if a state is established on the principle that the Emperor and his subjects are one." The naval reservist who had fired the first shot at Prime Minister Inukai expressed some slight regret: "I felt sorry but I thought his death unavoidable as he had to be sacrificed at the shrine of national reformation."

The civilian trial of twenty disciples of the Native-Land-Loving Society had commenced on September 26 and would continue until February 3, 1934. Tachibana, the Tolstoyan leader of the Land-Lovers, was allowed to explain himself in a harangue to the court which lasted for six days. "The nation," he said, in the course of his peroration, "must stand on the basis of farming villages. . . . Japan is a debtor nation, yet Tokyo and the cities grow larger year by year. Where does this strength come from? It is clear that if the villages were released from the burden of sustaining the cities, the national power of Japan would increase. At a stroke, we could exclude the influence of the United States from the Pacific, liberate China from the yoke of the war lords, set India free, and enable Germany to rise again. . . . It is necessary to get rid of capitalism in the interests of peace, and the people should oppose capitalism. The defense of Asia must be perfected. . . . The Japanese people must prepare for the day when all the men on the farms will go to the front to fight and the women will take the place of the men."

When the other civilian trial, that of Friar Inoue and his twelve disciples of the Blood Brotherhood, reconvened on March 26, 1934, there was little left to say. "Party politics in Japan," opined Friar Inoue humbly, "are politics of the privileged classes. In Germany, the politics of the right wing are politics of the gods. Party politics should be corrected, and the Emperor should give the final word. . . . I am thinking about the future society but I am not learned and cannot decide such important matters alone."

To these peculiarly Japanese polemics the Japanese people for the most part responded favorably. In particular the ideas of strength emanating from the farms and of religious virtue in direct rule by the Emperor struck responsive chords. A petition asking clemency for the Native-Land-Lovers was signed by 357,000 well-organized patriots. The officers of the various courts received over 110,000 letters in the same vein. Nine men of the town of Niigata chopped off their little fingers and sent them to War Minister Araki in alcohol together with a note saying that the defendants "broke the law but their motives were pure. We are profoundly impressed by their spirit of self-sacrifice." The Osaka Bar Association went so far as to pass a resolution declaring that the assassins, in the deepest sense, had merely acted in self-defense.

At the end of the trials the Army cadets, on September 19, 1933, were given four years in prison and were released for good behavior during the New Year celebrations of 1935. Then they were met at the prison gates by nine limousines and driven to the Double Bridge of the palace to do grateful obeisance. The naval flight officers of the Misty Lagoon, on November 9, 1933, were sentenced to from one to fifteen years, of which only their three ringleaders served more than a few months. The Native-Land-Lovers, sentenced on February 3, 1934, were immediately amnestied and set at liberty by Hirohito on February 17—all but Tachibana, their dangerously articulate leader. The Blood Brothers were sentenced in November 1934 and, except for Friar Inoue and the two who had actually pulled triggers, were amnestied in early 1935.

HOLY BIRTH

By a word from either Araki or Hirohito the trials might have been turned into a spectacle of recrimination between the Strike-North and Strike-South factions. Instead, while Araki watched with amazement, they slid by in months of perfectly disciplined oratory. Araki had hoped that the discontent expressed by the trial defendants over farm and labor conditions might be taken up by editorial writers and street demonstrators and turned into an outcry against Hirohito's policies in general. His hopes were dashed, however, on December 23, 1933, when Empress Nagako gave birth to another child—at long last a son, Crown Prince Akihito.

After the previous accouchement, in 1931, resulting in the birth of Princess Atsuko, Hirohito had grunted and gone out into the garden to collect specimens of moss. Now the cigar-smoking, philosophizing grand chamberlain, Admiral Suzuki Kantaro, burst into Hirohito's modest Western-style study in the Imperial Library and flapped his kimono sleeves like some great bat of good omen. "It is a boy," he cried. "I saw the honorable signs of manhood myself."

Hirohito arose in rumpled Army uniform from his small, Spartan desk and with a sigh and a smile ordered champagne to flow for the rest of the day for any visiting wellwishers who might need it. Saionji's Secretary-Spy Harada, informed by phone, came over for several glasses and, feeling somewhat tipsy, told Chief Aide-de-Camp Honjo how thankful everyone was that Honjo had made the Army understand and believe in "the Emperor's personal sagacity." The more temperate Kido announced to his diary, "Now, at last, the biggest problem has been solved."

The full significance of the blessed event was admitted two days later on Christmas Day when the Constitutionalist and anti-Constitutionalist parties overcame past differences and held a "purely social" get-together "for the sake of the nation." The birth of the crown prince gave the influence of the Throne a much needed infusion of sentimental popular support, and the two parties amicably agreed, on that December 25, 1933, that there was now no longer any way of standing against the Throne. On December 31 Prince Higashikuni arrived in Tokyo from his command in Sendai, went to the palace to pay his respects to the new-born crown prince, and then let it be known that "it is time for Araki to quit."

Two weeks of bitter infighting followed in which Araki tried at least to appoint his own successor. On January 3, Big Brother Kido and Secretary Harada called on old Saionji and found him exhausted.

Major General Nagata, the first of the Three Crows, at 1st Brigade headquarters in the Tokyo suburbs, collected an unofficial staff and renewed position-paper work on a policy of "first reorganize China, then renovate Japan."

On January 7 Marquis Kido, the ubiquitous Suzuki, and others of the Big Brothers' fraternity gathered by the inconspicous but slow transportation of private automobile at Prince Konoye's villa in Kamakura. They agreed that, whatever Araki might think, the next war minister had to be an officer who could manipulate the Army-Navy lobby which advocated friendship with China. Specifically they concluded that General Matsui Iwane, the later scapegoat "Butcher of Nanking," could best be led by a certain General Hayashi Senjuro, the man who had loyally sent troops from Korea into Manchuria before receipt of official orders in 1931.

Hirohito made one concession to Araki's sense of morality and personal face. He agreed, both for Araki's and Konoye's political comfort, to proclaim an amnesty for the civilian participants in the carefully aborted 5–15 coup d'etat which had killed Prime Minister Inukai. The amnesty would be given to the nation as a token of imperial magnanimity on the occasion of the birth of the crown prince.

"We will leave out thieves, murderers, and those who have committed lèse majesté," explained Prime Minister Saito to the Throne, "but the amnesty will bring commutation of sentence to the Blood Brotherhood and the men of 5–15."

Hirohito replied, "The dignity of the law must not be tarnished, but I think, within those limits, an amnesty is permissible."

The amnesty enabled Araki to go in peace and honor without toppling the entire Cabinet. It satisfied his private commitment to partisans who had gone to prison for him after the murderous 5–15 coup. And resignation would now satisfy his public commitment to believers in domestic reform and the Strike North.

Accordingly, on the next day, January 16, Araki sequestered himself in the hospital at the Military Medical School and announced himself stricken with pneumonia. He summoned to his bedside the generals, colonels, and majors of his faction and told them one by one that he intended to resign, at his doctor's suggestion, if a suitable replacement could be found for him. For the next five days he struggled to have General Mazaki, his blunt honest henchman, formerly vice chief of staff, put in his place. Hirohito said, however, that Mazaki had personality problems. And Prince Kanin, the sixty-eight-year-old chief of the Army General Staff, the last surviving brother of Prince Asahiko who had counseled Emperor Komei at Perry's coming eighty years earlier, emerged briefly from his veils to take personal responsibility for blackballing Mazaki.

Araki resigned the war ministership on January 22, 1934, and his loyal lieutenant, General Mazaki, was placated with the nominally important but substantially uninfluential post of inspector general of military education. The Prayer Meeting Plot had reached its benedictus. The strategic concept of a Strike North to meet the supposed international crisis of 1936 had passed behind a cloud of imperial frowns. The nation would now lapse into two years of full peace and hectic hard work. The mass of the people might suppress doubts; the peasants and privates might toil in positive resentment; but the majority of the Army's officer corps had retired to their corner to await fresh tocsins and another round before Araki would finally be counted out.

ZERO

Given a free hand to prepare for a Strike South, Hirohito acted first to create a good naval airplane. Up to now the only hot military planes made in Japan had been pieced together one by one, like racing cars, out of components which were largely imported. In January 1934, when Araki's retirement was imminent, the members of the Eleven Club made a personal effort to free the air force from dependence on Western parts and to develop consistent Japanese types of planes, designed domestically to meet specific Japanese requirements. On January 12 and again on February 9 and 13, Prince Higashikuni, Big Brother Kido, and Secretary-Spy Harada met with executives of aircraft plants and with officers of the two air force headquarters to found a joint Army-Navy-Tokyo Imperial University Aviation Institute. It came into being a few months later under the direction of Kido's brother, the aeronautic engineer Wada Koroku (who was Colonel Charles Lindbergh's friend), and of seventy-seven-year-old physics professor Tanakadate Aikitsu, lecturer on aviation to the Emperor. The institute at once procured the services of the British Sopwith company's talented designer, Herbert Smith, who was celebrated for his unstable but highly maneuverable Sopwith Camel fighter of World War I fame. In a year, with the help of Smith and a team at Mitsubishi, the experts at the institute had test-flown a superb Japanese fighter plane, the A5M, forerunner of the famous Zero which would terrorize Allied Hawk and Buffalo pilots in the opening months of World War II.

LET THEM EAT CAKE

On February 8, 1934, Chief Aide-de-Camp Honjo tried to tell Emperor Hirohito that the Strike-North Faction was still alive and that there was still much political unrest in the Army. Hirohito asked how it was that Army men, who were pledged to take orders—particularly men of a faction which professed a belief in direct rule by the Emperor—could think to cause unrest or have an interest at all in politics. Honjo replied that some interest in politics was desirable in an officer because it was his duty to inculcate his peasant soldiery with political morals and patriotism.

Hirohito understood at once where the conversation was heading—to another lecture on the plight of the farmers. It had been a disastrous year agriculturally. The northern part of Japan, from which the Army drew its stoutest recruits, was being ravaged by one of the worst famines in history. The old nineteenth century practice of farmers selling their daughters had come back into fashion. In 1932, the number of girls from the farms of the north bound over under contract to Tokyo labor heelers had been 12,-108. In 1933 the number had more than quadrupled to 58,173. Of these 19,244 had been indentured as nursemaids; 17,260 as factory hands; 5,952 as bar girls; 5,729 as odd-jobbists; 4,512 as common prostitutes; 3,271 as cabaret hostesses; and only 2,196 of the best looking for relatively honorable service as apprentice geisha. Hirohito had sent chamberlains to inspect the stricken farm areas and offer words of consolation. He had helped to apply pressure to the Mitsui cartel to set up a $10 million philanthropic fund for the re-education of dispossessed peasants. But he had done nothing material on his own behalf or that of the government to alleviate the farmers' lot.

To Honjo, Hirohito said: "It cannot be helped that officers, especially the noncoms who are closest to the men, should feel some concern and sympathy for the miserable conditions in farming villages. On the other hand, if in so doing their interest becomes excessive, it is harmful."

"I do not mean," replied Honjo, "that they should ever engage in political activity or have any taste for it. Indeed they should stop short of feeling any interest beyond what is required of them in the line of duty."

"Although one must naturally sympathize with the troubled condition of the farm villages," persisted the Emperor, "nevertheless the peasants have their own joy in the heaven of the land, and it is not to be said that a man of noble rank is always invariably happy. I, for instance, in visiting Europe, found the feeling of freedom there a great change for me. As long as I was able to enjoy it, it put me in a most pleasant frame of mind. It is presumptuous to speak of the former Emperor, but I recall that when my father was still a prince, he was extremely vigorous and healthy, and on visits to the villas of his aunts he was carefree and agile. Then after he ascended the throne everything became narrow and tight for him. As his physique was by nature frail, he finally fell sick. Believe me, it was an awesome thing to see. Reflecting on his example, the farmers should not talk on and on about the unpleasant aspects of their life but should concentrate rather on the enjoyment of nature around them. In sum, it should be emphasized in the guidance of peasants that a man must rely on moral effort and not dwell purely on the legality or logic of his lot."

"Full of awe and trepidation" at the Emperor's words of wisdom, Honjo, by his own account, then reminded Hirohito that in the case of the extremely poor, some concern for material welfare could not be overlooked in the course of giving the nation moral guidance.

18

ORGAN OR GOD?

(1934–1935)

UNCTION AND CONSOLIDATION

The ouster of the Strike-North Faction's General Araki from the war ministership ushered in a two-year period of quiet domestic struggle in which Hirohito consolidated his position and faced a growing swell of passive mass resistance. On the one hand the people began to feel the heel of police state tyranny and to appreciate that Japan was headed on a dangerous course. On the other hand Hirohito's inner circle of Big-Brother advisors, the friends and classmates of his uncles—now all men in their mid-forties—began to replace the elders of Japan, the carry-overs from Emperor Meiji's time, in positions of public responsibility. Concurrently the armament programs of the late 1920's and early 1930's neared completion and the control of Japan's modernized armed services passed from popular demagogic leaders to professional disciplinarians and technocrats.

A month after Strike-North War Minister Araki had fallen from power, Hirohito held a three-day celebration in the palace in honor of his two-month-old son, Crown Prince Akihito. On the first day, February 23, 1934, imperial princes and princesses, Cabinet ministers and foreign ambassadors in Tokyo all sat down at one big table to a luncheon with the Emperor and Empress. American Ambassador Grew described the occasion as "magnificent."

The food and wines were delicious. The servants bowed much lower than in Europe. An orchestra played softly from behind gold screens in front of which were arrayed artful displays of hothouse flowers and stunted pine trees. Mrs. Grew sat between two princes of the blood. Crimson saké cups embossed with the imperial crest in gold and small silver samurai helmets were presented to each guest. In an audience afterwards, Ambassador Grew found the Emperor "exceedingly cordial" and the Empress "beaming."

Not one of the Court diarists who were intimates of Hirohito jotted down any mention of this festivity. Their reality was the Hirohito in Army uniform, hunched over his desk in the Imperial Library. After Araki's ouster they were busy insinuating young men affiliated with the Eleven Club into all the key positions of the Japanese government; busy, too, trying to pacify the Strike-North Faction and keep it quiet. Ambassador Grew shrewdly guessed that there was far more afoot than met his eye and that "the great majority" of Japanese, themselves, were "astonishingly capable of really fooling themselves." Grew judged that the new Japanese foreign minister might be sincere and then again that his "moderation" might be "one of manner and strategy rather than substance." Grew concluded:

We shall sooner or later be seriously concerned as to whether the new generation will acquit itself successfully of the gigantic task to which the nation seems committed, because American and Japanese policy in the Far East will directly conflict—unless someone puts the helm over hard.

In giving up the war ministership in January 1934, General Araki had succeeded in having the number-two leader of the Strike-North Faction, the blunt, honest General Mazaki, appointed to the post of inspector general of military education. The inspector general, along with the war minister and chief of staff, was considered one of the Big Three of the Army. He was, however, the least powerful of the Big Three and the one who had least personal business with Hirohito.

As a further gesture to save the face of the Strike-North Faction,

Hirohito accepted as the new war minister a man who was known to be one of General Mazaki's best friends. This was General Hayashi Senjuro, the obedient commander who had bravely ordered his men to cross the Manchurian frontier without official sanction during the 1931 take-over of Mukden. Now, on assuming office, Hayashi quickly revealed that his loyalty to the Throne was far more important to him than old friendships. He began his term of office by issuing a blanket prohibition against use of the Strike-North slogan "Crisis of 1936" in all Army publications and speeches. He followed by purging Strike-Northists from the staff of the Kwantung Army and from the high command of the secret police.

Hayashi's purge and prohibition brought the secret struggle between Strike-North and Strike-South factions to the attention of the newspaper-reading public for the first time. As usual in that era, the real issues at stake were heavily veiled in the press accounts. The names of the Strike-North and Strike-South factions, in use previously only by top-level strategists and bureaucrats, were changed. The Strike-North Faction, of which the Emperor disapproved, was publicized as the Imperial Way Group. The Strike-South Faction, of which the Emperor was the guiding light, came out as the Control Clique—a name that implied manipulation of the Throne.

It would have been taboo, of course, for either faction to claim the personal backing of the Emperor. Instead the Imperial Way Group and its naval affiliate, the Fleet Faction, associated themselves with conservative samurai ideals, reliance upon force of numbers in the armed services, abhorrence of the regicidal creed of Bolshevism abroad, and a co-operative type of decentralized socialism at home. The Control Clique and its following in the Naval Air Force associated themselves with military mechanization, strict discipline, and a fascistic type of centralized national socialism.

In March 1934 Hirohito gave a hint as to which type of socialism he preferred by dispatching Empress Nagako's senior cousin, his own childhood playmate and near twin, Prince Kaya, on a six-month tour of observation in Europe. Major Kaya and his princess-wife, a niece of Hirohito's mother, scurried through most of the European capitals and then settled down to be wooed for the bulk of their holiday in Hitler's Berlin. There they witnessed one of the early meetings between Hitler and Mussolini, and Prince Kaya told the press, "I was deeply moved to see those two heroes taking a motorboat ride together."

A NOT-SO-MEDIEVAL SCANDAL

Almost immediately after War Minister Hayashi had commenced his regime, Constitutionalist party politicians, working under the tired but approving eyes of old Prince Saionji, began searching for an Achilles' heel in Hirohito's new body politic. They found one in the person of Commerce and Industry Minister Nakajima Kumakichi, a confidant of the Throne who had once been secretary for Emperor Taisho's favorite, Prime Minister Katsura. The Constitutionalists began by accusing Commerce Minister Nakajima of having written an appreciation of the shogun who had deposed the true emperors of the southern dynasty in the fourteenth century. Although Hirohito came of the northern dynasty and occupied the Throne because of this shogun's king-making, it was official doctrine that the shogun had been a traitor. The attack embarrassed Hirohito and brought him out in defense of Commerce Minister Nakajima. To and through his courtiers, Hirohito explained that northern and southern dynasties were both of the same blood and had had equal rights to the Throne.

As soon as Hirohito committed himself in defense of Nakajima, Saionji's cunning political henchmen leveled a more serious charge. They revealed that Nakajima was involved in a major stock swindle and had made millions on the market by manipulating government holdings of the Teikoku Rayon Company. What was more, the swindle had been devised in the geisha house of Child of the Carp, the former mistress of Emperor Taisho's favorite, Katsura. Not only was Katsura's former secretary, Commerce Minister Nakajima, involved in it, but also Katsura's natural son, Big Brother Colonel Marquis Inoue Saburo, who had brought the ubiquitous Suzuki into Hirohito's circle. As a result of the scandal Commerce Minister Nakajima had to resign his portfolio in April 1934, Saito his prime ministership in July, and Big Brother Marquis Inoue his colonel's commission in August.

As soon as the attack on Commerce Minister Nakajima looked as if it would be effective, old Saionji paid an unexpected visit to Tokyo. On May 9, 1934, he called at the palace to pay his belated respects to the infant crown prince and to meet briefly with Hirohito for the first time in almost two years. The encounter took place over tea and cookies in the crowded chamberlains' common room. A dozen courtiers' ears were bent to catch every nuance of the conversation.

"Your Majesty," observed the eighty-four-year-old Saionji, lighting one of his favorite imported Pall Malls, "does not smoke or drink saké at all."

"That's right," replied Hirohito. "When I was four or five years old, I was made drunk by saké and since then I have never liked the stuff."

"Your Majesty means to set a good example for his subjects in a natural manner without having to say a single word," noted Saionji dryly, before the congregated chamberlains. "But it makes for a subtle relationship with the people. Perhaps it would be better to express the virtues of the Throne in some more expansive way."

Chief Aide-de-Camp Honjo, who stood by, noted in his diary that Saionji's manner, as he delivered his remarks, "seemed full of loyalty and respect."

A SECOND NAVAL CABINET

Two weeks later, on May 23, 1934, Baron Harada, the secretary-spy assigned to Saionji, dined with Big Brother Marquis Kido, the secretary to the lord privy seal. The two young intimates of the Throne admitted to one another that the Nakajima scandal had emasculated the effectiveness of Prime Minister Saito. A new government would have to be organized which paid a nod to old Saionji's prejudices. Kido and Harada agreed that the best next prime minister would be another admiral, Okada Keisuke, a well-spoken former Navy minister with a long career in unconventional weapons development and an old friendship with Saionji. For

more than a month after Kido and Harada had reached this understanding, the Saito Cabinet died a lingering death while the
ramifications of the Teikoku Rayon case curled over the toes of
almost every government minister.

When the Cabinet finally resigned *en bloc* on July 4, 1934, old
Saionji, the official prime-minister-maker, had already been persuaded to accept the Big Brothers' choice and recommend Admiral Okada to the Throne as the next head of state. His
Secretary-Spy Harada had made it clear to him that the only alternative would be an imperial Cabinet headed by one of Hirohito's uncles or brothers. So sure was Hirohito of the arrangements which had been made that he first summoned his political
advisor, the nervous, soft-spoken Lord Privy Seal Count Makino,
and said to him, "Okada will suggest his own Cabinet members
and by then it will be impolite to comment on them, so please
take care now to keep out people who will cause problems."

Only then, secondarily, did Hirohito summon Saionji to come
to Tokyo and select a prime minister. The message to Saionji was
carried by the cigar-smoking Taoist, Grand Chamberlain Suzuki.
In it Hirohito wrote, "There is no need to ask you, Prince Saionji,
to abide by the Constitution when you arrange the new Cabinet,
but remember also that you must not achieve an unfavorable
result."

Saionji arrived in Tokyo the next day, made a perfunctory investigation of the political circumstances, and, in a frigid audience
with Hirohito that lasted less than five minutes, rubber-stamped
the arrangements which had already been made. A friend said to
Saionji afterwards, "You have covered a boil with ointment because you are afraid of drastic operations. It may be all right for
the time being, but I am afraid that in the long run the boil will
burst."

As soon as the Okada Cabinet took office, Hirohito required
the new prime minister to reratify the decision passed seven
months earlier by the Inner Cabinet—the prime, foreign, war,
navy, and finance ministers—to expand south as far as possible by
diplomacy and then to rely on force of arms. In asking for this
reaffirmation, Hirohito wanted the Navy to agree specifically to
certain goals it must pursue. The naval Strike-North group, the

Fleet Faction, had used the Strike-South decision as an excuse for demanding more capital ships and an increase in naval manpower. Hirohito wished it clearly understood that naval expenditures should be entirely dedicated to real aggressive striking power rather than showy dreadnoughts and masses of samurai in sailor suits.

The officers of the Naval General Staff found themselves in a difficult position, for in compromising with the Fleet Faction they had already allowed keels to be laid for ships which did not fit perfectly into the Emperor's plans. Hirohito wished to keep international naval limitations in force as long as possible as a cover for the building of the Japanese Naval Air Force. The ships under construction could not all be launched on schedule in 1937—at least not legally—unless Japan in late 1934 gave a year's notice to other nations that it would cease to abide by naval limitations after 1936.

To carry out the contemplated Strike South toward the riches of the Indies, the Naval General Staff officers sincerely believed that they needed the ships which they had planned. Hirohito suspected them of sympathizing with the Strike-North Fleet Faction and of trying to deceive him. To disabuse him they wrote a stack of position papers and entrusted them to Empress Nagako's cousin, Admiral Prince Fushimi, the chief of the Naval General Staff. Fushimi called at the palace impromptu on July 12, 1934, in order to present the Navy's case. Hirohito had been thinking of other matters and found the visit an intrusion. He and Fushimi exchanged hot words. Fushimi slapped down the sheaf of position papers on Hirohito's desk, told him to read and consider them, and then stormed from the palace. Hirohito, in anger, sent an aide-de-camp after him to give back the bundle of position papers unopened.

Then, for the next week, Hirohito reconsidered his position, cross-questioned his naval aides, and saw that he had been wrong. On July 17, squirming a little, he sighed to Prime Minister Admiral Okada, "If the treaty must be abrogated, how about handling the negotiations so that France will bear the brunt of the criticism?"

Hirohito had forehandedly appointed the chief Japanese delegate to the 1934 naval disarmament conference eight months earlier, in November 1933. He had chosen fifty-year-old Vice Admiral Yamamoto, the future architect of the daring raid on Pearl Harbor. Yamamoto had been detached full time since February 1934 to study the problems of the forthcoming conference, and it was his opinion that Japan's best weapon in the negotiations would be one he had used earlier, in 1929, during his unofficial bargaining with President Hoover. Why not disarm the disarmament conference by offering, on Japan's part, to abolish all such offensive vessels as aircraft carriers? Since there were few "stationary aircraft carriers"—few islands—in the California half of the Pacific, the proposal might force the United States to take upon herself the responsibility for abrogating the limitations treaty.

On July 21, nine days after his spat with Cousin Fushimi, Hirohito gave an audience to the Japanese ambassador to the United States, who was home for rebriefing. The ambassador told him that the United States took a hostile legalistic position toward Japan's aspirations but could still be managed for several more years by appropriate short-term political gestures. Hirohito asked the ambassador's opinion of Yamamoto's aircraft-carrier stratagem and the ambassador endorsed it enthusiastically.

SHEDDING LIMITATIONS

A month later, on August 24, Hirohito personally dictated to the Navy minister an outline of the instructions which he wished Yamamoto to carry with him to the limitations conference. On September 6, Hirohito approved the instructions as they had been drafted for the Cabinet. On September 11, Hirohito sanctioned the final draft of the instructions passed by the Cabinet.

Yamamoto set out on his mission a week later. The conference, once again, was to be held in London, and once again Yamamoto traveled by way of the United States. Crossing the Pacific he stayed in his cabin and played poker. Crossing the continent, he stayed in a locked compartment on the train. General Billy Mitchell was then making headlines with his demands that the United States equip herself with an air force for ultimate use against Japan. Newsmen pestered Yamamoto's aides for an interview.

Finally Yamamoto held one press conference. "I have never thought of America as a potential enemy," he declared in Japanese, "and the naval plans of Japan have never included the possibility of an American-Japanese war." American editorial writers applauded his calm good sense and branded Mitchell an alarmist. Refusing to say more on the grounds that he could not speak English, Harvard graduate Yamamoto sailed for England on the *Berengaria*. The day he arrived in Southampton he abruptly called a press conference and gave British reporters a frontpage story. "Japan," he said in his best New England accent, "can no longer submit to the ratio system. There is no possibility of compromise by my government on that point."

That same day in Tokyo—October 16, 1934—Hirohito authorized a telegram to be sent to Yamamoto instructing him to break off discussion and announce abrogation of the treaty "at the earliest convenient moment in the negotiations." Time was important because the treaty had to be abrogated by December 31 if Japan was to be allowed legally to launch the ships she was already building. Throughout November, Yamamoto held his carte blanche from the Throne close to his chest and did his utmost to seem earnest and likeable. Admiral Chatfield, the British Lord of the Admiralty, realized that Japan did not want to take responsibility for aborting the conference and brought pressure to bear on U.S. colleagues to be conciliatory. The American delegates complained that they represented a navy which had to be split between two oceans and that they could not, therefore, accept a total fleet strength exactly equal to Japan's. Yamamoto insisted on perfect parity. "I am smaller than you," he said at a dinner party, "but you do not insist that I eat three fifths of the food on my plate. You allow me to eat as much as I need."

Finally in early December, as time ran out, Yamamoto made his dramatic proposal to abolish aircraft carriers. Admiral Chatfield sounded out the U.S. delegates and found that they were willing to discuss absolute parity if all capital ships were abolished. As indication of good faith, the U.S. delegation canceled its bookings home and offered to stay on in London indefinitely for further unscheduled weeks of conversation. The British vied with the Japanese in pacifism by offering to give up a third of their destroyer tonnage. Poker player Yamamoto realized that his bluff was being called and raised. If the Western nations agreed to give up building capital ships, they might begin to spend their naval funds on the unconventional weapons—the one-man submarines and dive and torpedo bombers—in which Yamamoto saw the victories of the future. Much embarrassed, Yamamoto had his palace advisor and traveling companion, the father-in-law of Hirohito's brother Prince Chichibu, cable home for further instructions.

After consulting with Hirohito, Prime Minister Okada penned a long, noncommittal reply to Yamamoto's query, informing him that domestic politics were "extremely well in hand" and that therefore no repercussions at home need be considered in dealing with the British peace offensive. Yamamoto mulled this reply for twenty-four hours, then returned to the conference table with a fresh attitude and a suddenly hard concern for technical details. The American delegates responded in kind by booking passage home on a ship sailing December 29.

The American date of departure was an awkward one. Yamamoto did not wish, after his protestations, to announce abrogation of the limitations treaty while there was still any possibility that he might have to meet face to face with his opposite numbers from the United States. At the same time, abrogation must be announced before December 31. Yamamoto cabled home asking that notification of abrogation be postponed until the last minute. After consultation with the palace and with the Japanese ambassador in Washington, the Navy minister agreed that abrogation should be announced to the U.S. State Department on Saturday, December 29, a few minutes before commencement of the American New Year holiday. The plan worked to split-second perfection. The State Department received the notice of abrogation before it closed its doors, and Yamamoto was just able to see off the American delegation from Southampton before news came from Washington that abrogation had been declared. It was a close call in timing and one that would be re-enacted—unsuccessfully—seven years later when Japan sought to declare war with technical propriety a few seconds before Yamamoto's attack on Pearl Harbor.

DOMESTIC DISCIPLINE

During Yamamoto's abrogation of naval limitations—a challenge, incidentally, which failed to make the complacent United States build even her quota of naval vessels—Emperor Hirohito back in the palace had been seeking fresh ways of controlling the Strike-North-minded ranks of the Japanese Army. He had found a new Army leader in Lieutenant General Count Terauchi Hisaichi, an in-law of Secretary to the Lord Privy Seal Big Brother Marquis Kido. Terauchi was the son of one of Emperor Meiji's oligarch-generals, a dedicated believer in the Strike South, and the future World War II commander-in-chief for all of Southeast Asia.

In the summer of 1934 Terauchi founded a stern disciplinarian faction in the Army officer corps which was known as the Army Purification Movement. It stood for nonintervention in politics and strict obedience to orders. In August 1934, when Yamamoto was getting his instructions for the naval conference in London, Hirohito approved a set of summer repostings which greatly diminished the Strike-North Faction's influence at key desks and garrison outposts. At the same time Hirohito dispatched purification leader Terauchi to organize provisional Strike-South preparations on the island of Taiwan. As Terauchi set out on his mission, he told well-wishers, "The problem of the Army still remains that of having no work to do."

Two months later, from October 1 to October 18, 1934, the senior warrior of the imperial family, Prince Kanin, visited Terauchi's command in Taiwan and approved plans for setting up a top-secret intelligence organization there, recruited largely from civilian sources, which would begin to collect data from Japanese commercial travelers and emigrants about Malaya, Luzon, Java, and other points south. Under the name of the Southward Movement Society, the organization would later be funded publicly with money voted in the Diet. In late 1940, it would provide the maps and facts for the staff officers who drew up the operational plans for the conquest of Malaya and the Philippines.

To Yamamoto's efforts in London and Terauchi's in Taiwan,

Hirohito, during September 1934, added a reorganization in Manchuria. This Manchukuo Structure Plan formalized the malpractices already in use in Manchuria by bringing them all under the jurisdiction of a single organization loyal to the Emperor, the secret police. The first of the Three Crows of Baden-Baden, Major General Nagata Tetsuzan, surprised his intimates by coming out with members of the Strike-North Faction in opposition to the structure bill. Nagata insisted—pretense be damned—that Manchuria should be honestly annexed and given a decent administration such as it would enjoy if it were a part of the Empire and not merely a phony autonomous buffer zone. Nagata was defeated in his stand, and other members of Hirohito's cabal suggested in his defense that he had acted under the compulsion of blackmail. Retired War Minister Araki had possession of the plan—the "novel"—which Nagata had drawn up for the March Plot in 1931. Nagata was, therefore, subject to blackmail, but whether he resisted the Manchukuo Structure Plan because of political or conscientious pressure remained a moot point. Hirohito himself was not sure of the truth and thereafter dealt with Nagata cautiously.

No sooner had the Manchukuoan structure bill passed its hurdles than the Army publicity squad completed a project begun by its former director, the ubiquitous Suzuki Tei-ichi, and came out on October 1, 1934, with a booklet entitled "The True Meaning of National Strength and Proposals for Building It." Prepublication copies, containing return postcards for comment and criticism, were sent out to all leaders of the Army bureaucracy including the aides-de-camp at Court. Hirohito had glanced through the text and passed on it even earlier.

The booklet began with the words: "War is the father of creation and the mother of culture." It was a phrase brought back from Mussolini's Italy by a former attaché in Rome and aide-de-camp in the palace. The booklet went on in detail to explain what the slogan, "National Defense for Total War," would mean as distinct from Araki's slogan, "Crisis of 1936." Japan was a small backward nation in a commanding position. If she were to dominate Asia, every aspect of national life from the lowliest newspaper article to the mightiest industrial enterprise would have to come under "national defense discipline." The whole people must purge itself of Western individualism and work together for the glorious Armageddon ahead. Business leaders were naturally alarmed by this pronouncement, and War Minister Hayashi at a get-together on November 14 had to assure them in person that construction of the defense state would be gradual and that their vested interests would not be disregarded.

REBUFF ON MANEUVERS

On November 10, 1934, Hirohito went off into the rugged Gunma alps to attend the Army's annual grand maneuvers. All seemed well. The purge of the Army and building program of the Navy seemed settled. Hirohito did honor to the Imperial Guards Division by bivouacking with their commander, his uncle, Lieutenant General Prince Asaka, who would later rape Nanking.

However, the Strike-North Faction had an unpleasant surprise in store. The maneuvers were meant to demonstrate how Japanese forces would deal with a hypothetical attack by Soviet forces in Manchuria. This they failed to do because the "Army of the West," commanded by the former war minister, General Araki, and staff-officered by the second of the Three Crows, the brilliant, dissident Major General Obata, entirely rearranged itself on the opening night of the big show and by dint of forced marches surprised the "Army of the East" at the outset. In the two days that followed, the aristocratic "Eastern" General, Abe Nobuyuki, continued to be outwitted and outmaneuvered by the mock-Russian forces of Araki and Obata. At the close of the exercise Abe's "Eastern Army" had been reduced to scattered pockets. The Strike-North Faction had won a battle where it most counted—on the battlefield. Hirohito could see what the advice of aristocratic generals might lead to, and the men in the ranks had tangible evidence that preparations against Russia must not be suspended.

On November 15, the day after the Strike-North Faction's triumph at the maneuvers, several young officers broke into War Minister Hayashi's residence, seized one of his aides, and warned that if national policy were not redirected there would be, finally, a genuine Army coup d'etat in Japan. The young troublemakers belonged to a sub-faction of Araki's Strike-North following which believed that domestic reform must take precedence over foreign involvements, whether to the north or the south. Some of them had been parties to the earlier break-in at the war minister's residence, when, after the assassination of Prime Minister Inukai in May 1932, they had sought to prevent War Minister Araki from aborting the planned 5–15 coup d'etat. Now, in 1934, they once again returned to their billets in peace. No disciplinary action was taken against them because they knew far more than could be told publicly about the Army-palace plots of 1931 and 1932.

The tension generated by these latest Strike-North stratagems was indirectly revealed the next day, November 16, 1934, in "an unpleasant incident" which occurred during an official inspection by Hirohito of two schools in Nagano prefecture near the alpine site of the just completed maneuvers. First Hirohito was to visit Nagano Middle School, then the Nagano Higher Technical High School. On the way the security policeman who led the imperial cavalcade took the wrong road by accident and brought the Emperor to the technical school first. Being caught unprepared, the school faculty was embarrassed and Minister of Education Matsuda was not there to greet the Emperor. Hirohito was visibly put out by the delay, and a few minutes later the policeman in charge of guidance committed suicide. Then the Emperor hastily said, in a voice which could be heard by all around him: "Did you change the schedule? It is all right but it may disturb the school."

"Such a generous mind!" concluded Chief Aide-de-Camp Honjo in his diary account.[1]

THE MILITARY ACADEMY PLOT

On November 20, 1934, shortly after Hirohito's return from the maneuvers to Tokyo, a plot came to light at the military academy which discredited the Strike-North Faction in general

[1] A few days later, on November 23, 1934, Honjo wrote: "Today the Emperor officiated at the Harvest Festival. Last night he changed his underraiment and did not go to the Imperial bedchamber but slept instead on a couch outside his office. He is always extremely careful, I am told, on this particular point. About dawn he arose and sat down, solemn and motionless, for two hours of meditation."

and in particular the young domestic reformers who had broken into the war minister's residence five days earlier.

The plot was reported to the palace by Major General Yamashita Tomoyuki, the strategic genius and "Tiger of Malaya" who would later, in 1942, capture the supposedly impregnable British fortress of Singapore. Yamashita had been assigned since August by one of Hirohito's aides-de-camp to establish an undercover network in Araki's Strike-North circles. One of Yamashita's agents was a thirty-one-year-old captain named Tsuji Masanobu who would later serve as Yamashita's chief staff officer during the Singapore campaign. Brilliant, fanatic, colorful, and intensely puritanic, Tsuji would become famous during the war with China for going out at night in the streets of Shanghai with a lighted faggot in hand and burning down brothels which were supposed to be off-limits to Japanese troops. At war's end in 1945 he donned the clothes of a Buddhist priest and walked home "underground" from Burma. He resurfaced in Tokyo as an author in 1949, was elected to the Diet in 1952, and in 1958, when he was fifty-five and the United States had become involved in Vietnam, disappeared without trace in Hanoi.

Major General Tiger Yamashita had insinuated Captain Tsuji into the military academy as the morals instructor for a dissident company of cadets there. In line of duty Tsuji had learned that some of his cadets were in touch with the group of young domestic reformers in the officer corps who perennially broke into the war minister's residence. The young reformers, in fact, had asked the cadets to take part in an armed uprising intended to open Hirohito's eyes and persuade him to "renovate the nation." Morals instructor Captain Tsuji persuaded his charges to take no part in the plan. He warned them that they were being incited by mere talkers who had been involved in several fake coups already and would never carry out anything.

In the course of his counseling Tsuji learned that one of the officers who had tempted his cadets was a special student at the Army Staff College who had assisted Major General Obata, the second of the Three Crows, in drafting the brilliant plan which had confounded all at the Army grand maneuvers. This was information of value, for it implicated the top brass of the Strike-

North Faction with the sedition at the military academy. At the request of Major General Yamashita, Tsuji reported it to his friendly neighborhood secret police contact, who happened to be Captain Tsukamoto Makoto, the later watchdog of the fake coup in the palace on the night of August 14, 1945.

At 2 A.M. on November 20, 1934, morals instructor Tsuji and secret policeman Tsukamoto called at the official residence of the vice minister of war and roused him from bed to tell him their story. The vice minister, Lieutenant General Hashimoto Torano-suke, was one of the few partisans of the Strike-North Faction who was venal enough to make a deal with. He had been secret police commandant in Manchuria from August 1932 to August 1933 and was known to love money. Tsuji and Tsukamoto showed him an operations plan for the seizure of Tokyo which they told him had been proposed to the innocent cadets at the academy by the eager young reformers in General Araki's following of staff officers. After several hours of talk, Vice War Minister Hashimoto agreed to have three of the ringleading troublemakers kept under arrest in their quarters for the next three months.

During the three months in which the activists were detained, the reputed Strike-North plan for rebellion was bruited about Tokyo and used effectively to divide the Strike-North Faction and prevent it from exercising the influence it had won at the grand maneuvers. At least in part the plan was a forgery, put on paper by Tsuji and Tsukamoto. But having been forced to take the blame for it, the young Strike-North reformers finally adopted it as their own. And when they rose in insurrection over a year later they took with them, regiment by regiment and company by company, the units stipulated in the plan.

The plan included an excellent little list of a dozen palace advisors who were deemed worthy of assassination. In the event, fifteen months later, the most culpable villains on the list would escape unharmed, but during the interval, from November 1934 to February 1936, all men of influence in Japan walked a gossamer span of mounting tension and intrigue.

BETRAYING CHIANG KAI-SHEK

While the inciters of the Military Academy Plot were restricted to quarters, Hirohito pressed forward, ignoring all opposition. On December 7, 1934—seven years before Pearl Harbor and seven years after Chiang Kai-shek's last visit to Tokyo—Hirohito decided to turn his back on Chiang, to stand by no longer while Chiang attempted to unify classical China, and finally to take for Japan more than the outer Chinese provinces of Manchuria and Mongolia which had been stipulated in Japan's early bargains with Chiang and Sun Yat-sen. Specifically, on that fine winter Friday, Hirohito approved a resolution of the Inner Cabinet: "For the time being it is desirable to reduce to a minimum the influence of the Nanking government on the regimes in north China." A few days later the foreign minister informed Prime-Minister-Maker Saionji that a power play could be expected in north China the following spring.

Japanese moderates registered their disapproval of Hirohito's decision in their usual discreet ways. For instance, on December 30, 1934, the Supreme Court judge who was conducting the preliminary hearings in chambers for the pilgrims who had met at Meiji Shrine a year and a half earlier for Prince Higashikuni's Prayer Meeting Plot came in some bemusement to old Saionji's Secretary-Spy Harada and protested that it would be absolutely impossible ever to stage a public trial of the case. "Why!" he exclaimed, "names of the imperial family appear constantly . . . not only Prince Higashikuni's but Prince Chichibu's and Prince Fushimi's as well."

The most effective opposition to Hirohito's latest step forward was put up by the politicians of the Constitutionalist party in the Diet, and from December 1934 to February 1935, Hirohito's political agents fought the most protracted budgetary battle of their careers. The Constitutionalists and Strike-Northists tried to bleed the naval development program by drawing off from it funds for domestic famine and hurricane relief. Even when Lord Privy Seal Makino's henchmen had bought or bludgeoned all the venal Constitutionalist politicians they could, there still remained a majority which would not settle. Finally, when the Constitution-alist party had been split by inducements, its two halves met on separate floors of the same restaurant, both armed to the teeth with swords and pistols. In the course of a saké-steeped evening the two factions, upstairs and down, climbed back and forth and compromised without firing any shots. Once again a budget was passed containing not a drop of relief for the victims of drought and typhoon in the rice-root farming areas.

NATIONAL PRINCIPLE

During the budget battle and the continuing house arrest of the reform-minded staff officers, fellow dissidents in the Army organized themselves as a National Principle Group. On February 5, 1935, they published a catechism of questions and answers en-titled "Two Basic Movements for the Renovation of the Nation, the Fascistic Group and the National Principle Group."

The fascists [warned the pamphlet] are the National Socialists who wish to carry out a reformation under the slogan, so they say, of "National Defense." The National Principle Group, however, believes that our national defense is inadequate because the nation as a whole is not under the control of the true national principle. . . . If the people close their eyes to the national principle and dance to the flute of fascism, there will be a critical day for Imperial Japan. That is what you must be most concerned about.

During the two weeks after publication of this blunt manifesto, Lord Privy Seal Makino's secretary, the original Big Brother Mar-quis Kido, undertook a comprehensive research into the feelings and factions of the Army. He concluded that "the main trunk" of the Emperor's Strike-South following was still sound. Lieutenant General Tatekawa, who had stayed abed at the Literary Chrysan-themum during the seizure of Mukden in 1931, seemed faithful still to his patron, Prince Kanin, the chief of staff. So did Lieuten-ant General Koiso who had masterminded the March Plot paving the way for the Mukden Incident. Even War Minister Hayashi, despite years of friendship with the leaders of the Strike-North Faction, could now be considered dependable.

On the other hand First Crow Nagata, the original center of the Emperor's cabal in the Army, was under extreme pressure because Inspector General of Military Education Mazaki, the number-two leader of the Strike North, was threatening to make "disclosures about half a million past incidents." The ubiquitous Colonel Suzuki Tei-ichi was also in difficulties. Many of the young officers whom he had recruited for the imperial cabal in days gone by were weary of waiting for reform, indignant about peasant suffering, and fast becoming downright dangerous.

Kido cited several names and by way of illustration expatiated briefly on the feelings of a Lieutenant Colonel Mitsui Sakichi, a devout young Shintoist who the year before had pushed his way into the home of a namesake, the senior Mitsui of the Mitsui cartel, and had delivered a long sermon there. Such firebrands disliked the fact that at the Big Brothers' Eleven Club meetings Colonel Suzuki and Major General Nagata talked and bargained with politicians and industrialists—with corrupt and corrupting "plutocrats."

Big Brother Kido submitted his evaluation of Army loyalty to Hirohito and to a number of elder chamberlains close to Hirohito, including old Prime-Minister-Maker Saionji. With it, as documentation, he circulated a compendium of secret police intelligence briefs which he had collected from his sources in the bureaucracy. The briefs reported that the National Principle Group "believes only in righteousness," that it "has leagued itself" with Baron Hiranuma, the horse-faced lawyer of the Aristocratic National Foundation Society who would sit in judgment at the surrender scene in Hirohito's bunker in 1945, and that "with unusually grim determination, they have resolved to take political power."

THE ORGAN CONTROVERSY

All the various opposition groups which were springing up against Hirohito's increasingly explicit Strike-South policy were unified in early 1935 by an ingenious issue devised by one of Saionji's elderly cronies. It was an issue which police state methods could not combat, yet one that struck at the very root of Hirohito's power. Old Saionji received word of it on February 18, 1935, in a radiogram from his bohemian underworld agent, the artist Takuno Dempu. Takuno advised Saionji that now even the elders of the Black Dragon Society wished to reprimand Hirohito and embarrass the Throne. To this end they were planning to launch an attack on one of Hirohito's most loyal elder retainers: Ikki, the former minister of the imperial household and present president of the Privy Council. The charge against Ikki would be that in his youth he had advocated ideas "against the Constitution of the nation" and specifically that he had subscribed to "the theory that the Emperor is merely an organ of the state."

The attack was duly opened the next day, February 19, 1935, in the upper chamber of the Diet, the House of Peers. The speaker was Baron Kikuchi Takeo, the scion of a brilliant family of physicians, lawyers, and scientists, and the same man who had engineered the slur on Konoye's friends in the Kyoto Law School faculty two years earlier. Baron Kikuchi began his defamation quietly and obliquely by noting that Privy Council President Ikki was a follower of a certain Professor Minobe.

The accusation sounded harmless enough for Dr. Minobe was himself a member of the House of Peers, the Dean of Law at Tokyo Imperial University, and one of the most respected scholars in the land. He had delivered educational lectures frequently to Hirohito and his family in the Imperial Study. Only the year before he had written two magazine articles in support of the Throne. In one of them, which he had been asked to write by Secretary-Spy Harada, he had speculated on the role which political parties might play in a truly imperial Japan, united behind the Throne under a "whole-nation" prime minister such as Fujiwara Prince Konoye or one of the princes of the blood. In the second article, published later in 1934, Dr. Minobe had deplored the oversimplifications of militaristic thinking and had warned against the staff-officer approach to politics and economics.

Having asserted that Privy Council President Ikki was a disciple of Professor Minobe and having then established that Professor Minobe was a pedagogue of stature, valued highly by Hirohito, the cunning Baron Kikuchi began gradually and insidiously to explain to the House of Peers Professor Minobe's theories of constitutional law. He introduced quotation after quotation from

Minobe's own writings demonstrating that, in Minobe's view, the Emperor did not transcend the state or comprehend the state but was merely an organ of the state. Finally, in a crescendo of passion, Baron Kikuchi accused Professor Minobe and Privy Council President Ikki of heresy, sacrilege, and lèse majesté.

Professor Minobe did not appreciate the grave religious implications of the charges leveled against him. On February 25, 1935, when he arose in the House of Peers to answer, he spoke slowly, quietly, almost disdainfully, and carefully explained fundamental theories of constitutional law as set forth by learned men of many nations. When he had concluded, the applause was scattered. Neither his hearers nor the masses really cared about the academic fine points of constitutional law. The issue was the Emperor's leadership. Would Hirohito hide behind the Constitution as "an organ of state" and continue to manipulate the nation or would he come out into the open and take responsibility for his rule?

Popular clamor in opposition to the organ theory of the Emperor and in favor of "a clarification of the national structure" pre-empted headlines daily for six months and was not completely stilled until the shame of insurrection, exactly a year later, had dropped a stained mask over the nation's much prized "face." Hirohito did everything in his personal power to end the controversy without bloodshed. He compromised again and again with General Araki's Strike-North Faction and taxed his brain to find arguments which would impugn the motives of his metaphysical tormentors. But the Strike-North Faction had struck on an issue of devilish ingenuity, which united both patriots and pacifists. The great mass of the people, accustomed to shouting slogans on order, did not realize that they were crossing the Emperor's personal wishes. They were urged on by the same military officers and underworld labor leaders who had previously organized them in the Emperor's service. And the Emperor, of course—even if he had been willing to come so far out into the open—could hardly explain his own position without damaging the simple religious faith in which his power consisted. As for the rich and the educated who opposed imperial policy, they found themselves in a uniquely enjoyable position. By agreeing that it was sacrilege to call the living god an organ they could snipe at the Throne and at the same time utter sentiments that were impeccable.

As soon as Minobe had made his chilly answer to the House of Peers, retired Major General Eto Genkuro—one of those Choshu officers who had been purged from the Army in the 1920's—lodged a formal charge against Minobe for the capital offense of lèse majesté. Out of realism the charge was later reduced to one of press code violation, but nevertheless the case against Minobe was dragged through the courts for the next nine months. Moreover, similar charges were brought against eighteen other public figures who were alleged to have subscribed to Minobe's theories. Only two of the accused were professors; the other sixteen were bureaucrats and politicians who had been used by the Throne in the past as covert messengers or manipulators. They included even Okada, the prime minister.

The lawyers enjoyed a field day turning the phraseology of recent peace preservation and censorship laws against the pillars of propriety who had drafted them. The people participated in the controversy with back-street discussions. Now if ever was the time to remind Hirohito that he was "above the clouds" and that his "Voice of the Crane" should only be heard on earth infrequently as a kind of miracle. Poor Professor Minobe, who was a deluded academician rather than a deliberate villain, fought blindly for his status, his "face," and his means of livelihood.

GOD DEMURS

The Emperor's first reaction to the attack on Minobe verged on petulance. On February 18, the day before Baron Kikuchi's speech to the Peers, Hirohito had agreed that when Manchukuo's puppet emperor, Henry Pu-Yi, came to Tokyo on a ceremonial visit in April the soldiers on review would be excused from paying him the customary international courtesy of dipping their colors. As soon as Baron Kikuchi made his speech, however, Hirohito called in Chief Aide-de-Camp Honjo and abruptly attacked him about the non-dipping of the colors to which he had given routine consent the day before.

"I return the salute even of one soldier," he announced without prologue. "If the Army flag cannot be dipped in acknowledgment of my generosity to Henry Pu-Yi, then the Army flag is more respected by the soldiers than I am."

Honjo replied: "In general it is ruled that an officer must return the salute of a junior officer, but there is no rule like that for the Emperor. As I understand it, when the Emperor returns a salute he does so as a voluntary gesture, out of his infinite sympathy for the people. The Army's flag which is given to the Army by the Emperor is dipped only to the Emperor in person—not to the Empress, not even to the crown prince. In peace and war the flag is a symbol of the Emperor to which all men of all services give their full belief. Where it goes, they go, even to the water and the fire. The faith and courage of the national Army depend upon this severe respect for the flag."

"The Emperor," in Honjo's words, "nodded his silent understanding." Men could more easily die for a god who was a figurehead than for one who functioned materially as an organ of government. Hirohito summoned War Minister Hayashi to a private audience, and a few days later Hayashi gave a soothing speech to the Diet explaining that the doctrine of the Emperor as an organ of the state was merely a national convenience for dealing with other nations. Western states, he pointed out, could not conceive the true nature of the Emperor and preferred to contract treaties with a whole people rather than a deified individual.

On March 9, after reading the shorthand notes of Hayashi's remarks to the Diet, Hirohito called Chief Aide-de-Camp Honjo and said: "Of course my ranking is different but physically I am no different from you or anyone else. . . . Therefore, this is a most vexatious problem for me because the Army's attack on the organ theory may restrict my future movements, both physical and spiritual."

Honjo carefully dodged the obvious question—how anyone's freedom could be curtailed by being acknowledged absolute decision maker for the nation—and answered noncommittally: "The Army, Sire, intends no restriction on your movements." And with this Honjo backed his way out of Hirohito's workroom.

Up to this point Hirohito's Big Brothers had treated the organ-or-god controversy lightly. Prince Konoye's group in the House of Peers had prepared a resolution condemning anti-organ ideas as old-fashioned and reactionary. Now, however, after some canvassing, Konoye decided that the resolution could not safely be brought to a vote.

In March 1935 the Black Dragon Society launched a League for the Extermination of the Organ Theory and in co-operation with a lower-class religious sect, Omoto-kyo, a Movement for Modification of the National Structure. The Shinto fundamentalists of Omoto-kyo collected 400,000 signatures on a petition to the Emperor asking him to come out into the open, take responsibility for what was being done, and appoint a Cabinet composed of princes of the blood. Hirohito asked Lord Privy Seal Count Makino how to handle the petition if it were ever presented. Count Makino assured him that it would not be presented. The police and secret police began a vigorous persecution of the "heretical" Omoto-kyo sect and of the Black Dragon Society itself. No less than 515 Black Dragon hoodlums were arrested for crimes which had been previously overlooked. Two hundred of them were even brought to trial and sentenced.

On March 22, 1935, the lower house of the Diet resolved for "renovation of national thought" and "clarification of the nation's fundamental moral principle." Saionji's Secretary-Spy Harada observed to his diary that "the Diet should be burned to the ground."[2] The next day Privy Council President Ikki was set upon and beaten at his wife's funeral. The police, according to their files, determined that the thugs had been hired by a relative of Baron Kikuchi Takeo who had begun the accusations against the heretic Minobe in the House of Peers the month before.

Original Big Brother Marquis Kido, secretary to the lord privy seal, tried to persuade Professor Minobe to resign his chair at Tokyo Imperial University and apologize for the misunderstandings which his academic theories had caused. In vain Kido enlisted Minobe's brother and one of his richest friends in this endeavor. Professor Minobe offered to withdraw his works from print and

[2] Big Brother Harada, in fear of assassination at the hands of the Black Dragon Society or of the Strike-North Faction, had just moved to a villa in the country, near Saionji's home, and announced that temporarily, on doctor's orders, he would be performing his duties from retirement.

even to rephrase the most misunderstood statements in them but refused to resign or recant utterly. Privy Council President Ikki offered to resign in his stead, but courtiers agreed that this would seem too much of a personal concession on the part of Hirohito.

GOD ARGUES

On April 4, 1935, the commanders of Japan's seventeen divisions gathered at the palace for individual briefings from Hirohito on the objectives of Japan's forthcoming push through the Great Wall into north China. Now had arrived the moment of decision on which all the organ-theory controversy was predicated. The number-two leader of the Strike-North Faction, Inspector General of Military Education Mazaki, tried to subvert the proceedings by circulating in advance among the divisional commanders a memorandum which asked them to endorse flatly the statement: "The organ theory is incompatible with the fundamental principles of the nation."

Hirohito heard of the memo from one of the assistant aides-de-camp. He at once summoned Chief Aide Honjo. "Does the Army hope," he asked, "that I will sanction this statement?"

"No, never," said Honjo. "I have simply had it reported to the Throne. It is wholly Mazaki's responsibility."

In the five days that followed Hirohito saw the divisional commanders individually and impressed upon each of them the need to disregard Mazaki as a hothead and to serve loyally in the approaching north China crisis. At the same time Hirohito officiated over Manchukuoan Emperor Henry Pu-Yi's state visit to Tokyo.[3]

When the ceremonies were over on April 9 Hirohito called Honjo into his study and concluded their unfinished business by taxing him with semantic fine points. "In his statement," said Hirohito, "Mazaki calls me the *shutai* of the nation [the main constituent or grammatical subject of the national sentence]. . . . This is absolutely no different in fundamental interpretation from Professor Minobe's *kikan* [organ]. It is only unfortunate that

[3] He was both shocked and amused by Henry's servility to him. He told intimates that, on one reviewing stand, Henry had gone so far as to thank him effusively for making the sky clear and the sun shine that day.

Minobe improperly used the *kikan* meaning 'mechanical organ' instead of the *kikan* meaning 'body organ.' . . . In short, if we regard the Emperor as a brain in charge of the nation's life and if we regard the rest as hands, feet and so on which are activated by order of the master brain, then there is no dispute at all with Minobe's ideas. . . . On the other hand, if sovereignty is to reside exclusively in the Emperor rather than the nation as a whole, it will raise the suspicion of tyranny and make for all sorts of difficulties in international treaty and credit arrangements."

Hirohito felt that the farce of the organ-theory attack against him had now gone far enough. Through his Big Brothers he approached Lieutenant General Terauchi, the loyal martinet who had charge of early Strike-South preparations in Taiwan, and asked him for his help in disciplining the Army. Terauchi at first shook his head and said, "It is a difficult problem." But on April 12, 1935, he informed Hirohito's envoys that he had negotiated with War Minister Hayashi and that the war minister was now committed to a total purge of the Strike-North Faction from the Army, including the retirement of his friend, the number-two Strike-North leader Mazaki from his post as inspector general of military education.

In preparation for the showdown with the Strike-North Faction, Hirohito, on April 18, 1935, summoned his wife's cousin Prince Fushimi, the chief of the Navy General Staff, to the palace and demanded that the Navy must have a determination, unwritten but agreed upon, as to how far it was committed to go. Hirohito asked that it be a secret *hara* policy, or policy "in the guts." Prince Fushimi at first tried to equivocate but finally pledged that the Navy would go all the way with the Emperor, abandoning dreadnoughts, large crews, and political strength in preparation for aggressive war. Chief Aide-de-Camp Honjo, representing the Army, tried to find out what the Navy had agreed to. He was met with a blank look of ignorance by the Navy minister and by a security-conscious "no comment" from his friends on the Navy General Staff.

At about this same time, in mid-April 1935, the veterans clubs of retired Choshu-clan officers, organized by Strike-North leader

Araki after the great purge of 1924, began to circulate a petition explaining the evils of the organ theory and begging Hirohito to renounce it. On April 19, having just read the pamphlet, Hirohito asked Honjo playfully: "Will it be all right if I take this theory about the absolute sovereignty of the Emperor in earnest instead of as a mere theory on paper? During the Manchurian Incident when I tried to make the Cabinet conduct an appropriate investigation, Army officers frequented the aides-de-camp office and made all sorts of demands. They did not listen and try to understand."

Honjo recorded in his diary, "When I checked these assertions with aides-de-camp from General Nara's era, I could find no facts such as the Emperor mentioned." He returned to the Imperial Presence and said, "If someone believes that the Emperor could be wrong in a way that would injure his virtue, he is obliged to rebuke the Emperor with utmost virtue. Since the Army never did what you just told me, it will harm your virtue if I do not rebuke you."

For the first time since childhood, Hirohito had been called a liar to his face. He dismissed Honjo without a word and for six days mused or sulked behind a mask of formality. Then on April 25 he said very simply to Honjo, "The Army, in attacking the organ theory, is acting against my will. In so doing they are treating me as an organ. Is that not true?"

"Not absolutely," squirmed Honjo. "The reservists are merely circulating a small pamphlet and trying to unify their own thinking on the matter."

"If science is suppressed by emotion and conviction," declared Hirohito darkly, "the progress of the world will be retarded and the theory of evolution will be upset."

After further reflection, Hirohito called Honjo on April 27 and itemized his objections to the veterans' arguments in a veritable blizzard of learned hailstones. He spoke extremely tersely, without any attempt to explain his nuggets of thought. In the process, however, he gave the most complete and personal statement of his beliefs on record, and exposed in himself the young sheltered intellectual, sure of his unlimited power and convinced that sci-

entific rationalism could be applied to statecraft for the betterment of Japan and all Asia. He said:

In the first place the theory that a nation's sovereignty resides in the
nation itself is not necessarily the same as the theory of democracy and
it is utterly indefensible to argue that it is.

In the second place, it is a mistake to regard the trend in the world
at large as a trend toward individualism. It is correct to say that democracy in Europe and the United States is an outgrowth of individualism in the past. But how do you regard the enactment of the
prohibition law in the United States? As individualistic? How do you
account for the fact that men in England died for their nation in great
herds during the last world war?

In the third place your Army theorists in their discussion of constitutional theory speak much of the constitutions of England, France,
and other democracies but do not seem to have studied the German
constitution [of Bismarck] which was the model for the drafting of the
Imperial Constitution of Japan.

In the fourth place, though natural science is susceptible to proof
and though matters pertaining to life are not susceptible to proof, it
is impossible to point to the line of demarcation and say that thus
and so is outside the realm of scientific proof. For instance, there is
no distinction which can be made between physiology and philosophy.

In the fifth place, these veterans in their discussion of purely academic theories occasionally mention individual names like [Privy
Council President] Ikki's in a most personal way. In so doing, they
run the risk of inciting unexpected incidents.

Finally, in the sixth place, it is true that the Emperor of Japan is
the center of everything—of art, literature, and of the whole national
life as well as politics. But it is not correct to say, on the other hand,
that the kings of Europe are involved only in politics. I happen to
know for a fact that the king of England makes great contributions in
cultural areas.

Hirohito had turned his biggest intellectual guns on Chief Aide-
de-Camp Honjo, and Honjo was somewhat impressed. "Thus the
Emperor," he wrote in his diary, "gave his honorable explanation
and aired his views in detail. I felt particularly awed as to point
number five and cautioned the Army about it," that is, cautioned

the Army lest its theorists, by mentioning individual names, cause untoward incidents such as individual assassinations.

Three weeks later Chief Aide-de-Camp Honjo was still trying to maintain that anti-organ agitation was honest philosophical debate and not mere heckling of the Throne. On May 18 he went so far as to say that the controversy was sharpening and strengthening the people to resist insidious "Anglo-Saxon propaganda" of the type which had "speeded Germany's collapse during World War I."

Ignoring the silliness of the statement, Hirohito retorted tartly: "The prime reason for the fall of Germany was that, of all the German states, only Prussia gave full obedience and perfect trust to the kaiser." Hirohito added as an afterthought that the kaiser had compounded the disaster by his cowardice in retiring to Holland after the war instead of remaining in Berlin to see out his destiny. Then Hirohito reiterated his contention that the trend of the world in 1935 was not toward individualism but toward non-individualistic nationalism.

GOD SNARLS

Four days later, on May 22, 1935, Hirohito was shocked to discover that even some of his trusted Navy minions were joining the opposition to him. Navy Minister Osumi, who had been an attaché in Paris during Hirohito's visit in 1921 and had assisted the Throne faithfully during the conspiratorial military reorganizations of the 1920's, gave open notice of his disaffection by asking that Strike-North Admiral Kato Kanji be made governor general of Taiwan. In the context of government gossip at the time, it was like saying that Taiwan Commander Terauchi needed watching; that preparations were afoot in Taiwan that would not bear scrutiny by light of day.

Court officials dismissed the request summarily as an impractical one, and Hirohito that same morning summoned Chief Naval Aide-de-Camp Rear Admiral Idemitsu Mambei. "Men in the Navy," he declared, "are insisting on a non-organ theory of the Throne. This is a contradiction in terms, for in so doing they are disregarding my wishes."

Idemitsu replied recklessly: "Where affairs touching the position of the Emperor are concerned, the Navy may sometimes fail to respond to the hints of the Honorable All-including Mind. Nevertheless it is a mistake to confuse the main point by over-regard for trivia. In routine business, the Navy may sometimes follow badly, but this does not mean, as you imply, that there is any disobedience in the Navy or any contradiction in our faith that the Emperor is supreme. If you continue to speak this way about a matter as important as the national structure, it is a confusion on your part of major and minor issues. I, Idemitsu, in genuine humility, think that the Emperor should wait, should survey the arguments of his subjects from a vantage point, and should, for the time being, direct his mind to other matters than these theoretical ones."

That afternoon Hirohito had Aide Idemitsu reposted, at fifty-one, to the headmastership of the naval academy. Three years later Idemitsu would go further into exile and while away the last years of his blighted career as commander of a port arsenal. In his anger Hirohito did not even accept the Navy Personnel Bureau's first recommendation as to Idemitsu's successor. Confronted suddenly with the demand for a replacement, the bureau listed two names, one a brilliant man whom Honjo identifies only as Rear Admiral So-and-So, and the other a loyal plodder, Rear Admiral Hirata Noburo. Hirata was the son of the lord privy seal to Emperor Taisho during his mad declining years of 1922–1925. In his own right Hirata recommended himself by having long served as aide-de-camp for the Misty Lagoon's "Flying Prince" Yamashina.[4]

Navy Minister Osumi and Chief of the Naval General Staff Prince Fushimi both questioned Hirohito about his acceptance of Hirata as naval aide and pointed out that there was no precedent for demanding the second candidate. Hirohito refused to change his choice. Navy Minister Osumi withdrew from the Im-

---

[4] Yamashina, who was still ill from the "nervous breakdown" he had suffered after Prime Minister Inukai's murder in 1932, was troubling chamberlains at this time by having an affair with his nurse, a certain plebeian Miss Murayama.

perial Presence remarking, "There is nothing more to be said. It is the Emperor's decision."

THROUGH THE GREAT WALL

The emotional explosive which lobbed these metaphysical shells from room to room in the palace had been kindled by Hirohito's new tough policy toward Chiang Kai-shek. Instead of alliance with China, Hirohito was now demanding outright seizure of the Chinese facilities needed for a Strike South.

For two months, since March 1935, one of the Eleven Reliables chosen at Baden-Baden, Major General Isogai Rensuke, had been negotiating with Chiang in Nanking for what amounted to Japanese sovereignty over the whole of north China. Major General Isogai asked Chiang "to neutralize" north China. Japan, he said, had no territorial aims in the area, of course, but felt obliged to silence the anti-Japanese agitation there and deal once and for all with the Communist bandits of Mao Tse-tung with whom Chiang's forces had been fighting inconclusively for five years. Would Chiang please, therefore, withdraw all officials of the Nanking government from north China and leave administration of the area to local mayors and police subservient to Japan. It was as if a trusted major general of a victorious Kaiser Wilhelm had arrived in Philadelphia a few years after World War I and demanded that the area of the thirteen original states be neutralized by withdrawal of federal troops, tax agents, and party politicians to the west of the Appalachians.

Chiang Kai-shek still had no military power to set against Japan. And he owed many debts of kindness to the Japanese. He agreed with them, basically, that the Orient must someday stand united, on its own feet, as a single bloc of self-interests in the international arena. But he had made great strides since 1930 in uniting his shattered land. He had rid it partially of opium addiction and almost entirely of local war lords. He had driven the Communist armies of Mao Tse-tung into the badlands of the northwest.

Moreover, Chiang had found new sources of political strength in the coolie classes of his land. At the urging of Protestant missionaries from the West, he and Madame Chiang had launched a mass movement for spiritual and moral reform called The New Life. It was a simple, personal, evangelistic program emphasizing self-help and brotherhood. It drew its inspiration partly from Confucius and partly from the Oxford Group, the New Church, Seventh-Day Adventism, and other manifestations of the Second Protestantism in the West. It was intended, frankly, as a constructive supplement to Chiang's interminable "bandit suppression campaigns" against the Communists. In spite of the suspect Western influences and political motives behind it, the Chinese masses were taking to The New Life movement with surprising fervor.

Full of hope for his program, Chiang Kai-shek offered Japan nothing more, after six weeks of negotiation, than a pact of mutual nonaggression and friendship. Accordingly, in late April 1935, Hirohito set in motion the machinery for a show of strength. Because of the delicate situation domestically in his own army, he monitored the operation through a personal representative. On May 1, Prince Kaya, fresh from his recent holiday in Berlin with heroes Mussolini and Hitler, set off on a tour of north China and Manchukuo with a group of military academy cadets. Major Prince Kaya was their tactics instructor and proceeded to give them a routine demonstration of Japanese tactical intrigue. On his way to Manchukuo he stopped in Tientsin and visited with the Strike-South lieutenant general who was in command of the garrison there.

While feasting Prince Kaya, the staff officers of the Tientsin garrison accused a Chinese weekly magazine, *The New Life*, of committing lèse majesté against the Japanese Emperor. In consequence—by whose hand is not clear—two Chinese newspapermen who had been writing pro-Japanese propaganda were assassinated inside the Japanese concession in Tientsin. The Japanese staff officers blamed the murders on Chiang Kai-shek's counterespionage force, the Blue Shirts. And the Tientsin commander, as he left the city to accompany Prince Kaya to Manchuria, told his chief of staff that it might be well, in his absence, to issue the Chinese a stern warning. The chief of staff then visited the governor of Hopei, the province in which Peking is situated, and told him that his territory would be occupied by

Japanese troops unless all KMT party organs and security agents were promptly expelled from it.

Lest the governor of Hopei and his master, Chiang Kai-shek, take the warning lightly, Prince Kaya was joined in Manchukuo by everyone of importance in the Japanese Army—War Minister Hayashi, Chief of Staff Prince Kanin, and the commanders of the Korean and Formosan armies. The pretext was the dedication ceremony of a shrine in Long Spring Thaw, the Manchukuoan capital, to Amaterasu, the Japanese sun goddess. But the conclave was meant to appear, as indeed it was, a high-level consultation of the most ominous gravity. So much top brass was there that Secretary-Spy Harada complained to his diary that there was no one left in the Tokyo bureaucracy to gossip with and consult about Army matters.

Japanese noncommissioned officers on weekend passes swaggered through the streets of Tientsin and Peking looking for any pretext to start an "incident." On May 24, Prince Kaya and his class of tactics students from the military academy returned home from Long Spring Thaw, followed a week later by War Minister Hayashi and Army Chief of Staff Prince Kanin. When Chiang Kai-shek continued to seek face-saving terms, Prince Kanin and Hirohito, on June 6, 1935, signed combat orders and dispatched them to the Kwantung Army and the Tientsin garrison. On June 10, as anticipated, Chiang Kai-shek capitulated short of battle. His representative, General Ho, met with the Tientsin garrison commander, Lieutenant General Umezu Yoshijiro, and signed a document known to this day only as the Ho-Umezu Pact.

By the terms of the Ho-Umezu Pact, China promised to prevent her citizens from "scowling" at Japanese soldiers and to cede all but civil police powers in the bulk of north China to representatives approved by Tokyo. Hirohito's inner circle of Big Brothers hoped to use the pact to split north China into several autonomous regions, each governed by a puppet regime responsive to Tokyo. Then, through infiltration of Japanese economic and military advisors, north Chinese labor, raw materials, and railroads were to be integrated into the over-all "defensive structure of the Japanese Empire." Finally, said Japanese visionaries, the example of mutually beneficial Sino-Japanese co-operation in the area would make the rest of China sympathetic to Japan and would prepare the way for a Sino-Japanese alliance against the West.

Emperor Hirohito had long ceased to expect much of Sino-Japanese friendship. He was already preparing for a full-scale war with China and would launch it two years later, in July 1937. In the interim his advisors' dreams for north China would vanish like smoke, and officers of the Japanese Army opposed to war with China would stage a mutiny. On February 26, 1936, elements of Japan's two crack divisions would seize the center of Tokyo and lay siege to the palace in an effort to change Hirohito's mind. All Western writers up to now have ascribed the rebellion to Army extremists who wished to make Hirohito more rather than less militaristic. The story of the rebellion, however, and of the events leading up to it has become available in Japan only in the last few years.

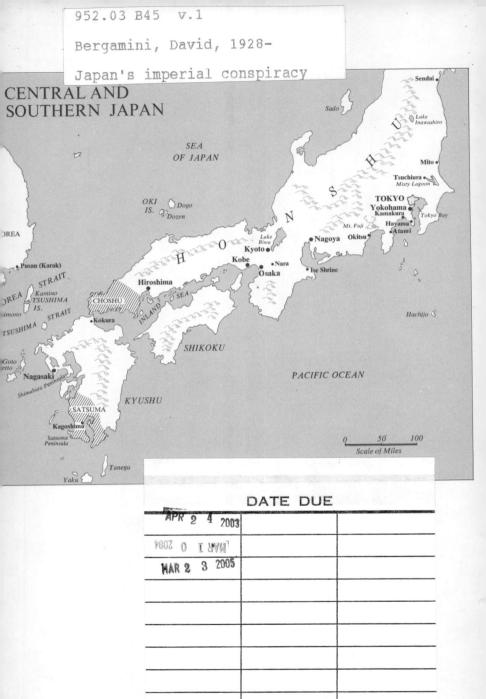

CENTRAL AND
SOUTHERN JAPAN